5th Edition

Law & Ethics in the Business Environment

Terry Halbert, J.D.
Professor of Legal Studies
Temple University Fox School of Business & Management

Elaine Ingulli, J.D., L.L.M.
Richard Stockton College

Australia · Brazil · Canada · Mexico · Singapore · Spain · United Kingdom · United States

Law and Ethics in the Business Environment, Fifth Edition
Terry Halbert and Elaine Ingulli

VP/Editorial Director:
Jack W. Calhoun

Publisher:
Rob Dewey

Acquisitions Editor:
Steven Silverstein, Esq.

Developmental Editor:
Brian Coovert

Marketing Manager:
Lisa Lysne

Production Editor:
Chris Sears

Web Coordinator:
Scott Cook

Technology Project Editor:
Christine Wittmer

Manufacturing Coordinator:
Charlene Taylor

Production House:
Interactive Composition Corporation

Art Director:
Anne Marie Rekow

Internal Designer:
Kathy Heming

Cover Designer:
Kathy Heming

Cover Images:
Photodisc

Printer:
Courier
Kendallville, IN

Printed in the United States of America
1 2 3 4 5 08 07 06 05

ISBN: 0-324-20490-6

Library of Congress Control Number: 2005923730

For more information about our products, contact us at:

Thomson Learning Academic Resource Center

1-800-423-0563

Thomson Higher Education
5191 Natorp Boulevard
Mason, OH 45040
USA

Brief Table of Contents

Table of Contents

PREFACE

"In civilized life, law floats in a sea of ethics," Supreme Court Chief Justice Earl Warren once wrote. We observe today that the smooth operation of our legal, and indeed our economic system, is contingent upon the assumption that most of us will behave ethically. The rule of law, no matter how exacting and fair, is not enough to sustain us. We must be able to do business with the expectation that, most of the time, most of the people we encounter will tell the truth, will keep their promises and will not hide from us information we need to protect ourselves from harm. If forced to live with the opposite assumption, our energies would be spent pursuing legal claims; our market economy would be drained of vitality.

This may sound simple and true, but what does it mean for managers at crunch-time, when the pressure of deadlines, quotas and quarterly statements makes it difficult to do the right thing? Given the demands of the market, whatever we can do to integrate ethics into business education becomes critical. According to corporate leadership researcher Judith Samuelson, "Business school is a primary environment where students shape their attitudes about corporate values." Samuelson was disturbed by the results of a 2001 study of some 2,000 graduates of top business schools. The study tracked a shift in their values during the two years of MBA training. They began as relative idealists—reporting the desire to create high-quality goods and services, to be of service to customers, and to give back to their local communities. But by the time of graduation, they were much more oriented to goals such as maximizing value for shareholders. For whatever reason, the experience of an MBA appears to educate people in reverse, where ethics is concerned.

Those of us who teach ethics in business courses are used to hearing the "oxymoron" joke, some version of "What? You teach business and ethics? Isn't that a contradiction in terms?" But these days—after Enron, Worldcom and Parmalat, and after global trade conferences where the plight of the world's poor is an urgent agenda item identified as a root cause of terrorism—we hear less about oxymorons, more about the pressing need to understand how business can operate profitably, legally, and ethically.

Our book takes on exactly this problem. It presents a set of flashpoints where business imperatives, legal rules and ethical concepts collide, creating difficult choices. Our goal has been to make these complex situations come alive, and to give students the tools to wrestle with them. It is, in a sense, a simulated minefield, where they can practice confronting some of the toughest decisions they will make as managers.

FOCUS ON TEACHING AND LEARNING

Our book can be used as a supplement or as a primary text. It works well in undergraduate business law and/or ethics courses, MBA and Executive MBA graduate courses.

It is impossible to effectively cover everything about the legal system—even everything about business law—in just one semester. The material itself is fluid; the vast "seamless web" is always in flux, as legislatures and courts channel the cultural, economic and political forces that impact upon it. We know that the law is, in fact, a kind of moving target, and we believe in learning it that way—in studying why and how it changes. We have selected readings that allow us to teach the process of the law as it evolves—at the pressure points, the places where controversy is brewing, where ethical issues tend to surface.

As much as content, we teach skills: how to read and write critically, how to discuss, debate and persuade. As ever, we have revised our book with an eye on these elements. Assuming that every student can be motivated to chase down a good question, we have conceived our job as a matter of laying out good questions, of equipping students with enough information to sustain their curiosity without giving them so much that they feel there is nothing left to discover.

We find our students respond well when they are presented with a highly contextualized story or fact pattern, the kind we provide in lightly edited cases, especially those we use to begin each chapter. Many of the students we teach these days have been staring at screens more than at the pages of books, but they know a good story when they see one. So we have tried to take advantage of what the law offers us, in the stylized, rich form of a case: a story—with protagonist, antagonist, dispute, and resolution.

Our mix of readings allows students to view the same problem through a series of disciplinary prisms. We believe a particular legal and ethical dilemma becomes richer to the extent it takes on new tints as seen from new angles, and so we have carefully selected a variety of material—from both scholarly and news media sources, from different areas of expertise, and from different cultural perspectives.

Continuity and Change: The Fifth Edition

In this revision we worked to preserve the best of past editions while responding to the wise suggestions of our reviewers.

Chapter 1 still begins with the Duty to Rescue, but now introduces ethical theory by looking at offshoring jobs to India. We have added new materials on corporate governance, the Sarbanes Oxley Law, and Enron (Chapters 2 and 6). Chapter 3 integrates the PATRIOT Act into its privacy coverage. Chapter 4 has been re-focused to center on stereotyping, weaving material on gay marriage into its discrimination theme. The pharmaceutical industry is prominent in several chapters, and the treatment of copyright in Chapter 9 is newly focused on the Internet.

Perhaps the biggest change, though, is an overall shift towards globalization. In our second decade of writing this textbook, we couldn't help noting that technological change and the world economy have marked every controversial issue that we track with a global imprint. In response, we threaded this new emphasis through every chapter, from offshoring to international patent law.

Much of this edition will be familiar to those who have been using it. While we have added new cases to most chapters, we have also included the most provocative, clearest, most teachable cases from prior editions. We have not altered the organizing framework of the original text. Each chapter presents a central issue in a lead case, often with majority and dissenting opinions. We then expand upon that central issue, offering its legal context, and tracing the policy and ethical issues that flow from it in a series of interdisciplinary readings. At the end of every chapter are problems and an interactive project. We have refined the chapter projects that work best and have added new ones.

In keeping with our goal to write a book that "teaches itself" we have once again included Appendices for the benefit of both students and instructors. Appendix A provides richer checklists to help students become more critical readers of media and Internet sources. Appendix E (new) provides background on alternative dispute resolution, and instructions for several experiential approaches to teaching ADR. Too, we have included instructions for a simulated Legislative Hearing in a new Appendix F.

Thanks

We thank our students and colleagues. Their response to our work gives us the incentive to treat each revision with attention and care.

We thank Diane Williams, secretary to the Department of Legal Studies at Temple University's Fox School of Business and Management and the library staff at Richard Stockton College, especially Mary Ann Trail and Carolyn Gutierrez, for their kind assistance.

We thank reviewers for giving us valuable mental traction for this revision.

De Vee E. Dykstra	University of South Dakota
George P. Generas, Jr.	University of Hartford
John Houlihan	University of Southern Maine
Thomas A. Klein	The University of Toledo
John McGee	Texas State University
Dr. Cliff Olson	Southern Adventist University
Judee A. Timm	Monterey Peninsula College
Diana Walsh	New Jersey Institute of Technology
John Anthony Wrieden	Florida International University

We thank the staff at West/Thomson Learning, especially our new team: developmental editor Bob Sandman and marketing guru Steve Silverstein, who convinced us we could do a valuable and timely revision by providing us with the support we needed; Chris Sears, who once again proved a delightful and efficient production manager; Brian Coovert, who stewarded us painlessly through the production process; Nancy Ahr, who did fine-toothed copyediting for us. This was an unusually pleasant team to work with, and we are delighted to have been a part of it.

We thank our husbands, Brian Ackerman and Bill Coleman, for staying out of the way and remaining as sweet as ever. And, once more, we give each other the happiest of high fives over this latest round of our long, productive and affectionate collaboration.

Chapter 1

Law, Ethics, Business: An Introduction

Law must be stable, and yet it cannot stand still.

— Roscoe Pound

Neither fire nor wind, birth nor death, can erase our good deeds.

— Buddha

Business has become, in the last half century, the most powerful institution on the planet. The dominant institution in any society needs to take responsibility for the whole. . . . Every decision that is made, every action that is taken, must be viewed in light of that kind of responsibility.

— David Korten

Law is not a static phenomenon, yet in certain ways it appears bounded and clear cut. Where it holds jurisdictional authority, law provides a set of rules for behavior. When these rules are broken, behavior is punishable. If you have been driving carelessly and hit another car, you might pay money damages. If you are caught stealing, you might go to jail. If you are caught polluting, you may be forced to stop. The creation of law and the delivery of sanctions for rule breaking are contested processes. How law is made, how it is enforced, and how it is interpreted are always in dispute, constantly changing, and responsive to the power relations that surround it. Still, we can identify its purposes: law both sets behavioral standards and sets up a system for compliance with them. Within the reach of a legal system, we are on notice that we must meet its standards or risk penalty. Chances are we were not directly involved in the making of the rules—we may even disagree strongly with them—but we understand that the legal system shadows us anyway. It may be the closest we can get to a shared reality.

Ethics, on the other hand, presents a menu of options, often disconnected from official sanctions.[1] While law concerns what we *must* do, ethics concerns what we *should* do. Suppose you work for an advertising agency and have just been offered a chance to work on a new ad campaign for a certain fast-food chain. Burgers, fries, and sodas are legal products. Under the First Amendment of the U.S. Constitution, fast-food companies have the legal right to get their messages out to consumers. But you may believe that their ads are particularly attractive to children, who are at risk of becoming accustomed and even addicted to the empty calories that make them fat and unhealthy. Although no law requires it, you may feel you should decline to participate in the campaign. Or suppose a company manufactures a pesticide that can no

1 We distinguish ethics from "professional ethics," which are binding on those with professional licenses for the practice of law or accounting, for example. Indeed, licensing authorities have enforcement powers not unlike those of legal authorities to sanction those who violate their professional codes of ethics.

longer be sold in the United States because the Environmental Protection Agency has banned its primary ingredient, but that *can* be sold in places like India or Africa, where environmental regulations are far less stringent. Legally, the company is free to sell its pesticide overseas; but should it?

Ethical preferences are not preselected for us by legislators or by judges; they involve critical consciousness, engaging each of us in a process of bringing reason and emotion to bear on a particular situation. The right way to behave is not necessarily a matter of aligning our actions with the norm—a community or religious norm, for instance—although it may be. Yet we struggle to carve out some form of consensus on ethics, especially in areas where law does not seem to cover the significant bases. In the above examples, where the law allows people to profit in the marketplace by selling highly dangerous products, we may want to say that certain "shoulds" are universally compelling.

The question of what should be done in a given situation, of the right way to live our lives, is complicated by divergent and overlapping cultural inputs. Within the borders of the United States, and in the global marketplace, we are confronted with a kaleidoscopic array of ethical traditions. Does this mean that there can be no such thing as consensus, no agreement about what is good behavior?

Then there is the "business environment." More than half of the 100 largest economies in the world are multinational corporations. Comparing corporate revenues to the gross domestic product of nations, ExxonMobil is generating more revenue than Turkey, Wal-Mart more than Austria, and DaimlerChrysler is about tied with Norway.[2] The largest 200 companies in the world account for more than one-fourth of the world's economic activity. By 2002, they had twice the economic clout of the poorest four-fifths of humanity. At this point in history, we witness the enormous impact of business, across the world, on virtually every part of life. Business is deeply intertwined with every important institution in our culture—politics, education, the media, the art world, and the sports world. It has powerful effects on our natural environment. It strongly affects what we eat, how we transport ourselves, what our communities look like, and how we take care of ourselves when we are sick. The few hundred largest multinational corporations of the global economy are such a force that they overshadow all other forms of human organization. In recent decades global corporate power has grown to rival or even surpass governmental power. To a certain extent, the impact of global business on society is beneficial. Multinationals pay increased taxes, provide new jobs, and produce new or less expensive goods and services. They introduce to their host countries technology, capital, and skills, ultimately raising living standards. They often donate their resources for charitable purposes. On the other hand, multinationals have been blamed for taking advantage of weak and/or corrupt governments in some of the countries where they do business, turning a blind eye to inadequate safety, environmental, and financial regulation, and ultimately intensifying the disparities between rich and poor. Whether we see progress or exploitation, innovation or destruction, in the power of multinational corporations, we will tend to turn on whatever our own personal experience or bias might be. Yet we might all agree that the power exists, and that it is expanding quickly.

As bearers of a diverse set of cultural achievements, we need to find points of agreement, both in legal and ethical terms, as to how human societies can best flourish. And as participants in the global economy—all of us in some way constrained by competitive market forces—we need to discover ways of tempering the tremendous power of the market, of shaping it to reflect those shared values.

2 "The World's Largest Corporations: Fortune 2000 Global 500," *Fortune,* July 23, 2001 (for corporate revenue); *World Development Report 2001* (Washington, D.C.: World Bank, 2001) (for country GDP).

Freedom vs. Responsibility: A Duty to Rescue?

Yania v. Bigan

Supreme Court of Pennsylvania, 1959
155 A.2d 343

JONES, Benjamin R., Justice.

. . . On September 25, 1957 John E. Bigan was engaged in a coal strip-mining operation in Shade Township, Somerset County. On the property being stripped were large cuts or trenches created by Bigan when he removed the earthen overburden for the purpose of removing the coal underneath. One cut contained water 8 to 10 feet in depth with side walls or embankments 16 to 18 feet in height; at this cut Bigan had installed a pump to remove the water.

At approximately 4 p.m. on that date, Joseph F. Yania, the operator of another coal strip-mining operation, and one Boyd M. Ross went upon Bigan's property for the purpose of discussing a business matter with Bigan, and, while there, [were] asked by Bigan to aid him in starting the pump. Bigan entered the cut and stood at the point where the pump was located. Yania stood at the top of one of the cut's side walls and then jumped from the side wall—a height of 16 to 18 feet—into the water and was drowned.

Yania's widow [sued], contending Bigan was responsible for Yania's death.

She contends that Yania's descent from the high embankment into the water and the resulting death were caused "entirely" by the spoken words . . . of Bigan delivered at a distance from Yania. The complaint does not allege that Yania slipped or that he was pushed or that Bigan made any physical impact upon Yania. On the contrary, the only inference deducible from the . . . complaint is that Bigan . . . caused such a mental impact on Yania that the latter was deprived of his . . . freedom of choice and placed under a compulsion to jump into the water. Had Yania been a child of tender years or a person mentally deficient then it is conceivable that taunting and enticement could constitute actionable negligence if it resulted in harm. However, to contend that such conduct directed to an adult in full possession of all his mental faculties constitutes actionable negligence is . . . completely without merit.

[The widow then claims] that Bigan . . . violated a duty owed to Yania in that his land contained a dangerous condition, i.e. the water-filled cut or trench, and he failed to warn Yania of such condition. . . . Of this condition there was neither concealment nor failure to warn, but, on the contrary, the complaint specifically avers that Bigan not only requested Yania and Boyd to assist him in starting the pump to remove the water from the cut but "led" them to the cut itself. If this cut possessed any potentiality of danger, such a condition was as obvious and apparent to Yania as to Bigan, both coal strip-mine operators. Under the circumstances herein depicted Bigan could not be held liable in this respect.

Lastly, [the widow claims] that Bigan failed to take the necessary steps to rescue Yania from the water. The mere fact that Bigan saw Yania in a position of peril in the water imposed upon him no legal, although a moral, obligation or duty to go to his rescue unless Bigan was legally responsible, in whole or in part, for placing Yania in the perilous position. "[The deceased] voluntarily placed himself in the way of danger, and his death was the result of his own act. . . . That his undertaking was an exceedingly reckless and dangerous one, the event proves, but there was no one to blame for it but himself. He had the right to try the experiment, obviously dangerous as it was, but then also upon him rested the consequences of that experiment, and upon no one else; he may have been, and probably was, ignorant of the risk which he was taking upon himself, or knowing it, and trusting to his own skill, he may have regarded it as easily superable. But in either case, the result of his ignorance, or of his mistake, must rest with himself and cannot be charged to the defendants." The law imposes on Bigan no duty of rescue.

Order [dismissing the complaint] affirmed.

• QUESTIONS •

1. What happened in this case? If Yania couldn't swim, why did he jump?
2. Identify each of the arguments made by Yania's widow. For each, explain how the judge dealt with it.
3. According to the judge, Bigan would have been liable in this case under certain circumstances that did not apply here. What are those circumstances?
4. Suppose you could revise the law of rescue. Would you hold people responsible for doing something to help others in an emergency? If so, what circumstances would trigger a duty to rescue? How much would be required of a rescuer?

HURLEY V. EDDINGFIELD

Supreme Court of Indiana, 1901
59 N.E.1058

DESMOND, Chief Judge.

The material facts alleged may be summarized thus: At and for years before decedent's death [Eddingfield] was a practicing physician at Mace, in Montgomery County, duly licensed under the laws of the state. He held himself out to the public as a general practitioner of medicine. He had been decedent's family physician. Decedent became dangerously ill, and sent for [Dr. Eddingfield]. The messenger informed [the doctor] of decedent's violent sickness, tendered him his fee for his services, and stated to him that no other physician was procurable in time, and that decedent relied on him for attention. . . . Without any reason whatever, [Dr. Eddingfield] refused to render aid to decedent. No other patients were requiring [his] immediate service, and he could have gone to the relief of decedent if he had been willing to do so. Death ensued. . . . The alleged wrongful act was [Dr. Eddingfield's] refusal to enter into a contract of employment.

Counsel do not contend that, before the enactment of the law regulating the practice of medicine, physicians were bound to render professional service to every one who applied. . . . The act regulating the practice of medicine provides for a board of examiners, standards of qualifications, examinations, licenses to those found qualified, and penalties for practicing without license. . . . The act is a preventive, not a compulsive, measure. In obtaining the state's license (permission) to practice medicine, the state does not require, and the licensee does not engage, that he will practice at all or on other terms than he may choose to accept. . . .

Judgment [dismissing the complaint] affirmed.

• QUESTIONS •

1. What happened in this case?
2. What reason did the judge give for his decision?

THE OATH OF HIPPOCRATES

I swear to Apollo the Physician, to the Goddess of Health and to all the Gods and Goddesses, that I shall fulfill, to the best of my ability and judgment, this Oath and Covenant.

My teacher who instructed me in this Art I will hold as equal to my parents, and his male descendants hold as my brothers, to teach them this Art and all the medical knowledge, should they ask me, without any reward or fee. I will do so too for all those that have taken the medical Oath, but for none others.

According to my ability and judgment, I will use my medical knowledge for the benefit of those that suffer, and avoid from doing any harm or injustice.

I will not give anyone a lethal drug, even if asked, and neither will I suggest such. I will not supply any woman with the means for abortion.

With purity and holiness I will pass my life and practice my Art. I will not render eunuch even those that may ask me to but to leave this to the manual laborers.

To any Homes I enter, I will go for the good and benefit of those that suffer and abstain from any voluntary act of mischief or corruption, and from the seduction of females or males, be they free citizens or slaves.

Anything that I may hear or see during the course of treatment, even outside the space where such treatment is conducted, I will not divulge, reckoning that all such should be kept secret.

While I continue to keep this Oath unviolated, may it be granted that I enjoy life and the practice of this Art, respected by all men, in all times. But should I ever transgress or violate it, may the reverse be my lot.

• QUESTIONS •

1. Can you identify any part of this Oath that would create a duty to take care of a dying patient such as Mr. Hurley? How would you re-write the Hippocratic Oath for the twenty-first century?
2. **Internet Assignment:** In a U.S. medical environment of managed care, in a world that includes AIDS and the threat of bio-terror, of what relevance is the Hippocratic Oath? Visit http://www.pbs.org/wgbh/nova/doctors/oath.html for comments from doctors and non-doctors on this question. What is your view?

Justifying the "No Duty to Rescue" Rule

The men who wrote the Bill of Rights were not concerned that government might do too little for the people, but that it might do too much to them.[3]

Although *Hurley v. Eddingfield* was decided in 1901, it is still "good law." Unless a doctor is already treating a patient, or is on duty in a medical facility offering treatment to patients, she is not legally required to assist, even in an emergency.[4] The ruling in *Yania v. Bigan* is also still valid. In general, in the U.S. legal system, we do not have a duty or responsibility to rescue those who are endangered.

There are both philosophical and practical reasons against imposing a duty to rescue. Traditionally, our society has tended to grant maximum leeway to individual freedom of choice. Requiring that people help one another in emergencies would infringe on that freedom by forcing people to act when they might choose not to. Further, imposing an affirmative duty to rescue presupposes that there is agreement that rendering assistance is always the right thing to do. Is there really such consensus? Opinions, beliefs, and concepts of the right way to behave in a given situation might vary radically between individuals and between cultures, particularly as they mix and clash in our diverse society. If we are to grant genuine respect to each person's freedom

3 *Jackson v. City of Joliet,* 715 F. 2d 1200, 1203 (7th Cir. 1983), in which Judge Richard Posner explains why someone in need of emergency assistance has no constitutional right to it.

4 On the other hand, should they become involved in a rescue attempt, doctors in the United States are protected from losses in malpractice suits by the so-called Good Samaritan statutes. Existing in every state, these laws ensure that doctors and other medically trained people who decide to help in an emergency will not be held responsible for errors unless they have been "grossly negligent." In approximately two-thirds of the states, the Good Samaritan laws protect even people who are not medically trained.

of conscience, shouldn't we insist on legal enforcement of "right" behavior only when it is unavoidable? Shouldn't we reserve punishment or liability for the times when people actively injure others, and allow rescue to be a matter of personal choice? In a sense, those who do not choose to rescue are not behaving badly; rather, they are merely doing nothing. As U.S. Supreme Court Justice Oliver Wendell Holmes once said, "While there is properly in law a duty not to harm, there is not . . . a negative duty not to allow harm to happen."

In the next excerpt, nineteenth-century philosopher John Stuart Mill describes the connection between individual freedom of choice and the law of the liberal democratic state.

ON LIBERTY

John Stuart Mill

Over himself, over his own body and mind, the individual is sovereign. . . .

This, then, is the appropriate region of human liberty. It comprises, first, the inward domain of consciousness; demanding liberty of conscience, in the most comprehensive sense; liberty of thought and feeling; absolute freedom of opinion and sentiment on all subjects, practical or speculative, scientific, moral, or theological. The liberty of expressing and publishing opinions may seem to fall under a different principle, since it belongs to that part of the conduct of an individual which concerns other people; but, being almost of as much importance as the liberty of thought itself, and resting in great part on the same reasons, is practically inseparable from it. Secondly, the principle requires liberty of tastes and pursuits; of framing the plan of our life to suit our own character; of doing as we like, subject to such consequences as may follow; without impediment from our fellow-creatures, so long as what we do does not harm them, even though they should think our conduct foolish, perverse, or wrong. Thirdly, from this liberty of each individual, follows the liberty, within the same limits, of combination among individuals; freedom to unite, for any purpose not involving harm to others: the persons combining being supposed to be of full age, and not forced or deceived.

No society in which these liberties are not, on the whole, respected, is free, whatever may be its form of government; and none is completely free in which they do not exist absolute and unqualified. The only freedom which deserves the name, is that of pursuing our own good in our own way, so long as we do not attempt to deprive others of theirs, or impede their effort to obtain it. Each is the proper guardian of his own health, whether bodily, or mental and spiritual. Mankind are greater gainers by suffering each other to live as seems good to themselves, than by compelling each to live as seems good to the rest.

Creating a legal duty to rescue would not only run into resistance on philosophical grounds. There would also be practical objections. How would we enforce such a rule? Where would we draw the line? Must a person attempt to rescue even if it would be terribly dangerous? Should a rescuer be compensated by the victim for any injuries suffered? Who, in a crowd, are the potential rescuers: The closest witnesses? Anyone at the scene? Anyone aware of the incident?

Radical Change?

> *Lawgivers make the citizens good by training them in habits of right . . . this is the aim of all legislation, and if it fails to do this it is a failure; this distinguishes a good form of constitution from a bad one.*
>
> — Aristotle, *Nichomachean Ethics*

While the Anglo-American tradition emphasizing individual freedom of choice is a major reason our legal system demands no duty to rescue, law professor Steven Heyman argues that recognition of a duty to rescue is in line with that very tradition. His article appeared in a communitarian journal. Communitarians are concerned with reviving the notion of shared responsibility and interconnectedness at a time when, they believe, too many people view social change solely in terms of defining and enforcing an ever-growing number of personal rights.

He begins his essay by mentioning two famous examples in which bystanders chose to ignore those who desperately needed help. The first incident happened one night in March 1964. Twenty-eight-year-old Kitty Genovese was returning home to her apartment complex in a quiet, respectable neighborhood in Queens, New York. Manager of a bar in another part of Queens, she was arriving late; it was 3:00 A.M. As she left her red Fiat and began walking to her apartment, she saw a man walking towards her. He chased her, caught up with her, and attacked her with a knife. She screamed: "Oh my God, he stabbed me! Please help me! Please help me!" People opened windows, someone called out "let that girl alone," and several lights went on. But as more than a half hour passed, none of the witnesses did anything more. The killer had time to drive away, leaving Ms. Genovese collapsed on the sidewalk, and then to drive back to stab her again. Thirty-eight people later admitted they had heard Ms. Genovese's screams, but no one even called the police until after she was dead.[5]

The second incident happened many years later. In 1983, in New Bedford, Massachusetts, young woman went into a bar to buy a pack of cigarettes. She was gang-raped on the pool table while customers watched and even cheered.[6]

The Duty to Rescue: A Liberal-Communitarian Approach

Steven J. Heyman[7]

Rescue and the Common-Law Tradition

Consider two notorious incidents: the 1964 slaying of Kitty Genovese and the 1983 New Bedford tavern rape. In both cases, neighbors or bystanders watched as a young woman was brutally and repeatedly assaulted, yet they made no effort to intervene or call for help. Under current doctrine, their inaction breached no legal duty, however reprehensible it may have been morally.

Suppose, however, that a police officer had been present at the time. Surely we would not say that the officer was free to stand by and do nothing while the attack took place. The state has a responsibility to protect its citizens against criminal violence. It performs this function largely through its police force. An officer who unjustifiably failed to prevent a violent crime would be guilty of a serious dereliction of duty, which might result in dismissal from the force or even criminal prosecution. Thus the officer would have a legal duty to act. But what if there is no officer on the scene? In that situation, the state can fulfill its responsibility to prevent violence only by relying on the assistance of those persons who *are* present.

Contrary to the conventional view, there is strong evidence that, for centuries, the common law of England and America did recognize an individual duty to act in precisely such cases. According to traditional legal doctrine, every person was entitled to protection by the government

5 A. M. Rosenthal, *Thirty-Eight Witnesses: The Kitty Genovese Case* (Berkeley, CA: University of California Press, 1999).

6 This incident became the basis of a film, *The Accused,* with Kelly McGinnis and Jody Foster.

7 *The Responsive Community,* Vol. 7, No.3, Summer 1997, pp. 44–49.

against violence and injury. In return for this protection, individuals had an obligation not merely to obey the law, but also, when necessary, to actively help enforce it. Ordinarily, of course, the government kept the peace through its own officers. When no officer was present, however, it was said . . . that "the law makes every person an officer" for the preservation of the peace. Thus, individuals at the scene of a violent crime had a duty to intervene if they could do so without danger to themselves. If they could not, they were required to notify the authorities.

With the development of modern police forces in the 19th century, this tradition of active citizen participation in law enforcement gradually declined. In recent decades, however, it has become increasingly clear that effective crime prevention requires the efforts of the whole community—a recognition that is reflected, for example, in neighborhood crime watch and community policing programs. As the Genovese and New Bedford cases show, there are situations in which a simple duty to call the police may be crucial. In response to these incidents, half a dozen states have recently passed laws requiring those present at the scene of a violent crime to notify the authorities or provide other reasonable assistance to the victim.

In the debate over a duty to rescue, [d]iscussion often focuses on the classic example of the drowning man. There the danger arises purely from natural forces, not from any human action. In that setting the potential rescuer and victim may appear to be mere "strangers" without any relationship or obligation to one another. . . . In the Genovese and New Bedford cases, by contrast, the threat comes from wrongful human conduct. In this context, it is easier to recognize that the parties do have a relationship—one of common citizenship—that can give rise to duty to aid.

Rescue and the Liberal Tradition

A duty to prevent violence finds support not only in the Anglo-American common-law tradition but also in liberal political theory. According to Locke and other natural rights theorists, individuals enter into society to preserve their lives, liberties, and properties. Under the social contract, citizens obtain a right to protection by the community against criminal violence. In return, they promise not only to comply with the laws, but also to assist the authorities in enforcing those laws. In this way, Locke writes, the rights of individuals come to be defended by "the united strength of the whole Society." In *On Liberty,* John Stuart Mill recognizes a similar duty on the part of individuals. . . . Mill agrees "that every one who receives the protection of society owes a return for the benefit," including an obligation to bear one's fair share of "the labours and sacrifices incurred for defending the society or its members from injury."

In addition to endorsing a duty to prevent violence, liberal thought suggests a way to expand that duty into a general duty to rescue. According to liberal writers, the community has a responsibility to preserve the lives of its members, not only against violence but also against other forms of harm. For example, Locke, Blackstone, and Kant all maintain that the state has an obligation to relieve poverty and support those who are unable to provide for their own needs. In Locke's words, both natural right and "common charity" teach "that those should be most taken care of by the law, who are least capable of taking care of themselves." Of course, this is also a major theme in contemporary liberal political thought. . . .

Rescue and Communitarian Theory

Communitarian theory supports and deepens the argument for a duty to rescue. On this view, community is valuable not merely as a means to the protection of individual rights, but also as a positive human good. Human nature has an irreducible social dimension that can be fulfilled only through relationships with others. The community has a responsibility to promote the good of its members. But this can be fully achieved only within a society whose members recognize a reciprocal obligation to act for the welfare of the community and their fellow citizens. A core instance is the duty to rescue.

Of course, some might doubt whether contemporary society is characterized by the kind of community required for a duty to rescue. Community is not simply given, however; it must be created. Common action, and action on behalf of others, plays a crucial role in creating relationships between people. Thus the adoption of a duty to rescue might not merely reflect, but also promote, a greater sense of community in modern society.

The Contours of a Duty to Rescue

Advocates of a duty to rescue usually propose that it be restricted to cases in which one can act with little or no inconvenience to oneself. But this does not go far enough. Because its purpose is to safeguard the most vital human interests, the duty should not be limited to easy rescues, but should require an individual to do anything reasonably necessary to prevent criminal violence or to preserve others from death or serious bodily harm. Rescue should not require self-sacrifice, however. Thus the duty should not apply if it would involve a substantial risk of death or serious bodily injury to the rescuer or to other innocent people.

This responsibility falls on individuals only in emergency situations when no officer is present. Moreover, the duty would often be satisfied by calling the police, fire department, or rescue services. . . .

In performing the duty to rescue, one acts on behalf of the community as a whole. For this reason, one should receive compensation from the community for any expense reasonably incurred or any injury suffered in the course of the rescue. Any other rule would mean that some people would be required to bear a cost that should properly be borne by the community at large, simply because they happened to be at a place where rescue was required. . . .

Far from diminishing liberty, the recognition of a duty to rescue would enhance it by strengthening protection for the most basic right of all—freedom from criminal violence and other serious forms of harm. And by requiring action for the sake of others, a duty to rescue also has the potential to promote a greater sense of community, civic responsibility, and commitment to the common good.

• QUESTIONS •

1. According to the writer, a change in our law—a new duty to rescue—might change the way people think, heightening their awareness of one another as members of a community, and leading them to be more responsive to one another. Do you think law can have such power? Can you think of any examples where a change in the law seemed to improve the moral climate of our society?
2. Do you think law should be used as a tool for shaping a shared moral climate? Why or why not?
3. **Internet Assignment:** What is the communitarian approach to the process of re-anchoring Americans to a sense of shared morality and community? Who are some communitarians? How would you describe their politics?

Exceptions to the Rule

The law recognizes a number of exceptions to the "no duty to rescue" rule. Many states impose criminal penalties, for example, for failing to report child abuse or an accident in which someone is killed. Only a few states—including Rhode Island, Vermont, and Minnesota—impose a more general duty to rescue by statute. In theory, violators would be fined. In fact, however, the statutes are rarely, if ever, invoked.

One means of finding a legal duty to rescue is through contract law. Certain persons assume contractual responsibilities to help others or to prevent them from being harmed. A lifeguard, for instance, cannot ignore a drowning swimmer, nor can a firefighter let a building burn. While a person could be disciplined or fired for refusing to attempt rescue under such circumstances,[8] to commit to a dangerous job such as policing or firefighting is itself a statement of willingness to risk one's life to save lives—to risk rescue as a part of an ordinary day's work. In fact, of the 343 firefighters killed on September 11, 2001, 60 were not on duty that day, but responded to the alarm as if they were.

When people—trained or not—volunteer to rescue, they become legally bound to take reasonable care in finishing what they have started. In one case, an 80-year-old woman had a stroke while she was shopping at a department store. A salesclerk led her to the store infirmary and left her unattended for six hours. By the time help arrived, her condition was irreparably aggravated, and the store was held liable for failing to carry through on the rescue attempt.[9] Liability is imposed in this kind of case for making a bad situation worse: the person in trouble may be lulled into a false sense of security, believing they will be helped, and other would-be rescuers may not realize assistance is needed.

Another exception to the "no duty to rescue" rule applies when a person has endangered another, even indirectly, or has participated in creating a dangerous situation. When professionals in a mental institution release a violent psychotic without taking measures to make certain he will be properly medicated, they may be putting members of the public in danger. When organizers of a rock concert sell general admission tickets to a performance of a wildly popular group and do not provide lane control, they may be held responsible for the fatal result as fans are suffocated in the crush to gain entry.

Finally, a set of exceptions is triggered when there is a "special relationship" between the person who needs help and the person who must take responsible action. Special relationships may be based on their custodial, rather intimate nature, such as that between a parent and child or between a teacher and young pupils. Or such relationships may exist because of an economic connection, such as that between an employer and employees or between a provider of public transportation and its passengers. In either type, the relationship involves a degree of dependency. The law allows those who are dependent to expect reasonable protection from harm, and requires the more powerful to provide it. A father must make some effort to save his drowning infant, and a city transportation system must take reasonable steps to protect its subway riders from criminal attacks.

Business Liability for Rescue and Protection

A business, then, has a "special relationship" with its customers that creates some responsibility for their safety, but what might be the parameters of that duty? The next case examines the scope of business liability to customers who are victimized by crime on the premises. When and how should a company act to prevent trouble in the first place?

ROGER L. MCCLUNG V. DELTA SQUARE

Supreme Court of Tennessee, 1996
937 S.W.2d 891

WHITE, Justice.

On September 7, 1990, thirty-seven-year-old Dorothy McClung, plaintiff's wife, went shopping at Wal-Mart in the Delta Square Shopping Center in Memphis. As she was returning to her parked car around noon, Mrs. McClung was abducted at gunpoint and forced into her car by Joseph

---

8 For reasons of public policy, however, civil lawsuits against police, fire, or other government workers are rarely permitted.

9 *Zelenko v. Gimbel Bros. Inc.*, 287 N.Y.S. 134 (1935).

Harper, a fugitive from Chattanooga. Later, Harper raped Mrs. McClung and forced her into the trunk of her car where she suffocated. Her body was found by hunters in a field in Arkansas the day after the abduction. Harper confessed, and was convicted of kidnapping, rape, and murder. He committed suicide after being sentenced to life in prison.

Plaintiff filed suit against defendants on his own behalf and on behalf of his and Mrs. McClung's three minor children. In his suit, he alleged that defendant Wal-Mart, the anchor tenant at the Delta Square Shopping Center, and defendant Delta Square, the owner and operator of the center, were negligent in failing to provide security measures for the parking lot. . . .

[Mr. McClung had lost in the lower courts of Tennessee where judges applied a rule set in an earlier (1975) case, *Cornpropst v. Sloan*. The *Cornpropst* court held that a merchant had no responsibility to protect customers from criminal attack, unless the merchant had advance warning that its customers were about to be attacked on their premises. Joseph Harper had made no indication to Wal-Mart or to Delta that he was about to assault Dorothy McClung, so her husband's claim failed. Since criminals do not make a habit of announcing their plans, the precedent established by *Cornpropst* effectively prevented recovery for plaintiffs in cases like *McClung*. Now, more than 20 years later, the Supreme Court of Tennessee notes that the majority of other states are using a different legal rule, more favorable to plaintiffs, focusing on whether a criminal attack was *foreseeable*. To determine when crime might be foreseeable, the court makes an effort to balance the interests of businesses and of customers.]

[A] business is not to be regarded as the insurer of the safety of its customers, and it has no absolute duty to implement security measures for the protection of its customers. However, a duty to take reasonable steps to protect customers arises if the business knows, or has reason to know, either from what has been or should have been observed or from past experience, that criminal acts against its customers on its premises are reasonably foreseeable, either generally or at some particular time.

In determining the duty that exists, the foreseeability of harm and the gravity of harm must be balanced against the commensurate burden imposed on the business to protect against that harm. In cases in which there is a high degree of foreseeability of harm and the probable harm is great, the burden imposed upon defendant may be substantial. Alternatively, in cases in which a lesser degree of foreseeability is present or the potential harm is slight, less onerous burdens may be imposed. By way of illustration, using surveillance cameras, posting signs, installing improved lighting or fencing, or removing or trimming shrubbery might, in some instances, be cost effective and yet greatly reduce the risk to customers. . . .

[The Tennessee Supreme Court goes on to apply its new approach to the facts at hand:]

[F]or the purpose of offering an illustration of the analysis required of courts in these type of cases, we return to the facts of the case at bar. Here, plaintiff's wife was returning to her car in defendants' parking lot when she was accosted. Plaintiff argues that because of past crimes committed on or near defendants' parking lot, a requisite degree of foreseeability to impose a duty to take reasonable precautions was established. To support this contention, plaintiff relies upon records from the Memphis Police Department, which indicate that from May, 1989 through September, 1990, when plaintiff's wife was abducted, approximately 164 criminal incidents had occurred on or near defendants' parking lot . . . includ[ing] a bomb threat, fourteen burglaries, twelve reports of malicious mischief, ten robberies, thirty-six auto thefts, ninety larcenies, and one attempted kidnapping on a parking lot adjacent to defendants' parking lot. . . . The record also establishes that defendants' premises were located in a high crime area, and that other nearby major retail centers utilized security measures to protect customers.[10] The manager of the Wal-Mart store at the time of the abduction testified that he would not hold "sidewalk sales" or place merchandise outside the store, except for "dirt," out of fear it would be stolen.

10 Although the measures varied, one business even posted guards in five separate watch towers located throughout its parking lot.

Considering the number, frequency, and nature of the crimes reported to police, management's acknowledgement of security problems, and other evidence in the record, we conclude that the proof would support a finding that the risk of injury to plaintiff's wife was reasonably foreseeable. . . .

[T]he court must also consider the burden which the duty would impose upon defendants. We note, for example, that defendants contend . . . that security measures are not effective in reducing crime; and that providing security is cost prohibitive. These arguments must be considered on remand in light of conflicting information supplied by one of Wal-Mart's senior security and loss prevention executives. . . . [11]

[T]he judgments of the lower courts are reversed. The case is remanded to the trial court for further proceedings consistent with this opinion. The principles set forth today apply to all cases tried or retried after the date of this opinion and all cases on appeal in which the issue in this case has been raised. Costs shall be taxed to defendants.

• QUESTIONS •

1. Dorothy McClung met a horrible fate that she didn't deserve. But isn't that just a matter of terrible luck? Why should terrible luck translate into legal liability?

2. In a negligence case, a plaintiff must first establish that the defendant owed the plaintiff a "duty of care," an obligation under law to behave in a reasonable manner towards the plaintiff. In a portion of the opinion not included above, the *McClung* court wrote that "a legal duty reflects society's contemporary policies and social requirements concerning the right of individuals and the general public to be protected from another's act or conduct." It went on to note that a legal duty is "frequently an expression by the court of evolving public policy." How does the *McClung* decision reflect the evolution of public policy? Is the court creating a "duty to rescue" here? If not, how would you describe the duty it creates?

3. If we look at *McClung v. Delta* in economic terms, what would be the most cost effective way to reduce criminal activity on business premises? Here is one scholar's analysis:

> *Of all the involved parties, the cost of crime reduction is cheapest to the landowner. For the criminal, imposing civil liability on him in addition to existing criminal sanctions does not deter him from committing the crime. Imposing duty on the patron, so that he must protect and compensate himself, may result in crime reduction, but only at the expensive cost of the patron staying home. While the patron can prevent crime by not going out at night, the price of staying home is high not only for him but also for society in general. As opposed to the transient patron, who has little information about the crime problem on the landowner's premises and little ability to directly influence it, the landowner can be much more effective in dealing with the problem. While the patron holds just one expensive option, staying home, the landowner holds many options ranging from installation of better lighting, fences, or guard service, to even varying hours of operation. All of these options should be less expensive and much more effective in deterring crime than the patron's sole choice of staying home.*
>
> —Bazyler*

11 In an article written for a trade publication, it was acknowledged that 80 percent of crime at Wal-Mart stores occurred in the parking lots or the exterior perimeter of the stores. The article praised newly implemented parking lot security measures ranging from roving patrols to employees wearing orange vests to surveillance cameras. These measures were said to produce "outstanding" results in reducing crime, helping "halt many crimes in progress," and providing "crucial evidence to local [law enforcement authorities]." The article also noted that the cost of these security measures "wasn't quite as expensive as what [the store] had been doing. So [the store] saved a little money and did much more effective work."

* "The Duty to Provide Adequate Protection: Landowner's Liability for Failure to Protect Patrons from Criminal Attack," 21 *Ariz L.Rev.* 727, 747–48 (1979)

Do you agree that, in these situations, it is the business owner who is best positioned to thwart on-premises crime? Does Bazyler overlook any options available to customers, other than staying home?

4. No one from Wal-Mart or Delta Shopping Center abducted or raped Dorothy McClung. Instead of blaming the business, why not blame the local police for failing to protect her? Isn't that the job of the police? **Internet Assignment:** Locate a case in which the police were sued for failing to protect someone from violent harm. What was the result?

5. The following is a quote from a 1962 New Jersey case, which had been relied upon by the Tennessee Supreme Court in deciding *Cornpropst*:

> *Everyone can foresee that commission of crime virtually anywhere and at any time. If foreseeability itself gave rise to a duty to provide police protection for others, every residential curtilage, every shop, every store, every manufacturing plant would have to be patrolled by the private arms of the owner. And since hijacking and attacks upon occupants of motor vehicles are also foreseeable, it would be the duty of every motorist to provide armed protection for his passengers and the property of others.*
>
> —*Goldberg v. Housing Auth. of Newark,* 186 A.2 291 (1962), at 293.[12]

Do you agree with this slippery slope argument presented here? How would the *McClung* court answer it?

Ethical Decision Making: A Toolkit

We have been looking at the way U.S. law addresses the question of balancing two important values, that of freedom—the freedom of individuals like Mr. Bigan or Dr. Eddingfield to choose not to help in an emergency—and that of responsibility—the responsibility of businesses like Wal-Mart to protect their shoppers from foreseeable crime. So far, we have been considering "bystander" situations; Dr. Eddingfield didn't cause Hurley to develop a fatal illness, and Wal-Mart didn't kidnap Dorothy McClung.

We now alter the scenario: suppose a cost-efficient, perfectly legal business strategy happens to be very hurtful to certain people? Again, there is an interplay between freedom and responsibility, but here the focus will be more on ethics than on law. We'll begin with a recent business news story.

The Ethics of Offshoring: Outsourcing IBM Jobs to India

In late 2003 the *Wall Street Journal* reported that IBM planned to move nearly 5,000 jobs overseas to save expenses, the latest twist in the "offshoring" phenomenon that had become pronounced in the U.S. high-tech industry. Employees at IBM facilities in Texas, North Carolina, New York, Colorado, and Connecticut would be affected; IBM had already hired hundreds of engineers in India to begin taking on their work. According to the *Journal,* IBM workers slated for replacement throughout 2004 would actually be expected to train their foreign replacements.

For years U.S. firms had been shifting manufacturing and other blue-collar jobs to Asia where labor costs are much lower, but IBM's plans made headlines because they were part of a newer trend, distressing to many: job losses would now affect well-educated, white-collar

12 The rule of *Goldberg* was abandoned by the New Jersey Supreme Court 20 years later in *Butler v. Acme Markets Inc.,* 445 A.2d 1141 (1982).

employees. Having begun with call centers and information technology positions, offshoring had mushroomed to include accountants, production control specialists, industrial engineers, medical transcriptionists, and others. By late 2003 the U.S. Bureau of Labor Statistics estimated that half a million high-tech professionals had lost their jobs since 2001, a figure expected to double by the end of 2004. Although many IT jobs had been eliminated due to the bursting of the dot-com bubble, U.S. corporate foreign outsourcing was predicted to be the main driver of future losses. Perhaps most disturbing was the statistic that only about 40 percent of the workers who had held those jobs would be "redeployed" by their employers.

Late in 2003, Sam Palmisano, chairman of IBM's board of directors and its chief executive officer, justified the company's decision to move to India for skilled labor in a speech to the Council on Competitiveness in Washington, D.C. He stated that the nations of Asia not only provide low-cost labor, but also have heavily invested in their educational and communication infrastructure. It would only be fair to respond to what they offer:

> *China, India, South Korea, and other rapidly developing nations are replicating the structural advantages that historically have made the U.S. the center of innovation. We can't—shouldn't—regret improvements in other nations' competitiveness. Their people deserve to participate fully in the benefits of innovations.*

Was Sam Palmisano's decision ethical?

There are many different ways to answer this question. Ethical analysis, unlike much quantitative analysis, can be a messy, complex business, without a clear and definitive outcome. However, we do have tools at our disposal to help us make these complicated assessments.

First, let's turn to an approach that will be familiar to you. It amounts to the bedrock principle of strategic management; it underlies the entire free market system. This value system is so embedded in both business theory and business reality that we might fail to recognize it as not only an economic perspective, but also as an ethical one.

Free Market Ethics

A basic assumption of classic microeconomic theory is that the overriding goal of any business is to be profitable. As trustees (**fiduciaries**) of the shareholders, managers have a primary responsibility to try to improve the value of shareholder investment. In fact, under the law of corporations, managers are answerable to the owners of a company—its stockholders—if they fail to take reasonable care in running it.

Milton Friedman, a well-known free market economist and a proponent of this view, has written:

> *In a free enterprise, private property system, a corporate executive is the employee of the owners of the business. He has a direct responsibility to his employers. That responsibility is to conduct the business in accordance with their desires, which generally will be to make as much money as possible while conforming to the basic rules of society, both those embodied in law and those embodied in ethical custom.*[13]

While it is not entirely clear what Friedman means by "ethical custom," he believes it is wrong for managers to use corporate resources to deal with problems in society at large. Decisions regarding what might be best for society should be made in the political arena, and implementation of policies agreed upon there should be funded by tax dollars. For managers to make those kinds of decisions themselves, and to use corporate monies to pay for them, is the equivalent of theft—theft of stockholders' resources.

13 "The Social Responsibility of Business is to Increase Its Profits," *New York Times*, September 13, 1970.

Friedman expresses strong disapproval of companies that take on socially beneficial tasks and then promote themselves as good corporate citizens. This he calls "hypocritical window-dressing."

> *Whether blameworthy or not, the use of the cloak of social responsibility, and the nonsense spoken in its name by influential and prestigious businessmen, does clearly harm the foundations of a free society.... This may gain them public praise in the short run. But it helps to strengthen the already too prevalent view that the pursuit of profits is wicked and immoral and must be curbed and controlled by external forces. Once this view is adopted, the external forces that curb the market will not be the social consciences, however highly developed, of the pontificating executives; it will be the iron fist of Government bureaucrats.*[14]

Friedman believes in minimal government interference in the private enterprise realm, and worries that managers are capable—if inadvertently—of undermining the very environment they need to operate within. He goes on:

> *In a free society, there is one and only one social responsibility of business—to use its resources and engage in activities designed to increase its profits so long as it stays within the rules of the game, which is to say, engages in open and free competition without deception or fraud.*[15]

Let's apply Friedman's thinking and free market ethical theory to Sam Palmisano's decision to move several thousand IBM jobs to India. First we must ask: Will this choice be profitable for the company? The answer is yes. In India, chemists with doctoral degrees and employees in high-tech jobs earn one-fifth of the salaries of their American counterparts; a software programmer in Bangalore will earn about one quarter of what someone with comparable skills in the United States would earn. Even with extra communication costs, IBM will save at least 50 percent by hiring overseas. There are other profit factors. Offshoring yields capacity increases, providing service more rapidly while taking advantage of time zone variations. Offshoring allows companies like IBM to concentrate on what they do best. Highly innovative work may still be done domestically, while maintenance chores, minor enhancements, and bug-fixing that make up most of what programmers do in a large software firm can be handled overseas.

Looking ahead, the flexibility offered by offshoring may be the best way for IBM to remain competitive. In 2003, offshore outsourcing increased by 60 percent. According to a marketing research firm for the Fortune 1000, by 2015, more than 3.3 million U.S. service-industry jobs and $136 billion in wages will have moved offshore. This is a conservative forecast; for many job categories there could be 30 percent losses to offshoring. If other high-tech companies are participating in this trend—and they are[16]—it would seem to be in IBM's best interests to position itself ahead of the curve.[17]

Using Friedman's analysis we would also need to know whether the process of moving jobs to India was legal. At this writing, there are no legal impediments to outsourcing, other than a federal rule passed in January 2004 stating that any private contracting done for a federal agency "may not be performed by the contractor at a location outside the United States" unless the

---

14 Ibid.

15 Ibid.

16 Cisco, Dell, General Electric, Accenture, EDS, Microsoft, and SAP are a few of these companies.

17 Offshoring is not just an IT phenomenon. According to a survey by Deloitte Research, insurance claim and mortgage application processing, accounting, and equity research positions are the types of jobs that 43 financial institutions across North America and Europe had been offshoring at a greatly quickened pace—from an average of 300 to an average of 1,500 from 2003 to 2004. Deloitte predicts that by 2010 the 100 biggest global financial institutions will have shifted $400 billion worth of services overseas, saving themselves some $150 billion.

work had been done outside the country previously. According to an IBM spokesperson, its federal government contracts generally do not involve offshore work.[18]

In microeconomic terms then, the decision to move jobs to India should focus on shareholder interests, and not be swayed by the interests of other stakeholders—except to the extent that these would impact profits. Sam Palmisano's choice should not be made out of concern for the families dependent on jobs at IBM, for example, or out of concern for possible degrading of educational systems dependent on local property taxes in those places—Dallas, Poughkeepsie, Boulder, and Raleigh—where the job losses will take place. Palmisano should not be troubled by the political storm that might be brewing as his company outsources to India. (Campaigning for president in 2004, John Kerry called executives who participated in offshoring "Benedict Arnolds," unpatriotic in the extreme.) He should not worry about controversy unless it reaches such a pitch that there is real public outrage. Only if offshoring becomes a focal point for consumer activism, and only if profits are likely to be significantly affected, would Friedman urge IBM to put the brakes on its plans.

The decision to move jobs to India could—in the long run—turn out better for all concerned. It allows IBM to react to market forces with minimal losses, to be flexible as it faces domestic and global competition, and may put the company in a better position to expand and create new jobs in the future. In other words, what works for IBM may have long-term benefits for many other stakeholders, but cost-benefit shareholder analysis of offshoring would not take such possibilities into account.

Notice that this analysis aligns with a belief in maximum freedom of choice for individuals—and minimal power of government to obstruct that freedom. This strand of thought, which we saw supporting the "no duty to rescue" rule, has been key in the development of both our market economy and our legal system. It would support both IBM's freedom to invest where it can best make a profit and the freedom of IBM's employees to leave their jobs and seek work elsewhere. The idea is that we can best progress as a society if we grant as much leeway as possible to private preference, allowing people (and private associations of people, like corporations) the right to do what they think is best with their property and their personal lives. This ethical perspective is deeply imprinted upon the economic and cultural lives of most people in the developed world.

Utilitarianism: Assessing Consequences

Through much of our history, the most influential ethical reference point was religious; the rules to be followed were "written in the heavens" and were guidelines for achieving immortality of the soul. It was a radical break with tradition, then, for eighteenth-century philosopher and social thinker Jeremy Bentham to suggest an entirely new frame of reference. Ethical behavior, he argued, was not a matter of pleasing God, but of bringing about as much happiness as possible for the greatest number of people. According to Bentham, the definitive moral standard is that of "utility," requiring us to consider the consequences of an act (or a social policy) for all those affected by it. One of Bentham's followers, nineteenth-century philosopher John Stuart Mill (see above), would become the best-known proponent of this ethical approach, known as **utilitarianism.**

According to the principle of utilitarianism, the right way to behave in a given situation is to choose the alternative that is likely to produce the greatest overall good. Cost-benefit analysis, the sort of efficiency calculation that is common to business decision making—what IBM CEO Sam Palmisano probably used as he chose to outsource thousands of jobs to India—is based on notions of utility. As an ethical theory, however, utilitarianism asks us to compare the harms and benefits of an action not just for the decider, but for *all persons who will be affected by the decision.* In the IBM scenario, this would mean, at the least, not only weighing the effects of offshoring upon

18 A politically hot topic in the election year of 2004, offshore outsourcing was the target of several proposed state laws banning or restricting such moves on the part of those contracting with government. At this writing, none of them had been enacted.

IBM shareholders, but also looking at the consequences to IBM employees whose jobs were lost (and their families) and at those in India who were hired to replace them (and their families). Since local communities in both the United States and India are affected, consequences to people in that wider circumference must also be assessed.

Hardest hit would have to be IT employees who are laid off. While job retraining programs exist for manufacturing workers when their jobs move overseas, there is no such safety net for workers in IT or in other white-collar fields. According to the December 8, 2003 issue of *Business Week,* only about one-third of those Americans displaced by offshoring found jobs at the same or higher pay. The utilitarian calculation asks us to consider not only the immediate and direct consequences, but also those that are indirect, and those that are foreseeable into the future. If the offshoring job exodus continues—and most experts forecast that it will—by 2005 some 600,000 IT jobs for American-based companies will be performed elsewhere. What will happen to a local community as many of its citizens lose well-paying jobs? As the tax base diminishes, will its libraries, schools, police and fire forces experience cutbacks? There is concern too about another major ripple effect: Offshoring, and the threat of offshoring, could become leverage, putting downward pressure on the the salaries and benefits of all U.S. workers.

Yet some analysts see a silver lining. As the *Washington Post* reported in September 2003, offshoring could be a "healthy trend":

> *Some IT workers here may be forced to leave the "computer industry" and move into non-offshorable jobs, but this may not mean they give up doing computer work, because as our economy continues to shift away from manufacturing and toward services, we may see . . . many non-portable IT "support" jobs created. . . . The upshot: Even though hundreds of thousands of programming and other IT jobs are likely to leave the U.S. over the next few decades, the vast majority of U.S. IT workers will survive, and possibly even prosper in the end, although they may have new employers and work in new fields.*

Quoting an editorial in the Silicon Valley's *San Jose Mercury News,* the *Post* article highlights how tricky it might be to track the consequences of offshoring for U.S. workers:

> *It is impossible to make a direct link between a job lost here and a job gained elsewhere. The economics of labor are more complex. First, the savings incurred by U.S. companies when they hire low-paid workers overseas help generate profits used to hire workers, or make new investments, here. Second, Valley companies sell nearly two-thirds of their products overseas, so the rise in overseas markets helps boost their fortunes.*

Offshoring may end up boosting the American economy overall. According to the McKinsey Global Institute, "at least two-thirds of the economic benefit from sending jobs offshore will flow back to the U.S. economy in the form of lower prices, expanding overseas markets for U.S. products, and fatter profits that U.S. companies can plow back into even more innovative businesses."[19]

---

19 Even within management ranks there is no consensus that offshoring makes sense long term, however. William J. Holstein, editor of *Chief Executive Magazine,* recently noted that direct labor costs represent a shrinking percentage of the overall costs of production for many businesses, making the savings from offshoring less significant. He also pointed to less tangible negative effects: "I don't think of many things as more intrinsic to the long-range thrust of a company, to the development of a company as a place of innovation and creativity . . . than the ability to design your own products and build your own products. You have to lovingly make them and care about their quality. It's difficult to wrap numbers around that and prove it, but I think it's central." "Does Outsourcing Cost More Than It Saves, "*New York Times,* June 6, 2004. Links to articles with similar import can be found at http://www.yourjobsisgoingtoindia.com, where a posted article included survey results of 100 executives representing New York's largest companies who were not finding offshoring to be as cost efficient as they had expected it would be. Linda Prospero, "New York Survey Finds Outsourcing Not a Panacea," *Reuters,* July 19, 2004.

Then there are the benefits of offshoring, both short and long range, overseas. In India, revenue from U.S. outsourcing shot up 50 percent through 2003 to $3.6 billion, and was predicted to do the same in 2004. Consider the positive effects as thousands of competent individuals begin to earn decent salaries in a country where half of the population lives on pennies a day. A critical mass of new wage earners materializes, each one in a position to produce significant benefits for themselves and their loved ones. As they rise into the middle class, they create markets for refrigerators, cars, computers, etc.—to the benefit of producers in India and elsewhere. And as this happens, there are cultural side effects. In her July 2004 *New Yorker* article, "The Best Job in Town," Katherine Boo writes about Office Tiger, a firm where college-educated Indians perform various types of data entry for U.S. companies:

> *[I]t was the possibility that one could rise up from a lowly position that had made Office Tiger one of the city's status employers, a firm whose workers were so pleased by their affiliation that they put it on their wedding invitations, just below their fathers' names. A foreign notion—that jobs should be distributed on the basis of merit—was amending the rules of society where employment had for millennia been allotted by caste, and great possibilities abounded.*[20]

The utilitarian weighing of pluses and minuses becomes complex, especially because it is not simply a matter of numerical quantifying. How to assess the harm—the emotional hurt and anxiety—that a person feels when they lose a well-paid job in a "jobless recovery"? How much weight to give the loss of a job in Dallas, Texas? Might that be a city with plenty of other options for IT professionals? Of the thousands of jobless in the United States, how can we know how each employee (and each family of each employee) will be affected? One person whose job has gone to Bangalore may be married to someone earning more than enough to comfortably support the family; another may be a single parent with no real backup. All of these immeasurables play havoc with neat measurement.

Although it is difficult to meaningfully assess comparative harms and benefits, our analysis does seem to suggest that IBM's decision is ethical, given all the actual and potential benefits of offshoring, and given that relatively few people are harmed by it. This outcome points to one of the problems with utilitarian theory. Consider another situation: The federal government requires that new drugs be tested on humans after they have been tested on animals. Drug companies must advertise widely and offer to pay as much as $250 a day to attract test subjects. But one company, Eli Lilly, does not have to advertise and pays only $85 per day, because most of its subjects are homeless alcoholics recruited through word-of-mouth from soup kitchens, shelters, and prisons across the country.[21] What happens when we run this arrangement through the utilitarian analysis? Where is the harm? New drugs are brought to market, benefiting the public—Lilly developed Prozac, for example. Cost savings may not be passed on to consumers, but they enhance corporate profits, benefiting the employees and stockholders. Alcoholism in volunteers does not skew the company's data, since those with severe liver disease will fail the initial screening process and be excluded in the first place. Even the test subjects are comfortable: interviews with those who have participated in Lilly's program describe themselves as happy with the "easy money" they can earn—as much as $4,500 when the testing continues over months. Is this an ethical outcome? Arguably it is, on utilitarian grounds. We might wonder if the homeless alcoholics are capable of making decisions that are truly voluntary. We may wonder if it is fair to use a small number of relatively desperate people in this way, even if the results benefit many more people.

---

20 July 5, 2004. More on the plus side: Some Indian companies have found that offshoring is creating a positive synergy, enabling them to do more hiring of their own—even in the United States. Infosys, an Indian firm with annual revenues over $1 billion, has set up its own consulting arm in America, and plans to hire 500 high-powered IT people within three years.

21 Laurie P. Cohen, "Stuck for Money," *Wall Street Journal,* November 14, 1996, pp. 1, 10.

Finally, consider the firemen rushing up into the World Trade Center towers on September 11, 2001. If we try to measure the overall usefulness of what they did, we come up empty. The towers fell; they were killed—the only "positive" would be the impossible-to-weigh fact of their heroism. Here, utilitarianism does not seem to "count" courage, or acts of pure altruism.

Deontology: Rights and Duties

In contrast to the utilitarian concern with maximizing social welfare, **deontological**[22] ethics is marked by steadfastness to universal principles—for example, respect for life, fairness, telling the truth, keeping promises—no matter what the consequences. At the core of this approach to making ethical choices is the understanding that moral action should be guided by certain overriding rights and duties.

The most famous deontological thinker, eighteenth-century German philosopher Immanuel Kant, believed that human beings could reason their way to a set of absolute rules for right behavior. A person should never lie, according to Kant, even when lying seems to produce a good result. Suppose someone running away from a murderer tells you where he is going to hide, and then the murderer rushes up to ask you where the first person went. Wouldn't this be a good time to lie? Kant would say there is never a good time, even in this example.

Moral behavior, then, is a matter of holding, without exception, to certain principles. Kant believed that each person has the right to be treated with respect as the equal of every other, and that each person has the corresponding duty to treat everyone else with respect as an equal.

He arrived at this by means of his **categorical imperatives.** The first of these states that a people should be willing to have the reasons for their actions become universal principles. That is, people should be willing to live in a world where an action they chose to take would be repeated for the same reasons whenever the same situation arose, even if they wound up on the receiving end of such actions.

Think of IBM and offshoring. If we apply Kant's first categorical imperative, the decision maker should ask: Would I want to live in a world where multinational corporations cut labor costs by replacing skilled white-collar U.S. employees with equally competent employees in other countries? Perhaps Mr. Palmisano would be comfortable with a universe of such behavior until it was his job that was eliminated. So, in Kantian terms, his action might not be an ethical one.

In another formulation of the categorical imperative, Kant states that we should have respect for the intrinsic value of other people, and not just use them as means to achieve our own purposes. By this Kant did not mean that people should *never* use other people at all. People "use" one another in mutually beneficial ways all the time. For example, in a typical contractual transaction, each party to the agreement gives something up to get what it wants. Each party "uses" the other to get what it wants; if you purchase gasoline, you "use" the oil company's product and it "uses" you to pay for it. Kant would have no objection here. Rather, he believed it was unethical for people to use others *only* as a means to accomplishing their own purposes, with no mutual benefit attached. So, if the oil company uses slave labor to build an oil pipeline in Southeast Asia, it would be violating this Kantian categorical. Here one party—the more powerful one—is able effectively to remove the free will of the other, to make it do what it wants the way a puppeteer would pulls a marionette's strings. What is lost—of great ethical value in deontology—is the right to autonomy, the right to make fully informed decisions for oneself about how to live one's life. Consider IBM and offshoring. Is IBM manipulating its U.S. engineers? Think of the way the company expects them to spend several weeks training their own replacements. This does appear to involve some manipulation. Are the engineers really in any position to make decisions for themselves?

In late 2003 the *Wall Street Journal* obtained IBM documents which indicated the company was also trying to conceal information as it offered pointers to its managers on how to "sanitize"

---

22 From the Greek *deon,* or duty.

the offshoring process. "The words 'offshore' or 'on-shore' should never be used," the company warned. "Do not be transparent regarding the purpose/intent" of offshore outsourcing. Assuming the *WSJ* report is accurate, if IBM was attempting to cover up what was really happening, we could say it was violating Kant's categorical imperative.

So far the deontological approach appears to be leaning against the decision to go ahead with the offshoring. There can be real murkiness within this moral framework, though, when it comes to interpreting those universal rights and duties that Kant considered "absolute"—beyond compromise. In the offshoring scenario, for example, how do we understand the duty to be "fair"? Sam Palmisano, we might say, is caught in a latticework of different versions of fairness. On the one hand, moving white-collar jobs away from well-educated American employees is unfair to them and to their families. But not to go through with the offshoring plan is arguably unfair to IBM's shareholders, who deserve the best possible return on investment, and to the well-qualified employees in India and their families. Recall how Palmisano himself used the concept of fairness when explaining offshoring:

> *China, India, South Korea, and other rapidly developing nations are replicating the structural advantages that historically have made the U.S. the center of innovation. We can't—shouldn't—regret improvements in other nations' competitiveness. Their people deserve to participate fully in the benefits of innovations.*

Another difficulty with deontology is the confusion created when different universal rights and duties crop up in the same ethical problem, and seem to conflict with one another. How does one decide which absolute value should prevail? These situations can get ugly. Consider the intensity of conflicting beliefs on the question of abortion. Both the right-to-life and the pro-choice factions are convinced that their points of view derive from natural rights; both embrace referents that they each consider beyond debate, beyond compromise. How do we resolve competing claims of this type? The "war on terror" presents us with other examples of clashing rights and duties, such as lengthy detentions under the USA Patriot Act of suspects not charged with any crime, proposals to allow the Pentagon to randomly monitor personal e-mail, and problems with prisoner abuse in Afghanistan and Iraq. Conflicting views here pit the right to life and safety against the right to privacy, the duty to be fair, and the categorical imperative to respect others—including those of Middle Eastern origin or beliefs—as equals.

Virtue Ethics: Habits of Goodness

For some critics, both the utilitarian and deontological frameworks are inadequate in a fundamental sense; while both set forth logical bases for deciding what might be called moral minima—the floor beneath which no one should drop in terms of ethical choices—they are silent on the concept of moral excellence. They also focus on the moral acceptability of *actions*. Virtue ethics, on the other hand, directs our attention to what human beings are capable of *being*, on how they can cultivate the habits of good character that will naturally lead them to their fullest potential.

This strand of thinking derives from Aristotle, who argued that people develop their moral abilities, called **virtues,** through training, by being repeatedly exposed to demonstrations of decent behavior within families and communities. We learn to become courageous, generous, just, honest, cooperative, and cheerful gradually, as we become habituated to living in social settings where these qualities are exhibited and valued. Ethics, then, is not a matter of teasing out the correct choice given a series of knotty dilemmas; it is instead a lifelong conditioning process. In harmonious relationship with their communities, people thrive, reaching the fullest unfolding of their potential, learning the habits that allow them to excel at everything they are capable of doing.

Consider this. Just before Christmas 1995, Malden Mills, the largest textile mill in New England, was ravaged by a severe fire. Its owner, Aaron Feuerstein, could have taken the insurance and retired comfortably. Instead, he decided to rebuild the plant. He also decided to draw down $1.5 million a week from accounts receivable to keep paying 1,400 idled workers, to give each of them a holiday bonus of $275, and to extend their health insurance for 90 days. Even before the fire, Feuerstein had a reputation for being committed to his employees and to the depressed Merrimac Valley. Bucking the trend, he would not move his business to the southern United States or to Asia. He paid what are reputedly the highest textile wages in the world: $12.50/hour. He called his labor force "the most valuable asset for the future." A devout Orthodox Jew, given to memorizing passages from Shakespeare and the Talmud, Feuerstein graduated from Yeshiva University in New York. Yet he did not explain his behavior in terms of his religious faith. As he put it, "I thought rebuilding was the right thing to do. And then people thought I did such a saintly thing. I did a normal thing."[23]

Feuerstein's reaction to the fire at his plant, which appears to be "knee-jerk" or instinctual, is more likely the result of training, of habits formed so long ago they seem automatic instead of deliberated—as in the virtue ethics model. We might recognize this kind of behavior formation in the firefighting community, where recruits learn total commitment to the saving of lives and to standing by one another as they do so. Of the 343 firefighters who died on September 11, 2001, 60 were not on duty, but responded to the alarm as if they were. It is unlikely that they took the time to measure the consequences of their actions, or to weigh conflicting rights and duties. They simply responded. It is difficult to imagine them assessing the pros and cons, or carefully matching their behavior to abstract rules.

Virtue ethics does raise its own set of questions, however. What does it mean to define moral character in term of one's community? What community? As the new millennium unfolds, too many Americans are living in family environments in which relatedness endures in spite of severe economic and psychological stresses. Half the population of the world lives in poverty. If children grow up in hardship, where the natural environment is harshly degraded and the social fabric is weakened, does the transmittal of virtuous habit become a luxury? If families cannot effectively teach virtue to their young, what are the alternatives? Schools? Religious communities? And when these are in such diverse forms—sometimes in sharp opposition—how do we judge which moral community is best? We call the men who flew into the World Trade Towers terrorists, but at some schools in the deserts of the Middle East, boys memorize the Koran and learn the heroic significance of being a suicide bomber. Which system can claim moral hegemony?

And what do we mean by community in the business context? Where is the community touchstone in the IBM scenario? To answer this question about a large company like IBM we must examine what is called "corporate culture." Here one scholar describes what that is meant by the culture of an organization:

> *The pattern of basic assumptions that a given group has invented, discovered, or developed in learning to cope with its problems of external adaptation and internal integration, and that have worked well enough to be considered valid, and, therefore, to be taught to new members as the correct way to perceive, think, and feel in relation to those problems.*[24]

More colloquially, a company might describe its culture as "the way we do things around here." In studies by Harvard corporate management guru John Kotter, as of 1987–1991, IBM was ranked at number 8 (out of the more than 2,300 firms studied) in terms of the strength of its

23 Malden Mills went bankrupt in early 2002. Feuerstein found himself fighting to buy his company back from General Electric, which had gained control of Malden Mills after the bankruptcy. In January 2004, after an intense lobbying campaign, the U.S. Export Import Bank agreed to provide $35 million in loan guarantees on more generous terms than had been expected, and Feuerstein was able to regain control of his company. In March 2002, during the bankruptcy period, he was interviewed by the CBS program "60 Minutes." When asked if, knowing how things played out, he would do the same thing he had done, Feuerstein answered, "Yes, it was the right thing to do. We are charged with acting not for the moment but rather for the larger goal."

24 Edgar H. Schein's definition. Professor Schein is a management expert at MIT.

corporate culture. We can see how it got that way by looking at its ascendancy under Thomas Watson, Sr., called "the greatest capitalist in history" by *Fortune Magazine*. It was Watson who named the company International Business Machines in 1924. Originally a manufacturer of tabulating machines, IBM would move into electric punch-card accounting and then into early computers. Though its growth in the 1920s and 1930s, Watson posted the motto "T-H-I-N-K" in all offices and required all his salesmen to wear blue suits and white shirts. An intense focus on sales and on a "buttoned-down" image would stay with the company through the twentieth century. Extremely charismatic, vain, and proud of his company, Watson built a corporate culture designed to instill loyalty and enthusiasm. IBM had company sports teams, family events, and was one of the first firms to offer workers paid vacations, life insurance, and survivor benefits. Through the Depression, even as sales weakened, it managed to avoid mass layoffs. By mid-century IBM had an unparalleled reputation as a fair employer. Salaries were paid continuously to employees serving in WWII, while the company used weapons manufacturing profits to help widows and orphans of IBM employees killed in the conflict.[25] The firm covered moving expenses for transferees, guaranteed minimum resale prices on their homes, and paid for retraining. Most impressively, during this time IBM guaranteed lifetime employment for all employees. For years Watson told his people: "The IBM is not merely an organization of men; it is an institution that will go on forever."

A powerhouse of the computer mainframe market, the company would continue to grow through the 1950s, 1960s, and 1970s, and "Big Blue" was ranked the most admired company in the United States year after year. By 1984 it was the most valuable company in the world, famous for consistent stock and dividend growth. It stood for the best of American big business—for its stockholders, its consumers, and its workforce.

Then—a crisis. As technology advanced, the computer market changed. Personal computers came to the fore, innovative upstarts like Apple entered the field, and by the 1990s IBM had suffered serious losses. As its stock lost half of its value, tens of thousands of workers were laid off. The very strength of IBM's culture was blamed, in part, for this catastrophe. As one commentator put it:

> *The company, it seemed, had become the epitome of an overgrown, anonymous, monopolistic, bureaucratic monster—outmatched in marketing and technology by swifter, nimbler competitors; too big to change, it appeared destined to collapse under its own ungainly weight.*[26]

Although it recovered profitability by the late 1990s, IBM would never recover its former image as a benevolent giant, with a strong, paternalistic and compassionate corporate environment.

Returning to our question: If virtue ethics is a matter of moral characteristics ingrained within a community, and if CEO Sam Palmisano attends to the culture of his corporate community, he would be guided by this ethical code, touted today by IBM:

---

25 There were less salutary aspects to IBM's activities during this period. Thomas Watson accepted a medal from the Nazi regime in 1937, an event featured in Edwin Black's recent book, *IBM and the Holocaust.* Although IBM was not alone in its willingness to do business with Hitler, Black tells how crucial its role was. IBM's German subsidiary, acting "with the knowledge of its New York headquarters," supplied the Nazis with a punch card system that organized, tabulated, and analyzed population data, making possible mass deportations and executions. From Black's introduction:

> [D]azzled by its own swirling universe of technical possibilities, IBM was self-gripped by a special amoral corporate mantra: If it can be done, it should be done. To the blind technocrat, the means were more important than the ends. The destruction of the Jewish people became even less important because the invigorating nature of IBM's technical achievement was only heightened by the fantastical profits to be made at a time when bread lines stretched across the world.

26 Steven Kotok, *St. James Encyclopedia of Popular Culture,* 2002 Gale Group. See http://articles.findarticles.com/p/articles/mi_g1epc/is_tov/ai_2419100611.

The IBM Principles

1. The marketplace is the driving force behind everything we do.
2. At our core, we are a technology company with an overriding commitment to quality.
3. Our primary measures of success are customer satisfaction and shareholder value.
4. We operate as an entrepreneurial organization with a minimum of bureaucracy and a never-ending focus on productivity.
5. We never lose sight of our strategic vision.
6. We think and act with a sense of urgency.
7. Outstanding, dedicated people make it all happen, particularly when they work together as a team.
8. We are sensitive to the needs of all employees and to the communities in which we operate.

As you review these guidelines, and Sam Palmisano's speech to the Council on Competitiveness, can you sense whether the culture of IBM supports offshoring?

What forces inside a company determine the type of culture that develops inside it? What forces outside a company might influence that process? Are there *business* virtues?[27] What might they be?

Ethic of Care

> *The elusive mystery of women's development lies in its recognition of the continuing importance of attachment in the human life-cycle . . . while masculine development litany intones the celebration of separation, autonomy, individuation and natural rights.*
>
> —Carol Gilligan

> *I hope I would have the guts to betray my country before I would betray my friend.*
>
> —E.M. Forster, *"What I Believe,"* 1938

The ethical theories we have looked at so far assume that a decision about the right thing to do is ultimately a private decision, made by an individual in isolation. Whether using their intellectual powers or responding to trained habit, people act as autonomous beings, as free agents in this process. A different approach to ethics assumes that people are deeply connected to one another in webs of relationships, and that ethical decisions cannot be made outside the context of those relationships. This alternative view holds that ethics is essentially a matter of nurturing and reinforcing the ties we have with one another. This has become known as the "ethic of care," as it is based on caring for others.

The notion of an ethic of care was developed by feminist theorists such as Carol Gilligan, a psychologist who studied moral development. Her research led her to believe that men and women approach moral issues from different perspectives. While most men have an individualistic focus on abstract rights and justice, women tend to focus on caring, on supporting human

27 Robert C. Solomon thinks so. He has written extensively about Aristotle and business. Included in his list of business virtues are friendliness, charisma, fairness, heroism, style, toughness, and wittiness. See his book, *A Better Way To Think About Business* (New York: Oxford University Press, 1999).

interconnectedness—an approach that Gilligan saw as undervalued, and which she characterized as "a different voice." Over time this understanding has shifted: rather than a split between male versus female ethics, it is thought that there are two different approaches to moral problem solving that can be accessed by either men or women.

In the following reading Leslie Bender, Professor of Law at Syracuse University, suggests a feminist reframing of negligence law and the "no duty to rescue" rule. She begins by referencing Gilligan's work.

A PRIMER OF FEMINIST THEORY AND TORT

Leslie Bender[28]

A Feminist Ethic of Caring and Interconnectedness

Gilligan recognized that there are two thematic approaches to problem solving that generally correlate with gender, although she makes no claims about the origin of the difference. . . . When she asked what characterizes the different methods for resolving and analyzing moral dilemmas, Gilligan found that the "right" answers (according to the traditionally formulated stages of moral development) involve abstract, objective, rule-based decisions supported by notions of individual autonomy, individual rights, the separation of self from others, equality, and fairness. Often the answers provided by women focus on the particular contexts of the problems, relationships, caring (compassion and need), equity, and responsibility. For this different voice "responsibility" means "response to" rather "obligation for." The first voice understands relationships in terms of hierarchies or "ladders," whereas the "feminine" voice communicates about relationships as "webs of interconnectedness. . . ."

While an ethic of justice proceeds from the premise of equality—that everyone should be treated the same—an ethic of care rests on the premise of nonviolence—that no one should be hurt.

Negligence Law: A Feminist Ethic of Care and Concern as a Basis for the Standard of Care

Our traditional negligence analysis asks whether the defendant met the requisite standard of care to avoid liability.

In tort law we generally use the phrase "standard of care" to mean "level of caution." How careful should the person have been? What precautions do we expect people to take to avoid accidents? We look to the carefulness a reasonable person would exercise to avoid impairing another's rights or interest. If a defendant did not act carefully, reasonably, or prudently by guarding against foreseeable harm, she would be liable. The idea of care and prudence in this context is translated into reasonableness, which is frequently measured instrumentally in terms of utility or economic efficiency.

When the standard of care is equated with economic efficiency or levels of caution, decisions that assign dollar values to harms to human life and health and then balance those dollars against profit dollars and other evidences of benefit become commonplace. . . . The risk of their pain and loss becomes a potential debit to be weighed against the benefits or profits to others. The result has little to do with care or even with caution, if caution is understood as concern for safety.

What would happen if we understood the "reasonableness" of the standard of care to mean "responsibility" and the "standard of care" to mean the "standard of caring" or "consideration of

28 38 *J. Leg. Educ.* 3 (1988), pp. 63–68.

another's safety and interests?" What if, instead of measuring carefulness or caution, we measured concern and responsibility for the well-being of others and their protection from harm? Negligence law could begin with Gilligan's articulation of the feminine voice's ethic of care—a premise that no one should be hurt. . . .

"No Duty" Cases

One of the most difficult areas in which questions of duty and the standard of care arise is the "no duty to rescue" case. The problem is traditionally illustrated by the drowning-stranger hypothetical and the infamous case of *Yania v. Bigan*.

How would this drowning-stranger hypothetical look from a new legal perspective informed by a feminist ethic based upon notions of caring, responsibility, interconnectedness, and cooperation?

If we put abstract reasoning and autonomy aside momentarily, we can see what else matters. In defining duty, what matters is that someone, a human being, a part of us, is drowning and will die without some affirmative action. That seems more urgent, more imperative, more important than any possible infringement of individual autonomy by the imposition of an affirmative duty.

If we think about the stranger as a human being for a moment, we may realize that much more is involved than balancing one person's interest in having his life saved and another's interest in not having affirmative duties imposed upon him in the absence of a special relationship. . . .

The drowning stranger is not the only person affected by the lack of care. He is not detached from everyone else. He no doubt has people who care about him—parents, spouse, children, friends, colleagues; groups he participates in—religious, social, athletic, artistic, political, educational, work-related; he may even have people who depend upon him for emotional or financial support. He is interconnected with others. If the stranger drowns, many will be harmed. It is not an isolated event with one person's interests balanced against another's. When our legal system trains us to understand the drowning-stranger story as a limited event between two people, both of whom have interests at least equally worth protecting, and when the social ramifications we credit most are the impositions on personal liberty of action, we take a human situation and translate it into a cold, dehumanized algebraic equation. We forget that we are talking about human death or grave physical harms and their reverberating consequences when we equate the consequences with such things as one person's momentary freedom not to act. . . .

Bender goes on to write:

> *The duty to act with care for another's safety, which under appropriate circumstances would include an affirmative duty to act to protect or prevent harm to another, would be shaped by the particular context.*

This is one of the hallmarks of the Ethic of Care, a willingness to be concerned with the particulars of a situation, and from there an interest in discovering compromise—creative ways to find a solution that might work for all the stakeholders.

How might the IBM offshoring decision look through the lens of the ethic of care? The strongest relational connection in the scenario must be between IBM and its employees. Some of them may have survived the deep job cuts of the 1990s, but even if not, they were probably well aware of the effort the company had recently made to turn itself around and become profitable again. What happens, though, when market pressures interfere with established relationships? How can we reconcile these apparently opposite forces, the urge to do the right thing for the people you know best, and the imperatives of business? The ethic of care suggests that the specific context of offshoring at IBM receive attention. Who are these people about to lose their positions? How can IBM ease their transition? From what we know of the facts—that many employees will be told to train their replacements for weeks, and that most cannot expect to be rehired anytime soon—these are a harsh set of particulars.

The ethic of care might lead Sam Palmisano to investigate *how* the offshoring process will be managed at IBM. If the process itself cannot be reversed, then the way it is to be implemented might be changed. What can IBM do to soften the blow? Are there any resources to retrain and/or rehire workers, to assist them in job searches? Open communication can be very important, both for laid-off employees and for local communities. The ethic of care suggests that creative efforts be made, not just for the sake of "damage control," but because there is value in relationships that have been nourished over time.

Ironically, putting relationships first can end up positively affecting the bottom line. Take Malden Mills, for instance. When the plant burned down, Aaron Feuerstein perceived the tragedy as one for a network of stakeholders, his family, his employees, and the surrounding community. As he responded by including all of those affected in his plans for rebuilding, the network responded in turn. Donations came in from local businesses; customers such as Patagonia and Lands' End pledged support and promised to wait for their Polartec; citizens from neighboring New Hampshire donated Christmas trees and toys for idled workers. Once the rebuilt factory was in operation, productivity rose 25 percent. But insurance had covered only three-quarters of the $400 million cost of rebuilding the plant, and by late 2001, Malden Mills faced bankruptcy. Just before Christmas that year though, the employees agreed to give up their personal paid days in 2002—saving the company $500 million—and to keep their salaries frozen through 2003. Massachusetts senators have promised to fight for more Defense Department contracts for the company, and Feuerstein is hopeful that Malden Mills will survive. "Consumers send me beautiful, compassionate and interesting letters every day with checks in them," he told his cheering employees, "They want us to win."[29]

Problems arise with the ethic of care, though, as with the other theories. Sometimes there are several relationships at stake, and it becomes difficult to rank and care for them. The ethic of care can be troubling in another way. Suppose you have the responsibility of recommending someone from your work team for promotion. One of the team members is your friend. She's a single parent and could really use the extra income. But she isn't the most deserving person in your group. If you are fair, you'll recommend the best person for the job—but the ethic of care might push you to recommend your friend, as care deteriorates into favoritism.

Why Ethical Theory?

Having explored several approaches to ethics, we have seen potential flaws in each. We may feel unsettled by the journey, uncertain how useful it has been. Yet this unresolved aftertaste may be exactly appropriate. There are no easy answers at the intersection of law, ethics, and business. The best we can hope for may be a reflective approach, combining one or more frameworks to reach several possible solutions, and then comparing the solutions to see if they "agree."

Ideally, familiarity with these theories will support you in at least two ways as you face business dilemmas in the future. First, the models for analysis can spark creative thinking, as you brainstorm ways of handling the dilemmas. Second, they offer you a means of explaining your decisions to others. Explanations can be useful. Suppose you are working for the pesticide manufacturer that cannot sell certain of its products in the United States because they are hazardous by U.S. standards, yet plans to sell them overseas. Knowing the theoretical basis for ethical decision making could help you understand your own position, and help you articulate it to your superiors, your co-workers, and those who report to you in the organization. There is a familiar "language" in the business world for most decision making: cost-benefit analysis. Ethical theory offers you another language, making you "bilingual" in complex situations.

---

29 "At Malden Mills, One Good Turn Deserves Another," *Christian Science Monitor,* December 19, 2001.

Chapter Problems

1. **Internet Assignment:**
   a. Although in the United States there is no general "duty to rescue," other countries do have such requirements. In France, Germany, and Russia, for example, bystanders may not legally ignore a fellow citizen who needs help in an emergency. What can you find about laws that require rescue in other parts of the world?
   b. Several states in the United States, including Wisconsin, Vermont, and Minnesota, also have such legislation. Many states require certain persons to report specific kinds of crimes, most often child abuse. Find and compare two state statutes.
   c. While rescue is not required in the United States, it is encouraged by the existence in every state of "Good Samaritan" laws, protecting people who assist in an emergency from liability in most circumstances. Locate the Good Samaritan law in your home state. Describe it in your own words. Does it protect those who do not have medical training?

2. Tidmore called his Auto Club for help in changing a flat tire. The Club sent a tow truck driver, Fiss, who carelessly jacked up the car so that it rolled off the jack, trapping her hand between the tire and the car body. When Fiss screamed, "Get it off me!" Tidmore lifted the car twice from the left rear bumper, injuring his shoulder and groin. (a) Does Tidmore have any basis for a lawsuit? Explain. (b) Suppose Tidmore had ignored Fiss's distress. Would there have been any basis for a legal claim against Tidmore? How ethical would that have been? (c) Suppose the Auto Club had refused to send aid to Tidmore. On what basis might he have made a claim? *Tidmore v. Automobile Club of Southern California,* 78 Cal.Rptr.2d 836 (Ct. of Appeal, 1999).

3. How much responsibility should a college have to protect its students from crime? Suppose college officials knew that there had been a number of assaults on or attempted rapes of female students in a certain area on campus, where a stairway was hidden by foliage and trees. Suppose they chose not to publicize these incidents and had not warned students in any way. Then another attack occurred, and the male assailant used a *modus operandi* similar to the one that had been used previously on the same stairway. Should the college be held liable for the victim's injuries? Check *Peterson v. San Francisco Community College District,* 685 P.2d 1193 (Calif. 1984). **Internet Assignment:** Find more recent cases involving college or university defendants being sued for on-campus crime. Is there a trend for or against holding them responsible? What are the arguments pro and con?

4. In the summer of 2004 the *New York Times* reported that the United States was losing its once dominant position in basic scientific research. The proportion of articles by U.S. experts in the best physics journals, for example, had dropped from 61 percent in 1983 to 29 percent in 2003. While in India, excellent science and math programs turn out some 40,000 computer science graduates annually, American science education–and education generally–is in a relatively weakened state. Today the U.S. high school drop-out rate is higher than it was in the 1970s. What might these figures suggest about offshoring of U.S. jobs? Should U.S. corporations respond? If so, how?

5. In late 2004, after some ten years of taking tax breaks and union concessions, Maytag closed its refrigerator manufacturing plant in Galesburg, Illinois (population 33,000) and relocated it in Mexico. The company had received more than $10 million from the town and the state. Galesburg District Attorney Paul Mangieri wanted to sue the firm to reclaim

tax money that the town would have spent on its schools: "We gave Maytag these incentives and they accepted them. We did it on faith and trust." Yet other locals believed such a strategy would backfire, driving away other potential business interests. "Maytag's leaving town has devastated our community," car dealer Jeff Klinck pointed out, "But I don't think any good comes from revenge. We want to move forward, not back." **Internet Assignment:** A final decision as to whether to sue Maytag was made in November 2004. What happened? Find out if any other communities in the United States went to court to catch up with corporations which had benefited from tax abatements but ended up closing down operations for more cost-efficient locations. See: *Township of Ypsilanti v. General Motors*, 1993 Wl 132385 (Michigan Cir. Ct.) and *Ypsilanti v. GM*, 506 N.W.2d 556 (Michigan Court of Appeals, 1993).

6. In mid-2004, a carpenter from Durham, North Carolina found out that his potentially fatal heart condition required surgery that would cost $200,000. As one of the 45 million uninsured American citizens, he could not afford it. So—he outsourced the job to India, flying to Delhi for a heart valve replacement that would cost only $10,000, including airfare and a side trip to the Taj Mahal! Approximately 150,000 so called "medical tourists" traveled to India for similar reasons in 2004, a growing number from the United States. They are taking advantage of lower costs and quality services—everything from airport pickups to private hospital rooms to treatments that include yoga and other traditional forms of healing. Overall, India's health care system is poor, but there is an increasing number of private medical facilities there which can provide services as good or better than those in the developed world. For example, while the death rate for heart bypass at Escorts Heart Institute and Research Centre in Delhi was just 0.8 percent, the 1999 death rate for the same procedure at the New York hospital where former president Bill Clinton had bypass surgery was 2.35 percent.[30] **Internet Assignment:** What can you find out about the trend to outsource high end services like these? Is it on the up tick? Is it expanding to include other services which require advanced professional training?

7. As companies increasingly do business around the world, they often must decide how to behave in developing countries where the legal system may be more lax than that of their home base. Some believe in the principle "when in Rome, do as the Romans do," justifying activities abroad that are illegal and unacceptable at home. Others argue that transnational companies must use their influence to nudge other businesses and nations towards higher standards, even attempting to make a difference in the way foreign governments handle human rights. In the 1980s many companies stopped doing business in South Africa, in an effort to pressure that government to end apartheid. In 1992 Levi Strauss withdrew operations from Burma, saying "it is not possible to do business [there] without directly supporting the military government and its pervasive violations of human rights." In 1994 Reebok and Liz Claiborne pulled out of Burma; in 1995 Eddie Bauer and Amoco also withdrew, citing growing opposition in the United States to company involvement there. Wal-Mart, Ikea, Crate and Barrel, Jones New York, and (under pressure from activists) Ames Department Stores have promised to stop sourcing products from Myanmar (formerly Burma). In 1998, after many strikes and negative press reports, Nike announced plans to improve conditions in Indonesia. It offered education and business loans to workers' families, promised to improve air quality in its plants, bringing them in line with U.S. OSHA standards, agreed to open its plants to inspections, and raised wages by 40 percent. Rejected at a 1998 shareholders' meeting was one proposal that Nike spend about 2 percent of its yearly advertising budget to double the wages of its workers in Indonesia, which would have provided them with what critics claim is a living wage.

Where should companies draw the line in their activities abroad? If they decide to go in the direction of challenging the moral climate, is that a form of "cultural imperialism?"

30 John Lancaster, "Surgeries, Side Trips for Medical Tourists," *Washington Post Foreign Service,* October 21, 2004.

How wide should they spread their net of rescue in these settings? Is it enough to raise their own employees' wages, or should they also be concerned with the behavior of their suppliers? Should they try to improve infrastructure (education, environment)? Should they try to influence government policies? What about boycotting products from an "outlaw" state?

8. Plato believed that the rulers of the ideal society should be paid no more than four times more than the lowliest member of that society. In the United States today, executives not uncommonly earn 700 times what the ordinary employees do. And corporate leaders are often recompensed heftily even after leading their companies into disaster. Senior executives and directors of 25 large companies that collapsed between 1999 and 2001 walked away with roughly $3.3 billion in salary, bonuses, and proceeds from the sale of stock options. Business reporter Cassidy traces the use of stock options as a form of executive compensation back to the "stockholder value credo," the notion that CEOs should act as agents for shareholders, and that a smart way to make them keep shareholders' best interests in focus would be to tie their financial rewards to their firm's stock performance. Stock options, granting the right to buy stock in the company at a certain price at a certain future date, became increasingly popular between 1980, when they were given to fewer than one-third of the CEOs of publicly traded companies, and 1997, when 92 of the top 200 CEOs received options with an average value of $31 million.[31] Suddenly these executives had very big incentives to drive stock prices up—at least temporarily, so they could realize enormous profits. The cascade of corporate scandals that included Enron was, experts now agree, at least in part caused by greedy senior executives who wanted to get the numbers up by any means necessary.

Analyze stock options and executive compensation with the ethical toolkit. How would Milton Friedman want to recompense corporate executives? How would a utilitarian? A deontological thinker? What would a virtue ethicist have to say about executive compensation? What would be the response of the ethic of care?

9. Although Aaron Feuerstein denied that he consciously referenced his religious training when he chose to rebuild Malden Mills, many people believe that religion is a crucial source of ethical guidance.[32] Think of the ethical dilemmas you have faced. Is religion important for you in dealing with them? Do you think religion should be the point of reference for the teaching of business ethics? Why or why not?

Stakeholder Ethics Role Play

Guidelines in Appendix C

Name the stakeholders in this business ethics dilemma. Discuss possible choices for Nash in the light of ethical theory.

31 John Cassidy, "The Greed Cycle," *The New Yorker,* 64, September 23, 2002.

32 In fact, the Jewish rabbinical tradition calls for no work to be done on the Sabbath, but there is an exception allowed for rescue in an emergency.

Desperate Air[33]

Desperate Air Corporation (DAC) flies routes along the U.S. East Coast. DAC acquired a number of hotels and undeveloped properties five years ago as part of a short-lived diversification strategy. DAC has recently experienced substantial losses, has a negative cash flow, and bankruptcy looms as a possibility unless high labor costs can be reduced and consumer confidence restored.

Benton Williams has just been brought in as CEO to revitalize DAC. Williams began by cutting back on middle management and by placing a one-year moratorium on hiring MBAs. Middle managers terminated by DAC and other airlines are having a tough time finding equivalent jobs.

DAC owns a large, undeveloped oceanfront property on the east coast of Florida. Williams directs George Nash, DAC's Vice President of Real Estate, to find a buyer for the property to generate badly needed cash. After some effort, Nash identifies Fledgling Industries, a relatively new developer of retirement villas, as a good prospect. Fledgling is interested in finding a property on which it could build a complex of high-rise retirement condos featuring elaborate walking trails and outside recreational facilities.

DAC had conducted a full environmental audit of the property six months earlier and had discovered no problems. A copy of this report was given to the Fledgling representative, who also walked over the property and discovered no problems. The representative asked, "Anything I should know about?" Nash replied, "No problems."

As the negotiations progressed with Fledgling, Nash was approached by a longtime friend at DAC, Laura Devitt, who told him that there was now some highly toxic waste on the property. She said she heard this might be true through the rumor mill at the firm and that she had been curious enough to check things out. Walking around on the property one day, she had found several partially buried metal containers marked DANGER/BIOHAZARD. RADIOACTIVE MEDICAL WASTE. The containers were rusted where they were exposed; two were cracked and their liquid contents was seeping onto the ground. Laura told Nash she wanted him to know about this because she was worried that innocent people could be hurt if the sale went through.

Nash contacted Williams, but before he could mention the containers to him, Williams interrupted and told him it was vital that the sale closed and that it be done as soon as possible. Nash consulted with a DAC lawyer who told him that under Florida law it is not necessary to disclose the existence of hazardous waste on commercial property as long as there hasn't been a fraudulent misstatement about the condition of the property.

Nash was troubled. Should he mention the hazardous materials to the Fledgling representative before he closed the sale? He knew Fledgling had been considering some other similar properties and Nash thought that if he mentioned the toxic spill problem Fledgling would probably not go through with the sale. At the least, disclosure could delay the sale for months while the spill was investigated and potential liability problems considered. Nash figured that he would be unlikely ever to deal with Fledgling again regarding future real estate deals because DAC did not own any other properties that fit Fledgling's business needs.

The question of whether to close the sale immediately bothered Nash enough that he talked to his wife about it, and then prayed about what to do.

33 Written by Thomas W. Dunfee, The Wharton School, University of Pennsylvania.

The Duty of Loyalty: Whistleblowing

Chapter 2

The men the American people admire most extravagantly are the most daring liars; the men they detest most violently are those who try to tell them the truth.

— H.L. Mencken

The woods were filled with smart people at Enron, but there were really no wise people, or people who could say "this is enough."

— John Olson, energy industry analyst

What matters . . . is not what a person is, but how closely his many personae mesh with the organizational ideal; not his willingness to stand by his actions, but his agility in avoiding blame; not what he stands for, but whom he stands with in the labyrinths of his organization.

— Robert Jackall, *Moral Mazes: Bureaucracy and Managerial Work*

This chapter is about people who feel morally driven to call attention to problems they see at work, at the risk of disturbing the status quo, alienating others, and bringing damaging repercussions upon themselves and their families. It is about being caught between conflicting loyalties—to one's employer, and to one's conscience—the dilemma faced by a person who must decide whether to become a "whistleblower."

Whistleblowers are people who decide to report unethical or illegal activities under the control of their employers. They may be working for private companies, nonprofit organizations, or for the government. They may disclose information inside or outside their organizations—to supervisors, regulators, or to the media. What unites all whistleblowing is the urge to bring a disturbing situation to light, the urge to bring about some corrective change. The motivating issues range from airline, nuclear, and environmental safety to the kinds of improper accounting practices that brought down Enron and Worldcom.

This chapter explains the legal doctrine known as **employment-at-will,** which gives employers broad discretion to fire employees "for a good reason, a bad reason, or no reason at all." Although twentieth-century exceptions to this rule have blunted its harshness, the cases demonstrate that whistleblowers often experience retaliation and have little recourse under the common law. Statutes passed in all 50 states provide some protection for employees, but wide variation exists among them; we will look at one of them. We turn to the Sarbanes-Oxley Act—passed in the wake of financial and accounting scandals—to assess the degree to which it protects corporate whistleblowers. And we consider how First Amendment freedom of speech has been interpreted by the Supreme Court to give public employees limited rights to blow the whistle.

We examine the complex concept of loyalty in the workplace—the crosscurrents of loyalty to an employer, to a professional code, to a personal moral compass. In the aftermath of the collapse of Enron, we ask why those with "watchdog" responsibilities, such as accountants and securities analysts, allowed their independent judgment to be compromised.

Whistleblowing can wreak havoc. Those who insist that bad news must be heard may damage the reputations of their employers; they risk having their own careers destroyed. In this chapter we see that in spite of the costs, we may yet appreciate the role of the dissenters in serving the public interest when the checkpoints of our systems fail us.

In 1993, Dr. Donn Milton was hired by a nonprofit scientific research organization, IIT Research Institute (IITRI), to oversee a contract with the federal government. By 1995, his responsibilities widened as he was promoted to vice president of IITRI's Advanced Technology Group. Like other nonprofits, IITRI had been established with a public mission and was classified as tax exempt. As Dr. Milton discovered, however, the organization was "abusing its tax-exempt status by failing to report . . . taxable income generated by the substantial portion of . . . business that did not constitute scientific research in the public interest."

DONN MILTON, DR., V. IIT RESEARCH INSTITUTE

Fourth Circuit Court of Appeals, 1998
138 F.3d 519

WILKINSON, Chief Judge.

Milton voiced his concerns to IITRI management, to no avail. In 1995, after similar allegations by a competitor, IITRI initiated an internal examination of the issue. In connection with this inquiry, IITRI received an outside opinion letter concluding that the IRS could well deem some of IITRI's projects unrelated business activities and that the income from these activities was likely taxable. Milton urged the President of IITRI, John Scott, to take action in response to the letter, but Scott refused. Milton raised the issue with IITRI's Treasurer, who agreed that IITRI was improperly claiming unrelated business income as exempt income and promised to remedy the problem after Scott's then-imminent retirement. However, this retirement did not come to pass. Finally, in November 1996, when Scott falsely indicated to IITRI's board of governors that IITRI had no problem with unrelated business income, Milton reported the falsity of these statements to Lew Collens, Chairman of the Board of IITRI, and informed Collens of the opinion letter.

On January 1, 1997, Scott called Milton at home and informed him that he had been relieved of his Group Vice President title and demoted to his previous position as supervisor of TSMI. On February 12, 1997, Milton's attorney contacted IITRI about the demotion, alleging that it was unlawful retaliation for informing management of IITRI's unlawful practices. Two days later . . . Milton received a letter from Collens terminating his employment with IITRI.

[The general legal rule is that employees can be fired with or without cause, but there is an exception: under the tort of "wrongful discharge," an employee can argue that the firing clearly conflicts with "public policy."]

Milton filed suit against IITRI . . . for wrongful discharge. . . .

Maryland has recognized a "narrow exception" to the general rule of at-will employment: "discharge may not contravene a clear mandate of public policy." Maryland courts have found such a mandate only in limited circumstances: (1) "where an employee has been fired for refusing to violate the law . . ."and (2) "where [an] employee has been terminated for exercising a specific legal right or duty. . . ."

Milton makes no claim that he was asked to break the law. He had no role in preparing IITRI's submissions to the IRS and no responsibility for their content. Instead, Milton claims he was fired for fulfilling his fiduciary duty as a corporate officer to inform IITRI's Board of activities injurious to the corporation's long-term interests. . . . Maryland law does provide a wrongful discharge cause of action for employees who are terminated because they perform their "statutorily prescribed duty." However, this exception to the norm of at-will employment has been construed narrowly by the Maryland courts and is not available in Milton's case. . . . [I]n *Thompson v. Memorial Hospital,* the . . . court . . . held that, because a hospital employee was not chargeable with the hospital's regulatory duty to report misadministration of radiation, he did not state a claim for wrongful discharge when he was fired for making such a report. By contrast, in *Bleich v. Florence Crittenden Services* (1993), the court recognized that an educator terminated for filing a report of child abuse and neglect, as she was explicitly required to do by Maryland law, did state a claim for wrongful discharge. These cases indicate that, for Milton to recover, it is not enough that *someone* at IITRI was responsible for correcting its tax filings or that the corporation may have been liable for tax fraud. This responsibility was never Milton's, nor did he face any potential liability for failing to discharge it, so his claim fails.

Milton argues that his fiduciary obligations as an officer of IITRI supply the legal duty that was missing in *Thompson* and that supported the cause of action in *Bleich.* But in fact Milton labored under no "specific legal duty," to report IITRI's tax fraud to the Board. He points to no statute or other legal source that imposes on him a specific duty to report, and the broad fiduciary obligations of "care and loyalty" he alleges are simply too general to qualify as a specific legal duty that will support the claim that his discharge violates a "clear mandate of public policy." Recognizing whistleblower protection for every corporate officer fired in the wake of a disagreement over an employer's business practices would transform this "narrow exception" into a broad one indeed.

This search for a specific legal duty is no mere formality. Rather it limits judicial forays into the wilderness of discerning "public policy" without clear direction from a legislative or regulatory source

[Judgment of dismissal affirmed.]

• QUESTIONS •

1. In legal terms, why did Milton lose?

2. The court here expresses concern that, if Dr. Milton were permitted to win, it would open a "Pandora's box," with "every corporate officer fired in the wake of a disagreement over an employer's business practices" a potential successful plaintiff. Reframe this argument. What is at stake here for employers?

3. This case is about conflicting loyalties. Make a list of the stakeholders (those primarily affected by the situation). Now describe the various links of loyalty—who felt responsible to whom? Analyze the situation using the ethical theories in Chapter 1. Did Milton do the right thing? How does the decision to fire him look through the lens of ethical theory?

4. In late 2001, the seventh largest corporation in the United States, Enron Corp., filed for the largest bankruptcy in U.S. history. The Texas energy conglomerate suffered a complete and sudden collapse—but not before a handful of its executives sold more than $1 billion of their shares. Meanwhile, thousands of Enron employees whose retirement plans were tied to the value of the company's stock were barred from selling, and had to watch their savings drain away. Enron had been overstating its profits by nearly $600 million over five years, in statements that its auditors, Arthur Anderson, approved. Within a series of complicated off-the-books partnerships, the company was able to conceal major losses, making Enron stock continue to seem a safe bet. Such "creative accounting" is often legal and not unusual; many businesses use these techniques to enhance their perceived financial health.

   A few months before Enron laid off more than 4,000 employees and filed for bankruptcy, Sherron Watkins, a 42-year-old vice president of corporate development at Enron, wrote to CEO Kenneth Lay, warning that improper accounting practices threatened to bring

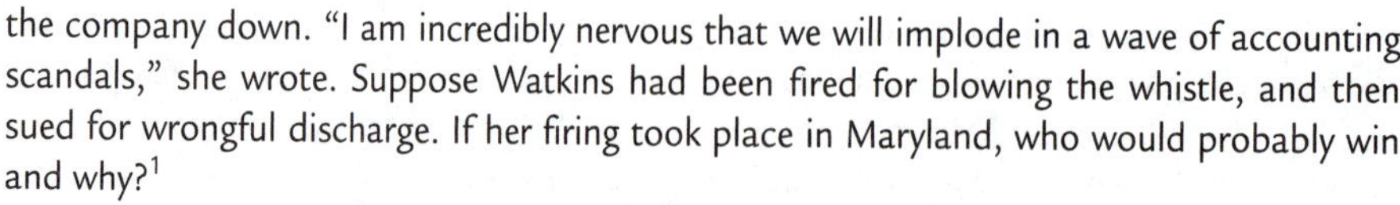

the company down. "I am incredibly nervous that we will implode in a wave of accounting scandals," she wrote. Suppose Watkins had been fired for blowing the whistle, and then sued for wrongful discharge. If her firing took place in Maryland, who would probably win and why?[1]

5. Should it make any difference how the whistle is blown—internally or externally? Dr. Milton tried to discuss his concerns inside his organization with the president, the treasurer, and eventually with the board of directors. Former Enron executive Maureen Casteneda gave an interview to ABC News in late January 2002, in which she described ongoing, large-scale document shredding at the company. When might it be ethically appropriate to blow the whistle (a) internally; (b) to the enforcing authorities, such as SEC regulators; and (c) to the media?

EMPLOYMENT-AT-WILL

> *I am in charge here. My word is law and your wishes mean nothing. If I dislike anything about you—the way you tie your shoes, comb your hair or fart, you're back in the streets, get it?*
>
> – Charles Bukowski, *Ham and Rye*

Employment-at-will is a relatively recent common law development. It gives employers unfettered power to "dismiss their employees at will for good cause, for no cause, or even for cause morally wrong, without being thereby guilty of a legal wrong."[2] The theory crystallized at the time of the industrial revolution in the United States when it became advantageous for employers to have the ability to bring on or to shed employees, depending on the fluctuating demands of the market.

The economic philosophy of laissez-faire provided theoretical support for employment-at-will. Its legal underpinnings consisted mainly of "freedom of contract," the idea that individuals are free to choose how to dispose of what they own, including their labor, as they see fit, and that the voluntary contractual promises they make are legitimately enforceable.

Employment-at-will is a "two-way street," allowing both employers and employees to sever their relationship without cause. As the Supreme Court put it in a 1908 case striking down early labor legislation:

> *The right of an employee to quit the service of the employer, for whatever reason, is the same as the right of the employer, for whatever reason, to dispense with the services of such employee.*[3]

Practically speaking, however, while a business may suffer temporary disruption when an employee quits, it is not uncommon for an employee to be devastated by dismissal; this has been

1 As a matter of fact, Watkins was not fired for sending the seven-page memo. The company decided to "investigate" her concerns, hiring for that purpose Vinson & Elkins, the same law firm that helped set up some of the transactions Sherron Watkins was challenging. Enron told this firm to limit its review, and not to examine the underlying accounting of the partnerships. Not surprisingly, the report concluded that the accounting procedures were "legitimate." Meanwhile, Mr. Lay and others continued to assure their employees about the stock values, although at the same time these executives were selling their own holdings.

2 *Payne v. Webster & Atlantic R.R. Co.*, 81 Tenn. 507, 519–20 (1884).

3 *Adair v. United States*, 208 U.S. 161, 174–75 (1908). This quote is reminiscent of Anatole France, who wrote: "The Law, in its majestic equality, forbids the rich, as well as the poor, to sleep under the bridges, to beg in the streets, and to steal bread."

described as the "organizational equivalent of capital punishment." While an employer faces the cost of finding and training a replacement, a dismissed employee faces greater, multifaceted costs. Most obvious is the loss of present income. There is, with loss of seniority and retirement benefits, future economic hardship.[4] The employee may be considered too old or too specialized to be hired anew, or may have to move to look for work. Interviewing for a new position may be an uphill battle with an uneven employment history. And in the case of a whistleblower, the ex-employer may have spread the word that he was a troublemaker; he may be blackballed throughout an entire industry.

Whatever the actual circumstances of a dismissal, it is not easy for employees to keep their self-respect intact. Isolated, having been taken off the "team," they may be anxious over an uncertain future.

Exceptions to the Rule

The earliest adjustments to the doctrine of employment-at-will were made as workers fought for the right to organize and form unions. In 1935, they were guaranteed these rights, and not long after, the U.S. Supreme Court announced that an employer could not use employment-at-will as a means of "intimidat[ing] or coerc[ing] its employees with respect to their self organization."[5] In other words, employees could not be fired as punishment for attempting to organize themselves into unions. Although at this writing only a fairly narrow slice of the U.S. workforce is unionized,[6]collective bargaining agreements typically cut against employment-at-will, protecting workers from being fired except for "good cause."

Beginning in the 1960s, federal civil rights laws created remedies against employers who fire workers because of their race, national origin, color, religion, sex, age, or disability.[7] In the 1970s and 1980s, federal and state statutes included protection from retaliation for employees who report violations of environmental or workplace safety laws, for example.[8] And in 2002 Congress passed corporate fraud reform legislation with whistleblower provisions protecting those who report financial misconduct in publicly traded companies. This law is known as Sarbanes-Oxley, or SOX.

The common law, too, has evolved to soften the harsher effects of employment-at-will. In some states, courts have set limits by means of contract law. There are two main approaches: (1) to imply a promise of "good faith and fair dealing" in the contract of employment, or (2) to imply contractual terms (not to dismiss except for good cause, for instance) from an employer's handbook, policy statement, or behavior. However, only a handful of states use the first approach. And, although the second approach has been recognized by most states, employers are on notice, and unlikely to make any express or implied promises that might be interpreted to cut

---

4 The National Bureau of Economic Research reports that those who change employers twice at ages 41 and 51 will reduce their pensions by 57 percent.

5 *NLRB v. Jones & Laughlin Steel Corp.*, 301 U.S. 1, 45–46 (1937).

6 According to the Bureau of Labor Statistics, for the past 20 years, union membership in the United States has been declining steadily. In 2003, under 13 percent of the U.S. workforce was unionized. http://www.bls.gov/news.release/union2.nr0.htm

7 For example, *Civil Rights Act of 1964*, 42 U.S.C. Sec. 2000e-2a (1976); *Age Discrimination in Employment Act of 1967*, 29 U.S.C. Sec. 623(a) (1976); *Americans with Disabilities Act*, 42 U.S.C. Sec. 12112(b)(5)(A). Civil rights laws are discussed more fully in Chapter 4. Most states have similar laws, and some of these go further than the federal statutes, protecting employees against discrimination on the basis of family status or sexual orientation, for example.

8 Federal laws include the *Toxic Substances Control Act*, 15 U.S.C. Sec. 2622(a) (1988); *Occupational Safety and Health Act*, Sec. 660(c)(1) (1988); *Water Pollution Control Act*, 33 U.S.C. Sec. 1367(a) (1988); *Safe Drinking Water Act*, 42 U.S.C.A. Sec. 300j-9(i)(1); *Energy Reorganization Act*, 42 U.S.C. Sec. 5851(a)(3) (1982); *Solid Waste Disposal Act*, 42 U.S.C. Sec. 6971(a) (1982); *Comprehensive Environmental Response, Compensation, and Liability Act*, Sec. 99610(a); *Clean Air Act* Sec. 7622(a).

against employment-at-will. In fact, they are more likely to promise the reverse, as in the following paragraph, recommended for inclusion in employment handbooks for law firms:

> *Your employment with the Firm is voluntarily entered into and you are free to resign at any time. Similarly, the Firm is free to conclude an employment relationship with you where it believes it is in the Firm's best interest at any time. It should be recognized that neither you, nor we, have entered into any contract of employment, express or implied. Our relationship is and will be always one of voluntary employment "at will."*[9]

Tort law has provided another means of making inroads into employment-at-will, offering a plaintiff the chance to convince a jury to award substantial money damages. For the past 35 years, most U.S. state courts have been shaping the tort of "wrongful discharge," a firing that contradicts "public policy"—in other words, a dismissal that undermines what is beneficial to society in general.

The problem has been how to define public policy.[10] As with contract law, this exception to employment-at-will has been developing simultaneously in different states, producing a crazy quilt of different rules. Most state courts are comfortable looking to the legislature—to laws that have already been passed—for guidance. For instance, they will protect from retaliation employees who have simply exercised their legal rights to file a worker's compensation or a sexual harassment claim,[11] or who have merely performed their legal duty to serve on a jury.[12] And, if employers put their employees "between a rock and a hard place," expecting them to participate in breaking the law or be fired, most courts would again see a violation of public policy, triggering the tort of wrongful discharge.[13] For example, suppose you were an employee of Arthur Andersen, and your supervisor told you to delete computer files related to the government investigation of Enron. Once the SEC subpoenas were issued, destroying those files would amount to obstruction of justice. So, if you refused to destroy then and were fired for that, you would succeed in a suit for wrongful discharge.

But some states do not recognize the tort at all. In New York, for instance, while an employer could be fined for refusing to allow an employee time for jury service, the employee could not then sue for wrongful discharge.[14] As we have seen, other jurisdictions, such as Maryland, are conservative in identifying violations of public policy.

Inconsistencies like these complicate the risk for whistleblowers. They have noticed a situation at work that troubles them. It may be illegal; it may be "merely" unethical; it may be one they are expected to participate in; it may be one they are expected to ignore; it may involve a statute that carries protection for whistleblowers; it may not. Whistleblowers react first, and must worry about the reach of "public policy" later. Characteristically unable to remain passive in the face of what they believe is wrong, they speak out. Research reveals that whistleblowers are typically long-term, highly loyal employees who feel strongly that their companies should do the right thing, and who tend to disclose to outsiders only after trying to make headway

9 Victor Schachter, "The Promise of Partnership," *National Law Journal,* October 8, 1984, p. 15.

10 Public policy is generally understood to mean that which benefits society as a whole. But this is a fuzzy concept indeed, and very likely to mirror the personal and political beliefs of individual judges. As one commentator put it, "Public policy is the unruly horse of the law."

11 *Frampton v. Central Indiana Gas Co.,* 297 N.E.2d 425 (Indiana 1973). Plaintiff fired for filing a worker's compensation claim.

12 *Reuther v. Fowler & Williams,* 386 A.2d 119 (Pa. 1978). Plaintiff fired for jury service.

13 For example, in *Petermann v. Int'l. Brotherhood of Teamsters,* 344 P.2d 25 (1969), plaintiff was instructed by his employer to lie when testifying before a legislative investigatory committee. He refused and was fired. The court allowed his suit for wrongful discharge, describing public policy as "that principle of law which holds that no citizen can lawfully do that which has a tendency to be injurious to the public or against the public good." *Id.* at 27.

14 *Di Blasi v. Traffax Traffic Network,* 681 N.Y.S.2d 147 (N.Y. App. Div 1998).

internally.[15] The whistleblower profile is such that, if nothing is done to respond to their internal complaints, they often feel compelled to disclose to authorities outside the company—even to the media. In any case, they are taking the chance that they will not be covered under the wrongful discharge exception to employment-at-will. As one commentator put it, effectively, those who blow the whistle "very often must choose between silence and driving over a cliff."[16]

The Mayor: *We shall expect you, on further investigation, to come to the conclusion that the situation is not nearly as pressing or as dangerous as you had at first imagined.*

Dr. Stockmann: *Oh! You expect that of me, do you?*

The Mayor: *Furthermore we will expect you to make a public statement expressing your faith in the management's integrity and in their intention to take thorough and conscientious steps to remedy any possible defects.*

Dr. Stockmann: *But that's out of the question, Peter. No amount of patching or tinkering can put this matter right; I tell you I know! It is my firm and unalterable conviction—*

The Mayor: *As a member of the staff you have no right to personal convictions.*

Dr. Stockmann: (With a start): *No right to—?*

The Mayor: *Not as a member of the staff—no! As a private individual—that's of course another matter. But as a subordinate in the employ of the Baths you have no right to openly express convictions opposed to those of your superiors.*

Dr. Stockmann: *This is too much! Do you mean to tell me that as a doctor—a scientific man—I have no right to—!*

The Mayor: *But this is not purely a scientific matter; there are other questions involved—technical and economic questions.*

Dr. Stockmann: *To hell with all that! I insist that I am free to speak my mind on any and all questions!*

— Henrik Ibsen, *An Enemy of the People*

In the next case, the plaintiff is a doctor caught in a conflict between what her employer expects her to do, and what she feels is in line with her professional ethical responsibilities.

PIERCE V. ORTHO PHARMACEUTICAL CORP.

Supreme Court of New Jersey, 1980
417 A.2d 505

POLLOCK, J.

This case presents the question whether an employee-at-will has a cause of action against her employer to recover damages for the termination of her employment following her refusal to continue a project she viewed as medically unethical. . . .

Ortho specializes in the development and manufacture of therapeutic and reproductive drugs. Dr. Pierce is a medical doctor who was first employed by Ortho in 1971 as an Associate Director of Medical Research. She signed no contract except a secrecy agreement, and her

---

15 Marlene Winfield, "Whistleblowers as Corporate Safety Net," in *Whistleblowing: Subversion or Corporate Citizenship?* 21, 22 (New York, NY: St. Martin's Press, 1994).

16 Joseph Henkert, "Management's Hat Trick: Misuse of 'Engineering Judgment' in the Challenger Incident," 10 *J. Bus. Ethics* 617, 619 (1991).

employment was not for a fixed term. She was an employee-at-will. In 1973, she became the Director of Medical Research/Therapeutics, one of three major sections of the Medical Research Department. Her primary responsibilities were to oversee development of therapeutic drugs and to establish procedures for testing those drugs for safety, effectiveness, and marketability. Her immediate supervisor was Dr. Samuel Pasquale, Executive Medical Director.

In the spring of 1975, Dr. Pierce was the only medical doctor on a project team developing loperamide, a liquid drug for treatment of diarrhea in infants, children, and elderly persons. The proposed formulation contained saccharin. Although the concentration was consistent with the formula for loperamide marketed in Europe, the project team agreed that the formula was unsuitable for use in the United States.[17] An alternative formulation containing less saccharin might have been developed within approximately three months.

By March 28, however, the project team, except for Dr. Pierce, decided to continue with the development of loperamide. That decision was made apparently in response to a directive from the Marketing Division of Ortho. This decision meant that Ortho would file an investigational new drug application (IND) with the Federal Food and Drug Administration (FDA), continuing laboratory studies on loperamide, and begin work on a formulation. . . .

Dr. Pierce . . . continued to oppose the work being done on loperamide at Ortho. On April 21, 1975, she sent a memorandum to the project team expressing her disagreement with its decision to proceed. . . . In her opinion, there was no justification for seeking FDA permission to use the drug in light of medical controversy over the safety of saccharin.

Dr. Pierce met with Dr. Pasquale on May 9 and informed him that she disagreed with the decision to file an IND with the FDA. . . . She concluded that the risk that saccharin might be harmful should preclude testing the formula on children or elderly persons, especially when an alternative formulation might soon be available. . . .

After their meeting on May 9, Dr. Pasquale informed Dr. Pierce that she would no longer be assigned to the loperamide project. On May 14, Dr. Pasquale asked Dr. Pierce to choose other projects. . . . She felt she was being demoted, even though her salary would not be decreased. Dr. Pierce [submitted a] letter of resignation. . . . [This is called "constructive discharge," the legal equivalent of being fired.]

Dr. Pierce claimed damages for the termination of her employment. Her complaint alleged: "The Defendant, its agents, servants and employees requested and demanded Plaintiff follow a course of action and behavior which was impossible for Plaintiff to follow because of the Hippocratic oath she had taken, because of the ethical standards by which she was governed as a physician, and because of the regulatory schemes, both federal and state, statutory and case law, for the protection of the public in the field of health and human well-being, which schemes Plaintiff believed she should honor. . . ."

Under the common law, in the absence of an employment contract, employers or employees have been free to terminate the employment relationship with or without cause. . . .

Commentators have questioned the compatibility of the traditional at-will doctrine with the realities of modern economics and employment practices. . . . The common law rule has been modified by the enactment of labor relations legislation [prohibiting employers from firing workers because they organize or join a union]. . . .

Recently [many] states have recognized a common law cause of action for employees-at-will who were discharged for reasons that were in some way "wrongful." The courts in those jurisdictions have taken varied approaches, some recognizing the action in tort, some in contract. Nearly all jurisdictions link the success of the wrongful discharged employee's action to proof that the discharge violated public policy. . . .

17 The group's toxicologist, for instance, noted that saccharin was a "slow carcinogen"; it had produced benign and malignant tumors in test animals after 17 years. The harm it might cause would be obvious only after a long period of time, and "any intentional exposure of any segment of the human population to a potential carcinogen is not in the best interest of public health of the Ortho Pharmaceutical Corporation."

In recognizing a cause of action to provide a remedy for employees who are wrongfully discharged, we must balance the interests of the employee, the employer, and the public. Employees have an interest in knowing they will not be discharged for exercising their legal rights. Employers have an interest in knowing they can run their businesses as they see fit as long as their conduct is consistent with public policy. The public has an interest in employment stability and in discouraging frivolous lawsuits by dissatisfied employees.

Although the contours of an exception are important to all employees-at-will, this case focuses on the special considerations arising out of the right to fire an employee-at-will who is a member of a recognized profession. One writer has described the predicament that may confront a professional employed by a large corporation: Consider, for example, the plight of an engineer who is told that he will lose his job unless he falsifies his data or conclusions, or unless he approves a product which does not conform to specifications or meet minimum standards . . . and the predicament of an accountant who is told to falsify his employer's profit and loss statement in order to enable the employer to obtain credit.

Employees who are professionals owe a special duty to abide not only by federal and state law, but also by the recognized codes of ethics of their professions. That duty may oblige them to decline to perform acts required by their employers. However, an employee should not have the right to prevent his or her employer from pursuing its business because the employee perceives that a particular business decision violates the employee's personal morals, as distinguished from the recognized code of ethics of the employee's profession.

We hold that an employee has a cause of action for wrongful discharge when the discharge is contrary to a clear mandate of public policy. The sources of public policy include legislation; administrative rules, regulations or decisions; and judicial decisions. In certain instances, a professional code of ethics may contain an expression of public policy. However, not all such sources express a clear mandate of public policy. For example, a code of ethics designed to serve only the interests of a profession or an administrative regulation concerned with technical matters probably would not be sufficient. Absent legislation, the judiciary must define the cause of action in case-by-case determinations. . . . [U]nless an employee-at-will identifies a specific expression of public policy, he may be discharged with or without cause.

[B]efore loperamide could be tested on humans, an IND had to be submitted to the FDA to obtain approval for such testing. The IND must contain complete manufacturing specifications, details of pre-clinical studies [testing on animals] which demonstrate the safe use of the drug, and a description of proposed clinical studies. The FDA then has 30 days to withhold approval of testing. Since no IND had been filed here, and even giving Dr. Pierce the benefit of all doubt regarding her allegations, it is clear that clinical testing of loperamide on humans was not imminent.

Dr. Pierce argues that by continuing to perform research on loperamide she would have been forced to violate professional medical ethics expressed in the Hippocratic oath. She cites the part of the oath that reads: "I will prescribe regimen for the good of my patients according to my ability and my judgment and never do harm to anyone." Clearly, the general language of the oath does not prohibit specifically research that does not involve tests on humans and that cannot lead to such tests without governmental approval.

We note that Dr. Pierce did not rely on or allege violation of any other standards, including the "codes of professional ethics" advanced by the dissent. Similarly, she did not allege that continuing her research would constitute an act of medical malpractice or violate any statute. . . .

The case would be far different if Ortho had filed the IND, the FDA had disapproved it, and Ortho insisted on testing the drug on humans. . . .

[I]mplicit in Dr. Pierce's position is the contention that Dr. Pasquale and Ortho were obliged to accept her opinion. Dr. Pierce contends, in effect, that Ortho should have stopped research on loperamide because of her opinion about the controversial nature of the drug.

Dr. Pierce espouses a doctrine that would lead to disorder in drug research. . . . Chaos would result if a single doctor engaged in research were allowed to determine, according to his or her individual conscience, whether a project should continue. An employee does not have a right to continued employment when he or she refuses to conduct research simply because it would contravene his or her personal morals. An employee-at-will who refuses to work for an employer in answer to a call of conscience should recognize that other employees and their employer might heed a different call. However, nothing in this opinion should be construed to restrict the right of an employee-at-will to refuse to work on a project that he or she believes is unethical. . . .

Under these circumstances, we conclude that the Hippocratic oath does not contain a clear mandate of public policy that prevented Dr. Pierce from continuing her research on loperamide. To hold otherwise would seriously impair the ability of drug manufacturers to develop new drugs according to their best judgment.

The legislative and regulatory framework pertaining to drug development reflects a public policy that research involving testing on humans may proceed with FDA approval. The public has an interest in the development of drugs, subject to the approval of a responsible management and the FDA, to protect and promote the health of mankind. . . .

[Appellate division judgment for the plaintiff is reversed and the case is remanded.]

PASHMAN, J., dissenting.

The majority's analysis recognizes that the ethical goals of professional conduct are of inestimable social value. By maintaining informed standards of conduct, licensed professions bring to the problems of their public responsibilities the same expertise that marks their calling. The integrity of codes of professional conduct that result from this regulation deserves judicial protection from undue economic pressure. Employers are a potential source of this pressure, for they can provide or withhold until today, at their whim, job security and the means of enhancing a professional's reputation. Thus, I completely agree with the majority's ruling that "an employee has a cause of action for wrongful discharge when the discharge is contrary to a clear mandate of public policy" as expressed in a "professional code of ethics."

The Court pronounces this rule for the first time today. One would think that it would therefore afford plaintiff an opportunity to seek relief within the confines of this newly announced cause of action. By ordering the grant of summary judgment for defendant, however, the majority apparently believes that such an opportunity would be an exercise in futility. I fail to see how the majority reaches this conclusion. There are a number of detailed, recognized codes of medical ethics that proscribe participation in clinical experimentation when a doctor perceives an unreasonable threat to human health. Any one of these codes could provide the "clear mandate of public policy" that the majority requires.

Three other points made by the majority require discussion. . . . The first is the majority's characterization of the effect of plaintiff's ethical position. It appears to believe that Dr. Pierce had the power to determine whether defendant's proposed development program would continue at all. This is not the case, nor is plaintiff claiming the right to halt defendant's developmental efforts. [P]laintiff claims only the right to her professional autonomy. She contends that she may not be discharged for expressing her view that the clinical program is unethical or for refusing to continue her participation in the project. She has done nothing else to impede continued development of defendant's proposal; moreover, it is undisputed that defendant was able to continue its program by reassigning personnel. Thus, the majority's view that granting doctors a right to be free from abusive discharges would confer on any one of them complete veto power over desirable drug development, is ill-conceived.

The second point concerns the role of governmental approval of the proposed experimental program. In apparent ignorance of the past failures of official regulation to safeguard against pharmaceutical horrors, the majority implies that the necessity for administrative approval for human testing eliminates the need for active, ethical professionals within the drug industry. But we do not know whether the United States Food and Drug Administration (FDA) would be aware of the safer alternative to the proposed drug when it would pass upon defendant's application for the more hazardous formula. The majority professes no such knowledge. We must therefore assume the FDA would have been left in ignorance. This highlights the need for ethically autonomous professionals within the pharmaceutical industry. . . .

The final point to which I must respond is the majority's observation that plaintiff expressed her opposition prematurely, before the FDA had approved clinical experimentation. Essentially, the majority holds that a professional employee may not express a refusal to engage in illegal or clearly unethical conduct until his actual participation and the resulting harm is imminent. This principle grants little protection to the ethical autonomy of professionals that the majority proclaims. Would the majority have Dr. Pierce wait until the first infant was placed before her, ready to receive the first dose of a drug containing 44 times the concentration of saccharin permitted in 12 ounces of soda?

I respectfully dissent.

• QUESTIONS •

1. The *Pierce* majority announces a new "cause of action in New Jersey for wrongful discharge when the discharge is contrary to a clear mandate of public policy." Such a mandate, it goes on to say, could be found in a professional code of ethics, yet Dr. Pierce had failed to identify one in her complaint with enough specificity. How does the dissenting judge respond to this point? Do Dr. Pierce's professional medical ethics resemble any of the ethical theories in Chapter 1?

2. What is the procedure for obtaining FDA approval of a new drug? Do you agree with the majority that when Dr. Pierce stopped working on the loperamide project the risk to human test subjects was not "imminent"?

3. Surveying the interests at stake in the case, the *Pierce* majority states:

   > *[W]e must balance the interests of the employee, the employer, and the public. Employees have an interest in knowing they will not be discharged for exercising their legal rights. Employers have an interest in knowing they can run their businesses as they see fit as long as their conduct is consistent with public policy. The public has an interest in employment stability and in discouraging frivolous lawsuits by dissatisfied employees.*

   Are there any important stakeholder interests not mentioned here?

4. The dissent mentions "past failures of official regulation to safeguard against pharmaceutical horrors." There have been more recent failures. Since 2000, the cholesterol-lowering Baycol caused muscle tissue breakdown, the diet drug Fen-Phen led to lung and heart disorders, antidepressants like Zoloft and Prozac caused some children to commit suicide, and the painkiller Vioxx was found to double the risk of heart attack. In each instance, there was evidence that the pharmaceutical firms had evidence suggesting serious problems with drugs that were in development or had already been brought to market. By the time Merck recalled Vioxx, in late 2004, there were congressional hearings underway. A doctor in the FDA's Office of Drug Safety, David Graham, told Congress that Vioxx may have caused as many as 55,000 deaths. Graham charged his agency with being "incapable of protecting America" against dangerous drugs. By November 2004 the American Medical Association was recommending that all clinical testing be made publicly available, and that a new regulatory body, independent of the FDA, be created to focus on the safety of drugs already approved for use. **Internet Assignment:** (a) Find out what happened to calls for overhaul of the FDA. (b) Fearing his job was at risk, Graham sought help from the whistleblower support organization, the Government Accountability Project. Find out what happened.

5. The regulatory apparatus of our government depends on ethical behavior on the part of corporations. It depends on corporations to generate accurate data for agencies such as the FDA, the FAA, and the EPA to use in analyzing safety risks. The government's resources are limited; it cannot perform all the necessary tests itself, but must rely on companies to do their

own tests, and to share all relevant results—particularly when those results point to safety problems. Business decisions to hold back adverse information from regulators can be both fatal and expensive. Consider the Bridgestone/Ford debacle of 2000. In the 1970s, the National Highway Traffic Safety Administration (NHTSA) collected safety data directly from a network of repair shops, but after the budget cuts of the 1980s, this agency began relying on data generated by industry. NHTSA also made reports of foreign car recalls voluntary. In 1999, both Bridgestone and Ford knew the Wilderness tire/Ford Explorer combo was dangerous; there had been dozens of tread separations and SUV rollover deaths abroad, particularly in hot climates. The two companies planned a recall in Saudi Arabia, but then made a joint decision not to alert NHTSA, fearing this would lead to a recall in the United States. By late 2000, after SUV rollovers caused more than 100 fatalities in the United States, Bridgestone was forced to recall more than 6 million tires, and both companies faced countless lawsuits.

The dissent in *Pierce* mentions the need to protect "professional autonomy." What does this phrase mean? What connection might professional autonomy have with the U.S. safety regulatory scheme?

6. In 1986, responding to the *Pierce* decision of its supreme court, the New Jersey legislature adopted *The Conscientious Employee Protection Act,*[18] shielding from retaliation employees who object to, or refuse to participate in, "any activity, policy or practice which the employee reasonably believes to be incompatible with a clear mandate of public policy concerning the public health, safety or welfare." What would have been the likely outcome had Dr. Pierce sued under this new law? **Internet Assignment:** By 2000, every state in the United States had adopted whistleblower protection statutes of some type. Locate one such law from your home state. Under what circumstances are whistleblowers protected? Are private sector as well as government employees covered? Does coverage under the statute exclude the possibility of suing in tort?

Statistics on Whistleblowers

> *Physical courage is remarkably widespread in [the U.S.] population. . . . Moral and intellectual courage are not in nearly so flourishing a state, even though the risks they entail—financial or professional disadvantage, ridicule, ostracism—are comparatively minor. . . . These forms of courage suffer from the disadvantage of requiring new definitions continually, which must be generated out of individual perception and judgment. They threaten or violate loyalty, group identity. . . They are, intrinsically, outside the range of consensus.*
>
> – Marilynne Robinson

Who are these people who blow the whistle? Are they informers, troublemakers, tattletales, or are they, as one sociologist has described them, "ethical resisters,"[19] brave dissenters, the watchdogs of the general good? Do they deserve to be ostracized or treated like heroes?

The next reading describes a survey of whistleblowers.

---

18 N.J.S.A. 34:19-1 et. seq.

19 Myron Peretz and Penina Migdal Glazer, *The Whistleblowers* (New York: Basic Books, 1989).

Survey of Whistleblowers Finds Retaliation but Few Regrets

C. H. Farnsworth[20]

Workers who reveal waste, fraud and abuse can expect retaliation, financial loss and high emotional and physical stress, according to a survey by two Maryland researchers.

Donald R. Soeken, a psychiatric social worker, and his wife, Karen L. Soeken, a statistician, found that whistleblowers win little more than increased self-respect. But they also found, in the first systematic effort to determine what actually happens to whistleblowers, that most of them would do it again.

A whistleblower who worked in a nuclear power plant wrote: "This has turned out to be the most frightening thing I have ever done. But it has been the most satisfying. I think I did the right thing, and I have caused some changes to be made in the plant."

Their study shatters a perception of whistleblowers as misfits. The average whistleblower in the survey was a 47-year-old family man who was employed seven years before exposing wrongdoing. Most were driven by conscience.

As a group, the whistleblowers were moderately religious. They tended to assume that the best could be achieved by following universal moral codes, which guided their judgments.

After exposing misdeeds, all those in the private sector reported they were dismissed. Because of Civil Service administrative appeals, it is more difficult to dismiss Government workers, but 51 percent of these whistleblowers reported they were no longer with the same agency.

One out of every five of those in the survey reported they were without a job, and 25 percent mentioned increased financial burdens on the family as the most negative result of their action. 17% lost their homes.

Fifty-four percent of the whistleblowers said they were harassed by peers at work. Mrs. Soeken said, "We got replies like 'People made fun of me,' or 'People who I thought were my best friends stopped associating with me. . . .'"

A Government worker said, "don't do it unless you're willing to spend many years, ruin your career and sacrifice your personal life." 15% view their subsequent divorce a result of their whistleblowing activity. 10% report having attempted suicide. Others admit having considered it.

But an engineer in private industry replied more positively: "Do what is right. Lost income can be replaced. Lost self-esteem is more difficult to retrieve."

Another Federal employee confided, "Finding honesty within myself was more powerful than I expected."

The whistleblowing experience took a high toll in physical and emotional health, the survey showed. 80% reported physical deterioration, with loss of sleep and added weight as the most common symptoms. 86% reported negative emotional consequences, including feelings of depression, powerlessness, isolation, anxiety and anger.

Montana's Statute on Wrongful Discharge

In 1987, Montana passed the following law, the first in the nation to override employment-at-will.

20 *New York Times,* February 21, 1988.

WRONGFUL DISCHARGE FROM EMPLOYMENT ACT[21]

Purpose

This part sets forth certain rights and remedies with respect to wrongful discharge. Except as limited in this part, employment having no specified term may be terminated at the will of either the employer or the employee on notice to the other for any reason considered sufficient by the terminating party.

Definitions

In this part, the following definitions apply:

(2) "Discharge" includes a constructive discharge . . . and any other termination of employment, including resignation, elimination of the job, layoff for lack of work, failure to recall or rehire, and any other cutback in the number of employees for a legitimate business reason.

(3) "Employee" means a person who works for another for hire. The term does not include a person who is an independent contractor. . . .

(5) "Good cause" means reasonable job-related grounds for dismissal based on a failure to satisfactorily perform job duties, disruption of the employer's operation, or other legitimate business reason. The legal use of a lawful product by an individual off the employer's premises during nonworking hours is not a legitimate business reason. . . .

(7) "Public policy" means a policy in effect at the time of the discharge concerning the public health, safety, or welfare established by constitutional provision, statute, or administrative rule.

Elements of Wrongful Discharge

A discharge is wrongful only if:

(1) it was in retaliation for the employee's refusal to violate public policy or for reporting a violation of public policy;

(2) the discharge was not for good cause and the employee had completed the employer's probationary period of employment; or

(3) the employer violated the express provisions of its own written personnel policy.

Remedies

(1) If an employer has committed a wrongful discharge, the employee may be awarded lost wages and fringe benefits for a period not to exceed 4 years from the date of discharge, together with interest thereon. . . .

(2) The employee may recover punitive damages otherwise allowed by law if it is established by clear and convincing evidence that the employer engaged in actual fraud or actual malice in the discharge of the employee [for refusing to violate public policy or for reporting a violation of public policy.]

Exemptions

This part does not apply to a discharge:

(1) that is subject to any other state or federal statute that provides a procedure or remedy for contesting the dispute. Such statutes include those that prohibit discharge for filing complaints, charges, or claims with administrative bodies or that prohibit unlawful discrimination

21 39 *Montana Code Annotated* Chapter 2, Part 9. Puerto Rico has been the only other U.S. jurisdiction that has passed equivalent legislation.

based on race, national origin, sex, age, handicap, creed, religion, political belief, color, marital status, and other similar grounds.

(2) of an employee covered by a written collective bargaining agreement or a written contract of employment for a specific term.

Preemption of Common-Law Remedies

Except as provided in this part, no claim for discharge may arise from tort or express or implied contract.

• QUESTIONS •

1. How would the *Milton* case have been decided had this law been in effect in Maryland? How would Dr. Pierce have fared under it?
2. What parts of this law seem to benefit employees? Employers?
3. The state laws protecting whistleblowers vary enormously, but none of them protect whistleblowers who turn to the media first. Why do you think that is so? Does that seem like sound policy to you? Does it encourage or discourage ethical behavior?

Global View: U.S., U.K., Japan

The United States stands virtually alone in the world, in that more than 200 million of its workers can be fired almost at the unfettered discretion of their employers. Nearly all of the developed nations who are our global competitors have laws protecting against wrongful discharge, establishing special tribunals where such claims can be adjudicated. Protective statutes exist in more than 60 countries, such as Japan, Canada, and the European Community.

The International Labor Organization of the United Nations (ILO) has a mandate to identify global labor problems, and to come up with standards—called "conventions"—for addressing them. Although compliance with its standards is voluntary, they do carry moral authority. A convention of the ILO calls upon all its members to adopt laws that would protect against wrongful discharge. The representative from the United States was the only one to vote against that convention.

While there is no general whistlebower legislation at the federal level in the United States, other nations have acted to protect whistleblowers. The United Kingdom adopted a law in 1998 after several widely publicized scandals. One involved the drowning of four children because of inadequate safety equipment and training at a recreational facility. Management had fired an employee who had complained about the conditions there. In a second incident, 18,000 elderly investors lost their savings when an investment firm collapsed. The U.K. legislation, the *Public Interest Disclosure Law,* protects employees with a reasonable, good faith belief that an illegality, a "danger to health or safety," or "damage to the environment" is occurring. Three types of disclosures are protected: internal (to the employer), regulatory (to the government) and wider (to the media or police). An employee must have escalating certainty about wrongdoing to be protected for these ascending levels of whistleblowing.

In Japan too, legislation was prompted by scandal, by widespread disillusionment with both corporate and governmental abuse of power. In 1999 the world's second worst nuclear accident happened when workers at a Japanese uranium processing plant mixed nuclear fuel in buckets, an extremely unsafe practice mandated by the facility's operating manual. In 2000 Japan's most famous dairy allowed unhygienic conditions to fester, and thousands were food poisoned. In 2002, during the mad cow scare, Nippon Meat Packers mislabeled product to get government subsidies. And in 2003 the public learned that, for 30 years, while it disowned responsibility for fatal car accidents, Mitsubishi was hiding evidence of safety defects. In each instance, insiders who complained were ostracized. Japanese culture values group stability and harmony ("wa") very highly, and whistle-blowing there is subversive in a deep way. One proverb says: "The nail that sticks up gets hammered." (When salesman Hiroaki Kushioka discovered evidence that his company was participating in price-fixing, he told his bosses, and was told to keep quiet. He then went to the regulators, and the media. Once the controversy died down, the company transferred Kushioka to a remote subsidiary, where his office was a room without a working telephone. For 27 years, he was given only humiliating tasks, like snow shoveling and weeding, and not a single promotion.) But cascading scandals finally led the Japanese Diet to act. As of June 2006, employees will be protected if they report illegal behavior to their superiors or to the government. They are not protected, however, when the behavior they report is unethical yet legal, or when they report to the media or to consumer groups. And while whistleblowers can sue to redress retaliation, the new law does not mete out fines for corporate wrongdoing. Critics worry that Japan has passed toothless legislation.

If you could write model legislation for all American employees, what would it look like? Would you make any change in employment-at-will? Would you provide protection for whistleblowers?

THE QUESTION OF LOYALTY

Mere blind obedience to every wish of the person who is the object of loyalty is not loyalty; it is a perversion of loyalty. There is no moral value to it, since it is not something that is morally due. A loyal Nazi is a contradiction in terms.

— Edwards, ed., *Encyclopedia of Philosophy,* p. 98

Tell tale tit
Your tongue shall be slit
And all the dogs in town
Shall have a little bit.

— Children's rhyme

Ms. Watkins is no whistleblower in the conventional sense. She was and is a loyal employee.

— Rep. James Greenwood (R., Pa.) Chairman of House Energy and Commerce Committee investigating the collapse of Enron Corp.

At the crux of the whistleblower's decision is the question of loyalty, and of divided loyalties. An employee like Dr. Pierce who blows the whistle experiences opposite pulls—allegiance to the employer and allegiance to a professional code of values. The same might be said of Sherron Watkins, the most well-known whistleblower associated with Enron Corporation.

Although Ms. Watkins was not the first or the only person inside Enron who raised concerns about shady accounting practices employed by the firm's CFO, she was the one in the spotlight at the time Enron collapsed. In the following article, law professor Leonard Baynes takes up the example of Sherron Watkins as a means of discussing the difficult position of the corporate insider who chooses to blow the whistle. He goes on to ask whether the Sarbanes-Oxley Act, the new federal law designed to prevent future Enrons, adequately addresses the quandary of the corporate whistleblower.

Just Pucker and Blow: An Analysis of Corporate Whistleblowers

Leonard M. Baynes[22]

> *You know how to whistle, don't you, Steve? You just put your lips together—and blow.*
>
> — Lauren Bacall to Humphrey Bogart in *To Have and To Have Not*

Ms. Watkins was a Vice-President at Enron Corp. She earned a master's degree in professional accounting from the University of Texas at Austin. In 1982, she began her career as an auditor with the accounting firm Arthur Andersen, spending eight years at its Houston and New York offices. In 1983, she became a certified public accountant. Enron Vice-President Andrew Fastow hired Ms. Watkins to manage Enron's partnership with the California Public Employee Retirement System. From June to August 2001, Ms. Watkins worked directly for Mr. Fastow. During this time, Ms. Watkins learned that Enron was engaging in accounting improprieties with certain affiliated entities. She believed that Enron was using its own stock to generate gains and losses on its income statement. [She] . . . failed to receive satisfactory explanations regarding these accounting transactions from Enron executives. . . . [S]he was troubled by the accounting practices but was uncomfortable reporting them to either Mr. Fastow or former Enron President Jeff Skilling, fearing termination. . . . On August 15, 2001, Ms. Watkins sent to Kenneth Lay, the CEO of Enron, a seven-page anonymous letter. In the letter, Ms. Watkins asked, "Has Enron become a risky place to work?" She also more specifically described the accounting improprieties and stated that "to the layman on the street [it will look like] we are hiding losses in a related company and will compensate that company with Enron stock in the future." She shared her prescient fears that Enron might "implode in a wave of accounting scandals." On August 22, 2001, Ms. Watkins met with Mr. Lay and outlined her concerns about the accounting improprieties, and requested a transfer from working for Mr. Fastow. In late August she was reassigned to the human resources group. Ms. Watkins reported that Mr. Lay assured her that he would investigate the irregularities. Ms. Watkins never reported her concerns to the SEC, the Department of Treasury, or any other governmental official. . . .

---

22 76 *St. John's L. Rev.* 875, Fall 2002.

Ms. Watkins is the prototypical whistleblower because she had knowledge of damaging information and she disclosed it to her supervisor's supervisor. At the same time, she is very atypical for several reasons. First, as an accountant, she had the expertise to know that her corporation was possibly breaking the law and defrauding the public. Second, her disclosure in and of itself to the president of the corporation did not lead to the type of investigation that was necessary to stop any wrongdoing. Her actions did not cause the immediate collapse of the Enron financial giant. Third, even though she "ratted" out her boss . . . her disclosure did not compromise her job security. In fact, Ms. Watkins has received a lot of positive press from her actions. . . . Ms. Watkins was even named Time magazine's "Person of the Week. . . ." A movie deal also is reportedly in the works that will paint Ms. Watkins as a "feminist icon," like Erin Brockovich. . . .

[Baynes next points to the dangerous tight-rope a corporate whistleblower typically walks, who may be "damned if she does 'just pucker and blow,' and damned if she does not." He explains that corporate executives must be responsive to two common law obligations. First, they are under a "duty of loyalty:"]

They must act in good faith and in a manner that they reasonably believe will be in the best interests of the corporation, including safeguarding corporate information. . . . The nature of the corporation requires it to rely on the officers and managers to run the day-to-day business. These employees have access to a very precious commodity, that is, vital and privileged corporate information. In the more mundane duty of loyalty cases, the senior executive has access to important corporate information dealing with customer lists, customer preferences, customer pricing, new opportunities, and secret formulas.

[T]hese principles still apply in the whistleblowing context. For example, the whistleblower may convert corporate proprietary information by taking corporate records and sharing them with the authorities. The whistleblower could disclose information that, at worst, could lead to civil or criminal liabilities for the corporation and its other senior officers and directors. At best, certain disclosures could lead to significant embarrassment or humiliation. In either case, deciding how to make such disclosures would usually be a decision of the board of directors and senior managers of the corporation. For example, if the disclosure might give rise to criminal or civil liability, the corporation under the best of circumstances would want to vest its decision with its attorneys in an effort to minimize its potential liability and maximize profits. If the whistleblower discloses the information, she may make it impossible for the corporation and other senior executives to obtain a good deal from prosecutors. If the information disclosed is not rooted in civil or criminal misconduct, but nevertheless is scandalous, the corporation may want to refrain from disclosing such information. The whistleblower may cause a great deal of public relations harm by disclosing such information. . . . [S]enior executives know where the corporation may be most vulnerable . . . [and] are in a position to inflict harm on the corporation in a way that strangers cannot.

[Baynes then outlines the other pole of responsibility for corporate executives.]

Corporate officers and senior executives have a duty of care to the corporation. They have an obligation to perform their duties with the care that a person in a like position would reasonably exercise under similar circumstances. This duty has been analogized to the diligence, care, and skill that ordinarily prudent individuals would exercise in the management of their affairs. . . .

In the case of whistleblowing, tension between the duty of loyalty and duty of care exists. The senior executive is required to disclose her objections to certain actions that she believes are illegal. But how is she supposed to do that? As a non-director officer, she could disclose her objections to her supervisor or her supervisor's supervisor like Sherron Watkins did at Enron. This objection may take the form of a "cover your ass" memo. But will this really stop wrongdoing? In some cases, such a memo may be insufficient to stop the wrongdoing, and the senior executive may have an obligation to report the matter to the authorities. She may, however, be in a bind because her contractual obligations and her duty of loyalty responsibilities may limit the type of information that she could give to the authorities. In addition, unless someone has real inside information allowing them to actually observe the wrongdoing and has the expertise to know that the wrongdoing is illegal, what safe harbor exists to protect the senior executive from mistakenly reporting wrongdoing?

[In 2002 the Sarbanes-Oxley Act was passed, in response to the wave of corporate scandals that began with Enron. As Baynes explains, it "was designed to promote investor confidence by ensuring that the public receives more information about possible corporate fraud. Such disclosures would ensure that the markets have perfect information so that investors could make informed investment choices."]

The Sarbanes-Oxley Act prohibits any public company from discriminating against any employee who lawfully provides information or otherwise assists in an investigation of conduct that the employee "reasonably believes" constitutes a violation of the federal securities laws. This provision was designed from the lessons learned from Sherron Watkins's testimony. As Senator Patrick Leahy stated, "'We learned from Sherron Watkins of Enron that these corporate insiders are the key witnesses that need to be encouraged to report fraud and help prove it in court.'" The legislation protects an employee from retaliation by an employer for testifying before Congress or a federal regulatory agency, or giving evidence to law enforcement of possible securities fraud violations. To secure this protection, the employee must have assisted in an investigation, which was conducted by Congress, a federal agency, the employee's supervisor, or anyone else authorized by the employer to conduct an investigation. . . .

[Baynes now asks whether the anti-retaliation provision of the new law adequately addresses the dilemma of the corporate whistleblower, caught in the "vortex" of the duty of loyalty and the duty of care.]

Undoubtedly, the Sarbanes-Oxley Act provides an extra level of protection for employees. Despite this . . . we must be cognizant that federal whistleblowers have low success rates in their suits before government agencies. The Whistleblowers Survival Guide reports that "the rate of success for winning a reprisal lawsuit . . . for federal whistleblower laws has risen to between 25 and 33 percent in recent years." Under the Act, the corporate senior executive or employee is likely . . . also [to] have a low rate of success under its whistleblowing provisions. First, the statute only affords protection against retaliations based on securities fraud. Whistleblowing of other kinds of wrongdoing remain unprotected under this Act. In these cases, the whistleblower then must rely on the vagaries of state law, which generally give preference to those allegations dealing with public safety. For example, a senior executive may overhear a high-ranking executive make disparaging remarks about a particular racial group and state that he would never hire or promote members of that group. The corporation employs very few members of this particular group and has none in senior management. The senior executive believes that the corporation is engaged in race discrimination. The senior executive has a fiduciary obligation to hold certain corporate information like employee demographics in confidence but has an obligation to resign or object from his position when confronting corporate wrongdoing. The Act provides protection only for those matters that involve security fraud. If this senior manager discloses, she would have to rely on the protections of the state laws.

Second, low-level employees are also relatively unprotected. They probably are unaware of these new protections. They may feel particularly oppressed by the many layers of management that may exist in some corporations. Some may be unsophisticated and may not know whether certain actions violate the law. Many of the wrongful or illegal activities that they observe may not rise to the level of securities fraud. For example, an employee at McDonald's may notice that large numbers of pre-packaged hamburgers disappear shortly after delivery. The disappearance may be the result of conversion by the store manager. The McDonald's employee might be in the best position to ascertain whether this wrongdoing is occurring, but she is unprotected by the Sarbanes-Oxley Act because this conversion does not involve securities fraud. . . . In addition, many of these employees rely very heavily on their paychecks; a high turnover rate exists in these jobs. Students and those re-entering the workforce hold many of these jobs. These individuals may be particularly reluctant to "rock the boat" and report wrongdoing unless they are guaranteed that their job is protected. The Act does nothing to address this population of whistleblowers.

Third, for both senior executives and low-level employees, the Sarbanes-Oxley Act gives little guidance as to the circumstances under which an employee is to disclose allegations of wrongdoing to her supervisor as opposed to law enforcement authorities. Senior executives also have an obligation to use "reasonable efforts" to disclose to the principal information which is "relevant to affairs entrusted to [the agent]" and which the principal would desire to have. . . . In some instances, however, the whistleblowing employee who reports wrongdoing to her supervisor might not be doing enough to stem the wrongdoing behavior. For instance, once she has made the report, the wrongdoing supervisor might exclude the employee from access to information that would allow her to continue to observe the wrongful behavior. In those cases, the reporting employee may have breached her duty of care to the corporation by using insufficient actions to stop the wrongdoing. . . . Conversely, if the whistleblowing employee reports the evidence of wrongdoing immediately to law enforcement authorities, she may be violating her duty of loyalty to the corporation. . . . She has an obligation to protect certain proprietary and confidential corporate information. Also by going to the law enforcement authorities right away, she may be depriving the corporation of the opportunity to resolve the matter or, in the case of wrongdoing, get the best deal for the corporation. In addition, the employee who jumps the gun and goes to law enforcement authorities may be putting herself in a difficult political situation at her corporation. Even though the terms of her position and employment may remain the same, she will always, to her detriment, be remembered for making that report.

Fourth, the Sarbanes-Oxley Act gives no guidance concerning whether the whistleblowing employee should disclose the information to her direct supervisor or her supervisor's supervisor. Who is the principal of senior executives? Is it the corporation? Is it the board of directors? Is it the senior executive's boss?

[Baynes writes that the same kinds of problems raised above arise here. If the report goes to a direct supervisor, the employee may not be doing enough to stop the behavior. But by going over his head, she prevents her direct supervisor from fixing the problem himself, and risks being "perceived as a 'rat fink,'" something Baynes euphemistically notes "may be a career-limiting move."

Fifth, the legislative history of the Sarbanes-Oxley Act states that the employee's actions have to be reasonable in making reports. . . . Most cases may not be as clear-cut as the one involving Sherron Watkins. Because she was an accountant, she had a very good idea that Enron's accounting policies were illegal. For most other whistleblowers, they may have only a slight inkling that something might be amiss. In those circumstances, what are they supposed to do? Depending on the nature of the corporation, they may have an obligation to investigate further. We then may require the senior executives of major corporations to be "Nancy Drew, Girl Detective." With downsizing, . . . many of these employees already have many additional responsibilities. If, however, they fail to properly investigate their suspicions, they may violate their duty of care to the corporation. [A]lthough Senator Leahy stated that the Act protects whistleblowers who report and disclose their reasonable suspicions, the statutory language fails to explicitly provide such protection. Whistleblowers who report and disclose their reasonable suspicions are in a tough spot if their allegations turn out to be unfounded. . . .

Sixth, the Sarbanes-Oxley Act prohibits a corporation from "discharg[ing], demot[ing], suspend[ing], threaten[ing], harass[ing], or in any other manner discriminat[ing] against an employee in the terms and conditions of employment" because she blew the whistle. Senator Leahy conceded, however, that "most corporate employers, with help from their lawyers, know exactly what they can do to a whistleblowing employee under the law." The types of retaliation that can occur include: (1) "attacking the [whistleblower's] motives, credibility, [or] professional competence"; (2) "build[ing] a damaging record against [the whistleblower]"; (3) threatening the employee with "reprisals for whistleblowing"; (4) "reassign[ing]" the employee to an isolated work location; (5) "publicly humiliat[ing]" the employee; (6) "set [ting] . . . up [the whistleblower] for failure" by putting them in impossible assignments; (7) "prosecut[ing the employee] for unauthorized disclosures [of information]"; (8) "reorganiz[ing]" the company so that the whistleblower's job is eliminated"; and (9) "blacklist[ing]" the whistleblower so she will be unable to work in the industry. Of course some methods on this list would clearly violate the Act. A deft supervisor, however, could "set up" the whistleblowing employee for failure. For instance, the employer may place the whistleblower in a job unsuitable to her skill level to ensure her failure. The employer could then document the employee's poor performance. The Act provides protections for whistleblowing employees except in cases where valid business reasons exist for their termination like inferior work performance. In addition, even if the employer refrains from discriminating against the whistle-blowing employee in the terms and conditions of her employment, the employer is unlikely to give that employee any opportunities for advancement. By blowing the whistle, she may have "tapped out" her career trajectory. . . . Her future supervisors will probably always worry that she is not a "team player" who may go over their heads when she suspects they are doing something wrong.

• QUESTIONS •

1. Describe the conflict faced by corporate insiders who discover unethical or illegal activities within their organizations.

2. Would the SOX law have protected Dr. Donn Milton? Dr. Grace Pierce? What kinds of corporate wrongdoing might a senior executive discover that would not be covered by SOX?

3. Baynes identifies these weaknesses in the SOX law:

"(1) non-securities fraud matters are not covered;
(2) low-level employees may not be aware of the protections;
(3) no guidance is given as to when to report wrongdoing to outside authorities or to a supervisor;
(4) no guidance is given as to when the whistleblower should go over his or her supervisor's head to senior management; and
(5) no protection is given to undercover retaliations that do not quite manifest themselves as a "discharge, demotion, suspension, threat, or other manner of discrimination."

Working with a group of classmates, tackle each of these issues. How would you amend the law to respond to them? Might some of these concerns be more effectively addressed by changes in corporate culture? If so, what changes would your group recommend?

4. In 1991 law professor Anita Hill gave congressional testimony implicating then Supreme Court nominee Clarence Thomas in sexually inappropriate behavior towards her when he was her supervisor at the EEOC. In 2002 she published an editorial in the *New York Times* noting that many prominent whistleblowers happened to be women. She suggested that women who have had the opportunity to rise to power within corporate or governmental organizations are more likely to blow the whistle, calling them insiders with "outsider values."[23] At the close of 2002, three women whistleblowers made the cover of *Time Magazine,* touted as "Persons of the Year:" Sherron Watkins was joined by Cynthia Cooper, who uncovered accounting improprieties at Worldcom, and Colleen Rowley, the FBI employee who pleaded unsuccessfully for the agency to investigate Zacarias Moussaoui, a co-conspirator in the attacks of September 11th. What do you think of the claim that women insiders are likely to have "outsider values"? What does that mean? How might it relate to a tendency to blow the whistle?

5. Sherron Watkins was lucky, in that she was a hero in the eyes of the public, but as Baynes notes elsewhere in his article, most whistleblowers do not receive accolades:

> *In Sophocles's Antigone, a messenger tells Creon that someone has given proper funeral rites to Polyneices' body and remarks "no[one] delights in the bearer of bad*

23 In a July 2002 *Washington Post* article citing Anita Hill's insider/outside thesis, Paul Farhi wrote:

> After years of tortured progress, women sit closer than ever to the inner circle of American corporations and government institutions. Close to it, but not in it. While the International Labor Organization estimated in 1998 that American women held about 43 percent of all managerial positions, a survey two years earlier of Fortune 500 companies indicated that women held only 2.4 percent of the highest management jobs and made up just 1.9 percent of the highest-paid officers and directors. So, a few women have gotten close to the summit—with access to sensitive information, authority over subordinates, a direct line to the boss—but generally aren't themselves at the top. The top remains a male preserve.

news." As evidenced by this ancient Greek play, society has often blamed and disliked the bearer of bad news. Even in our more recent American history, whistleblowers have often been portrayed as liars, sometimes vile or untrustworthy . . .

Why do you think society tends to react against dissenters?

6. **Internet Assignment:** Founded in 1977, the Government Accountability Project promotes "government and corporate accountability through advancing occupational free speech and ethical conduct, defending whistleblowers, and empowering citizen activists. What tips do they offer a would-be whistleblower? See http://www.whistleblower.org.

Ethical Corporate Culture Makes For Loyal Employees

According to a recent study of almost 10,000 business, governmental and non-profit employees from around the world, "people care deeply about the same few things. . . [P]eople everywhere ask: Am I fairly compensated for my work? Am I well suited for my work? Does my employer trust me to do that work?"

Employees were divided into four groups:

TRULY LOYAL (34%): those who work hard and late, "go the extra mile to delight the customer, and recommend the company to their friends as a good place to work."

ACCESSIBLE (8%): employees who are no less loyal to the company in their feelings or actions, but see themselves as possibly moving within two years for unrelated, personal reasons–such as following a spouse or taking on new family obligations.

TRAPPED: (31%): people who want to leave their jobs, but feel that they cannot.

HIGH RISK: (27%): those who are "spending their working hours clicking through Monster.com" and wouldn't recommend their company as a good place to work.

The study reported a connection between ethics and loyalty: "Employees who perceive their employers as ethical are more likely to be proud to be associated with the company. Of the employees who felt they were working for an ethical company, 55% were Truly Loyal. Only 9% of those who questioned their employer's ethics were Truly Loyal."

Researcher Marc Drizin had this advice: "Being an ethical company doesn't really cost money over the long term. What it does cost is cheap compared to the cost of replacing workers revolving through your door. Some U.S. statistics may help us to understand this: On average, it costs $8,000 to $10,000 to replace a manufacturing employee. It costs $15,000 to replace that kid on the front line who sells you hats and jackets. It costs $3,000 just to interview someone before actually hiring or training him or her. And the cost for an IT worker, on average, is astronomical: over 125% of that employee's annual compensation."

Drizin even suggests a pay-off from career-development programs that lead employees to better jobs at other companies: "[B]eing an exporter of talent is not a bad thing. . . . The person who leaves will tell everyone else, 'Man, that was a good place to work. Go apply for my job!'"[24]

24 Katherine J. Sweet, "Employee Loyalty Around the World," *MIT Sloan Management Review,* Vol. 42, No. 2, Winter 2001, p. 16.

PUBLIC EMPLOYEES AND FREEDOM OF SPEECH

What I was surprised at was the silence, the collective silence by so many people that had to be involved, that had to have seen something or heard something.

— Sgt. Samuel Provance, key witness in government investigation of Abu Ghraib prison abuse

People who work for the government or for any of its branches—such as police, air traffic controllers, and those employed by government-supported institutions like hospitals or schools—are called public employees. For almost 200 years, public employees were thought to have no greater speech rights than those who worked in the private sector. The leading case, which dates back to the nineteenth century, involved a policeman who was fired for publicly criticizing the management of his department. He sued to get his job back, relying on his free speech rights. Judge Oliver Wendell Holmes refused his claim, stating, "The petitioner may have a constitutional right to talk politics, but he has no constitutional right to be a policeman."[25]

Then, in 1968, the Supreme Court re-interpreted the First Amendment of the U.S. Constitution to give public employees limited speech protections. Marvin Pickering, a public school teacher, was fired for publishing a letter in the local paper critical of the Board of Education's allocation of funds to its athletic program. He sued, losing in the lower courts. On appeal, however, the Court ruled in his favor. In *Pickering v. Board of Education,*[26] the Court weighed "the interests of the teacher, as a citizen, in commenting upon matters of public concern" against the "interest of the State, as an employer, in promoting the efficiency of the public services it performs through its employees." On balance, Pickering's free speech interests were greater. In 1983, the Supreme Court re-affirmed and clarified the *Pickering* test as it decided *Connick v. Myers.*[27] Sheila Myers had distributed a questionnaire at her place of employment. The circular inquired not only about internal matters, such as an office transfer policy, but also about matters of legitimate public concern, including pressure put on employees to work on certain political campaigns. Based on its content, form, and context, the *Connick* Court determined that the questionnaire was tinged with just enough public interest to be examined under the *Pickering* test, although a statement limited to internal matters would not be. Myers lost her case, however, since the government demonstrated that her questionnaire interfered with working relationships by causing a "mini-insurrection" that could have disrupted the office. Had her speech been of greater importance to the public, the Court explained, the government may have had a harder case.

Today, to prevail on a First Amendment claim, a fired public employee must prove that the conduct at issue was constitutionally protected, and that it was a substantial or motivating factor in the termination. The government can still avoid liability by proving that the person would have been fired even in the absence of the protected conduct ("dual motive"), or that the firing was justified because the countervailing government interests are sufficiently strong. The Court also has ruled that the same balancing test applies to independent contractors who claim they lost government contracts in retaliation for exercising their free speech rights.[28]

---

25 *McAuliffe v. Mayor of New Bedford,* 29 N.E. 517 (1892).

26 391 U.S. 563 (1968).

27 *Connick v. Myers,* 461 U.S. 138 (1983).

28 *Board of County Commissioners, Wabaunsee County, Kansas v. Umbetter,* 116 S.Ct. 2342, 518 U.S. 668 (1996).

Try to apply these legal standards to the following recent current events. If these whistleblowers sued, would they succeed in their free speech claims?

- On February 1, 2003, as it was making its re-entry to land, the Columbia space shuttle burst into flame and broke apart over Texas. All 11 astronauts were killed. Two weeks later, scientists learned that foam tiles had broken away from the spacecraft, striking its left wing. A few NASA engineers strongly believed that images of the resultant damage should be created and analyzed. They met with institutional resistance, a "bureaucratic dead end," and the pictures were never taken. Suppose they had persisted in their requests, gone public when they were denied, and then been fired.[29]
- President Bush signed the Medicare bill on December 8, 2003, praising it as "the greatest advance in health care coverage for America's seniors since the founding of Medicare." While Democrats argued the law benefited drug companies and insurers more than the elderly, Republicans hoped to win votes from seniors with it in the November presidential election. In June 2003, as the bill was being considered by Congress, the Bush administration presented costs estimates for the prescription drug plan portion of the bill at $400 billion. However Richard Foster, the Medicare system's chief actuary, estimated those costs much higher—at $500–$600 billion. Foster was threatened with dismissal if he revealed this to Congress.
- In 2004, Richard Clarke, who had been in charge of counterterrorism under President Bush, published a book titled *Against All Enemies,* and went public with his opinion that the president had "done a terrible job in the war against terrorism." The Bush administration responded, arguing Clarke was both "out of the loop" and more interested in book sales than in truth. Suppose the Bush administration took further retaliatory steps against Clarke.
- In May 2004, a key witness in the military investigation into prisoner mistreatment at Abu Ghraib, Sgt. Samuel Provance, 30, told ABC News that dozens of soldiers—in addition to the seven military police reservists who have been charged—were involved in the abuse at the prison, and he said there is an effort under way in the Army to hide it. Provance said, "There's definitely a cover-up. People are either telling themselves or being told to be quiet." He spoke out in spite of orders from his commanders not to, was stripped of his security clearance, transferred to a different platoon, and officially "flagged," meaning he will never be promoted or receive honors within the military. In addition, Provance was told he might face prosecution because his comments were "not in the public interest."

CORPORATE GOVERNANCE AND THE GATEKEEPERS

At the heart of this chapter is the question of accountability. How might a large organization—business or government—police itself? Can we identify the forces that prevent complex organizations from effectively auditing themselves? Can we understand why the mechanisms that are supposed to monitor and punish wrongdoing are often ineffective? From there, can we imagine how to reduce the need for whistleblowing?

The Enron Story

> *As a partner in the communities in which we operate, Enron believes it has a responsibility to conduct itself according to certain basic principles. . . .*
>
> *Respect: We treat others as we would like to be treated ourselves. We do not tolerate abusive or disrespectful treatment. Ruthlessness, callousness and arrogance don't belong here.*

29 James Glanz and John Schwartz, "Dogged Engineer's Effort to Assess Shuttle Damage," *New York Times,* 2003.

Integrity: We work with customers and prospects openly, honestly and sincerely. When we say we will do something, we will do it; when we say we cannot or will not do something, then we won't do it.

Communication: We have an obligation to communicate. Here, we take the time to talk with one another . . . and to listen. We believe that information is meant to move and that information moves people.

— Enron's statement of Vision & Values

The business community tends to look at these things in terms of what can we get away with, rather than what's right. Optics has replaced ethics.

— Arthur Levitt, former SEC chairman,
commenting on Enron's collapse

Shortly after the collapse of Enron and as the Worldcom scandal was breaking, securities law scholar John C. Coffee, Jr. analyzed the key role played by corporate watchdogs such as auditors and securities analysts in these events. As Coffee views it, their failure to function effectively was more telling than the failure of the board of directors. It would be a mistake to expect insights from a close reading of the behavior of Enron's board, Coffee writes, since Enron itself was "maddeningly unique:"

> *Other public corporations simply have not authorized their chief financial officer to run an independent entity that enters into billions of dollars of risky and volatile trading transactions with them; nor have they allowed their senior officers to profit from such self-dealing transactions without broad supervision or even comprehension of the profits involved. . . . Precisely for this reason, the passive performance of Enron's board of directors cannot fairly be extrapolated and applied as an assessment of all boards generally. . . . Enron is an anecdote, an isolated data point that cannot yet fairly be deemed to amount to a trend.*

Below he explores why the guardians of objectivity—paid whistleblowers, in a sense—did not do their jobs.

Understanding Enron: "It's About the Gatekeepers, Stupid"

John C. Coffee, Jr.[30]

. . . Behind [Enron] is the market's discovery that it cannot rely upon the professional gatekeepers—auditors, analysts, and others—whom the market has long trusted to filter, verify and assess complicated financial information. Properly understood, Enron is a demonstration of gatekeeper failure, and the question it most sharply poses is how this failure should be rectified.

30 57 *Bus. Law* 1403, August 2002. Coffee's title is a play on a phrase that was commonly heard as Bill Clinton was campaigning for president: "It's about the economy, stupid!"

Although the term "gatekeeper" is commonly used, here it requires special definition. Inherently, gatekeepers are reputational intermediaries who provide verification and certification services to investors. These services can consist of verifying a company's financial statements (as the independent auditor does), evaluating the creditworthiness of the company (as the debt rating agency does), assessing the company's business and financial prospects vis-a-vis its rivals (as the securities analyst does), or appraising the fairness of a specific transaction (as the investment banker does in delivering a fairness opinion). . . .

Characteristically, the professional gatekeeper essentially assesses or vouches for the corporate client's own statements about itself or a specific transaction. This duplication is necessary because the market recognizes that the gatekeeper has a lesser incentive to lie than does its client and thus regards the gatekeeper's assurance or evaluation as more credible. To be sure, the gatekeeper as watchdog is typically paid by the party that it is to watch, but its relative credibility stems from the fact that it is in effect pledging a reputational capital that it has built up over many years of performing similar services for numerous clients. In theory, such reputational capital would not be sacrificed for a single client and a modest fee. Here, as elsewhere, however, logic and experience can conflict. Despite the clear logic of the gatekeeper rationale, experience over the 1990s suggests that professional gatekeepers do acquiesce in managerial fraud. . . .

[Coffee goes on to cite statistics demonstrating the extent of gatekeeper failure.]

[T]he number of earnings restatements by publicly held corporations averaged 49 per year from 1990 to 1997, then increased to 91 in 1998, and finally skyrocketed to 150 and 156, respectively, in 1999 and 2000. . . .

As late as October 2001, sixteen out of seventeen securities analysts covering Enron maintained "buy" or "strong buy" recommendations on its stock right up until virtually the moment of its bankruptcy filing. . . .

According to a study by Thomson Financial, the ratio of "buy" to "sell" recommendations increased from 6 to 1 in 1991 to 100 to 1 by 2000.

Explaining Gatekeeper Failure

None of the watchdogs that should have detected Enron's collapse—auditors, analysts or debt rating agencies—did so before the penultimate moment. This is the true common denominator in the Enron debacle: the collective failure of the gatekeepers. Why did the watchdogs not bark in the night when it now appears in hindsight that a massive fraud took place? Here, two quite different, although complementary, stories can be told. The first will be called the "general deterrence" story, and the second, the "bubble" story. The first is essentially economic in its premises, and the second, psychological.

The Deterrence Explanation: The Underdeterred Gatekeeper

[Here Coffee explains that auditors had lower incentives to resist pressure from clients to use aggressive accounting techniques, because, throughout the 1990s as those demands increased, the risks of legal liability decreased. He mentions several specific changes in relevant law, including a 1994 Supreme Court decision which eliminated liability for "aiding and abetting" securities fraud, and a federal law passed in 1995 that made it more difficult for plaintiffs to succeed in securities fraud claims. As the legal environment became considerably more permissive, particularly for auditor defendants, the benefits of caving in to management pressures became greater.]

. . . [T]he Big Five learned during the 1990s how to cross-sell consulting services and to treat the auditing function principally as a portal of entry into a lucrative client. Prior to the mid-1990s, the provision of consulting services to audit clients was infrequent and insubstantial in the aggregate. Yet, according to one recent survey, the typical large public corporation now pays its auditor for consulting services three times what it pays the same auditor for auditing services. Not only did auditing firms see more profit potential in consulting than in auditing, but they began during the

1990s to compete based on a strategy of "low balling" under which auditing services were offered at rates that were marginal to arguably below cost. The rationale for such a strategy was that the auditing function was essentially a loss leader by which more lucrative services could be marketed.

Appealing as this argument may seem that the provision of consulting services eroded auditor independence, it is subject to at least one important rebuttal. Those who defend the propriety of consulting services by auditors respond that the growth of consulting services made little real difference, because the audit firm is already conflicted by the fact that the client pays its fees. More importantly, the audit partner of a major client, such as Enron, is particularly conflicted by the fact that such partner has virtually a "one-client" practice. Should the partner lose that client for any reason, the partner will likely need to find employment elsewhere. In short, both critics and defenders of the status quo tend to agree that the audit partner is already inevitably compromised by the desire to hold the client. From this premise, a prophylactic rule prohibiting the firm's involvement in consulting would seemingly achieve little.

While true in part, this analysis misses a key point: namely, how difficult it is for the client to fire the auditor in the real world. Because of this difficulty, the unintended consequence of combining consulting services with auditing services in one firm is that the union of the two enables the client to more effectively threaten the auditing firm in a "low visibility" way. To illustrate this point, let us suppose, for example, that a client becomes dissatisfied with an auditor who refuses to endorse the aggressive accounting policy favored by its management. Today, the client cannot easily fire the auditor. Firing the auditor is a costly step, inviting potential public embarrassment, public disclosure of the reasons for the auditor's dismissal or resignation, and potential SEC intervention. If, however, the auditor also becomes a consultant to the client, the client can then easily terminate the auditor as a consultant, or reduce its use of the firm's consulting services, in retaliation for the auditor's intransigence. This low visibility response requires no disclosure, invites no SEC oversight, and yet disciplines the audit firm so that it would possibly be motivated to replace the intransigent audit partner. In effect, the client can both bribe (or coerce) the auditor in its core professional role by raising (or reducing) its use of consulting services.

Of course, this argument that the client can discipline and threaten the auditor/consultant in ways that it could not discipline the simple auditor is based more on logic than actual case histories. But it does fit the available data. A recent study by academic accounting experts, based on proxy statements filed during the first half of 2001, finds that those firms that purchased more non-audit services from their auditor (as a percentage of the total fee paid to the audit firm) were more likely to fit the profile of a firm engaging in earnings management.

The Irrational Market Story

Alternatively, Enron's and Arthur Andersen's downfalls can be seen as consequences of a classic bubble that overtook the equity markets in the late 1990s and produced a market euphoria in which gatekeepers became temporarily irrelevant. Indeed, in an atmosphere of euphoria in which stock prices ascend endlessly and exponentially, gatekeepers are largely a nuisance to management, which does not need them to attract investors. Gatekeepers are necessary only when investors are cautious and skeptical. . . . Arguably, auditors were used [in the 1990s] only because SEC rules mandated their use or because no individual firm wished to call attention to itself by becoming the first to dispense with them. [T]he rational auditor's best competitive strategy, at least for the short term, was to become as acquiescent and low cost as possible.

For the securities analyst, a market bubble presented an even more serious problem. It is simply dangerous to be sane in an insane world. The securities analyst who prudently predicted reasonable growth and stock appreciation was quickly left in the dust by the investment guru who prophecized a new investment paradigm in which revenues and costs were less important than the number of "hits" on a Web site. Moreover, as the initial public offering (IPO) market soared in the 1990s, securities analysts became celebrities and valuable assets to their firms; indeed, they became the principal means by which investment banks competed for IPO clients, as the underwriter with the "star" analyst could produce the biggest first day stock price spike. But as their salaries thus soared, analyst compensation came increasingly from the investment banking side of their firms. Hence, just as in the case of the auditor, the analyst's economic position became increasingly dependent on favoring the interests of persons outside their profession (i.e., consultants in the case of the auditor and investment bankers in the case of the analyst) who had little reason to respect or observe the standards or professional culture within the gatekeeper's profession.

The common denominator linking these examples is that, as auditors increasingly sought consulting income and as analysts increasingly competed to maximize investment banking revenues, the gatekeepers' need to preserve their reputational capital for the long run slackened. . . .

Toward Synthesis

These explanations still do not fully explain why reputational capital built up over decades might be sacrificed or, more accurately, liquidated once legal risks decline and/or a bubble develops. Here, additional factors need to be considered.

The Increased Incentive for Short-Term Stock Price Maximization

The pressure on gatekeepers to acquiesce in earnings management was not constant over time, but rather grew during the 1990s [when] executive compensation shifted from being primarily cash based to being primarily equity based. The clearest measure of this change is the growth in stock options. Over the last decade, stock options rose from five percent of shares outstanding at major U.S. companies to fifteen percent—a three hundred percent increase. The value of these options rose by an even greater percentage and over a dramatically shorter period: from $50 billion in 1997 in the case of the 2000 largest corporations to $162 billion in 2000—an over three hundred percent rise in three years. Stock options create an obvious and potentially perverse incentive to engage in short-run, rather than long-term, stock price maximization because executives can exercise their stock options and sell the underlying shares on the same day. . . . Thus, if executives inflate the stock price of their company through premature revenue recognition or other classic earnings management techniques, they could quickly bail out in the short term by exercising their options and selling, leaving shareholders to bear the cost of the stock decline when the inflated price could not be maintained over subsequent periods. Given these incentives, it becomes rational for corporate executives to use lucrative consulting contracts, or other positive and negative incentives, to induce gatekeepers to engage in conduct that made the executives very rich. The bottom line is then that the growth of stock options placed gatekeepers under greater pressure to acquiesce in short-term oriented financial and accounting strategies.

The Absence of Competition

The Big Five obviously dominated a very concentrated market. Smaller competitors could not expect to develop the international scale or brand names that the Big Five possessed simply by quoting a cheaper price. More importantly, in a market this concentrated, implicit collusion develops easily. Each firm could develop and follow a common competitive strategy in parallel without fear of being undercut by a major competitor. Thus, if each of the Big Five were to prefer a strategy under which it acquiesced to clients at the cost of an occasional litigation loss and some public humiliation, it could more easily observe this policy if it knew that it would not be attacked by a holier-than-thou rival stressing its greater reputation for integrity as a competitive strategy. This approach does not require formal collusion but only the expectation that one's competitors would also be willing to accept litigation losses and occasional public humiliation as a cost of doing business. Put differently, either in a less concentrated market where several dozen firms competed or in a market with low barriers to entry, it would be predictable that some dissident firm would seek to market itself as distinctive for its integrity. But in a market of five firms (and only four for the future), this is less likely. . . .

[At this point Coffee notes that the two stories—the deterrence story and the market bubble story—are not necessarily mutually exclusive, but when we begin to think about how to reform the system, it matters which one we think is dominant. If we buy into the bubble story, we may believe that as the bubble bursts the market self-corrects; if we have more faith in the deterrence story, we would want to regulate to make change.]

Conclusion

Reasonable persons can always disagree over what reforms are desirable. But the starting point for an intelligent debate is the recognition that the two major, contemporary crises now facing the securities markets (i.e., the collapse of Enron and the growing controversy over securities analysts, which began with the New York Attorney General's investigation into Merrill Lynch) involve at bottom the same problem—both are crises motivated by the discovery by investors that reputational intermediaries upon whom they relied were conflicted and seemingly sold their interests short. Neither the law nor the market has yet solved either of these closely related problems.

• QUESTIONS •

1. **Internet Assignment:** "Neither the law nor the market" had solved the problem of gatekeeper failure, Coffee wrote at the end of his article. It was published in 2002. Find out what you can about events since then. Have shifting market conditions made a difference in terms of the pressures on gatekeepers to be independent and objective? Has the legal system responded to the Enron/Worldcom scandals in a way that encourages them to do their work more effectively?

2. The accounting profession is self-policed by a professional group, the American Institute of Certified Public Accountants (AICPA). The industry has successfully warded off enhanced government oversight in recent years, as its political campaign contributions burgeoned. Contributing more than $14 million in 2000, for example, the profession is now in the same league as the biggest donors, such as the telecommunications industry and trade unions. **Internet Assignment:** In the wake of the Enron scandal, what is the accounting industry doing to police itself?

3. Coffee states that Enron's board of directors was up against a uniquely bizarre situation. But since Enron/Worldcom, many have a argued for the presence of "independent" directors on corporate boards. **Internet Assignment:** Has there been progress or implementation of this concept?

4. Most large companies have an ethical code, such as Enron's statement of Vision and Values. And we might safely assume that most people who work for large companies are ethical human beings who would not consciously commit illegal or unethical acts. Why, then, do we so often observe a disconnect between corporate ethical codes and business practice?

A 1995 Ethics Resource Center study suggests that ethical codes are overshadowed by other priorities. Of 10,000 employees who responded, 55 percent "never or only occasionally" found their company standards useful in guiding their decisions and actions, reporting corporate underemphasis on ethics as opposed to business goals. While an ethics compliance officer might make an annual attempt to discuss ethics, performance is measured on a quarterly, monthly, or even a daily basis. This disturbing reality is consistent with the findings of Harvard Professor Joseph L. Badaracco, Jr., who interviewed 30 recent graduates of Harvard's MBA program. These young managers were "dubious" about ethics codes and programs, explaining that the values contained in them "seemed inconsistent with 'what the company was about.'" Here, Badaracco summarizes what he learned:

> *First, in many cases [they] received explicit instructions from their middle-manager bosses or felt strong pressures to do things they believed were sleazy, unethical, or sometimes illegal. Second, corporate ethics programs, codes of conduct, mission statements, hotlines, and the like provided little help. Third, many of the[m] believed that their company's executives were out of touch on ethical issues, either because they were too busy or because they sought to avoid responsibility. Fourth, the[y] resolved the dilemmas they faced largely on the basis of personal reflection and individual values, not through reliance on corporate credos, company loyalty, [or] the exhortations of senior executives.*

Badaracco's interview subjects, who worked in banking, consulting, accounting, and advertising, came to believe they had to respond to the following "powerful organizational commandments:"

> *First, performance is what really counts, so make your numbers. Second, be loyal and show us you're a team player. Third, don't break the law. Fourth, don't over-invest in ethical behavior.*[31]

What do these findings suggest about the role of whistleblowers inside large corporations?

CHAPTER PROBLEMS

1. What should be the result when an employee-at-will is fired for being a Good Samaritan? Kevin Gardner had a job driving an armored car. At a scheduled stop at a certain bank in Spokane, Washington, he waited in the vehicle while his co-worker was in the bank. Suddenly he spotted a woman, whom he recognized as the manager, running out of the bank screaming, "Help Me!" Chasing her was a man with a knife.

> *Gardner described the expression on her face: "It was more than fear. There was a real—it was like a horrified kind of a look, like you—I can't describe it other than that, I mean she—she was horrified, not just afraid." Gardner looked around the parking lot and saw nobody coming to help the manager. After the manager and the suspect ran past the front of the truck, Gardner got out, locking the door behind him. As he got out of the truck, he temporarily lost sight of the manager and the suspect, who were both on the passenger side of the truck. While out of Gardner's view, the manager reached a drive-in teller booth across the parking lot, where she found refuge. It is unclear whether the manager was safe before Gardner left the truck, but by the time Gardner walked forward to a point where he could see the suspect, the suspect had already grabbed another woman who was walking into the bank. Gardner recognized the second woman as Kathy Martin, an employee of Plant World, who watered plants at the bank. The suspect put the knife to Ms. Martin's throat and dragged her back into the bank. Gardner followed them into the bank where he observed his partner with his gun drawn and*

31 Joseph L. Badaracco, Jr. and Allen P. Webb, "Business Ethics: A View From The Trenches," *California Management Review*, Vol. 37, No. 2 (Winter 1995).

> *aimed at the suspect. When his partner distracted the suspect, Gardner and a bank customer tackled the suspect and disarmed him. The police arrived immediately thereafter and took custody of the suspect. Ms. Martin was unharmed.*

Gardner's employer had a company rule forbidding armored truck drivers from leaving the truck unattended. Even if pulled over by someone who appears to be a police officer, drivers were instructed to show a card explaining that the driver would follow the police to the stationhouse. Gardner was fired for violating this absolute rule. He sued for wrongful discharge. What would be the arguments of the employer? Of the employee? See *Gardner v. Loomis Armored Inc.*, 913 P.2d 377 (Washington 1996).

2. The 2001 Enron Corporate Responsibility Annual Report contains this statement:

> *Enron employees . . . are trained to report without retribution anything they observe or discover that indicates our standards are not being met.*

In December 2001, using company equipment on company premises, an Enron employee posted a comment on an Internet message board revealing that Enron had paid $55 million in bonuses to its top people just before it filed for bankruptcy and laid off 4,000 workers. The employee who wrote this was fired. What ethical issues arise in this situation?

Enron's headquarters are in Houston. In Texas, wrongful discharge claims succeed only when an employee has refused to perform an illegal act, so if this whistleblower sues he would lose. What would be the legal result in Maryland? In New Jersey? In Montana?

3. **Internet Assignment:** New Jersey's whistleblower law states that an employee cannot be fired for refusing to participate in an activity that he reasonably believes violates a law, is fraudulent or criminal, or goes against a clear mandate of public policy concerning the public health, safety, or welfare. William Scholtz was a security guard for Garden State Park. The park was hosting a prom when it received a bomb threat. Scholtz's supervisor told him to check the premises for a bomb, but he refused, claiming he had had no training in responding to bomb threats or in bomb detection. He was fired. Does Scholtz's argument fit within CEPA? What did the court decide? How would Scholtz have fared if he had worked in Maryland? In Montana?

4. Daniel E. Greer, who had spent nearly three decades studying technology and computer security, was chief technology officer for AtStake Inc., a firm that provides consulting services to Microsoft. In 2003, Greer was one of seven experts who wrote a report criticizing the U.S. government for relying too heavily on Microsoft software, claiming that the widespread dominance of the Windows "monoculture" made it too easy for hackers to spread viruses and to make trouble. Shortly after their report was published, Greer's job with AtStake ended. If he was terminated, what arguments might he make in a lawsuit? How might AtStake respond? What would be the most likely outcome if the company was located in Maryland? New Jersey? Montana? **Internet Assignment:** Find out what actually happened to Greer.

5. Ten months before the Enron debacle, a 30-year-old reporter with *Fortune* magazine, Bethany McLean, wrote an expose of the company, called "Is Enron Overpriced?" The most disturbing fact she revealed was the absence of solid information in Enron's financial reports. Three Enron Executives were flown to New York to try to convince the magazine not to publish the piece; Enron executive Jeffrey Skilling questioned Ms. McLean's research, calling her unethical; and Enron's CEO Kenneth Lay placed a call to the magazine's editor, claiming McLean was relying on a source who would benefit if Enron stock lost value. None of this pressure worked; the article was published anyway–although its message was largely ignored. What is at stake when corporate power attempts to silence the media?

6. Cindy Schlapper was responsible for advertising and promotion for Ran Ken, a corporation that ran a chain of 24 restaurants and bars called Chelsea Street Pubs. In 1994, the company cosponsored a nationwide contest with Remy-Amerique, a liquor company. The manager of a Chelsea Pub in Texas won a trip to Las Vegas by selling the most margaritas containing Cointreau, a Remy-Amerique product. Although everyone involved at the time thought it was illegal under Texas law for a liquor company to pay for the promotion, Schlapper's boss ordered her to prepare a fake invoice, charging Remy-Amerique for table tents:

> *Knowing that no such table tents had been prepared for . . . Remy-Amerique, Ms. Schlapper inquired about the purpose for the invoice . . . [H]er supervisor told Ms. Schlapper that the invoice would allow Ran Ken to be reimbursed for the Las Vegas trip-prize which had cost the company $630. However, Ms. Schlapper was instructed to make the invoice out in the uneven amount of $631.80 to make the invoice "look good, make it look real." Ms. Schlapper was even ordered to include some phony sales tax to make the invoice look authentic. Recognizing that this whole transaction did not pass the "smell test," Ms. Schlapper expressed discomfort and refused to prepare the invoice. After her supervisor called her a "bitch" and ordered her to take the matter up with the company vice-president, Ms. Schlapper's inquiry, which ultimately got her fired was, "Exactly what are the legalities of doing this?"*

Ms. Schlapper sued for wrongful discharge. As it turned out, the Texas law applied to beer companies, not liquor companies. Because of this fluke, the invoice would not have been illegal, and Schlapper lost her case.

What is the "smell test?" Can you think of an argument against relying upon intuitive tools like the "smell test" as a moral compass?

7. The following is a quote from Johnson & Johnson's corporate "Credo":

> *We are responsible to our employees, the men and women who work with us throughout the world. Everyone must be considered as an individual. We must respect their dignity and recognize their merit. They must have a sense of security in their jobs. Compensation must be fair and adequate, and working conditions clean, orderly and safe. Employees must feel free to make suggestions and complaints. There must be equal opportunity for employment, development, and advancement for those qualified. We must provide competent management, and their actions must be just and ethical.*

As vice president of R&D for Therakos, a subsidiary of Johnson & Johnson, Daniel Tripoldi was responsible for the development of a new device called Centrinet. The company had already developed a device that had been approved to treat lymphoma. Centrinet was the name it chose for an improved version of the device, which Therakos now wanted to market as a means of treating another condition known as scleroderma. Tripoldi began to have reservations about these plans. In his opinion the already-approved device and the Centrinet were "sufficiently different in structure and operation that, under FDA regulations, new clinical tests would be required to establish Centrinet's efficacy." But the new tests would delay the marketing of the product. Tripoldi continued to raise his concerns with the company president—who was not a scientist—and others, insisting that what Therakos planned to do would violate FDA regulations. He was fired.

Tripoldi sued, claiming that his termination violated the Johnson & Johnson Credo, which, ironically, he had helped write! Look at the Credo. Would it support Tripoldi's claim that the company had made an implied promise to him not to fire him except for a good reason? A promise not to retaliate against him for expressing his concerns? Is there any other claim he might make? How should the court rule? *Tripoldi v. Johnson & Johnson and Therakos, Inc.*, 1877 F.Supp. 233 (D.N.J. 1995).

8. In this chapter, we have looked at how the law may operate to protect employees who have been punished for blowing the whistle. But another approach is to give people an incentive to become whistleblowers in the first place—to encourage them to take the risk of coming forward. The federal False Claims Reform Act gives any citizen the right to file a civil suit against any company he knows is cheating the government. The government prosecutes the claim, and the whistleblower is then eligible for between 15 and 25 percent of whatever the government is able to collect, while being protected against retaliation by the company.[32]

A plaintiff under this law is called **qui tam,** an abbreviation of a Latin phrase that may be translated as "who sues on behalf of a king as well as for himself."[33] The law has been amended three times, with the most significant change in 1986 when it was strengthened to help the government fight fraud, particularly in defense and health care contracts. The most recent qui tam successes have been focused on the health care industry. In 1998 SmithKline Beecham settled for $325 million the charge that it had defrauded the government by performing unnecessary tests, double-billing, and paying in-kind kick-backs to doctors in exchange for Medicare patients' business. In October 2001, qui tam whistleblowers made possible an $840 million settlement against the largest hospital chain in the United States—the biggest fraud settlement to date.

Qui tam cases are mutually advantageous to the Justice Department, which can receive triple damages, and to the whistleblowers. As the scope of such recoveries increases, industry representatives have expressed frustration with the law. They argue it cuts against company loyalty by discouraging employees from using internal reporting mechanisms to stop wrongdoing, and by offering huge incentives for employees to bring their employers down.

Is the False Claims Act a sensible response to the problem it seeks to address? Or does it turn employees into bounty hunters, too eager to turn against their employers? To help you think about this, check http://www.quitam.com or http://www.taf.org.

9. Seven months after the Columbia shuttle crashed, in August 2003, a report on the causes of the disaster was released. It had been a gargantuan effort. Some 25,000 workers had gathered more than 84,000 pieces of debris by walking slowly across eastern Texas and western Louisiana, collecting evidence. According to the final report, the "broken safety culture" inside NASA was at least as much to blame for the crash as the chunk of foam tile that blew a hole in the wing of the Columbia just after liftoff. Engineers, hoping a high-risk rescue might be possible, had asked management for outside assistance in getting photos of the damage, but these requests were rejected:

> *As much as the foam, what helped to doom the shuttle and its crew, even after liftoff, was not a lack of technology or ability . . . but missed opportunities and a lack of leadership and open-mindedness in management. The accident "was probably not an anomalous, random event, but rather likely rooted to some degree in NASA's history and the human spaceflight program's culture."*[34]

Similar problems appear to have affected the CIA in the months leading up to the U.S. invasion of Iraq. According to a scathing congressional report released in July 2004, key assessments used to justify the war were not supported by the government's own evidence:

> *Among the central findings, endorsed by all nine Republicans and eight Democrats on the committee, were that a culture of "group think" in intelligence agencies left unchallenged an institutional belief that Iraq had illicit weapons; . . . and that intelligence agencies too often failed to acknowledge the limited, ambiguous and even contradictory nature of their information about Iraq and illicit arms.*[35]

Studies have shown that, within large organizations, there is a tendency to go along with the majority. Most people are not likely to challenge the worthiness of the task at hand, or the way

32 31 U.S.C. Sec. 3730.

33 *Black's Law Dictionary,* 1251 (6th ed., 1990).

34 John Schwartz and Matthew Wald, "Report on Loss of Shuttle Focuses on NASA Blunders," *New York Times,* August 27, 2003.

35 Douglas Jehl, "Senators Assail C.I.A. Judgments on Iraq's Arms as Deeply Flawed, *New York Times,* July 10, 2004.

in which the task at hand is being accomplished. This reality, combined with the pressures that affect an organization from the outside—time and money pressures in the case of NASA's Columbia shuttle, political pressures in the case of the United States in Iraq—can obscure good judgment.

Could there be advantages, for large corporations, in countering the "group think" tendency? Could employees who challenge the status quo be valuable? If so, how might corporate culture make room for them without risking destructive effects?

CHAPTER PROJECT

Enron Stakeholder Role Play

You will be a member of one of these teams:

- Board of Directors: Enron board of directors, excluding management
- Accountants: Arthur Andersen, and the accounting industry as a whole
- Management: senior management at Enron (Fastow, Skilling, Lay, etc.)
- Government: regulatory agencies (OPIC, FERC, FCC, SEC), Congress
- Banks: investment banking firms and their research analysts
- Lawyers: Enron's in-house counsel and their principal firm, Vinson & Elkins

Part 1: SELF STUDY: What part did your team play?

Research and write (approximately 3–4 pages double-spaced) a "self study," an explanation of your stakeholder group's role in the collapse of Enron. What did your group do (or fail to do) that contributed to the final outcome?

Part 2: DISCUSSION: Why did Enron collapse?

Preparation: Team self studies are distributed to all teams. All read them.

With your instructor as moderator, hold a discussion with representatives from each team about the question of why Enron went bankrupt. The goal is to put forward your team's best foot. Try to either justify any behavior that appeared to contribute to the downfall of the company or shift blame to other teams.

Part 3: THE CURE: What should be done?

In smaller mixed groups, in which there is one person representing each team, talk about the best way to prevent another Enron. Record your primary recommendations.

Part 4: EPILOGUE: Best Cure?

As individuals, evaluate the "cures" recommended by the different mixed groups. Select the one you believe best alleviates the circumstances that led to Enron. Now compare that with what actually happened. Look at the Sarbanes-Oxley Act, at litigation, at shareholder activism, and at any other developments that followed and responded to the collapse of Enron. Write your findings. Which looks like it would work best, the cure you selected or what has happened since 2001? Why?

Privacy and Technology

Chapter 3

A wonderful fact to reflect upon, that every human creature is constituted to be that profound secret and mystery to every other. A solemn consideration, when I enter a great city by night, that every one of those darkly clustered houses encloses its own secret; that every room in every one of them encloses its own secret; that in every beating heart in the hundreds of thousands of breasts there is, in some of its imaginings, a secret to the heart nearest to it!

— Charles Dickens

You already have zero privacy—get over it.

— Scott McNealy, *CEO*, Sun Microsystems

There is indeed a whole lot a scannin' goin' on. People surreptitiously intercept, record, and disclose the usual suspects for the usual reasons, in the perpetual parade of human perfidy. Popular motivations are love, sex, drugs, crime, politics, business, and employment. And if we reflect, we quickly see that none of us is perfect and that all of us are potential victims. Who among us does not sometime, somewhere, have something they would prefer to keep to themselves?

— Rodney A. Smolla, "Information as Contraband,"
96 *Nw. Univ. L Rev* 1099 (2002)

Human beings must experience a degree of privacy to thrive. Yet, as they act inside organizations, they frequently need information about one another, information that may be sensitive and confidential. Employers want to find out if their workers are productive and loyal. Corporations want to know the preferences of potential customers or the strategies of their competitors. Health insurers want access to patient medical histories and genetic profiles. Governments want to thwart terrorists. Tension between privacy and the need to know is heightened as computer technology revolutionizes information gathering. The process has never been so fast, so efficient, so omnipresent.

This chapter highlights the conflict between the sweeping power of technology to access and assemble information and the ongoing concerns about privacy we all share. Opening with a case involving the interception of e-mail by an employer, it broadens to look at electronic surveillance more generally, and at the legal framework that might address it. We read about the value of privacy, both for individuals and for communities. Next, we look at efforts employers are making to control employees' off-the-job behavior. Should employers be able to fire you for unhealthy habits? For dating someone who is married? We consider workplace testing of various types, such as psychological and drug tests. Readings on consumer privacy follow. We move on to explore both constitutional privacy protection and the manner in which the war on terrorism appears to justify enhanced technologies for government surveillance and data collection. The chapter ends with a focus on the collection of sensitive health data through genetic testing.

SURVEILLANCE AT WORK

E-mail Interception

Ninety percent of all companies with more than 1,000 employees currently use e-mail, putting about 40 million workers on e-mail systems and sending some 60 billion messages annually. Because they use passcodes, employees may believe their e-mail messages are private, but the reality is that they are not. Even deleted messages are stored in archives easily accessible to employers and others. In 1996, a district court in Philadelphia was faced with the following situation. A Pillsbury employee and his supervisor were sending e-mail messages to one another. One message, referring to sales management, mentioned plans to "kill the back-stabbing bastards." Another message described a holiday party as the "Jim Jones Kool-Aid affair." These messages fell into their boss's hands, and both men were fired for sending "inappropriate and unprofessional comments" over Pillsbury's e-mail system. One of the employees sued, claiming he was "wrongfully discharged" when he lost his $62,500 per year job as a regional manager.

MICHAEL A. SMYTH V. THE PILLSBURY COMPANY

United States District Court, 1996
914 F. Supp. 97

WEINER, District Judge.

Defendant [Pillsbury Company] maintained an electronic mail communication system ("e-mail") in order to promote internal corporate communications between its employees. Defendant repeatedly assured its employees, including plaintiff, that all e-mail communications would remain confidential and privileged. Defendant further assured its employees, including plaintiff, that e-mail communications could not be intercepted and used by defendant against its employees as grounds for termination or reprimand.

In October 1994, plaintiff [Michael Smyth] received certain e-mail communications from his supervisor over defendant's e-mail system on his computer at home. In reliance on defendant's assurances regarding defendant's e-mail system, plaintiff responded and exchanged e-mails with his supervisor. At some later date, contrary to the assurances of confidentiality made by defendant, defendant, acting through its agents, servants and employees, intercepted plaintiff's private e-mail messages made in October 1994. On January 17, 1995, defendant notified plaintiff that it was terminating his employment . . . for transmitting what it deemed to be inappropriate and unprofessional comments over defendant's e-mail system. . . .

[Smyth argued wrongful discharge, claiming his employer had violated public policy by committing a tort known as "invasion of privacy." One version of invasion of privacy is called "intrusion." In the first step of his analysis, the judge defines the tort of "intrusion":]

"One who intentionally intrudes, physically or otherwise, upon the solitude or seclusion of another or his private affairs or concerns, is subject to liability to the other for invasion of his privacy, if the intrusion would be highly offensive to a reasonable person. . . ."

[To determine if the facts of the case fit the definition above, the judge uses a "balancing test," weighing the employee's privacy interests against the employer's need to discover information.]

[W]e do not find a reasonable expectation of privacy in e-mail communications voluntarily made by an employee to his supervisor over the company e-mail system notwithstanding any assurances that such communications would not be intercepted by management. Once plaintiff communicated the alleged unprofessional comments to a second person (his supervisor) over an e-mail system which was apparently utilized by the entire company, any reasonable expectation of privacy was lost. Significantly, the defendant did not require plaintiff, as in the case of a urinalysis or personal property search, to disclose any personal information about himself. Rather, plaintiff voluntarily communicated the alleged unprofessional comments over the company e-mail system. We find no privacy interests in such communications.

Secondly, even if we found that an employee had a reasonable expectation of privacy in the contents of his e-mail communications over the company e-mail system, we do not find that a reasonable person would consider the defendant's interception of these communications to be a substantial and highly offensive invasion of his privacy. . . . [T]he company's interest in preventing inappropriate and unprofessional comments or even illegal activity over its e-mail system outweighs any privacy interest the employee may have in those comments.

In sum, we find that the defendant's actions did not tortuously invade the plaintiff's privacy and, therefore, did not violate public policy.

• QUESTIONS •

1. How does Judge Weiner explain why Michael Smyth lost any "reasonable expectation of privacy" in his e-mail comments?

2. Is there any difference between a password-protected message sent on company e-mail and a handwritten memo sealed in an envelope marked private sent through company mail? Consider the judge's reasons for his ruling that you articulated above. Would they also apply to the memo? Suppose Pillsbury began covert audio monitoring of the area near the coffee station in order to screen employee conversations on break time. How would the judge's reasoning apply?

3. From a Kantian perspective, how ethical were the actions of Smyth? Of Pillsbury? What appears to be the ethical framework underlying judge's ruling?

4. Corporate culture varies, and with it, corporate surveillance policies. Some companies give notice to employees that their e-mail communications are not private. Kmart's policy, for example, introduced at every employee orientation, states that "misuse of the e-mail system could result in denial of access to the Kmart computing environment or dismissal." Apple Computers, on the other hand, has an explicit policy of not monitoring employee e-mail. What might be the advantages and disadvantages of such policies from an employee's viewpoint? An employer's?

5. Suppose you were responsible for developing a surveillance policy where you worked. How would you go about setting its parameters? How would you implement it?

6. Judge Weiner points out that Smyth's e-mail messages were "voluntarily" placed on the Pillsbury system, and that Pillsbury never forced the kind of disclosure that goes along with urine testing for drugs, for example. In a sense, the judge is saying that Smyth consented to the monitoring. Do you agree?

7. Hi-tech surveillance is not solely directed by employers at workers. American businesses have always been interested in capturing confidential information and trade secrets from competitors. Today, thanks to computer technology, they are able to spy on one another with more sophisticated means than ever before. What are some of the latest developments in this

area? How far can a company go in this direction without crossing the line? Visit the Web site of the Society of Competitive Intelligence Professionals at http://www.scip.org.

8. Should educational institutions be free to randomly monitor student and faculty e-mail? What is your school's policy on e-mail privacy? Review it and discuss it with others. Are there elements of the policy that you would change, in the light of what you have read? Rewrite it.

Electronic Surveillance: The Debate

Employers have long had an interest in scrutinizing their workforces. In the 1880s, Frederick Taylor invented an approach to industrial efficiency that broke each job into many separate, measurable components. He monitored every part of the process—time per task; hand and eye movements; spacing between workers, machines, and products—developing a system that gave managers the ability to track both the speed and the intensity of work very closely. And in the early twentieth century, Ford Motor Company hired social workers to investigate employees, to check that they had the right habits of cleanliness, thriftiness, and churchgoingness to deserve what was then an impressive $5/day wage. What is different about present-day workplace monitoring is the introduction of technology that allows workers to be observed secretly and in newly intrusive ways.

Statistics make it clear that our workplace is pervaded with electronic oversight. According to a 2001 American Management Association study, "more than three quarters of major U.S. firms (77.7 percent) record and review employee communications and activities on the job, including their e-mail, Internet connections, and computer files," a figure that has doubled since 1997.[1] The 2003 American Management Association survey shows more than 50 percent of companies monitoring e-mail, up from fewer than 15 percent in 1997. Most companies carry out electronic monitoring on a spot-check basis, but there is a growing interest in the use of software that puts employees under continuous surveillance. Such software is evolving quickly and becoming increasingly sophisticated. Programs exist that can take surreptitious "screen shots" of employee computers or that can hunt for particular images. A product called Pornsweeper examines pictures attached to e-mails and picture files for anything that looks like flesh. Software can monitor keystrokes and can retrieve documents, even those that employees did not save. Telemate.Net can track Web site visits by individuals and rank them by categories—games, humor, pornography, cults, shopping, and job-hunting—instantly generating logs that reveal precisely who went where and when. SuperScout produces bar charts that show which workers are sending the longest e-messages, and who is sending or receiving the most e-mail. XVmail facilitates searching the actual text of e-mail messages. As of July 2001, the Privacy Foundation reported that about one-third of the U.S. online workforce and one-quarter of the world's online workforce is being monitored in these ways.[2]

Businesses justify electronic surveillance in a number of ways. It is a form of quality control, enabling supervisors to better correct and improve employee performance. It both measures and encourages efficiency. (When employees realize they are being monitored, they may spend less time surfing the Net and more time getting their work done.) It enhances the completeness and fairness of personnel evaluations. It can uncover employee disloyalty, which can take the form of stealing tangible items like products and supplies, or intangibles like trade

---

1 If other forms of surveillance are included—telephone logs and videotaping, for example—the figure jumps to 82 percent, up from 67 percent in 2000.

2 Andrew Schulman, chief researcher for the Privacy Foundation study, reports that, more than concerns over low productivity or vicarious liability, employers are driven to use continuous surveillance software because it is cheap. It costs less than $10/year to monitor each worker.

secrets. It can flag racially or sexually harassing e-messages. (In 1995, Chevron Corporation paid more than $2 million to settle claims brought by female employees who had received pornographic e-mail.) And recent legislation, such as the federal Health Insurance Portability and Accounting Act of 1996 and the anticorruption Sarbanes-Oxley law of 2002, may add to the reasons companies already have to track and investigate their people.

Countering all this, employees claim that electronic monitoring puts them under dehumanizing pressure, in which computers, instead of people, judge their output. Because computers measure quantity better than quality, employees who work fast might look better than those who work best. The "electronic sweatshop," they say, causes psychological stress and physical symptoms.[3] Apart from the more measurable costs, employees emphasize their need to preserve at work what they expect to maintain elsewhere—a sense of dignity and self-respect.

Electronic Surveillance: The Law

> *The right of the people to be secure in their persons, houses, papers and effects, against unreasonable searches and seizures, shall not be violated.*
>
> — Fourth Amendment, U.S. Constitution

America lacks a comprehensive, uniform legal standard protecting privacy. No express "right to privacy" was written into the U.S. Constitution. While the Fourth Amendment does protect citizens from "unreasonable searches," it is triggered only when the *government* is conducting a search; there is no constitutional protection against searches or surveillance by private corporations. And while government employees might argue that electronic surveillance is a "search" in violation of the Fourth Amendment, their constitutional rights are limited by a balancing test: judges must decide which counts more weightily, an employee's privacy interest or the need of the government (as employer) to search. Once government concerns are placed on the scale, the result will typically favor the employer.

In the private sector, privacy law is determined by a variety of federal and state statutes and by the common law of torts.[4] Employees may claim that electronic monitoring amounts to "intrusion," a variation on the tort of invasion of privacy. As the *Pillsbury* case indicates, intrusion involves invading another person's solitude in a manner considered highly offensive—unauthorized prying into a personal bank account, or a landlord bugging the wall of his tenants' bedroom, for example. Most courts consider two main factors: (1) the obnoxiousness of the means used to intrude, that is, whether it is a deviation from the normal, accepted means of discovering the relevant information; and (2) the reasons for intruding. In one Oregon case the employer had secretly taken 18 rolls of film of a worker suspected of filing a fraudulent worker's compensation claim. The film showed him taking out his trash, mowing his lawn, and otherwise looking fit and able. Dismissing his claim for intrusion, the court mentioned that once he filed his worker's compensation claim he had to expect a reasonable investigation.[5] Because electronic monitoring is now commonplace, it may be considered "normal," if not "accepted," and, as long as employers can point to a legitimate purpose for monitoring, it will be difficult for employees to win cases against them.

---

3 Peter Blackman and Barbara Franklin, "Blocking Big Brother: Proposed Law Limits Employers' Right to Snoop," *N.Y.L.J.*, August 19, 1993, p. 5, citing University of Wisconsin study that found monitored telecommunications workers suffered more depression, anxiety, and fatigue than their non-monitored counterparts at the same facility.

4 As of 2004, only one state, Connecticut, passed a law to protect employees against e-mail monitoring without notice. Conn. Gen. Stat. Sec. 31-48d.

5 *McClain v. Boise Cascade Corporation,* 533 P.2d 343 (1975).

The 1968 federal Wiretap Law, as amended by the Electronic Communications Privacy Act 1986 (ECPA), making it illegal to intercept, disclose, or access messages without authorization, would appear to protect workers from electronic eavesdropping. But some courts have held that e-mail archives may be searched without triggering this statute, because there has been no "interception."[6] And there are a number of exemptions to the ECPA. For example, there is no protection for communications that are "readily accessible to the general public," such as public chat room exchanges. The law does not apply to the extent that employees give "consent" to monitoring, which would seem to eliminate ECPA coverage in the many workplaces where people are told that their communications are not private. The ECPA also allows employers to listen in on communications made in the "ordinary course of business." In other words, where business interests such as efficiency or legal liability are at stake, the surveillance would be allowed.

THE VALUE OF PRIVACY

> *Privacy is much more than just a possible social technique for assuring this or that substantive interest. . . . it is necessarily related to ends and relations of the most fundamental sort: respect, love, friendship and trust. Privacy is not merely a good technique for furthering these fundamental relations, rather without privacy they are simply inconceivable. They require a context of privacy or the possibility of privacy for their existence. . . . To respect, love, trust, feel affection for others and to regard ourselves as the objects of love, trust and affection is at the heart of our notion of ourselves as persons among persons, and privacy is the necessary atmosphere for those attitudes and actions, as oxygen is for combustion.*
>
> — Charles Fried, "Privacy," 77 Yale L.J. 475 (1968)

The following excerpt describes how privacy serves a set of important human needs. The author, Columbia University professor emeritus Alan Westin, now a corporate consultant on privacy issues, has been in the forefront of research on the effects of technology on privacy in our society, particularly in the workplace.

THE FUNCTIONS OF PRIVACY

Alan Westin[7]

[T]he functions privacy performs for individuals in democratic societies . . . can [be] . . . grouped conveniently under four headings—personal autonomy, emotional release, self-evaluation, and limited and protected communication. . . .

Personal Autonomy

In democratic societies there is a fundamental belief in the uniqueness of the individual, in his basic dignity and worth as a creature of God and a human being, and in the need to maintain

---

6 *United States v. Councilman*, 373 F.3d 197(1st Cir. 2004).

7 Alan Westin, *Privacy and Freedom* (New York: MacMillan, 1967).

social processes that safeguard his sacred individuality. Psychologists and sociologists have linked the development and maintenance of this sense of individuality to the human need for autonomy—the desire to avoid being manipulated or dominated wholly by others.

[Scholars describe a] "core self,". . . pictured as an inner circle surrounded by a series of larger concentric circles. The inner circle shelters the individual's "ultimate secrets"—those hopes, fears, and prayers that are beyond sharing with anyone unless the individual comes under such stress that he must pour out these ultimate secrets to secure emotional relief. . . . The next circle outward contains "intimate secrets," those that can be willingly shared with close relations, confessors, or strangers who pass by and cannot injure. The next circle is open to members of the individual's friendship group. The series continues until it reaches the outer circles of casual conversation and physical expression that are open to all observers.

The most serious threat to the individual's autonomy is the possibility that someone may penetrate the inner zone and learn his ultimate secrets, either by physical or psychological means. Each person is aware of the gap between what he wants to be and what he actually is, between what the world sees of him and what he knows to be his much more complex reality. In addition, there are aspects of himself that the individual does not fully understand but is slowly exploring and shaping as he develops. Every individual lives behind a mask in this manner; indeed, the first etymological meaning of the word "person" was "mask". . . .

Emotional Release

Life in society generates such tensions for the individual that both physical and psychological health demand periods of privacy for various types of emotional release. At one level, such relaxation is required from the pressure of playing social roles. . . . On any given day a man may move through the roles of stern father, loving husband, car-pool comedian, skilled lathe operator, union steward, water-cooler flirt, and American Legion committee chairman—all psychologically different roles. . . . [N]o individual can play indefinitely, without relief, the variety of roles that life demands. There have to be moments "off stage" when the individual can be "himself:" tender, angry, irritable, lustful, or dream-filled. Such moments may come in solitude; in the intimacy of family, peers or woman-to-woman and man-to-man relaxation; in the anonymity of park or street; or in a state of reserve while in a group. Privacy in this aspect gives individuals, from factory workers to Presidents, a chance to lay their masks aside for rest. . . .

Another form of emotional release is provided by the protection privacy gives to minor non-compliance with social norms. . . . [A]lmost everyone does break some social or institutional norms—for example, violating traffic laws, breaking sexual mores, cheating on expense accounts, overstating income tax deductions, or smoking in restrooms when this is prohibited. Although society will usually punish the most flagrant abuses, it tolerates the great bulk of the violations as "permissible" deviations. . . . [I]f all transgressions were known—most persons in society would be under organizational discipline or in jail, or could be manipulated by threats of such action. The firm expectation of having privacy for permissible deviations is a distinguishing characteristic of life in a free society. At a lesser but still important level, privacy also allows individuals to deviate temporarily from social etiquette when alone or among intimates, as by putting feet on desks, cursing, letting one's face go slack, or scratching wherever one itches.

Another aspect of release is the "safety valve" function afforded by privacy. Most persons need to give vent to their anger at "the system," "city hall," "the boss," and various others who exercise authority over them, and to do this in the intimacy of family or friendship circles, or in private papers, without fear of being held responsible for such comments. This is very different from freedom of speech or press, which involves publicly voiced criticism without fear of interference by government. . . .

Still another aspect of release through privacy arises in the management of bodily and sexual functions. . . .

Self-evaluation

Every individual needs to integrate his experiences into a meaningful pattern and to exert his individuality on events. To carry on such self-evaluation, privacy is essential. At the intellectual level, individuals need to process the information that is constantly bombarding them, information that cannot be processed while they are still "on the go. . . ." This is particularly true of creative persons. Studies of creativity show that it is in reflective solitude and even "daydreaming" during moments of reserve that most creative "non-verbal" thought takes place. At such moments the individual runs ideas and impressions through his mind in a flow of associations; the active presence of others tends to inhibit this process. . . .

The evaluative function of privacy also has a major moral dimension—the exercise of conscience by which the individual "repossesses himself." While people often consider the moral consequences of their acts during the course of daily affairs, it is primarily in periods of privacy that they take a moral inventory of ongoing conduct and measure current performance against personal ideals. For many persons this process is a religious exercise. . . . Even for an individual who is not a religious believer, privacy serves to bring the conscience into play, for, when alone, he must find a way to continue living with himself.

Limited and Protected Communication

The greatest threat to civilized social life would be a situation in which each individual was utterly candid in his communications with others, saying exactly what he knew or felt at all times. The havoc done to interpersonal relations by children, saints, mental patients, and adult "innocents" is legendary.

In real life, among mature persons all communication is partial and limited. . . . Limited communication is particularly vital in urban life, with its heightened stimulation, crowded environment, and continuous physical and psychological confrontations between individuals who do not know one another in the extended, softening fashion of small-town life. . . .

Privacy for limited and protected communication has two general aspects. First, it provides the individual with the opportunities he needs for sharing confidences and intimacies with those he trusts. . . . "A friend," said Emerson, "is someone before . . . [whom] I can think aloud." In addition, the individual often wants to secure counsel from persons with whom he does not have to live daily after disclosing his confidences. He seeks professionally objective advice from persons whose status in society promises that they will not later use his distress to take advantage of him. To protect freedom of limited communication, such relationships—with doctors, lawyers, ministers, psychiatrists, psychologists, and others are given varying but important degrees of legal privilege against forced disclosure. In its second general aspect, privacy through limited communication serves to set necessary boundaries of mental distance in interpersonal situations ranging from the most intimate to the most formal and public. In marriage, for example, husbands and wives need to retain islands of privacy in the midst of their intimacy if they are to preserve a saving respect and mystery in the relation. . . . In work situations, mental distance is necessary so that the relations of superior and subordinate do not slip into an intimacy which would create a lack of respect and an impediment to directions and correction. . . .

Psychological distance is also used in crowded settings. . . . [A] complex but well-understood etiquette of privacy is part of our social scenario. . . . We learn to ignore people and to be ignored by them as a way of achieving privacy in subways, on streets, and in the "non-presence" of servants or children. . . .

• QUESTIONS •

1. What are the functions of privacy, as described by Westin? For each, can you think of examples from your own experience?

2. Law professor and journalist Jeffrey Rosen, author of *The Unwanted Gaze: The Destruction of Privacy in America,*[8] offers this description of one of the primary values of privacy:

> *Privacy protects us from being misdefined and judged out of context. . . . [W]hen your browsing habits or e-mail messages are exposed to strangers, you may be reduced, in their eyes, to nothing more than the most salacious book you once read or the most vulgar joke you once told. And even if your Internet browsing isn't in any way embarrassing, you run the risk of being stereotyped as the kind of person who would read a particular book or listen to a particular song. Your public identity may be distorted by fragments of information that have little to do with how you define yourself. In a world where citizens are bombarded with information, people form impressions quickly, based on sound bites, and these brief impressions tend to oversimplify and misrepresent our complicated and often contradictory characters.*

   Does Westin come close to mentioning this aspect of privacy?

3. Which functions of privacy may have been served by the e-mail messages that Michael Smyth sent while working for Pillsbury?

4. To what extent can we describe privacy as an ethical imperative? Think of the *Smyth v. Pillsbury* scenario. Who are the most affected stakeholders? Under the utilitarian approach to ethics, was intercepting the e-mail the right thing to do? Now consider the case from the deontological perspective. Again, was Pillsbury's action ethical?

5. In 1890, in a first attempt to conceptualize privacy within the common law, U.S. federal judges Samuel Warren and Louis Brandeis described it as the right "to be let alone." They believed the law should not consider "a man's house as his castle" and then "open wide the back door" to invasions of privacy, particularly those enabled by the prying, gossip-mongering news media.[9] More recently, theorists have conceptualized privacy not so much as a right possessed by individuals, but more in terms of a public good, a benefit to society at large. Consider the Internet as an incubator of political awareness and debate, for instance. Legal scholar Paul Schwartz sees this potential, but warns:

> *In the absence of strong rules for information privacy, Americans will hesitate to engage in cyberspace activities—including those that are most likely to promote democratic self-rule. Current polls already indicate an aversion on the part of some people to engage even in basic commercial activities on the Internet. Yet, deliberative democracy requires more than shoppers; it demands speakers and listeners. But who will speak or listen when this behavior leaves finely-grained data trails in a fashion that is difficult to understand or anticipate?. . . The Internet's interactive nature means that individuals on it simultaneously collect and transmit information. As a result, merely listening on the Internet becomes a speech-act. A visit to a Web site or a chat room generates a record of one's presence. . . . [O]ne leading computer handbook, the Internet Bible, concludes its description of the low level of privacy in cyberspace with the warning, "Think about the newsgroups you review or join—they say a lot about you."*

   Schwartz goes on to argue that a vibrant democracy depends not only on robust public deliberation but also on the ability of each person to figure out who they are and what they believe. This process of self-determination, he writes, is also compromised by lack of online privacy:

> *George Orwell carried out the classic analysis of how surveillance can exert this negative pressure. In the novel* 1984 *. . . he imagined a machine called the "telescreen." This omnipresent device broadcasted propaganda on a nonstop basis and allowed the*

8 New York: Random House, 2000.

9 "The Right to Privacy," 4 *Harv. L. Rev.* 193, 214 (1890).

state officials, the "Thought Police," to observe the populace. Computers on the Internet are reminiscent of the telescreen; under current conditions, it is impossible to know if and when the cyber-Thought Police are plugged in on any individual wire. To extend Orwell's thought, one can say that as habit becomes instinct and people on the Internet gain a sense that their every mouse click and key stroke might be observed, the necessary insulation for individual self-determination will vanish.[10]

Do you agree that privacy is essential to the flourishing of a healthy democracy? Do other areas of our collective life depend on privacy protection?

LIFESTYLE CONTROL

When he opened up his assembly line 80 years ago, Henry Ford issued a booklet, called "Helpful Hints and Advice to Employees," warning against drinking, gambling, borrowing money, taking in boarders, and poor hygiene, advising workers to "use plenty of soap and water in the home and upon their children, bathing frequently." As we read, Ford even employed 100 investigators to do door-to-door checks to make sure his advice was being followed. Today we find such a story quaint. We might think we have reached some sort of societal consensus that what employees do on their own time, away from the workplace, should be entirely their own business.

In 1968, then-chairman of IBM, son of its founder, Thomas Watson Jr. notified his managers that off-the-job-behavior should concern them only when it impaired a person's ability to perform on-the-job. He wrote:

> *The line that separates an individual's on-the-job business life from his other life as a private citizen is at times well-defined and at other times indistinct. But the line does exist, and you and I, as managers in IBM, must be able to recognize that line. . . . Our primary objective as IBM managers is to further the business of this company by leading our people properly and measuring quantity and quality of work and effectiveness on the job against clearly set standards of responsibility and compensation. This is performance—and performance is, in the final analysis, the one thing that the company can insist on from everyone. . . .*

The line that Tom Watson felt he could recognize and define has become much fuzzier since his memo was circulated at IBM. At this point, one of the most contested areas of workplace privacy involves the extent to which an employer may exercise control over a worker's life outside of working hours. Employers want to curb habits that drive up the cost of health care premiums.[11] From this perspective, smokers are much more expensive than nonsmokers,[12] and so businesses have tried to cut their losses with a number of strategies. Ford Meter Box Co. of Wabash, Indiana, fired one of its payroll clerks after a drug test revealed traces of nicotine in her urine—their policy was to forbid smoking anywhere, anytime. Turner Broadcasting in Atlanta, Georgia, also refuses to hire smokers. Some companies use disincentives (Texas Instruments adds a monthly $10 surcharge on health insurance for employees who smoke); others offer incentives (Southern California Edison rebates each nonsmoking worker $120 annually). Policies like these have been aimed at a range of behaviors: workers must keep their blood pressure and cholesterol at healthy levels, avoid being overweight, wear seat belts, join corporate wellness programs. One Georgia developer will not employ anyone who engages in "high risk" recreational activities such as motorcycling or skydiving. The Best Lock Corporation will hire no one who admits to drinking.

10 "Privacy and Democracy in Cyberspace," 52 *Vand. L. Rev.* 1609 (1999).

11 Lifestyle-related illnesses are estimated to cost employers as much as $100 billion annually.

12 According to one Florida case, where a job applicant sued because Miami city government would not hire her as a smoker, health care and productivity costs of more than $4,611/year were cited as associated with employees who smoke. *Kurtz v. City of North Miami,* 653 So.2 1025 (S. C. Florida 1995).

While companies say they are cutting health care costs and lowering rates of absenteeism in these ways, organizations such as the American Civil Liberties Union (ACLU) are troubled by this drift to control off-site behavior. Former ACLU President Ira Glasser has said:

> *If an employer believes your capacity to take care of yourself is in his interest, then you become like a piece of equipment. He gets to lock it up at night and control the temperature and make sure dust doesn't get into the machine, because what happens when it's not working affects how long it's going to last.*

In fact, a peculiar alliance between the ACLU and the tobacco industry was extremely effective in lobbying state legislatures for laws that protect employees who smoke when they are not at work.[13] Today, a majority of states have some version of off-the-job privacy protection laws. In New York, for instance, it is illegal to fire an employee for engaging in off-hours sports, games, hobbies, exercise, reading, movie- or TV-watching.

This was the law at issue in the case that follows. Laurel Allen was married but separated from her husband when she began dating Samuel Johnson, a co-worker at Wal-Mart. When the store manager found out, they were both fired. Wal-Mart's anti-fraternization policy prohibited such relationships as inconsistent with the company's "strongly held belief in and support of the family unit." The New York Attorney General entered the case on behalf of the dating couple, alleging that firing them violated the state law protecting employees' right to engage in off-duty, off-premises recreational activity.

State of New York v. Wal-Mart Stores, Inc.

N.Y. App. Div., 1995
621 N.Y.S.2d 158

MERCURE, Justice.

In February 1993, defendant discharged two of its employees for violating its "fraternization" policy, which is codified in defendant's 1989 *Associates Handbook* and prohibits a "dating relationship" between a married employee and another employee, other than his or her own spouse. In this action, plaintiff seeks reinstatement of the two employees with back pay upon the ground that their discharge violated Labor Law § 201-d(2)(c), which forbids employer discrimination against employees because of their participation in "legal recreational activities" pursued outside of work hours. . . .

[The court must decide whether "a dating relationship" is meant to be included within the statutory definition of "recreational activities."]

Labor Law § 201-d(1)(b) defines "recreational activities" as meaning:

> *. . . any lawful, leisure-time activity, for which the employee receives no compensation and which is generally engaged in for recreational purposes, including but not limited to sports, games, hobbies, exercise, reading and the viewing of television, movies and similar material.*

In our view, there is no justification for proceeding beyond the fundamental rule of construction that "[w]here words of a statute are free from ambiguity and express plainly, clearly and distinctly the legislative intent, resort may not be had to other means of interpretation" . . . . To us, "dating" is entirely distinct from and, in fact, bears little resemblance to "recreational activity." Whether characterized as a relationship or an activity, an indispensable element of "dating," in

13 By 1996, such laws were in effect in 28 states. Virginia, a "tobacco state," was the first to pass one. It reads: "No employee or applicant . . . shall be required . . . to smoke or use tobacco products on the job, or to abstain from smoking or using tobacco products outside of the course of his employment." *VA Code Ann.* 15.1-29, 18 (1990).

fact its raison d'etre, is romance, either pursued or realized. For that reason, although a dating couple may go bowling and under the circumstances call that activity a "date," when two individuals lacking amorous interest in one another go bowling or engage in any other kind of "legal recreational activity," they are not "dating."

Moreover, even if Labor Law § 201-d(1)(b) was found to contain some ambiguity, application of the rules of statutory construction does not support [the trial court's] interpretation. We agree with defendant that . . . the voluminous legislative history to the enactment, including memoranda issued in connection with the veto of two earlier more expansive bills, [shows] an obvious intent to limit the statutory protection to certain clearly defined categories of leisure-time activities. Further, in view of the specific inclusion of "sports, games, hobbies, exercise, reading and the viewing of television, movies and similar material" within the statutory definition of "recreational activities," . . . personal relationships fall outside the scope of legislative intent. . . .

[Order in defendant's favor affirmed.]

YESAWICH, Justice, dissenting.

I respectfully dissent, for I find defendant's central thesis, apparently accepted by the majority, that the employment policy at issue only prohibits romantic entanglements and not other types of social interaction, to be wholly without merit. While the majority encumbers the word "dating" with an "amorous interest" component, there is nothing in defendant's fraternization policy, its application—defendant does not allege that its two former employees manifested an intimate or amatory attitude toward each other—or even in defendant's own definition of a "date", "a social engagement between persons of opposite sex" (*Webster's Ninth New Collegiate Dictionary,* 325 [1988]), that leads to such a conclusion.

More importantly, I do not agree that "dating," whether or not it involves romantic attachment, falls outside the general definition of "recreational activities" found in [the law]. The statute, by its terms, appears to encompass social activities, whether or not they have a romantic element, for it includes any lawful activity pursued for recreational purposes and undertaken during leisure time. Though no explicit definition of "recreational purposes" is contained in the statute, "recreation" is, in the words of one dictionary, "a means of refreshment or diversion" (*Webster's Ninth New Collegiate Dictionary,* 985 [1985]); social interaction surely qualifies as a "diversion. . . ."

In my view, given the fact that the Legislature's primary intent in enacting Labor Law § 201-d was to curtail employers' ability to discriminate on the basis of activities that are pursued outside of work hours, and that have no bearing on one's ability to perform one's job, and concomitantly to guarantee employees a certain degree of freedom to conduct their lives as they please during nonworking hours, the narrow interpretation adopted by the majority is indefensible. Rather, the statute, and the term "recreational activities" in particular, should be construed as broadly as the definitional language allows, to effect its remedial purpose. . . . Here, the list, which includes vast categories such as "hobbies" and "sports," as well as very different types of activities (e.g., exercise, reading), appears to have been compiled with an eye toward extending the reach of the statute. This, coupled with the explicit directive that the definition is not to be limited to the examples given, provides further indication that the term "recreational activities" should be construed expansively.

• QUESTIONS •

1. The judges in this case—both majority and dissenting—are engaging in what is called **statutory construction;** they are determining the outcome of the case by trying to understand the meaning of the law passed by New York's legislature. Note the differences between them. One gives the statute a "broad" reading, the other gives it a "narrow" one. Which is which? What tools do the two judges use to interpret the law? Which interpretation do you think is most in keeping with the intent of the legislators?

2. Try to imagine yourself in Albany as this New York law was being debated. What policy issues might have been raised in favor of the passing the law? Against?

3. Suppose you had the ability to rewrite the New York law, or even delete it from the statute books. How would you change it?

4. **Internet Assignment:** For your state, find out if there is any legislation protecting employees' rights to engage in off-worksite activities. If so, are there any cases interpreting the law? Then, go back to the Montana Wrongful Discharge statute in Chapter 2. What similarities can you see between your state's law and it? What differences?

Testing

Are you a homosexual?
Do you know of any reason why you could be blackmailed?
Do you get along with your spouse?
Are you a communist?
Do you have any money in the bank?
Have you ever stolen anything and not been caught?

These are a few of the questions asked in a polygraph test used by the Coors Brewing Company as a pre-employment screening device. The intrusive nature of that test was part of the reason for a wildcat strike at Coors in 1977. In 1986, as the U.S. Congress was considering a law that would make the use of polygraphs by employers illegal,[14] Coors replaced its polygraph with a lengthy psychological test and background check.

Today, the use of such "pen and pencil" (as opposed to electronic polygraph) honesty or integrity tests is common among employers. One major reason is that employee theft costs U.S. businesses about $10 billion annually. In addition, companies claim an interest in the ability to identify people who are not only competent and honest, but who also fit a certain psychological or moral profile.

In the next case, applicants for security guard positions at a chain of stores objected to many of the questions on a psychological test they had to take.

Soroka v. Dayton Hudson Corporation

Court of Appeal, First District, California, 1991
1 Cal.Rptr.2d 77

REARDON, Associate Justice.

Dayton Hudson Corporation owns and operates Target Stores throughout California and the United States. Job applicants for store security officer (SSO) positions must, as a condition of employment, take a psychological test that Target calls the "Psychscreen." An SSO's main function is to observe, apprehend and arrest suspected shoplifters. An SSO is not armed, but carries handcuffs and may use force against a suspect in self-defense. Target views good judgment and

14 *The Polygraph Act of 1988* bans such tests except for security personnel and others in extremely sensitive positions. Applicants for police force jobs, for instance, are often faced with the kinds of intrusive questions asked in the Coors polygraph test.

emotional stability as important SSO job skills. It intends the Psychscreen to screen out SSO applicants who are emotionally unstable, who may put customers or employees in jeopardy, or who will not take direction and follow Target procedures.

The Psychscreen is a combination of the Minnesota Multiphasic Personality Inventory and the California Psychological Inventory. Both of these tests have been used to screen out emotionally unfit applicants for public safety positions such as police officers, correctional officers, pilots, air traffic controllers and nuclear power plant operators.[15] The test is composed of 704 true-false questions. . . .

The test includes questions about an applicant's religious attitudes, such as: "I feel sure that there is only one true religion. . . . I have no patience with people who believe there is only one true religion. . . . My soul sometimes leaves my body. . . . A minister can cure disease by praying and putting his hand on your head. . . . Everything is turning out just like the prophets of the Bible said it would. . . . I go to church almost every week. . . . I believe in the second coming of Christ. . . . I believe in a life hereafter. . . . I am very religious (more than most people). . . . I believe my sins are unpardonable. . . . I believe there is a God. . . . I believe there is a Devil and a Hell in afterlife."

The test includes questions that might reveal an applicant's sexual orientation, such as: "I wish I were not bothered by thoughts about sex. . . . I have never been in trouble because of my sex behavior. . . . I have been in trouble one or more times because of my sex behavior. . . . My sex life is satisfactory. . . . I am very strongly attracted by members of my own sex. . . . I have often wished I were a girl. (Or if you are a girl) I have never been sorry that I am a girl. . . . I have never indulged in any unusual sex practices. . . . I am worried about sex matters. . . . I like to talk about sex. . . . Many of my dreams are about sex matters."

An SSO's completed test is scored by the consulting psychologist firm of Martin-McAllister. The firm interprets test responses and rates the applicant on five traits: emotional stability, interpersonal style, addiction potential, dependability and reliability, and socialization—i.e., a tendency to follow established rules. Martin-McAllister sends a form to Target rating the applicant on these five traits and recommending whether to hire the applicant. Hiring decisions are made on the basis of these recommendations, although the recommendations may be overridden. Target does not receive any responses to specific questions. . . .

Appellants Sibi Soroka, Susan Urry and William d'Arcangelo were applicants for SSO positions when they took the Psychscreen. All three were upset by the nature of the Psychscreen questions. Soroka was hired by Target. Urry—a Mormon—and d'Arcangelo were not hired. . . .

Soroka alleged causes of action for violation of the right to privacy [under the state constitution], invasion of privacy, disclosure of confidential medical information, fraud, negligent misrepresentation, intentional and negligent infliction of emotional distress, [and violations of state antidiscrimination law].

[Concerning Soroka's state constitutional right to privacy claim, the court wrote:]

The California Constitution explicitly protects our right to privacy. "All people are by nature free and independent and have inalienable rights. Among these are enjoying and defending life and liberty, acquiring, possessing, and protecting property, and pursuing and obtaining safety, happiness, and privacy. . . ."

[W]e turn to the voter's interpretation of [the privacy guarantee]. The ballot argument—the only legislative history for the privacy amendment—specifically states that one purpose of the constitutional right to privacy is to prevent businesses "from collecting . . . unnecessary information about us. . . ." It also asserts that the right to privacy would "preclude the collection of extraneous or frivolous information." Thus, the ballot language requires that the information collected be necessary to achieve the purpose for which the information has been gathered. . . .

15 We view the duties and responsibilities of these public safety personnel to be substantially different from those of store security officers.

While Target unquestionably has an interest in employing emotionally stable persons to be SSOs, testing applicants about their religious beliefs and sexual orientation does not further this interest. To justify the invasion of privacy resulting from use of the Psychscreen, Target must demonstrate a compelling interest and must establish that the test serves a job-related purpose. In its opposition to Soroka's motion for preliminary injunction, Target made no showing that a person's religious beliefs or sexual orientation have any bearing on the emotional stability or on the ability to perform an SSO's job responsibilities. It did no more than to make generalized claims about the Psychscreen's relationship to emotional fitness and to assert that it has seen an overall improvement in SSO quality and performance since it implemented the Psychscreen. This is not sufficient to constitute a compelling interest. . . . Therefore, Target's inquiry into the religious beliefs and sexual orientation of SSO applicants unjustifiably violates the state constitutional right to privacy.

[The court also forecasts that Soroka's claim that the test violates state antidiscrimination law is likely to succeed.]

• QUESTIONS •

1. A $400 million industry, psychological testing is used by 89 of the Fortune 100 companies. Yet it has been criticized on many fronts. There's the problem of unreliability. At the *Soroka* trial, for instance, expert witnesses had thrown into question both the validity and the reliability of Psychscreen. One of the tests on which it was based had been designed only for use in hospital or clinical settings, and there was a 61 percent false positive rate; in other words, more than 6 of every 10 *qualified* applicants fail Psychscreen. Too, recent studies reveal a very low correlation between good tests results and effective performance at work. Some wonder if American employers put so much stock in psychological testing out of an urge to get a quick fix on something that is impossible to quantify. As one writer put it: "We have personality in the sense that we have a consistent pattern of behavior. But that pattern is complex . . . personality is contingent: it represents an interaction between our internal disposition and tendencies and the situation that we find ourselves in."[16] Assuming psychological testing is rife with problems, what could employers do instead to screen job applicants?

2. The *Soroka* case was decided in California. This makes it unusual, because California is unique. One of the eleven states with a privacy amendment in its state constitution, California is the only state to apply it to *private* (not just government) employment. A different and perhaps more typical outcome occurred in a 1982 Massachusetts case where salespeople for Bristol-Myers were fired for resisting an integrity test. Here the judge describes what happened:

> *The questionnaire, entitled Biographical Summary, sought information which, it represented, would be held in strict confidence. The subjects covered included business experience, education, family, home ownership, physical data, activities, and aims. . . . Questions . . . concerned (a) serious illnesses, operations, accidents, or nervous disorders, (b) smoking and drinking habits, (c) off-the-job problems, and (d) principal worries, if any. . . . [Employee] Cort, however, gave limited answers, one of which he admitted was wrong. He was not married in 1960, 1961, and 1962. He listed his dog as a dependent. He gave no information, as the others did, about parents or siblings, if any.*
>
> *Cort answered [other] questions . . . largely in a flippant manner. . . . He wrote as to his principal strengths: "Able to leap tall bldg. at a single bound." As to his principal weaknesses: "Can't land on my feet." Activities in which he would prefer not to engage: "Filling in questions on forms of very personal nature that are no one's business but*

16 Malcolm Gladwell, "Personality Plus," *The New Yorker*, September 20, 2004.

> *mine." He suggested "$1,000,000" as the income he would need to live the way he would like to. Answering concerning plans for the future, he wrote, "Depends on who reads this." He followed his questionnaire with a memorandum to his superiors asking the value to Bristol-Myers of answers to the following questions: "what medications I may be taking, the age and health of my mother and father, the occupations of my brothers and sisters, the value of my house and the amount of mortgage, whose support outside of my immediate family I contribute to, how much I smoke and drink each day, my wife's maiden name, and what personal problems I have outside of business."*

The court decided Cort and his co-workers were at-will employees with no cause of action for privacy invasion:

> *Questions about family and home ownership were probably not of much significance to Bristol-Myers, but those questions were not improperly intrusive, sought information mostly available in public records, and . . . were no more intrusive than those asked on an application for life insurance or for a bank loan.*
>
> *Cort v. Bristol-Myers Co.*, 431 N.E. 2d 908 (1982).

Internet Assignment: In your state, are there any cases dealing with psychological or honesty testing? What was the outcome?

3. Some tests measure abilities:

- Can you type 200 words a minute?
- Can you run 1.5 miles in 12 minutes?
- Are you comfortable using Excel?

Clearly, employers need the results of ability tests to make good hiring and promotion decisions. More controversial is the use of another type of test, one that asks whether you are what you say you are. These are called authenticity tests:

- You say you don't use illegal drugs, but are you really drug-free?
- You say you are honest, but are you really honest?

4. In his 1993 book *Testing Testing: Social Consequences of the Examined Life,* anthropologist F. Allan Hanson explores this form of testing. He begins with history from the period before the scientific method, when authenticity tests took the form of torture and witch burning. He then moves forward to modern forms of testing for truth—the polygraph, honesty test, and urinalysis drug test. Hanson is concerned with the "metamessage," the message that is an inevitable byproduct of authenticity testing. He writes:

> *[T]he metamessage of distrust conveyed by the demand that employees take authenticity tests is unmistakable, and it often erodes loyalty and morale. Essentially they are being told, regardless of your record of service, reliability, and safety, you are suspected of theft, dishonesty, or drug use, and that suspicion will be suspended only by your passing this test, and even if you pass, you will be trusted only until the next test. This engenders hostility against the company and may even spur some workers to take steps to confound or subvert the tests purely as a way to maintain a sense of autonomy and dignity in the face of a system that is aimed at systematically humiliating them. . . . Much more commonly, the metamessage . . . destroys employee motivation to take pride in one's work and perform at a high level and engenders a passive-aggressive response marked by smoldering resentment and diminished productivity.*

Hanson goes on to mention the problem of false positives, where innocent people are wrongly judged guilty. Which ethical theory would attach significance to the points Hanson makes?

Next, Hanson links his argument to a basic privacy concern:

> *To the claim that only those with something to hide need fear . . . authenticity tests, the proper response is that there is a little crook in all of us. . . . [Social interaction consists largely of a series of dramaturgical performances in which people don many masks in an effort to present themselves artfully—concealing certain elements of the self while highlighting and tinting others. The aim is to exercise some control over social situations by influencing others' perception of the self and thereby of the situation. . . . [A]uthenticity testing erodes this distinctive feature of social life. Whether test results are positive or negative is, at this level, irrelevant. The point is that testing opens the self to scrutiny and investigation in ways that the self is powerless to control. So far as the areas of knowledge covered by the tests are concerned, this transforms the person from autonomous subject to passive object.*

What similarities to Alan Westin's description of the functions of privacy do you detect here?

Some may claim that the fact that test results can be kept confidential changes the picture, but Hanson argues the reverse. For him, confidentiality is not a safeguard of privacy, but "yet another ingenious and highly effective technique for exercising power and discipline over the individual":

> *Although it is advertised as a protective measure for test takers, confidentiality completes the domination of test givers over test takers. It assures that each individual confronts the organizations that mandate testing utterly alone and therefore in the weakest possible state. Here disciplinary power has achieved the remarkable feat of perfecting the domination of people by dividing them and dealing with them singly, all the while convincing them that the arrangement is for their own good.*

Do you agree with Hanson's analysis?

Consumer Privacy

> *Advertisers and publishers want a better eyeball, and a better eyeball is a more targeted eyeball.*
>
> — Richard Baumer, president of a company that sells ads on behalf of Web sites

> *The big long-term concern about privacy is the surreptitious compilation of every site you click, every page you download, every product you order into a single database.*
>
> — Marc Rotenberg, President, Electronic Privacy Information Center

According to a study by the research firm Privacy and American Business, 86 percent of Internet users want to be able to trade their personal data online as long as they are properly informed as to how the information would be used and are offered benefits in exchange for it. In the next case, bank customers object after their personal data was taken without their consent.

TIMOTHY V. CHASE MANHATTAN BANK

New York Supreme Court, 2002
741 N.Y.S.2d 100

The plaintiffs, who purport to represent a class of similarly-situated persons, are holders of credit cards and mortgages issued by Chase Manhattan Bank USA, N.A. . . . The complaint alleges that Chase violated its commitment to protect customer privacy and confidentiality and not to share customer information with any unrelated third party. . . . This confidentiality commitment was contained in a printed document entitled "Customer Information Principles," which was distributed to the plaintiffs. Allegedly unbeknownst to the plaintiffs, without their consent and without giving the plaintiffs an opportunity to opt-out, Chase sold information to non-affiliated third-party vendors, including the plaintiffs' names, addresses, telephone numbers, account or loan numbers, credit card usage, and other financial data. The third-party vendors used this information and created lists of Chase customers, including the plaintiffs, who might be interested in their products or services. These lists were then provided to telemarketing and direct mail representatives to conduct solicitations. In return for the information, the third-party vendors agreed to pay Chase a commission (of up to 24% of the sale) in the event that a product or service offered were purchased. . . .

To establish a cause of action under [New York's] General Business Law § 349, a plaintiff must prove that the challenged act or practice was consumer-oriented, that it was misleading in a material way, and that the plaintiff suffered injury as a result of the deceptive act. Whether a representation or omission, the deceptive practice must be likely to mislead a reasonable consumer acting reasonably under the circumstances. In addition, to recover under the statute, a plaintiff must prove actual injury, though not necessarily pecuniary harm.

[T]he plaintiffs have not alleged, and cannot prove, any "actual injury" as is necessary under General Business Law § 349. . . . [despite their claim that]:

> *the products and services offered to class members as a result of [Chase's] practices of selling class members' confidential financial information included memberships in discount shoppers' clubs, emergency road service plans, dental and legal service plans, travel clubs, home and garden supply clubs, and credit card registration and magazine subscription services.*

Thus, the "harm" at the heart of this purported class action, is that class members were merely offered products and services which they were free to decline. This does not qualify as actual harm.

The complaint does not allege a single instance where a named plaintiff or any class member suffered any actual harm due to the receipt of an unwanted telephone solicitation or a piece of junk mail.

[The state GBL claim was dismissed.]

The plaintiffs seek to recover damages for unjust enrichment based on the profits Chase earned as commissions on the purchases made by members of the plaintiffs' class. "To state a cause of action for unjust enrichment, a plaintiff must allege that it conferred a benefit upon the defendant, and that the defendant will obtain such benefit without adequately compensating plaintiff therefor" [cite] The plaintiffs failed to state a cause of action to recover damages for unjust enrichment since the members of the plaintiffs' class who made purchases of products and/or services received a benefit. There being no allegation that the benefits received were less than what these purchasers bargained for, it cannot be said that the commissions paid by the third-party vendors to Chase belong to the plaintiffs.

[The claim for unjust enrichment was also dismissed.]

• QUESTIONS •

1. Why was plaintiffs' claim under the New York General Business law dismissed? Their claim regarding unjust enrichment?
2. What similarities are there between this case and *Smyth v. Pillsbury*? Differences? **Internet Assignment:** Find out what happened when consumers sued American Express in Illinois for selling information much as Chase Manhattan had done in this case.
3. If you had to write a dissenting opinion to the *Smith v. Chase Manhattan* case, what would you argue?
4. In August 2002, the New York Attorney General sued Student Marketing Group (SMG) for violating the state's consumer protection laws. SMG had given surveys to high school teachers across the United States to be handed out to students, who would then fill in their names, e-mail addresses, age, gender, religious affiliation, ethnicity, grade point average, and career interests. SMG claimed it was going to distribute this information to colleges and universities for admissions and financial aid purposes, but in fact they turned it over to marketers. How would you analyze this scenario from a utilitarian ethical perspective? A deontological one? **Internet Assignment:** What happened in this case?
5. **Internet Assignment:** In 1999, the U.S. Congress passed the Gramm-Leach-Bliley Act, requiring banks and other financial institutions to tell consumers when they plan to share or sell their personal financial information, and to give consumers the power to stop such a transfers. Has there been adequate compliance with this recent law? Start here: http://www.ftc.gov.
6. Low-fare, no-frills JetBlue airlines had a scandal on its hands in the fall of 2003 when it admitted it had released information about more than one million of its passengers at the request of a private company working on antiterrorism with the Pentagon, Torch Concepts. The disclosure of customer names, addresses, phone numbers, and flight information was in violation of JetBlue's own privacy policy. **Internet Assignment:** What was the fallout of this incident? Investigation? Lawsuits?
7. **Internet Assignment:** Are U.S. consumers concerned about privacy as they shop online? Find a recent poll.

Europe vs. America: Dignity vs. Liberty

Yale law professor James Q. Whitman makes this broad distinction between conceptions of privacy in Europe versus America:

> *Continental privacy protections are, at their core, a form of protection of a right to respect and personal dignity. [They] . . . are rights to one's image, name, and reputation, and . . . to informational self-determination—the right to control the sorts of information disclosed about oneself . . . all rights to control your public image—to guarantee that people see you the way you want to be seen. They are, as it were, rights to be shielded against unwanted public exposure—to be spared embarrassment or humiliation.*
>
> *By contrast, America, in this as in so many things, is much more oriented toward values of liberty, liberty against the state. The American right to privacy still takes much of the form that it took in the eighteenth century: It is the right to freedom from intrusions by the state, especially in one's own home. The prime danger, from the American point of view, is that the . . . [home] will*

be breached by government actors. American anxieties . . . tend to be about maintaining a kind of private sovereignty within our own walls.[17]

Perhaps this distinction explains the strength of the protections given to personal information by the European Privacy Directive. A "Directive" protecting the privacy of personal information as it moves across national borders was passed by the European Union on July 24, 1995. Under the Privacy Directive, each member nation must pass laws guaranteeing that personal data gathered is accurate, up-to-date, relevant, and not excessive. Information collected may be used only for the purpose for which it was collected, and can be processed only with the consent of the subject, when required by law, or to protect the "public interest" or the "legitimate interests" of a third party, unless those interests are superseded by the "fundamental rights and freedoms of the data subject." The Directive sharply limits the collection of information about "racial or ethnic origin, political opinions, religious or philosophical beliefs, trade-union membership [or] concerning health or sex life." Data subjects must be informed that data will be taken about them, and must be notified how it will be used. Perhaps most striking of all, given the very different legal rules in the United States, the EU Directive gives Europeans the right of access to information collected about themselves, and the opportunity to correct inaccuracies. Further, each member nation must establish a data privacy "commissioner," and a national agency that monitors enforcement.

Internet Assignment: Look up the "safe harbor" provision that allows U.S. multinational corporations some flexibility in complying with this Directive as they do business in Europe. How does it function?

Privacy Under the Constitution

The Fourth Amendment protects the "reasonable expectations of privacy" of both individual and corporate citizens against unwarranted and unreasonable government searches or seizures. Whenever the government searches a person's body for drugs or alcohol, or searches business premises for evidence of wrongdoing, there is a potential "privacy" Fourth Amendment claim.

That is why those who work for the government—public school teachers, IRS agents, police, firefighters, regulators at the FTC, and attorneys in the Justice Department, for example—can be subject to electronic surveillance or genetic testing only when their employer's justification outweighs the individual's privacy interests. Case law developed over the past two decades has made it clear that the government interest in a drug-free workplace almost always trumps an employee's desire to avoid drug-testing, so long as the procedures are fair and reasonable.

In 1987, the Supreme Court decided a case involving the search of a public employee's office. Magno Ortega, a psychiatrist at State Hospital, was suspected of stealing a computer and of sexually harassing female workers. While he was on vacation, his employer had his desk and file cabinets searched thoroughly. Investigators found, among other items, a valentine card, a book of love poetry, and a semi-nude photograph of a female doctor.

The Court found that this search did not violate the Fourth Amendment. It explained that the employment context itself both (1) lowered the employee's legitimate privacy expectations, and (2) created a strong need on the employer's part to discover work-related misconduct:

An office is seldom a private enclave free from entry by supervisors, other employees and business and personal invitees. Instead in many cases offices are continually entered by

17 "The Two Western Cultures of Privacy: Dignity v. Liberty," 113 *Yale L. J.* 1151 (2004).

fellow employees and other visitors during the workday for conferences, consultations, and other work-related visits. Simply put—it is the nature of government offices that others . . . may have frequent access to an individual's office. . . .

While police . . . conduct searches for the primary purpose of obtaining evidence for use in criminal . . . proceedings, employers most frequently need to enter the offices and desks of their employees for legitimate work-related reasons wholly unrelated to illegal conduct. Employers and supervisors are focused primarily on the need to complete the government agency's work in a prompt and efficient manner. An employer may have need for correspondence, or a file or report available only in an employee's office while the employee is away from the office. Or, as is alleged to have been the case here, employers may need to safeguard or identify state property or records in an office in connection with a pending investigation into suspected employee malfeasance.[18]

The Court went on to hold that a search of a government employee would be viewed as reasonable as long as (1) the search was justified at its inception, as it was in Ortega's case because they suspected him already, and (2) the search was carried out in an appropriate manner.

Suppose the government wants to search the site of a business to look for possible violations of the law? At about the time the Justice Department began to investigate them for possible securities fraud, employees at Enron and Arthur Andersen deleted many computer files. To locate stored copies of those files, government investigators may need to search the hard drives of computers at those firms. To do so, they must have consent, or probable cause to get a search warrant. More often, however, businesses are subject to what are known as "administrative searches" conducted by regulatory agencies such as the Occupational Safety and Health Administration or the Environmental Protection Agency, rather than the local police or FBI. In those situations, warrants are easier to get. Instead of the kind of specific facts required to establish "probable cause" that a crime has been committed, an administrative search warrant can be issued for routine inspections done as part of a reasonable legislative or administrative plan. [*Marshall v. Barlows*, 98 S.Ct. 1816 (1978).] And, in "closely regulated industries"—mining, liquor, and pawnshops, for example—even warrantless searches or records inspections generally pass the reasonableness test of the Fourth Amendment, because the high degree of regulation creates a greatly diminished expectation of privacy.

Counter-Terrorism: Security vs. Privacy

In the immediate aftermath of the attacks of September 11th, as American citizens were newly expected to remove their shoes for inspection at airports, or to empty their purses on entry to museums and other public buildings, they seemed not to mind letting go of some old assumptions about their personal privacy. Most U.S. citizens trusted their government as it gave itself heightened ability to fight terrorism. The USA Patriot Act of 2001—more than seven hundred pages of amendments to a whole range of federal statutes—expanded the government's statutory surveillance powers, making it easier for it to eavesdrop, share information among various agencies, and find out such things as what books library patrons have checked out.

In 2001, roughly one-third of Americans polled were "very confident" and more than half were "somewhat confident" that federal authorities were handling their enlarged powers properly. In early 2003 the citizen comfort level remained about the same, even as civil liberties groups challenged some of the provisions of the USA Patriot Act as violations of the Fourth Amendment. By the end of that year, Congress further expanded the FBI's authority to demand

18 *O'Connor v. Ortega,* 107 S.Ct. 1492 (1987).

business records without court approval in national security investigations. Under what some have called Patriot II, it is now easier for the FBI to get an administrative subpoena known as a "national security letter" to search more kinds of businesses, including car dealerships, pawnbrokers, the Postal Service, travel agents, and casinos.

Kari Lydersen writes for the *Washington Post* and is an instructor for the Urban Youth International Journalism Program in Chicago. In this article she explains the intermeshing of the public and the private sector in the war on terror.

SPYING FOR FUN AND PROFIT

Kari Lydersen[19]

New technology has become ubiquitous in the post-Sept. 11 world. Biometric devices record the facial bone structures, iris scans, voices and other physical attributes of every person who walks by in an airport, stadium or park. Electronic monitors track web page visits or bank transactions. Even good old-fashioned video surveillance cameras are being used more than ever in conjunction with facial recognition software.

All these technologies raise serious questions about invasions of privacy and violations of civil liberties. They also cost a lot of money. Taxpayers fund this massively beefed up security. Private corporations and even individuals are also paying large amounts to boost their own security procedures in light of the war on terrorism. Naturally, someone is also profiting off this boom.

Market analysts and corporate watchdog groups note that there have been a raft of upstart companies jumping into the security/surveillance market, and existing major security and defense companies have expanded their product lines and sales. . . .

The Spy-Tech Boom

One of the first widespread security technologies to be discussed after the Sept. 11 attacks was face recognition software in airports. Almost immediately after the terrorist attacks, two providers of this software—Visionis and Viisage—started marketing their products as terror prevention solutions.

"Their publicity stunt worked," said Chris Hoofnagle of the Electronic Privacy Information Center (EPIC) in a Nov. 2001 interview with the Multinational Monitor. "Their stock prices doubled very quickly, and it appeared as though different public transportation centers would adopt the technology. In fact, Oakland International Airport has." Since then, various other airports including Dallas, Rhode Island and Boston and other tourist destinations including the Virginia Beach oceanfront and a Tampa nightlife district have purchased facial recognition systems. One of the main beneficiaries has been Pelco Inc., the world's largest maker of video security systems.

The growth in demand for software alone to comply with the PATRIOT Act has been huge—the act requires financial institutions, including banks, credit card companies and insurance carriers, to closely monitor customer activity. Cisco, Sybase, Sun Microsystems and Oracle are just a few of the various software companies ready to meet these demands, often by expanding their existing lines of anti-money laundering (or AML) software. "Compliance with the USA PATRIOT Act has never been easier, thanks to Sybase's PATRIOT compliance solution," says a promo on the company's web site.

There has been some small protest within the companies; in March 2003, Groove Networks Inc. board member Mitch Kapor quit in protest over Groove selling its software to the government for anti-terrorism surveillance. And one vendor refused to sell its software to the government. But, for the most part, companies have jumped at the chance of government contracts.

19 AlterNet, May 27, 2003.

Veni, Vidi, Vendors

In a report called "The USA PATRIOT Act: Impact on AML Vendors and the Market," financial services analyst Breffni McGuire wrote that, "although the law imposes new burdens on banks, it is proving to be a boon for vendors of AML and related products and technology. . . ." Many are hesitant to question the necessity or efficiency of security-related expenditures, but the fact is this may be more a matter of companies capitalizing on opportunity to create a demand rather than developing products that genuinely offer a needed service. In reality, much of the now-popular security technology had been developed and marketed for other purposes before Sept. 11. . . .

[I]n 2002 the Food and Drug Administration approved the long-in-development sale of subdermal microchips which would allow someone's location to be tracked at any moment. While now these chips are mentioned as parts of a hazy plan to keep tabs on all residents at all times, in the past they were marketed to parents on the basis that they could help them find their children should they be kidnapped.

"Lots of these technologies have been in the works and looking for a justification for a long time," said Charlie Cray of the group Citizen Works. "Then some news event comes along and they find someone to push it. For example, every once in a while you see a national story about some kid getting kidnapped. Then someone says that's a reason why parents should get their kids registered in some kind of national database. Of course, what they don't tell you is the corporate motive behind this fear-mongering. That Oracle just happens to own the national ID database that would be used."

Biometric Bungles

A report released by the General Accounting Office (GAO) in spring of 2002 said that government agencies had spent more than $50 million in the past five years on camera surveillance technology, with a notable increase in spending proposals after Sept. 11. A big chunk of this money was funneled toward facial recognition programs, which made up 90 percent of government surveillance budgets since 1997 according to the GAO report. In the pre-terrorism era, significant surveillance funds were also designated for catching and fining red light runners. In nabbing red light runners, surveillance technology has been highly effective. But for catching would-be terrorists, it is a different story.

While biometrics is currently all the rage for everything from scanning for terrorists in crowds at public events to recording participants at demonstrations, the fact is the technology is highly error-prone and not well-suited for these functions. A study by the National Institute for Standards in Technology showed that face recognition biometric technology turned up false positives in matching scans with a database 43 percent of the time. . . ." If a terrorist really wants to get into the country they'll just hire a marijuana smuggler to get them in a boat into the swamps in Louisiana," [according to Leon Tien, staff attorney for the Electronic Frontier Foundation].

Defense CEOs' Cash Crop

David Martin, a researcher and media coordinator at the non-profit United for a Fair Economy, noted that as with surveillance technology, increased government spending as well as speculation is leading to major profiteering for defense companies—and even more so for their CEOs. A recent report Martin co-authored, called "More Bucks for the Bang," found that the salaries of CEOs of the top 37 publicly traded defense companies have mushroomed way out of proportion to other CEOs and also out of proportion to the companies' actual profits. . . .

While these companies are primarily involved with manufacturing weapons, many of them, including Dell Computers, also develop electronic or other surveillance-related technologies. The defense company CEOs' pay increased an average of 79 percent from 2001 to 2002, compared to 6 percent for CEOs in general. The CEO of Lockheed Martin, the country's largest defense contractor, increased 400 percent.

The study also found that the amount of a company's campaign contributions are in direct correlation (statistically .90) with the size of the defense contracts they receive.

As with most of the legislation and political programs that have come to pass since Sept. 11, the growing market for security and surveillance isn't likely to go away even if our country goes years without suffering a terrorist attack. Even before most people had ever heard of Al Qaeda, Americans were becoming more and more obsessed with both locking themselves in and finding ways to sneak peeks at others—witness the parallel growth in both gated communities and voyeuristic web cams and reality TV shows. "You can't totally differentiate between what's going on now and the natural trends before Sept. 11," Tien said, noting the long-time grassroots popularity of low-level surveillance gadgets. "People are very interested in security and watching each other—we're all watched by Big Brother, but we're also all little brothers watching each other." Now, with security as the excuse for all kinds of surveillance, there are a few companies who stand to make a large profit—and a lot of citizens who will lose something even more precious—their privacy.

• QUESTIONS •

1. What are the drivers of surveillance technology sales?
2. To what extent do you think enhanced surveillance technology will make our society safer?
3. What are some of the ethical issues suggested by this article?
4. As Lydersen notes, a major problem with surveillance technology has been false positives. Even the most sophisticated systems have been problematic in this way, especially when operating out of doors, and especially when applied to younger people. The top three systems had a less than 65 percent accuracy rate with people between the ages of 18 and 27, for example. What can you find out about the accuracy rates of the latest surveillance technologies? Are they improving?
5. The article mentions the curious paradox that Americans seem to be "more and more obsessed with both locking themselves in and finding ways to sneak peeks at others." Do you think it's a coincidence? Or is there some relationship between these trends?

PRIVACY IN MEDICAL INFORMATION

> *Whatsoever things I see or hear concerning the life of men, in my attendance on the sick or even apart therefrom, which ought not to be noised about, I will keep silence thereon, counting such things to be as sacred secrets.*
>
> — Hippocratic Oath

One of the most disturbing flashpoints where technology has outstripped privacy protection involves the health care industry. Profoundly confidential medical information is accessible to thousands of strangers, as physicians, hospitals, HMOs, insurers, pharmacies, government agencies, pension funds, and employers find themselves generating and/or processing it.

Genetic testing of tiny amounts of human tissue—strands of hair, a few drops of blood—can reveal tremendous amounts of sensitive health data. In the next case, medical privacy issues come up in the context of genetic testing. A research facility in California required all job applicants to undergo health examinations to be eligible for clerical and administrative positions. The applicants, seven African-Americans and one Latino, had completed questionnaires and given blood and urine samples, but did not realize that theirs would be among those selected to be tested for such conditions as syphilis, sickle cell trait, and pregnancy. Here, the Ninth Circuit, in a case of first impression, must decide whether citizens have a right to genetic privacy.

Norman-Bloodsaw v. Lawrence Berkeley Laboratory

U.S. Court of Appeals, Ninth Circuit, 1997
135 F.3d 1260

REINHARDT, Circuit Judge.

[The named plaintiffs] are current and former administrative and clerical employees of defendant Lawrence Berkeley Laboratory ("Lawrence"), a research facility operated . . . pursuant to a contract with the United States Department of Energy (the Department). The Department requires federal contractors such as Lawrence to establish an occupational medical program. Since 1981, it has required its contractors to perform "preplacement examinations" of employees as part of this program, and until 1995, it also required its contractors to offer their employees the option of subsequent "periodic health examinations." The mandatory preplacement examination occurs after the offer of employment but prior to the assumption of job duties. The Department actively oversees Lawrence's occupational health program, and, prior to 1992, specifically required syphilis testing as part of the preplacement examination.

[All but one of the named plaintiffs] received written offers of employment expressly conditioned upon a "medical examination. . . ." All accepted these offers and underwent preplacement examinations. . . . In the course of these examinations, plaintiffs completed medical history questionnaires and provided blood and urine samples. The questionnaires asked, [among other things,] whether the patient had ever had any of sixty-one medical conditions, including "[s]ickle cell anemia,"[20] "[v]enereal disease," and, in the case of women, "[m]enstrual disorders."[21]

The blood and urine samples given by all employees during their preplacement examinations were tested for syphilis; in addition, certain samples were tested for sickle cell trait; and certain samples were tested for pregnancy. Lawrence discontinued syphilis testing in April 1993, pregnancy testing in December 1994, and sickle cell trait testing in June 1995. Defendants assert that they discontinued syphilis testing because of its limited usefulness in screening healthy populations, and that they discontinued sickle cell trait testing because, by that time, most African-American adults had already been tested at birth. Lawrence continues to perform pregnancy testing, but only on an optional basis. Defendants further contend that "for many years" signs posted in the health examination rooms and "more recently" in the reception area stated that the tests at issue would be administered.

Plaintiffs allege that the testing of their blood and urine samples for syphilis, sickle cell trait, and pregnancy occurred without their knowledge or consent, and without any subsequent

20 Sickle cell anemia is a physical affliction in which a large proportion or majority of an individual's red blood cells become sickle-shaped. Sickle cell trait is a genetic condition in which an individual carries the gene that causes sickle cell anemia. The sickle cell gene is only semi-dominant; if the carrier of the gene is heterozygous (meaning that the gene is paired with a non-sickle cell gene), some of his or her red blood cells may sickle, but usually not to a sufficient degree to result in actual sickle cell anemia.

21 The section of the questionnaire also asks women if they have ever had abnormal pap smears and men if they have ever had prostate gland disorders.

notification that the tests had been conducted. They also allege that only black employees were tested for sickle cell trait and assert the obvious fact that only female employees were tested for pregnancy. Finally, they allege that Lawrence failed to provide safeguards to prevent the dissemination of the test results. They contend that they did not discover that the disputed tests had been conducted until approximately January 1995, and specifically deny that they observed any signs indicating that such tests would be performed. Plaintiffs do not allege that the defendants took any subsequent employment-related action on the basis of their test results, or that their test results have been disclosed to third parties.

On the basis of these factual allegations, plaintiffs contend . . . that the defendants violated the federal constitutional right to privacy by conducting the testing at issue, collecting and maintaining the results of the testing, and failing to provide adequate safeguards against disclosure of the results. They [also]contend that the testing violated their right to privacy under Article I, s 1 of the California Constitution. Finally, plaintiffs contend that Lawrence and the Regents violated Title VII by singling out black employees for sickle cell trait testing and by performing pregnancy testing on female employees generally.

Federal Constitutional Due Process Right of Privacy

The constitutionally protected privacy interest in avoiding disclosure of personal matters clearly encompasses medical information and its confidentiality. [cites] Although cases defining the privacy interest in medical information have typically involved its disclosure to "third" parties, rather than the collection of information by illicit means, it goes without saying that the most basic violation possible involves the performance of unauthorized tests—that is, the non-consensual retrieval of previously unrevealed medical information that may be unknown even to plaintiffs. These tests may also be viewed as searches . . . that require Fourth Amendment scrutiny. Accordingly, we must balance the government's interest in conducting these particular tests against the plaintiffs' expectations of privacy. Furthermore, "application of the balancing test requires not only considering the degree of intrusiveness and the state's interests in requiring that intrusion, but also 'the efficacy of this [the state's] means for meeting' its needs."

One can think of few subject areas more personal and more likely to implicate privacy interests than that of one's health or genetic make-up. . . . Furthermore, the facts revealed by the tests are highly sensitive, even relative to other medical information. With respect to the testing of plaintiffs for syphilis and pregnancy, it is well established in this circuit "that the Constitution prohibits unregulated, unrestrained employer inquiries into personal sexual matters that have no bearing on job performance." The fact that one has syphilis is an intimate matter that pertains to one's sexual history and may invite tremendous amounts of social stigma. Pregnancy is likewise, for many, an intensely private matter, which also may pertain to one's sexual history and often carries far-reaching societal implications. Finally, the carrying of sickle cell trait can pertain to sensitive information about family history and reproductive decision making. Thus, the conditions tested for were aspects of one's health in which one enjoys the highest expectations of privacy.

[T]here was little, if any, "overlap" between what plaintiffs consented to and the testing at issue here. . . . That one has consented to a general medical examination does not abolish one's privacy right not to be tested for intimate, personal matters involving one's health—nor does consenting to giving blood or urine samples,[22] or filling out a questionnaire. As we have made clear, revealing one's personal knowledge as to whether one has a particular medical condition has nothing to do with one's expectations about actually being tested for that condition. Thus, the intrusion was by no means [insignificant]. . . .

---

22 Indeed, the Supreme Court has recognized that while the taking of a bodily fluid sample implicates one's privacy interests, "[t]he ensuing chemical analysis of the sample to obtain physiological data is a further intrusion of the tested employee's privacy interests." *Skinner v. Railway Labor Executives' Ass'n,* (1989) (allowing urine testing of railway workers for drugs).

Title VII Claims

Section 703(a) of Title VII of the Civil Rights Act of 1964 provides that it is unlawful for any employer:

> *to fail or refuse to hire or to discharge any individual, or otherwise to discriminate against any individual with respect to his compensation, terms, conditions, or privileges of employment, because of such individual's race, color, religion, sex, or national origin. . . .*

The Pregnancy Discrimination Act further provides that discrimination on the basis of "sex" includes discrimination "on the basis of pregnancy, childbirth, or related medical conditions."

[P]laintiffs' Title VII claims fall neatly into a Title VII framework: Plaintiffs allege that black and female employees were singled out for additional nonconsensual testing and that defendants thus selectively invaded the privacy of certain employees on the basis of race, sex, and pregnancy.

It is well established that Title VII bars discrimination . . . in the "terms" and "conditions" under which individuals may obtain employment. See, e.g., *Griggs v. Duke Power Co.* (1971) (facially neutral educational and testing requirements that are not reasonable measures of job performance and have disparate impact on hiring of minorities violate Title VII). Thus, for example, a requirement of preemployment health examinations imposed only on female employees, or a requirement of preemployment background security checks imposed only on black employees, would surely violate Title VII.

In this case, the term or condition for black employees was undergoing a test for sickle cell trait; for women it was undergoing a test for pregnancy. It is not disputed that the preplacement exams were, literally, a condition of employment: the offers of employment stated this explicitly. Thus, the employment of women and blacks at Lawrence was conditioned in part on allegedly unconstitutional invasions of privacy to which white and/or male employees were not subjected. An additional "term or condition" requiring an unconstitutional invasion of privacy is, without doubt, actionable under Title VII.[23]

[Judgment of the lower court dismissing the claims is reversed.]

• QUESTIONS •

1. On what basis did the Ninth Circuit find that the federal Constitution had been violated by the laboratory in this case? The federal Civil Rights Act?

2. Why do you think employers are interested in the results of genetic testing of their employees?

3. There have many documented instances of employers and insurance companies denying health coverage based on knowledge of genetic dispositions.[24] The *Bloodsaw* case raises the specter of such data being gathered in a discriminatory way. Can you think of some of the other potential problems with genetic testing?

4. **Internet Assignment:** Since the *Bloodsaw* case, Congress passed the Health Information Portability and Accountability Act, or HIPAA, which took effect in 2004. Would the type of testing that occurred in *Bloodsaw* violate the HIPAA statute?

5. Gary Avary worked for Burlington Northern Santa Fe Railroad. He had developed carpal tunnel syndrome there, and had filed a workers compensation claim. The railroad then told him he had to have a medical exam. When his wife, Janice, found out that this exam required

---

23 An exception exists for pregnancy testing in those "instances in which . . . pregnancy actually interferes with the employee's ability to perform the job." No such exception is asserted here.

24 A Georgetown University survey of people with genetic-based disorders in their families found that 43 percent claimed they were denied health insurance, life insurance, or a job because of disclosures of potential genetic problems.

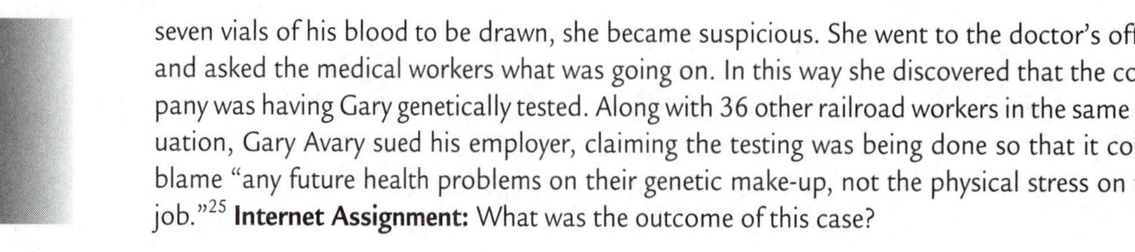

seven vials of his blood to be drawn, she became suspicious. She went to the doctor's office and asked the medical workers what was going on. In this way she discovered that the company was having Gary genetically tested. Along with 36 other railroad workers in the same situation, Gary Avary sued his employer, claiming the testing was being done so that it could blame "any future health problems on their genetic make-up, not the physical stress on the job."[25] **Internet Assignment:** What was the outcome of this case?

Genetic Testing: Economics and Ethics

> *Ladies and gentlemen, progress is like a storekeeper. You can have anything you want, but you have to pay the price. You can have the telephone, but you will lose some of your privacy, and the charm of distance. You can have the airplane, but the birds will lose their wonder and the clouds will smell of gasoline.*
>
> — Clarence Darrow in *Inherit the Wind,* about the Scopes trial

The next reading is a speech given by Lewis Maltby, President of the National Workrights Institute. Mr. Maltby is a lawyer. At the beginning of his career he was a corporate attorney; later he managed an engineering company. His experiences with business and law combined with his personal interest in social policy led him to volunteer time with the ACLU. In 2000 he formed his own nonprofit organization focused on the rights of employees.

BRAVE NEW WORKPLACE: GENETIC BREAKTHROUGHS AND THE NEW EMPLOYMENT DISCRIMINATION[26]

Lewis Maltby, President, National Workrights Institute

In the long run, the genetic revolution may prove to be a historic blessing. . . . Think what the post-genetic world could be like. A world in which vibrant young men no longer turn into human statues and die. A world in which young women aren't forced to mutilate themselves and still die before their children are out of elementary school. A world in [which] we don't have to watch our parents slowly losing their minds while we stand by helpless.

But these utopian changes are years in the future, probably decades. The immediate future looks much more grim. What happens during the time when we can identify the genes linked to disease, but have no prevention or cure? What happens to those among us who have been identified as carrying the gene for Huntington's or cancer, but whose medical future we cannot affect?

---

25 "Genetic Tests Outpace Efforts to Safeguard People's Data," *USA Today,* August 19, 2002, p. A10.

26 Lynda M. Fox Memorial Keynote Address, University of Colorado Medical School, Aspen, Colorado, July 21, 2000.

Employment Discrimination

The sad truth is that these people will probably be subjected to a lifetime of employment discrimination. The economic cost incurred by a person with Huntington's disease is approximately $50,000. What employer will hire a person who comes with that kind of liability? What employer will willingly hire a woman who carries the genetic marker for breast cancer?

It's true, of course, that the math isn't that simple. With the exception of Huntington's, having a genetic marker represents only an increased probability of contracting the disease. . . . And the best candidate for a job brings more value than the other candidates. But the bottom line is still the same, unless you're a superstar, you won't get the job.

What's worse, you won't get any job. If you're denied a job because of your race or your gender, at least you have the chance to keep applying at other places until you find an employer that isn't biased against you. But it's totally different with genetic discrimination. An employer who refuses to hire someone with a genetic marker isn't acting on irrational bias. In some cases the discrimination really is cost-justified. It may be bad ethics, but it's not bad economics. . . . We are facing the prospect of thousands of young, capable people being denied the opportunity to have a career and contribute to society.

Fortunately, genetic discrimination is still uncommon. According to the American Management Association, only 1% of employers have a genetic testing program. The reason for this is not ethics, but money. At the present time, genetic testing is not generally cost-justified. An employer would have to test thousands of potential employees to find a single person with the Huntington's gene. The cost of testing so many people is greater than the amount that would be saved by excluding the person with Huntington's.

But this could easily change, and very soon. The cost of technology always drops dramatically once it moves from the laboratory to the factory. Genetic testing technology will be no exception. Tests have already been developed that will reduce the cost of testing for HD by an order of magnitude. Even more important are the implications of the development of tests for more common genetic markers. For example, the incidence of breast cancer is 30 times that of Huntington's. An employer can get 30 times the financial payoff from screening for breast cancer genetic markers than it can by testing for Huntington's. While the numerical dust hasn't settled yet, there are many who believe that genetic screening will soon be cost-justified. When this occurs, genetic testing may become as common as drug testing is today.

Legal Status

To make matters worse, the law doesn't protect us against genetic discrimination. The only relevant federal law, the Americans with Disabilities Act, defines "disability" as being "substantially limited in the ability to carry out major life activities." While a person who currently has a genetic disease may well meet this definition, someone who merely carries the gene associated with a disease does not. They are not at all limited in their abilities because they have no symptoms.

There is another definition of "disability" under the ADA. The act also protects people who are "perceived as" being disabled. But this doesn't really fit either. Employers don't mistakenly think that asymptomatic carriers of a genetic mutation are limited. Employers know that a woman with the breast cancer gene is just as capable as anyone else. They just know that she has a higher than average likelihood of running up a big medical bill in the future and want to avoid the expense.[27]

27 As an indicator of how federal courts will rule on this issue, the Supreme Court's decision in *Bragdon v. Abbott,* while holding that people who are HIV positive are covered by the ADA, is disappointing. This was a textbook case of discrimination based on future disability. But the Court refused to decide it that way. Instead, the Court conjured up a tortured claim that a person who is HIV positive, although totally asymptomatic, is already disabled (because she is unable to perform the major life activity of reproduction).

Many states have enacted statutes that address this problem by specifically prohibiting genetic discrimination in employment. Fourteen states now prohibit genetic discrimination by employers. Unfortunately, many of these laws provide little or no protection in practice.

For example, some state laws outlaw genetic discrimination, but do not address employer access to genetic information. Employers will still be able to learn which potential employees are at risk for future disease and the attendant medical bills. Where these risks are substantial employers will often find that it is more cost effective to discriminate.

Other legislatures recognized this problem and prohibited genetic testing as well. But this too falls short because most employers who acquire genetic information do not get it by testing themselves. Rather, they obtain it by examining applicants' medical records and checking their family history and tests they have taken privately. Employers are able to see these records because there is a gaping hole in the ADA that allows employers to see an applicant's entire medical history once a conditional job offer has been made, including information that is not job related in any way.

The only effective formula is to prohibit both discrimination and employer access to genetic information. Several states, including New Jersey, have taken this approach in their statutes, as does pending federal legislation.

While we may be able to deal with the direct threat of genetic discrimination by employers, our growing ability to see into the medical future raises broader issues that are not easily answered, even in theory.

Health Insurance

The greatest of these is whether we can maintain the model of providing health insurance through employment. There is no compelling reason why health insurance should be provided in this manner. Most advanced industrial nations do not do it this way, and the United States' decision to do so was a historical accident. During World War II, there was a shortage of employees because most of the workforce was in uniform. But strict wage and price controls prevented employers from competing for workers by raising salaries. Clever employers realized that they could escape this trap by providing other benefits such as medical insurance. Workers liked this change and it became standard operating procedure for American employers.

Despite its strange beginning the model worked well for decades. Employers knew that some of their employees would ultimately prove to be medically expensive, but had no way of knowing who they were. So employers . . . trusted in the law of averages to avoid competitive disadvantage.

But as it becomes possible to know which employees are at increased risk for future disease, everything changes. Employers are by nature profit maximizers. That is what they do. That is what they are supposed to do. Employers do not maximize profit by deliberately hiring people whom they know are likely to incur higher than average medical costs. And even if an individual employer was willing to take that course, it would be under great pressure to change if its competitors did not follow suit. There is an inherent tension between the way employers make decisions in a market economy and our collective desire to see people with genetic markers have equal employment opportunities. This may be one of those contradictions we simply choose to live with in an imperfect world. Or we may have to reconsider the way we provide medical care, such as the single payer model which Canada has adopted.

Insurance Discrimination

. . . Health insurers today lose money on individuals who contract serious expensive diseases such as cancer. The premiums the policyholder pays don't even come close to covering the cost of their care. Insurers are able to make money by charging people with good health a premium that more than covers their costs. The excess pays the loss the insurer incurs on those who contract expensive medical conditions and the profit. The dream of every insurer is to be able to issue policies only on people who won't file claims.[28] That's the world that genetic testing begins to make possible. Insurers can determine in advance which applicants are likely to be unprofitable and refuse to insure them. . . .

. . . [T]his could be changed through legislation prohibiting discrimination. Health insurers could easily function under such a regime. They have always insured people with genetic markers, and made a profit in the process, by pooling risks and costs. There is no reason they cannot continue to do so. . . . Several states have already outlawed genetic discrimination by health insurers, and the industry has continued to function well. . . .

If life insurers are forced to sell policies without genetic underwriting an individual who knows that they carry a gene that puts them at elevated risk has an opportunity and incentive to game the system. For example, I'm a 52 year old male. If I were to learn tomorrow that I had the Huntington's gene, I'd know that I was lucky to have lived this long, and that I would probably die within the next 5 years. If I could buy life insurance at standard rates, I'd be a saint or a fool not to hock everything I own and buy millions of dollars in coverage. My wife and kids could mourn my loss in a castle on the Riviera.

But if genetic underwriting is allowed, life insurers will refuse coverage to people with genetic markers, or will offer it at rates no one can afford. This would leave thousands of families destitute if the breadwinner dies, especially now that the welfare system has been dismantled.

One answer to this dilemma might be to set up risk pools, similar to those that are used in auto insurance. Individuals who need coverage, but cannot afford the rate called for by actuarial computations, could obtain a modest amount of coverage (perhaps $250,000) at an affordable premium (but perhaps not the standard rate).

But even if this were worked out, the fundamental tension remains. It is the nature of insurers to calculate premiums according to risk. That's why safe drivers pay lower liability premiums and smokers pay more for health insurance. . . .

The Bigger Picture

. . . The knowledge we gain from the genetic revolution chips away at our very sense of community. Our willingness to think of ourselves as members of a community and to act as such has two deep roots. The first is that we are inherently social animals. Nature has wired us that way. The second is people have generally been better off as members of a community.

But our sense of community is unraveling before our eyes. Millions of upper middle class parents have abandoned the public schools. This phenomenon is not limited to urban areas where the public schools leave much to be desired. Even in affluent communities, with excellent public schools, many middle class families send their children to private schools. We don't even live in the same towns anymore. When I grew up, there was a rich side of town and a poor side of town. But at least it was the same town and people freely crossed from one side of the tracks to another. But today we see the rise of gated communities. These private towns not only have their own police and other municipal services, but you can't even enter these new towns unless the security guard at the gate lets you in.

Our growing ability to peer into the medical future only makes things worse. When we don't know who among us will be struck by calamity, it makes sense to stick together and take care of each other. But when we know that the curses of Job are likely to befall someone else rather than ourselves, our incentive to be a community diminishes. All of a sudden, we're not in the same boat

28 It is possible that the health insurance industry's dreams of increased profits through genetic underwriting are an illusion. An individual insurer would make more money if it could exclude applicants with genetic markers without changing its premiums. But the insurance industry is fiercely competitive, and competition is largely based on price. If we continue to allow genetic discrimination, all insurers will practice it. Any competitive advantage will disappear, and price competition will force profits back to traditional levels.

anymore. The genetic revolution did not create this sea change. Widespread accumulation of wealth and growing economic inequality are the primary causes. But predictive genetics adds fuel to the fire.

The greatest challenge we face entering a new century may be how to maintain our sense of community as the economic foundation of community disappears.

• QUESTIONS •

1. **Internet Assignment:** As Maltby assures us, as of 2000 when he gave this speech, genetic testing by employers was relatively uncommon because it was not cost effective. Only 1 percent of employers used such techniques. Update this statistic.
2. **Internet Assignment:** Maltby mentions "pending" federal legislation related to genetic discrimination. (a) Has any law been passed that addresses this issue head-on? Any bills in the works? Find out and compare their provisions with those advocated by Maltby. (b) Find out if your home state is one of the 27 that, by 2003, had passed legislation banning genetic discrimination in the workplace. Again, compare its provisions with Maltby's recommendations.
3. **Internet Assignment:** How does the HIPAA Act limit genetic testing? Do these limitations effectively counter Maltby's concerns about employer access to genetic test results?
4. Maltby links the disintegration of community and the genetic testing phenomenon. How does he do that? Do you agree with his thesis? **Internet Assignment:** Research the "science" of eugenics. Is there any connection between that history and the issues Maltby addresses?

CHAPTER PROBLEMS

1. When Vernon Clayton, a Texan and self-described "political progressive" started working at Enron in 1999, he was attracted to the idea that the company was diverse—a meritocracy. His job involved designing computer models to estimate the value of Enron's energy trades. In an online discussion inside the company, Vernon asked CEO Kenneth Lay about the "supposedly independent partnerships" that were used to hide huge company losses. His question was "brushed off." Vernon became frustrated, as reported by *The New York Times:*

   > *By mid-November, with Enron's stock plunging, Mr. Vernon had begun to post dozens of messages a day on the Yahoo discussion board under the screen name "utlonghornsrule," referring to the University of Texas, where he received a master's degree in economics. His messages warned investors away from Enron's stock, and many sharply criticized Enron and Mr. Lay. "We were just sitting there with nothing to do," Mr. Vernon said, ". . . watching our stocks go down."*
   >
   > *The final straw for him came on November 19th . . . when Enron canceled its Christmas party. At 5:16 p.m. that day, in a . . . message sprinkled with vulgarities, Mr. Vernon wrote that Mr. Lay had "just cancelled the Enron Christmas party so he wouldn't have to show up for his own party with armed bodyguards." ". . . Nobody*

believes a word" that Mr. Lay says, the posting said, using a vulgar epithet. "People have enjoyed the company spending a few dollars on them and giving them a chance to laugh and dance a bit. Esp since most of us adore our coworkers... Ken Lay is the sorriest sack of garbage I have ever been associated with, a truly evil and satanic figure."[29]

Vernon was using company equipment at the Houston headquarters when he wrote his online complaints. Enron tracked his identity and fired him the day after the "satanic figure" posting. A company representative refused to comment, except to say, "We're not going to discuss internal security actions, but we will... protect very vigorously the corporation's property." In what way is Vernon's firing factually similar to Smyth's in the Pillsbury case? Factually different? Suppose Vernon sues for wrongful discharge. Would the legal outcome be the same, using the rule of the *Smyth* case? How would you analyze the Enron firing in ethical terms?

2. James Gleick, in *What Just Happened*, writes this about privacy:

> *In public opinion surveys, Americans always favor privacy. Then they turn around and sell it cheaply. Most vehemently oppose any suggestion of a national identification system yet volunteer their telephone numbers and mothers' maiden names and even—grudgingly or not—their social security numbers to merchants bearing discounts or Web services offering "membership" privileges. For most, the abstract notion of privacy suggests a mystical, romantic cowboy-era set of freedoms. Yet in the real world it boils down to matters of small convenience. Certainly where other people's privacy is concerned, we seem willing to lower our standards. We have become a society with a cavernous appetite for news and gossip. Our era has replaced the tacit, eyes-averted civility of an earlier time with exhibitionism and prying. Even borderline public figures must get used to the nation's eyes in their bedrooms and pocketbooks. That's not Big Brother watching us. It's us.*

Do you agree that Americans seem to be willing to sell their own privacy cheaply while simultaneously craving private information about one another? If so, what role do you think technology has played in all of this? Can you imagine technology being used in new and different ways that might affect these trends?

3. Virginia Rulon-Miller had been an IBM employee for years, starting in 1967 as a receptionist in Philadelphia, and working her way up through a series of promotions to marketing manager in San Francisco by 1978. She began dating Matt Blum, who was an accountant with IBM when they met, but who left to work for a competitor. Ms. Rulon-Miller continued to see Mr. Blum, and to flourish in her management position. In 1979 she received a $4,000 merit raise and was praised by her supervisor, Philip Callahan. Then one day Callahan left a message that he wanted to meet with her. Rulon-Miller testified:

> *I walked into Phil's office and he asked me to sit down and he said, Are you dating Matt Blum? and I said What? I was kind of surprised he would ask me and I said: Well, what difference does it make if I'm dating Matt Blum?... And he said, well, something to the effect: I think we have a conflict of interest, or the appearance of a conflict of interest here. And I said, Well, gee, Phil, you've pointed out to me that there are no problems in the office because I am dating Matt Blum, and I don't really understand why that would have any, you know, pertinancy to my job. You said I am doing an okay job. I just got a raise. And he said: No and he said: I'll tell you what. He said: I'll give you a couple of days to a week. Think this whole thing over. I said: Think*

29 Alex Berenson, "Enron Fired Workers For Complaining Online," *New York Times*, January 21, 2002.

> *what over? And he said: You either stop dating Matt Blum or I'm going to take you out of your management job. And I was just kind of overwhelmed.*

The next day Callahan called her in again, told her "he had made up her mind for her," and when she protested, dismissed her. . . .

Ms. Rulon-Miller sued and won $300,000—in large part (and ironically) due to IBM's own policy. Developed by its Chairman Thomas Watson, Jr. (see page 74), the policy protected her from exactly the kind of treatment she had received. According to Watson, there should be a clear distinction between an individual's on and off-the-job life. Performance—"the one thing the company can insist on from everyone"—should be measured; private life should remain private. See *Rulon-Miller v. IBM,* 208 Cal.Rptr. 524 (1984). **Internet Assignment:** (a) Find a case from your state in which an employee claims an employer has overstepped the line between work and private life. What happened? What was the legal basis for the court's decision? (b) In 2003 the Supreme Court ruled that there is a fundamental right for consenting adults to engage in private sexual activity, as it ruled a state anti-sodomy law unconstitutional. *Lawrence v. Texas,* 538 U.S. 918, 123 S.Ct. 1512 (2003). How might someone in Rulon-Miller's position today use that precedent to save her job? How would the employer likely respond?

4. In June 1998, the FTC reported to Congress that 89 percent of 212 children's Web sites collected personal information about children without requiring some form of parental control over the process. According to a University of New Hampshire study, 20 percent of young people between the ages of 10 and 17 received unwanted sexual solicitations online in 2000, and only a quarter of them told their parents. Nancy Willard, a psychologist-attorney who directs Responsible Netizen, has this to say about the invasion of a child's online privacy:

> *The emergence of an understanding of the appropriate boundaries of personal privacy is clearly a developmental process, tied to the child's emerging cognitive development. Technically proficient children are using the Internet before they have the cognitive ability to appreciate the possible consequences of disclosure of personal information. Dot.com companies can use this to their advantage in seeking to mold the children's perceptions about personal privacy. They are able to accomplish this largely outside of parental influence because most parents do not know about the actions and intentions of these companies.*
>
> *Dot.com companies are asking children to disclose personal information and then using that information to develop a close relationship with the child for the purpose of influencing consumer behavior. . . . Children raised in such an environment will likely fail to develop an understanding of the appropriate boundaries of personal privacy. They will be extremely vulnerable to all manner of manipulation and exploitation, not only from corporate marketers, but also from scam artists, cults, and sexual predators.*[30]

Do you agree that there are special concerns regarding privacy for children online? **Internet Assignment:** Has there been a legislative response to this problem? Check http://www.ftc.gov.

5. Do Americans have a reasonable expectation of privacy that is violated when they are videotaped on public streets? In store dressing rooms? In motel rooms? In cybercafes? On what basis might they be challenged?

When cybercafes began to proliferate in Garden Grove, California, they seemed to bring with them gang activity. The police chief pushed for some control, and the city council

30 "Capturing the 'Eyeballs' and 'E-wallets' of Captive Kids in School: Dot.com Invades Dot.edu," http://www.responsiblenetizen.org.

responded by passing a law that required cybercafes to install a video surveillance system that could be inspected by the city during business hours. When a California court denied a constitutional challenge to the video-surveillance law, one judge dissented:

> *Do my colleagues not realize the—there is no other word for it—Orwellian implications of their ruling today? They approve an ordinance which* literally *forces a "Big Brother" style* telescreen *to look over one's shoulder while accessing the Internet. . . .*
>
> *Cybercafes are not just your ordinary "retail establishment." . . .*
>
> *Cybercafes allow people who cannot afford computers . . . the freedom of the* press. *They can post messages to the whole world, and, in theory (if they get enough "hits") can reach more people than read the hard copy of the New York Times every morning. . . . [They allow them] to access the global bulletin board of the Internet, i.e. the ability to* receive *what others have posted. Logging on is an exercise of free speech.*
>
> *Consider that totalitarian governments have always cracked down on unrestricted access to the* means *of communication. When the Communists were in control of countries such as Albania and Bulgaria, each* typewriter *was licensed. . . .*
>
> *And consider that the governments of both Communist China and Vietnam have recently cracked down on cybercafes in an effort to curb the freedom of ideas that they promote—an effort that has entailed learning the identity of cybercafe owners. . . .*
>
> *Given the constitutional ramifications of the very nature of cybercafes, I will go so far as to say that there is an expectation of privacy even as to one's* identity *when using a cybercafe. . . .* Vo v. City of Garden Grove, *9 Cal.Rptr.3d 257 (Court of Appeal, 2004) (Sills, Concurring and Dissenting).*

Do a constitutional analysis of the video surveillance requirement passed by Garden Grove.

6. Since the Columbine tragedy, there has been a general crackdown on high school student freedoms, with the use of metal detectors, locker searches, Internet use monitoring, and even discipline of students for expressing their thoughts about violence. Drug testing is part of this trend. In 1995, the U.S. Supreme Court held that a high school could test its student athletes for drug use without violating their Fourth Amendment rights. The Court based this decision partly on the lowered expectation of privacy that would exist in a locker room shared by students who had volunteered to play football—in a school where the drug problem seemed centered on the football team. **Internet Assignment:** What about students in Tecumsah, Oklahoma, who have volunteered to sing in the choir, and who are not suspected of any drug-oriented activity? Do they have the right to resist school drug tests? Check the Supreme Court for 2002.

7. **Internet Assignment:** In May 2004, a federal advisory committee headed by former FCC Chair Newton N. Minow made its recommendations to Secretary of Defense Donald Rumsfeld: Congress should pass laws to protect civil liberties when the government sifts through computer records and data files for information about terrorists. Find out whether Congress has acted to safeguard privacy when the Department of Defense uses data mining to fight terrorism.

8. In a poll conducted in 2001, 68 percent of Americans favored the use of a national ID, while 86 percent supported the biometric scanning idea. Libertarian pundit William Safire worried that a national ID would become a tightly focused information bank, a "single dossier . . . supposedly confidential but available to any imaginative hacker":

> *[I]n the dreams of Big Brother and his cousin, Big Marketing, nothing can compare to forcing every person in the United States—under penalty of law—to carry what the totalitarians used to call "papers." The plastic card would not merely show a photograph, signature and address, as driver's licenses do. . . . In time, and with*

> *exquisite refinements, the card would contain not only a fingerprint, description of DNA and the details of your eye's iris, but a host of other information about you. Hospitals would say: How about a chip providing a complete medical history in case of emergencies? Merchants would add a chip for credit rating, bank accounts and product preferences, while divorced spouses would lobby for a rundown of net assets and yearly expenditures. Politicians would like to know voting records and political affiliation. Cops, of course, would insist on a record of arrests, speeding tickets, E-Z pass auto movements and links to suspicious Web sites and associates.*

For Safire, the central problem with this system is that those who resist it on principle will become suspicious to the authorities.

> *What about us libertarian misfits who take the trouble to try to "opt out?" We will not be able to travel or buy on credit. . . . Soon enough, police as well as employers will consider [us] . . . to be suspect. The universal use and likely abuse of the national ID—a discredit card—will trigger questions like: When did you begin to subscribe to these publications and why were you visiting that spicy or seditious Web site? Why are you paying cash? What do you have to hide?*

(a) Compare Safire's concerns with those of the Communitarians. Find out what their position is on the national ID.
(b) Analyze the national identity card concept from a utilitarian ethical perspective. Now look at it through the lens of deontology.
(c) Oracle chairman and CEO Larry Ellison has offered to supply the government with the software it would need to create a national identity card system "absolutely free." He has said:

> *This privacy you're concerned about is largely an illusion. . . . All you have to give up is your illusions, not your privacy. Right now you can go onto the Internet and get a credit report about your neighbor, and find out where your neighbor works, how much they earn, and if they had a late mortgage payment and loads of other information.*

Does Ellison's comment effectively counter Safire's concerns?

CHAPTER PROJECT

Mock Trial

Guidelines in Appendix D

My name is Lily Kim. I am 35 years old, a divorced parent of two boys, and I have an advanced degree in molecular biology. I've been working for six years for a rapidly expanding biotechnology company called Greengenes. The company hired me because I had exactly the right training to do what they needed: research in the field of food irradiation. Treating food with small doses of radiation increases crop yields and nutritional value. I did my Ph.D. thesis in this area, so the position at Greengenes has been perfect for me. I started as head of one lab, but by last year I was supervising three labs—one in North Carolina, one in California, and one in Atlanta. There was a lot of travel involved, but I really loved my work, and I'd been receiving excellent performance evaluations and salary increases. Last year I made $200,000.

But here's the bad news. Last week Greengenes announced that it intended to do genetic testing on all of its full-time employees, no matter what their rank. The tests they want to run would isolate DNA from a few skin cells and ultimately detect whether a person has the genetic tendency to develop any serious disease in the future.

I know that DNA tests can be used to reveal this type of information, forecasting the ways people can get sick. Some people want to have themselves tested so they can try to prevent or minimize potential illnesses. Suppose they predict you are likely to get heart disease. You can take precautions—be extra careful of your diet and exercise, even go on blood thinners. But I'm not like that kind of person. *I don't want to know* if I am going to get—say—cancer! That's the kind of news I would really rather *not* get. I *don't want to know* whether or not I have a predisposition to get Alzheimer's disease! I want to live my life the best way I can, without trying to "play god" with my future. And I don't want anyone else to know my private health story either. What gives Greengenes the right to read my future? What business is it of theirs? And how do I know they'll keep secret whatever they find out about me? As a scientist I hate to admit it, but there are times when cutting-edge technology can be used clumsily, and the net result is not a benefit.

I've also heard of companies finding out that an employee might be a bad risk, and then deciding they don't want to carry the higher costs of health insurance. So they find an excuse to lay you off—it's easy to do. Suppose it turns out that I am genetically inclined to get cancer? Greengenes might start claiming I am underperforming, and that would be the end of my wonderful job. Once Greengenes has my data, I don't see how I can be certain the whole world won't find out—or at least the world of biotech companies. Which could mean I can't get another job—or health insurance. Imagine being unable to get insurance *because* you desperately need it?

So I told them I didn't want to be tested. The company responded immediately. I was called into the Human Resource office one day. There was someone there I didn't know—a Cary Packer. Packer wouldn't look me in the eye; said that Greengenes had a policy, a clear-cut rule, and because I was failing to obey it, I was to be terminated.

Now I am suing. I am concerned—not only for myself but for anyone else who is forced to make this kind of choice. Why should a company be able to demand that someone with a great background and a terrific job record reveal so much to keep their job? What controls are there on their use of that kind of information? If it is OK for employers to require genetic tests, what else can they force people to do? This is where technology is running away with privacy—it's just scary.

I am Cary Packer, Human Resource manager of Greengenes, Inc. We are a new and flourishing company, one of only about 1,000 biotechnology companies worldwide. Biotechs are among the fastest growing companies of the twenty-first century. We are at the center of nearly every effort to improve healthcare, agriculture, industrial manufacturing, and the environment today.

Greengenes focuses on products for agricultural markets, on methods of altering plants to make them more beneficial for humans. We began operating in 1997 with about 20 employees; now, ten years later, we employ over 300. And almost all of the people we hire are experts, with advanced research or clinical backgrounds. Like software and computer companies, biotech employers like us attract top applicants through compensation packages that include stock options. And once we have made a hiring decision, we like to keep our employees happy, assuming they prove themselves to be valuable to us. We provide an on-site gym and squash courts, high-quality childcare at a reduced cost, and excellent health and retirement benefits. We believe that a happy workforce is an efficient one, and that it only makes good sense to do right by our employees.

As a high-tech company, we feel especially comfortable trusting in technology to help us make smart and efficient business decisions.

As part of that, we have decided to implement a policy of genetically testing everyone who works for the company. We feel we need to discover whether our people have the tendency to develop cancer and other life-threatening illnesses.

We have three simple reasons for this. First, we compete in a global marketplace, and many of our competitors are operating in countries where the government bears most of the cost of health care. But we are based in the United States, where the spiking costs of health care fall increasingly on employers. Our testing program is an effort to control losses in this area. Second, we want to employ the best, and the best means the best qualified, both mentally and physically. Employers should have the right to know if the people they hire, train, and trust with big responsibilities will someday become seriously ill and have their productive capacities cut short. This is nothing new—it's a matter of using technology that has existed for many years to give us a better handle on how to invest our resources.

The third reason we have for the testing is really for Ms. Kim's own good. Like many of our employees, Kim will be exposed to chemicals and radiation on the job. Not a lot—but even in small amounts those exposures could have nasty effects over the long term, especially if the person already has a tendency to become ill. Suppose an employee is susceptible to getting cancer? We may want to move her out of the lab and into some other division of the company. In this sense we would actually be doing her a favor. Of course, like any business, we have our shareholders' interests to consider. There's the potential to be sued at some later date by dozens of people who claim that they got cancer because we put them at risk on the job. Even when you win a case like that you lose in the court of public opinion.

We are sorry that Ms. Kim is so upset. But any employee who doesn't feel comfortable with our testing procedures should work somewhere else. It's a free country, after all!

Valuing Diversity: Discrimination, Accommodation, and Affirmative Action

Chapter 4

Like and difference are quickening words, brooding and hatching. Better and worse are eggsucking words. They leave only the shell.

— Ursula Le Guin

The case is simple. A woman with pre-school children may not be employed, a man with pre-school children may. The distinguishing factor seems to be motherhood versus fatherhood. The question then arises: Is this sex-related? To the simple query, the answer is just as simple: Nobody—and this includes Judges, Solomonic or life tenured—has yet seen a male mother. A mother, to oversimplify the simplest biology, must then be a woman.

—Justice Brown, dissenting,
Phillips v. Martin Marietta Corp.

Three and a half decades after federal civil rights laws barred discrimination, the remnants of past practices survive. They can be seen in the difficulties that continue to plague small businesses owned by minorities and women, in the wage gap between men and women, people of color and whites, and in a national workforce in which jobs are still by and large segregated by race and gender. Stereotypes continue to create social and economic hardships for many in our society.

The chapter opens with a case that is one of the most controversial in years: the ruling by the high court of Massachusetts in favor of same-sex marriage. Federal laws against discrimination based on sex and disability, and current interpretation of the Equal Protection Clause of the U.S. Constitution, provide the legal backdrop to the case. A look at affirmative action in higher education and the debate about the fairness of preferring one race or gender over another provide the ethical context.

If, as some argue, the time has come to end the programs labeled affirmative action, are there other ways to move toward greater equality? That question sets the stage for our exploration of various accommodations of work and family at home and abroad.

In 2001, gay and lesbian couples in Massachusetts—including some who had lived together for many years—applied for licenses to marry. Denied by the town clerks, they filed a lawsuit seeking a judicial declaration that the Department of Public Health's policy violated the Massachusetts state constitution. When the lower court ruled against them, the plaintiffs appealed.

GOODRIDGE V. DEPARTMENT OF PUBLIC HEALTH

Supreme Judicial Court of Massachusetts, 2003
798 N.E.2d 941

MARSHALL, C. J. (with whom IRELAND and GREANEY, J. J. Concur)

. . . Marriage is a vital social institution. The exclusive commitment of two individuals to each other nurtures love and mutual support; it brings stability to our society. For those who choose to marry, and for their children, marriage provides an abundance of legal, financial, and social benefits. In return it imposes weighty legal, financial, and social obligations. The question before us is whether, consistent with the Massachusetts Constitution, the Commonwealth may deny the protections, benefits, and obligations conferred by civil marriage to two individuals of the same sex who wish to marry. We conclude that it may not. The Massachusetts Constitution affirms the dignity and equality of all individuals. It forbids the creation of second-class citizens. In reaching our conclusion we have given full deference to the arguments made by the Commonwealth. But it has failed to identify any constitutionally adequate reason for denying civil marriage to same-sex couples.

We are mindful that our decision marks a change in the history of our marriage law. Many people hold deep-seated religious, moral, and ethical convictions that marriage should be limited to the union of one man and one woman, and that homosexual conduct is immoral. Many hold equally strong religious, moral, and ethical convictions that same-sex couples are entitled to be married, and that homosexual persons should be treated no differently than their heterosexual neighbors. . . . "Our obligation is to define the liberty of all, not to mandate our own moral code."*. . .

The plaintiffs are fourteen individuals from five Massachusetts counties. As of April 11, 2001 . . . Gloria Bailey, sixty years old, and Linda Davies, fifty-five years old, had been in a committed relationship for thirty years; . . . Hillary Goodridge, forty-four years old, and Julie Goodridge, forty-three years old, had been in a committed relationship for thirteen years and lived with their five year old daughter; . . . Gary Chalmers, thirty-five years old, and Richard Linnell, thirty-seven years old, had been in a committed relationship for thirteen years and lived with their eight year old daughter and Richard's mother. . . .

The plaintiffs include business executives, lawyers, an investment banker, educators, therapists, and a computer engineer. Many are active in church, community, and school groups. They have employed such legal means as are available to them—for example, joint adoption, powers of attorney, and joint ownership of real property—to secure aspects of their relationships. Each plaintiff attests a desire to marry his or her partner in order to affirm publicly their commitment to each other and to secure the legal protections and benefits afforded to married couples and their children. . . .

The benefits accessible only by way of a marriage license are enormous, touching nearly every aspect of life and death. The department states that "hundreds of statutes" are related to marriage and to marital benefits. . . . [S]ome of the statutory benefits conferred by the Legislature on those who enter into civil marriage include. . . : joint Massachusetts income tax filing; tenancy by the entirety (a form of ownership that provides certain protections against creditors and allows for the automatic descent of property to the surviving spouse without probate); extension of the benefit of the homestead protection. . . to one's spouse and children; [inheritance rights]. . . ; entitlement to wages owed to a deceased employee; eligibility to continue certain businesses of a deceased spouse; the right to share the medical policy of one's spouse; . . . access to veterans' spousal benefits and preferences; financial protections for spouses of . . . fire fighters, police officers, and prosecutors . . . killed in the performance of duty; [property rights upon divorce or separation]; . . . the right to bring claims for wrongful death and loss of consortium; . . . the presumptions of legitimacy and parentage of children born to a married couple; . . . evidentiary

* *Lawrence v. Texas,* 123 S.Ct. 2472, 2480 (2003) (*Lawrence*), quoting *Planned Parenthood of Southeastern Pa. v. Casey,* 505 U.S. 833, 850 (1992)
(obtained at *http://news.findlaw.com/hdocs/docs/conlaw/goodridge111803opn.pdf*)

rights, such as the prohibition against spouses testifying against one another about their private conversations; . . . qualification for bereavement or medical leave to care for [relatives]. . . ; an automatic "family member" preference to make medical decisions for an incompetent or disabled spouse; . . . and the right to interment in the lot or tomb owned by one's deceased spouse. . . .

It is undoubtedly for these concrete reasons, as well as for its intimately personal significance, that civil marriage has long been termed a "civil right." . . .

Without the right to marry—or more properly, the right to choose to marry—one is excluded from the full range of human experience and denied full protection of the laws for one's "avowed commitment to an intimate and lasting human relationship." . . .

For decades, indeed centuries, in much of this country (including Massachusetts) no lawful marriage was possible between white and black Americans. That long history availed not when the . . . United States Supreme Court . . . held that a statutory bar to interracial marriage violated the Fourteenth Amendment, *Loving v. Virginia*, (1967). . . .

The individual liberty and equality safeguards of the Massachusetts Constitution protect both "freedom from" unwarranted government intrusion into protected spheres of life and "freedom to" partake in benefits created by the State for the common good. Both freedoms are involved here. Whether and whom to marry, how to express sexual intimacy, and whether and how to establish a family—these are among the most basic of every individual's liberty and due process rights. . . .

Under both the equality and liberty guarantees, regulatory authority must, at very least, serve "a legitimate purpose in a rational way.". . . Any law failing to satisfy the basic standards of rationality is void.

. . . The [lower court held] that "the state's interest in regulating marriage is based on the traditional concept that marriage's primary purpose is procreation." This is incorrect. Our laws of civil marriage do not privilege procreative heterosexual intercourse between married people above every other form of adult intimacy and every other means of creating a family. . . . Fertility is not a condition of marriage, nor is it grounds for divorce. . . .

There is . . . no rational relationship between the marriage statute and the Commonwealth's proffered goal of protecting the "optimal" child rearing unit. . . . People in same-sex couples may be "excellent" parents. These couples have children for the reasons others do—to love them, to care for them, to nurture them. . . . Excluding same-sex couples from civil marriage will not make children of opposite-sex marriages more secure, but it does prevent children of same-sex couples from enjoying the immeasurable advantages that flow from the assurance of "a stable family structure in which children will be reared, educated, and socialized."

The department [also argues that] broadening civil marriage to include same-sex couples will trivialize or destroy the institution of marriage as it has historically been fashioned. Certainly our decision today marks a significant change in the definition of marriage as it has been inherited from the common law, and understood by many societies for centuries. But it does not disturb the fundamental value of marriage in our society.

Here, the plaintiffs seek only to be married, not to undermine the institution of civil marriage. . . .

The history of constitutional law "is the story of the extension of constitutional rights and protections to people once ignored or excluded.". . . As a public institution and a right of fundamental importance, civil marriage is an evolving paradigm. The common law was exceptionally harsh toward women who became wives: a woman's legal identity all but evaporated into that of her husband. . . . Alarms about the imminent erosion of the "natural" order of marriage were sounded over . . . the expansion of the rights of married women, and the introduction of "no-fault" divorce. Marriage has survived all of these transformations, and we have no doubt that marriage will continue to be a vibrant and revered institution.

The marriage ban works a deep and scarring hardship on a very real segment of the community for no rational reason. The absence of any reasonable relationship between, on the one hand, an absolute disqualification of same-sex couples who wish to enter into civil marriage and, on the other, protection of public health, safety, or general welfare, suggests that the marriage restriction is rooted in persistent prejudices against persons who are (or who are believed to be) homosexual. "The Constitution cannot control such prejudices but neither can it tolerate them. . . ." Limiting the protections, benefits, and obligations of civil marriage to opposite-sex couples violates the basic premises of individual liberty and equality under law protected by the Massachusetts Constitution.

SPINA, J. (dissenting, with whom Sosman and Cordy, JJ., join).

. . . The power to regulate marriage lies with the Legislature, not with the judiciary. . . . Today, the court has transformed its role as protector of individual rights into the role of creator of rights, and I respectfully dissent. . . .

CORDY, J. (dissenting, with whom Spina and Sosman, JJ., join).

. . . Because a conceivable rational basis exists upon which the Legislature could conclude that the marriage statute furthers the legitimate State purpose of ensuring, promoting, and supporting an optimal social structure for the bearing and raising of children, it is a valid exercise of the State's police power.

The marriage statute . . . does not intrude on any right that the plaintiffs have to privacy in their choices regarding procreation, an intimate partner or sexual relations. The plaintiffs' right to privacy in such matters does not require that the State officially endorse their choices in order for the right to be constitutionally vindicated. . . .

While the institution of marriage is deeply rooted in the history and traditions of our country and our State, the right to marry someone of the same sex is not. No matter how personal or intimate a decision to marry someone of the same sex might be, the right to make it is not guaranteed by the right of personal autonomy. . . . [nor by the] right to freedom of association. . . .

Paramount among its many important functions, the institution of marriage has systematically provided for the regulation of heterosexual behavior, brought order to the resulting procreation, and ensured a stable family structure in which children will be reared, educated, and socialized.

. . . The alternative, a society without the institution of marriage, in which heterosexual intercourse, procreation, and child care are largely disconnected processes, would be chaotic. . . .

It is undeniably true that dramatic historical shifts in our cultural, political, and economic landscape have altered some of our traditional notions about marriage, including the interpersonal dynamics within it, the range of responsibilities required of it as an institution, and the legal environment in which it exists. Nevertheless, the institution of marriage remains the principal weave of our social fabric. . . . A family defined by heterosexual marriage continues to be the most prevalent social structure into which the vast majority of children are born, nurtured, and prepared for productive participation in civil society.

It is difficult to imagine a State purpose more important and legitimate than ensuring, promoting, and supporting an optimal social structure within which to bear and raise children. At the very least, the marriage statute continues to serve this important State purpose. . . .

. . . [T]he Legislature could conceivably conclude that declining to recognize same-sex marriages remains prudent until empirical questions about its impact on the upbringing of children are resolved. . . .

As long as marriage is limited to opposite-sex couples who can at least theoretically procreate, society is able to communicate a consistent message to its citizens that marriage is a (normatively) necessary part of their procreative endeavor; that if they are to procreate, then society has endorsed the institution of marriage as the environment for it and for the subsequent rearing of their children; and that benefits are available explicitly to create a supportive and conducive atmosphere for those purposes. If society proceeds similarly to recognize marriages between same-sex couples who cannot procreate, it could be perceived as an abandonment of this claim, and might result in the mistaken view that civil marriage has little to do with procreation: just as the potential of procreation would not be necessary for a marriage to be valid, marriage would not be necessary for optimal procreation and child rearing to occur. In essence, the Legislature could conclude that the consequence of such a policy shift would be a diminution in society's ability to steer the acts of procreation and child rearing into their most optimal setting. . . .

• QUESTIONS •

1. On what basis does the majority strike down the Massachusetts marriage license law? How does the dissent respond?
2. **Internet Question:** The dissent mentions "empirical questions" about the impact of same-sex marriage on children. What can you find out about the impact–positive or negative–on those who have been raised by same-sex parents?
3. **Internet Question:** Find *Loving v. Virginia,* the 1967 Supreme Court case which held that statutes barring marriage across racial lines were unconstitutional. Did the Court employ any of the same arguments made by the majority in *Goodridge*?
4. In your view, what is marrige really about? An intimate relationship? An economic partnership? A way to raise children? An institution that allows the state to "privatize dependancy" by making spouses legally responsible for caring for each other and their children? Which judge in *Goodridge* comes closest to your own vision? To what extent does your vision affect how you feel about same sex-marriage?
5. Do you think the majority in *Goodridge* would have a problem with the following: (a) A statute declaring divorce illegal? (b) A law lowering the age for legitimate marriage to 11?
6. What impact would wide-scale recognition of same-sex marriage likely have on business?
7. **Internet Assignment:** In 2002, the Netherlands became the first country in the world to open up civil marriage to same-sex couples. Since then, Belgium, Denmark, Sweden, Iceland, Finland, France, and Germany have allowed marriage-like partnerships.[1] Find out how your state deals with same-sex marriages or partnerships.

Equal Protection

> *[N]or shall any State deprive any person of life, liberty or property, without due process of law; nor deny to any person within its jurisdiction the equal protection of the law.*
>
> – Fourteenth Amendment, United States Constitution

Equal protection requires government to treat different groups of people that are in the same situation similarly. As with all constitutional rights, however, the right to equal protection is not absolute. If government can show that it has strong enough justification for treating different–but "similarly situated"–groups unequally it may do so. The justification the government must give varies depending on the type of discrimination involved.

Suppose the state of California passed a law that allowed all 16-year-olds, except those of Mexican ancestry, to apply for drivers' licenses. This law would discriminate between groups

1 Kees Waaldijk, "Others May Follow: The Introduction of Marriage, Quasi-Marriage and Semi-Marriage for Same Sex Couples in European Countries," 38 *N. Eng. L. Rev.* 569 (2004).

(Mexicans vs. non-Mexicans) that are similarly situated: They are all 16 years old and they all want to get a driver's license. It distinguishes them based on a characteristic that people can do nothing to change, and one that has been used historically to oppress groups of people: their ethnicity. This kind of discrimination can only pass the standard of equal protection if California can show its law serves a very strong or "**compelling**" **state interest,** and if it is narrowly tailored to do so. In other words, if California can achieve its important goal(s) in a less discriminatory way, it must. This equal protection test is called **strict scrutiny.** It has been applied only to **suspect classifications,** such as race and ethnicity, and in cases where the classification infringes on such **fundamental freedoms** as the right of free speech or the right to vote. It sets such a high barrier that a few cases in our entire history have met the strict scrutiny standard. The best known case was the *Korematsu* decision, in which the Supreme Court upheld an executive order issued by President Franklin Roosevelt that sent Japanese-Americans to live in internment camps during World War II.[2]

When the government discriminates in a way that is neither based on race or ethnicity nor involves a fundamental right, equal protection analysis is much looser and permits the **state action** so long as it has a **rational relationship** to a valid government purpose. For example, suppose Chicago passed a law specifying that restaurants of more than 1,000 square feet must be inspected by the Department of Health twice a year, while smaller restaurants need be inspected only annually. The classification—larger versus smaller eating establishments—is not suspect, and there is no fundamental right to operate an unclean restaurant. The law will probably be upheld as well tailored to promote a legitimate state goal. Most legislation can pass the rational relationship test.

Some classifications—notably gender—receive what has come to be known as **intermediate** or **heightened scrutiny,** a level of judicial inquiry that falls somewhere between strict scrutiny and the minimal rational relationship. When government treats males one way and females another, the courts must determine if there is a substantial government reason for the difference. If not, it will rule that the classification violates equal protection.

> *I know this film well. "Easter '62" was the home movie Dr. Luce talked my parents into giving him. This was the film he screened each year for his students at Cornell University Medical School. This was the thirty-five second segment that, Luce insisted, proved out his theory that gender identity is established early on in life. This was the film Dr. Luce showed to me, to tell me who I was. And who was that? Look at the screen. My mother is handing me a baby doll. I take the baby and hug it to my chest. Putting a toy bottle to the baby lips, I offer it milk.*
>
> —Jeffrey Eugenides, *Middlesex**

When Elana Back was denied tenure as a school psychologist, the school district claimed it was because she lacked organizational and interpersonal skills. Back had a different perception: She claimed that the real reason had to do with stereotypes about mothers. That, she insisted, violated her constitutional right to equal protection of the laws.

---

2 *Korematsu v. United States,* 323 U.S. 214 (1944). In an effort to ameliorate the results of this later-regretted decision, Congress in 1988 ordered $20,000 in reparations to be paid to each living survivor of the detention camps. 50 U.S.C. App. Sect. 1989(b) (1988).

* (NY: Farrar, Strauss & Giroux, 2002) p. 226.

BACK V. HASTINGS ON HUDSON UNION FREE SCHOOL

U.S. Court of Appeals, Second Circuit, 2004
365 7.3d. 107

CALABRESI, Circuit Judge.

. . . This appeal . . . poses an important question, one that strikes at the persistent "fault line between work and family—precisely where sex-based overgeneralization has been and remains strongest.". . . It asks whether stereotyping about the qualities of mothers is a form of gender discrimination, and whether this can be determined in the absence of evidence about how the employer in question treated fathers. We answer both questions in the affirmative. . . .

. . . [In her first two years as a school psychologist, Elana Back's supervisors] Brennan and Wishnie consistently gave her excellent evaluations. In her first annual evaluation, on a scale where the highest score was "outstanding," and the second highest score was "superior," Back was deemed "outstanding" and "superior" in almost all categories, and "average" in only one. . . . Narrative evaluations completed by Wishnie and Brennan during this time were also uniformly positive, [noting that she] . . . had "successfully adjusted to become a valued and valuable member of the school/community."

In her second year at Hillside, Back took approximately three months of maternity leave. After she returned, she garnered another "outstanding" evaluation from Brennan. . . ." In her annual evaluation, Back received higher marks than the previous year, with more "outstandings" and no "averages." . . .

Back asserts that things changed dramatically as her tenure review approached. The first allegedly discriminatory comments came . . . shortly after Back had returned from maternity leave, [when Back claims that Brennan] (a) inquired about how she was "planning on spacing [her] offspring," (b) said "[p]lease do not get pregnant until I retire," and (c) suggested that Back "wait until [her son] was in kindergarten to have another child."

Then, a few months into Back's third year at Hillside . . . Brennan allegedly told Back that she was expected to work until 4:30 p.m. every day, and asked "What's the big deal. You have a nanny. This is what you [have] to do to get tenure." Back replied that she did work these hours. . . . Brennan also indicated that Back should "maybe . . . reconsider whether [Back] could be a mother and do this job which [Brennan] characterized as administrative in nature," and that Brennan and Wishnie were "concerned that, if [Back] received tenure, [she] would work only until 3:15 p.m. and did not know how [she] could possibly do this job with children."

A few days later . . . Brennan allegedly told Back for the first time that she might not support Back's tenure because of what Back characterizes as minor errors that she made in a report. . . . [B]oth Brennan and Wishnie reportedly told Back that this was perhaps not the job or the school district for her if she had "little ones," and that it was "not possible for [her] to be a good mother and have this job." The two also allegedly remarked that it would be harder to fire Back if she had tenure, and wondered "whether my apparent commitment to my job was an act. They stated that once I obtained tenure, I would not show the same level of commitment I had shown because I had little ones at home. They expressed concerns about my child care arrangements, though these had never caused me conflict with school assignments.". . .

Back claims that in March, Brennan and Wishnie reiterated that her job was "not for a mother," that they were worried her performance was "just an 'act' until I got tenure," and that "because I was a young mother, I would not continue my commitment to the work place.". . .

. . . Individuals have a clear right, protected by the Fourteenth Amendment, to be free from discrimination on the basis of sex in public employment. . . .

To show sex discrimination, Back relies upon a *Price Waterhouse* "stereotyping" theory. [The gender stereotypes method for proving same-sex sexual harassment is based on *Price Waterhouse v. Hopkins* (1989), a case in which the Supreme Court reviewed the sex discrimination claim of a woman who had been denied partnership in an accounting firm at least in part on the basis that she was "macho," "overcompensated for being a woman," needed "a course in charm school," was "masculine," and was "a lady using foul language." A partner advised the plaintiff that if she wished to improve her chances of earning partnership, she should "walk more femininely, talk more femininely, dress more femininely, wear make-up, have her hair styled, and wear jewelry."... The Court noted that "we are beyond the day when an employer could evaluate employees by assuming or insisting that they matched the stereotype associated with their group, for '[i]n forbidding employers to discriminate against individuals because of their sex, Congress intended to strike at the entire spectrum of disparate treatment of men and women resulting from sex stereotypes.'" *Bibby v. Phila. Coca Cola Bottling Company,* 260 F.3d 257 (3d Cir. 2001).]

Accordingly, she argues that comments made about a woman's inability to combine work and motherhood are direct evidence of such discrimination. . . .

. . . The principle of *Price Waterhouse* . . . applies as much to the supposition that a woman *will* conform to a gender stereotype (and therefore will not, for example, be dedicated to her job), as to the supposition that a woman is unqualified for a position because she does *not* conform to a gender stereotype. . . .

. . . [I]t takes no special training to discern stereotyping in the view that a woman cannot "be a good mother" and have a job that requires long hours, or in the statement that a mother who received tenure "would not show the same level of commitment [she] had shown because [she] had little ones at home." . . .

Moreover, the Supreme Court itself recently took judicial notice of such stereotypes. In an opinion by Chief Justice Rehnquist, the Court concluded that stereotypes of this sort were strong and pervasive enough to justify prophylactic congressional action, in the form of the Family Medical Leave Act:

> *Stereotypes about women's domestic roles are reinforced by parallel stereotypes presuming a lack of domestic responsibilities for men. Because employers continued to regard the family as the woman's domain, they often denied men similar accommodations or discouraged them from taking leave. These mutually reinforcing stereotypes created a self-fulfilling cycle of discrimination that forced women to continue to assume the role of primary family caregiver, and fostered employers' stereotypical views about women's commitment to work and their value as employees. Those perceptions, in turn, Congress reasoned, lead to subtle discrimination that may be difficult to detect on a case-by-case basis.*
>
> — *Nevada Dept. of Human Resources v. Hibbs,* 123 S.Ct. 1972 (2003)

Hibbs makes pellucidly clear, however, that, at least where stereotypes are considered, the notions that mothers are insufficiently devoted to work, and that work and motherhood are incompatible, are properly considered to be, themselves, gender-based. *Hibbs* explicitly called the stereotype that "women's family duties trump those of the workplace" a "*gender* stereotype," and cited a number of state pregnancy and family leave acts—including laws that provided *only* pregnancy leave—as evidence of "pervasive sex-role stereotype that caring for family members is women's work."....

[We find that] stereotyping of women as caregivers can by itself and without more be evidence of an impermissible, sex-based motive.

• QUESTIONS •

1. Is there a difference—ethically speaking—between denying someone tenure because she is a woman and denying her tenure because she is a mother and might spend less time on her job responsibilities? Is it unethical to allow stereotypes to affect employment decisions? Why or why not?

2. How would you define stereotyping? What are some common stereotypes of women besides the one Elana Back had to confront? Of Hispanics? Asians? Muslims? African-Americans? What is the heart of the difference between stereotyping and outright discrimination?

3. **Internet Assignment:** Only those who are employed by the government can argue that the Constitution entitles them to equal protection in a situation like Elana Back's. Find a case in which a private sector employee claims discrimination or wrongful discharge based on stereotyping. On what law did the plaintiff rely? What happened?

4. Feminist lawyer Nancy Dowd argues that "family is such a strong cultural construct it can change the law, but law cannot change family. . . . It may facilitate change or support change, but it cannot force change in family culture."[3] Nearly one-third of all families with minor children are single-parent families; marriage is neither a lifelong partnership nor the only form of committed partnership; there are increasing numbers of "independent" adoptions by persons other than a married husband and wife. All of these, she points out, are examples of "culture subverting [the legal definition of] family." Does the *Back* case help support or refute Dowd's claim? The *Goodrich* case? Should the law be used to facilitate or support change in family culture? To try to stifle such changes?

Joan C. Williams directs the Program in Gender Work and Family at American University. In the following reading, she discusses some of what psychologists and sociologists have learned about stereotyping and cognitive bias against caregivers.

Beyond the Glass Ceiling: The Maternal Wall as a Barrier to Gender Equality

Joan C. Williams[4]

My subject is motherhood. More specifically, the intertwining of motherhood, economic vulnerability, and social stigma. We've all heard about the glass ceiling and I'm sad to say that the glass ceiling is alive and well in America. But most women never get near it because they are stopped long before by the maternal wall.

Over eighty percent of women become mothers. And although the wage gap between men and women is actually narrowing, the wage gap between mothers and other adults has actually risen in recent decades. Although young women now earn about ninety percent of the wages of men, mothers still earn only about sixty percent of the wages of fathers. This is what's called the family gap, as distinguished from the wage gap.

Much of this family gap stems from the ways we organize the relationship of market work to family work. We still define the ideal worker as someone who starts to work in early adulthood and works full-time, full force, for forty years straight, taking no time off for childbearing, childrearing, or really anything else. That's not an ungendered norm. . . .

. . . [T]here is no federal statute that forbids discrimination against adults with caregiving responsibilities. . . .

[Let me tell you about] two lawyers, a husband and wife, who worked for the same firm. After they had a baby, the wife was sent home like clockwork at 5:30—after all, she had a baby to take care of. The husband was kept late almost every night—after all, he had a family to support. That's called benevolent stereotyping. It's stereotyping done in a very different tone of voice than hostile stereotyping, but the effect is much the same: the employer polices men and women into traditionalist bread-winner/housewife roles—clearly an inappropriate role for an employer to play.

---

3 Nancy E. Dowd, "Law, Culture, and Family: The Transformative Power of Culture and the Limits of Law," 78 *Chi.-Kent L. Rev.* 785 (2003).

4 26 T. Jefferson L. Rev. 1 (2003). This article was part of the 1st Annual Ruth Bader Ginsburg Lecture on Women and the Law Conference, Thomas Jefferson School of Law, April 25, 2003.

In the caregiver context, one key study by Susan Fiske and her colleagues ranked stereotypes by perceived competence. Fiske and her colleagues found that businesswomen were rated as very high in competence, similar to businessmen and millionaires. Housewives, on the other hand, were rated as very low in competence– similar to–(here I quote the researchers) the elderly, blind, "retarded," and "disabled."

To see how the caregiver stereotype operates in practice, let's recall the famous story of the Boston attorney who returned from maternity leave and found she was given the work of a paralegal. She said, "I wanted to say, 'Look I had a baby, not a lobotomy.'" What happened? She was taken out of the high competence "business woman" category and put into the low competence caregiver category.

Understanding this process is very important for understanding the kinds of problems mothers often experience at one of three particular moments in time: when they get pregnant, return from maternity leave, or go on a flexible work arrangement. . . .

[Sociologists] Monica Biernat and Diane Kobrynowicz . . . compared the "good father" to the "good mother," and they found a lot of overlap. But they also found one key difference, in the time culture of parenthood. The "good mother" was viewed as someone who was always available to her children. . . . When a woman cuts back her hours, she may trigger stigma of various sorts and cease to be considered an ideal worker, at least she'll often be considered an ideal mother. The same is not true of many fathers. Nick Townsend, in a wonderful recent book, *The Package Deal,* pointed out that our ideals of fatherhood retain a strong emphasis on fathers as the providers. And studies of masculinity by Scott Coltrane and others document how we still tie masculinity very tightly into the size of a paycheck. These studies help us understand why the chilly climate for mothers at work often becomes a frigid climate for fathers who take an active role in family care. This frigid climate can give rise to some troubling situations. . . .

The stigma that's associated with flexible work arrangements also reflects various patterns of unexamined bias. [One person I interviewed told me:] "Before I went part-time and people called and found that I wasn't at my desk, they assumed I was somewhere else at a business meeting. But after I went part-time, the tendency was to assume that I wasn't there because of my part-time schedule, even if I was out at a meeting. Also, before I went part-time, people sort of gave me the benefit of the doubt. They assumed that I was giving them as fast a turn-around as was humanly possible. This stopped after I went part-time. Then they assumed that I wasn't doing things fast enough because of my part-time schedule. As a result, she said, she used to get top-of-the-scale performance reviews, but now she didn't, "even though, as far as I can tell, the quality of my work has not changed." Here we can identify three types of unexamined bias.

The first is attribution bias. When she was full-time and was not there, her co-workers attributed her absence to legitimate business reasons. But when she was part-time, and they found her not there, they attributed her absence to family reasons—even if she was at a business meeting.

The second kind of bias is called in-group favoritism. The in-group for this purpose is full-timers, and the out-group is part-timers, who are almost exclusively female. When the informant was in the in-group, she was given the benefit of the doubt. But after she went part-time, she was in the out-group and that stopped. . . .

Finally . . . women employed part-time were viewed similar to "housewives."

The implication of all these studies is that the chilly climate for family caregivers at work, including the stigma that attaches to many part-time and other flexible work arrangements, stems in part from gender stereotyping. . . .

• QUESTIONS •

1. Elsewhere in this reading, Williams asks: "Should feminists seek to empower in traditionally feminine roles or should they seek access to the preserves of masculinity?" What do you think? What would be involved in each goal?

2. According to Williams, how do employers define the "ideal worker"? How would you reinvent the ideal worker in an ungendered fashion? How might the law be used to support such a worker?

3. **Internet Assignment:** Find a company that has tried to create a corporate culture that supports men or women in part- or "flex" time employment. What are the characteristics of its program? Now check the company's financials. Is the "progressive" firm you've located also a successful one?

THE CIVIL RIGHTS ACT OF 1964

> *It shall be unlawful for an employer to fail or refuse to hire or to discharge any individual or otherwise discriminate against any individual with respect to his compensation terms, conditions, or privileges of employment because of such individual's race, color, religion, sex or national origin.*
>
> — Title VII, the Civil Rights Act of 1964[5]

Gradually, over time, the courts began to expand the meaning of equal protection—ruling in *Brown v. Board of Education* in 1954, for example, that segregated schools were unequal. But the Constitution applies only to discrimination by government. There was no federal law against discrimination in private sector employment, and state laws were uneven in their scope and application.

After a decade of protest against segregation and in the wake of the assassination of President John F. Kennedy, the U.S. Congress passed comprehensive civil rights legislation that, for the first time, would address discrimination on the part of private businesses and individuals. It outlawed discrimination in public accommodations (hotels, motels, restaurants), housing, public education, federally assisted programs, and employment.

Title VII, the provision dealing with employment, has no mention of the hot-button issues that emerged in the decades after its passage—affirmative action, sexual harassment, same-sex marriage. Its mandate appears to be relatively straightforward: to end discrimination. Yet Title VII has been interpreted as banning not only outright differential treatment, but also practices that appear to be neutral (height and weight standards, educational requirements, for example), but which disproportionately disadvantage members of one race, sex, or religion ("disparate impact discrimination"). It empowers courts to correct discrimination when they find it; to order companies to hire, promote, adjust raises or benefits, or otherwise compensate those who have been wronged.

Sex Discrimination

Sex, gender, and **sexuality** are terms whose meanings have been contested and re-conceptualized in the past few decades. Psychologists and feminist theorists, for example, generally use "sex" to refer to one's biological sex, labeling people "male" or "female" depending on their chromosomes, hormones, and anatomical features. Sex, they argue, is distinguishable from "gender" (whether one is masculine or feminine), because gender is the meaning that a particular society gives to one's sex. Whether one is "feminine" may depend, for example, on whether one takes care of children—even though, biologically, both males and females are capable of caring for children. This is often called the **social construction of gender.**

5 42 U.S.C.A. Sect. 2000(e).

Interpreting the Civil Rights Act's ban on "discrimination on the basis of sex," courts have had to decide what Congress meant by sex. Federal courts have consistently held that "sex" refers to one's biological sex, whether discrimination occurred because one is male or female, or because of the kind of gender-stereotyping that Elana Back confronted. The statute has not been interpreted to protect against discrimination based on one's sexual orientation or affiliations (homosexuality, bisexuality, heterosexuality). This means that, except in those states and localities with laws banning discrimination based on sexual orientation, an employer can refuse to hire a woman because she is a lesbian.

The next case presents yet another nuance in the realm of sex discrimination. Peter Oiler alleges that he was fired from his job because he cross-dresses and impersonates a woman when he is off duty. This, he claims, illegally discriminates on the basis of sexual stereotyping.

OILER V. WINN-DIXIE LOUISIANA, INC.

U.S. District Court, Louisiana, 2002
2002 WL 31098541

AFRICK, District Judge.

In 1979, plaintiff, Peter Oiler, was hired by defendant, Winn-Dixie, as a loader. In 1981, he was promoted to yard truck driver and he later became a road truck driver. As a road truck driver, plaintiff delivered groceries from Winn-Dixie's grocery warehouse in Harahan, Louisiana, to grocery stores in southern and central Louisiana and Mississippi.

Plaintiff is a heterosexual man who has been married since 1977. The plaintiff is transgendered. He is not a transsexual and he does not intend to become a woman. . . . He is a male crossdresser [or] transvestite.

When he is not at work, plaintiff appears in public approximately one to three times per month wearing female clothing and accessories. In order to resemble a woman, plaintiff wears wigs and makeup, including concealer, eye shadow, foundation, and lipstick . . . skirts, women's blouses, women's flat shoes, and nail polish. He shaves his face, arms, hands, and legs. He wears women's underwear and bras and he uses silicone prostheses to enlarge his breasts. When he is crossdressed as a woman, he adopts a female persona and he uses the name "Donna".

. . . While crossdressed, he attended support group meetings, dined at a variety of restaurants in Kenner and Metairie, visited night clubs, went to shopping malls, and occasionally attended church services. He was often accompanied by his wife and other friends, some of whom were also crossdressed.

On October 29, 1999, plaintiff told Gregg Miles, a Winn-Dixie supervisor, that he was transgendered. . . . [W]hen plaintiff did not resign voluntarily, Winn-Dixie discharged him . . . because [of concerns that] if Winn-Dixie's customers learned of plaintiff's lifestyle, i.e., that he regularly crossdressed and impersonated a woman in public, they would shop elsewhere and Winn-Dixie would lose business. Plaintiff did not crossdress at work and he was not terminated because he violated any Winn-Dixie on-duty dress code. He was never told . . . that he was being terminated for appearing or acting effeminate at work, i.e., for having effeminate mannerisms or a high voice. Nor did any Winn-Dixie manager ever tell plaintiff that he did not fit a male stereotype or assign him work that stereotypically would be performed by a female. . . .

In *Ulane v. Eastern Airlines, Inc.* (7th Cir. 1984) a male airline pilot was fired when, following sex reassignment surgery, she attempted to return to work as a woman. . . . The *Ulane* court stated that:

> *The phrase in Title VII prohibiting discrimination based on sex, in its plain meaning, implies that it is unlawful to discriminate against women because they are women and against men because they are men. The words of Title VII do not outlaw discrimination*

> *against a person who has a sexual identity disorder,* i.e., *a person born with a male body who believes himself to be a female, or a person born with a female body who believes herself to be male; a prohibition against discrimination based on an individual's sex is not synonymous with a prohibition based on an individual's sexual identity disorder or discontent with the sex into which they were born. . . .*

In 1964, when Title VII was adopted, there was no debate on the meaning of the phrase "sex." In the social climate of the early sixties, sexual identity and sexual orientation related issues remained shrouded in secrecy and individuals having such issues generally remained closeted. Thirty-eight years later, however, sexual identity and sexual orientation issues are no longer buried and they are discussed in the mainstream. Many individuals having such issues have opened wide the closet doors.

Despite the fact that the number of persons publicly acknowledging sexual orientation or gender or sexual identity issues has increased exponentially since the passage of Title VII, the meaning of the word "sex" in Title VII has never been clarified legislatively. From 1981 through 2001, thirty-one proposed bills have been introduced in the United States Senate and the House of Representatives which have attempted to amend Title VII and prohibit employment discrimination on the basis of affectional or sexual orientation. None have passed. . . .

Plaintiff argues that his termination by Winn-Dixie was not due to his crossdressing as a result of his gender identity disorder, but because he did not conform to a gender stereotype. . . .

After much thought and consideration of the undisputed facts of this case, the Court finds that this is not a situation where the plaintiff failed to conform to a gender stereotype. Plaintiff was not discharged because he did not act sufficiently masculine or because he exhibited traits normally valued in a female employee, but disparaged in a male employee. Rather, the plaintiff disguised himself as a person of a different sex and presented himself as a female for stress relief and to express his gender identity. The plaintiff was terminated because he is a man with a sexual or gender identity disorder who, in order to publicly disguise himself as a woman, wears women's clothing, shoes, underwear, breast prostheses, wigs, make-up, and nail polish, pretends to be a woman, and publicly identifies himself as a woman named "Donna.". . .

This is not just a matter of an employee of one sex exhibiting characteristics associated with the opposite sex. This is a matter of a person of one sex assuming the role of a person of the opposite sex. . . .

In holding that defendant's actions are not proscribed by Title VII, the Court recognizes that many would disagree with the defendant's decision and its rationale. The plaintiff was a long-standing employee of the defendant. He never crossdressed at work and his crossdressing was not criminal or a threat to public safety.

Defendant's rationale for plaintiff's discharge may strike many as morally wrong. However, the function of this Court is not to raise the social conscience of defendant's upper level management, but to construe the law in accordance with proper statutory construction and judicial precedent. The Court is constrained by the framework of the remedial statute enacted by Congress and it cannot, therefore, afford the luxury of making a moral judgment. . . .

• QUESTIONS •

1. On what basis did Oiler lose his case?

2. Assume that this case was appealed and that the appeals court agreed with Judge Africk. Write a dissenting opinion.

3. Women who worked for Winn-Dixie were allowed to wear jeans, plaid shirts, and work shoes while working in the warehouse or in refrigerated compartments. How might that information be used to make another kind of sex discrimination claim? What arguments might Winn-Dixie make to defend itself?

Highlights in the Evolving Laws of Sexual Harassment

- **Congress Sets the Stage:** In 1964, Title VII of the Civil Rights Act was passed, outlawing discrimination in hiring, firing, and terms and conditions of employment based on race, color, religion, sex, or national origin. There is no mention of sexual harassment.
- **Early Lower Court Cases:** The first reported case of sexual harassment is filed by two women who resigned because of constant sexual advances from their boss. The court denied their claim, describing the supervisor's conduct as "nothing more than a personal proclivity, peculiarity or mannerism." *Corne v. Bausch & Lomb,* 380 F. Supp.161 (D. Ariz., 1975). But in a breakthrough case, a woman whose job was abolished after she repulsed the sexual advances of her boss sued and won. ("But for her womanhood the woman would not have lost her job.") *Barnes v. Costle,* 561 F.2d 983 (D. C. Cir. 1977).
- **EEOC Drafts Guidelines:** By 1980, EEOC announced that two types of illegal sexual harassment existed: **quid pro quo** and **hostile environment.** Quid pro quo refers to demands for sexual favors with threats attached; either the victim gives in or loses a tangible job benefit—even the job itself. Hostile environment refers to behavior that creates an intimidating or abusive workplace atmosphere.
- **Supreme Court Speaks:** Recognizing the hostile environment form of sexual harassment, the Supreme Court allows a suit where behavior is "sufficiently severe or pervasive to alter the conditions of the victim's employment and create an abusive working environment," in *Meritor Savings Bank v. Vinson,* 106 S.Ct. 2399 (1986). In a later case, the Supreme Court explains that a victim need not prove psychological injury to win, "so long as the environment would reasonably be perceived, and is perceived, as hostile or abusive." *Harris v. Forklift Systems,* 114 S.Ct. 367 (1993).
- **Supreme Court and Employer Liability:** The Court clarifies that employers are liable for misuse of supervisory authority—whether or not threats are carried out. Where tangible employment retaliation—for example, termination, demotion, or undesirable reassignment—is carried out or even threatened, the employer is automatically liable. In cases where a plaintiff claims a hostile environment exists, the employer can successfully defend by proving (1) it took reasonable care to prevent and correct promptly any sexually harassing behavior, and (2) the employee "unreasonably failed to take advantage of any preventive or corrective opportunities." *Faragher v. City of Boca Raton* 118 S.Ct. 2275 (1998) and *Burlington Industries v. Ellerth,* 118 S.Ct. 2257 (1998).
- **Same-Sex Harassment:** In 1999, the Supreme Court held that Title VII protects men as well as women, and that the fact that both plaintiff and defendant are of the same sex does not necessarily prevent a claim of sex discrimination. *Oncale v. Sundowner Offshore Services, Inc.,* 118 S.Ct. 998 (1999).
- **Constructive Discharge:** When a supervisor's official act precipitates a constructive discharge—making the abusive working environment so intolerable that a reasonble person would be compelled to resign—the employer is strictly liable ("aggravated hostile environment"), *Pennsylvania State Police v. Suders,* 124 S.Ct. 2342 (2004).

Sexual Harassment

Sexual harassment has a familiar ring today. But the notion that any type of private discrimination based on sex could be grounds for lawsuits was new at the time the Civil Rights Act of 1964 was under consideration by Congress. Then, opponents of the law attempted to block its passage by amending it to cover "sex," a ploy they believed would expose the whole concept of the law as absurd. Their strategy backfired; the Civil Rights Act did pass, and sex discrimination became illegal almost as an ironic afterthought. Yet the law made no mention of sexual harassment and never identified it as a form of sex discrimination. By the late 1970s, successful plaintiffs had convinced the courts that what feminist lawyer Catharine MacKinnon described as the "unwanted imposition of sexual requirements in the context of a relationship of unequal power" must indeed be classified as sex discrimination—an understanding that receives widespread support today.

Hostile Environment: Proving a *Prima Facie* Case

What has been called "quid pro quo" harassment—sexual favors in exchange for something concrete such as a job or a raise—is generally easily identifiable as illegal sex discrimination and employers are automatically responsible for such "tangible" employment retaliation. Much harder to define and far more controversial are situations involving what has come to be known as "hostile environment" sexual harassment.

As is true in every civil lawsuit, a plaintiff's first burden is to demonstrate the *possibility* of winning by offering evidence to support each element of her claim. This is called a ***prima facie*** case. The defendant will then offer contrary evidence, witnesses who can discredit the plaintiff's allegations or support the defendant's own claims and affirmative defenses. To make out a *prima facie* case of hostile environment sexual harassment, a plaintiff must show that (1) she is a **member of a protected group,** (2) she was the subject of **unwelcome** sexual harassment, (3) the harassment occurred **because of her sex,** and, in cases involving hostile environment, (4) the harassment was **sufficiently severe or pervasive** to alter the **terms and conditions** of her employment.

Member of a Protected Group

The first element is easy to prove in most cases. The Supreme Court has made clear that men, as well as women, are "protected" by Title VII—so long as they are targeted based on their maleness or femaleness—and that a supervisor can be responsible for sexually harassing a person of the same sex. Each of the other elements, however, have created knotty problems for the lower courts.

Unwelcomeness

Plaintiffs must prove that the behavior that creates such an environment is not welcomed. As courts try to determine "welcomeness," they consider the entire range of circumstances. They may take into account, for example, a plaintiff's manner of speaking, behaving, or dressing. For a female plaintiff, this could mean that the tight fit of her sweaters or her taste in jokes may be viewed as "provocative," as inviting the behavior of which she complains. Even after-hours behavior could be examined: Does she go to bars alone? Have intimate relationships outside of marriage?

Some have argued that the standard used to measure hostile environment and whether a victim found it unwelcome is male-biased. While studies have repeatedly demonstrated that there is a great disparity between the way men and women view being approached sexually at work—men are typically flattered; women insulted—many in our society make the assumption that women tend to enjoy and welcome sexualized behavior. The law allows that assumption to be overcome, but the burden of proof is on the plaintiff. While in the context of a rape case the victim must prove non-consent, in the context of a claim of sexual harassment she must prove unwelcomeness.

Making such proof even more difficult is the tendency of females in our culture to avoid direct confrontation, to find ways to avoid conflict. In the following, a consultant who trained hundreds of New York City firefighters to identify and prevent sexual harassment describes how women typically deal with unwanted advances:

> *[W]omen respond to sexually harassing behavior in a variety of reasonable ways. The coping strategy a woman selects depends on her personal style, the type of incident, and her expectation that the situation is susceptible to resolution. . . . Typical coping methods include: (1) denying the impact of the event, blocking it out; (2) avoiding the workplace or the harasser, for instance, by taking sick leave or otherwise being absent; (3) telling the harasser to stop; (4) engaging in joking or other banter in the language of the workplace in order to defuse the situation; and (5) threatening to make or actually making an informal or formal complaint. . . .*
>
> *Of these five categories, formal complaint is the most rare because the victim of harassment fears an escalation of the problem, retaliation from the harasser, and embarrassment in the process of reporting. . . . Victims also often fear that nothing will be done and they will be blamed for the incident. . . . Thus, the absence of reporting of sexual harassment incidents cannot be viewed as an absence of such incidents from the workplace. . . .*
>
> *An effective policy for controlling sexual harassment cannot rely on ad hoc incident-by-incident reporting and investigation. . . .*
>
> *A study by the Working Women's Institute found that ninety-six percent of sexual harassment victims experienced emotional stress. . . . Sexual harassment has a cumulative, eroding effect on the victim's well-being. . . . When women feel a need to maintain vigilance against the next incident of harassment, the stress is increased tremendously. . . . When women feel that their individual complaints will not change the work environment materially, the ensuing sense of despair further compounds the stress.*
>
> – Testimony of K. C. Wagner*

Because of . . . One's Sex

Since hostile environment suits are essentially claims of sex discrimination, a plaintiff must establish that whatever harassment took place did so "because of" her sex. John Bibby, a gay man, worked at the Philadelphia Coca-Cola Bottling Company for fifteen years. There he suffered from what he believed to be discriminatory–but nonsexual–problems with supervisors. They harassed him by yelling at him, ignoring his reports of problems with machinery, and arbitrarily enforcing rules against him in situations where infractions by other employees would be ignored. Bibby also objected to graffiti of a sexual nature, some bearing his name, written in the bathrooms and allowed to remain there far longer than other graffiti. The trial court rejected his hostile environment claim, finding that he was harassed because of his sexual orientation, not his sex. On appeal, the Third Circuit must decide whether or not Bibby has demonstrated that he is a victim of illegal same-sex harassment.

BIBBY V. PHILA. COCA COLA BOTTLING COMPANY

U.S. Court of Appeals, Third Circuit, 2001
260 F.3d 257

BARRY, Circuit Judge.

. . . The question of how to prove that same-sex harassment is because of sex is not an easy one to answer. . . . [W]hen a heterosexual man makes implicit or explicit proposals of sexual activity to a woman co-worker or subordinate, it is easy to conclude or at least infer that the behavior is motivated by her sex. Similarly, if a man is aggressively rude to a woman, disparaging her or sabotaging her work, it is possible to infer that he is acting out of a general hostility to the presence of women in the workplace. These inferences are not always so clear when the harasser and victim are of the same sex.

**Robinson v. Jacksonville Shipyards,* 760 F. Supp.1486 (M. D. Fla. 1991).

There are several situations in which same-sex harassment can be seen as discrimination because of sex. The first is where there is evidence that the harasser sexually desires the victim. Thus, when a gay or lesbian supervisor treats a same-sex subordinate in a way that is sexually charged, it is reasonable to infer that the harasser acts as he or she does because of the victim's sex.

Same-sex harassment might also be found where there is no sexual attraction but where the harasser displays hostility to the presence of a particular sex in the workplace. For example, a woman chief executive officer of an airline might believe that women should not be pilots and might treat women pilots with hostility amounting to harassment. Similarly, a male doctor might believe that men should not be employed as nurses, leading him to make harassing statements to a male nurse with whom he works. In each of these hypothetical situations, it would be easy to conclude that the harassment was caused by a general hostility to the presence of one sex in the workplace or in a particular work function, and, therefore, amounted to discrimination because of sex.

Further, although it is less clear, a plaintiff may be able to prove that same-sex harassment was discrimination because of sex by presenting evidence that the harasser's conduct was motivated by a belief that the victim did not conform to the stereotypes of his or her gender. . . .

. . . Bibby simply failed [to prove the discrimination was because of his sex]; indeed, he did not even argue that he was being harassed because he was a man. . . . There was no allegation that his alleged harassers were motivated by sexual desire, or that they possessed any hostility to the presence of men in the workplace or in Bibby's particular job. Moreover, he did not claim that he was harassed because he failed to comply with societal stereotypes of how men ought to appear or behave or that as a man he was treated differently than female co-workers. His claim was, pure and simple, that he was discriminated against because of his sexual orientation. No reasonable finder of fact could reach the conclusion that he was discriminated against because he was a man.

For the foregoing reasons, we will affirm the judgment of the District Court [dismissing the case].

• QUESTIONS •

1. A sixteen-year-old man was harassed because his voice was soft, his physique slight, his hair long, and he wore an earring. Does he have a valid claim for sexual harassment?

2. What advice would you give to a young woman entering the workforce in terms of how best to present herself? A young man?

Sufficiently Severe or Pervasive

Case law tells us that an employee does not have to put up with discriminatory intimidation, ridicule, and insult so severe or pervasive that it creates an abusive working environment. Courts are supposed to determine when this standard has been met by looking at all—the "totality" of—the circumstances including:

> *[The] frequency of the discriminatory conduct; its severity; whether it is physically threatening or humiliating, or a mere offensive utterance; and whether it unreasonably interferes with an employee's work performance. [S]imple teasing, offhand comments, and isolated incidents (unless extremely serious) will not amount to discriminatory changes in the terms and conditions of employment.*[6]

But, which factors to consider, and how to weigh them, is a matter of dispute among the various federal courts of appeals. One federal trial judge explains:

> *The question of what is "sufficiently severe" sexual harassment is complicated because: (a) courts routinely remind plaintiffs that "Title VII is not a federal civility*

6 *Harris v. Forklift Systems, Inc.*, 114 S. Ct. 367 (1993).

*code," (b) the modern notion of acceptable behavior—as corroded by instant-gratification driven, cultural influences (*e.g., *lewd music, videos, and computer games, "perversity-programming" broadcast standards, White House "internal affairs" and perjurious coverups of same, etc.) has been coarsening over time; therefore, (c) what courts implicitly ask the "Title VII victim" to tolerate as mere "boorish behavior" or "workplace vulgarity" must, once placed in the contemporary context, account for any "Slouch Toward Gomorrah" societal norms might take.*

At the same time, this entire area of law is enervated by vague, almost circular standards: Title "VII affords employees the right to work in an environment free from discriminatory *intimidation, ridicule and insult." Hence, intimidation, ridicule and insult can be actionable if they reach a "discriminatory"* (i.e., *"sufficiently severe") level. But that's just another way of saying that if behavior offends the particular judge . . . then it must be "discriminatory." . . .*

[C]ourts decide what is "sufficiently severe" by resorting to "crudity comparables." That is, judges must compare the crudity and "lewdity" found in one case with that deemed sufficient to [allow the case to go to trial] in another.

Thus, not only must patterns or (in some cases) mere spasms of offensive behavior be judicially dissected and quantified, but also the "surrounding circumstances" in which they occurred. . . . Often this compels judges to painstakingly recite and analyze the "real" meaning of every last passing glance, raised eyebrow, comment, double entendre, grunt, sniff, etc. even if—especially where the victim has maintained a "journal" or "diary"—such occurred over long periods of time.

To that end, some judges simply recount a "parade of horribles," then announce that the line has been crossed . . . ("Here, Plaintiffs were subjected to a continual, sustained barrage of unwelcome comments and touchings, including requests for sex and unwelcome grabbing of their hips, buttocks, breasts, and genitalia.).

Consulting the case law could *lead one to think that only cases involving sexual touching will cross the actionability line. But in fact, sexual touching, grabbing, fondling (etc.) is simply not necessary.* See R&R Ventures. *(Restaurant . . . manager allegedly directed sexually pointed comments exclusively to young women who worked for him, closely examined female employees' bodies, inquired about their pant size, and made references to size of female employee's buttocks and breasts.)*

As the case law has grown to show, determining the intensity/quantity of sexual gesturing, touching, bantering and innuendo that it takes to render a work environment sexually hostile is now no less difficult than "trying to nail a jellyfish to the wall." . . .

Vicki Schultz has been a strong advocate for changes that would make the workplace more equitable and hospitable to women. In the next reading, Schultz is critical of employer attempts to wipe out sexual harassment by harshly and promptly punishing harassers—a process she dubs "sanitization," and which she believes causes problems of its own, further distancing us from real solutions to gender inequality.

THE SANITIZED WORKPLACE

Vicki Schultz[7]

. . . [T]he focus on sexual conduct has encouraged organizations to treat harassment as a stand-alone phenomenon—a problem of bad or boorish men who oppress or offend women—rather than as a symptom of larger patterns of sex segregation and inequality. . . .

---

7 112 *Yale L. J.* 2061 (2003).

. . . [T]he emphasis on eliminating sexual conduct encourages employees to articulate broader workplace harms as forms of sexual harassment, obscuring more structural problems that may be the true source of their disadvantage. Thus, women may complain about sexual jokes, when their real concern is a caste system that relegates them to low-status, low-pay positions. . . . Even more worrying is the prospect that some employees may make allegations of sexual harassment that disproportionately disadvantage racial and sexual minorities. . . . [W]hite women who enjoy sexual banter and flirtation with their white male coworkers may regard the same conduct as a form of sexual harassment when it comes from men of color. Heterosexual men who willingly engage in sexual horseplay with men whom they regard as heterosexual may be quick to label the same overtures as harassment when they come from openly gay men. [This suggests] that one-size-fits-all, acontextual prohibitions on sexual conduct may give individual employees, and management as a whole, too much power to enforce sexual conformity in the name of pursuing a project of gender equality that has been all but abandoned.

The truth is that managers cannot succeed in banishing sexuality from the workplace: They can only subject particular expressions of it to surveillance and discipline. Although some groups suffer more than others when this occurs, everyone loses. . . . With the decline of civil society, the workplace is one of the few arenas left in our society where people from different walks of life can come to know one another well. Because people who work together come into close contact with each other for extended periods for the purpose of achieving common goals, work fosters extraordinarily intimate relationships of both the sexually charged and the more platonic varieties. . . . We cannot expect diverse groups of people to form close bonds and alliances—whether sexual or nonsexual—if they must be concerned that reaching out to one another puts them at risk of losing their jobs or their reputations. . . .

. . . The larger question is whether we as a society can value the workplace as a realm alive with personal intimacy, sexual energy, and "humanness" more broadly. The same impulse that would banish sexuality from the workplace also seeks to suppress other "irrational" life experiences such as birth and death, sickness and disability, aging and emotion of every kind. But the old Taylorist dream of the workplace as a sterile zone in which workers suspend all their human attributes while they train their energies solely on production doesn't begin to reflect the rich, multiple roles that work serves in people's lives. For most people, working isn't just a way to earn a livelihood. It's a way to contribute something to the larger society, to struggle against their limits, to make friends and form communities, to leave their imprint on the world, and to know themselves and others in a deep way. . . . [W]ork isn't simply a sphere of production. It is also a source of citizenship, community, and self-understanding.

. . . Just as individual employees may express themselves or embroider intimate relations through sexual language and conduct, so too may employees as a group resort to sexual interactions to alleviate stress or boredom on the job, to create vital forms of community and solidarity with each other, or to articulate resistance to oppressive management practices. Research suggests that workplace romance may even increase productivity in some circumstances.

Contrary to prevailing orthodoxy, such uses of workplace sexuality do not always harm or disadvantage women: A lot depends on the larger structural context in which the sexuality is expressed. As a well-accepted body of systematic social science research demonstrates, women who enter jobs in which they are significantly underrepresented often confront hostility and harassment from incumbent male workers, and in some settings the men use sexual conduct as a means of marking the women as "different" and out of place. However, a new body of sociological research suggests that women who work in more integrated, egalitarian settings often willingly participate and take pleasure in sexualized interactions—probably because their numerical strength gives them the power to help shape the sexual norms and culture to their own liking. Rather than presuming that women will always find sexual conduct offensive, this research suggests that we should ensure that women are fully integrated into equal jobs and positions of authority, thus giving them the power to decide for themselves what kind of work cultures they want to have.

. . . I would like to see organizations abandon sensitivity training in favor of incorporating their harassment policies into broader efforts to achieve integration and equality throughout the firm. Along similar lines, I urge that employers forgo measures to prohibit or discourage sexual or dating relationships among employees and refuse to intervene, just as they do with nonsexual friendships, unless there is clear evidence that a particular relationship is undermining specific organizational goals. . . . In my view, employees and supervisors should be free to work together to create a variety of different work cultures–including more and less sexualized ones–so long as that process occurs within a larger context of structural equality that provides all women and men the power to shape those cultures. . . .

The contemporary drive to sanitize the workplace came about through a complex interplay of forces in which feminists, judges, HR managers, lawyers, and the news media all helped create an understanding that sexuality disadvantages women and disrupts productivity. In my view, we can only hope to halt the sanitization process by articulating a more appealing vision in which sexuality and intimacy can coexist with, and perhaps even enhance, gender equality and organizational rationality. . . .

• QUESTIONS •

1. What does Schultz mean by "the decline of civil society"?
2. Schultz favors broad efforts to achieve integration and equality throughout the firm. What do you think she means by this? Can you give examples?
3. **Internet Assignment:** Schultz mentions "the old Taylorist dream of the workplace as a sterile zone." Who was Frederick Taylor? What about his life's achievement would lead Schultz to describe his dream as "sterile"?

REASONABLE ACCOMMODATION OF DISABLED WORKERS

Society first confined people with disabilities in almshouses, and then in institutions. Alone and ignored, people with disabling conditions experienced life in a Hobbesian state of nature: an existence, "solitary, poor, nasty, brutish, and short.". . . Until 1973, Chicago prohibited persons who were "deformed" and "unsightly" from exposing themselves to public view. . . . In 1975, when federal legislation finally required states receiving federal educational funds to serve all school-aged children with disabilities, 1.75 million children were not receiving any schooling, and an estimated 2.5 million were in programs that did not meet their needs.

— Mark C. Weber[8]

8 "Exile and the Kingdom: Integration, Harassment, and the Americans with Disabilities Act," 63 *Md. L. Rev.* 162 (2004).

Hailed by some as the most important legislation since the Civil Rights Acts of 1964, in 1990 Congress adopted the **Americans with Disabilities Act (ADA).** Patterned on an earlier law that prohibited discrimination against persons with handicaps in government-funded programs, the ADA is a bold stroke to eliminate barriers in employment, education, housing, transportation, and public accommodations. Wherever reasonably possible, physical obstacles—the absence of ramps to enter buildings, narrow seating in theatres, the arrangement of furniture and machinery in some workplaces—must be replaced to make business and public places accessible to disabled customers, clients, and employees. The ADA also takes aim at another problem: society's accumulated myths and fears about disability and disease.

Of particular importance to business are the provisions that not only outlaw discrimination as such, but require firms to make "reasonable accommodation" so that the disabled are given more opportunity to enter the mainstream. The concept of reasonable accommodation is broad and flexible—but is not intended to impose an "undue hardship" on the employer. It encompasses both physical changes to buildings (e.g., broadening aisles and doorways and lowering shelves to make them accessible to those in wheelchairs) and adjustments in the ways people work (e.g., flexible work schedules or modified job descriptions). While Title VII speaks of ending discrimination, the ADA does that and more: it sometimes requires employers to alter the jobs themselves.

The following is excerpted from the law:

Equal Opportunity for Individuals with Disabilities (Americans with Disabilities Act)

42 United States Code Annotated Sect. 12101

The term **disability** means, with respect to an individual (A) a physical or mental impairment that substantially limits one or more of the major life activities of such individual; (B) a record of such an impairment; or (C) being regarded as having such an impairment.

The term **qualified individual with a disability** means an individual with a disability who, with or without reasonable accommodation, can perform the essential functions of the employment position that such individual holds or desires. . . . [C]onsideration shall be given to the employer's judgment as to what functions of a job are essential, and if an employer has prepared a written description before advertising or interviewing applicants for the job, this description shall be considered evidence of the essential functions of the job.

The term **reasonable accommodation** may include (A) making existing facilities used by employees readily accessible to and usable by individuals with disabilities; and (B) job restructuring, part-time or modified work schedules, reassignment to a vacant position, acquisition or modification of equipment or devices, appropriate adjustment or modifications of examinations, training materials or policies, the provision of qualified readers or interpreters, and other similar accommodations. . . .

The term **undue hardship** means an action requiring significant difficulty or expense, when considered in light of the [following]: In determining whether an accommodation would impose an undue hardship on a covered entity, factors to be considered include (i) the nature and cost of the accommodation needed under this chapter; (ii) the overall financial resources of the facility or facilities involved in the provision of the reasonable accommodation; the number of persons employed at such facility; the effect on expenses and resources, or the impact otherwise of such accommodation upon the operation of the facility; (iii) the overall financial resources of the covered entity; the overall size of the business of a covered entity with respect to the number of its employees; the number, type, and location of its facilities; and (iv) the type of operation or operations of the covered entity, including the composition, structure, and functions of the workforce of such entity; the geographic separateness, administrative, or fiscal relationship of the facility or facilities in question to the covered entity.

• QUESTIONS •

1. Alcoholism is considered an "impairment" within the meaning of the ADA, although the law explicitly allows a company to hold an alcoholic employee to the same standards of behavior as other employees, even if the employee's inability to perform is related to her alcoholism. A salesman with a generally good sales record also had a long history of alcoholism (including experiences with Alcoholics Anonymous and in-patient rehabilitation). (a) Suppose his employer fires him after a supervisor found an empty liquor bottle in his desk. How might he frame a complaint under the ADA? (b) In *Toyota Motor Manufacturing, Kentucky, Inc. v. Williams,*[9] the Supreme Court ruled that "major" life activities refers to those that are of central importance to daily life, such as walking, seeing, and hearing. What impact would that ruling have on the salesman's chances of winning? See *Sullivan v. Nieman Marcus Group, Inc.,* 358 F. 3d 110 (1st Cir. 2004) for a discussion of the "alcoholic's conundrum."

2. **Internet Assignment:** Persons with mental illness are among the most stigmatized Americans. Yet there are few court cases finding ADA protection for mentally ill claimants. In what ways are mental impairments different from physical ones? How might the ADA apply to the following: Steele, who suffered from obsessive compulsive disorder, was taunted by co-workers who called him "psycho-Bob." He requested transfers, but the teasing continued in his new position and his superiors did not believe him when he tried to give notice of his disability. Find out what happened in *Steele v. Thiokol Corp.* 241 F 3d 1248 (10th Cir. 2001).

3. Under regulations promulgated by the EEOC to implement the ADA, a claimant cannot prove discrimination based on a "record of impairment" unless she can show her past impairment had substantially limited a major life activity. So, for example, a temporary stay in a psychiatric hospital, alone, would not be enough to establish that a person was protected under the ADA. Does that rule seem designed to further the goal of ending practices based on stereotypes about the disabled?

4. The Supreme Court has directed lower courts to determine whether a person is disabled by taking into account "measures that mitigate the impairment." This means, for example, that a person who has 20-20 vision with glasses is not considered disabled no matter how poor her unimproved vision [*Sutton v. United Air Lines,* 527 U.S. 471 (1999)]. Should the same analysis apply if a person chooses not to use hearing aids because he is disturbed by the background noise? Or does not take blood pressure medication because of its side effects? Asthma medication because of feared—but not scientifically proven—side effects? See *Finical v. Collections Unlimited, Inc.,* 65 F. Supp. 2d 1032 (D. Ariz. 1999), *Hein v. All American Plywood,* 232 F.3d 482 (6th Cir. 2000) and *Tangires v. Johns Hopkins,* 79 F. Supp. 2d 587 (D. Md. 2000), aff'd 230 F.3d 1354 (4th Cir. 2000). How should the courts evaluate a severely depressed person who does not want to take psychotropic drugs because they make him impotent? [*McAlindin v. County of San Diego,* 192 F 3d 1226 (9th Cir. 1999)].

AFFIRMATIVE ACTION

Four decades ago, when the Civil Rights Act was first enacted, some believed that to achieve equality within a reasonable time, the nation would have to do more than simply end past discriminatory practices. In September 1965, President Lyndon B. Johnson signed Executive Order 11246, requiring companies that contracted with the federal government to "act affirmatively" to alter the effects of race discrimination. Many employers, either because they sought federal

9 122 S.Ct. 681 (2002).

contracts or because they wanted to avoid Title VII liability, devised plans inviting those making hiring or promotion decisions to take race and gender into account.

Race In America in the New Millennium

Unemployment Rates: Among white Americans were 3.7 percent in 1999, 3.5 percent in 2000, and 4.2 percent in 2001; among African-Americans was 8.0, 7.6, and 8.7 percent, respectively; among Hispanics, 6.4, 5.7, and 6.6 percent).[10]

Health Insurance: In 2000, 9.7 percent of non-Hispanic whites were without health insurance, as compared to 18.5 percent of African-Americans, 18.0 percent of Asian-Americans, and 32.0 percent of Hispanics.[11]

Segregation: Whites are the most segregated group in the nation's public schools; they attend schools, on average, where eighty percent of the student body is white. "[A]lmost three-fourths of black and Latino students attend schools that are predominantly minority. . . . More than one in six black children attend a school that is 99–100% minority. . . . One in nine Latino students attend virtually all minority schools."[12]

Poverty: Blacks, Hispanics, and Native Americans each have poverty rates almost twice as high as Asians and almost three times as high as whites.[13]

The seminal case on affirmative action in industry reached the U.S. Supreme Court in 1979. It grew out of an affirmative action plan adopted by Kaiser Aluminum and its unions five years earlier. At the time, fewer than 2 percent of Kaiser's skilled craft workers were black, even though the local workforce was approximately 39 percent black, largely due to past discriminatory practices. As a remedy, Kaiser agreed to establish a program to train production workers to fill craft openings and to earmark 50 percent of the openings for blacks. During the first year, seven black and six white trainees were selected from the plant. Brian Weber, a white man, was not, despite the fact that he had more seniority than any of the seven black trainees. He sued, arguing for a literal interpretation of the Civil Rights Act that would outlaw Kaiser's affirmative action plan because it did not treat whites the same as blacks. The Court rejected his claim in an opinion by Justice Brennan:

> *The purposes of [Kaiser Aluminum's affirmative action] plan mirror those of [Title VII of the Civil Rights Act]. Both were designed to break down old patterns of racial segregation and hierarchy. Both were structured to "open employment opportunities for Negroes in occupations that have been traditionally closed to them. . . ."*
>
> *At the same time, the plan does not unnecessarily trammel the interests of the white employees. The plan does not require the discharge of white workers and their replacement with new black hires. . . . Nor does the plan create an absolute bar to the advancement of white employees; half of those trained in the program will be white. Moreover, the plan is a temporary measure; it is not intended to maintain racial balance, but simply to eliminate a manifest racial imbalance.*
>
> —*Steelworkers v. Weber,* 443 U.S. 193 (1979)

10 U.S. Dept. of Commerce, Bureau of Census, *Statistical Abstract of the United States: 2002,* p. 368 (2002) (Table 562).

11 U.S. Dept. of Commerce, Bureau of Census, *Health Insurance Coverage: 2000,* p. 391 (2001) (Table A).

12 U.S. Dept. of Commerce, Bureau of Census, *Racial and Ethnic Residential Segregation in the United States: 1980–2000* (2002) (documenting residential segregation).

13 S. Staveteig and A. Wigton, *Racial and Ethnic Disparities: Key Findings from the National Survey of America's Families 1* (Urban Institute Report B-5, 2000).

A decade later, in *Johnson v. Santa Clara County Transportation Authority,*[14] the Supreme Court extended its decision in *Weber* to allow voluntary programs designed to benefit women as well as men of color. But the *Santa Clara County* case did little to end the controversy over affirmative action. As new justices were appointed to the Supreme Court, the Court itself began to chip away at its earlier decisions. A series of rulings in the late 1980s restricted the protections of the Civil Rights Act and fed a national debate that did not subside even after Congress passed the 1991 Civil Rights Act amendments, reversing some of the Supreme Court's narrow interpretations.

One section of the 1991 Act required U.S. employers operating abroad to obey the anti-discrimination provisions of Title VII, unless doing so put them in violation of another nation's laws. So, an American-owned company doing business in Saudi Arabia could not discriminate against the women in its workforce, even if such treatment was acceptable under Saudi tradition or tolerated by the Saudi legal system. Another provision makes it clear that no employer would be required to grant preferences based on race, religion, sex, or national origin to meet at any numerical "quota" based on workforce statistical demographics.

When private firms choose to undertake affirmative action initiatives, they must be certain they are consistent with the goals and spirit of the civil rights laws. Government employees however, must do more than that. Cities, states, and federal agencies must be concerned not only with statutes passed by Congress; they must also be sure that their actions comply with the equal protection mandates of the U.S. Constitution.

Prior to 1989, the Court had never applied strict scrutiny to an affirmative action plan. It had reasoned that although such programs may involve different treatment on the basis of race or ethnicity, they were well intentioned and "benign." After all, when the majority sets up an affirmative action plan, it voluntarily gives up privileges to compensate for wrongs done in the past. The impulse is remedial, not oppressive.

Encouraged by language that seemed to allow, if not encourage, such efforts, universities tried to undo years of segregation and exclusion with recruitment efforts aimed at minorities and women. In one well known case, *University of California Board of Regents v. Baake,*[15] the Supreme Court struck down "racial quotas" in medical school admissions, but indicated that race could be one consideration among many.

In the decades following *Baake* schools across the nation, including the Law School and the College of Literature, Science, and the Arts (LSA) at the publicly supported but highly selective University of Michigan, adopted affirmative action plans. The Law School's admissions policy focuses on academic ability coupled with a flexible assessment of applicants' talents, experiences, and potential to "contribute to the learning of those around them." The policy reaffirms the Law School's commitment to racial and ethnic diversity by enrolling a critical mass of underrepresented minority students. To achieve that goal, it uses a "highly individualized, holistic review of each applicant's file."

LSA, on the other hand, allowed race to be taken into account in its admissions policies in two specific ways. First, admissions counselors had discretion to "flag" applicants based on certain qualities–including race–to keep applicants below the initial admit threshold in the review pool for further consideration. Second, in calculating an applicant's "selection index score"–a combination of high school GPA and SAT scores–certain applicants could be given additional points: 6 for geographic factors; 4 for alumni relationship; 3 for outstanding essays; 5 for leadership and service skills; and 20 for athletic talent, socioeconomic status, or minority racial status. LSA justified this system because diversity "increased the intellectual vitality of [its] education, scholarship, service and communal life."

14 *Johnson v. Transportation Agency Santa Clara County,* California, 107 S. Ct. 1442 (1987).

15 *University of California Regents v. Bakke,* 438 U.S. 265 (1978). Allen Bakke was a white man who brought a race discrimination claim when he was rejected by the University of California Medical School. The Supreme Court agreed that he had been denied his right to equal protection of the laws, and ordered the school to admit him.

Both Michigan programs came under attack by opponents of affirmative action in the 1990s.[16] Barbara Grutter, a white woman with a 3.8 grade point average, had been rejected by Michigan's law school. She sued, claiming that Michigan violated her right to equal protection. Another white woman, Jennifer Gratz, filed a separate class action lawsuit against the LSA when she, too, was denied admission.

Fearing that the courts might overturn Michigan's policies, 360 institutional members of the professional higher education community joined with the University of Michigan in defense of affirmative action admissions programs. It soon became clear that the Supreme Court would take another look at affirmative action in higher education. By the time the Michigan cases were decided, a record number (107) of *amicus curiae* briefs had been filed with the Court. Major corporations, states, retired military officers, and 60 congresspersons were among the overwhelming majority of those siding with the University of Michigan.

Decisions in the two cases were handed down on the same day, with the Court seeming to give something to everyone. Writing for the majority in the *Grutter* case, Justice Sandra Day O'Connor explained why the Law School's program passes strict scrutiny:

> *. . . Our conclusion that the Law School has a compelling interest in a diverse student body is informed by our view that attaining a diverse student body is at the heart of the Law School's proper institutional mission, and that "good faith" on the part of a university is "presumed" absent "a showing to the contrary.". . .*
>
> *The Law School's admissions policy promotes "cross-racial understanding," helps to break down racial stereotypes, and "enables [students] to better understand persons of different races." These benefits are "important and laudable," because "classroom discussion is livelier, more spirited, and simply more enlightening and interesting" when students have "the greatest possible variety of backgrounds.". . .*
>
> *These benefits are not theoretical but real, as major American businesses have made clear that the skills needed in today's increasingly global marketplace can only be developed through exposure to widely diverse people, culture, ideas, and viewpoints. . . . What is more, high-ranking retired officers and civilian leaders of the United States military assert that "[b]ased on [their] decades of experience," a "highly qualified, racially diverse officer corps . . . is essential to the military's ability to fulfill its principle mission to provide national security."*
>
> — *Grutter v. Bollinger,* 539 U.S. 306 (2003)

For now, O'Connor wrote, the individualized evaluation of applicants made the school's race-conscious admissions program sufficiently narrow in scope to satisfy strict scrutiny. But, she warned, "we expect that 25 years from now, the use of racial preferences will no longer be necessary to further the interest approved today."

As the following companion case to *Grutter* indicates, the undergraduate admissions policy would not be given the same deference.

Gratz v. Bollinger

Supreme Court of the United States, 2003
123 S.Ct. 2411

Chief Justice REHNQUIST delivered the opinion of the Court.

. . . It is by now well established that "all racial classifications reviewable under the Equal Protection Clause must be strictly scrutinized.". . .

---

16 They were spurred on by Supreme Court decisions that require all racial classifications to be strictly scrutinized and by *Hopwood v. Texas,* a 1996 federal appeals court ruling that struck down the admissions program at the University of Texas law school.

To withstand our strict scrutiny analysis, respondents must demonstrate that the University's use of race in its current admission program employs "narrowly tailored measures that further compelling governmental interests." Because "[r]acial classifications are simply too pernicious to permit any but the most exact connection between justification and classification . . . our review of whether such requirements have been met must entail "'a most searching examination.'". . . We find that the University's policy, which automatically distributes 20 points, or one-fifth of the points needed to guarantee admission, to every single "underrepresented minority" applicant solely because of race, is not narrowly tailored to achieve the interest in educational diversity that respondents claim justifies their program.

In *Bakke,* Justice Powell reiterated that "[p]referring members of any one group for no reason other than race or ethnic origin is discrimination for its own sake." He then explained, however, that in his view it would be permissible for a university to employ an admissions program in which "race or ethnic background may be deemed a 'plus' in a particular applicant's file.". . .

Justice Powell's opinion in *Bakke* emphasized the importance of considering each particular applicant as an individual, assessing all of the qualities that individual possesses, and in turn, evaluating that individual's ability to contribute to the unique setting of higher education. . . .

[U]nlike Justice Powell's example, where the race of a "particular black applicant" could be considered without being decisive, . . . the LSA's automatic distribution of 20 points has the effect of making "the factor of race . . . decisive" for virtually every minimally qualified underrepresented minority applicant.

Even if [an applicant's] . . . "extraordinary artistic talent" rivaled that of Monet or Picasso, the applicant would receive, at most, five points under the LSA's system. At the same time, every single underrepresented minority applicant . . . would automatically receive 20 points for submitting an application. Clearly, the LSA's system does not offer applicants the individualized selection process [described with approvaal by Justice Powell in the *Bakke* decision.] . . .

[The University r]espondents] contend that "[t]he volume of applications and the presentation of applicant information make it impractical for [LSA] to use the . . . admissions system" upheld by the Court today in *Grutter.* But the fact that the implementation of a program capable of providing individualized consideration might present administrative challenges does not render constitutional an otherwise problematic system. . . . Nothing in Justice Powell's opinion in *Bakke* signaled that a university may employ whatever means it desires to achieve the stated goal of diversity without regard to the limits imposed by our strict scrutiny analysis.

We conclude, therefore, that because the University's use of race in its current freshman admissions policy is not narrowly tailored to achieve respondents' asserted compelling interest in diversity, the admissions policy violates the Equal Protection Clause of the Fourteenth Amendment. . . .

Justice GINSBURG, with whom Justice SOUTER joins, dissenting.

Educational institutions, the Court acknowledges, are not barred from any and all consideration of race when making admissions decisions. . . . But the Court once again maintains that the same standard of review controls judicial inspection of all official race classifications. This insistence on "consistency," would be fitting were our Nation free of the vestiges of rank discrimination long reinforced by law. But we are not far distant from an overtly discriminatory past, and the effects of centuries of law-sanctioned inequality remain painfully evident in our communities and schools.

In the wake "of a system of racial caste only recently ended," large disparities endure. Unemployment, poverty, and access to health care vary disproportionately by race. Neighborhoods and schools remain racially divided. African-American and Hispanic children are all too often educated in poverty-stricken and underperforming institutions. Adult African-Americans and Hispanics generally earn less than whites with equivalent levels of education. Equally credentialed job applicants receive different receptions depending on their race. Irrational prejudice is still encountered in real estate markets and consumer transctions. "Bias both conscious and unconscious, reflecting traditional and unexamined habits of thought, keeps up barriers that must come down if equal opportunity and nondiscrimination are ever genuinely to become this country's law and practice."

The Constitution instructs all who act for the government that they may not "deny to any person . . . the equal protection of the laws." In implementing this equality instruction, as I see it, government decisionmakers may properly distinguish between policies of exclusion and inclusion. . . .

Our jurisprudence ranks race a "suspect" category, "not because [race] is inevitably an impermissible classification, but because it is one which usually, to our national shame, has been drawn for the purpose of maintaining racial inequality." But where race is considered "for the purpose of achieving equality," no automatic proscription is in order. For, as insightfully explained, "[t]he Constitution is both color blind and color conscious. To avoid conflict with the equal protection clause, a classification that denies a benefit, causes harm, or imposes a burden must not be based on race. In that sense, the Constitution is color blind. But the Constitution is color conscious to prevent discrimination being perpetuated and to undo the effects of past discrimination.". . . Contemporary human rights documents draw just this line; they distinguish between policies of oppression and measures designed to accelerate *de facto* equality. . . .

Examining in this light the admissions policy employed by the University of Michigan's College of Literature, Science, and the Arts. . . . I see no constitutional infirmity. . . .

The stain of generations of racial oppression is still visible in our society, and the determination to hasten its removal remains vital. One can reasonably anticipate, therefore, that colleges and universities will seek to maintain their minority enrollment—and the networks and opportunities thereby opened to minority graduates—whether or not they can do so in full candor through adoption of affirmative action plans of the kind here at issue. Without recourse to such plans, institutions of higher education may resort to camouflage. For example, schools may encourage applicants to write of their cultural traditions in the essays they submit, or to indicate whether English is their second language. Seeking to improve their chances for admission, applicants may highlight the minority group associations to which they belong, or the Hispanic surnames of their mothers or grandparents. . . . If honesty is the best policy, surely Michigan's accurately described, fully disclosed College affirmative action program is preferable to achieving similar numbers through winks, nods, and disguises.

• QUESTIONS •

1. Compare the admissions policies challenged in the *Grutter* and *Gratz* cases. How does the Court explain the different outcomes? On what basis does Justice Ginsberg dissent from the ruling in *Gratz*?

2. Does a program designed to ensure diversity further "the greatest good for the greatest number," if we look at it from a utilitarian perspective? And what does it do to rights within a deontological framework?

3. California, Florida, and Texas all have "percentage plans," under which the top 10 or 20 percent of high school graduates are guaranteed admission to state universities. To what extent is such an approach more "race-neutral" than Michigan's? What advantages can you see to such plans? What disadvantages? Do you think such plans could help create diversity in graduate and professional schools?

4. Find out if your school has an admissions policy designed to boost diversity of any kind. If so, what kind? Do you think it is of value? Is it working? Have you experienced any of the benefits of "heterogeneous groups" in classrooms? In work or social settings?

AFFIRMATIVE ACTION: THE PRICE OF PREFERENCE

Shelby Steele[17]

In a few short years, when my two children will be applying to college, the affirmative action policies by which most universities offer black students some form of preferential treatment will present me with a dilemma. I am a middle-class black, a college professor, far from wealthy, but also well-removed from the kind of deprivation that would qualify my children for the label "disadvantaged." Both of them have endured racial insensitivity from whites. They have been called names, have suffered slights, and have experienced firsthand the peculiar malevolence that racism brings out in people. Yet, they have never experienced racial discrimination, have never been stopped by their race on any path they have chosen to follow. Still, their society now tells them that if they will only designate themselves as black on their college applications, they will likely do better in the college lottery than if they conceal this fact. . . .

[After] twenty years of implementation, I think affirmative action has shown itself to be more bad than good and that blacks—whom I will focus on in this essay—now stand to lose more from it than they gain. . . .

[The] essential problem with [affirmative action mandates that give preferences on the basis of race are] the way [they] leap over the hard business of developing a formerly oppressed people to the point where they can achieve proportionate representation. This may satisfy some whites of their innocence and some blacks of their power, but it does very little to truly uplift blacks. . . .

Too often the result of this on campuses (for example) has been a democracy of colors rather than of people, an artificial diversity that gives the appearance of educational parity between black and white students that has not yet been achieved in reality. . . .

Racial representation is not the same thing as racial development, yet affirmative action fosters a confusion of these very different needs. Representation can be manufactured; development is always hard-earned. . . . None of this is to say that blacks don't need policies that ensure our right to equal opportunity, but what we need more is the development that will let us take advantage of society's efforts to include us. . . .

The effect of preferential treatment—the lowering of normal standards to increase black representation—puts blacks at war with an expanded realm of debilitating doubt, so that the doubt itself becomes an unrecognized preoccupation that undermines their ability to perform, especially in integrated situations. . . . Preferential treatment, no matter how it is justified in the light of day, subjects blacks to a midnight of self-doubt, and so often transforms their advantage into a revolving door.

Another liability of affirmative action comes from the fact that it indirectly encourages blacks to exploit their own past victimization as a source of power and privilege. Victimization, like implied inferiority, is what justifies preference, so that to receive the benefits of preferential treatment one must, to some extent, become invested in the view of one's self as a victim. In this way, affirmative action nurtures a victim-focused identity in blacks. The obvious irony here is that we become inadvertently invested in the very condition we are trying to overcome. Racial preference sends us the message that there is more power in our past suffering than our present achievements—none of which could bring us a preference over others. . . .

But, I think, one of the worst prices that blacks pay for preference has to do with an illusion . . . [that] overlooks a much harder and less digestible reality, that it is impossible to repay blacks living today for the historic suffering of the race. If all blacks were given a million dollars tomorrow morning it would not amount to a dime on the dollar of three centuries of oppression,

17 This article originally appeared in the May 13, 1990, issue of the *New York Times Magazine* under the title "A Negative Vote on Affirmative Action." Reprinted with permission of the author.

nor would it obviate the residues of that oppression that we still carry today. The concept of history reparation grows out of man's need to impose a degree of justice on the world that simply does not exist. Suffering can be endured and overcome, it cannot be repaid. Blacks cannot be repaid for the injustice done to the race, but we can be corrupted by society's guilty gesture of repayment.

Affirmative action is such a gesture. . . .

Racial preferences implicitly mark whites with an exaggerated superiority just as they mark blacks with an exaggerated inferiority. They not only reinforce America's oldest racial myth but, for blacks, they have the effect of stigmatizing the already stigmatized. . . .

The mandates of black power and white absolution out of which preferences emerged were not wrong in themselves. What was wrong was that both races focused more on the goals of these mandates than on the means to the goals. Blacks can have no power without taking responsibility for their own educational and economic development. Whites can have no racial innocence without earning it by eradicating discrimination and helping the disadvantaged to develop. Because we ignored the means, the goals have not been reached, and the real work remains to be done.

Shelby Steele expresses misgivings about affirmative action because of the way it gives a false sense of innocence to whites while keeping blacks mired in self-doubt and victimhood. The next excerpt, also authored by a black, middle class, college professor, offers an even deeper critique of affirmative action.

Charles Lawrence begins by telling us about a lawsuit. The setting is California, which has one of the best state-supported university systems in the nation. In the California system, the Berkeley campus is the crown jewel, offering a top-quality education at low cost. As a result of a California voter initiative ending affirmative action in state higher education, Berkeley had discontinued mechanisms like those used at Michigan's LSA and Law School, and was instead using a color-blind numerical score to determine admissions. Lawrence opens by describing the effects of this on three applicants of color who were turned down.

Two Views of the River: A Critique of the Liberal Defense of Affirmative Action

Charles R. Lawrence III[18]

On February 2, 1999, Jesus Rios, Gregory McConnell, Justine Certeza, and five other named individuals filed a class action suit against the University of California Regents and the University of California (UC) at Berkeley. Jesus Rios, a Latino, is the son of farm workers. For as long as he can remember, Jesus worked beside his parents picking apples and apricots and digging ditches from sunup to sundown. Despite the travails of migrant life, Jesus graduated from high school in the top four percent of his class. But when Jesus applied to Berkeley, he was told, "You don't belong here."

Gregory McConnell, an African American, is a Presidential Scholar. In high school he played soccer and varsity tennis, participated in numerous community service activities, and was a Junior Statesman of America. When Gregory applied to Berkeley he was told, "You don't belong here."

Justine Certeza, a Filipina American, will be the first in her family to graduate from college. In high school, she was sophomore senator, junior class secretary and senior class president. During her junior year she participated on her high school's Academic Decathlon team, which placed

18 This is an excerpt from an article that originally appeared in 101 *Colum. L. Rev.* 928 (2001). Reprinted with permission of *Columbia Law Review* and Charles R. Lawrence III, professor of law, Georgetown University Law Center.

second in Salano County. She was also an "A" student. When Justine applied to Berkeley she was told, "You don't belong here."

In the year that Berkeley turned down Jesus, Gregory, and Justine, over 750 other black, Latino and Filipino-American students with similarly superior academic records were denied admission. Berkeley is the UC system's most selective school, and of the 25,796 applicants for the 1999 freshman class, 9,858 had GPAs of 4.0. But a white applicant with a straight "A" average has a much better shot at getting into Berkeley than a black, Latino or Filipino applicant with the same grades.

How could this be? How could a university committed to diversity exclude so many of the state's brightest and most talented minority students? The complaint in *Rios* reveals a troubling, if unsurprising, answer. The so-called "color-blind" post-affirmative action admissions process at Berkeley has resurrected the old preferences for the sons and daughters of the privileged. . . . The current Berkeley admissions process creates a preference for white folks in two very concrete ways: First, it gives bonus points to high school students who are enrolled in advanced placement courses; and second, it relies in a determinative and exclusionary way on insignificant differences in standardized test scores.

Advanced placement courses are not available in every California high school. . . . The higher the concentration of black, Latino and Filipino-American students, the fewer the number of AP offerings. . . . [Berkeley's current admissions] policy . . . assigns an extra grade point for grades achieved in AP courses. Many of the 750 Latino, black and Filipino-American students with 4.0 GPAs who were denied admission to Berkeley in the fall of 1998 attained the highest possible grades in their school, a rare and remarkable achievement, but they did not stand a chance in competition against a student from Beverly Hills or Palo Alto when the Berkeley admissions policy boosted the other student's straight "A" average to as much as a 5.0. . . .

The student who takes more AP courses has the additional advantage of learning information and practicing academic skills that will significantly increase her chances for higher standardized test scores. Furthermore, the school that offers more AP courses typically has superior resources, such as higher quality of teaching, lower class size, and more books, labs, and computers.

Berkeley also discriminated against the *Rios* plaintiffs by relying in a determinative way on the SAT. Blacks and Latinos have consistently scored more poorly on these tests than white and Asian-American students. An extensive body of research challenges the usefulness of standardized tests in predicting the performance of poor and minority students, and finds that the SAT does a better job predicting the socio-economic status of the test taker's parents than predicting college performance. Yet, SAT scores often become the decisive factor in admissions in a competitive environment like Berkeley, where so many applicants have equally excellent high school grades. . . .

The *Rios* suit reveals a state school system that continues to provide most young people of color with a separate and unequal education. California schools remain segregated in fact, if not by law. Non-white children are concentrated in the worst of those schools. The *Rios* plaintiffs' claim that the state's premier university campus replicates and perpetuates a race-based distribution of educational opportunity and privilege by choosing to make the very opportunities denied to black, Latino, and Filipino-American children the prerequisites for admission. No matter how bright and talented Jesus Rios is, and no matter how hard he has worked, he cannot inherit the race and class privilege passed on by parents who can move to wealthy white suburbs or pay for fancy private schools. This suit makes the legal and moral claim that when Berkeley chooses to make inherited privilege the determining criteria of admission, it violates Jesus and Gregory and Justine's rights to equal citizenship. . . .

[Lawrence is a self-described advocate for affirmative action; he admits to have benefited from it and to have enjoyed watching others succeed by the same means. But he is concerned that the primary justification given for affirmative action by its supporters—the hope that it will make our campuses more diverse—has had the effect of displacing more important reasons for its existence. Lawrence calls the diversity argument the "liberal defense of affirmative action," and here he explains why it doesn't go far enough.]

Liberal theory focuses on guarding the liberty of an autonomous, disconnected human being. It holds that "power should be exercised in accordance with the rule of law, that government should recognize and respect rights, and that freedom, rather than equality, should be the highest political value." Liberal legality sees the equality principle as primarily concerned with protecting individuality, and views racial discrimination as unjust because when we judge a person based on her race we disregard her unique human individuality. For the liberal legal theorist, racism consists of isolated prejudicial discriminatory practices in an otherwise nondiscriminatory world. Identifiable perpetrators who have purposefully or intentionally caused harm to identifiable individual victims violate the moral and constitutional command of equality, not historical or institutional conditions of group subordination. . . .

[The] liberal defense of affirmative action is grounded in liberal theory. Rather than defend affirmative action as necessary to insure equal opportunity in a world where a variety of social structures, institutional practices, and unconscious racist beliefs conspire to deny minorities equal consideration and respect, the liberal defense justifies diversity as a way to help privileged whites better understand people of color in a nation that may soon have a non-white majority. This social utility argument leaves in place our current measures of merit and defends minor adjustments in those measures because racial integration of elite universities and professions will benefit the community as a whole.

Critics of liberal theory, including critical race theorists, have offered another way to think about promoting equality and human dignity, one that reflects the perspective of the subordinated. Consider the constitutional and moral command of equal protection as one requiring the elimination of society's racism rather than mandating equal treatment as an individual right. Critical race theorists have called this theory "substantive equality" or "antisubordination" theory. . . . [It] focuses on the persistence of conditions created by and traditionally associated with racist practice. Racism as traditionally practiced led to discriminatory exclusions from employment, from "white" neighborhoods, from politics, from government contracts, and from universities like Texas, Michigan, and Berkeley. If those same conditions of exclusion exist in virtually identical form after antidiscrimination laws have prohibited overt racial discrimination, the law has not yet done its job. . . . The *Rios* suit speaks from the vantage point of the subordinated. . . .

[Lawrence goes on to charge that by focusing narrowly on the "forward-looking" diversity goal, the liberal defense of affirmative action refuses to consider the weight of the past, as if to deny history and the legacy of discrimination.]

By looking only forward, [the University] avoids any direct admission or acknowledgement of the institution's past discriminatory practices. . . . It makes no effort to inquire into the ways that current facially neutral practices may have a foreseeable and unjustifiable discriminatory impact or to account for unconscious bias in their administration. This denial concurs in and reiterates "the big lie," the anti-affirmative action argument that pretends that white supremacy is extinct and presupposes a color-blind world, a world in which race-conscious remedies become invidious discrimination. . . . It is a defense that . . . [ignores]the university's long history of de jure and de facto segregation; segregation that continued until disruptive student protests and the fires of urban rebellions forced a change. . . .

By contrast, the underlying moral claim of the Civil Rights Movement and of the demand for affirmative action that grew therefrom, contested the university's historic role as palace guard for the power elite. It challenged the university to make racial justice central to its mission and to expand its constituency to include those most in need. Great universities like Yale, Chicago, and Columbia were asked to look out at the blocks surrounding their campuses, where human suffering and urban decay stood as a challenge to the greatest intellects of the day. . . .

Ultimately, by failing to examine how conventional procedures and standards for admissions reinforce race and class subordination, the liberal defense leaves unchallenged a definition of the university's primary mission as gatekeeper for and producer of a professional elite . . . [and] sidesteps the debate over whether our institutions are truly meritorious. . . .

The liberal argument for race-sensitive admissions is, in part, a utilitarian one. It is premised on a widely shared belief that the primary mission of colleges and universities is to educate those students who are likely to become the leaders of society in an increasingly diverse world. . . . Education for leadership, however, is more than skills training for business executives, doctors, and lawyers. Our best colleges and universities have always played a central role in shaping our society's moral vision. We socialize our students. We teach them values by engaging them in moral discourse, but even more importantly, we teach by the example of our own leadership in the construction of our nation's conscience.

The argument for racial diversity cannot in the end rest only upon a university's choice to expose its students to a more colorful, more culturally diverse universe, or on a cost-benefit analysis of the need for an integrated elite in a soon-to-be majority non-white nation, or, as the *Bakke* Court argued, on the faculty's First Amendment right to academic freedom. We must integrate our universities because we cannot fulfill our democratic ideal until we have conquered the scourge of American apartheid. And we cannot teach and learn about racism in classrooms where only white folks are present. . . .

• QUESTIONS •

1. As Charles Lawrence points out, most students admitted to Berkeley come from only 5 percent of California high schools. He explains that the non-elite schools lack resources—from computers to strong teachers—to give their students the advantages of the elite schools. Why do these disparities exist? Articulate the connection Lawrence or the critical race theorists might make between these disparities and affirmative action.

2. Lawrence suggests that liberal theory has been used to provide the moral underpinning to the diversity defense of affirmative action. What does he mean? Can you frame this in terms of ethical theory? Now look at the moral basis for critical race theory. What is it? Can you frame it in terms of ethical theory as well?

3. In May 2004, National Public Radio reported that less than 5 percent of students at America's top colleges and universities come from low-income families, with nearly three-quarters of the students at those schools coming from the wealthiest families. William Bowen, once president of the University of Michigan and now head of the Andrew W. Mellon Foundation, suggests that "if admissions departments gave low-income applicants the same credit based on their economic status as they do to the children of alumni, the percentage of disadvantaged students at elite schools would rise from 11 percent to 17 percent."[19] Is it time for affirmative action based on economic status?

FAMILIES AND WORK

To achieve equity, we cannot ignore the complicated relationship between family and work. Some economists argue that the wage gap between men and women is explained neither by discrimination nor by occupational segregation, but by the fact that many women choose to spend more time with their families than in developing their careers. They point to human capital studies that show that workers who take time off (e.g., to have or raise children, to care for elderly parents) earn less money than workers who don't interrupt their careers. Not surprisingly, it is more often women who leave their jobs, work part time and work less, and so earn lower wages.[20] If they are right, what, if anything, should employers do to fairly accommodate the differing family roles of men and women?

---

19 "Elite Universities Eye Economic Affirmative Action," National Public Radio, *All Things Considered,* May 22, 2004.

20 See J. Wenger, "Issue Briefing #155," April 24, 2001, Economic Policy Institute.

U.S. Family Realities

In 2000 31.1 percent of women compared to 19.5 percent of men earned poverty level wages or less.

Of the 72.3 million families reported in the 2000 U.S. Census, 7.4 million were headed by single mothers, 2.2 million run by single fathers.[21]

Since passage of the Family and Medical Leave Act in 1993, 42 percent of those taking leave have been men; roughly three of five U.S. workers meet the law's eligibility criteria.[22]

3.3 million Americans aged 65 and older are severely impaired, requiring some kind of caregiving.[23] Two-thirds of those providing care for elders are employed.[24]

Two-fifths of all employed Americans work mostly at nonstandard times–in the evening, at night, on a rotating shift or during the weekend; single and low-educated mothers are more likely than married or better educated mothers to work nonstandard schedules.[25]

The average working woman in the United States spends about twice as much time as the average working man on household chores and the care of children. On average, men spend more time than women at their jobs and on leisure and sports.[26]

Legislating Family Leave

While Title VII made it illegal for employers to discriminate on the basis of gender ("sex"), the courts interpreted it as allowing employers to single out and discriminate on the basis of pregnancy. In one highly criticized case, the Supreme Court upheld an employee disability plan that provided insurance for sickness and accidents, but excluded coverage for complications arising from pregnancy. The Court explained why Title VII's ban on sex discrimination was not violated:

> *[A]n exclusion of pregnancy from a disability-benefits plan providing general coverage is not a gender-based discrimination at all. . . . [T]he selection of risks covered by the Plan did not operate, in fact to discriminate against women. . . . The Plan, in effect . . . is nothing more than an insurance package, which covers some risks, but excludes others. . . .*[27]

---

21 Marianne Sullivan, "Paid Sick Leave is Rare for Low Income Women," Women's eNews, May 10, 2004, http://www.womensenews.org/article.cfm/dyn/aid/1809/context/archive. (Site visited May 10, 2004.)

22 Ibid.

23 Barbara R. Stucki and Janemarie Mulvey, "Can Aging 'Boomers' Avoid Nursing Homes?," 83 *Consumers' Research Mag.* 20, Aug. 1, 2000, available at 2000 WL 12692361.

24 Katherine Elizabeth Ulrich, "Insuring Family Risks: Suggestions for a National Family Policy and Wage Replacement," 14 *Yale J.L. & Feminism* 1, 6 (2002).

25 Harriet B. Presser, Working in a 24/7 Economy (NY: Russell Sage Foundation, 2003), p.1.

26 Time-Use Survey, Bureau of Labor Statistics, September 14, 2004, http://www.bls.gov/news.release/pdf/atus.pdf. (Site visited December 18, 2004.)

27 *General Electric Co. v. Gilbert,* 429 U.S. 125 ('1976).

Congress reacted to the Court's interpretation of Title VII by amending the law in 1978 to make it clear that discrimination on the basis of pregnancy was illegal. The amendments, known as the **Pregnancy Discrimination Act of 1978,** provide:

> *Women affected by pregnancy, childbirth, and related medical conditions shall be treated the same for all employment-related purposes, including receipt of benefits under fringe benefit programs, as other persons not so affected but similar in their ability or inability to work.*

Under this law, pregnant workers are to be treated like any other workers. But an argument can be made that a law that makes it illegal to fire a woman simply because she is pregnant does not go far enough. It affords no protection, for example, to a pregnant employee who is fired for excessive absenteeism by a company that similarly dismisses ill or injured workers who miss too many days at work. Nor does it address the need for time to care for a healthy newborn or accommodate other family responsibilities. In 1993, Congress passed, and President Clinton signed into law, the Family and Medical Leave Act, excerpted as follows:

FAMILY AND MEDICAL LEAVE ACT

29 United States Code Annotated 2601, et seq.

Findings and Purposes

(1) the number of single-parent households and two-parent households in which the single parent or both parents work is increasing significantly;

(2) it is important for the development of children and the family unit that fathers and mothers be able to participate in early childrearing and the care of family members who have serious health conditions;

(3) the lack of employment policies to accommodate working parents can force individuals to choose between job security and parenting;

(4) there is inadequate job security for employees who have serious health conditions that prevent them from working for temporary periods;

(5) due to the nature of the roles of men and women in our society, the primary responsibility for family caretaking often falls on women, and such responsibility affects the working lives of women more than it affects the working lives of men; and

(6) employment standards that apply to one gender only have serious potential for encouraging employers to discriminate against employees and applicants for employment who are of that gender.

Leave Requirements

(a.)(1) Entitlement to leave

[A]n eligible employee shall be entitled to a total of 12 workweeks of leave during any 12-month period for one or more of the following:

(A) Because of the birth of a son or daughter of the employee and in order to care for such son or daughter.

(B) Because of the placement of a son or daughter with the employee for adoption or foster care.

(C) In order to care for the spouse, or a son, daughter, or parent, of the employee, if such spouse, son, daughter, or parent has a serious health condition.

(D) Because of a serious health condition that makes the employee unable to perform the functions of the position of such employee.

[Other sections of the law guarantee that an employee who returns from a leave can go back to his or her position, or one with equivalent benefits, pay, and employment conditions, without losing any benefits that had accrued prior to the leave, and without gaining any seniority while they were on leave.]

Exceptions and Special Rules

[There are some exceptions. Those within a firm's top 10 percent of salaried employees within a 75-mile radius, for example, can be denied restoration to the job after a leave if:]

(A) such denial is necessary to prevent substantial and grievous economic injury to the operations of the employer;

(B) the employer notifies the employee of the intent of the employer to deny restoration on such basis at the time the employer determines that such injury would occur; and

(C) in any case in which the leave has commenced, the employee elects not to return to employment after receiving such notice.

[The law also provides that employees have a right to use their leave time by taking intermittent or reduced time health leaves if medically necessary. The employer, however, may temporarily transfer the employee to a different, comparably paid position. Leave for new-child care must be taken all at once, unless both employee and employer agree to some other arrangement. Employees must give whatever notice of their intention to give leave is possible and reasonable considering the circumstances (e.g., 30 days notice before birth or placement of an adopted child), and make reasonable efforts to schedule medical treatment to cause the least possible disruption to the employer. Employers are required to maintain coverage under group health plans for employees on leave.]

• QUESTIONS •

1. Look at the statutory provisions that explain the leave requirements. Do they seem well crafted to respond to the findings set forth by Congress in the law?

2. Does Congress address any stereotypes about caregivers? How responsive is the law to changes in our ideas about family? Who benefits from the law? Is anyone harmed? Can you think of any changes that would make it more equitable?

3. **Internet Assignment:** In 2002, California became the first state to enact a comprehensive paid family leave law. The National Partnership for Women and Families has drafted a bill for a similar law. Find out the current status of the law or proposals in your state or in Congress.

4. **Internet Assignment:** *Working Mother* magazine identified Eli Lilly, IBM, General Mills, and Wachovia as among the top ten family-friendly companies in 2003. Find one of the Web sites for one of the top-ten companies and compare its work/family programs and benefits to those of other companies in the same business sector. What are the relative merits of legislation such as the Family and Medical Leave Act versus purely voluntary efforts by business?

International Perspectives

The working woman shall have the same rights and, for equal work, receive the same remuneration as the working man. Working conditions must allow the fulfillment of her essential family function and assure the mother and child a special protection.

— Italian Constitution, Article 7

According to researchers for the Economic Policy Institute (EPI), U.S. employers expect employees to act as "unencumbered workers,"—that is, as employees who function as if they had a full-time partner or caregiver at home—ignoring the reality of an economy in which most mothers work and most married couples are dual wage-earners. Experiences in other countries can yield insights for new U.S. workplace policies, making it easier for American workers to balance the demands of career and family. In a report issued on January 9, 2002, EPI highlighted the findings of a study of global policies.

POLICIES THAT MAKE WORK MORE FAMILY FRIENDLY

Economic Policy Institute[28]

Reduced Hours and Job Sharing/*The Netherlands and Sweden*

At an elder care facility in the Netherlands, only five of the 100 employees work full time. Part-time employees are paid the same hourly rate that full-time employees are paid, and their benefits are prorated.

Workers can reduce their hours when their children are young and increase them later. Despite a national nursing shortage, this facility has had little trouble attracting younger nurses who must combine work and family responsibilities and older nurses who need a slower pace.

A Dutch multinational company with 90,000 employees worldwide introduced a job-sharing program in response to requests from employees for part-time hours. Between 30 and 40 percent of part-time employees are now participating, usually by pairs of workers alternating two and three day weeks.

A cardiac hospital in the Netherlands with 2,500 workers maintains full-time work weeks of 32 or 36 hours. Shifts are eight hours a day, so workers achieve a 36-hour week by working five days one week and four days the next, or by alternating between six and three days. They may also work a permanent 32-hour week for prorated pay.

Under Swedish law, workers at a steel company that the authors visited can opt to work a six-hour day instead of an eight-hour day, until their children are eight years old or in the first grade. The company pro-rates the workers' pay, with the balance covered by social insurance for eligible workers.

Greater Flexibility at Work Schedules/*Australia*

Nurses at an Australian hospital enjoy greater flexibility by arranging their own work schedules. The nurses all indicate their desired four-week schedule, and then the nurses in a department negotiate among themselves. A manager then settles any conflicts and determines a final schedule. This is feasible partly because of the large number of permanent part-time nurses the hospital employs, who are often willing to pick up an extra shift (for which they are rewarded with a 15 percent premium).

Paid Parental Leave/*Sweden*

At a Swedish electronics facility, workers may choose to work any eight hours between 6:00 a.m. and 9:00 p.m. Swedish law provides social insurance that replaces up to 80 percent of wages for

28 The full report by Eileen Appelbaum, Thomas Bailey, Peter Berge, and Arne Kalleberg, "Shared Work, Valued Care: New Norms for Organizing Market Work and Unpaid Care Work" is available through the Economic Policy Institute, http://www.epinet.org.

parental leave; this firm has also adopted a policy to make sure that its workers always reach that 80 percent cap if they choose to take parental leave.

Career-Track Jobs for Women and On-Site Day Care/*Japan*

A Japanese publishing firm promotes career track jobs for women employees with a range of incentives, including reduced work hours, child and family leave, career development and on-site day care.

Since the 1980s, American feminists have debated how to achieve gender equity. One side insists that if women want to be equal to men they should support laws treating them just as men are treated. Others believe that it does no good to ignore the inherent biological differences between men and women. Equality will not be achieved, according to this view, unless there is special accommodation for women's "differences," particularly regarding childbearing and rearing.

Joan Williams contrasts the American and European experience in her call for feminists to refocus this "sameness vs. difference" debate. She does not underestimate the difficulty American feminists face in challenging the "traditional allocation of child-rearing to the privatized realm of the family." She notes, for example, that for a long time the United States was the only Western industrialized country with no parental leave laws; that even today, compared to European countries, there are few public resources devoted to child care outside the home. In the excerpt that follows, she draws on the experiences of many nations to suggest some new approaches to gender equity.

Unbending Gender: Market Work and Family Work in the 21st Century

Joan Williams[29]

If the goal is to redesign the relationship of market work to family work, three possibilities exist. The first is to change either the allocation of family work within the household or the entitlements that flow from it: I call this gender redistribution. The next is to shift some of the responsibilities from the private to the public sphere. The third is to challenge employers' entitlement to marginalize all employees who have responsibility for family work, thereby redefining the relationship between employers and employees.

Gender Redistribution

The first strategy consists of policies that redistribute household work and the entitlements that spring from it. On the family side, this involves redefining who owns the wealth generated by the dominant family ecology. On the work side, it involves redistributing responsibilities within the household. . . . Although redistributing entitlements between ex-husbands and wives is an important feminist project, it is not one that will help all women. . . . [It is] estimated that sixty-five percent of all new cases of poverty among black women who go from a married-couple to a female-headed family are "reshuffled poverty": in others words, the women were impoverished even while they were married. In contrast, only twenty-five percent of white women were impoverished during

---

29 (Oxford University Press, 2000). This excerpt is reprinted from an early version that appeared in *Journal of Contemporary Issues,* 1998.

their marriages. Using gender redistribution as the only feminist strategy, therefore, helps white women as a group more than black women. It also does not help women in families where poverty results not from an unfair distribution of assets between them and their former husbands, but from a lack of assets overall.

Gender redistribution strategies must be linked with income redistribution strategies if all women are to be helped out of poverty. . . . Women, on average, still do eighty percent of the housework and two-thirds of the child care.

U.S. feminists need to recognize that many men cannot afford, economically or emotionally, to do more family work as long as they have to pay for caregiving in the coin of marginalization. Most families rely on men's wages, so most men cannot afford to [risk] marginalization at work. Moreover, men's identity is built around work roles, which makes them psychologically unable to risk marginalization. . . .

Reconfiguring the Public and Private Spheres

A major reason American feminists have focused so heavily on gender redistribution is that they face such serious obstacles in their attempts to shift childrearing into the public arena. . . . [M]any countries in Europe have had extensive systems of child care facilities as well as other forms of direct public support for childrearing such as child allowances and generous provisions for paid maternity disability and/or parental leaves. Latin American feminists are astonished, indeed disbelieving, to learn how recently American women gained the right to maternity leaves, and the fact that such leaves are unpaid. In Chile, for example, an employer must provide a child care facility if he employs more than twenty women workers; in Sweden, parents can work part-time until the child has completed the first year of school. In Norway, employees can take one year's parental leave paid at a rate of eighty percent of their earnings for the past 52 weeks. In France, high-quality government funded child-care facilities are widespread.

For single parents, and many married ones, child care remains an important part of the solution. . . . Child care in the U.S. is both under funded and under regulated, with the result that the quality of child care is not what it should be: child care workers are paid less than garbage collectors, and turnover is among the highest for any job in the country. . . .

Currently, mothers' marginalization depresses the wages of women: because families typically compare the costs of child care to the salary potential of the mother, it also keeps child care salaries low.

Our political culture is resistant to providing public funds or public provision of anything at all. In addition, there are particular problems in the U.S. with child care: Our status as a middle class nation reinforces the notion that children need parental care so they can build up the human capital they need to "succeed." These are political facts of life . . . [and for now] it seems foolhardy to link hopes for feminist transformation to expansion of the government sphere. . . .

Redistributing Entitlements Between Employers and Employees

[I have advocated a third alternative strategy:] to renegotiate rights between employers and employees, using the language of family values. . . . [I]t has two chief drawbacks. The first is the low rate of union membership, for unions are an obvious arena in which to push for a shift in employee entitlements. The second is that most unions traditionally have placed work/family issues low on their list of priorities. . . . Unions in Europe have often played a key role in gaining entitlements related to family work for men as well as women; a revitalized union movement in the U.S. could play a similar role if it has the will to do so. . . .

Feminists need to demand not accommodation but their due—which includes a world not designed around the bodies and life patterns of men.

• QUESTIONS •

1. What three strategies for achieving gender equity does Williams identify? Which would require changes in U.S. law? Which would depend on changes in individual relationships? Could any be achieved by voluntary business initiatives?

2. Review the Family and Medical Leave Act. Does it seem to fit with any of the approaches outlined by Williams?

3. Tax law can be a tool for changing behavior. For example, a provision that penalizes married couples may encourage some to live together without marrying. What changes in tax law could we adopt if we wanted to place greater social value on caretaking? If we instead wanted to take greater public responsibility for it?

4. Economists Deborah M. Figart and Ellen Mutari raise concerns about the European response to the work/family dilemma:

   > *In country after country, observers are noting a similar trade-off. Unions are giving in to employers' desire for flexibility in exchange for work redistribution policies that save jobs. As part of this compromise, unions are accepting the expansion of both part-time and overtime work. . . . This compromise only reinforces a Europe in which gender roles are defined not by whether a man or woman has a job, but by the amount of time men and women spend on the job.*[30]

   Internet Assignment: Compare part-time employment in the United States and the EU. What benefits are available to the part-time workforce? Should the law require companies to accommodate family life by restricting mandatory overtime? By limiting involuntary night or weekend hours? By mandating flex-time for parents—or for all workers?

5. Americans worked 4 percent more hours per year in 2000 than they did in 1980, with overtime—often mandatory—reaching a record high in the 1990s. **Internet Assignment:** What impact would you expect overtime to have on each of the following: (a) male workers, female workers; (b) family relationships; (c) business profitability and competitiveness. Find out about legislative initiatives regarding overtime using http://thomas.loc.gov.

CHAPTER PROBLEMS

1. Has the war on terrorism created or exacerbated ethnic/religious stereotyping? Consider the case of American Brandon Mayfield, a Muslim convert, married to an Egyptian woman, and living in Portland, Oregon. Mayfield is a lawyer. He represented a man who was later convicted of conspiracy to aid the Taliban and Al Qaeda in a custody case. In Spring 2004, Mayfield was arrested as a material witness in connection with the terrorist attack on Madrid's railway that killed hundreds of civilians. The FBI held Mayfield for two weeks based on a fingerprint "match" that was later discredited. His lawyer told news reporters that

30 Deborah M. Figart and Ellen Mutari, "It's About Time: Will Europe Solve the Work/Family Dilemma?" *Dollars and Sense,* January/February 1998, p. 27.

"very early in the investigation, the FBI examiner met with Spanish fingerprint examiners [who told them] "We do not agree with your analysis [of the fingerprints] and we don't see a connection."[31] What role do you think stereotypes might have played in the Mayfield case?

2. Employers are generally allowed to enforce dress and appearance standards so long as they do not discriminate on the basis of race, sex, religion, etc. Gender-specific rules are acceptable if based on social norms, unless they place an unfair burden on one sex. So, for example, having a "business dress" rule that requires men to wear ties and women to wear dresses or skirts would be legal, but requiring only one sex to wear a uniform would not. What problems can you identify with any of the following? (a) A pizza company will make no exceptions to its rule that drivers must be clean shaven. Sixty percent of African-American men have a skin condition characterized by severely painful shaving bumps. The condition is cured by growing a beard. (b) UPS prohibits its workers from wearing dreadlocks. (c) Famous Bank does not allow male employees to wear earrings. (d) Casino hires men and women as cocktail waiters. Women are required to wear three-inch high heels; men are allowed to wear any "dress shoe." (e) Imperial Palace wants to hire only slim, young women who look good in their geisha-girl costumes to serve cocktails. But some of the waitresses have complained that the costumes are sexually provacative to customers and invited unwanted attention.

3. It is estimated that in 2005, 25 percent of the American workforce will be telecommuting. Advocates predict that telecommuting will decrease the gendered division of unpaid labor in the home, and enhance women's access to a wider variety of jobs. However, researchers point to several problems: Working from home is often seen as a tool for greater autonomy and flexibility for mostly male, high-level professionals in the information and service-related jobs. But telecommuting women most often find themselves in low-paying jobs without benefits, without job security, and with few training and advancement opportunities. In addition, there is little evidence that the practice leads to fathers spending proportionately more time with their children.[32] What role might stereotyping play in these findings?

4. **Internet Assignment:** Under the **Equal Pay Act** as interpreted by the courts, employers may not pay men and women different wages for doing the same job except to the extent that wage differentials are based on seniority, merit, or factors "other than sex." Title VII of the Civil Rights Act of 1964 prohibits discrimination in pay and other compensation based on race, sex, color, religion, or national origin. Yet there are still wage gaps.
   (a) What is the current gap between male and female wages in your state? In the nation?
   (b) Find out what you can about the "glass ceiling" that prevents women and men of color from reaching the highest ranks in America's largest companies.
   (c) What evidence can you find of continued income/wage disparities based on race?

5. **Internet Assignment:** Proponents of **comparable worth** suggest that even if we achieve equal pay for the same jobs, there remains a deeper unfairness: the high correlation between the market wage for some kinds of jobs and the gender and race of most people who hold them. In 1998, for example, Los Angeles paid its mostly male probation officers close to $20,000 a year more than it paid its primarily female social workers; in most places, 911 dispatchers are women who earn less than emergency operators (largely men) for the fire departments. Pay equity laws—introduced but not yet passed in most states— would require all employers to adjust wage scales to pay men and women equally for work of comparable value. Nationally, bills have been introduced that would require employers to identify employment categories; look at the education, skill, working conditions, effort, and responsibilities required for each; and pay the same for different jobs of comparable worth. Check

31 Sara Kershaw and Eric Lichtblau, "Bomb Case Against Lawyer is Rejected," *New York Times,* May 25, 2004, p. A16, col. 1.

32 Michelle A. Travis, "Telecommuting: The Escher Stairway of Work/Family Conflict," 55 *Me.L.Rev.* 261 (2003).

out the Web site run by the National Committee on Pay Equity, a coalition of more than 80 labor, women's, and civil rights organizations, to find out the current status of pay equity laws in your home state.

6. **Internet Assignment:** Find out what has happened to the nationwide class action suit filed against Wal-Mart for its employment practices. On what do plaintiffs base their claim of sex discrimination? How has Wal-Mart defended itself? If there are court rulings, what are they? Compare and contrast the Wal-Mart suit to one brought against the big warehouse chain Costco Wholesale Corporation in August 2004.

7. According to the research group Catalyst, in 2002 only 15.7 percent of corporate-officers, 5.2 percent of top earners at Fortune 500 companies, and 9.9 percent of line corporate-officers were women. What might account for these gender differences at the highest levels? In June 2004, a survey conducted by Catalyst reported that a majority of senior executives, both male and female, at Fortune 1000 companies want to become their employer's CEO.[33] Yet, another study, this by the international group ISR, found "critical differences in workplace opinions between male and female executives" in the United States. Women focus on working relationships, communications and the overall health of the workplace, while men are driven by their own career development and personal financial reward.[34] How might you reconcile these findings? How might they be used by a company seeking to promote gender equity?

8. Abercrombie & Fitch, the clothing retailer whose catalogs featured predominantly white models, was charged with racial discrimination in employment. By November 2004 the company and the EEOC reached an unusual settlement. Abercrombie agreed to increase diversity not only in hiring and promotions, but also in its catalogs and advertisements, and to broaden its recruitment focus beyond predominantly white fraternities and sororities. What impact might this case have on breaking down stereotypes?

Chapter Project

Alternative Dispute Resolution: Accommodating Parents

Guidelines in Appendix E

Witness Statement for Donna Coke, the ER Nurse:

When I had our third child, my husband and I planned things carefully. He's a full-time student, so it made sense that he'd stay home taking care of the kids, and I'd go back to work and support us.

As a nurse, I know experts strongly recommend breast-feeding as the healthiest way to nourish infants. I've learned there is real evidence showing that children who have been breast-fed for at least a year turn out physically and psychologically healthier than other children. So I

33 Joann S. Lublin, "Women Aspire to be Chief as Much as Men Do," *The Wall Street Journal,* June 23, 2004, P D2.

34 ISR Press Release, August 3, 2004. Available at http://www.isrsurveys.com. (Site visited December 19, 2004.)

made a decision to breast feed our baby Meghan. I took the two months maternity leave, and then I was ready to go back to work. Using a breast pump, I expressed enough milk in a bottle for the baby to be fed while I was at work. But the first night we tried this, the baby wouldn't accept the bottle. She started yelling and shaking—my husband called all upset. I could hear her screaming in the background. I had to tell my supervisor Lee Gibbon that there was a family emergency, and I had to go home that night.

The next day, my supervisor meets me as I'm coming in. She says: What are you going to do about the situation? I tell Gibbon my husband and I have come up with an idea: He'll drive the baby up to the ER entrance door each time I'm on mid-shift break, and I'll go out and sit in the car and feed the baby. The supervisor doesn't go for this. She says my patients might need me. I say, "Hey, other nurses go outside the building for their breaks. They smoke cigarettes, they go shopping. You don't do anything to stop them." She says, "This isn't going to work." So I make other suggestions. I even tell her I'm willing to go to part-time. She doesn't really answer me. She says, "Go home. I need to think this over."

I called the next day and Gibbons told me that she didn't think I should come back until she had figured out a better solution. She said she'd call me but didn't. It's been almost five months now, and they still haven't called me, not even to tell me I won't be called back in. I can't believe they were making me make a choice between caring for my baby and caring for my patients. I loved my job, and we need me to have that job. I was good at it, just like I'm good at being a mother. I think I should have a right to breast feed—that Meghan has the right to be breast-fed. I think we should sue the hospital.

Witness Statement: Lee Gibbon, the Supervisor:

Donna Coke is an excellent nurse. I'd never argue with that. But what I do argue with is her assumption that she should be accommodated by the hospital on this. Donna made a choice to breast feed her baby. She has a right to do that. What she doesn't have a right to do is force her employer to make allowances for that choice. She and her husband have to live with it.

When Donna came in to tell me she wanted special arrangements to feed her baby in the parking lot at break, it took me 15 seconds to imagine all the ways that plan could go wrong. What if her baby demanded more time than Donna's break allowed? What if the baby was not ready to feed when Donna was on break? Anything can happen with small babies, we all know that. Donna and her husband seemed to expect the hospital—and its critically ill patients—to cut her some slack. We just aren't in a position to do that. This is a business, no different from anyplace else.

If women keep on expecting the government to protect them in every single individual situation like this, where will it end? Pretty soon we'll be hearing from women, that they should have extra paid time off to go to PTA meetings, because evidence shows that children whose mothers are involved in schools do better academically—and psychologically! It's time we stopped acting like victims all the time, and took on the world of work like everyone else. We can handle it. In fact, it would serve the cause of feminism better if we women got to proving that we too know how to "take it like a man!"

Workers Rights as Human Rights: Health and Safety in the Workplace

Chapter 5

There was another interesting set of statistics that a person might have gathered in Packingtown—those of the various afflictions of the workers. . . . [E]ach one of these lesser industries was a separate little inferno, in its way as horrible as the killing-beds, the source and fountain of them all. The workers in each of them had their own peculiar diseases. And the wandering visitor might be skeptical about all the swindles, but he could not be skeptical about these, for the worker bore the evidence of them about on his own person generally he had only to hold out his hand.

— Upton Sinclair, *The Jungle* (1906)

Everyone has the right to work, to free choice of employment, to just and favourable conditions of work and to protection against unemployment.

— Universal Declaration of Human Rights (1948)

From the time of the industrial revolution through today's increasingly global economy, there has been little consensus in the United States regarding the appropriate balance between risk and security in the workplace. Just how healthy and safe must a workplace be? Whose responsibility is it to set the standards to minimize harm to life, limb, and pocketbook caused by industrial accidents, occupational disease, and toxic exposures? Free-market economists believe regulation tends to stifle competition and detract from efficiency, while reformers look to the state to rein in the harshest effects of unrestrained capitalism. Some are wary of both big business and big government, arguing for maximal freedom for individuals. Similar questions arise on a transnational scale, with some clinging to national sovereignty while others point to universal norms and international bodies for guidance.

This chapter begins with a look at workers' compensation laws adopted at the start of the twentieth century to address the seemingly unavoidable: accidental injuries and deaths on the job. Next we look at the watershed Occupational Health and Safety Act of 1970, which created a national policy to try to prevent workplace injuries and disease. In the final section we explore the twenty-first century global dimensions of the problem.

Workers' Compensation

Workers' compensation schemes were first adopted in the United States during the period 1911 to 1925, first in the more industrialized states and gradually throughout the nation. Effective in ameliorating some of the conflict between management and employees over the social and economic costs of accidental injuries, the details varied from state to state. In general, however, they were designed to provide a limited, "no-fault" recovery, regardless of who was responsible for the injury. The New Mexico statute at issue in the first case was typical. So, too, was the plaintiff: a widow of a man killed at work who wanted to bypass the limited benefits of workers' compensation and instead bring a tort suit for "wrongful death." If allowed a tort claim, and if she won it, a jury would be free to award large damages.

DELGADO V. PHELPS DODGE CHINO, INC.

Supreme Court of New Mexico, 2001
34 P.3d 1148

FRANCHINI, Justice.

[Factual Background]

In the summer of 1998 . . . Reynaldo Delgado . . . had been working at the Phelps Dodge smelting plant in Hurley, New Mexico, for two years. The smelting plant distills copper ore from rock, called "slag," by superheating unprocessed rock to a temperature in excess of 2,000 degrees Fahrenheit. During the process, the ore rises to the top, where it is harvested, while the slag sinks to the bottom of the furnace where it drains through a valve called a "skim hole." From there, the slag passes down a chute into a fifteen-foot-tall iron cauldron called a "ladle," located in a tunnel below the furnace. Ordinarily, when the ladle reaches three-quarters of its thirty-five-ton capacity, workers use a "mud gun" to plug the skim hole with clay, thus stopping the flow of molten slag and permitting a specially designed truck, called a "kress-haul," to enter the tunnel and lift and remove the ladle.

On the night of June 30, Delgado's shorthanded work crew . . . was being pressured to work harder in order to compensate for the loss of production and revenue incurred after a recent ten day shut down. Suddenly, the crew experienced an especially dangerous emergency situation known as a "runaway." The ladle had reached three-quarters of its capacity but the flowing slag could not be stopped because the mud gun was inoperable and manual efforts to close the skim hole had failed . . . in the worst runaway condition that many of the workers on the site had ever experienced. [Plant managers] could have shut down the furnace, thereby allowing the safe removal of the ladle of slag. However, in order to avoid economic loss, [they] chose instead to order Delgado, who had never operated a kress-haul under runaway conditions, to attempt to remove the ladle alone, with the molten slag still pouring over its fifteen-foot brim.

When Delgado entered the tunnel, he saw that the ladle was overflowing and radioed [his supervisor] White to inform him that he was neither qualified nor able to perform the removal. White insisted. . . . Shortly after Delgado entered the tunnel, the lights shorted out and black smoke poured from the mouth of the tunnel. Delgado's co-workers watched as he emerged from the smoke-filled tunnel, fully engulfed in flames. He collapsed before co-workers could douse the flames with a water hose. . . . [Delgado] died three weeks later in an Arizona hospital. . . .

[New Mexico Worker's Compensation Act]

When a worker suffers an accidental injury and a number of other preconditions are satisfied, the [New Mexico Worker's Compensation] Act provides a scheme of compensation that affords profound benefits to both workers and employers. The injured worker receives compensation quickly, without having to endure the rigors of litigation or prove fault on behalf of the employer. . . . The employer, in exchange, is assured that a worker accidentally injured, even by the employer's own negligence, will be limited to compensation under the Act and may not pursue the unpredictable damages available outside its boundaries. The Act represents the "result of a bargain struck between employers and employees. In return for the loss of a common law tort claim for accidents arising out of the scope of employment, [the Act] ensures that workers are provided some compensation. . . .

The Act is subject to abuse from both sides of this quid pro quo. An unscrupulous worker, for example, might seek recovery from a self-induced injury, knowing that the Act generally awards compensation regardless of fault. An employer, on the other hand, may abuse the Act by subjecting a worker to injury after determining that the economic advantage of the injurious work outweighs the limited economic detriment that the Act will impose upon the employer after the injury occurs. In part to prevent against such bilateral abuse, the Act limits the availability of compensation only to those workers "injured by accident arising out of and in the course of his [or her] employment."

[Analysis]

[The court then addresses the defense raised by Phelps-Dodge: that workers' compensation covers workplace injury except in those rare cases where an employer actually sets out to hurt someone. In other words, only deliberate wrongdoing will provide a way out of workers' compensation. Despite the fact that there is "near unanimity" among the states in allowing suits only when there is an "actual intent" to injure, the court finds this rule bizarre:]

[T]he actual intent test encourages an employer, motivated by economic gain, to knowingly subject a worker to injury in the name of profit-making. As long as the employer is motivated by greed, rather than intent to injure the worker, the employer may abuse workers in an unlimited variety of manners while still enjoying immunity from tort liability. . . .

We expressly overrule all case law that has required allegation or proof of an employer's actual intent to injure a worker as a precondition to a worker's tort recovery. . . . We hold that when an employer intentionally inflicts or willfully causes a worker to suffer an injury that would otherwise be exclusively compensable under the Act, that employer may not enjoy the benefits of exclusivity, and the injured worker may sue in tort.

[W]e hold that willfulness renders a worker's injury non-accidental, and therefore outside the scope of the Act, when: (1) the worker or employer engages in an intentional act or omission, without just cause or excuse, that is reasonably expected to result in the injury suffered by the worker; (2) the worker or employer expects the intentional act or omission to result in the injury, or has utterly disregarded the consequences; and (3) the intentional act or omission proximately causes the injury.

To the extent that this case reflects an adverse development for employers, we remind [Phelps-Dodge] that workers, whose families may depend for their livelihood on the compensation received under the Act, have consistently been, and will continue to be, deprived of compensation under the same standard we now apply to employers. We also note that under the test presently adopted, employers may avert tort liability by simply refraining from intentionally or willfully injuring workers. Finally, we seriously doubt that employers are willfully injuring their workers with such frequency that the consequence of our decision to expose such employers to tort liability will be to "wreak havoc" with the workers' compensation system. The greater the impact this opinion has on the workers' compensation system, the more profound will have been its need.

[Order dismissing the complaint is reversed and case remanded.]

• QUESTIONS •

1. What is the workers' compensation "exclusivity" rule? Who benefits from it?
2. In deciding this case, the highest court in New Mexico becomes one of the few states to allow employees to bring tort suits against their employers, even when there is no proof that the employer actually intended to harm them. What reasons does the court give for doing so?

3. Look at the three-part test the court sets forth for deciding when an injury is "willful," and thus outside the scope of workers' compensation. How would it apply to each of the following?
   (a) an employee who refuses to wear safety equipment
   (b) an employer who insists that a worker do a task without needed safety equipment
   (c) firefighters or police injured during a rescue attempt

4. **(a)** **Internet Assignment:** Find the workers' compensation statute in your home state. Under what circumstances can a person file a claim?
   (b) Look for a case in which an injured worker is suing for tort, and the employer is arguing that workers' compensation covers the claim. Compare its facts to those of Delgado. Does the motivation appear to involve "actual intent" to harm, willful injury, or mere greed?

Before workers' compensation was available, an employee bringing a negligence suit against her company would have to prove that her injury was caused by unreasonably risky conduct traceable to her employer. Even then, she might still lose if the company successfully argued one of the defenses to negligence:

(a) **contributory negligence,** that is, the employee herself was partly at fault,
(b) **assumption of risk,** that is, the employee voluntarily worked in an environment known to be dangerous, or
(c) **fellow servant rule,** that is, the employee's injury was caused by the negligence of a co-worker

Under workers' compensation, firms contribute to a fund that is used to pay benefits to employees accidentally injured in the workplace. Instead of suing, an employee's legal task is simplified; she need only file a claim indicating that she was hurt in the course of her employment; the company cannot raise any of the "defenses to negligence" to defeat it.

Employers are willing to accept this "no fault" approach because there is a trade-off: If workers' compensation covers an injury, the employee cannot go before a jury with a negligence claim. This is the **exclusivity rule** that was at issue in *Delgado,* so-called because the employee's only—or "exclusive"—remedy lies with workers' compensation. Payments are set by a formula that generally provides less than the actual wages lost, and no provision is made for the kind of money damages that could reach high numbers in a tort suit—pain and suffering, loss of consortium, or punitive damages.

When an employee is killed or severely injured, however, the limited benefits of workers' compensation may seem inadequate and the trade-off unfair. In some states (for example, New Mexico and California) the worker or worker's family may sue, arguing that the harm was not covered by workers' compensation, as Delgado's family did.

The workers' compensation system was originally set up to deal with accidental and sudden injuries. Gradually, statutes were amended to include occupational diseases caused by exposure to workplace toxins and chemicals. Labor leaders together with the insurance industry pressed for disease coverage, especially after the publicity surrounding a tunnel disaster in West Virginia in the 1930s, where as many as 1,500 workers—mostly rural Southern blacks—may have been killed by exposure to silica dust.

But claiming benefits for occupational illness is not as simple as for accidental injury. It is often difficult and costly to prove that a disease is work-related. There is often a long latency period before symptoms appear, and limited scientific and medical understanding of the health effects of most environmental and occupational exposures to toxins are also problems. Consider the high-tech industry. James Moore made component parts for more than 20 years at IBM, working with chemicals such as trichloroethylene and sulfuric acid. Although he complained of headaches, blurred vision, and blackouts, it was not until he was diagnosed with non-Hodgkin's lymphoma in 1995 that he sued his employer. Another long-time IBM employee, Alida Hernandez, believes her breast cancer was a result of exposure to similarly toxic chemicals. Both claim they were never warned by IBM's doctors that their symptoms might reflect chemical poisoning. In October 2003, Moore and Hernandez became the first of more than 200 employees to bring suit against IBM. (a) What will they have to prove to win a tort suit? (b) **Internet Assignment:** Find out what has happened in the suits against IBM. (c) **Internet Assignment:** Check out what the Silicon Valley Toxics Coalition has to say about health problems in the high tech industry.

Today, workers' compensation is widely criticized as anachronistic and unworkable. Besides the claim that the exclusivity rule is unfair where harm is intentional, there are other contentious issues: whether an injury occurred in the "course of employment;" whether a work-related disability is whole or partial, temporary or permanent; and whether an employer should pay for items not covered by workers' compensation statutes, such as property damage or mental anguish in the absence of physical harm. Whenever these issues arise, there is a chance that one party will insist on judicial resolution. In some states, workers' compensation cases languish in the courts for as many as ten years. And, critics point out, because most disability, health, and life insurance policies offer far more extensive coverage than the limited amounts available under workers' compensation, many firms are required to carry liability insurance to cover acts of negligence, forcing them to pay separate premiums for duplicative policies that may not even provide employees with the intended coverage.

Risk in the Workplace

> *For most people in our society, work is unavoidable. If individual workers find themselves facing unacceptable occupation risks they cannot simply withdraw from the market. . . . Adequate information is often lacking; the power to insist on less risk does not exist; and there is no possibility of mobility. These limitations on choice characterize occupational as opposed to recreational or aesthetic risks.*[1]

From sudden accidents with dangerous machinery on the assembly line to the gradual onset of carpal tunnel syndrome from repetitive motions like data processing or butchering, workers face a wide array of risks. Many of the worst hazards are invisible, like the chemical exposures that threaten the productive capacities of both men and women. Those who work in dry cleaners and laundries face carbon disulfide and benzene. Health workers—in hospitals, clinics, and dentist offices—are exposed to infectious diseases and X rays. Mercury, cadmium, coal tar, carbon tetrachloride, and vinyl chloride are risks for production line workers. Computer assemblers breathe toxic dust; taxi drivers breathe carbon monoxide.

Dr. George Friedman-Jimenez, who directs the New York University-Bellevue Occupational and Environmental Medical Clinic and teaches environmental medicine discusses the intersection of workplace hazards, race, ethnicity, and class distinctions in the following reading.

1 Mark McCarthy, "A Review of Some Normative and Conceptual Issues in Occupational Safety and Health," 9 *Boston College Env'tl Affairs L. Rev.* 773, 778–80 (1980–82).

Achieving Environmental Justice: The Role of Occupational Health

George Friedman-Jimenez, M.D.[2]

[P]ublished evidence suggests that African-American, Latino and probably Asian, Pacific Islander, Caribbean, and Native American workers in the United States, especially those in low-paying agricultural, manufacturing, service, and manual labor jobs, tend to be at higher risk for occupational diseases, injuries, and disability than the general population. . . .

Occupational diseases are caused by exposure to toxic substances or hazardous conditions in the workplace. . . . The best available estimate indicates that 350,000 workers develop new onset occupational diseases and 50,000–70,000 active, disabled, or retired workers die of occupational diseases each year in the United States. . . .

Occupational diseases and injuries are almost completely preventable and create avoidable costs not adequately reflected in published data, budgets, or cost-effectiveness analyses. . . . Low wage workers and workers of color may be less able than the general population to leave or refuse dangerous or obviously health-damaging jobs. If the occupational cause of the illness remains unrecognized and is not eliminated early, a worker who is reluctant to request improved working conditions or leave the job can suffer severe and prolonged disease. . . .

A study of steel mill workers found that long-term, full-time, topside coke oven work, one of the least pleasant and most hazardous plant jobs, had a ten-fold increase in risk of lung cancer. Of these workers, 88% were "Nonwhite", while only 21% of non-coke oven workers in the entire plant were "Nonwhite." A recent California study reported that Hispanic men had 2.21 times the risk of occupational disease and injury of White men. Black men had 1.41 times the risk of White men, Hispanic women had 1.49 times the risk of White women, and Black women had 1.31 times the risk of White women. This effect was only partially explained by differences in educational level and length of employment.

A toxic liver disease epidemic in a coated fabric factory in Connecticut was found to have been caused by skin contact with dimethylformamide (DMF), a solvent used in the production process. Seventy-six percent of the production workers, some of whom had to dip their arms into vats of DMF, were found to have abnormal liver function tests. Only eight percent of non-production workers had abnormal liver function tests. Latinos comprised over ninety percent of the production workers, but only thirty-three percent of non-production workers. This epidemic apparently existed for over ten years before being discovered and represents a failure of both the medical care system and the occupational health surveillance system to identify a severe and long standing occupational disease epidemic. . . .

Sweatshops are businesses that regularly violate health and/or safety laws, as well as wage or child labor laws. These workplaces are often hazardous and employ many low wage workers and workers of color. Sweatshops are found in the apparel, restaurant, meat packing, and other labor intensive industries. . . .

Two U.S. General Accounting Office studies of sweatshops reported that most sweatshop workers are Latino, Asian, and African-American, and estimate that in New York City, 50,000 people work in some 3,000–4,500 apparel factories classified as sweatshops. In addition, only one percent of the 17,000-plus apparel and restaurant sweatshops in New York City had been inspected by the Occupational Safety and Health Administration over a five year period.

Greater exposure to hazards on the job is the single most likely reason for increased risk of occupational disease and injury among low wage workers and workers of color. . . . [I]ntensity,

2 21 *Fordham Urban Law Journal* 605 (Spring 1994).

duration, and frequency of exposure to hazards in the workplace remain the main modifiable risk factors for occupational disease.

Lack of health and safety training, lack of English fluency, and newness on the job (the "last hired, first fired" phenomenon) can greatly increase risk of exposure. . . . Often, workers are unwilling to take steps to improve working conditions which they feel may label them as "troublemakers" and possibly jeopardize their jobs. . . .

Another factor is the employer's degree of commitment to providing healthy and safe working conditions. . . . Businesses that pay low wages and hire recent immigrants tend not to invest in workplace safety. OSHA only regulates businesses with more than ten employees and does not cover employees of smaller businesses or farm workers.

Asbestos abatement is a relatively new industry with potential for asbestos exposure. . . . In discussions with Latino students working in the industry, it became apparent that the protective methods and equipment were frequently unavailable. Workers described having to reuse the same dusty disposable coveralls for many days, lack of showers on site, difficulty obtaining replacement filter cartridges for their respirators, being issued a respirator without a proper fitting, and lack of enforcement of other OSHA-mandated preventive practices. Many workers reported finding white dust inside their respirators. . . . Several workers who had complained about these violations lost their jobs, and others feared that if they complained the same would happen to them. Several unemployed workers were always waiting to take each of these jobs as soon as it became available, which added to workers' feelings of vulnerability. In addition, some employers assist workers in obtaining legal residency status. This practice contributes to workers' reluctance to complain about unsafe working conditions. Asbestos abatement could be a safe industry since effective protective methods are available and required by OSHA. . . .

• QUESTIONS •

1. To what extent are occupational risks similar to the risks of "extreme" sports like bungee jumping or night skiing? Different?
2. What obstacles to environmental equity does the author describe? What can be done to overcome those problems? What role should business play?

The Right to Take Workplace Risk

Risks never exist in isolation. They are part of systems. For that reason, any effort to reduce a single risk will have a range of consequences, some of them likely unintended. . . .

If the Occupational Safety and Health Administration ("OSHA") increases regulation of benzene, a carcinogenic substance, it might lead companies to use a less safe, or perhaps even an unsafe, substitute; it might also decrease the wages of affected workers, and decrease the number of jobs in the relevant industry. People who have less money, and who are unemployed, tend to live shorter lives and hence occupational regulation might, under certain circumstances, sacrifice more lives than it saves. Of course the unintended consequences of risk regulation might be desirable rather than undesirable as, for example, when regulation spurs new pollution-control technologies.

— Cass R. Sunstein[3]

In the following case, the court must weigh an individual's willingness to risk his own health against a company's efforts to ensure a safe working environment.

ECHAZABAL V. CHEVRON USA, INC.

United States Court of Appeals, Ninth Circuit, 2000
226 F.3d 1063

REINHARDT, Circuit Judge.

Mario Echazabal first began working at Chevron's oil refinery in El Segundo, California in 1972. Employed by various maintenance contractors, he worked at the refinery, primarily in the coker unit, nearly continuously until 1996, when the events that gave rise to this litigation occurred.

In 1992, Echazabal applied to work directly for Chevron at the same coker unit location. . . . A preemployment physical examination conducted by Chevron's regional physician revealed that Echazabal's liver was releasing certain enzymes at a higher than normal level. Based on these results, Chevron concluded that Echazabal's liver might be damaged by exposure to the solvents and chemicals present in the coker unit. For that reason, Chevron rescinded its job offer. Nevertheless, Echazabal continued to work for Irwin, a maintenance contractor, throughout the refinery including at the coker unit. Chevron made no effort to have him removed from his assignment.

In 1995, Echazabal again applied to Chevron for a position at the coker unit. Again, the job offer was rescinded because of the risk that his liver would be damaged if he worked in the coker unit. This time, however, Chevron wrote Irwin and asked that it "immediately remove Mr. Echazabal from [the] refinery or place him in a position that eliminates his exposure to solvents/chemicals."

[Echazabal claimed that Chevron's refusal to allow him to work in the coker unit was illegal discrimination under the Americans with Disabilities Act (ADA) based on his disability—his diagnosed Hepatitis C. Chevron disagreed with Echazabal's interpretation of a provision in the ADA that creates what is called the "direct threat defense." Here, Chevron argued, it did not have to allow Echazabal to work in the coker unit because his presence would present a "direct threat" to his own health. The court disagrees:]

The direct threat defense permits employers to impose a "requirement that an individual shall not pose a direct threat to the health or safety of other individuals in the workplace." On its face, the provision does not include direct threats to the health or safety of the disabled individual himself. . . .

Although we need not rely on it, the legislative history of the ADA also supports the conclusion that the direct threat provision does not include threats to oneself. The term "direct threat" is used hundreds of times throughout the ADA's legislative history in the final conference report, the various committee reports and hearings, and the floor debate. . . . In nearly every instance in which the term appears, it is accompanied by a reference to the threat to "others" or to

3 "Cost-Benefit Default Principles," 99 *Mich. L. Rev.* 1651 (2001).

"other individuals in the workplace." Not once is the term accompanied by a reference to threats to the disabled person himself. . . .

Congress's decision not to include threats to one's own health or safety in the direct threat defense makes good sense in light of the principles that underlie the ADA in particular and federal employment discrimination law in general. . . . [T]he ADA was designed in part to prohibit discrimination against individuals with disabilities that takes the form of paternalism. . . .

More generally, courts have interpreted federal employment discrimination statutes to prohibit paternalistic employment policies. . . . In *Johnson Controls,* the Court . . . held that the threats of lead exposure to female employees' own reproductive health did not justify the employer's decision to exclude women from certain positions at a battery manufacturing plant. Given Congress's decision in the Title VII context to allow all individuals to decide for themselves whether to put their own health and safety at risk, it should come as no surprise that it would enact legislation allowing the same freedom of choice to disabled individuals.

Chevron suggests that we must ignore Congress's clear intent because forcing employers to hire individuals who pose a risk to their own health or safety would expose employers to tort liability. . . . [G]iven that the ADA prohibits employers from refusing to hire individuals solely on the ground that their health or safety may be threatened by the job, state tort law would likely be preempted if it interfered with this requirement. Moreover, we note that Chevron's concern over an award of damages reflects a fear that hiring a disabled individual will cost more than hiring an individual without any disabilities. The extra cost of employing disabled individuals does not in itself provide an affirmative defense to a discriminatory refusal to hire those individuals. . . .

[W]e conclude that the ADA's direct threat defense means what it says: it permits employers to impose a requirement that their employees not pose a significant risk to the health or safety of other individuals in the workplace. It does not permit employers to shut disabled individuals out of jobs on the ground that, by working in the jobs at issue, they may put their own health or safety at risk. Conscious of the history of paternalistic rules that have often excluded disabled individuals from the workplace, Congress concluded that disabled persons should be afforded the opportunity to decide for themselves what risks to undertake. The district court's grant of summary judgment to Chevron on Echazabal's ADA claim is reversed.

TROTT, Circuit Judge, dissenting.

Mario Echazabal sues over not getting a job handling liver-toxic substances, i.e., "hydrocarbon liquids and vapors, acid, caustic, refinery waste water and sludge, petroleum solvents, oils, greases, and chlorine bleach." He was denied the job because he suffers from a chronic, uncorrectable, and life-threatening viral liver disease Hepatitis C that most likely will be aggravated by exposure to these hazardous materials to the extent that his life will be endangered.

[Under the ADA, employers are not required to hire disabled individuals unless they are "otherwise qualified" to handle the "essential functions" of the job.] . . . Mr. Echazabal simply is not "otherwise qualified" for the work he seeks. Why? Because the job most probably will endanger his life. I do not understand how we can claim he can perform the essential functions of the position he seeks when precisely because of his disability, those functions may kill him. To ignore this reality is bizarre. . . .

Our law books, both state and federal, overflow with statutes and rules designed by representative governments to protect workers from harm long before we rejected the idea that workers toil at their own peril in the workplace. "Paternalism" here is just an abstract out-of-place label of no analytical help. Whether paternalism or maternalism, the concept is pernicious when it is allowed to dislodge longstanding laws mandating workplace safety. That battle was fought and lost long ago in our legislatures. In many jurisdictions, it is a crime knowingly to subject workers to life-endangering conditions. . . . In effect, we repeal these laws with respect to [Echazabal], and to other workers in similar situations. So much for OSHA. Now, our laws give less protection to workers known to be in danger than they afford to those who are not. That seems upside down and backwards. Precisely the workers who need protection can sue because they receive what they need. . . .

Chevron correctly points out that the majority's holding leads to absurd results: a steelworker who develops vertigo can keep his job constructing high rise buildings; a power saw operator with narcolepsy or epilepsy must be allowed to operate his saw; and a person allergic to bees is entitled to be hired as a beekeeper. . . .

I believe it would be an undue hardship to require an employer to place an employee in a life-threatening situation. Such a rule would require employers knowingly to endanger workers. The legal peril involved is obvious, and as a simple human to human matter, such a moral burden is unconscionable.

• QUESTIONS •

1. Look again at the facts offered by both the majority and the dissent. Why do you think Echazabal was willing to risk his health by working in the coker unit? Assuming he had a complete grasp of the risks involved, is it ethical to allow him to work there? For this, re-examine the frameworks for ethical decision making in Chapter 1.

2. Chevron gave certain reasons for refusing to allow Echazabal to work in the coker unit. Name them. Can you think of any other reasons the company may have had for that decision?

3. **Internet Assignment:** On appeal, the Supreme Court reversed. Justice Souter explained why: "The EEOC was certainly acting within the reasonable zone when it saw a difference between rejecting workplace paternalism and ignoring specific and documented risks to the employee himself, even if the employee would take his chances for the sake of getting a job." *Chevron USA Inc. v Echazabal,* 536 U.S. 73, 122 S.Ct. 2045 (2002). The "direct threat defense" is allowable, according to the Court, when it is based on a "'reasonable medical judgment that relies on the most current medical knowledge and/or the best available objective evidence,' and upon an expressly 'individualized assessment of the individual's present ability to safely perform the essential functions of the job. . . .'" Find out how the lower courts applied the test when they revisited *Echazabal* on remand from the Supreme Court. Are you satisfied that Chevron's decisions were not based on the kind of pretextual stereotypes at which the ADA is aimed?

4. In this case, we see both the company and the employee between a rock and a hard place. Echazabal must choose to either further endanger his health or lose a coveted opportunity, while Chevron is caught between liability under the ADA and liability for unsafe work conditions. Suppose you were a top manager inside Chevron, responsible for strategic planning on workplace safety. Is there anything you and your firm can do to prevent or minimize the risk of this type of scenario from developing in the future?

5. Mentioned in the *Echazabal* case is *International Union v. Johnson Controls,* 111 S.Ct. 1196, a 1991 Supreme Court decision in which—again—a company was accused of paternalism for restricting access to hazardous jobs. In *Johnson Controls,* fertile women were not permitted to work on a battery-making production line where exposure to lead could cause harm to their offspring. The Supreme Court held that this restriction amounted to illegal sex discrimination under Title VII, stating that the female workers should "not be forced to choose between having a child and having a job." The company had argued it was concerned about harm to future generations, but the Court wrote: "Decisions about the welfare of future children must be left to the parents who conceive, bear, support and raise them rather than to the employers who hire those parents." Is there a group of stakeholders (affected individuals) whose preferences have not been considered in the *Johnson Controls* case? How might the absence of such voices alter an ethical analysis of this situation?

Occupational Safety and Health Administration (OSHA)

I build ships for a living. When I'm working on a particular job and the company needs something done fast, they tell me to go to work without the staging and the service I need to do the work safely. When they don't need a job done right away, then I get service. Sometimes it takes longer to provide me with a staging than it does for me to do the job itself, so when they want it fast, safety goes by the wayside. . . .

— Charley Richardson, Shipbuilder's Local 5 Quincy, Massachusetts, 1985[4]

The guiding principle regarding OSHA penalties must be this: it should cost an employer more to break the law than to observe it.

— Nancy Lessin, Mass. Coalition for OSH

OSHA Today

- More than 4.3 million nonfatal workplace injuries and illnesses were reported in 2003.
- 5,559 persons lost their lives due to work-related injuries in 2003 (Bureau of Labor Standards, http://www.bls.gov).
- In 2001, there were only 2,122 federal and state OSHA inspectors responsible for enforcing the law at some eight million workplaces. At these staffing and inspection levels, it would take OSHA 109 years to inspect each workplace under its jurisdiction just once. In some states with low staffing levels and numerous workplaces, it would take up to 150 years to make a single visit to them all (*The Boston Globe,* August 29, 2001).
- In 26 states, OSHA does not automatically cover more than eight million workers in the public sector.
- Some 874 immigrant occupational deaths nationwide were not investigated by OSHA during a six-year period studied. New York has the nation's highest rate of immigrants killed in the workplace, with foreign-born workers accounting for three of every ten such deaths, but OSHA never reviewed 143 of the 161 immigrants killed in retail jobs in New York (*Newsday,* 2001).
- Twenty-two percent of all immigrant occupational deaths during the six-year period took place in retail jobs at places such as late-night restaurants, gas stations, and other small, cash-only businesses. Yet only a small percentage of all OSHA fatality investigations occurred in this area (*Newsday,* 2001).

4 From a panel discussion published in "Chemical Hazards at Work: Whose Business?" 9 *Harvard Env't Law Rev.* 331, 351–2 (1985).

Although there is an element of risk reduction inherent in the way state workers' compensation premiums are set,[5] the primary focus of such schemes is on paying those who have been injured or made ill. But this is not the only possible approach. From their earliest days, labor unions have sought greater protections for their members. During the 1937 National Silicosis Conference, for example, industry representatives argued that because exposure to silicon dust was being minimized and minimal exposure was not disabling, there was no longer a real crisis. Representing organized labor, John Frey of the American Federation of Labor disagreed. As historians Rosner and Markowitz explain:

> *Frey argued silicosis was a problem for workers even before they became disabled . . . because any silica in the lungs was pathological. . . . He maintained that . . . emphasis on disability and impairment led management to rely on pre-employment physicals and periodic screening as a means of denying employment or firing diseased workers. . . . The real issue was not to eliminate diseased workers from the workplace but to "eliminate the silica from the air, and prevent additional infections."*
>
> *Unlike industry spokespeople, who sought to reduce the problem of silicosis to an engineering and cost-benefit issue that balanced the health of the work force against the cost to industry, Frey based his argument upon the older public health reformers' analysis, which emphasized protecting communities rather than individuals. "Silicosis is an industrial disease which can be eliminated as effectively as typhoid germs can be removed from the city's drinking water.". . . The cost of protecting the work force was a public obligation. . . . Just as modern city administrators had decided that the very high cost of purifying the water supply was justified by the improvements in health of the population, so too the cost of purifying the work environment was justified by the need to protect all workers from risk of contracting a preventable condition.*[6]

The union perspective did not prevail. It would be another 40 years before the AFL's goal of an expanded federal responsibility for workplace regulation and standard-setting would be realized.

With the adoption of the **Occupational Safety and Health Act of 1970** (OSH Act),[7] the emphasis shifted from compensation for inevitable harm to preventing workplace accidents and health hazards.

The OSH Act created a general duty on the part of every covered employer to maintain a work environment free from "recognized hazards causing or likely to cause death or serious physical harm to employees." It also created a federal agency, the Occupational Safety and Health Administration (OSHA), empowered to oversee safety and health standards, by enforcing the general duty clause and by writing and enforcing detailed health and safety standards for each industry.

OSHA was never provided with the enormous resources it would need to accomplish its mission—the regulation of several million work sites. From the beginning, monitoring had to be done on a random basis. The agency was also expected to identify an ever-growing number of toxic substances and to determine "Permissible Exposure Limits" (PELs) for them. Stymied by a cumbersome rulemaking procedure, requiring 22 separate steps, its decisions were often strongly contested by both industry and labor. By the end of OSHA's first decade, only 23 toxic substance standards had been set. Even when new findings raise new concerns about particular toxins or chemicals, the agency has been unable to respond quickly. When studies convinced

5 Most states use two methods for determining a firm's accident premiums. Small companies are "manually rated" so their premiums reflect the norm for all similar businesses. Larger companies are "experience rated"; payments are tied to their actual history of workplace injuries, providing an economic incentive to reduce accident rates.

6 David Rosner and Gerald Markowitz, *Deadly Dust: Silicosis and the Politics of Occupational Disease in Twentieth Century America* (Princeton U. Press, 1991).

7 29 U.S.C. Sections 651–678 (1970).

the Oil, Chemical and Atomic Workers Union that chromium exposures caused a grave risk of harm, they joined with Public Citizen's Health Research Group to pressure the government to adopt lower PELs than those set in 1971. In 1993, they filed an unsuccessful court action to force OSHA to act. As late as 1998, with the standards still "under review," the court deferred to the agency's judgment. OSHA could not do everything at once, it reasoned, and delays were justifiably explained by election results, government shutdowns, budget cuts, the need to consult with small businesses, and agency re-prioritizing of other OSHA projects.[8] Four years later, however, the court had had enough, and determined it would take the extraordinary action of mediating a deadline for new PELs due to the grave risk to public health.[9] But faced with a similarly long delay in adopting PELs for machining fluid—which would impact on some 1.2 million workers—the same court refused to second-guess OSHA's right to set its own priorities.[10]

Judicial reluctance to force the agency to speed up its standard setting is one thing, but what about lax enforcement? If someone is injured because OSHA fails to enforce its own rules and regulations, why shouldn't the employee be able to sue the government? The answer lies in a concept deeply embedded in our legal system. Under medieval common law, it was assumed that the king could do no wrong and, therefore, could not be sued. Today, the general notion of **sovereign immunity** still limits the kinds of lawsuits that can be brought against the government. Related doctrines of qualified and official immunity provide similar protection to government agents.

For most of our history, a person who wanted to bring a tort action against the United States had to request an exception from Congress. As requests mounted for the right to sue federal employees for their negligent behavior, pressure built for legislative change. Then, in 1945, a U.S. Army bomber, flying in dense fog, crashed into the Empire State Building, killing and seriously injuring many people in the building and on the streets. The pilot had been flying too low, yet sovereign immunity prevented victims or their families from suing. In response, in the following year Congress passed the Federal Tort Claims Act (FTCA). Still in effect today, the FTCA authorizes suits against the United States when a government worker, acting within the scope of his employment, wrongfully or negligently causes property damage, personal injury, or death.

But much of the old protection from suit remains in the "exceptions" set forth in the FTCA. For example, the government still cannot be sued for injuries that arise out of "discretionary functions." Discretionary functions are those that involve an element of judgment or choice; they are policy-making decisions where the government official must weigh political, economic, or social considerations. Coast Guard officials perform a "discretionary duty" when they decide whether to operate a lighthouse on a particular site. If they choose not to, and a ship crashes in the darkness, the government cannot be sued. But once the decision is made to open the lighthouse, if an official leaves it unattended or negligently allows it to dim, the government can be held legally responsible.[11]

The case that follows is one of the few reported tort cases brought against the government for OSHA's failure to assure a safe workplace. After Gail Merchant Irving was horrifically injured in a workplace accident, she sued the United States, blaming her suffering on the negligence of two OSHA compliance officers. After almost two decades of litigation, the trial court awarded Irving $1,000,000 in damages. The government appealed, claiming it was immune from suit

8 *Oil, Chemical & Atomic Workers Union v. Occupational Safety and Health Administration,* 145 F.3d 120 (3d Cir. 1998).

9 *Public Citizen Health Research Group v. Chao,* 314 F.3d 143 (3d Cir. 2002).

10 *International Union, United Autoworkers, Aerospace & Agricultural Implement Workers of America v. Chao,* 361 F.3d 249 (3d Cir. 2004).

11 *Indian Towing Company v. United States,* 350 U.S. 61 (1955).

because, at most, OSHA employees had failed to adequately perform a "discretionary function or duty." In the excerpts that follow, the majority and dissent give conflicting views on the discretionary function exception to the Federal Tort Claims Act.

IRVING V. UNITED STATES

United States Court of Appeals, First Circuit, 1998
146 F.3d 12

SELYA, Circuit Judge.

In 1979, Somersworth Shoe Company operated a manufacturing plant in New Hampshire. On October 10 of that year, the plaintiff, a Somersworth Shoe employee, was stamping innersoles by means of a marker machine. At one point, she went behind her workbench to obtain materials from the die rack. In the process, she dropped a glove. When she stooped to retrieve it, her hair was drawn into the vacuum created by the high-speed rotation of a drive shaft that delivered power to an adjacent "die-out" machine. She sustained grievous injuries.

OSHA compliance officers twice had inspected the plant (once in 1975 and again in 1978) under the auspices of OSHA's authority to conduct general administrative inspections, but had not noted any hazard in connection with the placement or guarding of the die-out machine in the stock fitting room or the bench assembly associated with it. Six days after Irving's mishap, OSHA conducted an inspection focused on the accident and concluded that the arrangement violated OSHA standards in three separate respects, and that all three conditions were "serious." The most important of these was the company's failure to guard the drive shaft component of the die-out machine. . . .

OSHA conducts both programmed general administrative inspections known in the bureaucratic argot that OSHA so readily attracts as "full-scope" or "wall-to-wall" inspections and more focused efforts pinpointed to threats of imminent danger. Aside from a reasonableness limitation on the time and manner of inspections, the statute places virtually no constraint on the Secretary's discretion to conduct such inspections in any way that she deems fit.

[Next, the majority finds that OSHA's implementing regulations delegate to compliance officers the authority to inspect and discretion to decide how. Here it quotes the OSHA Field Manual on full-scope inspections:]

> *The conduct of effective inspections requires identification, professional evaluation, and accurate reporting of safety and health conditions and practices. Inspections may vary considerably in scope and detail, depending upon the circumstances of each case. . . .*

Importantly, the Manual contains no specific prescription mandating OSHA inspectors to proceed item by item or to cover every nook and cranny of a facility during a general administrative inspection. . . .

[In order for the discretionary function exception to the FTCA to come into play, the court must find that the discretion is "grounded in policy":]

[W]e believe that the discretion granted to OSHA inspectors is deeply rooted in policy considerations. The OSH Act's purpose is to provide for a satisfactory standard of safety, not to guarantee absolute safety. . . . A corollary to this observation is that OSHA may legitimately devote its limited enforcement resources to monitoring workplaces and working conditions that pose the most serious threats to worker health and safety . . . by adopting inspection priorities and an administrative plan . . . [for] general inspections. . . .

The function of an OSHA compliance officer is an integral part of OSHA's enforcement policies. When conducting inspections under the auspices of an administrative plan, OSHA compliance officers are expected to study the layout of the facility they are about to investigate, to review its health and safety records, and to interview employer and employee representatives during the inspection about working conditions. One might expect that as a result of such study, OSHA inspectors will make daily judgments about what risks and safety issues most urgently require their attention. At bottom, OSHA inspectors must visit numerous workplaces, all of which present different challenges and issues, and they simply cannot be expected to inspect every item in every plant. The day-to-day decisions made by compliance officers thus further OSHA's enforcement policy of ensuring adequate safety in workplaces with a view toward efficient and effective use of limited enforcement resources, and are thus grounded in policy. . . .

We are not persuaded by the plaintiff's contention that all inspections ought to be painstakingly comprehensive because individual companies rely on OSHA inspections to improve their health and safety conditions. The OSH Act, in no uncertain terms, places primary responsibility for workplace safety on employers, not on the federal government. . . .

This case has disturbing aspects. The government's inspectors appear to have been negligent and the plaintiff suffered grievous harm. Arrayed in opposition, however, is the core policy that underlies the discretionary function exception: an abiding concern about exposing the government to far-flung liability for action (or inaction) in situations in which it has reserved to its own officials the decision about whether or not to act. Even if the decision may seem wrong in retrospect, or if its implementation is negligent, such decision making by its nature typically requires a balancing of interests (e.g., how to deploy scarce government resources in the accomplishment of worthwhile but expensive public needs). . . . Were the law otherwise, there would be scant likelihood of precision or uniformity, and local supervisors would have a perverse incentive to refrain from laying down any rules at all.

Reversed. No costs.

STAHL, Circuit Judge, dissenting.

Congress's purpose in enacting the discretionary function exception was to "prevent judicial 'second-guessing' of legislative and administrative decisions grounded in social, economic, and political policy through the medium of an action in tort.". . . Thus, the exception was designed to protect government agents' exercise of policy-based discretion, to prevent individual government agents from having to look over their shoulders worrying about a potential lawsuit when they are truly exercising policy-based discretion.

The same protective rationale does not apply when government agents are merely carrying out mandatory directives, whatever the basis of those mandatory orders. If a government employee has no choice about how to act whether because a statute, regulation, or agency policy mandates particular actions for all such employees, or for whatever other reason (here, because his supervisor explicitly ordered him to conduct a wall-to-wall inspection) then "there is no discretion in the conduct for the discretionary function exception to protect.". . .

[T]he two inspectors who actually visited the Somersworth plant had no choice about how extensively to inspect; [or] whether to skip any machines. . . . They had orders and they were to follow them. The fact that OSHA's upper management had a great deal of discretion to choose various methods of enforcement in deciding which plants around the country to inspect, whether to do spot checks for some and wall-to-wall inspections for others, is quite irrelevant. . . .

The majority . . . rewards the agency when it undertakes to conduct a comprehensive safety inspection and then does so carelessly. Such a decision violates the letter and spirit of the FTCA. I respectfully dissent.

• QUESTIONS •

1. What are the legal and policy arguments the majority uses to support its conclusion that the case must be dismissed? How does the dissent respond?

2. The majority decides that the government cannot be sued for inspectors' negligence. Does the decision create a "perverse incentive"? In other words, can you think of any possible long-term negative consequences of this ruling on OSHA inspectors? On workplace safety?

Critics of OSHA have long attacked the agency as either too aggressive or not aggressive enough. Some have complained of its slowness in standard-setting, infrequent inspections, and miniscule fines. Others argued that uniform standards resulted in inefficient allocation of limited resources, that reasonable regulations could not possibly be written with enough specificity for five million workplaces, that there could never be enough inspectors to make inspections truly reliable. Still, the rate of workplace deaths in the United States fell from 7.4 deaths per 100,000 in 1980 to 4.1 deaths in 1997—due in part to stricter safety regulations, in part to new technology, and in part to a shift in the economy toward safer service-industry jobs.

Under both the Clinton and Bush administrations, OSHA transformed itself into a more business-friendly agency, with an emphasis on joint business-government efforts, highlighted on their Web site. On January 1, 2002, for example, revised OSHA rules that were a decade in the making went into effect. The goal: to simplify record-keeping requirements so employers might spend less time struggling to understand complicated red tape and more on using the information to improve their own safety and health programs. Yet there continues to be widespread public skepticism about the agency.

Richard Parker argues that the scathing critiques of government's ability to regulate rationally have been fueled by "regulatory scorecards"—studies that try to "reduce hundreds of pages [of analysis] to a few summary statistics across hundreds of rules in order to generate what appears to be a concise, precise, and comprehensive picture of the cost-benefit rationality of programs, agencies and regulations overall." In particular, Parker critiques a widely cited report by Office of Management and Budget economist John Morrall, which claims that government regulations cost up to $72 billion per life saved, and a group of scorecards, compiled by Robert Hahn of the AEI-Brookings Joint Center for Regulatory Studies, which claimed over half of all major regulations passed since 1981 fail cost-benefit tests.

GRADING THE GOVERNMENT

Richard W. Parker[12]

Introduction

The Office of Management and Budget (OMB) estimates that federal government regulation costs businesses or consumers over $500 billion per year. Millions of Americans—as well as many scholars, pundits, think tank analysts, President [George W. Bush], his staff, and a majority or near majority of the House and Senate—believe the costs of these regulations often outweigh their benefits. . . .

The remarkable ascendancy of the anti-regulatory movement derives from two main empirical sources. One is a stream of well-publicized "horror stories" of government zealotry and caprice: companies forced to clean up Superfund sites to the point where children can eat the soil 245 days a year; air quality regulations issued in total disregard of costs; property owners denied development rights when the footprints of cows were declared wetlands, and so forth.

This Article will not have much to say about these stories, except that they need to be treated with caution. Anyone who begins to investigate these stories quickly finds out that some are true; others are exaggerated; many are simply fabricated. Most are published (or repeated) as stories with little or no investigation of the facts. Even if the story turns out to be true, one has no way of knowing whether the incident is typical of agency practice or an aberration. . . .

How do scorecards fare when judged by the standards of their own professional discipline? . . . [T]hey fail badly. [The most influential studies] rely on undisclosed data and non-replicable calculations; use regulatory samples that are biased against a finding of rationality; misrepresent ex ante guesses of costs and benefits as actual measurements; and grossly underestimate the value of lives saved, or the number of lives saved, or both. . . .

12 70 *U. Chi. L. Rev.* 1345 (2003).

Avoidable Errors

[Parker explains that some errors are avoidable. He gives two examples. The first is a study that counts the pages in the Federal Register to prove that regulations are too long and burdensome. Had the author read the Register, he would have known that one "105 page rule" was actually only five pages long, with 100 published pages providing notice, background, and public comments on the proposed rule. Another avoidable error: arbitrarily altering data, as Parker claims Morrall did when he unilaterally "revised" agency estimates on which his report was based because "regulatory agencies . . . tend to overstate the effectiveness of their actions."]

Generic Errors

[Another] group of equally serious shortcomings . . . could not have been avoided because they are inherent in the enterprise of compiling numerical scorecards. First and foremost, regulatory scorecards ignore virtually all benefits that are not quantified and/or monetized—thereby excluding most environmental benefits, many health benefits, and all intangible benefits ranging from the avoidance of pain and suffering or familial and societal disruption to the promotion of a public sense of security, fairness, confidence in markets, etc. Scorecards also ignore the impact of regulations on the distribution of social cost and risk, and the fairness of such impacts. Finally, scorecards ignore and conceal the large uncertainties that are present in virtually every regulatory impact assessment. (That, ironically, is the key to their influence: their use of speciously precise numbers lends them a scientific air which impresses the unsuspecting media and the public, but is quite unwarranted by the data.)

[Parker uses two examples to illustrate the first kind of "generic" scorecard errors: ignoring benefits that cannot be quantified:]

In 1992, EPA promulgated an agricultural worker protection standard for pesticides. Noting that the rule would help protect 3.9 million agricultural workers across the United States who [are] exposed to pesticides in their work, EPA predicted the following benefit:

> *(A)voiding 8,000–16,000 physician-diagnosed (non-hospitalized) acute and allergic pesticide poisoning incidents, (while) avoiding about 300 hospitalized acute and allergic pesticide poisoning incidents, and avoiding potentially important numbers of cancer cases, serious developmental defects, stillbirths, persistent neurotoxic effects and nondiagnosed acute and allergic poisoning incidents.*

Hahn's scorecard, however, does not recognize any "health benefit" other than "reducing the risk of cancer, heart disease, and lead poisoning." Since avoiding stillbirths, persistent neurotoxic effects, and pesticide poisoning does not fit within any of these categories, the regulation is assigned a zero benefit. Protecting 3.9 million workers from the risk of acute pesticide poisoning thus fails Hahn's cost-benefit test.

. . . Zeroing out unquantified benefits is not unique to Hahn. Morrall practices it, too, with consequences that can best be illustrated by examining the rule at the bottom of Morrall's table: OSHA's proposed formaldehyde exposure rule, which, according to Morrall, would cost an incredible $72 billion per life saved. How could any rational agency even propose such a preposterously expensive rule? The answer is found in a combination of Morrall's questionable accounting and the agency's concern with unquantifiable risks.

The rule in question involved a proposal to reduce the Permissible Exposure Level (PEL) for formaldehyde in the workplace from 3.0 parts per million (ppm) to either 1.0 or 1.5 ppm. OSHA anticipated that employers would meet this goal primarily by installing ventilators in work areas where formaldehyde is present in high concentrations. In addition to these "engineering" precautions, employers would be asked to better monitor exposures and conduct exposure risk and reduction training programs for employees. . . . OSHA predicted that compliance with the 1.5 ppm PEL would cost [those industries primarily impacted by the rule] about $22.5 million per year, while compliance with the 1.0 ppm limit would cost $36 million per year . . . [or roughly] 0.1 percent of revenues.

On the benefit side, OSHA predicted that the 1.5 ppm standard would avert anywhere from 5 to 42 fatal cancers over a career of exposure, while the 1.0 ppm standard would avoid 6 to 52 fatal cancers. But OSHA's proposed rule preamble also devotes many pages to the clinical evidence of the non-cancer benefits of a lower standard: reducing or avoiding burning eyes or noses, sore or burning throats, asthma attacks, chronic bronchitis, allergic reactions, dermatitis, and skin sensitization. OSHA noted that over 500,000 American workers are regularly exposed to formaldehyde at concentrations that have been found to cause one or more of these illnesses or discomforts. Is avoiding such discomforts and health hazards for 500,000 American workers—as well as 6 to 52 lifetime cancers—"worth" the expenditure of roughly 0.1 percent of revenues for a $30 billion group of industries? Will installing ventilators in the workplace also reduce employee exposure to other irritating and possibly hazardous chemical vapors besides formaldehyde? These are the central questions of the formaldehyde rulemaking. They are quite unlike (they are far more nuanced than) the question implicitly posed by the Morrall table: how could OSHA be so stupid as to propose a rule that will cost $72 billion for every life saved?

• QUESTIONS •

1. Are scorecards ethical from a free market ethical perspective? How would a utilitarian approach the notion of scorecards? A deontologist? How would someone using the ethic of care evaluate them?
2. In his own evaluation of health and safety laws, Parker includes as an intangible benefit "the impact of regulations on the distribution of social cost and risk." What does he mean? Can you think of examples?
3. Parker argues that "scorecards cannot be salvaged. They should simply be abandoned. . . . Instead, Congress should establish an independent ombudsman to investigate alleged regulatory failures (and failures to regulate) one intervention at a time—mixing ordinal and quantitative analysis to produce a full picture of costs, benefits, distributive impacts, and all relevant uncertainties." Can you identify any potential problems with Parker's approach? What would be the benefits? Can you think of other alternatives to the scorecards?
4. **Internet Assignment:** Choose an area where there is controversy over government regulation (workplace safety, health care, environmental protection), and locate the arguments in favor of dismantling or sharply limiting government action. (a) Find out what you can about the identities of those who take that position. Are they scientists? What is their political affiliation? How is their research published? Where is it funded? (b) Do the same kind of analysis for arguments advanced by those advocating to preserve or strengthen government regulation. (c) Look carefully at the arguments you have found to consider the *kinds* of issues that are being debated. Is Parker right that in the current climate "the only question of interest is how to accomplish sweeping reforms, not whether the regulatory system needs reforming"?

Corporate Criminal Liability

OSHA is empowered by law to bring criminal actions against violators, but has rarely done so: Willful violations of specific OSHA standards that result in employee deaths carry a maximum fine of $10,000 and/or six months imprisonment for a first offense. From 1982 to 2002, OSHA investigated 1,242 cases involving worker deaths due to employer willful safety violation, yet declined to prosecute in 93 percent of those cases. While there are criminal sanctions for giving advance notice of OSHA inspections ($1,000 fine and/or six months imprisonment), OSHA has not referred any cases of this nature for criminal prosecution. OSHA fines and prison terms are dwarfed by those in other government agencies, such as the EPA: Employers faced $106 million in civil OSHA fines and jail sentences totaling less than 30 years for all workplace deaths from 1982–2002; 20 of those years were attributable to the 1991 chicken-plant fire in North Carolina that killed 25 workers. In 1991 alone, 72 persons were jailed for a total of 256 years for violating environmental protection laws.[13]

In the face of such weak criminal enforcement at the federal level, some state prosecutors have sought indictments under state criminal laws to address the most horrific situations. The first state prosecution, *People v. O'Neil,*[14] was brought after a worker extracting silver from used x-ray film died of cyanide poisoning. The employees, most of whom were illegal immigrants who knew little English, were deceived about the hazards of working with cyanide. They were working in an area with inadequate ventilation and were supplied with virtually none of the safety equipment required by law. Both the company and its owners were initially found guilty of murder, but the convictions were overturned on technical grounds.

No other employers have been found guilty of murder, and relatively few have been convicted under any state criminal codes. The president, plant manager, and foreman of Chicago-Magnet were charged with aggravated battery when they exposed 42 employees to poisonous and stupefying substances in the workplace. But, after the longest trial in Illinois history, they were acquitted. In another widely publicized case, *People v. Pymm Thermometer,* a jury found the owners of a Brooklyn-based silver reclamation company guilty of assault with a deadly weapon for knowingly exposing workers to mercury. Their sentence: weekend jail for six months and a $10,000 fine.

Like almost half of the states, California runs its own workplace safety program. A special California-OSHA unit, mostly made up of former police officers, investigates every workplace death or serious injury and reports deliberate safety violations to local prosecutors. California has prosecuted more employers for safety violations than all of the other states combined and has a workplace death rate substantially lower than that of the rest of the nation.[15]

Fire Deaths: 1911, 1991, 2001

On Saturday, March 25, 1911, on the eighth floor of the building that housed the Triangle Shirtwaist Factory in New York, a pile of oily rags burst into flames. The fire quickly raged through the top floors of the building, where nearly 600 young immigrant women, some barely teenagers, toiled on sewing machines in overcrowded workrooms. The building's water hose was rotted through and one exit door was bolted shut from the outside. One tiny elevator—reserved for management—was the only line of escape. One hundred and forty-six women perished; many were trapped behind the locked doors; 62 jumped 100 feet to their deaths; and others were crushed when the

13 David Barstow, "When Workers Die," *The New York Times,* December 22, 2003.

14 550 N.E.2d 109 (Ill. App. Ct. 1990).

15 See David Barstow, "California Leads in Making Employer Pay for Job Deaths," *The New York Times,* December 23, 2003, p. A1.

only fire escape collapsed. The owners of the factory were indicted for manslaughter. At the end of a highly publicized trial, the jury returned a verdict of not guilty. Several years later, after collecting almost $65,000 from their insurance company for property damages, the owners settled suits filed on behalf of those whose lives were lost at a rate of $75 per life.[16]

Eighty years after the Triangle Shirtwaist fire, the American public was outraged by an eerily similar tragedy. A blaze in a chicken-processing plant in North Carolina left 25 people dead and 56 injured. Most of them were women. The building had no fire alarms and no sprinkler system; workers could not escape because exits were unmarked; and doors were locked shut from the outside to prevent theft. The last visit by state inspectors had been nearly 11 years earlier. This time, the company's owner entered a guilty plea to state criminal charges and was sentenced to nearly 20 years imprisonment. In return, the prosecutor agreed to drop charges against two managers at the plant.[17]

The country of Bangladesh has some of the world's cheapest labor. Since the mid-1980s, a new apparel industry has added 1.5 million jobs to its economy and is now this nation's leading exporter. Sweatshop conditions prevail: 12- to 18-hour days, wages sometimes as low as six cents an hour, gates locked from the outside to prevent workers from leaving. On November 25, 2001, 52 people, mostly young women, ten of them children, were killed in a fire in a polo-shirt factory at the Chowdhury Knitwears in Narsingdi. Trapped inside the burning building—gates locked from the outside, lights out—most of the victims fell or were trampled in a rush to escape. After a period of public mourning and outcry, the factory reopened. Almost all the surviving workers returned to a building that had been upgraded with smoke alarms, heat detectors, and a sprinkler system. While the Chowdhury fire was the most shocking, it was not an isolated incident; between 1995 and 2001, some 30 factory fires, 17 involving fatalities, occurred in Bangladesh.

Internet Assignment: New York responded to the Triangle Shirtwaist fire by creating a safety commission and a statewide agency to investigate factory conditions. Led by Frances Perkins, who became the first woman to head the U.S. Department of Labor, the factory commission's labor standards laws eventually became the model for the nation.[18] Find out what happened in North Carolina after the poultry fire and in Bangladesh after the Chowdhury blaze.

SAFETY CONCERNS IN THE GLOBAL ECONOMY

As capital, labor, and data cross national boundaries with increasing ease, products may be designed in one country, built in another (with components from still others), and then marketed around the world. Few would quarrel with the International Covenant on Economic, Social and Cultural Rights—that everyone has a right to safe and healthy working conditions, to form and join trade unions, to take other appropriate steps to safeguard the right to a livelihood. Yet, as the next series of readings makes clear, there is little consensus as to how to ensure those rights.

16 See Eric G. Behrens, "The Triangle Shirtwaist Company Fire of 1911," 62 *Tex. L. Rev.* 361 (1983).

17 "Meat Plant Owner Pleads Guilty in a Blaze that Killed 25 People," *The New York Times,* September 15, 1992, p. A-20.

18 See Jeanine Ferris Pirro, "Reforming the Urban Workplace: The Legacy of Frances Perkins," 26 *Fordham Urb. L.J.* 1423 (1999).

Fundamentally, there are only two ways of coordinating the economic activity of millions. One is central direction involving the use of coercion—the technique of the army and of the modern totalitarian state. The other is voluntary cooperation of individuals—the technique of the marketplace.

— Milton Friedman (1962)

Sweatshop exploitation is modern globalized capitalism stripped bare.

— http://www.nosweat.org.uk (2004)

The International Battle Against Sweatshop Labor

During the 1990s, student and labor activists fueled an international movement to end sweatshop labor. Tactics ranged from lobbying efforts and boycotts to street demonstrations during meetings of such established free trade groups as the World Trade Organization (WTO) and the International Monetary Fund (IMF). American-based multinationals have responded to such pressure in a variety of ways.

Nike, for example, engaged in a public relations campaign to enhance its image. Some activists, however, were not convinced that genuine change was underway. Claiming that Nike's press releases and letters to newspaper editors misrepresented the actual working conditions under which its products were made, one activist sued Nike for unlawful and unfair business practices and false advertising.

Kasky v. Nike

Court of Appeals, California, 2000
93 Cal. Rptr. 2d 854

SWAGER, Associate Justice.

Nike, Inc., a marketer of athletic shoes and sports apparel, has grown into a large multinational enterprise through a marketing strategy centering on a favorable brand image, which is associated with a distinctive logo and the advertising slogan, "Just do it." To maintain this image, the company invests heavily in advertising and brand promotion, spending no less than $978,251,000 for the year ending May 31, 1997. The promotional activities include product sponsorship agreements with celebrity athletes, professional athletic teams, and numerous college athletic teams. . . .

Like other major marketers of athletic shoes and sports apparel, Nike contracts for the manufacture of its products in countries with low labor costs. In Nike's case, the actual production facilities are owned by South Korean and Taiwanese companies that manufacture the products under contract with Nike. The bulk of Nike products are manufactured in China, Thailand, and Indonesia, though some components or products involving more complex technology are manufactured in South Korea or Taiwan. In 1995, a Korean company opened up a major new facility in Vietnam, giving that country also a significant share of Nike's production. The record indicates that between 300,000 and 500,000 workers are employed in Asian factories producing Nike products. The complaint alleges that the vast majority of these workers are women under the age of 24.

The company has sought to foster the appearance and reality of good working conditions in the Asian factories producing its products. All contractors are required to sign a Memorandum of Understanding that, in general, commits them to comply with local laws regarding minimum wage, overtime, child labor, holidays and vacations, insurance benefits, working conditions, and other similar matters and to maintain records documenting their compliance. To assure compliance, the company conducts spot audits of labor and environmental conditions by accounting firms. Early in 1997, Nike retained a consulting firm, co-chaired by Andrew Young, the former ambassador to the United Nations, to carry out an independent evaluation of the labor practices in Nike factories. After visits to 12 factories, Young issued a report that commented favorably on working conditions in the factories and found no evidence of widespread abuse or mistreatment of workers.

Nevertheless, Nike was beset in 1996 and 1997 with a series of reports on working conditions in its factories that contrasted sharply with the favorable view in the Young report. An accounting firm's spot audit of the large Vietnamese factory, which was leaked to the press by a disgruntled employee, reported widespread violations of local regulations and atmospheric pollution causing respiratory problems in 77 percent of the workers. . . . And the Hong Kong Christian Industrial Committee released an extensively documented study of several Chinese factories, including three used by Nike, which reported 11- to 12-hour work days, compulsory overtime, violation of minimum wage laws, exposure to dangerous levels of dust and toxic fumes, and employment of workers under the age of 16.

These reports put Nike under an unusual degree of public scrutiny as a company exemplifying a perceived social evil associated with economic globalization the exploitation of young female workers in poor countries. . . .

Nike countered with a public relations campaign that defended the benefits of its Asian factories to host countries and sought to portray the company as being in the vanguard of responsible corporations seeking to maintain adequate labor standards in overseas facilities. . . .

The complaint alleges that, in the course of this public relations campaign, Nike made a series of six misrepresentations regarding its labor practices including . . . that Nike products are made in accordance with applicable laws and regulations governing health and safety conditions. . . .

[These misrepresentations, plaintiff claimed, constituted unlawful and unfair business practices and false advertising. Next, the court addresses the defense raised by Nike: that its press releases are protected by the First Amendment to the Constitution.]

Since extending First Amendment protection to commercial speech . . . the United States Supreme Court has "been careful to distinguish commercial speech from speech at the First Amendment's core. . . . A line of decisions . . . has sanctioned restraints on commercial speech that is false, deceptive or misleading. . . .

[T]he speech at issue here was intended to promote a favorable corporate image of the company so as to induce consumers to buy its products. A Nike executive expressed this business objective in a letter to the editor [of a newspaper]: "Consumers . . . want to know they support companies with good products and practices. . . . During the shopping season, we encourage shoppers to remember that Nike is the industry's leader in improving factory conditions."

[W]e think that a public relations campaign focusing on corporate image, such as that at issue here, calls for a different analysis than that applying to product advertisement.

[T]he case at bar lies in familiar First Amendment territory public dialogue on a matter of public concern. Though drafted in terms of commercial speech, the complaint in fact seeks judicial intervention in a public debate.

The "heart of the First Amendment's protection" lies in "the liberty to discuss publicly and truthfully all matters of public concern. . . . Freedom of discussion, if it would fulfill its historic function in this nation, must embrace all issues about which information is needed or appropriate to enable the members of society to cope with the exigencies of their period." . . . [I]n the industrial society of 1940, the . . . constitutionally protected "area of free discussion" embraced the dissemination of information about labor disputes. . . . By the same logic, the labor practices of foreign contractors of domestic companies come within the "exigencies" of our times.

Nike exemplifies the perceived evils or benefits of labor practices associated with the processes of economic globalization. . . . Nike's strong corporate image and widespread consumer market places its labor practices in the context of a broader debate about the social implications of employing low-cost foreign labor for manufacturing functions once performed by domestic workers. We take judicial notice that this debate has given rise to urgent calls for action ranging from international labor standards to consumer boycotts. Information about the labor practices at Nike's overseas plants thus constitutes data relevant to a controversy of great public interest in our times.

Freedom of "expression on public issues" has always rested on the highest rung of the hierarchy of First Amendment values. . . . The constitutional safeguard . . . "was fashioned to assure unfettered interchange of ideas for the bringing about of political and social changes desired by the people." And, it represents a "profound national commitment to the principle that debate on public issues should be uninhibited, robust, and wide-open. . . ."

It follows that "under the free speech guaranty the validity and truth of declarations in political disputes over issues of public interest must be resolved by the public and not by a judge." . . .

The fact that Nike has an economic motivation in defending its corporate image from such criticism does not alter the significance of the speech to the "listeners" the consumers or other members of the public concerned with labor practices attending the process of economic globalization.

[The court affirms the decision of the trial judge to dismiss the complaint against Nike].

• QUESTIONS •

1. The court refused to order Nike to cease its public relations campaign. Why?

2. The Supreme Court of California reversed this case. "Because the messages in question were directed by a commercial speaker to a commercial audience, and because they made representations of fact about the speaker's own business operations for purposes of promoting sales of its product," the majority found they were commercial speech, subject to California's ban on false advertising. Dissenters argued that that the ruling would prohibit a business from speaking out on issues of public importance or from vigorously defending its own labor practices. *Kasky v. Nike, Inc.,* 119 Cal.Rptr. 2d 296 (2002). What arguments can you make to defend the decision of the lower court? Of the state's Supreme Court? Frame your argument in terms of ethical theory.

3. **Internet Assignment:** After granting a right to appeal, the United States Supreme Court issued a one-sentence unsigned order declaring that certiorari had been "improvidently granted." In other words, the matter was left to the California courts, where Nike would have to defend itself under the commercial speech standard adopted by the state's highest court. Instead, in September 2003 the company agreed to pay $1.5 million to the Fair Labor Association to settle the case. In a joint statement, Nike and the FLA said the money would be used for worker education and to develop a global standard on corporate responsibility. Find out what progress has been made.

4. At the time of the settlement, Nike indicated that it would not disseminate its corporate responsibility report outside the company and would continue to limit its participation in public events and media engagements in California. Use ethical theory to defend Nike's decisions.

5. **Internet Assignment:** Nosweatapparel.com is a "virtual mall" where all the vendors sell goods made by union workers. American Apparel, a company that moved from Mexico to Los Angeles in 2001, publicizes its sweat-free ethos by including photo essays of immigrant cutters and sewers at work in its catalog. Find out about current trends in the global movement against sweatshop labor.

Transnational Codes of Conduct

Pressure from students and consumers may well lead corporations to change their behavior, but their responses can have problematic ripple effects. As Claire Dickerson explains in the next reading, alterations of corporate practice can sometimes make a bad situation worse.

Dickerson uses the phrase "virtual organization" to describe a multinational organized around a "hub" that controls its "core competencies"—usually design and marketing—linked by contract to its spokes, the suppliers. Wal-Mart is one of the biggest of these virtual organizations. The twelfth largest corporation in the world, it has economic resources that would rank it thirtieth among the world's 191 countries, ahead of Poland and Greece. Dickerson critiques Wal-Mart's use of its tremendous power.

Leveling the Playing Field for Developing-Country Workers

Claire Moore Dickerson[19]

In 1992, the NBC program "Dateline" broadcast a story about children working in Bangladeshi garment factories that sold products to Wal-Mart. Children as young as eleven years old were sewing Wal-Mart products in these factories. Two years previously, a fire in one of the factories had killed twenty-five workers, including several children.

At that time, Wal-Mart had contracted with third-party suppliers located throughout the world, including in Bangladesh, for the manufacture of its products. The evidence suggests that, embarrassed by the broadcast in the United States, Wal-Mart began canceling its agreements with Bangladeshi suppliers. Other retailers similarly cancelled contracts with their suppliers, complaining that the bad publicity was adversely affecting business. The multinationals ultimately adopted codes of conduct imposing minimum standards of conduct on the remaining suppliers.

Meanwhile, the Bangladeshi Garment Manufacturers and Exporters Association (BGMEA) learned that proposed legislation before the United States Congress would ban importation into the United States of garments manufactured with child labor. The concern of the BGMEA was heightened by the fact that garment exports represented the single largest export industry of Bangladesh and that more than half of these goods were exported to the United States. In July 1994, the BGMEA announced that the use of child labor would cease after October 1994, a mere three months later.

At first blush, this appears to be a story about the might of the Western economy brought to bear in favor of human rights, particularly those of children. Available information indeed confirms that, after October 1994, significantly fewer children were working in factories manufacturing exports. However, the story is more complicated; the dismissed children did not merely retire to go to school. Thousands of children were fired between July and October of 1994, and the evidence reflects that these children found new jobs, working for underground subcontractors, or even working as beggars or prostitutes.

[S]hortly after the Bangladesh debacle, Wal-Mart unilaterally adopted a more formal so-called code of conduct that defined not only the multinational's behavior but also that of its suppliers. . . . [M]ultinationals imposing the codes have the power to expect compliance, or at least they have sufficient power to seek to transfer the public relations risk to their suppliers.

[T]he modern organizational form, the virtual organization, is premised on that dominance of the multinational hub over its suppliers. . . . [I]f the hub exercises that power in order to reduce

19 Excerpted from Claire Moore Dickerson, "Transnational Codes of Conduct Through Dialogue: Leveling the Playing Field for Developing-Country Workers," 53 *Fla. L. Rev.* 611 (2001). Reprinted with permission.

its costs, developing-country workers will suffer the impact. . . . As costs are pushed onto the third-party suppliers, the suppliers can control those costs either by firing the workers, or by impoverishing the working conditions for existing employees.

Because the vast majority of a virtual organization's services and supplies are by definition sourced from a third-party supplier under contract, there is both psychological and physical distance between the supplier and the hub. . . .

[T]he workers are not employees of the hub; they are employees of a supplier related to the hub by contract. When the hub ostensibly seeks to improve its standing with its industrialized-country market, it is instructing the suppliers how to treat the suppliers' own employees, persons who have no direct relationship to the hub. . . . Because the workers do not belong to the hub, they are not part of the same unit, not part of the same corporate culture. The virtual organization's structure enhances the hub's indifference to the actual consequences imposed on the developing-country workers, because these are structurally as well as literally foreign.

Because of its power, Wal-Mart was able to implement in Bangladesh what it perceived to be its developed-country customer market's anti-child-labor value. It was because of its psychological distance that it could do so without focusing on the consequences to the developing-country workers and, thus, cause devastating harm to the workers. . . .

[Next, Dickerson argues for creation of a "norm of good-faith relationship" between multinationals and workers in developing countries. The goal, as she sees it, is to allow the workers to be involved in the implementation of a universal norm or ethic such as the elimination of child labor. She recommends adoption of a "top-down optional code," where the only punishment for noncompliance would be adverse publicity. Dickerson cites the labor standards recommended by the International Labor Organization (ILO) as an example of an "optional code." Unless ratified by a country, the standards are not legally enforceable. Yet, she argues, they are valuable, in part because the ILO sought input from non-governmental organizations (NGOs), independent, private associations, before drafting the guidelines. By consulting NGOs that represent developing-national workers and their families, the ILO was able to incorporate those voices and concerns into its recommendations.]

[The ILO] has a long history of promoting absolute standards. However, recent studies and recommendations of the ILO emphasize the importance of empowering peoples and, specifically, of educating workers and their families. Educated workers are more likely to know what questions to ask and what the alternatives are, and thus are less likely to be abused. Further, educated families are less likely to place their children in abusive working situations.

The ILO's use of the NGOs, when it works correctly, has the workers speaking by proxy through the NGOs. . . .

What the ILO can do through the NGOs is facilitate, and doubtless influence, the multinationals' extension of the good faith norm to workers . . . [in part by helping] the multinationals to see the changes resulting from the codes as a gain, and even a short-term gain, rather than a loss, thus increasing the likelihood that they will support such changes. . . . [A]s developing-country workers and their families and descendants become consumers, they may remember how they have been treated, and multinationals with a record of tolerating abusive work conditions will find future markets relatively closed to them, and their overcapacity consequently relatively difficult to correct. . . .

Further, because the code is optional, the multinationals' voices, too, will be part of the process. And, the more the multinationals are included in that process, the more they will view the codes as damage control. Although, initially, the multinationals may have to increase expenditures to conform to the new obligations to workers, there is perhaps less likelihood of upside (expensive) defection than would be the case with a purely market-driven, optional code. . . . That is, with an ILO code, multinationals may feel protected from having to offer even better working conditions. . . .

[Next, Dickerson explores how a system of top-down, optional codes could have avoided the disaster that Wal-Mart triggered in Bangladesh.]

If the supranational organization were, for example, the ILO, it would first engage the NGOs on the one hand, and the multinationals on the other. Assuming an anti-child-labor norm, the ILO would seek the eradication of child labor by helping the multinationals to realize the articulated needs of the developed-country workers. . . . Instead of reacting suddenly and even brutally to the latest story generated by the media, Wal-Mart could report to its customers in the industrialized countries that it is taking all the steps that the ILO, after careful study, recommends. As just noted, these steps would include dialogue with affected workers so that Wal-Mart understands, before acting, the likely consequences of its actions.

Wal-Mart would receive an immediate double benefit. The ILO would provide an answer to negative publicity in the developed-country customer market, and, so long as all multinationals conform to the minimum standard of the top-down code, the ILO would also allow Wal-Mart and all other multinationals to contain costs. . . .

By ensuring that the developing-country workers are consulted in the implementation of the anti-child-labor norm, the ILO would be reinforcing the enhanced good faith norm within the transnational commercial community. The better established that enhanced norm, the less necessary will be the supranational structure's intervention. . . .

Organizing Labor for a Safer Global Workplace

The (ILO), the organization referred to by Dickerson, was created at the Versailles Conference at the end of WWI for the purpose of assuring that workers would be treated fairly as global trade evolved. Today, it continues its work under the umbrella of the UN.

The author of the next reading suggests an alternative route to higher labor standards: organizing labor unions that cross national boundaries.

THE PERILS AND PROMISES OF TRANSNATIONAL LABOR SOLIDARITY

James Atleson[20]

In recent years, the subject of international trade has tended to dominate any assertion or discussion of international labor rights. The creation of new trading blocks and, especially, the World Trade Organization (WTO), have moved the possible linkage of worker rights and trade to the front page. Unions, and some developed nations, have argued that a natural connection exists. . . .

The WTO, however, has greatly restricted a nation's ability to implement or enforce provisions for worker protection. Thus, a nation cannot, consistent with WTO standards, set labor or environmental standards which the WTO determines masks an intent to protect domestic industries. Nor may a nation bar the import of goods made in conditions it feels violate its own norms or standards, for instance, goods made by young children or produced in unsafe or unhealthy conditions. (The one exception is goods made by forced labor, which has led to a recent federal statute barring such goods from the United States market.) Even if a [nation] internally bars the manufacture and transport of goods made, for instance, by children under a specific age, it may not bar such goods made elsewhere despite the effect on its own labor standards. Current WTO rules, in short, provide significant barriers to state-based methods for the protection of human rights.

. . . [D]espite the history of attempts to set international standards for labor and employment, legal regimes are intensely local in character. As Lord Wedderburn noted, "one is struck by

20 James Atleson, "The Perils and Promises of Transnational Labor Solidarity," 52 *Buff. L. Rev.* 85 (2004).

the contrast between the facility of the internationalization of capital and the obstacles that obstruct international trade union action. Capital is not tied, but each trade union movement is tied to the particular social history of the country in which it operates.". . . Although labor law is basically national just as labor is still primarily based nationally, Lord Wedderburn's comments in 1973 are still valid:

> *. . . It is not free movement of labour but free international trade union action which is the true counterpart to free movement of capital.*

. . . Since the nineteenth century unions have attempted to gain control over the supply of labor, and their ideology stressed the international solidarity of workers. . . .

[But] international labor solidarity activists should . . . be prepared for the possibility that labor activity or social clauses in future trade agreements will ameliorate the often appalling conditions in many workplaces around the world to a more limited extent than is often believed. For instance, many of the workers now toiling in terrible conditions, including sweat shops in the first world like the United States, work for domestic, not international, markets. Attaching labor rights to international trade agreements may not help all the workers that should be aided. . . .

Moreover, many of the world's workplaces are populated by workers who have limited choices. Diane Wolf has discussed women factory workers in rural Java. Women workers, she found, worked for less than subsistence wages because they said they wanted money of their own to buy things like their own soap, they thought their status would be enhanced because the work would be cleaner and cooler than agricultural work, they could leave their parents' homes, and they could meet young men. Interestingly, these workers moved to factories for the same reason women traveled in the nineteenth century to places like Lowell, Massachusetts: to acquire some income, get away from agricultural work and their families, find a husband, and acquire some modern, hip belongings. Importantly, a large number of workers like these, including child laborers around the globe, work in industries that produce for the domestic market.

• QUESTIONS •

1. Dickerson argues that if Wal-Mart had used good-faith norming to resolve its Bangladesh problem, there would have been a different resolution. Instead of dismissing the child workers en masse, Wal-Mart would have helped to create access to education and some income to children and their families. Evaluate that outcome from a deontological perspective and from a utilitarian one.
2. What does Dickerson mean by "damage control"? Is it ethical from the point of view of Milton Friedman? From that of deontology?
3. According to Atleson, what are some of the advantages and limitations of transnational unions?
4. Atleson notes that the WTO rules prevent a country from banning imported goods made by young children or in unsafe conditions "despite the effect on its own labor standards." What does this mean?

Twenty-first Century Slavery

There are an estimated 27 millions slaves in the world today, more than ever before in human history. Kevin Bales, a scholar and activist trying to build a global coalition to end slavery, explains that this count does not include sweatshop workers or those who are just extremely poor, but "people who are controlled by violence, who cannot walk away." While this is a definition that would encompass slavery in the American pre-Civil War South, Bales notes the important difference between slavery then and now:

> *Historically, the investment of purchasing a slave gave incentive for the master to provide a minimum standard of care, to ensure the slave would be healthy enough to work and generate profit for the long term. Today, slaves are extremely cheap and abundant, and thus disposable. Today the interest is not in "owning" slaves, only in controlling them—through violence or the threat of. A slave is exploited for as long as he or she is profitable; then discarded.*

The lack of legal ownership, Bales has written, is a benefit to slaveholders today, "because they get total control without any responsibility for what they own."

In the following interview, Kevin Bales discusses modern slavery, and what can be done to end it. He begins by talking about why we are facing a situation where there are so many so-called "disposable people":

> *Vulnerability is the key here. When subsistence farmers are driven out of the countryside because they've been replaced by cash crop agribusiness, and they end up in cardboard shacks in shantytowns around developing world cities. . . . They don't have their temple or church, their extended family or the village network—all that gets lost. . . . [T]hey're economically vulnerable because they can't get work. . . . They're physically vulnerable because they can't protect themselves from people who have weapons, and they're legally vulnerable because the police won't enforce the law. . . .*

SLAVERY: ALIVE AND THRIVING IN THE WORLD TODAY

Interview with Kevin Bales[21]

What Are the Most Typical Types of Modern Slavery?

Debt bondage is the most common kind of enslavement around the world, concentrating in South Asia, [most commonly] . . . "collateral" debt bondage: when you borrow money, you and all of your family . . . become collateral. . . . In India I've met families in their fourth generation of bondage—a great-grandfather borrowed $20 worth of rupees . . . and because the family and all their work is collateral against the debt, there's no way that you can get the money to pay it back. . . .

In the developing world, particularly in small communities that are not necessarily literate, a person's word and reputation are extremely important to them. It means that there's a culture of honesty . . . and slaveholders will use that to trick people, to talk to them in a way that makes it sound like there's just a loan . . . and it's all fair. . . . [Even though they] . . . recognize the fact they're enslaved, they feel a responsibility to keep their word. . . .

What Are Some Examples of Modern Slavery?

Thailand is an excellent example because it has gone through rapid changes and is highly integrated into the global economy. Here you have young women enslaved into brothels who clearly demonstrate the impact of the low cost of slaves. In world terms, they're pretty expensive—one of these women, 14 to 15 years old, costs $800 to $2,000. At that price, and because they are forced to have sex with ten to 15 people a day—what is really a kind of serial rape—they generate enormous

21 Rachel Cernansky, *Satya Magazine,* December 2002/January 2003.

profits, something like 850 percent profit a year for the people who procured them. But these girls . . . only last two, three or four years. They become HIV positive or a cocktail of sexually transmitted diseases, they are brutalized or their mental health diminishes to the point where they can't function anymore, or all of those things mixed together. So after three or four years, they are, in a sense, useless and are just thrown away. . . .

It Seems so Far Removed, How Does Slavery Touch Our Own Lives?

. . . When you go to Wal-Mart, for example, the stuff you find there is really cheap, so cheap that if you think about it, you think how on earth could this be?

In Brazil, we know that people are enslaved making charcoal used by the steel industry, which is a major export from Brazil. We know that American companies are invested in Brazilian steel and in the land where forests are destroyed to make charcoal. American companies are invested in beef and timber from Brazil; and slaves are used to log timber and to prepare the land for the cattle and care for them and so forth. There's two, three, five—who knows how many—links in that chain, and it's hard for us to actually trace them.

There's a parallel here with multinational corporations that subcontract out to factories using sweatshop labor, which distances them from exploitation and shifts the blame.

Slavery is even further down the line than the factories. It occurs in very small units; you rarely—if ever—find a factory full of slaves. The factory may be a sweatshop, but the raw materials or bits coming into a factory may have come up from slave labor.

Can You Give a More Specific Example of How Slavery is Linked to Our Daily Lives?

Cocoa's an easy one—the Ivory Coast is the world's largest exporter of cocoa, and it flows directly into the U.S. . . . [We've] discovered horrific enslavement of young men, mostly economic migrants from Mali, who'd come down looking for work and had been forced into slavery on farms growing cocoa. . . .

Hasn't Legislation Related to that Been Passed by Congress?

This is extremely interesting. There was an amendment that would have required labeling of chocolate as slave-free; but it was withdrawn because it would have been impossible to determine—it's this problem again of tracing the product chains. It is currently impossible to determine precisely which cocoa is slave-free. Anybody who has that label wouldn't actually be able to prove that. It was also withdrawn because the chocolate industry agreed to work directly with human rights groups, anti-slavery organizations, and trade unions to eradicate the problem. . . . Now we finally have an industry that says, Yes, we take moral, economic, social responsibility for our product chain. . . .

[A]nti-Globalization Activists . . . Attack the Globalized Economy for Driving the Bottom Line at the Expense of Human Rights. Is Slavery the Epitome of that Type of Human Exploitation?

. . . Slavery is not essential to the global economy. The productive capacity of slaves, as I calculate it, is something like $13 billion a year in the global economy, which is nothing. . . . There's a positive side to globalization as well. . . . [T]he concepts of human rights are becoming globalized. . . . [W]hen I'm in rural India, where people are illiterate, and they blurt out in English, "Universal

Declaration of Human Rights." They know what it means—they don't know precisely what those English words mean, but they think about human rights.

What Are International Bodies Doing?

There's a new UN convention on human trafficking giving every country that adopts it . . . an agreed definition of what they're working on and suggests ways for it to be effective. A lot of countries are rewriting their laws so that they match each other's.

How Receptive Has the U.S. Government Been? What Kind of Success Have You Seen?

. . . Administrations change, but . . . the people who actually manage the projects and programs, who work overseas, or work in the customs service to inspect for slave-made goods—to them it doesn't matter which political party's in power. They're trying very hard, they're doing very good things about slavery.

What Do You See as Hope for Change?

The number of slaves is very high, but the cost of actually helping people out of slavery is very low. Sending an activist around India, for example, to talk to people about alternatives to their bondage is very cheap. When the resources are there it can be done. It may sound crazy after talking about such huge numbers, but with sufficient mobilization this really could be the generation that brings slavery virtually to an end—for the first time in human history. . . .

• QUESTIONS •

1. What impact might global slavery have on the health and safety conditions of ordinary workers?
2. **Internet Assignment:** According to Bales, there are some 150,000 to 200,000 slaves in the United States. Find out what kinds of work they are doing. Is anything being done to abolish this trade? Start at http://www.iAbolish.com, the Web portal of the American Anti-Slavery Group.
3. **Internet Assignment:** Elsewhere in this interview, Bales talks about the fair trade movement as a means of altering the demand component of the global economic equation, and of helping to eradicate modern slavery. What is the fair trade movement? How exactly might its activities impact slavery today?
4. In the mid-1990s villagers brought suit against the multinational energy giant, Unocal, for atrocities committed during the laying of a pipeline in Southeast Asia. There were allegations of forced land compensation and forced labor, with the Myanmar military threatening to kill those who would resist. There was testimony that one man was shot as he tried to escape the project, and in retaliation his wife and child were thrown into a fire; the baby died. Other witnesses described how villagers who would not work or who became too weak to work were summarily executed.

Plaintiffs brought suit under a federal statute, the Alien Tort Claims Act (ATCA), which allows non-citizens to sue in the U.S. courts for wrongs committed in violation of the law of nations. The defendants in most ATCA cases are foreign states or officials. For example, the statute was the basis of large—though uncollected—awards for human rights abuses committed by the former dictator of the Philippines Ferdinand Marcos and the Bosnian Serb leader

Radovan Karadic. The case against Unocal, however, was an attempt to hold global business interests responsible for allowing human rights violations to occur. The claim was that the firm knowingly looked the other way as the military regime in Myanmar oversaw the construction of their pipeline, using rape and torture to intimidate the local villagers into working on the project.

As the *Unocal* case was ongoing, in 2004 the U.S. Supreme Court held that ATCA cases had to involve human rights violations that are "specific, universal and obligatory" under international law—crimes like genocide, enslavement, or torture. Both sides in the *Unocal* case described the Supreme Court ruling as boding well for them. Defense attorneys stated that, in the absence of any direct involvement in atrocities, their clients were not responsible under ATCA, while plaintiffs' lawyer Dan Stormer forecasted the case would move on to trial: "We have slavery, we have torture, we have crimes against humanity as part of our claim. They can pound the table all they want but we are going to get to argue this case." The outcome of the case against Unocal would be closely watched, partly because several other corporations were facing charges under ATCA, including ExxonMobil, Royal Dutch/Shell, and ChevronTexaco.

(a) Is there any ethical theory we have looked at that you could use to justify the use of U.S. courts to punish corporations for indirect involvement in human rights abuses?

(b) **Internet Assignment:** Press reports in December 2004 indicated that Unocal had settled the suits in California state and federal courts. What can you find out about the settlement terms?

In the next reading, Henry Shue provides a framework for analyzing the ethics of exporting old, unsafe technology to developing nations.

Exporting Hazards

Henry Shue[22]

[A] general statement of the liberal no-harm principle is, "It is wrong to inflict avoidable harm upon other people, and it ought often to be prohibited by law." While harming oneself may sometimes be immoral, it is harming others that ought generally to be illegal. . . .

No one may hurt or endanger others, except in cases of genuine necessity, in the course of justified warfare, in punishment for heinous crime, or in other quite special circumstances. Even the most one-sided advocates of freedom have rarely advocated the freedom to injure and danger. . . .

[Shue discusses the argument that the general no-harm principle does not apply where the costs of exporting old, unsafe technology is overbalanced by the benefit to foreign workers. He distinguishes mere costs from true "harms," which he finds unacceptable.]

Yes, it is granted, there are costs to the foreign workers in the form of new dangers to health and safety, but there are also new benefits that are, so to speak, part of the same package. And—this is the point—although the costs to the workers are undeniably real . . . the benefits are real too and they are greater than the costs. . . . The worker might be safer sitting at home, but he or she might also be unemployed. . . .

[A cost, according to Shue, is a true harm when it involves all six of the following factors:]

The first factor is that the damage done is physical: it is life, limb and vitality that are at stake, not, for example, reputation or life style only, but the adequate, continued functioning of parts of one's body. . . .

Second, the potential damage is not simply physical; it is serious, possibly fatal. . . . The bodily threat is to vital organs. Some of the malignancies are still untreatable and certainly fatal.

22 From *Boundaries: National Autonomy & Its Limits,* P. Brown and H. Shue, Eds. (New Jersey: Rowan & Littlefield, 1981).

Third, besides being serious physical damage, the damage that is risked is irreversible. It does not "clear up," and damaged portions do not grow back. . . .

[Fourth], the potential physical damage to the workers is undetectable for the victim without a level of medical care to which the workers have no access and [fifth] is unpredictable for the victim, even probabilistically, without a level of knowledge to which the workers have no access. . . .

[Sixth,] the undetectability and unpredictability are avoidable at the choice of the firm's management. . . . This double point is simple but quite significant: people poor enough to work readily in the conditions we are considering will not have enough money—even if doctors are available, which is unlikely given the low effective demand—to afford routine medical examinations. . . . So "early detection by a doctor is out of the question. . . . This is what I mean by saying the damage is undetectable for the victim: it is, for the person who has undergone it, discoverable only when it is so serious as to interfere with normal overall functioning, if not to threaten life. It is readily detectable by a physician with standard X-ray equipment. This is why the damage seems to be avoidably undetectable. . . .

Even people who have never before seen or heard about mining . . . do not need to be told that shafts sometimes collapse and so might this one. . . . But they would not—and generations of miners did not—realize that there is such a thing as "black lung" and that they might well be developing it. . . . This fifth factor is that potential victims do not know, and cannot figure out for themselves, how high the risk is, although their employers know the probabilities and keep them quiet. Thus, once again, we appear to have avoidable unpredictability. . . .

[Finally, Shue addresses the argument that, even if harm is being inflicted in a manner that ought to be stopped, it cannot be the responsibility of individual firms acting alone to stop it: this would amount to a form of forced heroics or martyrdom. Again, Shue finds this position unpersuasive.]

It may be also be suggested that firms are not in the business of protecting the interests of their workers, except when this is a means to their own goals . . . [and that] if the government of a poor country wants the citizens of the country to enjoy safer workplaces, the government ought to impose uniform standards upon all firms, instead of expecting isolated firms to raise their own costs while their competitors are allowed to undercut them by retaining the cheaper, less safe technology. . . .

[B]ut no institution, including the corporation, has a general license to inflict harm, even if the infliction of harm holds down production costs. In order to maintain otherwise one must reject the traditional liberal no-harm principle. Protecting people against harm is another matter. . . . What the corporation is being asked to do is simply not to inflict harm: not to prefer to a safer process a manufacturing process that harms a higher percentage of the people subjected to it than other readily available processes do.

Second, the national governments of poor countries that try to protect their workers against such harms face precisely the same problem that the firms invoke—and the governments face it because of the reasoning that the firms use. They first complain that they cannot be expected to go it alone (by unilaterally introducing more expensive, safer processes) because this would put them at a competitive disadvantage. But governments of poor countries that compete for foreign investment face an exactly analogous choice. . . .

[In the final section of this piece, Shue discusses the allocation of responsibility for preventing harms.]

Whom does this leave to defend the victims of the harm who at present cannot defend themselves? It leaves us, fellow American consumers. Why us, or, to be precise, why me?

To some degree the question answers itself. Why should I defend defenseless human beings? Because they are human beings and they are defenseless. . . .

But there are additional . . . reasons. The main reason why one particular Samaritan must decide whether to do "good" is no better a reason than that this Samaritan happened to come along this road at this time, when (a) the victim was already in the ditch and (b) the previous travelers had already passed by on the other side of the road. To this Samaritan's "why me?" there is no cosmic explanation, and there is no better answer than: "You are here and therefore in a position to help this victim—is there a stronger claim upon you now?"

The firm that has retained control . . . of the harmful process [that] has inflicted the wound, and the victim's own government has usually passed by on the other side of the road. Whoever is next in a position to assist the victim has some obligation to do so, irrespective of whether he or she was previously involved, unless some stronger obligation overrides. A previous involvement with the case is not required. Call this responsibility through ability—ability to make a positive difference.

We have been considering a case in which products consumed by U.S. purchasers and formerly made by U.S. workers are now made by Mexican workers as the result of a U.S.-based firm's decision to continue to use a less safe process to which U.S. workers cannot legally be subjected. United States consumers are hardly Samaritans who just happen to be passing by an asbestos factory on the other side of the border. We pay lower prices, suffer less inflation, etc., because the health costs of the retention of the less safe technology are now borne by the Mexican workers and Mexican society. It is true, that most of us did not ask to have this arrangement made. But once we understand it, we are no longer unwilling (because unknowing) beneficiaries. We now must choose whether to continue to accept these benefits on these terms. In such situations, knowledge is not only power but also responsibility, because it places us in a position to act. Call this responsibility through complicity—complicity by continuing acceptance of benefits.

• QUESTIONS •

1. According to Shue, what are the six indicators that a "cost" is actually a "harm" where use of foreign labor is concerned? What does he mean by describing a harm as "unavoidably undetectable"?
2. What does Shue mean when he writes that poor countries face an "analogous choice" as they compete for foreign investment?
3. Shue mentions (a) responsibility through ability and (b) responsibility through complicity. Consider the *Unocal* case. Did the company possess either form of responsibility in Myanmar? What could it have done that would be in line with the "no-harm principle?"
4. Who do you think bears responsibility for the maintenance of safe working conditions in American-owned firms located in foreign countries: the workers themselves? The corporate owners or managers? The foreign government? The American government? An international safety and health organization? The individual American consumer?
5. Can you articulate connections between Shue's essay and any aspects of the ethical theories mentioned in Chapter 1?

Chapter Problems

1. **Internet Assignment:** In 1972 a bipartisan national commission found state workers' compensation laws to be generally inadequate and inequitable, leading to state increases in benefits throughout the 1970s and 1980s. Beginning in the late 1980s, however, states began to reduce benefits and make procedural reforms to reduce costs. What has happened in your state

in the past five years? Check to see what arguments were made by proponents/opponents of the amendments before they were passed. Have any studies been done since the changes that would help you to evaluate their effectiveness?

2. In *Hoffman Plastics Compounds, Inc. v. NLRB,*[23] decided in 2002, the Supreme Court ruled that an undocumented "alien" worker fired for union organizing was not entitled to the monetary remedy otherwise available under the NLRA. Critics viewed this as another blow to "ghost workers"—those 8 million immigrants who toil in the shadow of our economy, with few recognized rights. What impact might *Hoffman Plastics* have on the rights of undocumented workers to apply for and receive worker's compensation? Is it ethical to prevent recovery by injured workers who are in violation of American immigration laws? Use the different frameworks in Chapter 1 (stockholder theory, utilitarianism, deontology, virtue ethics, and ethic of care) for this analysis.

3. Homicide is the leading cause of workplace fatalities in five states, the nation's capitol, and New York City. Street-front shops in high crime areas, convenience stores, and taxicabs are particularly high-risk sites. (a) What obligation, if any, should an employer have to protect employees from intentional assaults by other employees? (b) Should workers' compensation laws cover workplace assault and battery? In recent years, OSHA has made workplace violence a major priority. **Internet Assignment:** What has OSHA done to draw attention to this problem? Start here: http://www.osha.gov.

4. How much discretion should government agencies have to not make rules? Consider the following: In 1989, the Mine Safety and Health Administration (MSHA) proposed a comprehensive rule that would establish lists of hazardous substances: PELs for more than 600 chemical substances that might be present in a mine, 165 of which would have been regulated for the first time. While one phase of the rule was adopted after public hearings and comments in 1994, the MSHA withdrew the remainder of its rule in September 2002. Its primary reason was the "result of changes in agency priorities." The United Mine Workers union challenged the withdrawal of the proposed Air Quality Rule as arbitrary and capricious. Find out if the court agreed in *International Union, United Mine Workers of America v. United States Department of Labor,* 358 F. 3d 40 (D.C.Cir. 2004).

5. In what some have called the "feminization of migration," increasing proportions—probably close to half—of the world's 120 million legal and illegal migrants are believed to be women, who overwhelmingly take up work as maids, domestics, and nannies.

> *Imagine you are locked away in a strange home. You do not speak your captor's language. On the rare occasions when you are escorted off the premises, you are forbidden to speak to anyone. You are often fed the leftover food of the children you are required to watch while completing your around-the-clock household duties. You have never been paid for your labors, and the woman of the house physically abuses you.*
>
> *While the scenario seems to hark back to an earlier time in U.S. history, it describes Noreena Nesa's recent working conditions in the Washington, D.C. area. Tucked behind the manicured lawns and closed doors of our wealthiest residents live some of the most vulnerable people in the United States: abused migrant domestic workers, who are sometimes the victims of slavery and human trafficking.*
>
> —Joy M. Zarembka, "America's Dirty Work: Migrant Maids and Modern-Day Slavery"[24]

23 535 U.S. 137 (2002).

24 *Global Woman: Nannies, Maids, and Sex Workers in the New Economy,* Barbara Ehrenreich and Arlie Russell Hochschild, Eds. (NY: Henry Holt, 2002).

The extremes—slavery and human trafficking—are criminal offenses that can be prosecuted and punished. (Indeed, the Thirteenth Amendment to the U.S. Constitution bans slavery and involuntary servitude.) But more common abuses—long hours, inadequate pay, unsafe conditions in the home itself—are more difficult to police since domestic servants are not covered by most American labor laws. Should they be?

6. Is collective bargaining by unions a better way to improve workplace safety and health than pervasive government regulation? Law professor Thomas Kohler believes that anti-union attitudes are one of the few areas of conservative-liberal agreement, but argues that this is a strange time in American history for such attitudes, given the degree to which wage and earnings distribution has become increasingly unequal, and the middle class has shrunk. He writes:

> *Along with these developments has come a significant loosening of the employment bond. So-called contingent employment arrangements—part-time, temporary and contract arrangements—are on the rise, and many analysts expect the number of part-time employees to double in the next few years. These "just-in-time" employees typically have at best highly restricted claims to pension, health and other benefits incident to employment. . . .*
>
> *[He looks, as well, at developments on the international level:]*
>
> *. . . [T]he remarkable transformation of what used to be called the Easternbloc was spearheaded by an independent trade-union movement, which improbably survived despite the forces arrayed against it. Nor were the Poles left to go it alone. At a time when our own government took a wait-and-see attitude, the AFL-CIO and other unaffiliated American unions supported Solidarity from the first with funds, equipment and expertise. American unions also lobbied Western governments on Solidarity's behalf, and worked to keep the Polish situation before the public's eye. . . .*
>
> *There is also a pronounced tendency today to overlook, or to be absolutely unaware of, the domestic contributions made by the union movement. The support of unions, for example, was crucial to the passage of the Civil Rights Act of 1964. Unions also have been in the forefront of efforts to improve workplace safety and public health and to ensure pay equality for the sexes. . . .*

Kohler speculates that unions might be more valued if people better understood the importance of collective bargaining. It is, he argues, a system of "private-law making." This is important because:

> *Individuals and societies alike become and remain self-governing only by repeatedly and regularly engaging in acts of self-government. It is the habit that sustains the condition. . . . [I]t is through their involvement in the collective bargaining process that average citizens can take part in deciding the law that most directly determines the details of their daily lives.*[25]

Internet Assignment: Find out what unions are doing today to support safe and healthy workplaces, in the United States and abroad.

7. Internet Assignment: While OSHA uses its Web site to provide statistical information about injury rates, the agency refused to release the injury rates for each of the 13,000 sites

---

25 Thomas C. Kohler, "Civic Virtue at Work: Unions as Seedbeds of the Civic Virtues," 36 *B.C. L. Rev.* 279 (1995).

it had identified as having unusually high numbers of worker injuries and illnesses. In 2002, the *New York Times* filed a request for that information under the Freedom of Information Act for the specifics. In August 2004 a federal court judge in New York granted the newspaper's request. OSHA was ordered to make public for the first time the names of the most dangerous worksites. Find out what has happened since then. Did OSHA appeal the lower court ruling? Has the Agency identified which employers are the worst offenders? How important is it that the public have such information? How hard or easy was it for you to find this information?

8. Reba Rudkin began working for Johns-Manville's California asbestos plant in 1946. There, for 29 years, he was exposed to and ingested asbestos. Although the company knew since 1924 that long exposure to asbestos is dangerous to health, it concealed that knowledge from its employees. Manville failed to provide adequate protective devices and allowed dust levels that exceeded federal and state exposure limits. Rudkin consulted company doctors, but they had not been told what the company knew about the risk of asbestos exposure or that Rudkin's pulmonary disease was the result of working conditions at the plant. Nor did the company file a report with the state—required by law—regarding Rudkin's occupational illness. In the late 1970s, Rudkin sued Johns-Manville for causing and concealing his asbestos-related illnesses. (a) What defense might the company raise? (b) How might Rudkin respond? (c) **Internet Assignment:** Find and read the Rudkin case. What was the outcome? In your own words, summarize the majority's reasons for its ruling and the gist of the concerns raised by the dissent.

9. Who should bear the health risks of volunteers? Consider this: After the attack on the World Trade Center, many were concerned about the environmental and health risks to rescue and clean-up crews working at Ground Zero. In October 2003, the directors of a medical screening program at Mount Sinai Medical Center in N.Y. told Congress that 75 percent of the 8,000 rescue workers they saw had persistent respiratory problems, and 40 percent suffered from mental health problems. But 40 percent had no health insurance, and one-third were unemployed. Although 250,000-400,000 people who were living, working, attending school, visiting or responding to the attack were exposed to toxic dust, as this book goes to press there is no federal treatment program for those suffering from related health problems. Dr. Stephen Levin, director of the Mount Sinai program is blunt in his criticism: The government prioritized re-opening the financial markets and showing the world that America would not be cowed, over people's health.[26] (b) **Internet Assignment**: Find out if the federal government has taken action to address these concerns.

10. Internet Assignment: China leads the world in producing low- and medium-tech goods, and most of the major multinational manufacturers have a presence in the country. Activists point out that workers are not free to form their own unions, and there are frequent abuses of health and safety standards. Union and business leaders from around the world hoped to pressure China to do more to protect workers' rights when the Organization for Economic Cooperation and Development met in Beijing in December 2004. But, only weeks before the planned meeting, China rescinded visas and the meeting was effectively blocked. Activists insisted that the pressure on behalf of workers' rights in China would continue. Find out what has happened. Was the meeting rescheduled? What improvements in working conditions in China, if any, have been reported?

26 Miriam Hill, "Grade zero for cleanup workers' care," *The Philadelphia Inquirer,* October 11, 2004, p. E1.

Chapter Project

Evaluating Workplace Health and Safety

Choose any company that you have some connection to that produces a product for the global market. (One that you or a family member have worked for, own stock in, purchased goods from, get a catalog from, etc.)

Begin by finding out as much as you can about the working conditions of their employees (at home and abroad). Pay particular attention to issues of safety and health. Find out if the company has an occupational health and safety office, clinic or committee, and whether employees are unionized.

Evaluate the company's practices in light of its own policies/statements, its human rights obligations (including the Norms on the Responsibilities of Transnational Corporations and Other Business Enterprises with Respect to Human Rights, adopted by the UN in 2002), and using the kind of ethical analysis basis on theory that we have done throughout this text.

Complete your analysis by making recommendations—for example, publicizing accolades for a company that is highly ethical or specific actions to change the conduct of one that is not.

Chapter 6 Justice and a Sustainable Economy: Environmental Protection

God, who hath given the world to men in common, hath also given them reason to make use of it to the best advantage of life, and convenience. The earth, and all that is therein, is given to men for the support and comfort of their being.

— John Locke

[My] story is of all life . . . and of us two-leggeds sharing in it with the four-leggeds and the wings of the air, and all green things; for these are children of one mother and their father is one Spirit.

— Black Elk

We need to have our senses transgressed, and to find life pasturing freely where we never wander.

— Henry David Thoreau

We begin this chapter with what is termed "environmental justice," looking at how race and class issues, as they have played out in our history and as they are structurally present today, affect the way environmental hazards are distributed in our society. We then focus on the legal response to environmental concerns in the United States: from the comprehensive legislative approach launched in the 1970s, to more recent innovations allowing market incentives to play a role in regulation, to the virtual dismantling of the regulatory apparatus in favor of voluntary stewardship of the environment.

A selection of readings presents different philosophical points of view on the relationship between humans and their natural surroundings. We resume the legal theme with a case in which environmental regulation is arguably a "taking" of property requiring "just compensation" under the Fifth Amendment to the U.S. Constitution.

We end with a reading about environmental justice and global free trade.

Environmental Equity

There's always likely to be some people who don't want you to be there. The best you can do is ask if you're doing what's right under the laws in effect and on an economic basis.

— Brian S. Montag, lawyer for St. Lawrence Cement Co.

The Civil Rights Act started in '64. I was there. There was bleeding and dying to get us rights. Why shouldn't we pick up where they left off? Everyone keeps saying our children are our future. What future do we have if they kill our children?

— Bonnie Sanders, resident, Camden Waterfront South

In this first case, a community organization in Camden, New Jersey, sues the state environmental agency, arguing that its decision to issue permits to a cement processing facility had a racially discriminatory impact on a poor neighborhood already burdened by the by-products of many industrial sites. The community, with a population of about 2,000, nearly half of whom are children, is asking the court to grant a preliminary injunction to rescind the permits and halt the project. A preliminary injunction is an order that takes effect until a full-scale trial occurs. It is only granted in special circumstances, after a plaintiff has successfully argued that irreversible harm will occur otherwise.

SOUTH CAMDEN CITIZENS V. NEW JERSEY DEP

U.S. Dist. Court, New Jersey, 2001
145 F.Supp.2d 446

ORLOFSKY, District Judge.

Plaintiffs' application for preliminary injunctive . . . relief presents . . . issues arising under Title VI of the Civil Rights Act of 1964, which prohibits discrimination based on race and national origin by recipients of federal funding. . . .

Plaintiff, South Camden Citizens In Action ("SCCIA"), is an unincorporated community organization, whose members are residents of a neighborhood in Camden, New Jersey, known as "Waterfront South." Defendant, the New Jersey Department of Environmental Protection ("NJDEP"), . . . receives federal funding and is thus obliged to conform its operations to the restrictions imposed by Title VI. . . . Defendant Intervenor, St. Lawrence Cement Co. ("SLC"), manufactures . . . cement products. . . .

[T]he NJDEP granted the necessary air permits to SLC to allow its proposed facility to begin operations. In doing so, the NJDEP considered only whether the facility's emissions would exceed technical emissions standards for specific pollutants, especially dust. Indeed, much of what this case is about is what the NJDEP failed to consider. It did not consider the level of ozone generated by the truck traffic to and from the SLC facility, notwithstanding the fact that the Waterfront South community is not currently in compliance with the National Ambient Air Quality Standard ("NAAQS") established by the EPA for ozone levels, nor did it consider the presence of many other pollutants in Waterfront South. It did not consider the pre-existing poor health of the residents of Waterfront South, nor did it consider the cumulative environmental burden already borne by this impoverished community. Finally, and perhaps most importantly, the NJDEP failed to consider the racial and ethnic composition of the population of Waterfront South.

SLC's Proposed Facility

SLC plans to use the proposed Camden facility to grind and process granulated blast furnace slag. . . . SLC plans to import, by barge, and process approximately 850,000 tons of [slag] and 16,500 tons of gypsum annually. . . . Trucks will then transport the [slag] and gypsum three miles to the SLC facility, where they will be offloaded into large, open piles. Front-end loaders will transfer the [slag] to a feed hopper. From the feed hopper, the [slag] will be transported by conveyor belt to a vibrating screen, which will sift out oversize materials. The remaining material will proceed via conveyor belt to the roller mill, where it will be heat dried and then ground into smaller particles. . . .

Before processing, [slag] particles are the size and texture of beach sand. After processing, the ground [slag] ("GGBFS") material will be the size and texture of powdered sugar.

Inbound truck deliveries to the facility will occur about 80 days per year, with approximately 500 truck deliveries per day; outbound truck departures will occur approximately 225 days per year, with approximately 200 trucks departing per day. The contemplated truck route passes through residential areas of the Waterfront South community. . . .

SLC's Permit Applications and Construction of the Facility

[After five months of discussion with the NJDEP, and having retained the services of environmental engineers and consultants, SLC submitted its permit application. Its main focus was on air permits. In November 1999, the NJDEP informed SLC that its application was "administratively complete"—in other words, all of the paperwork SLC had to submit was in order, but had not yet been reviewed. At this point, SLC could—and did—decide to go ahead with construction.]

SLC was very eager to have the facility operational in order to: (1) off-set construction expenses; and (2) beat its competitors in accessing and providing product to East Coast markets. . . .

SLC's Community Outreach

In July 1999, shortly before submitting its final air permit applications to the NJDEP, SLC began to solicit public support for the facility from the residents of Waterfront South [through its hired consultant, Morris Smith].

Smith arranged meetings between SLC representatives and municipal officials, local business leaders, community organizations, and residents. The purpose of these meetings was to share information about the facility and obtain community input.

[Initially, members of Waterfront South's SCCIA attended the meetings set up by SLC, but by January 2000, it had decided to stop participating.]

Applicable Environmental Standards

With the passage of the Clean Air Act ("CAA"), Congress delegated the authority to establish primary and secondary National Ambient Air Quality Standards ("NAAQS") to the EPA. . . . The CAA requires that new stationary sources of air pollutants, such as the proposed SLC facility, must meet established NAAQS. "Stationary sources" include buildings, structures, facilities, and installations.

Presently, the EPA has established NAAQS for the following six pollutants: (1) particulate matter less than 10 microns in diameter ("PM-10"); (2) ozone; (3) sulfur dioxide; (4) carbon monoxide; (5) nitrogen dioxide; and (6) lead. . . . [S]tates are charged under the CAA with the primary responsibility for implementing the NAAQS within their borders and monitoring compliance. . . .

Waterfront South

. . . In 1990, the median household income of residents of Waterfront South was $15,082, and the per capita income was $4,709. Over 50% of the residents of Waterfront South live at or below the federal poverty level.

Camden County is one of twenty-one counties in the State of New Jersey. The residents of the State of New Jersey are 79.4% non-Hispanic white and 20.6% non-white.

Many pollutant-producing municipal and industrial facilities are located in near Waterfront South . . . [including][a municipal] sewage treatment plant, which treats sewage for approximately 35 municipalities in Camden County; (2) the County trash-to-steam incinerator; and (3) a cogeneration facility, which converts waste energy to produce heat or electricity . . . the G-P Gypsum Corporation . . . and the Coastal Eagle Point Oil Company Refinery.

There are two Superfund sites located in Waterfront South. . . . There are four sites within one-half mile of the proposed SLC facility that the EPA has identified and has already or is currently investigating for the release or threatened release of hazardous substances. . . . The NJDEP has identified fifteen known contaminated sites in the Waterfront South neighborhood. . . .

Current Health of the Community

[According to Plaintiffs' medical expert], in Camden County:

(1) The age-adjusted cancer rate for black females is higher than 90% of the rest of the state;
(2) The age-adjusted cancer rate for black males is higher than 70% of the rest of the state;
(3) The rate of cancer is significantly higher for black males than for white males;
(4) The age-adjusted rate of death of black females in Camden County from asthma is over three times the rate of death for white females from asthma in Camden County;
(5) The age-adjusted rate of death of black males in Camden County from asthma is over six times the rate of death for white males from asthma in Camden County.

Furthermore, the self-reported asthma rate for Waterfront South residents is 33%, more than twice the self-reported rate of asthma in other parts of the City of Camden. It is undisputed that as many as 61% of Waterfront South residents have problems coughing and catching their breath, compared to 36–39% of the residents in North Camden. . . .

Effects of PM Inhalation

Because inhalation of particulate matter is a known health hazard, the EPA has established a NAAQ standard for particulate matter emissions. . . . The currently enforceable NAAQ standard for PM-10 was set in 1987.

[W]ith all proposed emissions controls in place . . . the SLC facility will emit 59.1 tons of particulate matter size PM-10 or smaller per year . . . in compliance with the current NAAQ standard. . . .

[Plaintiffs insist that just complying with the present standards will not prevent negative health consequences, however. They] argue that: (1) when the totality of the circumstances is considered, the addition of the SLC facility's PM-10 emissions to the existing environmental conditions in Waterfront South will have an adverse impact on the health of residents of Waterfront South; and (2) [small particle PM-10 emissions] not currently regulated by a NAAQ standard, will adversely affect the health of residents of Waterfront South. . . .

[A second medical expert for the plaintiffs] Dr. Lavietes testified that there is a statistically significant relationship between PM-10 emissions and mortality, even where PM-10 emissions are *well below* the level set by NAAQS.

Furthermore, Dr. Lavietes testified that exposure to PM-10 is also related to morbidity or incidence of disease. Specifically, Dr. Lavietes cited numerous studies which link high PM-10 concentrations to increased emergency room visits for asthma, impaired lung function, and the general state of respiratory health, particularly of children and the elderly. Inhalation of fine particulate matter . . . is also linked to other respiratory symptoms such as bronchitis, coughing, runny nose, and burning eyes. . . .

SLC estimated that "approximately half" of the emissions from the production of [ground slag] are PM-2.5. . . . In his certification, Dr. Lavietes testified that PM-2.5, because it is smaller, can lodge more deeply in the lungs than coarser components of PM-10 . . . [and] is the most dangerous component of PM-10. . . .

As the NJDEP is well aware, on July 18, 1997, the EPA issued a final agency rule setting new NAAQS for particulate matter, and specifically setting NAAQS for PM-2.5. . . . [T]he EPA explained that "[t]he most significant new evidence on the health effects of PM is the greatly expanded body of community epidemiological studies . . . [which] provide 'evidence that serious health effects' (mortality, exacerbation of chronic disease, increased hospital admissions, etc.) are associated with exposures to ambient levels of PM found in contemporary U.S. urban airsheds even at concentrations below current U.S. PM standard."

The EPA specifically noted that "[s]ensitive subpopulations appear to be at greater risk to such effects, specifically individuals with respiratory disease and cardiovascular disease and the elderly (premature mortality and hospitalization), children (increased respiratory symptoms and decreased lung function), and asthmatic children and adults (aggravation of symptoms). . . ."

[Implementation of these standards has been delayed by litigation brought by industry and other groups. The judge finds that PM-2.5 poses "unique dangers to human health."]

Effects of Ozone

Plaintiffs' second major complaint regarding the impact of the proposed SLC facility involves the emissions of nitrogen oxides and volatile organic compounds ("VOCS"). Both the facility and the approximately 77,000 diesel trucks that will traverse the Waterfront South neighborhood annually, delivering materials to and from the SLC facility, will emit these materials. Nitrogen oxide and VOCS are precursors to ozone; ozone is created when these materials combine with heat and sunlight.

Ozone and its precursors are hazardous to human health. Dr. Lavietes testified that diesel truck emissions, which produce PM-10, hydrocarbons, carbon monoxide, and other toxic chemicals, are carcinogenic and aggravate respiratory ailments. Ambient, or airborne, ozone aggravates respiratory ailments and causes irritation of the eyes, lungs and breathing passages. Ground level ozone contributes to decline in pulmonary function and has been linked to cancer. . . .

According to the NJDEP's statistics, the County of Camden is in "severe" or "very severe" nonattainment, or noncompliance, with the ozone NAAQS. In fact, eighteen of New Jersey's twenty-one counties are in noncompliance with the 1987 ozone NAAQS.

EPA promulgated new, more restrictive ozone NAAQS in 1997. . . . The new ozone NAAQS, were [also] challenged in litigation brought by industry groups against the EPA. When the Court of Appeals . . . issued its ruling on May 14, 1999 . . . vacating the proposed ozone NAAQS, NJDEP Commissioner Shinn issued the following press release:

> *New Jersey was the first state to support the more protective, eight-hour standard. . . . By forcing the reduction of smog-forming emissions, it will provide greater protection for some of our most vulnerable citizens: young children, the elderly, and those with respiratory and heart problems. We in New Jersey will not relent in our pursuit of cleaner air. We will continue to seek the emission reductions needed to achieve this health-based standard. . . .*

I find NJDEP's argument [in the case at bar] to be disingenuous. . . .

Legal Standard for Preliminary Injunction

An injunction is an extraordinary remedy granted only in limited circumstances. . . . [A] court must weigh the following four factors: (1) the likelihood of the movant's success on the merits; (2) whether the movant will be irreparably injured if relief is not granted; (3) whether the party to be enjoined will suffer irreparable injury if the preliminary relief is granted; and (4) whether the public interest will be served by the preliminary injunctive relief. . . .

Likelihood of Success on the Merits

(1) Adverse impact

[The court now must forecast "whether the operation of the proposed SLC facility will have an adverse, disparate impact on the Waterfront South Community based on the race, color, or national origin of the residents of that community."]

The operation of the proposed facility will impact the health of the residents of the Waterfront South community in two specific ways. First, particulate matter emitted from the proposed SLC facility will affect respiratory function in the members of the surrounding community, a disproportionate number of whom already suffer from asthma and other respiratory conditions which will be aggravated. . . . Second, the ozone generated by the annual migration of 77,000 trucks making deliveries to and from the SLC facility will impact residents' health because it aggravates respiratory function and causes cancer. The Court has also found that the Waterfront South community in general, and African-American members of the community in particular, already suffer disproportionately high rates of cardiovascular disease and respiratory disease such as asthma.

(2) Disparate impact

To support their claim that pollutant-producing facilities in New Jersey are disproportionately located in communities of color, Plaintiffs rely primarily on the expert report of Dr. Michel Gelobter.

Dr. Gelobter analyzed the correlation between race and the distribution of facilities that emit air pollution in New Jersey . . . using two different analyses. First, he gathered data on the number of air pollution emitting facilities [from a publicly available database called AIRS/AFS. Then he] gathered data on the racial composition of New Jersey ZIP Code areas using the 1990 U.S. Census results. Comparing these data, Dr. Gelobter found a statewide average of 7.8 AIRS/AFS facilities per ZIP Code. Dr. Gelobter further found that ZIP Codes with higher than the state-wide average of 20.6% non-white residents had an average of 13.7 AIRS/AFS facilities per ZIP Code, or 105% more AIRS/AFS facilities, than those with a below-average number of non-white residents, which had an average of 6.7 AIRS/AFS facilities per ZIP Code. [Waterfront South has 21 AIRS/AFS facilities or] 230% of the statewide average. . . .

[Using a second analytical method, Dr. Gelobter found that Waterfront South is in a ZIP Code area with 70 EDA-regulated facilities—almost double the statewide average per ZIP Code.]

Finally, Dr. Gelobter performed a regression analysis of the relationship between EPA-regulated facilities and the percentage of non-whites in a ZIP Code area. . . . [H]e concluded that "the odds that there is no relationship between the percentage of non-white residents and the number of facilities in a ZIP Code area are less than 3 in 10 million. . ."

I find that Dr. Gelobter's basic conclusion that in the State of New Jersey there is "a strong, highly statistically significant, and disturbing pattern of association between the racial and ethnic composition of communities, the number of EPA regulated facilities, and the number of facilities with Air Permits," to be sound. . . .

Irreparable Harm

[Next, the court must decide whether granting or denying an injunction will cause irreparable harm to plaintiffs, the NJDEP, the SLC, or the public:]

I note that injury to the environment . . . has been found by courts to be especially difficult to remedy and usually irreparable . . . [making injunctive relief] appropriate when a defendant's conduct poses a continued threat to environmental well-being."

[T]he NJDEP failed to consider important factors which it is mandated by law to consider, namely, the health status and cumulative environmental burdens in a receptor community. . . .

The harm alleged by SLC is entirely economic. Specifically, SLC argues that it has expended more than $50 million to construct the facility, and will lose $200,000 for each week that the facility does not operate. . . . [H]owever . . . purely economic injury is not irreparable harm. Furthermore . . . SLC was aware of the NJDEP's Title VI obligations and of the demographics of the neighborhood and the residents' concerns about potential civil rights violations prior to its construction of the facility, yet chose to proceed with construction of the facility. SLC cannot now argue that it will suffer irreparable harm based on its own assumption of the risk in constructing the facility. . . .[1]

Finally, SLC argues that a preliminary injunction is against the public interest because it would "thwart the public interest in a revitalized Camden." [H]owever . . . the already poor health of the community in which the facility is located is likely to be adversely affected by the operation of the facility, and . . . the NJDEP did not consider either the health status or the cumulative environmental burdens in this community prior to issuing the permits. . . .

Conclusion

[Plaintiff's application for a preliminary injunction is granted and the air permits vacated.]

• QUESTIONS •

1. The case you have just read is a groundbreaking one. It represents the first time civil rights law was applied in the context of environmental justice. It was the first time a federal judge ruled that a state agency, as a recipient of federal funds, had an obligation to investigate the ways a private project might have unfair and discriminatory effects on a subset of the community. When this case was appealed to the Third Circuit,[2] a record number of **amicus** ("friend of the court") briefs were filed on behalf of all litigants. Both business and civil rights groups had a high stake in the outcome. **Internet Assignment:** Find and read some of these amicus briefs. What were some of the policy arguments brought forward by the different groups as they attempted to influence the Court of Appeals?

2. On appeal, the Third Circuit found that the plaintiffs had no right to enforce Title VI's disparate impact regulations, the only enforceable right to be free of intentional discrimination. What kind of evidence would convince you that the permit-granting process was intentionally discriminatory? How do you imagine plaintiffs in a case like SCCIA would get such evidence?

3. Camden is not the only relatively powerless minority community with a concentration of heavily polluting industrial sites. In recent years, for example, toxic waste operators have considered Indian reservations and developing countries as potential disposal sites. Sometimes environmental justice advocates are able to pressure their way towards a more equitable outcome. Living through decades of industrial explosions and toxic leaks from the Royal Dutch/Shell-affiliated plants near her neighborhood in Norco, Louisiana—and watching cancer rates there rise sharply—brought Margie Eugene-Richard to the point of activism. She spearheaded negotiations that, by 2002, resulted in Shell buying the homes of the mostly low-income African-Americans in her community, enabling them to move away. Shell also agreed to upgrade its Norco facilities. **Internet Assignment:** Find out about an ongoing environmental justice project as near to where you live as possible. Which strategy is being employed—litigation, negotiation, or both?

4. Olga Pomar, the lead lawyer for the Waterfront South plaintiffs, has worked for a nonprofit organization that offers legal help to the poor for all but two of her twenty years in practice. She moved to Camden in 1994 to do hands-on community development, in search of the "immersion experience you get from this kind of work." She first helped build a neighborhood organization to identify local problems, then she provided the legal support to try to solve them.

---

1 In September 1999, well before SLC began construction, the NJDEP wrote a letter to the company warning that, since it would "be operating in an economically depressed area which has a substantial minority population, the Department will evaluate the need to conduct an Environmental Justice analysis." As Justice Orlovsky mentions in a footnote to his 120-page ruling, the "inexplicable" fact that such analysis was never performed was what triggered the whole lawsuit.

2 274 F.3d 771(3rd Cir. 2001).

Pomar has said that each of the attorneys in the team representing Waterfront South had different motivations for wanting to work on this difficult and time-consuming case:

> *For Luke [Cole of the Center on Race, Poverty and the Environment in San Francisco] and Jerry [Balter of the Public Interest Law Center of Philadelphia] it's an important environmental justice precedent. For Michael [Churchill—also of Philadelphia's PILC], it affects all other Title VI litigation. I'm so invested because I'm so invested in Camden.*

Think back to the different ethical frameworks described in Chapter 1. Now look again at the quote above. Can you identify the different ethical orientations that seem to be motivating the attorneys?

5. The analyses performed by both SLC and the NJDEP regarding levels of contamination caused by air pollution and the degree of benefits created by SLC's development of the Camden area were based on a regional—as opposed to a local—perspective. Does this make sense? What are the pros and cons of looking at polluting enterprise through the eyes of those closest to the point of impact?

6. **Internet Assignment:** (a) Go to http://www.epa.gov/airtrends/non.html and find out whether your city or county is located in one of the "nonattainment" areas, out of compliance with the EPA NAAQs. If it is, find out what is being done. Do you see involvement by the federal EPA? State EPA? Nonprofit organizations? Community groups? Is the situation trending towards better air?

7. **Internet Assignment:** Recent moves by the federal EPA have provoked reaction. In 2002, when George W. Bush signed a rule allowing thousands of industrial facilities to make upgrades without having to install new antipollution equipment, states like New York and New Jersey, which have to deal with much of the pollution that drifts from mid-Western power plants, moved to make their own regulations tighter. They are part of a fifteen-state lawsuit against the EPA to overturn the Bush rule. Find out what has happened to this suit. (b) In 2003, the EPA caused a stir when it determined that carbon dioxide, the main cause for global warming, could not be regulated as a pollutant. How did Congress respond?

8. **Internet Assignment:** A recent study tracking 500,000 people in 116 American cities for 16 years revealed that fine particulate air pollution is linked with higher rates of lung cancer and heart disease.[3] Experts note that this thorough and long-term research provides the strongest evidence so far that microscopic soot has dire human health consequences. It shows that the risk of developing lung cancer faced by many urban residents is comparable to that faced by people who live with smokers. In February 2001, the Supreme Court upheld the EPA's authority to set revised standards for ozone and particulate matter. Under a consent agreement with nine environmental groups, the EPA must issue a proposal on particulates by March 31, 2005. What was the result?

Environmental Protection Strategies

Statutory Law

Galvanized on the first Earth Day—April 22, 1970—the environmental movement helped create the political climate that would lead the U.S. Congress to mandate a new federal agency, the Environmental Protection Agency (EPA), and pass a series of laws protecting the environment. Over the ensuing years, the legislative framework in the United States—federal, state, and local regulations

3 *Journal of the American Medical Association,* March 6, 2002.

addressing pollution of the air, water, and land—grew to be the most comprehensive in the world. Yet this regulatory network is relatively new and, as of this writing, the head of the EPA is still not a cabinet level position. Below we briefly describe several federal environmental laws.

- The **Clean Air Act,**[4] first passed in 1970, regulates the emission of pollutants into the atmosphere. Under this law, national ambient air-quality standards (NAAQs) are set, and the release of certain major pollutants—particulates, toxins, and compounds that deplete stratospheric ozone, contribute to acid rain, and are dangerous to human health—are limited. As the *Camden Waterfront South* case demonstrates, the Clean Air Act is carried out and monitored by the states, which must submit "state implementation plans" (SIPS) for approval by the EPA. In the 1990 amendments to the Clean Air Act, Congress addressed "nonattainment" areas, the parts of the country that are not in compliance with the NAAQs, and new deadlines were set—from 5 to 20 years for compliance on ozone, for example.
- The **Clean Water Act (CWA)**[5] sets a goal of ending the discharge of pollutants into navigable waters, and provides federal funding of sewage treatment plants nationwide. Although CWA requires discharge permits, an April 2004 report by the Public Interest Research Group revealed that 60 percent of all major facilities discharged pollution in excess of their permits at least once between January 1, 2002 and June 30, 2003.[6] Regulations implementing the CWA were hotly contested throughout the Bush administration. The EPA first proposed, then abandoned, a re-definition of navigable waters that would have restricted the federal government's ability to regulate discharges into isolated wetlands and streams.
- The **Resource Conservation and Recovery Act (RCRA)**[7] sets up a "cradle-to-grave" program for the control of hazardous waste, regulating labeling, containers, transport and disposal sites.
- The **Comprehensive Environmental Response, Compensation, and Liability Act (CERCLA)**[8] is a liability scheme rather than a monitoring program. CERCLA created a $1.6 billion fund—**Superfund**—to finance the cleanup of toxic waste sites. For decades the government would collect from polluting companies to reimburse Superfund, but under the Bush administration most of the resources for cleanup will come from taxpayers. **Potentially responsible parties** include (1) owners or operators of hazardous waste sites, (2) those who owned or operated the sites when the hazardous material was deposited, (3) the "generators," or those who create the wastes, and (4) the transporters—those who carry it to the sites.

Other environmental laws deal with endangered species; pesticides; coastal management; the timber, mining, and oil industries; marine life; and so on. For many of these statutes, the federal version of each is either mirrored or implemented by legislation at state level. The EPA homepage, http://www.epa.gov, updates statutes and regulations.

Market-Based Incentives

By 1995, after 25 years overseeing thirteen extremely complicated laws, the Environmental Protection Agency could boast of many accomplishments. The number of Americans served by modern sewage treatment plants doubled. Sewage flow into waterways was cut by about one-third, and the proportion of waterways meeting clean water standards rose from 36 to 72 percent. Air pollution was improved by 25 percent—while our population increased by about

4 42 U.S.C. 7401 (1998).

5 33 U.S.C. sec. 7413(a)(2)(Supp. V 1993).

6 *Environmental Laboratory Washington Report,* Vol. 15, No.8, April 23, 2004.

7 42 U.S.C. Sec. 6901-6992k (1988 & Supp. V 1993).

8 42 U.S.C. Sec. 9601-9675 (1988 & Supp. V 1993). Amended in 1984 and 1986.

25 percent, vehicle miles traveled rose 111 percent, and our gross domestic product went up by 90 percent. The work still to be done by the EPA, though, is enormous, and differs somewhat from the kind of task it first faced. In the early years the agency dealt mainly with the type of environmental degradation—dirty smoke emitted from factory smokestacks, Love Canals, oil spills—that was blatant, and traceable to a few major industrial sources. At this point the problems are more insidious, and diffuse. They are generated by large firms but also by thousands of small businesses, by millions of individual consumers—and they surface here and transnationally as threats to forests, oceans, biodiversity and to global climate itself.

Over recent years, the comprehensive statutory scheme designed to protect our environment has come under attack. Its critics have been generally unopposed to the concept of environmental protection. Rather, they became convinced that the so-called "**command and control**" regulatory network was too complex, expensive, and inflexible. Some believed that costly regulation diminished the global competitiveness of American firms and was inefficient. Instead of forcing polluters to comply with preset governmental standards, they argued, why not integrate the profit motive into the mechanism for environmental protection, to drive change more effectively?

Such thinking was behind the **tradeable permit system** for sulfur dioxide emissions authorized by the 1990 Amendments to the Clean Air Act. Sulfur dioxide is a key culprit in producing acid rain, which not only defaces buildings, but lowers the pH levels in lakes, making them uninhabitable for fish and plants. Under the tradeable permit plan, the EPA auctions a set number of sulfur dioxide emission allowances annually, with each allowance permitting one ton of emissions. Companies can then use up their allowances for that year (by releasing sulfur dioxide), save them for future use, or sell their allowances to other companies. In this way pollution-reduction can occur in the most efficient way possible, because firms for whom emission-reduction is cheapest have the incentive to do more than meet the minimum standards, while those for whom it is too expensive to improve pollution controls will purchase more permits. Meanwhile, the overall emissions levels are held constant. While the so called "cap-and-trade" system appears to offer a desirable way to reduce certain pollutants such as sulfur dioxide and smog, it may not be the best way to handle others. Mercury, for example, affects the nervous system and is particularly harmful to children and developing fetuses. In its outgoing months, the Clinton administration EPA recommended that mercury not be traded, because of the danger of contamination "hotspots" developing around power plants that might choose to buy the right to emit mercury instead of installing technology to avoid mercury emissions. As of 2003, the Bush EPA was recommending tradeable permits for mercury. **Internet Assignment:** Find out what happened here.

Through the 1990s, regulators took advantage of "carrots" (market-based incentives) as well as "sticks" (injunctions, penalties) to bring environmental goals into focus. For example, Stone Container was first fined $244,800 by the EPA in 1992 for violations of RCRA at its plant in Panama City, Florida. Yet by October of that year the EPA and the company had reached a settlement for the payment of just $100,000. This was a result of Stone Container's suggestion that it should be allowed to invest much of the would-be fine into installing a new device that would reduce the use of sulfuric acid in the plant by 25 to 50 percent and would make use of recycled materials. The new system would cost about half a million dollars, but over time would save the firm money. So the settlement was a "win-win" all around—for Stone Container, for the government, and for the air. Such alternative enforcement measures may take the form of pollution prevention or reduction, restoration of damage to the environment, performing an "environmental audit" (a company studies and corrects its own environmental management practices) and public awareness projects (a company disseminates information about cleaner technologies to the public at large or within an industry).

Another alternative approach to environmental protection involves creative use of taxes. Traditionally, we tax many of the things we value; we levy taxes on paychecks, income, property, sales, businesses. But because taxation tends to discourage productive activity, why not use the power to tax for what it is: a reverse incentive? Why not, many argue, tax that which we do *not* value, such as pollution, congestion, sprawl, and resource depletion? Nine European governments do just that: Reducing taxes on the "goods," they instead tax the "bads," like toxic waste. This is called "tax shifting." A "green tax" is one that uses government taxing power to build sustainable economies and benefit the environment. **Internet Assignment:** Find an example of green taxes or environmental tax shifting, both in the United States and abroad. Compare the two. Which seems to offer the most promising solution? Which scheme generates "the greatest good for the greatest number"?

Consider these three means of controlling air pollution:

- @ Fines levied on companies that exceed set emission levels
- @ Taxing emissions
- @ Allowing a tradeable permit system for emissions

Compare and contrast the three approaches. Which would you want in your neighborhood? Which would you favor if you owned a polluting business?

Green Capitalism

> *The lesson is plain: pollution prevention works; pollution control does not. Only where production technology has been changed to eliminate the pollutant has the environment been substantially improved. Where it remains unchanged, where an attempt is made to trap the pollutant in an appended control device—the automobile's catalytic converter or the power plant's scrubber—environmental improvement is modest or nil. When a pollutant is attacked at the point of origin, it can be eliminated. But once it is produced, it is too late.*
>
> — Barry Commoner, 1989

Noted television journalist Bill Moyers speaks with Hunter Lovins in the next segment, taken from his show *Now With Bill Moyers,* aired on PBS on January 18, 2002. Lovins co-founded the Rocky Mountain Institute, an organization that describes itself as "independent, nonadversarial and transideological," with a mission to look to the free market system for ways to solve the energy needs of our society while sustaining the natural environment. As Moyers begins this interview, he asks Lovins if she believes the energy problem is a matter of U.S. dependence on foreign oil.

BILL MOYERS INTERVIEW OF HUNTER LOVINS

Lovins: People tend to define the energy problem as we're running out. And therefore we have to get more energy of any type from any source. In fact, the world is awash in energy.

As Pogo once said "we're confronted by insurmountable opportunities." What we really ought to be doing is choosing the best technologies to meet our needs for energy services at the least cost, in the ways that are most benign. And when you ask the question that way, the answer comes up energy efficiency and the various diverse renewable supplies of energy, which are what's winning in the marketplace today.

Moyers: The marketplace? You think the market can get us there?

Lovins: The market will absolutely get us there. Markets do work, but it will take a while. And if we care about getting off of imported oil, there are ways to do that. For example, just increasing the efficiency with which our cars burn gasoline by about three miles a gallon would eliminate our need to import any oil from the Mideast.

Moyers: But you hear all this talk in Washington that the answer to getting off dependence on oil is to develop fossil fuels at home. We'll use our oil to be free of foreign oil.

Lovins: The United States uses about 25% of the world's oil. We have reserves of about 3% or less. You do the math.

What has been proposed, for example, of drilling in the Arctic National Wildlife Refuge—assume that all the oil that the proponents hope is there is, in fact, there and it can be lifted economically. Those are two big assumptions that are probably not true. Assume they're true. It would provide about 1% of the oil that this country needs.

Moyers: For how long?

Lovins: For maybe a decade or so. Not very long.

Moyers: So it's not going to really liberate us from Middle Eastern oil.

Lovins: No. Now maybe the Gulf War in the early '90s was fought for other reasons. But myself, I think if Kuwait only grew broccoli, we would not have had our young men and women there in 0.7-mile-per-gallon tanks and 17-feet-per-gallon aircraft carriers. And if we had put our people in 32-mile-a-gallon cars, we wouldn't have needed any oil from the Middle East at all.

Moyers: And immediately, after 9/11, someone I respect very much in the environmental community called and said, "You know, this proves that our dependence on foreign oil, fossil fuels, is the Achilles Heel of American foreign policy." Do you think that's true?

Lovins: Clearly, our dependence on imported oil is costing us a lot of money; and it certainly contributed to that. And it's unnecessary.

Communities across the country have demonstrated alternatives. About ten years ago, Sacramento, California, voted to shut down its then-operating nuclear plant because it wasn't operating very well and it was costing a lot. That cut off about half the capacity to that community.

Instead, the utility invested in efficiency and in a diverse array of supply—solar, a little bit of wind, fuel cells, co-generation—all of this was relatively small scale, but collectively it made up all the energy they needed. Ten years later, the economics are in; the community is healthier. It has generated about $185 million, just this investment in efficiency and new supply. And it has generated hundreds of new jobs. . . .

Some of the American companies [are developing renewable energy resources. T]ake a look at Shell Oil, which recently created Shell Hydrogen. And as the head of it, Don Hubert, said the Stone Age didn't end because we ran out of stones; the Oil Age won't end because we ran out of oil. And Shell recently announced the end of oil and the beginning of the transition to Shell being an energy company supplying renewable energy—there's Shell renewables—and to ultimately an economy based on hydrogen. This would be a much more benign economy to have.

Hydrogen is the most plentiful element in the universe other than perhaps stupidity.

Now, suppose you drove a car that's powered by hydrogen. And most of the big car companies have hydrogen car programs already well in development. You will start to see hydrogen cars on the road within the next three to four years. So you drive your hydrogen car up to the building that has the fuel cell in it and the reformer making hydrogen. You plug your car into the reformer to get your hydrogen and into the grid. Your car, which has previously been an idle large asset, is now making electricity and selling it to the grid at the real time price, making you money.

The car fleet running around on the road is probably about ten times the generating capacity of all of the power plants of the electric utilities. You could displace all fossil plants just with this one measure. And these technologies exist and they're entering the marketplace.

Moyers: So the answer, as I read you, is not to hug a tree if you want to save the environment, but to hug an economist.

Lovins: (laughs) . . . Hug an entrepreneur. Hug somebody who's bringing these technologies into the marketplace and making money doing it.

• QUESTIONS •

1. **Internet Assignment:** Lovins claims that hydrogen-powered cars already exist, and that "they're already entering the marketplace." Is this true? What can you find regarding this technology? Which automakers seem to be most invested? Is the trend even across U.S., European, and Japanese manufacturers? What are the downsides to hydrogen-powered cars?
2. **Internet Assignment:** In the summer of 2004, the Apollo Alliance, a coalition of labor, community, business and environmental groups, released a commissioned study finding that if the United States invested $30 billion a year over 10 years in energy efficiency—updating older factories and using renewable fuels, for example—3.3 million jobs, $905 billion in personal income and $284 billion in energy savings would result. While there would be losses in the fossil fuel industries, America would dramatically reduce dependence on foreign oil and its economy would gain 10 times more jobs overall. As the country ramped up towards the election of 2004, energy policy was a hot topic. What happened in that election? Have there been changes in U.S. policy since then?
3. **Internet Assignment:** What are some of the most recent business applications for alternative energy resources? What applications can you find in the public sector? The Rocky Mountain Institute Web site is a good place to start.

George W. Bush and Environmental Policy

The next article argues that in its first three years the Bush administration was actively dismantling four decades worth of regulatory protections for the environment, a reversal of direction that could only be accomplished out of public view. The author writes: "No president has gone after the nation's environmental laws with the same fury as George W. Bush—and none has been so adept at staying under the radar."

DIRTY SECRETS

Osha Gray Davidson[9]

The Bush administration has been gutting key sections of the Clean Water and Clean Air acts, laws that have traditionally had bipartisan support and have done more to protect the health of Americans than any other environmental legislation. It has crippled the Superfund program, which is charged with cleaning up millions of pounds of toxic industrial wastes such as arsenic, lead, mercury, and vinyl chloride in more than 1,000 neighborhoods in 48 states. It has sought to cut the EPA's enforcement division by nearly one-fifth, to its lowest level on record; fines assessed for environmental violations dropped by nearly two-thirds in the administration's first two years; and criminal prosecutions—the government's weapon of last resort against the worst polluters—are down by nearly one-third.

The administration has [become] . . . the first not to voluntarily add a single species to the endangered species list. It has opened millions of acres of wilderness—including some of the nation's most environmentally sensitive public lands—to logging, mining, and oil and gas drilling. . . .

[T]he White House has all but denied the existence of what may be the most serious environmental problem of our time, global warming. After campaigning on a promise to reduce emissions of the greenhouse gas carbon dioxide, Bush made an abrupt about-face once elected, calling

9 *Mother Jones*, September/October 2003.

his earlier pledge "a mistake" and announcing that he would not regulate CO_2 emissions from power plants—even though the United States accounts for a fourth of the world's total industrial CO_2 emissions. Since then, the White House has censored scientific reports that mentioned the subject, walked away from the Kyoto agreement to reduce greenhouse-gas emissions, and even, at the behest of ExxonMobil, engineered the ouster of the scientist who chaired the United Nations Intergovernmental Panel on Climate Change.

So why aren't more people aware that George W. Bush is compiling what is arguably the worst environmental record of any president in recent history? The easy explanations—that environmental issues are complex, that war and terrorism push most other concerns off the front pages—are only part of the story. The real reason may be far simpler: Few people know the magnitude of the administration's attacks on the environment because the administration has been working very hard to keep it that way.

[The author claims that Bush has seeded the EPA with "anti-regulatory zealots," people who are "politically savvy and come from the very industries they're charged with regulating, [enabling the administration to implement] its ambitious pro-industry agenda—with a minimum of public notice."]

Take the case of mountaintop-removal coal mining. As the name implies, this method—the predominant form of strip mining in much of Appalachia—involves blasting away entire mountaintops to get at coal seams below and dumping the resulting rubble, called "spoil," into adjacent valleys. In some cases, valleys two miles long have been completely filled with spoil. Opponents had hoped that a court-ordered Environmental Impact Statement (EIS) would crack down on the practice, which has buried at least 1,000 miles of Appalachian streams and destroyed tens of thousands of acres of woodland that the EPA describes as "unique in the world" for their biological diversity. But when the Bush administration released the EIS [in spring 2003], it not only gave mountaintop removal a clean bill of health; it also relaxed what few meaningful environmental protections existed and focused on how to help mining companies obtain permits more easily.

So how did a process mandated by a federal judge "to minimize, to the maximum extent practicable, the adverse environmental effects" from mountaintop removal become a vehicle for industry? Two words: Steven Griles. . . . Before coming to work as deputy secretary of the Interior, Griles was one of the most powerful lobbyists in Washington, with a long list of energy-industry clients, including the National Mining Association and several of the country's largest coal companies. On August 1, 2001, Griles signed a "statement of disqualification," promising to stay clear of issues involving his former clients. Despite that promise . . . Griles met repeatedly with coal companies. . . . [O]n August 4, 2001—three days after signing his recusal letter—he gave a speech before the West Virginia Coal Association, reassuring members that "we will fix the federal rules very soon on water and spoil placement." Two months later, Griles sent a letter to the EPA and other agencies drafting the EIS, complaining that they were not doing enough to safeguard the future of mountaintop removal and instructing them to "focus on centralizing and streamlining coal mine permitting. . . ."

With key positions in the hands of industry veterans, the administration has been able to . . . steer clear of legislative battles and work instead within the difficult-to-understand, yawn-producing realm of agency regulations. . . .

[The author mentions the energy task force convened by Vice President Dick Cheney early in the Bush administration. The energy industry, which had given $2.8 million to the 2000 Bush campaign, had 63 representatives at those meetings; there was virtually no one present who might have offered an alternative view. Not surprisingly, the government's energy policy, when it was later announced, was strikingly pro-industry. The author believes the secretive Cheney task force was responsible for a strategy to weaken the Clean Air Act.]

Some 30,000 Americans die each year because the federal government is unwilling to take meaningful steps to enforce the Clean Air Act's standards for coal-fired power plants. Nearly 6,000 of those deaths are attributable to plants owned by a mere eight companies, according to a study by ABT Associates, which frequently conducts assessments for the EPA. (The companies are American Electric Power, Cinergy, Duke, Dynegy, FirstEnergy, SIGECO, Southern Company, and the Tennessee Valley Authority.)

When Congress passed the current air-pollution standards in 1977, it grandfathered in these aging plants and some 16,000 other industrial facilities. . . . Under a provision known as New Source Review, the plants could perform routine maintenance without having to install cleaner technologies, but any substantive changes or expansions leading to increased emissions would force the operators to meet the new standards. The grace period was expected to last just a few years—a reasonable compromise, it must have seemed to Congress at the time. Yet, for nearly three decades these facilities have gotten around the New Source Review rules by continually expanding and calling it "routine maintenance."

In 1999, the EPA's then-director of enforcement, Eric Schaeffer [began to] actually enforce the law. The agency filed suit against eight power companies that together emitted one-fifth of the nation's total output of sulfur dioxide, . . . the leading cause of acid rain. Soon, violators started lining up to negotiate settlements. By the end of 2000, two of the largest power companies had agreed to cut emissions by two-thirds. And then George W. Bush took office. The new administration immediately leaked its intentions to expand, rather than close, the New Source Review loophole. . . . Not surprisingly, the two tentative agreements the EPA had worked out evaporated.

Meanwhile, in a classic bit of greenwashing, the White House has released a plan called "Clear Skies" that will, in President Bush's words, "dramatically reduce pollution from power plants." In fact, Clear Skies would gut the standards of the Clean Air Act, allowing companies to wait 15 more years to install state-of-the-art pollution-control equipment—and even then, power plants would be emitting far more pollution than allowed under current law, for a total of 450,000 tons of additional nitrogen oxide, 1 million tons of sulfur dioxide, and 9.5 tons of mercury annually. . . .

In January 2003, the administration proposed new rules for managing the nation's wetlands, removing 20 percent of the country's remaining swamps, ponds, and marshes from federal protection. And wetlands are only the beginning: A close reading of the proposed rules shows that the administration is attempting to change the definition of "waters of the United States" to exclude up to 60 percent of the country's rivers, lakes, and streams from protection, giving industries permission to pollute, alter, fill, and build on all of these waterways. . . . "No president since the Clean Water Act was passed has proposed getting rid of it on the majority of waters of the U.S.," notes Joan Mulhern of Earthjustice—and Bush might not have tried either, had he been forced to justify the move in congressional debate rather than burying it in bureaucratic rule-making. . . .

By using stealth tactics to pursue a corporate agenda, the Bush administration is undermining the very landscape of democracy, which depends on an informed citizenry, transparency in government, and lively public debate. A culture of deception and deceit erodes all of these—and that is probably the most serious "environmental" damage of all.

• QUESTIONS •

1. **Internet Assignment:** The writer believes that the Bush administration has achieved its undoing of the apparatus of environmental protection "under the radar," largely because it placed pro-industry people in key bureaucratic positions. What can you find out about the backgrounds of the following members of the Bush administration? How were they educated? What kinds of jobs did they hold before they joined the government? What kind of expertise did they develop?

   @ James L. Connaughton, Council on Environmental Quality
   @ Allan Fitzsimmons, Wildlands Fuels Coordinator, Dept. of the Interior
   @ Dale Bosworth, Chief, U.S. Forest Service

- @ Rebecca Watson, Ass't. Sec'y for Land & Minerals Management, Dept. of the Interior
- @ Kathleen Clarke, Director, Bureau of Land Management
- @ David Bernhardt, Director of Congressional & Legislative Affairs, Dept. of the Interior
- @ Jeffrey Holmstead, Ass't. Administrator, Air & Radiation, EPA
- @ Marriane Horinko, Acting Administrator, EPA
- @ Bennett Raley, Ass't. Sec'y for Water & Science, Dept. of the Interior
- @ Patricia Lynn Scarlett, Ass't. Sec'y Policy, Management & Budget, Dept. of the Interior

2. **Internet Assignment:** Find out what you can about the author, Osha Gray Davidson. What background does he bring to this exposé? Has he written for other publications? Find out about *Mother Jones.* What is the history of the magazine? Who is on its editorial board? What impact has its investigatory reporting had on policies and politics?

3. In the area of the environment, as with so many public policy issues, views are sharply at odds. In the article you just read, Osha Gray Davidson makes a strong argument against the Bush administration as a steward of the environment. (a) What evidence does he cite to support his views? How convincing is it? (b) Identify the ethical conflicts mentioned by Davidson. Use ethical analysis from Chapter 1 to evaluate each. (c) **Internet Assignment:** Visit a Web site that favors the Bush approach to environmental policy. How does it answer some of the charges made by the author of the article? What positive claims are made on behalf of legislation such as the "Clear Skies" or the "Healthy Forests" initiatives? Select one environmental area, such as clean air or wetlands. Investigate it from differing views. Which perspective seems most convincing? Why? Try the Heritage Foundation for information about the Bush administration and http://www.nrdc.org for the opposition.

4. **Internet Assignment:** As of June 2004, the EPA reported that the amount of toxic pollutants in U.S. land, air, and water had risen by 5 percent, the biggest increase since the agency began tracking toxins in 1988. Industry released almost 5 billion tons of toxins into the environment in 2002. Mercury and lead levels rose 10 and 3 percent respectively, according to the report. Find out about current levels nationally or in your area.

5. In February 2002, in the wake of the Enron scandal, the U.S. General Accounting Office of the U.S. Congress requested the names of those who had attended the secret meetings of the National Energy Policy Development Group (NEPDG). Led by Vice President Cheney in 2001, NEPDG was a task force charged with formulating the Bush administration's energy policy. Cheney refused to disclose names or the subjects discussed, claiming a right to privacy. To be forced to reveal such information, he said, would interfere with need of the executive branch to get "unvarnished" advice from its chosen advisors. Congress backed down, but Judicial Watch and other public interest groups sued to get the information. **Internet Assignment:** Find out if the "who"s and "what"s of this Task Force have been identified.

6. **Internet Assignment:** Although the United States emits one-quarter of the world's carbon dioxide, the Bush administration has rejected the terms of the Kyoto Protocol, an international effort to limit greenhouse gases and address climate change. Signed by 130 countries and international blocs, and effective February 16, 2005, the treaty is not without its critics. Why did the U.S. government refuse to sign? What counterarguments can you make?

7. **Internet Assignment:** Investigate Davidson's claims about censorship by the Bush administration. Were scientific reports on global warming changed or kept from the public? What reports? If they were changed, how? If language was omitted, what language? Did the U.S. government act to unseat the scientist who chaired the UN panel on climate change? Did it take any other actions to sway public knowledge about global warming?

Catching Up to the Cost of Global Warming[10]

In July 2004 a financial analyst at Merrill Lynch held a teleconference to discuss a disturbing issue for the U.S. auto industry: the risk associated with new global warming regulations. According to one reputable forecast, domestic firms like Ford and G.M. had much to worry about.

Factors driving this analysis include existing and pending environmental regulation in the U.S. and abroad. In 2004 China, the fastest-growing auto market in the world, was preparing to introduce fuel economy standards, while the EU and Japan were already phasing in cuts on car emissions. Although the Bush administration had refused to sign the Kyoto Protocol, California had its own regulations and there was the possibility that many states in the U.S. Northeast would follow suit.

According to the analyst's report, for American automakers, the costs of responding to global warming regulation would be much more than for their competitors in Europe and Japan:

> *Ford would have to spend $403 more on each vehicle to meet the expected new standards, the report estimates, and G.M. would have to spend $377 more. By contrast, the added cost to Honda would be just $24.*
>
> *Car for car, BMW would have to spend even more than Ford or G.M., $649 on each vehicle, the report found, but because its prices are much higher, it would not be as difficult for it to absorb the cost.*

Perhaps the most troubling finding for G.M. and Ford, the last two major automakers based in the United States, is that some foreign competitors, particularly Toyota, may actually be helped by tougher regulations because they have already invested much more in fuel-efficiency technologies, like hybrid gas-electric engine systems, that could generate profits.

The analyst expressed real concern about the risks of major policy adjustments:

> *There's the potential for a confluence of events to occur. Americans could be more concerned about climate change, while at the same time we try to reduce our dependence on the Middle East for oil, for national security or political reasons. If these two strands come together, that would put a lot of pressure on policy makers, which would invariably lead back to higher fuel-economy standards.*

In the U.S., car manufacturers experience strong sales of SUVs and pickup trucks—the least fuel efficient vehicles. The analyst noted that fuel economy was "not high on the agenda of the U.S. consumer," adding, "Are these companies going to have successful strategies to compete in countries like China, where fuel prices are higher, and incomes are certainly lower and road space is considerably more limited?"

In 2004 the Carbon Disclosure Project revealed that of the world's 500 largest companies, only 35 to 40 percent were doing anything to address the risks posed by global warming to their financial viability. Particularly noted for their inaction were American firms, including auto manufacturers, utilities and gas and oil producers.

10 Danny Hakim, *The New York Times,* July 25, 2004. The Merrill Lynch U.S. auto analyst was John A. Casesa.

Corporate Governance: Shareholder Activism

Shareholders have the right to attempt to influence the actions of the management. They can do this by putting nonbinding proposals forward—called resolutions—to be voted upon at annual shareholder meetings. Until the 1970s, shareholder resolutions tended to focus on bottom line concerns. But in 1971, the Episcopal Church filed the first church-sponsored shareholder resolution, challenging General Motor's operations in the apartheid regime in South Africa, and sparking others to make proposals related to corporate social responsibility. Today, shareholder activism continues to grow, with proposals each year on a range of issues, from executive compensation to diversity to the environment.

The Proxy System

In advance of each annual meeting, shareholders are sent form ballots listing the items that are up for vote, including membership on the board of directors, choice of an outside auditor, and resolutions brought by the board or shareholders. Each share of stock generally counts as one vote.[11] Shareholders have the right to come to the annual meetings in person to cast their ballots, but few do. If they prefer, shareholders can vote by returning the "proxy card" that is mailed along with the notice of the meeting. The board of directors has the right to vote the shares of those who neither appear nor return a completed proxy vote. Given the large number of individuals who own stock in the typical publicly owned corporation, few of whom have a big block of shares, this system assures corporate control of the majority of the votes.

Preliminary Management Resistance

Getting a shareholder resolution voted upon is not automatic. Management may strongly disagree with the proposal, and has the right to write a statement in opposition (with no length limit) that will appear on the ballot ("proxy statement"), effectively killing the proposal. In the face of outright opposition from management, shareholder proposals are often withdrawn before a vote.

Broad Policy Proposals Only

According to SEC rules regarding shareholder proposals, there are thirteen circumstances under which a corporation may "omit" or ignore the resolution.[12] For example, resolutions may not deal with "the conduct of the ordinary business operations" of a company. This means that shareholders may not make proposals dealing with how the firm is actually run, but may only offer suggestions regarding overall corporate policy. Shareholders may propose that the company review its human resource policies with regard to homosexuals, for example, but may not propose that human resource personnel hire a certain proportion of gay men and women; shareholders may propose that a company conduct an audit of its practices regarding recycling and renewable energy use, but they may not offer specifics outlining how it would carry out such a plan.

In the wake of Enron and other corporate scandals, large institutional investors—controlling the pension funds for employees of an entire city or state, for example—have taken a self-protective interest in corporate governance, and in the shareholder resolution process. For example, they have focused on that fact that, in many firms, the CEO is also the Chairman of the Board,

---

11 Most states permit corporations to issue several classes of stock. Traditionally, only common stock had voting rights, although that law has changed in some states.

12 17 *Code of Federal Regulations (CFR)* Ch. II, Sec. 240.14a-8.

creating an inherent conflict of interest: The legal, fiduciary and ethical obligations belonging to top management can be at odds with those of the board, with its watchdog function. In a sharply contested proxy fight in 2004, institutional investors backed a proposal that Walt Disney, Inc. oust its CEO Michael Eisner. He was removed as CEO—although he remained as Chairman of Disney's Board.

Mere Recommendations, but with Moral Authority

Even if a proposal makes it onto the ballot, and even if an impressive proportion of shareholders votes for it, the result is merely advisory—or "nonbinding." Management still has the right to respond to the issue in some different way, or to ignore the resolution altogether. However, most corporate boards realize the appropriateness of making some kind of compromise with popular shareholder measures, and shareholder resolutions have been an effective means of forcing change even in the absence of majority shareholder approval. Recently, resolutions have brought on changes in corporate governance, accounting practices and environmental policies. For example, in 2003, Ford Motor Company opened a dialogue with sponsors of a shareholder proposal that the company report on its greenhouse gas emissions; at Occidental Petroleum shareholders agreed to withdraw their proposal once the company promised to report its carbon emissions and climate change data more fully. Spurred on by environmental organizations and socially conscious investment funds, shareholders filed dozens of global warming resolutions with U.S. firms in 2004, a trend that appears to be building. Many of these proposals garnered upwards of 20 percent approval, a high proportion, given the process.

Below is a sample shareholder resolution. It was put forward in 2004 by investors in American International Group, Inc. (AIG—Chubb Insurance its subsidiary), requesting that it assess the risks to its business presented by global climate change. The lead sponsors included "socially responsible" investment funds.[13] The insurance company decided to omit this resolution from its proxy statement.

SHAREHOLDER RESOLUTION ON CLIMATE CHANGE

Resolved:

The shareholders request that the Board of Directors prepare a report, at reasonable cost and omitting proprietary information, made available to shareholders by September 30, 2004, providing a comprehensive assessment of Chubb's strategies to address the impacts of climate change on its business.

Supporting Statements:

- We believe the human contribution to climate change has become widely accepted among the scientific community. Legislation, regulation, litigation, and other responses to climate change seem likely.
- "In global warming, we are facing an enormous risk to the U.S. economy and retirement finds that Wall Street has so far chosen to ignore." (Philip Angelides, Treasurer of California). . . .
- In November 2003, as a part of the Carbon Disclosure Project, 87 institutional investors representing over $9 trillion in assets wrote to the 500 largest companies by market

13 (Walden Asset Management, Calvert Asset Management Company, Progressive Investment Management), religious investors (Community Church of New York, Congregation of the Sisters of St. Joseph of Brighton), environmental groups (Conservation Land Trust, Tides Foundation) and government pension funds (State of Connecticut Treasurer's Office, State of Maine, Office of the Treasurer).

capitalization asking for relevant information concerning greenhouse gas emissions. According to the Project Coordinator, "There are potential business risks and opportunities related to actions stemming from climate change that have implications for the value of shareholdings in corporations worldwide."

- Munich Re's 2002 Annual Report states that climate related catastrophes are the greatest cost to the industry. Of the 35 largest natural catastrophes that cost insurers over €1 billion, only two were not climate related. Climate change may lead to increased erratic and extreme weather events, resulting in serious environmental and public health impacts.
- Swiss Re sees inaction on climate change as a possible liability for directors and officers (D&O), and is considering potential coverage implications for insured companies that do not address climate change risks. As D&O liability insurance is a significant part of Chubb's business, we believe investors should know how the company is addressing this issue.

We believe proactive behavior in the European Union, Japan and elsewhere may put U.S. companies at a competitive disadvantage globally. Of 84 signatories to the United Nations Environmental Programme Financial Initiatives Insurance Industry Initiative, only three are North American companies. Chubb is not a signatory.

- "Catastrophe insurers can't simply extrapolate past experience. If there is truly 'global warming,' for example, the odds would shift, since tiny changes in atmospheric conditions can produce momentous changes in weather patterns." (Warren Buffet, Chairman, Berkshire Hathaway, 1993)
- With property and casualty customers in 29 countries, we believe Chubb is exposed to climate risks. . . .
- Chubb's Annual Report has, since 1997, stated under the heading *Catastrophe Exposure*, "We also continue to explore and analyze credible scientific evidence, including the impact of global climate change, that may affect our potential exposure under insurance policies." Chubb has not responded to investor requests for additional information.

Environmental Philosophy

> *All the animals which can be taken upon the earth, in the sea, or in the air, that is to say, wild animals, belong to those who take them.*
>
> — Digest of Justinian

> *Every man . . . has an equal right of pursuing and taking to his own use all such creatures as are [wild].*
>
> — W. Blackstone, *Commentaries* 411 (1766)

The quotes above reflect the traditional Western Judeo-Christian understanding of the virtually unqualified right of men to control, to own, to "take" whatever can be taken from the natural world. In the late seventeenth century, political theorist John Locke wrote a justification of the natural right of each person, by dint of the labor he invested in it, to unlimited private property. Locke's thinking would greatly influence those who conceptualized and brought into existence the modern liberal democratic state, particularly those who established the American Republic.

SECOND TREATISE OF GOVERNMENT

John Locke

Of Property

§ 27. Though the earth, and all inferior creatures, be common to all men, yet every man has a property in his own person: this no body has any right to but himself. The labour of his body, and the work of his hands, we may say, are properly his. Whatsoever then he removes out of the state that nature hath provided, and left it in, he hath mixed his labour with, and joined to it something that is his own, and thereby makes it his property. It being by him removed from the common state nature hath placed it in, it hath by this labour something annexed to it, that excludes the common right of other men: for this labour being the unquestionable property of the labourer, no man but he can have a right to what that is once joined to, at least where there is enough, and as good, left in common for others.

§ 28. He that is nourished by the acorns he picked up under an oak, or the apples he gathered from the trees in the wood, has certainly appropriated them to himself. . . . That labour put a distinction between them and common: that added something to them more than nature, the common mother of all, had done; and so they became his private right. . . .

§ 30. . . . [W]hat fish any one catches in the ocean, that great and still remaining common of mankind . . . is by the labour that removes it out of that common state nature left it in, made his property . . . . And . . . the hare that any one is hunting, is thought his who pursues her during the chase . . . whoever has employed so much labour . . . as to find and pursue her, has thereby removed her from the state of nature, wherein she was common, and hath begun a property. . . .

§ 32. . . . As much land as a man tills, plants, improves, cultivates, and can use the product of so much is his property. He by his labour does, as it were, inclose it from the common. Nor will it invalidate his right, to say every body else has an equal title to it; and therefore he cannot appropriate, he cannot inclose, without the consent of all his fellow-commoners, all mankind. . . . God and his reason commanded him to subdue the earth, i.e. to improve it for the benefit of life. . . .

§ 33. Nor was the appropriation of any parcel of land, by improving it, any prejudice to any other man, since there was still enough, and as good left. . . . So that, in effect, there was never the less left for others because of his inclosure for himself: for he that leaves as much as another can make use of, does as good as take nothing at all. No body could think himself injured by the drinking of another man, though he took a good draught, who had a whole river of the same water left him to quench his thirst. . . .

§ 46. The greatest part of things really useful to the life of man, and such as the necessity of subsisting made the first commoners of the world look after, as it doth the Americans now, are generally things of short duration; such as, if they are not consumed by use, will decay and perish of themselves: gold, silver and diamonds, are things that fancy or agreement hath put the value on, more than real use, and the necessary support of life. Now of those good things which nature hath provided in common, every one had a right . . . to as much as he could use, and property in all that he could effect with his labour; all that his industry could extend to, to alter from the state nature had put it in, was his. He that gathered a hundred bushels of acorns or apples, had thereby a property in them, they were his goods as soon as gathered. He was only to look, that he used them before they spoiled, else he took more than his share, and robbed others. And indeed it was a foolish thing, as well as dishonest, to hoard up more than he could make use of. If he gave away a part to any body else, so that it perished not uselessly in his possession, these he also made use of. And if he also bartered away plums that would have rotted in a week, for nuts that would last good for his eating a whole year, he did no injury; he wasted not the common stock; destroyed no part of the portion of goods that belonged to others, so long as nothing perished uselessly in his hands. Again, if he would give his nuts for a piece of metal, pleased with its colour; or exchange his sheep for shells, or wool for a sparkling pebble or a diamond, and keep those by him all his life, he invaded not the right of others, he might heap up as much of these durable things as he pleased; the exceeding of the bounds of his just property not lying in the largeness of his possession, but the perishing of any thing uselessly in it.

§ 47. And thus came in the use of money. . . .

Of Paternal Power

§ 57. So that, however it may be mistaken, the end of law is not to abolish or restrain, but to preserve and enlarge freedom: for in all the states of created beings capable of laws, where there is no law, there is no freedom: for liberty is to be free from restraint and violence from others; which cannot be, where there is no law: but freedom is not, as we are told, a liberty for every man to do what he wishes: (for who could be free, when every other man's humour might domineer over him?) but a liberty to dispose, and order as he wishes, his person, actions, possessions, and his whole property, within the allowance of those laws under which he is, and therein not to be subject to the arbitrary will of another, but freely follow his own. . . .

Of the Ends of Political Society and Government

§ 123. If man in the state of nature be so free, as has been said; if he be absolute lord of his own person and possessions, equal to the greatest, and subject to no body, why will he part with his freedom? Why will he give up this empire, and subject himself to the dominion and control of any other power? To which it is obvious to answer, that though in the state of nature he hath such a right, yet the enjoyment of it is very uncertain, and constantly exposed to the invasion of others: for all being kings as much as he . . . and the greater part no strict observers of equity and justice, the enjoyment of the property he has in this state is very unsafe, very unsecure. This makes him willing to quit a condition, which, however free, is full of fears and continual dangers: and it is not without reason, that he seeks out, and is willing to join in society with others. . . .

§ 124. The great and chief end, therefore, of men's uniting into commonwealths, and putting themselves under government, is the preservation of their property. . . .

Of the Extent of the Legislative Power

§ 138. Thirdly, The supreme power cannot take from any man any part of his property without his own consent: for the preservation of property being the end of government, and that for which men enter into society, it necessarily supposes and requires, that the people should have property, without which they must be supposed to lose that, by entering into society, which was the end for which they entered into it; too gross an absurdity for any man to own. Men therefore in society having property, they have such a right to the goods, which by the law of the community are theirs, that no body hath a right to take their substance or any part of it from them, without their own consent: without this they have no property at all; for I have truly no property in that which another can by right take from me, when he pleases, against my consent. Hence it is a mistake to think, that the supreme or legislative power of any common-wealth, can do what it will, and dispose of the estates of the subject arbitrarily, or take any part of them at pleasure. . . .

• QUESTIONS •

1. According to Locke, what gives a person the right to own property? Is there any limitation on that right?
2. Why does Locke believe people form government?

Deep Ecology

> *A human being is part of the [W]hole, . . . a part limited by time and space. We experience ourself . . . as something separated from the rest—a kind of optical delusion of our consciousness. This delusion is a kind of prison for us, restricting us to our personal desires and to affection for a few persons nearest to us. Our task must be to free ourselves from this prison by widening our circle of compassion.*
>
> — Albert Einstein

Science and common sense tell us that human communities are ultimately deeply embedded within the natural world, that we must understand and nourish our interconnectedness with nature because our survival depends upon it. Businesses, just like other human groupings, depend on the continued existence of the natural world for the resources that allow them to continue. One way to understand the need for sustainable development, then, is purely instrumental. That is, the natural world is of value to humankind because humankind wants to use it to meet its various needs—material, and also psychological, spiritual. Some would go further and place environmentalism on a rights-based foundation. Although the U.S. Constitution does not name the right to a livable environment, arguably we each have such a right.[14]

Whether viewed as a means to human ends or as a right we each possess, we tend to conceptualize the importance of preservation of our natural world in terms of what it means to human beings. This is an **androcentric** perspective, experiencing, explaining and reasoning always from the human vantage point.

Some criticize this human-centeredness, and urge that we become **biocentric** in our approach to the environment. For them, the ethical stance is one that values the continued existence of the entire natural world for its own sake, not because of anything it can do for us. Supporters of what is sometimes called **deep ecology** insist that the rich diversity of life in all forms has intrinsic value, and that human beings have no right to threaten or reduce it, but rather have the obligation to change policies and behaviors that do so.

A SAND COUNTY ALMANAC

Aldo Leopold

Wilderness

For the first time in the history of the human species, two changes are now impending. One is the exhaustion of wilderness in the more habitable portions of the globe. The other is the world-wide hybridization of cultures through modern transport and industrialization. Neither can be prevented, and perhaps should not be, but the question arises whether, by some slight amelioration of the impending changes, certain values can be preserved that would otherwise be lost.

---

14 Some states have amended their constitutions to mention such rights. The *Constitution of Pennsylvania,* for instance, now reads:

> The people have a right to clean air, pure water, and to the preservation of the natural, scenic, historic and aesthetic values of the environment. Pennsylvania's natural resources . . . are the common property of all the people, including generations yet to come. As trustee of these resources, the Commonwealth shall preserve and maintain them for the benefit of all the people.

To the laborer in the sweat of his labor, the raw stuff on his anvil is an adversary to be conquered. So was wilderness an adversary to the pioneer.

But to the laborer in repose, able for the moment to cast a philosophical eye on his world, that same raw stuff is something to be loved and cherished, because it gives definition and meaning to his life.

This is a plea for the preservation of some tag-ends of wilderness, as museum pieces, for the edification of those who may one day wish to see, feel, or study the origins of their cultural inheritance.

The Ethical Sequence

This extension of ethics, so far studied only by philosophers, is actually a process in ecological evolution. Its sequences may be described in ecological as well as in philosophical terms. An ethic, ecologically, is a limitation on freedom of action in the struggle for existence. An ethic, philosophically, is a differentiation of social from anti-social conduct. These are two definitions of one thing. The thing has its origin in the tendency of interdependent individuals or groups to evolve modes of co-operation. The ecologist calls these symbioses. Politics and economics are advanced symbioses in which the original free-for-all competition has been replaced, in part, by co-operative mechanisms with an ethical content.

The complexity of co-operative mechanisms has increased with population density, and with the efficiency of tools. It was simpler, for example, to define the anti-social uses of sticks and stones in the days of the mastodons than of bullets and billboards in the age of motors.

There is as yet no ethic dealing with mans' relation to land and to the animals and plants which grow upon it. Land, like Odysseus' slave-girls, is still property. The land-relation is still strictly economic, entailing privileges but not obligations.

Individual thinkers since the days of Ezekiel and Isaiah have asserted that the despoliation of land is not only inexpedient but wrong. Society, however, has not yet affirmed their belief. I regard the present conservation movement as the embryo of such an affirmation.

Animal instincts are modes of guidance for the individual in meeting such situations. Ethics are possibly a kind of community instinct in-the-making.

The Community Concept

All ethics so far evolved rest upon a single premise: that the individual is a member of a community of interdependent parts. His instincts prompt him to compete for his place in that community, but his ethics prompt him also to co-operate (perhaps in order that there may be a place to compete for).

The land ethic simply enlarges the boundaries of the community to include soils, waters, plants, and animals, or collectively: the land.

This sounds simple: do we not already sing our love for and obligation to the land of the free and the home of the brave? Yes, but just what and whom do we love? Certainly not the soil, which we are sending helter-skelter downriver. Certainly not the waters, which we assume have no function except to turn turbines, float barges, and carry off sewage. Certainly not the plants, of which we exterminate whole communities without batting an eye. Certainly not the animals, of which we have already extirpated many of the largest and most beautiful species. A land ethic of course cannot prevent the alteration, management, and use of these "resources," but it does affirm their right to continued existence, and, at least in spots, their continued existence in a natural state.

In short, a land ethic changes the role of Homo sapiens from conqueror of the land-community to plain member and citizen of it. It implies respect for his fellow-members, and also respect for the community as such.

In human history, we have learned (I hope) that the conqueror role is eventually self-defeating. Why? Because it is implicit in such a role that the conqueror knows . . . just what makes the community clock tick, and just what and who is valuable, and what and who is worthless, in community life. It always turns out that he knows neither, and this is why his conquests eventually defeat themselves. . . .

Free Market Ideology

A being has rights only if it is a rational, free moral agent with the ability to regulate and guide its life in accordance with some overall conception it chooses to accept.

— Robert Nozick

WHY I AM NOT AN ENVIRONMENTALIST

Steven E. Landsburg[15]

Economics is the science of competing preferences. Environmentalism goes beyond science when it elevates matters of *preference* to matters of *morality*. A proposal to pave a wilderness and put up a parking lot is an occasion for conflict between those who prefer wilderness and those who prefer convenient parking. In the ensuing struggle, each side attempts to impose its preferences by manipulating the political and economic systems. Because one side must win and one side must lose, the battle is hard-fought and sometimes bitter. All of this is to be expected. . . .

Economics forces us to confront a fundamental symmetry. The conflict arises because each side wants to allocate the same resource in a different way. Jack wants his woodland at the expense of Jill's parking space and Jill wants her parking space at the expense of Jack's woodland. The formulation is morally neutral and should serve as a warning against assigning exalted moral status to either Jack or Jill.

The symmetries run deeper. Environmentalists claim that wilderness should take precedence over parking because a decision to pave is "irrevocable." Of course they are right, but they overlook the fact that a decision *not* to pave is *equally* irrevocable. Unless we pave today, my opportunity to park tomorrow is lost as irretrievably as tomorrow itself will be lost. The ability to park in a more distant future might be a quite inadequate substitute for that lost opportunity.

A variation on the environmentalist theme is that we owe the wilderness option not to ourselves but to future generations. But do we have any reason to think that future generations will prefer inheriting the wilderness to inheriting the profits from the parking lot? That is one of the first questions that would be raised in any honest scientific inquiry.

Another variation is that the parking lot's developer is motivated by profits, not preferences. To this there are two replies. First, the developer's profits are generated by his customers' preferences; the ultimate conflict is not with the developer but with those who prefer to park. Second, the implication of the argument is that a preference for a profit is somehow morally inferior to a preference for a wilderness, which is just the sort of posturing that the argument was designed to avoid.

It seems to me that the "irrevocability" argument, the "future generations" argument, and the "preferences not profits" argument all rely on false distinctions that wither before honest scrutiny. . . .

---

15 Steven Landsburg is Associate Professor of economics at the University of Rochester. The excerpt is from *The Armchair Economist: Economics and Everyday Life* (New York: MacMillan, 1993), pp. 224-227.

The hallmark of science is a commitment to follow arguments to their logical conclusions; the hallmark of certain kinds of religion is a slick appeal to logic followed by a hasty retreat if it points in an unexpected direction. Environmentalists can quote reams of statistics on the importance of trees and then jump to the conclusion that recycling paper is a good idea. But the opposite conclusion makes equal sense. I am sure that if we found a way to recycle beef, the population of cattle would go down, not up. If you want ranchers to keep a lot of cattle, you should eat a lot of beef. Recycling paper eliminates the incentive for paper companies to plant more trees and can cause forests to shrink. If you want large forests, your best strategy might be to use paper as wastefully as possible—or lobby for subsidies to the logging industry. Mention this to an environmentalist. My own experience is that you will be met with some equivalent of the beatific smile of a door-to-door evangelist stumped by an unexpected challenge, but secure in his grasp of Divine Revelation.

This suggests that environmentalists—at least the ones I have met—have no real interest in maintaining the tree population. If they did, they would seriously inquire into the long-term effects of recycling. I suspect that they don't want to do that because their real concern is with the ritual of recycling itself, not with its consequences. The underlying need to sacrifice, and to compel others to sacrifice, is a fundamentally religious impulse.

Environmentalists call on us to ban carcinogenic pesticides. They choose to overlook the consequence that when pesticides are banned, fruits and vegetables become more expensive, people eat fewer of them, and cancer rates consequently rise. If they really wanted to reduce cancer rates, they would weigh this effect in the balance.

Environmentalism has its apocalyptic side. Species extinctions, we are told, have consequences that are entirely unpredictable, making them too dangerous to risk. But unpredictability cuts both ways. One lesson of economics is that the less we know, the more useful it is to experiment. If we are completely ignorant about the effects of extinction, we can pick up a lot of valuable knowledge by wiping out a few species to see what happens. I doubt that scientists really *are* completely ignorant in this area; what interests me is the environmentalists' willingness to *plead* complete ignorance when it suits their purposes and to retreat when confronted with an unexpected consequence of their own position.

In October 1992 an entirely new species of monkey was discovered in the Amazon rain forest and touted in the news media as a case study in why the rain forests must be preserved. My own response was rather in the opposite direction. I lived a long time without knowing about this monkey and never missed it. Its discovery didn't enrich my life, and if it had gone extinct without ever being discovered, I doubt that I would have missed very much.

There are other species I care more about, maybe because I have fond memories of them from the zoo or from childhood storybooks. Lions, for example. I would be sorry to see lions disappear, to the point where I might be willing to pay up to about $50 a year to preserve them. I don't think I'd pay much more than that. If lions mean less to you than they do to me, I accept our difference and will not condemn you as a sinner. If they mean more to you than to me, I hope you will extend the same courtesy.

In the current political climate, it is frequently taken as an axiom that the U.S. government should concern itself with the welfare of Americans first; it is also frequently taken as an axiom that air pollution is always and everywhere a bad thing. You might, then, have expected a general chorus of approval when the chief economist of the World Bank suggested that it might be a good thing to relocate high-pollution industries to Third World countries. To most economists, this is a self-evident opportunity to make not just Americans but *everybody* better off. People in wealthy countries can afford to sacrifice some income for the luxury of cleaner air; people in poorer countries are happy to breathe inferior air in exchange for the opportunity to improve their incomes. But when the bank economist's observation was leaked to the media, parts of the environmental community went ballistic. To them, pollution is a form of sin. They seek not to improve our welfare, but to save our souls. . . .

Biodiversity and Habitat Preservation

> *Extinction is irreversible, we lose diversity, beauty, a genetic resource, a natural wonder, a souvenir of the past. But more underlies these, really a religious reason. Life is a sacred thing, and we ought not to be careless about it. This applies not only to experienced life, but to preservation of the lesser zoological and botanical species. Species enter and exit the natural theater, but only over geologic time and selected to fit evolving habitats. Individuals have their intrinsic worth, but particular individuals come and go, while that wave of life in which they participate overleaps the single lifespan millions of times.*[16]
>
> — Rolston Holmes III

At this point in history, the destruction of habitat is the primary cause of species loss, not the actual hunting and killing of individual creatures. Although poachers still hunt the rare black rhino, for instance,[17] much more damage to animals, birds, fish and plants occurs indirectly, as the rapidly expanding human population of the globe makes way for itself and its drive for a high-consumption existence. This is why habitat preservation is so important—the maintenance of wetlands, forests, prairies, oceans and rivers that naturally cleanse the water, air and soil.

In the 1995 Supreme Court case *Babbitt v. Sweet Home,* loggers who had lost income and jobs for the sake of preserving the northern spotted owl and the red-cockaded woodpecker argued that the Endangered Species Act should not be interpreted to protect habitat—in this situation the ancient woods where the birds lived—but should be used only to keep people from hunting and killing the birds themselves. The Supreme Court disagreed. Describing the ESA as "the most comprehensive legislation for the preservation of endangered species ever enacted by any nation," the Court ruled that it could indeed cover habitat. Dissenting, Justice Scalia argued for a more narrow interpretation of the ESA. The law prevented outright killing of individual endangered creatures, but if government wanted to go further and protect habitat on privately owned land, it should use government funds to buy that land and set it aside for conservation purposes. To do otherwise would "impose unfairness to the point of financial ruin—not just upon the rich, but upon the simplest farmer who finds his land conscripted to national zoological use." Scalia refused to view the destruction of breeding grounds as the equivalent of injury to the species:

> *[S]urely the only harm to the individual animal from impairment of [the breeding function] is not the failure of issue (which harms only the issue), but the psychic harm of perceiving that it will leave this world with no issue (assuming, of course, that the animal in question, perhaps an endangered species of slug, is capable of such painful sentiments). If it includes that*

16 *Environmental Ethics: Duties to and Values in the Natural World* (Philadelphia: Temple University Press, 1988).

17 Not that these "truly egregious, even macabre" hunting practices don't still happen, including "the decimation of tigers to produce tiger penis soup at $300 a plate." Christopher Stone, "What to Do about Biodiversity: Property Rights, Public Goods, and the Earth's Biological Riches," 68 *S. Cal L. Rev.* March 1995, p. 592.

psychic harm, then why not the psychic harm of not being able to frolic about—so that the draining of a pond used for an endangered animal's recreation, but in no way essential to its survival, would be prohibited by the Act?

It was just this point that Justice O'Connor had taken up in her concurring opinion. "Breeding, feeding, and sheltering are what animals do," she wrote:

> *To raze the last remaining ground on which the piping plover currently breeds, thereby making it impossible for any piping plovers to reproduce, would obviously injure the population (causing the species' extinction in a generation). But by completely preventing breeding, it would also injure the individual living bird, in the same way that sterilizing the creature injures the individual living bird. To "injure" is, among other things, "to impair."* Webster's Ninth New Collegiate Dictionary *623 (1983). One need not subscribe to theories of "psychic harm," to recognize that to make it impossible for an animal to reproduce is to impair its most essential physical functions and to render that animal, and its genetic material, biologically obsolete. This, in my view, is actual injury.*[18]

Private Property, Regulation, and the Constitution

The **Fifth Amendment** to the U.S. Constitution states that "private property [may not] be taken for public use, without **just compensation.**" The power to take private property for public use is called **eminent domain.** It may be exercised by local as well as federal and state government. Historically it has enabled public projects—such as the construction of highways, utility lines, parks and rapid transit systems—to move forward in spite of private property interests that might otherwise have blocked them. Suppose your state government determines that the most appropriate route for a new expressway is right through your living room. Your family may not refuse to cooperate with the state, but the state must pay your family for this "taking" of your property; government should not be able to force a small number of citizens to bear the brunt of activities that benefit the public generally.

The Fifth Amendment is the only part of the Constitution that explicitly protects private property owners' economic interests, and it has been an important battleground over the years as courts have had to define "public use," "just compensation," and, especially in recent environmental cases, the concept of a "**taking.**"

Early cases typically dealt with the confiscation of private land—as in the highway example above. By the early twentieth century, though, many of the conflicts involved local zoning laws that prevented owners from enjoying economically optimal use of their property. In a 1926 case,[19] for instance, land that had been zoned for industrial development was restricted by a new zoning ordinance to residential use, reducing its value to the owner by 75 percent. Yet the Supreme Court found that this did not amount to a taking, and the city did not have to compensate the owner for it. The Court viewed the rezoning as an exercise of the **police power,** the power of state and local governments to make laws for public health, safety and welfare.

---

18 *Babbitt v. Sweet Home,* 115 S.Ct. 2407 (1995).

19 *Village of Euclid v. Ambler Realty Co.,* 272 U.S. 365 (1926).

Pointing out that commercial use of land might, in shifting circumstances under that police power, wear out its welcome and become a **nuisance,** the Court wrote:

> *A nuisance may be merely a right thing in the wrong place—like a pig in the parlor instead of in the barnyard.*[20]

The result in *Euclid* was reached by balancing public benefits against private loss brought on by the regulation. In a more recent test of the police power to zone, the Supreme Court held that the benefit to the public derived from preserving the beauty and historic value of a train station in New York City outweighed the cost imposed on the private owner who had planned the construction of a 53-story building on top of it.[21] Again, there was no "taking," and no need to compensate the owner.

Since the passage of the National Environmental Protection Act in 1970, **regulatory takings** challenges have been brought by private property owners who believe that environmental regulations unfairly burden them as individuals with the costs of protecting our natural resources. Here is how these cases have arisen: a government regulation designed to protect the environment impinges on an owner's freedom to use that property in some way. For instance, farmers are directed not to use certain pesticides harmful to groundwater, ranchers are told they must put their cattle at risk to protect grizzly bears, the owners of "wetlands," the marshes that harbor delicate ecosystems crucial to the natural cleansing cycle, are directed not to drain or build on their land. In each situation, the owner alleges that the environmental regulation is the equivalent of a "taking," and demands compensation. Environmentalists view these claims with alarm, because, if they succeed, they have the potential of undercutting the entire regulatory network; government will not be able to afford to regulate.

In the next case, the Supreme Court deals with one of these challenges, and in the process recasts its mechanism for defining a taking under the Fifth Amendment.

LUCAS V. SOUTH CAROLINA COASTAL COUNCIL

Supreme Court of the United States, 1992
112 S.Ct. 2886

Justice SCALIA delivered the opinion of the Court.

In 1986, David H. Lucas paid $975,000 for two residential lots on the Isle of Palms . . . South Carolina, on which he intended to build single-family homes. In 1988, however, the South Carolina Legislature enacted the Beachfront Management Act (Act), which had the direct effect of barring [him] from erecting any permanent habitable structures on his two parcels. . . . This case requires us to decide whether the Act's dramatic effect on the economic value of Lucas's lots accomplished a taking of private property under the Fifth and Fourteenth Amendments requiring the payment of "just compensation."

South Carolina's expressed interest in intensively managing development activities in the so-called "coastal zone" dates from 1977 when, in the aftermath of Congress's passage of the federal Coastal Zone Management Act of 1972, the legislature enacted a Coastal Zone Management Act of its own. [This law] required owners of coastal zone land that qualified as a "critical area" (defined in the legislation to include beaches and immediately adjacent sand dunes), to obtain a permit from the newly created South Carolina Coastal Council prior to committing the land to a [new use].

---

20 In the *Euclid* case, the pig did not wander into the parlor. By varying the zoning, the town was moving its "parlor" to surround the "pig." Even so, the Supreme Court held that a common law "nuisance" existed.

21 *Penn Central Transportation Co. v. New York City,* 98 S.Ct. 2646 (1978).

In the late 1970's, Lucas and others began extensive residential development of the Isle of Palms, a barrier island situated eastward of the City of Charleston. . . . Lucas in 1986 purchased the two lots at issue in this litigation. . . . No portion of the lots, which were located approximately 300 feet from the beach, qualified as a "critical area" under the 1977 Act; accordingly, at the time Lucas acquired these parcels, he was not legally obliged to obtain a permit from the Council in advance of any development activity. His intention with respect to the lots was to do what the owners of the immediately adjacent parcels had already done: erect single-family residences. He commissioned architectural drawings for this purpose.

[But in 1988 new legislation directed the Council to create a line beyond which no "occupiable improvements" could be built. When this "baseline" was drawn, Lucas found he was prohibited from building on his land.]

[In *Pennsylvania Coal Co. v. Mahon* (1922), Justice Holmes recognized] that . . . if . . . the uses of private property were subject to unbridled, uncompensated qualification under the police power, "the natural tendency of human nature [would be] to extend the qualification more and more until at last private property disappear[ed]." These considerations gave birth in that case to the oft-cited maxim that, "while property may be regulated to a certain extent, if regulation goes too far it will be recognized as a taking."

[The Court explains that in the 70 years since the *Mahon* case, it has avoided the use of any "set formula" for determining "how far is too far," instead examining the specific facts of each case.]

We have, however, described at least two discrete categories of regulatory action as compensable without case-specific inquiry into the public interest advanced in support of the restraint. The first encompasses regulations that compel the property owner to suffer a physical "invasion" of his property. In general (at least with regard to permanent invasions), no matter how minute the intrusion, and no matter how weighty the public purpose behind it, we have required compensation. For example, in *Loretto v. Teleprompter Manhattan CATV Corp.* (1982), we determined that New York's law requiring landlords to allow television cable companies to emplace cable facilities in their apartment buildings constituted a taking, even though the facilities occupied at most only 1 1/2 cubic feet of the landlords' property.

The second situation . . . is where regulation denies all economically beneficial or productive use of land. . . .

[R]egulations that leave the owner of land without economically beneficial or productive options for its use—typically, as here, by requiring land to be left substantially in its natural state—carry with them a heightened risk that private property is being pressed into some form of public service under the guise of mitigating serious public harm. . . .

We think, in short, that there are good reasons for our frequently expressed belief that when the owner of real property has been called upon to sacrifice *all* economically beneficial uses in the name of the common good, that is, to leave his property economically idle, he has suffered a taking. . . .

[There are many precedent cases establishing that government may halt a use of property that is harmful to the public without paying compensation to the owner. However, Scalia argues, since none of those precedents involved regulations that completely removed all economic value from the land, that principle does not apply to the case before him. In *Lucas*-like situations, he reasons, the regulation must count as a taking—unless it simply forbids a use already forbidden under the common law.]

On this analysis, the owner of a lake bed, for example, would not be entitled to compensation when he is denied the requisite permit to engage in a landfilling operation that would have the effect of flooding others' land. Nor the corporate owner of a nuclear generating plant, when it is directed to remove all improvements from its land upon discovery that the plant sits astride an earthquake fault. Such regulatory action may well have the effect of eliminating the land's only economically productive use, but it does not proscribe a productive use that was previously permissible under relevant property and nuisance principles. The use of these properties for what are now expressly prohibited purposes was always unlawful, and . . . it was open to the State at any point to make the implication of those background principles of nuisance and property law explicit. . . .When, however, a regulation that declares "off-limits" all economically productive or beneficial uses of land goes beyond what the relevant background principles would dictate, compensation must be paid to sustain it.

The "total taking" inquiry we require today will ordinarily entail (as the application of state nuisance law ordinarily entails) analysis of, among other things, the degree of harm to public lands and resources, or adjacent private property, posed by the claimant's proposed activities, the social value of the claimant's activities and their suitability to the locality in question, and the relative ease with which the alleged harm can be avoided through measures taken by the claimant and the government (or adjacent private landowners) alike. The fact that a particular use has long been engaged in by similarly situated owners ordinarily imports a lack of any common-law prohibition (though changed circumstances or new knowledge may make what was previously permissible no longer so). So also does the fact that other landowners, similarly situated, are permitted to continue the use denied to the claimant.

[Judgment against Lucas is reversed. The case goes back to the state courts to determine if common law principles would prevent him from building on his property. If not, he must be compensated for the environmental restriction.]

Justice KENNEDY, concurring in the judgment.

The rights conferred by the Takings Clause and the police power of the State may coexist without conflict. Property is bought and sold, investments are made, subject to the State's power to regulate. Where a taking is alleged from regulations which deprive the property of all value, the test must be whether the deprivation is contrary to reasonable, investment-backed expectations. . . . .

In my view, reasonable expectations must be understood in light of the whole of our legal tradition. The common law of nuisance is too narrow a confine for the exercise of regulatory power in a complex and interdependent society.

Justice BLACKMUN, dissenting.

Today the Court launches a missile to kill a mouse.

The State of South Carolina prohibited Lucas from building a permanent structure on his property from 1988 to 1990. Relying on an unreviewed (and implausible) state trial court finding that this restriction left Lucas' property valueless, this Court granted review to determine whether compensation must be paid in cases where the State prohibits all economic use of real estate. . . .

I, like the Court, will give far greater attention to this case than its narrow scope suggests—not because I can intercept the Court's missile, or save the targeted mouse, but because I hope perhaps to limit the collateral damage.

In 1972 Congress passed the Coastal Zone Management Act. The Act was designed to provide States with money and incentives to carry out Congress' goal of protecting the public from shoreline erosion and coastal hazards. In the 1980 Amendments to the Act, Congress directed States to enhance their coastal programs by "[p]reventing or significantly reducing threats to life and the destruction of property by eliminating development and redevelopment in high-hazard areas."

South Carolina began implementing the congressional directive by enacting the South Carolina Coastal Zone Management Act of 1977. Under the 1977 Act, any construction activity in what was designated the "critical area" required a permit from the Council, and the construction of any habitable structure was prohibited. The 1977 critical area was relatively narrow.

This effort did not stop the loss of shoreline. In October 1986, the Council appointed a "Blue Ribbon Committee on Beachfront Management" to investigate beach erosion and propose possible solutions. In March 1987, the Committee found that South Carolina's beaches were "critically eroding," and proposed land-use restrictions. In response, South Carolina enacted the Beachfront Management Act on July 1, 1988. The 1988 Act did not change the uses permitted within the designated critical areas. Rather, it enlarged those areas to encompass the distance from the mean high watermark to a setback line established on the basis of "the best scientific and historical data" available.

Petitioner Lucas is a contractor, manager, and part owner of the Wild Dune development on the Isle of Palms. He has lived there since 1978. In December 1986, he purchased two of the last four pieces of vacant property in the development. The area is notoriously unstable. In roughly half of the last 40 years, all or part of petitioner's property was part of the beach or flooded twice daily by the ebb and flow of the tide. Between 1957 and 1963, petitioner's property was under water. . . . Between 1981 and 1983, the Isle of Palms issued 12 emergency orders for sandbagging to protect property in the Wild Dune development. Determining that local habitable structures were in imminent danger of collapse, the Council issued permits for two rock revetments to protect condominium developments near petitioner's property from erosion; one of the revetments extends more than halfway onto one of his lots. . . .

The Court creates new Takings jurisprudence based on the trial court's finding that the property had lost all economic value. This finding is almost certainly erroneous. [Lucas] can still enjoy other attributes of ownership, such as the right to exclude others, "one of the most essential sticks in the bundle of rights that are commonly characterized as property." [Lucas] can picnic, swim, camp, in a tent or live on the property in a moveable trailer. . . . Petitioner also retains the right to [sell] the land, which would have value for neighbors and for those prepared to enjoy proximity to the ocean without a house. . . .

The Court . . . takes the opportunity to create a new scheme for regulations that eliminate all economic value. From now on, there is a categorical rule finding these regulations to be a taking unless the use they prohibit is a background common-law nuisance. . . .

I first question the Court's rationale in creating a category that obviates a "case-specific inquiry into the public interest advanced," if all economic value has been lost. If one fact about the Court's taking jurisprudence can be stated without contradiction, it is that "the particular circumstances of each case" determine whether a specific restriction will be rendered invalid by the government's failure to pay compensation. This is so because . . . the ultimate conclusion "necessarily requires a weighing of private and public interests." When the government regulation prevents the owner from any economically valuable use of his property, the private interest is unquestionably substantial, but we have never before held that no public interest can outweigh it. . . .

This Court repeatedly has recognized the ability of government, in certain circumstances, to regulate property without compensation no matter how adverse the financial effect on the owner may be. More than a century ago, the Court explicitly upheld the right of States to prohibit uses of property injurious to public health, safety, or welfare without paying compensation . . . *Mugler v. Kansas* (1887). On this basis, the Court upheld an ordinance effectively prohibiting operation of a previously lawful brewery, although the "establishments will become of no value as property." *Mugler* was only the beginning in a long line of cases. . . . In *Miller v. Schoene* (1928), the Court held that the Fifth Amendment did not require Virginia to pay compensation to the owner of cedar trees ordered destroyed to prevent a disease from spreading to nearby apple orchards. . . .

In none of the cases did the Court suggest that the right of a State to prohibit certain activities without paying compensation turned on the availability of some residual valuable use. Instead, the cases depended on whether the government interest was sufficient to prohibit the activity, given the significant private cost. . . .

[T]he Court seems to treat history as a grab-bag of principles, to be adopted where they support the Court's theory, and ignored where they do not.

• QUESTIONS •

1. The image of David Lucas that emerges from majority Justice Scalia's description is strikingly different from the one that Justice Blackmun creates in his dissent. What are the two contrasting stories in this case? Do you think that when Lucas bought the land at issue here, in 1986, he had reason to know that by building on it he would soon be the owner of a "pig in a parlor"?

2. According to the majority, what two types of regulatory action automatically trigger compensation as takings, without a court needing to examine the circumstances in a case-specific way? Why does the dissent object to this approach?

3. Included in the bundle of rights that go with land ownership are those of occupation, use and sale. When something is done to affect those rights—making them less valuable to the owner—the common law allows a suit for **nuisance.** A nuisance is an activity or condition that creates an unreasonable interference with a person's use and enjoyment of property. So, for example, a nuisance is created when a service station allows gasoline to leak from its holding tanks onto adjourning residential property[22] or when a farmer's seasonal irrigation system spews waste water onto his neighbors' farmlands.[23] What role does nuisance play in the majority opinion in this case? In the other *Lucas* opinions?

4. **Internet Assignment:** When *Lucas* was first decided, environmentalists worried that its interpretation of the Takings Clause would so often require compensation that it would cripple virtually any attempt to rescue habitat from development. But case law developments since *Lucas* have muddied the waters. Some experts insist that what looked like a **per se** rule has been ignored by the lower courts. Find a federal court case involving regulatory takings that cites *Lucas.* (a) What test does the court use to determine whether there was a taking? Must the government compensate the landowner? (b) In 2004, the Supreme Court ruled that regulations do not require a property owner to "sacrifice *all* economically beneficial uses" if the sacrifice is only temporary. So, for example, a two-year moratorium on building would not constitute a per se taking.[24] Find out how environmentalists reacted to the *Tahoe-Sierra* case.

5. A ballot initiative passed by Oregon voters in the November 2004 election reverses a trend in that state, which has some of the most restrictive land-use rules in the country. The new measure allows owners to prove that zoning or environmental regulations will reduce the investment value of their property, forcing the government to either compensate them for those losses or exempt them from the rules. Describing Oregon's strict regulation, co-author of the ballot measure Ross Day said, "If Enron does something like this, people call it theft. If Oregon does it, they all it land-use planning." Think of a way to counter his point.

6. Can cities take private property and transfer it to private developers for the sake of economic revitalization? This is the question before the Supreme Court in one of the most closely-watched cases of the spring 2005 term. New London, Connecticut planned to use its power of eminent domain to condemn a neighborhood at its waterfront—a mix of small businesses and homes—and then turn it over to a private developer a hotel, conference center, office space, and upscale residences. The city hoped to create a synergy with a research facility being built nearby by the pharmaceutical giant Pfizer. When some of the original homeowners sued, the Connecticut Supreme Court ruled that New London had a valid public use, based on projections that thousands of jobs and significant revenue would be generated. On appeal, the homeowners wanted "to stop the use of eminent domain to take away their most sacred and important of possessions: their homes." What ethical issues surface in this dispute? **Internet Assignment:** Find out how the Supreme Court ruled in *Kelo v. City of New London*.

22 *Golovach v. Bellmont,* 4 A.D.3d 730 (App.Div, N.Y. 2004); *Felton Oil Company v. Gee,* 2004 WL 119486 (Ark. 2004).

23 *King v. Van Setten,* 2004 WL 1447736 (Mont. 2004).

24 *Tahoe-Sierra Preservation Council, Inc. v. Tahoe Regl. Plan. Agency,* 335 U.S.302 (2002).

GLOBALIZATION, FAIRNESS AND THE ENVIRONMENT

Vandana Shiva is a well-known activist for sustainable development and social justice. She holds a doctorate in theoretical physics, and in 1993 she received the prestigious Right Livelihood Award, an alternative to the Nobel Prize.[25] She writes and lectures about the damage done to democracy and to the natural environment by corporate globalization. This essay illuminates the essence of her critique. She begins by identifying what she calls the "myths of globalization." One myth is that trade integration will lead to a world where "everyone will have more goods, everyone will consume goods without limits, and everyone will be happy." This "trickle-down" theory, she writes, wrongly assumes that free trade will eventually benefit all, even the poor. A corollary "myth," according to Shiva, is that globalization is the path not only to universal prosperity, but to environmental stability: "The poor are hungry and will destroy the environment; only rich people will protect the environment; when everyone's rich the environment will prosper." In the essay that follows Shiva debunks these beliefs.

THE MYTHS OF GLOBALIZATION EXPOSED: ADVANCING TOWARD LIVING DEMOCRACY

Vandana Shiva[26]

[In India w]e were repeatedly told by organizations such as the International Monetary Fund (IMF) and the World Bank that Third World countries should not grow staple crops. They did not have competitive advantage, and the comparative advantage of feeding themselves should wait upon the development of a new market for farmers from the Midwest of the United States. In the meantime, Third World nations should grow flowers and shrimp and vegetables. If you look at any trade agreement-based structural adjustment prescription for any Third World country in the last decade, that is what it is supposed to do.

Basic or subsistence foods are, in general, low-valued goods. Shrimp and flowers are high-value commodities, so you can supposedly sell them on the export markets, and make a lot of money, with which your country can buy food, and so have growth. Unfortunately, it does not work that way, because when every country starts to grow shrimp, shrimp become cheap. When you import products such as rice and meat, they keep rising in cost. In India, we have had a four-fold rise in food prices in recent years, this in a country where 300 million are already hungry, where 90 percent of the income of the poor was for buying food. If they were already spending 90 percent buying food and were half-fed, when the food is four times more costly, you can imagine what they are doing—eating less. That is where malnutrition [and disease] comes from. . . .

This industry has been moved [from temperate zones] to the Third World by the global food corporations partly because of the environmental costs, which are heavy. . . . In trying to recreate the sea on land, using huge pumps to bring seawater into fields, there is the danger of seepage: The sea water seeps into the local groundwater, and soon the area has no drinking water. I came to know about this issue because the women in the costal area of India started to destroy the shrimp farm ponds in protest, and when they were arrested, they wrote to me and said, "We've done this, we think it is an environmental problem . . . come and help us." So I came to investigate and saw major environmental disaster areas: coconut trees dying and paddy fields wiped out because of salinization. . . .

Swedish environmentalists have done a tremendous job of assessing these shrimp farms and their environmental footprints. These studies, and ours in India, have examined the

25 Given annually by the Swedish parliament, the Right Livelihood Awards focus on visionary work on behalf of the planet and its people.

26 From James Gustave Speth, ed., *Worlds Apart: Globalization and the Environment* (Washington, DC: Island Press, 2003).

destruction of agriculture, water, and mangroves. Only 13 percent of the feed given to a shrimp converts into protein. The rest goes to waste and becomes pollution, which is then pumped out daily into the sea and, of course, is degrading sea fisheries. So more fishermen lose their occupations. . . . For every dollar traded globally by exporting shrimp, between seven to ten dollars is destroyed locally in resources. Shrimp farming also required that you catch 15 times more fish at sea than the weight of shrimp that will be produced: the sea fish are used to make the food fed to the farmed shrimp. Thus a "sustainable" industry requires even more unsustainable sea fishing. There are many such shadow costs to globalized industries. . . .

The Danish Environmental Ministry did a fascinating study some years ago that showed that 1 kilogram of food traded globally generates 10 kilograms of carbon dioxide. Thus, imports that replace local crops have the shadow cost of increased carbon emissions. . . . The Gujarat earthquake of January 2001 followed the Orissa cyclone of 2000, a storm of about 300 kilometers per hour. India never had cyclones of that kind of speed before. We did a study and found that it was approximately 50 percent higher in speed than past cyclones. . . . Because the shrimp farms had destroyed the costal mangroves, there was no natural buffer. As a result, the Orissa cyclone had a serious impact, and communities that had never been affected in the past did not know how to deal with it. Thirty thousand people died, along with about 1000,000 cattle. To the degree that global climate events may be linked to the environmental destruction brought about by globalization—and I believe that this link will be increasingly well demonstrated—we will see a vicious cycle: more globalized trade leading to more global environmental destruction that will require more global trade, and so on.

The government of India is now proposing a superhighway around the coast. We already have a highway and a train track. The new superhighway's only advantage would be that it is even closer to the sea and therefore it would supposedly save a few cents per ton in the transport of goods. [But] what happens when you have a highway wall 40 feet high hit by a cyclone driving a tidal wave 50 feet high: All that salt water sits on the inland side of the road and cannot drain out. We have already have examples of seawater rendering agricultural land infertile in this way; a new superhighway, combined with continuing climate change, is a recipe for further disasters.

Globalization has definitely meant the globalization of nonsustainable industrial agricultural, such as higher use of pesticides and more expensive seeds, which means debt, unpayable debt in the context of national poverty. In India, the land of karma, where we always believed that things got sorted out in the next janam (rebirth), for the first time people realize that we have to sort it out today with the moneylender. And who is the moneylender? The agent of the same global company that sells the pesticide and the seed. So, in India we see multinational corporations serving as moneylender and seed/pesticide agent in one, withdrawing traditional low-interest credit—another destructive element of globalization. These private moneylenders/sales agents charge for credit at 30 percent to 100 percent. . . . This is absolutely outrageous. . . . [M]ore than twenty thousand peasants have been driven to suicide due to high costs of seeds and pesticides in a deregulated market for agricultural inputs. . . .

I want to stress that none of this can happen without real violence against people. . . . In protests against the aquaculture movement, six people were shot dead in various parts of India by the police. These numbers may seem small on their face, but they indicate a much larger population driven to the edge by undemocratic changes imposed on them from without and an increasing level of state-sanctioned repression in response to legitimate protest. In 1993, before the conclusion of the Uruguay Round, we saw a protest of half a million farmers in Bangalore, basically telling the Indian government not to sign the treaty because it would destroy our agriculture, upon which 75 percent of Indians depend. . . . Almost every day there is a protest somewhere in India, and some are dealt with violently by corporate security forces and the police. . . . I believe that protest is the first step in resistance but that the second and bigger step is building concrete alternatives institutionally in both production systems and consumption systems.

. . . [H]ow do we make the transition to sustainability? We are in an unstable situation in which three upside-down pyramids—our global economic system, our global political system, and our global environmental systems—have the least powerful in their shadows. The economic pyramid assigns high value to markets, but little or none to local economies. Regarding the environmental pyramid, most natural resources should remain unexploited, to maintain nature's vital processes; instead, most natural resources are being sucked into global markets. Little is being left for the sustenance of the people, and next to nothing is being left for nature's maintenance. In politics, democracy requires that people be empowered locally because that is where they can truly act and influence, and through local action address national issues. People want secure ways to influence their representatives. Since most people live and work at local levels, that is where the democracy should be the strongest. . . . [W]hat should be a tip of the political pyramid is now at the base, a far-reaching erosion of democratic power at the national and local levels.

These three upside-down pyramids need to be put back in order because they are thoroughly unstable, ready to fall at any time. Our current global systems are explosive—economically, environmentally, and politically.

For me, the use of the term "sustainability" is very clear. It is the maintenance of the ecosystem over time so that our rivers are not dead, our lakes are not polluted, our species are not extinct. It is also social sustainability: People must be able to maintain their cultures and diversity, maintain their livelihoods, and maintain their economic security. We have to bring nature and people into the picture.

The way we have started in India is through a movement we called the "Jaya-Panchayat," which means, literally, "living democracy." It is spreading like wildfire. We started it in twenty villages. We have reached four thousand villages in a year, and they are shaping their own systems of what they call free colonies, freedom zones. We will not have patents on life, we seek to resurrect sustainable systems that we had, and we will learn to advance new, sustainable technologies.

The success in India that we have had with the Panchayat grows out of three things. First, we have a constitutional amendment recognizing decentralized democracy as the highest form of democracy, one where the local village community or town community has more powers than the parliamentarians regarding major areas of the law, especially natural resources use, development planning, and the like. It is an example of true self-rule; the people in these communities are saying, "We rule in our village and we will negotiate with government about what powers we want to delegate to them." The national government makes decisions on the basis of the principle of subsidiarity already enshrined in our constitution. And global investments and trade have to respect local democracy. . . .

Second, the Panchayati-Raj is an elected body, and a panchayat by law has to have 30 percent women . . . a more inclusive, less sexist, more balanced form of governance.

[Third], we are widening that concept to converge with the deep consciousness that we call "Vasudhaiv Kutumbkam," the earth community. This is not just the panchayat in the formal sense but the panchayat in the ecological sense of community, of all lives that must work together. The building of these new freedom zones, which ensure the protection of all species as well as the livelihoods of the poor, is creating a new potential and challenging the idea that you need to destroy the planet before you can save it. A new vision of a globalized world can come out of this potential; a globalization based not on free trade (that is not free) or open markets (which are not open), but on the true community of living things on a living planet.

• QUESTIONS •

1. Outline the many-faceted harms associated with shrimp aquaculture in India.
2. According to Shiva, rampant globalization has created "three upside-down pyramids." What are they?
3. **Internet Assignment:** What can you learn about the Jaya-Panchayat movement? Why was there resistance to DuPont's planned nylon plant in Goa? Why have grassroots activists been protesting Coca-Cola in Kerala? What happened in these instances?

CHAPTER PROBLEMS

1. Class actions have been brought against the chemical giant Monsanto Company (and its spin-off Solutia) for its longtime practice of dumping polychlorinated biphenyls (PCBs) in the landfills and sewage systems of a largely African-American community in Anniston, Alabama. The claim is that, over 40 years, exposure to PCB-polluted soil and water has caused children and adults to suffer from cancer, neurological and liver problems, skin disorders and learning disabilities. Plaintiffs located a 1938 report of an experiment done for Monsanto showing that rats exposed to PCBs developed skin cancer, and a 1955 letter from Monsanto's medical director stating, "Our main worry is what will happen if any individual develops any type of liver disease and gives a history of [PCB] exposure. I am sure a jury would not pay a great deal of attention to MACS [maximum allowable concentrations of PCBs.]" Plaintiffs also point to a 1975 company-sponsored study that revealed PCBs caused tumors in rats; Monsanto officials asked its researchers to change the language of the report from "slightly tumorigenic" to "does not appear to be carcinogenic," and they complied.

   On its Web site, Solutia has responded that, although PCBs have been banned since 1979, there is no scientific consensus that they cause cancer:

   > *There is no credible evidence that PCBs caused, or will cause, any of the plaintiffs to be sick. Studies of industrial workers have shown no illnesses attributable to PCB exposure, other than an acne-like skin rash....*

   Meanwhile, federal and state investigators began finding high levels of PCBs in the backyards, household dust and people of Anniston.

   How does the legal strategy for environmental equity in the Solutia case differ from that used in the *Waterfront South* case? **Internet Assignment:** Track the progress of the *Abernathy v. Monsanto* and *Tolbert v. Monsanto* cases, both class actions begun in 2002.

2. **Internet Assignment:** The **CERES (Coalition for Environmentally Responsible Economies) Principles** were crafted in the hope that corporations would adopt them and "seek profits only in a manner that leaves the earth healthy and safe." They include commitments to sustainable use of natural resources, reduction of wastes, cleanup and compensation for environmental damage, and yearly self-evaluations of progress, made available to the public. **Internet Assignment:** Check the Ceres Project Web site (http://www.ceres.org) to find out:

   - What are the Ceres Principles?
   - Which companies have signed them?
   - Have shareholders resolutions to adopt the CERES Principles been put forward at any corporations?
   - What new Ceres projects have been initiated in the past year?

3. The World Trade Organization was established in 1995 pursuant to the Uruguay Round of negotiations under the GATT to ensure the "optimal use of the world's resources in accordance with the objective of sustainable development." In 1998 the WTO ruled that the United States was wrong to prohibit shrimp imports from countries that fail to protect sea turtles from deadly entrapment in the trawls of shrimp boats. The large,

nearly extinct turtles had been getting tangled up and drowned in shrimping nets, so the U.S. Congress had passed a law requiring that domestic shrimpers use metal grills to keep the turtles from danger. In addition, any shrimp sold in the United States would have to be caught in nets equipped with turtle-excluders. India, Thailand, Pakistan and Malaysia protested to the WTO, calling this a barrier to trade. "Our shrimp exports are one of our significant items on our export list," said one Indian official, who also pointed out that shrimping employs hundreds of thousands of people in the developing world. **Internet Assignment:** What can you find about the role of the WTO (or the International Monetary Fund) in conflicts between free trade and environmental protection policies? Try the WTO's site at http://www.wto.org, the World Wildlife Fund (http://www.wwf.org), the Friends of the Earth (http://www.foe.org), or Greenpeace (http://www.greenpeace.org).

4. Species have been disappearing into extinction since they first existed on this planet, but the last 100 years has seen the rate of extinction leap alarmingly. At the time of the dinosaurs it is estimated that one species became extinct every 1,000 years, while today we lose one every day.[27] The predictions are dismal: within 30 years we will have lost 15 to 20 percent of all forms of life. Extinction should worry us for both practical and philosophical reasons. More than 50 percent of our pharmaceuticals come from various species. Until the bark of Pacific yew was discovered to contain a cure for ovarian cancer, it was considered a worthless scrub tree, and was almost wiped out. We do not know what other precious essences are yet to be discovered in the multitude of species now existing, but scientists are sure that by ruining their habitats, we are cheating ourselves and our descendants of their benefits. In fact, it seems likely that the more exotically diverse habitats, such as those in the rain forests, are likely to yield, if gradually, substances of highest priority for human well being.

The **Endangered Species Act** (ESA), a federal law that went into effect in 1973, has been remarkably effective so far. Eight species have been removed from the endangered list, including the American bald eagle. Twenty-five are almost recovered, close to being "unlisted." Of the more than 700 species on the current list, approximately 38 percent are either stable or improving. **Internet Assignment:** What is now happening with the Endangered Species Act? Which seems closer to passage, one that would weaken it, or one that would strengthen it? Try http://www.epa.gov, or one of the Web sites run by advocacy groups, such as http://www.pirg.org.

5. Bob Jackson, a ranger for the National Park Service at Yellowstone, became a whistleblower on behalf of grizzly bears. Hunters were placing salt licks just outside the park's boundaries to lure elk out to where they could shoot them. The elk carcasses would in turn attract grizzly bears, and they too were often shot. The ESA protects the bears, but hunters can kill them in self-defense. Ranger Jackson was been suspended from his post at Yellowstone, and told not to discuss the matter with the media. What legal claim might he make? **Internet Assignment:** What happened in this situation?

6. **Internet Assignment:** Consensus is real among the vast majority of the world's scientists, including those who wrote the UN Intergovernmental Panel on Climate Change (IPCC), that global warming is happening, that it has serious negative impacts on human health and the environment, and that human activity is one of its causes. In August 2004, for

27 In March 1996 the World Wildlife Fund announced a much higher die-off rate: 50,000 species of plants and animals disappear each year, most because of destruction of the world's forests.

instance, the European Environmental Agency reported that the carbon dioxide in the lower atmosphere is now at its highest level in 420,000 years, and is 34 percent above where it was at the start of the Industrial Revolution. Yet there are many who want to blunt that message. The Global Climate Coalition, for example, with membership largely made up of corporations and trade associations from the energy and auto manufacturing industries, ran a multi-million dollar ad campaign in the late 1990s arguing that the Kyoto Protocol would severely undermine the U.S. economy. Find out what you can about the other organizations which disfavor doing anything about global warming:

- @ George Marshall Institute
- @ Science and Environmental Policy Project (SEPP)
- @ Greening Earth Society
- @ Center for the Study of Carbon Dioxide & Global Change

Who funds them? Investigate the individuals who are prominent within the organizations. What is their expertise? What awards or achievements do they possess that would lend them credibility on this issue? If they have done research, how was it funded?

7. **Internet Assignment:** Some 155,000 seal-hunting people scattered around the Arctic have asked the Inter-American Commission on Human Rights to declare that United States is threatening their existence, by contributing substantially to global warming. Evidently the warmer water is inhospitable to much of the wildlife upon which that these communities depend. While the Commission has no enforcement powers, there may be a lawsuit filed in international court. Has this happened? If so, against whom was it filed? What result?

8. **Internet Assignment:** Find out what you can about indigenous environmental activists in other countries. What has been going on, for example, with the Mapuche Indians' fight for control of the forests on their ancestral lands in Chile? What was the result of the "water wars" in the Cochabamba region of Bolivia?

9. On half a million acres of the Mojave desert of California, U.S. soldiers stage mock battles, using real tanks and fake ammunition, the most extensive war games in the world. In December 2001, Congress gave the Army 10,000 more acres of federal land to expand this training area. Military bases already occupy more than a quarter of the habitat for the endangered desert tortoise, and the recently added land is inhabited by two-thirds of the known population of Lane Mountain milkvetch, an endangered plant species. Although sensitive to the political momentum favoring the military since September 11, environmentalists point out that expanding the training site will likely violate the ESA. What ethical arguments can you make on either side of this one?

10. More than 83,000 snowmobilers ride in Yellowstone National Park each winter, bringing tourist dollars to the surrounding communities, but disturbing wildlife habitat and forcing park rangers to wear gas masks to keep from getting headaches. But who is to say how people should appreciate nature? As one snowmobile enthusiast put it: "The environmentalists want to know how I can enjoy this beautiful scenery with all the noise. Well I may not hear it, but I can see it. I can be riding on this noisy thing and I got my solitude."
    (a) How would a utilitarian assess the consequences of snowmobiling in the national parks?
    (b) **Internet Assignment:** A five-year environmental impact assessment from the 1990s recommended banning snowmobiles from the national parks system. The day before he left office, President Clinton approved the ban. One of the first things President Bush did in office was reverse it. What is going on now with snowmobiling in our national parks?

Chapter Project

Business Ethics Fairy Tales

For the purposes of this exercise, a fairy tale is a story about how a single company was able to accomplish something "socially responsible" in the context of environmental quality. In other words, you will need to find an example of a company that has done what Milton Friedman would rail against–an activity that is not designed solely to increase stockholder return on investment, but is instead designed to benefit stakeholders who are not stockholders. The example you choose may in fact enhance the company's image and/or its bottom line, but the point of the exercise is to tell the story of a business which focused on environmentally and socially responsible goals, and achieved them.

The class will be divided into teams. Each team will research and then tell a business ethics "fairy tale." Then the class will vote to select the best team product.

The Contest

This is a contest, on two levels. First, your team is competing to locate the fairy tale you wish to tell.[28] Choose carefully–don't rush it. Consider a small or medium-sized company, and try to find one whose story has not been told as often as Ben & Jerry's. (Nonprofits don't count, for purposes of this assignment.) You may want to do some "dirt-digging" on a company before your team selects it. A company's own public relations description of its achievements may look wonderful, but often a little research reveals another reality. One Web site that offers a perspective that is not susceptible to greenwashing is http://www.corpwatch.org.

The second level of competition involves presenting your fairy tale to the rest of the class. Your team can tell its tale by making an oral report, distributing a written report, or by constructing a Web site. Once everyone has reviewed all the fairy tales, the class votes to see which team has done the best job, based on the evaluative criteria listed below.

Evaluative Criteria

1. **Effectiveness:** The company's program appears to be well designed to address the goal it is trying to meet. (Evidence that the company is succeeding in its efforts would help.)
2. **Ethical consistency:** The company's behavior in any area of its enterprise does not appear to undercut its fairy tale project. The project itself has substance beyond pure greenwashing. (This is where checking for critical commentary matters.)
3. **Originality:** The company's efforts are unusual or fresh in some way.
4. **Presentation:** The fairy tale is told clearly and colorfully.

28 To avoid duplication, communicate to your instructor in advance for approval of your selection.

Chapter 7 Marketing and Information: Advertising

In the lab I make cosmetics; in the store I sell dreams.

—Charles Revson, Revlon, Inc.

The drive for material goods . . . may be less admirable than a different . . . set of goals. The fact is that the system works, and that it does both motivate and reward people. If it appears to critics that the motivations are inferior, and rewards are vulgar, it must be remembered that at least the people have their own choice of what these rewards will be. . . . It is essentially a democratic system, and the freedom of individual choice makes it valuable to the people who do the choosing.

—John Crichton, *Morals and Ethics in Advertising*[1]

The average American sees about 20,000 TV ads annually and between 1,700 and 3,000 ads on all media per day. In the United States, more than $200 billion is spent annually on advertising. According to a United Nations report, global ad spending outstrips the growth of the world economy by one-third.

In this chapter, we consider marketing and advertising and how they affect our culture and our polity. We begin with an explanation of the U.S. Constitution First Amendment protection available to advertisers—their right to free "commercial speech." In the first case, this right is pitted against Congress' decision to ban a certain malt liquor label. We move on to consider consumer demand: Is it created and sustained by the advertising industry, or is it already present, just waiting to be appropriately educated and informed by advertising?

The chapter continues by introducing legislation responsive to deception in advertising, the Federal Trade Commission Act. The advertising business regulates itself, and we include a recent revision of the Association of American Advertising Agencies' Standards of Practice.

In classical microeconomic terms, wages and prices fluctuate in response to millions of preferences expressed by consumers as they make their purchasing choices. But do some marketing strategies warp optimal marketplace functions by manipulating consumer perceptions? We read about the history of the tobacco industry, where advertising and public relations techniques have successfully reconfigured consumer perception of risk. In the same vein, we consider direct-to-consumer advertising of pharmaceutical drugs.

We may be witnessing a sea of change in the marketing world, where what matters is less the relative qualities of a product or service, and more the mystique of its *brand*. We look at the impact branding may be having, on young consumers in particular, and we close this chapter with a reading about the use of the Internet to sell to children.

1 In *Ethics, Morality and the Media: Reflections on American Culture,* Lee Thayer, Ed. (New York: Hastings House, 1980), p. 113.

Commercial Speech

Freedom of speech is guaranteed by the First Amendment of the U.S. Constitution. For the first 200 years of our history, the Supreme Court refused to apply First Amendment protection to advertising, or **"commercial speech,"** distinguishing between the "marketplace of ideas," where the open exchange of opinion has traditionally been protected from most governmental restraint, and the marketplace of goods and services. Then, in 1976, a group of discount pharmacies in Virginia claimed that a state law that prevented them from advertising cut-rate drug prices violated their First Amendment rights. The Supreme Court agreed. Apart from the advertisers' economic interest, the Court recognized the consumers' interest in hearing what the advertisers had to say. "[T]hose whom the suppression of prescription drug price information hits the hardest are the poor, the sick and particularly the aged," it wrote. So, in *Virginia Board,*[2] the Court appeared to link the "right to receive information and ideas" with the traditional values that underlie free speech, as if well-educated consumers were the equivalent of well-educated voters. Commercial speech was protected mainly to ensure that "numerous private economic decisions" would be made on as well-informed a basis as possible. In contrast to pure speech, though, commercial speech was considered "hardier," better able to bounce back if regulated: "Since advertising is the *sine qua non* of commercial profits, there is little likelihood of its being chilled."

Two years after the *Virginia Board* case, the Supreme Court again struck down a state law as a violation of the First Amendment rights of a commercial speaker. In *First National Bank v. Bellotti,*[3] a Massachusetts bank wanted to publicize its opposition to proposed legislation for a graduated income tax. State law made it a crime for a corporation to advertise to influence voters on issues that did not "materially affect" its business, adding that no law regarding taxation would "materially affect" a corporation. The Supreme Court held that this law infringed upon the bank's First Amendment rights. Drawing from its reasoning in *Virginia Board,* it found the law limited the "stock of information from which the public may draw." And, in another case upholding the right to First Amendment protection for commercial speech—this time for lawyers' advertising—the Court stated that regulation restricting the flow of information to consumers fosters the "assump[tion] that the public is not sophisticated enough to realize the limitations of advertising, and that the public is better kept in ignorance than trusted with correct but incomplete information."[4]

The following case grew out of the furor caused by a marketing decision. Hornell Brewing Company chose to adopt the name Crazy Horse for one of its products, a malt liquor. Here the federal court must analyze a congressional ban on that label as a possible violation of commercial free speech.

Hornell Brewing Co., Inc. v. Brady

U.S. District Court, New York, 1993
819 F.Supp. 1227

AMON, District Judge.

Plaintiff Hornell Brewing Company ("Hornell") . . . produces and markets alcoholic and non-alcoholic beverages including "The Original Crazy Horse Malt Liquor" ("Crazy Horse"). . . . In February, 1992, the Bureau of Alcohol, Tobacco and Firearms ("BATF") issued a Certificate . . . authorizing the bottling and distribution of the Crazy Horse product. The certification process of

---

2 *Virginia State Board of Pharmacy v. Virginia Citizens Consumer Council, Inc.*, 96 S.Ct. 1817 (1976).

3 435 U.S. 765 (1978).

4 *Bates v. State Bar of Arizona*, 97 S.Ct. 2691 (1977).

BATF includes the consideration of whether the label is misleading, fraudulent, or obscene. Hornell introduced Crazy Horse in fourteen states in March 1992. To date, Crazy Horse is distributed in thirty-one states through over 200 wholesalers who resell to over 100,000 retailers. Hornell claims that Crazy Horse Malt Liquor was to be the first product in a series of Hornell beverages that celebrate the American West.[5]

The introduction of the product caused a surge of indignation throughout Congress, seemingly initiated by the United States Surgeon General Antonia Novello . . . [who] criticized the choice of the name Crazy Horse for a malt liquor. She accused Hornell of "insensitive and malicious marketing" and encouraged the leaders of Indian nations to use public outrage to force Crazy Horse off the market. Subsequently, members of Congress joined the effort. . . . South Dakota Senator Larry Pressler directed Hornell to change the product's name or donate its proceeds to Native American causes because "defamation of this hero is an insult to Indian culture." . . . Representative Patricia Schroeder called [a] hearing to consider legislation to prohibit use of the name Crazy Horse on alcoholic beverages. No representative of Hornell was permitted to appear at the hearing. . . .

[As Congress was gearing up to respond to this situation, a Senate committee adopted a resolution directing Hornell to negotiate with Sioux leaders, reach an agreement, and make it unnecessary for Congress to act. Hornell met with the Sioux to "protect its investment, distributors, suppliers, and work force," but Sioux leaders insisted on a general ban of Native American names and symbols in the marketing of all goods and services. Because Hornell had no power to make that happen, negotiations broke down. Then, in October 1992, Congress passed a law "banning the use of the name Crazy Horse on alcoholic products." Here the court discusses whether this law violates Hornell's First Amendment rights.]

The fundamental principle of the First Amendment is that the government may not prohibit speech because the ideas expressed therein are offensive. . . . When the government does regulate to prohibit speech based on its content, the regulation is presumptively invalid unless the speech falls into an unprotected category to which lesser standards apply. Commercial speech is not considered unprotected, but it does enjoy a lesser degree of First Amendment protection than protected speech. . . .

Commercial speech is defined as that speech which proposes a commercial transaction. In order to regulate commercial speech the government must satisfy a four-pronged test. *Central Hudson Gas & Electric Corp. v. Public Serv. Comm'n,* 100 S.Ct. 2343 (1980). First, the expression must be protected by the First Amendment; that is, it must concern lawful activity and not be misleading. Second, the government must establish a substantial interest. Third, the regulation must directly advance the governmental interest asserted. Finally, the regulation must be no more extensive than necessary to serve the interest asserted. . . .

a. Crazy Horse Label Is Lawful and Is Not Misleading

First, the Crazy Horse label, as commercial speech, is entitled to First Amendment protection because it concerns lawful activity and is not misleading. The sale and distribution of labeled malt beverage is a lawful activity under federal law. . . .

b. Substantial Interest

. . . It bears repeating that the desire to protect society or certain members of society from the purported offensiveness of particular speech is not a substantial interest which justifies its prohibition. *Texas v. Johnson,* 109 S.Ct. 2533 (1989) (overturning conviction for flag desecration); *Bolger v. Youngs Drug Products Corp.,* 103 S.Ct. 2875 (1983) (striking ban on mailing contraceptive advertisements). . . .

5 Crazy Horse was a highly revered Oglala Sioux leader.

Illustrative of this in the context of commercial speech are lower court decisions addressing governmental efforts to prohibit commercial use of "Sambo's," an appellation with patently offensive connotations to African Americans. In *Sambo's of Ohio, Inc. v. City Council of Toledo,* 466 F. Supp. 177 (N.D. Ohio 1979), the city of Toledo revoked permits to display the name Sambo's on the premises of a restaurant. . . . [The court held] that the government did not have a substantial interest in prohibiting use of the name merely because it was offensive to some. [Quoting the district court:] "One of the basic premises of advertising is that if it is too offensive to too many people, its use will be counterproductive, for those who are offended will not only refuse to buy the product, but also, if they are sufficiently offended, they will attempt to persuade others to refuse also."

The legislative history . . . clearly suggests that the government's initial objective in enacting the Crazy Horse statute was to protect Native American communities from what it perceived to be an offensive exploitation of the revered Sioux leader's name. . . . If the only interest asserted by the government were its desire to abate or avert the perceived offensiveness of the Crazy Horse name, it would not constitute a substantial interest under the *Central Hudson* test.

But that is not the end of our inquiry. . . .

[Congress] assert[s] that the government's substantial interest in enacting [the law] is the protection and preservation of the health, safety, and welfare of Native Americans by preventing the enhanced appeal of alcohol use among Native Americans due to the use of the name Crazy Horse on a malt liquor. This argument is based on the premise that the use of the name Crazy Horse will stimulate the demand for malt liquor in Native American communities. . . .

Courts have repeatedly held that the government has a substantial interest in protecting citizens from the problems associated with alcohol. Plaintiffs have even conceded that the government does have a substantial interest in the asserted health concerns related to alcohol.

At [a] hearing entitled "Confronting the Impact of Alcohol and Marketing on Native American Health and Culture," which was held before the House Select Committee on Children, Youth, and Families in May 1992, research was presented documenting alcohol related health problems that afflict Native American society. The alcoholism rate among Native Americans is six times higher than that of the general population. Native American infants are twenty times more likely than other United States infants to be born with Fetal Alcohol Syndrome. High rates of alcohol use and abuse among Native American teenagers are also reported. Given the serious nature of these problems, the government does have a substantial interest in preventing further use of alcohol among Native Americans. . . .

c. Direct Advancement

Although [the government has] asserted a substantial interest, [it has] not established that [the law] directly advances that interest. *Central Hudson* requires that the restriction must be narrowly drawn and that it "extend only as far as the interest it serves." This burden requires the government to demonstrate an "immediate connection" between the prohibition and the government's asserted interest. . . .

Here, the [government] failed to offer any evidence that suggests that [the law]—prohibiting only the use of the Crazy Horse label on liquor products—directly advances [its] interest in preventing the enhanced appeal of alcohol use among Native Americans. Indeed, the legislative record as to the offensiveness of the Crazy Horse label would seem as likely to suggest the contrary proposition, that Native Americans would be discouraged from consuming an alcoholic beverage that dishonors the name of a revered Native American leader. . . .

The government asks the Court to make a leap of faith and logic on the point by concluding that because advertising may increase consumption and a product label is a form of advertising, the mere use of the Crazy Horse label product will enhance consumption. It is true that in a general sense of the word "advertising," a product label is a form of advertising. But that is not to say that a product label, standing alone, can have a remotely comparable effect on product consumption as would all advertising, such as print ads, billboards, and radio and television commercials.

The Court [in fact], is not at all convinced that the use of a revered Native American name may cause any discernible increase in alcohol consumption among Native Americans, particularly when . . . Crazy Horse has not been marketed specifically toward Native Americans and [Hornell's] use of this name, according to legislative findings is, if anything, offensive to Native Americans.

d. Proportion to the Interest Asserted

The fourth prong that the government must satisfy is that the regulation must be in proportion to the interest asserted. A regulation is in proportion if it is no more extensive than necessary to further the government's interest. . . . [T]here must be a "reasonable fit" between the regulation and the government's interest. . . ."

It is the government's claim that the use of the name Crazy Horse, on its own, will have adverse effects on the Native American population by increasing alcohol use and thereby exacerbating the problems correlated with alcohol abuse. [Even assuming this for the sake of argument, however], complete revocation of the Crazy Horse Malt Liquor label is not a reasonable fit to this interest. The prohibition prevents use of the label anywhere simply to protect a relatively small segment of the population. The prohibition is not, as it could have been, limited to Native American reservations or narrow geographic areas where there is a demonstrably high concentration of Native Americans.

Nor does this sweeping prohibition take into account sensible alternatives that would not require any direct limit on use of the Crazy Horse label, such as education programs to inform Native Americans of the dangers of alcohol. Another possibility is an additional warning on the Crazy Horse bottle informing Native Americans of the dangers of alcohol or of the high incidence of alcoholism and its effects in Native American communities. . . . With obvious alternatives available that do not hinder speech in any way, or hinder it far less, the statute is not, by any means, a reasonable fit.

In sum, it is the finding of this Court that [the law banning Crazy Horse] is more extensive than necessary to serve the interest asserted by the government, and as such also fails the fourth prong of the *Central Hudson* test. . . .

Although this Court has found that [the law] violates the First Amendment, . . . this decision should not be read as either condoning or endorsing [Hornell's] choice of name for their product Crazy Horse Malt Liquor. The Court can well appreciate that the use of the name of a revered Native American leader, who preached sobriety and resisted exploitation under the hand of the United States government, is offensive and may be viewed as an exploitation of Native Americans throughout this country. The choice may be particularly insensitive given the ample documentation of alcohol abuse and its destructive results among Native Americans. Nevertheless, a price we pay in this country for ordered liberty is that we are often exposed to that which is offensive to some, perhaps even to many. It is from our exposure to all that is different that we best learn to address it, change it, and sometimes tolerate and appreciate it. "Freedom of speech may best serve its high purpose when it induces a condition of unrest, creates dissatisfaction with conditions as they are, or even stirs people to anger." To those who are offended by the use of the Crazy Horse Malt Liquor label, the directive of the district court in *Sambo's of Ohio, Inc. v. Toledo* is particularly apt:

> *If they are offended . . . not only can they refuse to patronize the plaintiffs, but they, too, can erect signs, carry placards, or publish advertisements designed to persuade others to refuse to patronize the plaintiffs. That is what freedom of speech is all about. . . .*

[The court granted Hornell's request for an injunction preventing the government from enforcing the ban on their label.]

• QUESTIONS •

1. Why do you think Hornell chose the name Crazy Horse for its malt liquor?

2. Should the law protect expression that is deeply offensive? Should there be an exception made for offensive advertising that hurts a minority group? Should it ban commercials that portray women and girls as sex objects?

3. As written, the ban on the Crazy Horse label violated the plaintiff's First Amendment rights. Could the law have been amended so that it would not run afoul of the Constitution? This court acknowledges that the government had a "substantial interest" in decreasing the rate of alcoholism among Native Americans. How could the government have served that interest without violating Hornell's rights?

4. Hornell argued that the choice of Crazy Horse was not mere "commercial speech" (which would receive less protection under the First Amendment), but was a matter of personal expression on the part of Don Vultaggio, the chairman and co-owner of Hornell Brewing, and so it deserved the strongest constitutional protection. But the court would not buy that:

   > *Plaintiff cannot seriously liken Vultaggio's freedom of expression in decorating his home in Southwestern style to the use of the name Crazy Horse on a nationally marketed alcoholic beverage.*

   Do you agree there should be a distinction in law between "pure speech," that is, expressions of opinion, and "commercial speech," that is, communications of the marketplace? How are they similar? Different?

5. **Internet Assignment:** In recent years, the U.S. Supreme Court and lower federal courts have been dealing with several First Amendment challenges to regulation of tobacco and alcohol ads. In 2002, a community college's ban on ads on its property for alcohol, tobacco, guns and illegal drugs was found to violate the First Amendment.[6] Using a legal search database, find out how the *Central Hudson* test was applied in the following cases:

   a. The city of Baltimore passed an ordinance banning billboard advertising of alcoholic beverages and cigarettes near schools and playgrounds.
   b. The state of Rhode Island passed a law banning the mention of price from all advertising of alcoholic beverages.
   c. The New York State Liquor Authority banned the Bad Frog Brewery label that showed a frog with the second of its four unwebbed fingers extended in a gesture of insult.

6. In a recent Supreme Court case, Coors Brewing Company claimed a government regulation prohibiting beer labels from displaying alcoholic content violated its First Amendment rights. Writing for the majority, Clarence Thomas agreed. In a footnote to the case, he addressed a very important question: Was the *Central Hudson* test itself too high a barrier to put in the way of government regulation of commercial speech? Should government have more latitude in its attempts to regulate advertising of products or services that are harmful or often generate socially harmful consequences? Thomas rejected that suggestion.[7] What do you think?

---

6 *Khademi v. S. Orange Co. College,* 194 F. Supp. 2d 1011 (Cal. 2002).

7 *Rubin v. Coors,* 115 S.Ct. 1585, 1589–90, fn2 (1995).

ADVERTISING AND ECONOMICS

Left wing economists, ever eager to snatch the scourge from the hand of God, hold that advertising tempts people to squander money on things they don't need. Who are these elitists to decide what you need? Do you need a dishwasher? Do you need a deodorant? Do you need a trip to Rome? I feel no qualms of conscience about persuading you to do that. [B]uying things can be one of life's more innocent pleasures, whether you need them or not. Remember your euphoria when you bought your first car?

— David Ogilvy, *Ogilvy on Advertising*

[T]he illusion arises that it is good to accumulate it without limit. By doing so, man harms both the community and himself because, concentrating on such a narrow aim, he deprives his soul and spirit of larger and more rewarding experiences.

— Aristotle

Advertising ministers to the spiritual side of trade. . . . It is a great power . . . part of the greater work of the regeneration and redemption of mankind.

— Calvin Coolidge, 1926

Which came first, the advertising or the consumer craving? And what's so wrong about consumer craving? Is advertising destructive of our polity? Or is it an essential driver of a healthy economy, even a form of artistic expression?

THE DEPENDENCE EFFECT

John Kenneth Galbraith[8]

The theory of consumer demand, as it is now widely accepted, is based on two broad propositions, neither of them quite explicit but both extremely important for the present value system of economists. The first is that the urgency of wants does not diminish appreciably as more of them are satisfied or, to put the matter more precisely, to the extent that this happens it is not demonstrable and not a matter of any interest to economists or for economic policy. When man has satisfied his physical needs, then psychologically grounded desires take over. These can never be satisfied or, in any case, no progress can be proved. The concept of satiation has very little standing in economics. It is neither useful nor scientific to speculate on the comparative cravings of the stomach and the mind.

The second proposition is that wants originate in the personality of the consumer. . . .

8 From John Kenneth Galbraith, *The Affluent Society* (Boston: Houghton Mifflin, 1958). Galbraith is a Harvard University economist.

Were it so that a man on arising each morning was assailed by demons which instilled in him a passion sometimes for silk shirts, sometimes for kitchenware, sometimes for chamber-pots, and sometimes for orange squash, there would be every reason to applaud the effort to find the goods, however odd, that quenched this flame. But should it be that his passion was the result of his first having cultivated the demons, and should it also be that this effort to allay it stirred the demons to ever greater and greater effort, there would be question as to how rational was his solution. Unless restrained by conventional attitudes, he might wonder if the solution lay with more goods or fewer demons.

So it is that if production creates the wants it seeks to satisfy . . . then the urgency of the wants can no longer be used to defend the urgency of the production. Production only fills a void that it has itself created. . . .

The even more direct link between production and wants is provided by the institutions of modern advertising and salesmanship. These cannot be reconciled with the notion of independently determined desires, for their central function is to create desires—to bring into being wants that previously did not exist. This is accomplished by the producer of the goods or at his behest. A broad empirical relationship exists between what is spent on production of consumers' goods and what is spent in synthesizing the desires for that production. A new consumer product must be introduced with a suitable advertising campaign to arouse an interest in it. The path for an expansion of output must be paved by a suitable expansion in the advertising budget. Outlays for the manufacturing of a product are not more important in the strategy of modern business enterprise than outlays for the manufacturing of demand for the product. None of this is novel. All would be regarded as elementary by the most retarded student in the nation's most primitive school of business administration. . . .

But such integration means recognizing that wants are dependent on production. It accords to the producer the function both of making the goods and of making the desires for them. It recognizes that production, not only passively through emulation, but actively through advertising and related activities, creates the want it seeks to satisfy.

The businessman and the lay reader will be puzzled over the emphasis which I give to a seemingly obvious point. The point is indeed obvious. But it is one which, to a singular degree, economists have resisted. They have sensed, as the layman does not, the damage to established ideas which lurks in these relationships. As a result, incredibly, they have closed their eyes (and ears) to the most obtrusive of all economic phenomena, namely modern want creation.

This is not to say that the evidence affirming the dependence of wants on advertising has been entirely ignored. It is one reason why advertising has so long been regarded with such uneasiness by economists. Here is something which cannot be accommodated easily to existing theory. More pervious scholars have speculated on the urgency of desires which are so obviously the fruit of such expensively contrived campaigns for popular attention. Is a new breakfast cereal or detergent so much wanted if so much must be spent to compel in the consumer the sense of want? But there has been little tendency to go on to examine the implications of this for the theory of consumer demand and even less for the importance of production and productive efficiency. These have remained sacrosanct. More often the uneasiness has been manifested in a general disapproval of advertising and advertising men, leading to the occasional suggestion that they shouldn't exist. Such suggestions have usually been ill received. . . .

The fact that wants can be synthesized by advertising, catalyzed by salesmanship, and shaped by the discreet manipulations of the persuaders shows that they are not very urgent. A man who is hungry need never be told of his need for food. If he is inspired by his appetite, he is immune to the influence of Messrs. Batten, Barton, Durstine and Osborn. The latter are effective only with those who are so far removed from physical want that they do not already know what they want. In this state alone men are open to persuasion. . . .

As a society becomes increasingly affluent, wants are increasingly created by the process by which they are satisfied. This may operate passively. Increases in consumption, the counterpart of increases in production, act by suggestion or emulation to create wants.

Or producers may proceed actively to create wants through advertising and salesmanship. Wants thus come to depend on output. In technical terms it can no longer be assumed that welfare is greater at an all-round higher level of production than at a lower one. It may be the same. The higher level of production has, merely, a higher level of want creation necessitating a higher level of want satisfaction. There will be frequent occasion to refer to the way wants depend on the process by which they are satisfied. It will be convenient to call it the Dependence Effect. . . .

The final problem of the productive society is what it produces. This manifests itself in an implacable tendency to provide an opulent supply of some things and a niggardly yield of others. This disparity carries to the point where it is a cause of social discomfort and social unhealth. The line which divides our area of wealth from our area of poverty is roughly that which divides privately produced and marketed goods and services from publicly rendered services. Our wealth in the first is not only in startling contrast with the meagerness of the latter, but our wealth in privately produced goods is, to a marked degree, the cause of crisis in the supply of public services. For we have failed to see the importance, indeed the urgent need, of maintaining a balance between the two.

This disparity between our flow of private and public goods and services is no matter of subjective judgment. On the contrary, it is the source of the most extensive comment which only stops short of the direct contrast being made here. In the years following World War II, the papers of any major city—those of New York were an excellent example—told daily of the shortages and shortcomings in the elementary municipal and metropolitan services. The schools were old and overcrowded. The police force was under strength and underpaid. The parks and playgrounds were insufficient. . . . Internal transportation was overcrowded, unhealthful, and dirty. So was the air. . . .

The family which takes its mauve and cerise, air-conditioned, power-steered, and power-braked car out for a tour passes through cities that are badly paved, made hideous by litter, blighted buildings, billboards, and posts for wires that should long since have been put underground. They pass on into a countryside that has been rendered largely invisible by commercial art. (The goods which the latter advertise have an absolute priority in our value system. Such aesthetic considerations as a view of the countryside accordingly come second. On such matters we are consistent.) They picnic on exquisitely packaged food from a portable icebox by a polluted stream and go on to spend the night at a park which is a menace to public health and morals. Just before dozing off on an air-mattress, beneath a nylon tent, amid the stench of decaying refuse, they may reflect vaguely on the curious unevenness of their blessings. Is this, indeed, the American genius?. . . .

The case for social balance has, so far, been put negatively. Failure to keep public services in minimal relation to private production and use of goods is a cause of social disorder or impairs economic performance. The matter may now be put affirmatively. By failing to exploit the opportunity to expand public production we are missing opportunities for enjoyment which otherwise we might have had. Presumably a community can be as well rewarded by buying better schools or better parks as by buying bigger cars. By concentrating on the latter rather than the former it is failing to maximize its satisfactions. . . .

The conventional wisdom holds that the community, large or small, makes a decision as to how much it will devote to its public services. This decision is arrived at by democratic process. Subject to the imperfections and uncertainties of democracy, people decide how much of their private income and goods they will surrender in order to have public services of which they are in greater need. Thus there is a balance, however rough, in the enjoyments to be had from private goods and services and those rendered by public authority.

It will be obvious, however, that this view depends on the notion of independently determined consumer wants. In such a world one could with some reason defend the doctrine that the consumer, as a voter, makes an independent choice between public and private goods. But given the dependence effect—given that consumer wants are created by the process by which they are satisfied—the consumer makes no such choice. He is subject to the forces of advertising and emulating by which production creates its own demand. Advertising operates exclusively, and emulation mainly, on behalf of privately produced goods and services. Since management and emulative effects operate on behalf of private production, public services will have an inherent tendency to lag behind. Car demand which is expensively synthesized will inevitably have a much larger claim on income than parks or public health or even roads where no such influence operates. The engines of mass communication, in their highest state of development, assail the eyes and ears of the community on behalf of more beer but not of more schools. Even in the conventional wisdom it will scarcely be contended that this leads to an equal choice between the two.

The competition is especially unequal for new products and services. Every corner of the public psyche is canvassed by some of the nation's most talented citizens it see if the desire for some merchantable product can be cultivated. No similar process operates on behalf of the non-merchantable services of the state. . . . The scientist or engineer or advertising man who devotes himself to developing a new carburetor, cleanser, or depilatory for which the public recognizes no need and will feel none until an advertising campaign arouses it, is one of the valued members of our society. A politician or a public servant who dreams up a new public service is a wastrel. Few public offenses are more reprehensible.

So much for the influences which operate on the decision between public and private production. The calm decision between public and private consumption pictured by the conventional wisdom is, in fact, a remarkable example of the error which arises from viewing social behavior out of context. The inherent tendency will always be for public services to fall behind private production. We have here the first of the causes of social imbalance.

• QUESTIONS •

1. What are the two assumptions of consumer demand theory as Galbraith explains it? How does Galbraith undermine those assumptions?
2. According to Galbraith, the notion that production is dependent on consumer demand, which is dependent on advertising, is dangerous, because most economists would sense "the damage to established ideas which lurks in these relationships." What does he mean by this?
3. Some would say that advertising does not create the desire to buy things, but simply taps into desires that already exist within us. According to Professor Hugh Rank, "If advertisers are often accused of peddling dreams, we must recognize first that they are *our* dreams: they are all genuine human desires; they are the benefits we seek." Do you agree?
4. Galbraith writes that we are paralyzed by a blitz "on behalf of more beer but not of more schools." Do you agree with him that advertising affects us so that we don't "want"—don't vote for—more and improved public goods and services? What would Milton Friedman and other free market economists say to this? How might a utilitarian thinker respond?

Federal vs. Industry Self-Regulation

The Federal Trade Commission

The Federal Trade Commission (FTC), one of the first federal agencies, has two broad mandates: to promote competition through its enforcement of the Sherman and Clayton Antitrust Acts, and to protect consumers. The agency was established by the Federal Trade Act of 1914, which outlawed "unfair methods of competition and unfair or deceptive acts and practices," including false or misleading advertising. Since then, the FTC has issued detailed regulations that outline its interpretation of the FTC Act and later consumer-protection laws.

Deceptive advertising claims are those likely to mislead reasonable consumers, causing them to change their conduct. These can take several forms. Obvious, or "express" claims must be truthful. An ad that appears to offer firsthand evidence of a product's qualities, for example, must be what it appears to be. The FTC pursued Campbell's Soup Company for having ad photos taken in which glass marbles were added to the bottom of bowls of soup, making it seem like they were brimming with vegetables.[9]

Advertisers are responsible, too, for suggested, or "implied" claims—the misleading messages that consumers are led to believe. In one case, the makers of Anacin invited consumers to discover whether "medically proven" Anacin would "work better" for them. While it was true the company had proved that Anacin contained more aspirin than other nonprescription analgesics, and that Anacin was as effective as its leading competitor, the ad was deceptive because it left the reasonable consumer with the wrong impression that Anacin had been "medically proven" to work better than any other analgesic.[10]

Some ads that are literally true are deceptive because of what they *don't* say; they fail to disclose information a consumer would consider important. Internet service providers America Online (AOL), Prodigy and CompuServe, for example, were all accused of deceptive advertising when their offers of "free trials" failed to mention that after the trial period, consumers would be automatically enrolled—and charged a monthly membership fee—unless they affirmatively cancelled during the free period.

Endorsements and testimonials must reflect the honest opinions or findings of the endorser. Ads that feature a named man identified as an "ordinary consumer" are deceptive unless, for example, his experience with weight loss is typical of what users of the product generally achieve. When an ad suggests that an endorser is an expert, she must have relevant expert qualifications and experience. It would be deceptive, for example, to have an "engineer" endorse a car if she were a chemical engineer and not an automotive engineer.

The FTC will typically investigate a complaint and attempt to settle it. One possible result is a **consent decree** that stops the ad from appearing. For example, the manufacturer of a well-known aerosol spray deodorant promoted the product as "ozone-friendly" because it did not contain or produce chlorofluorocarbons during its manufacture. What it failed to reveal was that butane, another air pollutant, was used as a substitute. The FTC barred the company from making "green" claims for products that add to air pollution. Where necessary, advertisers may be required to run new ads to correct misinformation in the original ad.

Opponents claim the FTC's process is much too slow; its preferred method of confronting false and misleading advertising is to proceed on a case-by-case basis, and a single case may take as long as 20 years to wend its way through the system. The FTC was relatively active during the 1970s, but in the early 1980s, President Ronald Reagan severely cut staff at the FTC and elsewhere in the federal government. In recent years, the agency has opened about 50 investigations and issued just 10 to 15 orders each year.

In 1996, still in its trimmed-down form, the FTC joined with state attorneys general to conduct a series of "sweeps"—investigations and enforcement actions against telemarketers, including "Operation Copycat," which attacked sellers of office and cleaning supplies, and "Operation Missed Fortune," aimed at fraudulent get-rich-quick schemes. On "American Health Claim Surf Day" in the fall of 1997, the agency joined with public health and consumer protection officials from Canada, Mexico, and the United States to surf the Internet for potentially false claims concerning medical treatments. Hundreds of warnings were sent out announcing that "cures"

9 *In re Campbell's Soup Co.*, 77 FTC 664 (1970).

10 *American Home Products Corp. v. FTC*, 695 F.2d 681 (3d Cir. 1982).

had to be substantiated. In 2001, the FTC partnered with the SEC and Commodities Futures Trading Commission in a coordinated crackdown on online firms offering the secrets to "easy cash," and with state and federal officials to end illegal online chain letters.

The following case was brought by the FTC against a company and its owner for making false and deceptive claims on Spanish-language television as it advertised that its product would eliminate cellulite.

FTC v. Silueta Distributors, Inc. and Stanley Klavir

United States District Court, California, 1995
1995 WL 215313

ARMSTRONG, District Judge.

Defendants promoted the sale of a product known as Sistema Silueta through advertisement broadcasts on KDTV, Channel 14, and on other Spanish-language stations across the country. Sistema Silueta consists of a moisture lotion and diuretic tablets. . . . [T]he advertisement represents that Sistema Silueta will eliminate cellulite from the body and that consumer testimonials support this assertion.

The Sistema Silueta advertisement features an unidentified man sitting on the edge of a desk, positioned in front of book-lined shelves. The man states: "I would like to talk to you for a few moments. Sistema Silueta is the scientific miracle of the moment." During this introduction, there is a subscript which reads: "We do not specify a determined weight loss with this product." The subscript disappears as the man continues: "Silueta is an astonishing treatment in two steps which penetrates the skin and attacks and dissolves the fat cells which are the cause of those ugly cellulite bumps, and later expels them from your body."

The commercial then switches to a swimsuit-clad woman who states: "We all know that neither diets nor strenuous exercises can get rid of cellulite, but with Sistema Silueta I did achieve it when I applied it on those areas I wanted to reduce." During the time the woman speaks, there is a subscript that reads: "To lose weight with this product, you need to eat less and follow the instructions."

The advertisement then moves into its third phase, which is comprised of illustration and narration. The illustration is of an overweight woman's body in a swimsuit. The figure rubs a cream onto corpulent and bumpy thighs. The figure then transforms and becomes thin. The next illustration apparently represents fat cells. Arrows are depicted entering into the spaces between the fat cells and the cells become smaller. Then a liquid pours over the picture, apparently washing the residue away. During this illustration phase, the narration is as follows: Step number one—the Silueta cream penetrates underneath the surface of the skin breaking those fat and cellulite deposits and converts them into liquids that step number two takes care of by expelling them from your body.

The advertisement then returns to the unidentified man's office. He is now sitting behind the desk and the swimsuit-clad woman is perched on the edge of the desk. The woman states: "Nothing could be easier. Start today to get the figure you have always dreamed about." During this last scene, there is a subscript that reads: "Testimonials on file."

At this point, the advertisement shows an 800 number. When a consumer calls the 800 number, the consumer is told that it is possible to order the Sistema Silueta products by C.O.D. Although the advertised cost of the Sistema Silueta regimen is $34.95 plus $5.00 shipping and handling, the C.O.D. cost of the regimen is $43.95.

Liability

Section 5(a) of the FTC Act declares unlawful "unfair or deceptive acts or practices in or affecting commerce" and empowers the Federal Trade Commission (the "Commission") to prevent such acts or practices. Section 12 of the FTC Act is specifically directed to false advertising. This section prohibits the dissemination of "any false advertisement" in order to induce the purchase of "food, drugs, devices, or cosmetics. . . ." The FTC Act defines "false advertisement" as "an advertisement, other than labeling, which is misleading in a material respect." An advertisement is misleading or deceptive if (1) there is a representation, omission, or practice that (2) is likely to mislead consumers acting reasonably under the circumstances, and (3) the representation, omission, or practice is material. Express product claims are presumed to be material. Furthermore, the use of a consumer endorsement violates Section 5 if the endorsement misrepresents that the alleged results are what consumers typically achieve.

FTC asserts that defendants' advertisement violated the FTC Act because it expressly and falsely represented that Sistema Silueta will eliminate cellulite, that Sistema Silueta has caused cellulite elimination in actual use, and that consumer testimonials support the conclusion that Sistema Silueta eliminates cellulite. Because these representations were expressly made in the advertisement, the materiality of the representations is presumed. Furthermore, because these representations relate to the very reason a consumer would purchase the product (i.e., to eliminate cellulite), these representations, if false, would clearly mislead consumers acting reasonably under the circumstances. Thus, the only issue here is whether the representations are false. . . .

Plaintiff provides ample evidence by way of expert declaration testimony establishing that Sistema Silueta cannot eliminate cellulite. This evidence reveals that the "cream is nothing more than a moisturizer, the ingredients of which are those found in body lotions and creams generally." Furthermore, the diuretic tablets contain an herbal diuretic that cannot cause the loss of cellulite, only water loss, which will be replaced immediately upon the ingestion of water.

Because defendants have presented no evidence contradicting plaintiff's contentions regarding any of the three representations, no genuine issue of fact exists as to whether defendants' Sistema Silueta advertisement was false and violated the FTC Act. Thus, this Court grants summary judgment in favor of plaintiff on this issue.

Klavir's Liability

Klavir asserts that he is not individually liable for the violations because he did not know and should not have known of the misrepresentations. Klavir maintains that he bought Silueta from Juan Perez, who created the advertisement for Sistema Silueta. Klavir claims that Perez stated he had verified the statements in the advertisement and Klavir had no reason to believe that Perez's verification was not accurate. Klavir claims that, except for products returned under the money-back guarantee, Klavir received no complaints about the product. Finally, he asserts that, as soon as plaintiff notified him of possible infractions of the FTC Act, defendants voluntarily stopped advertising the product. Based on these contentions, Klavir disclaims any individual liability in this case.

The policy behind the imposition of individual liability is to ensure that an individual defendant does not benefit from deceptive activity and then hide behind the corporation. Individual liability . . . can be predicated either on (1) having participated directly in the violative conduct, or (2) having had the authority to control the conduct. The parties do not dispute Klavir's authority to control Silueta's conduct, as he is the sole owner of Silueta. Disputed here is the issue of whether Klavir must have had knowledge of the conduct before liability attached. . . .

. . . Courts requiring a showing of knowledge before imposition of individual liability apply the following standard: The Commission must show that the individual defendant possessed one of the following: (1) actual knowledge of material misrepresentations, (2) reckless indifference to the truth or falsity of such misrepresentations, or (3) an awareness of a high probability of fraud along with an intentional avoidance of truth. . . .

The evidence presented here reveals that 63 percent of the consumers who ordered Sistema Silueta returned the product. Such an extraordinarily high rate of return should have placed Klavir on notice that the product did not eliminate cellulite as claimed by the advertisements. This evidence causes the Court to conclude that Klavir acted with a reckless indifference to the truth or falsity of the advertisement's misrepresentations, or, at a minimum, that Klavir had an awareness of a high probability of fraud and intentionally avoided the truth. Consequently, the Court finds that imposition of individual liability on Klavir is appropriate. . . .

Before moving on, the Court addresses Klavir's assertions that his reasonable reliance on the alleged verification made by Perez saves him from individual liability. The Court finds Klavir's argument to be unpersuasive for several reasons. . . . [N]othing in the record establishes Perez as a reliable source for an endorsement of Sistema Silueta. . . . [I]t was unreasonable for Klavir to rely on Perez's alleged verification, as this took place during a sales transaction between Klavir and Perez. It is unlikely that Perez would have informed Klavir, a prospective purchaser, that the advertisement was deceptive. . . . [T]he evidence reveals that the advertisement being challenged here was not the one created by Perez, but was one that was materially altered by Klavir. Klavir significantly edited the advertisement from a 1-minute running time to a 30-second running time. Finally, good faith reliance on another's representation is no defense to liability under the FTC Act.

[The defendant also objected to the remedy the government was seeking: not just a permanent injunction preventing Klavir from deceptively selling his product, but also "restitution and disgorgement," forcing him to give back his profits. The court ruled against Klavir on this issue also. Restitution and disgorgement are intended to prevent unjust enrichment, that is, to keep a company from benefiting from a deceptive trade practice. Klavir's firm had shipped 10,399 units of Silueta, but 6,546 were returned. Multiplying the unreturned shipments by the cost of each unit, the court required Klavir to "disgorge" $169,339.35. Then, using names and addresses provided by the defendant, the government would reimburse cheated consumers and keep in the U.S. Treasury whatever was left over.]

• QUESTIONS •

1. Why did Klavir claim he was not liable as an individual? How did the court respond? Note the treatment of Klavir's relationship with Perez, the creator of the actual ad. Why couldn't Klavir shift the responsibility for the Silueta commercial to Perez?

2. If you are led into making a contract by fraud or deception, you may sue to rescind the agreement and get your money back. Given that each of the misled customers for Silueta could have brought such a claim and won, do we need the FTC to pursue false advertisers also?

3. The Silueta ad appeared on Spanish-language television. Do you think this influenced the outcome of the case?

4. **Internet Assignment:** In the wake of September 11, the FTC has sent warnings to dozens of Web sites, ordering them to stop making unsubstantiated claims that their products would protect consumers from bioterrorism. Peddling such items as gas masks, mail sterilizers, protective suits, biohazard test kits, and a device called the "deGERMinator," which supposedly killed anthrax with ultraviolet light, the sites were told that they could be shut down, fined, or forced to reimburse their customers. What action has been taken since then by the FTC? Has the Food and Drug Administration (FDA) done anything to aid consumers?

5. **Internet Assignment:** Go to the FTC Web site, http://www.ftc.gov. Look for Advertising Policy Statements and Guidance. How does the agency define "deception"? "Unfairness"? What guidance is offered regarding advertising and marketing on the Internet?

Lanham Act

The Lanham Act was passed by Congress in 1946, one of a series of laws regulating business that were passed in reaction to the Great Depression. While the focus of the Lanham Act is trademark registration and protection, Section 43(a) gives competitors the right to sue for false or misleading advertising damaging to them. It has been interpreted to allow suits for false claims about either a company's own products or those of its rivals, and to include not only traditional advertising campaigns but infomercials, labels, and messages on telephone-answering systems.

To succeed under the Lanham Act, a plaintiff must prove that the defendant made a "factual misrepresentation" about a product or service, something more than sales "puffery." (The claim that a pregnancy test kit works "in as fast as ten minutes" is asserted as a fact and must be true. The claim that a pregnancy test kit is "the most advanced equipment available" is considered mere puffery, a general statement inflating the positive quality of what is for sale.) If a company can show that its rival's ads are actually false, or likely to confuse consumers, it can win a court order stopping the ads; to win money damages it must prove that it actually lost customers because of a rival's misleading claims.[11]

GlaxoSmithKline Consumer Healthcare (GSKCH) is in the nicotine replacement therapy (NRT) market. GSKCH sells two products–Nicorette, a nicotine gum, and a skin-patch called NicoDerm CQ. In 2002, it aired two TV commercials aimed at its competitor, Pharmacia, maker of Nicotrol.

The first ad, "Revised Tough Decision," features an actor portraying a consumer deciding whether to buy Nicorette or Nicotrol. A voice-over asks: "Trying to quit smoking? According to the labels, Nicorette gum can be used whenever you need it, day or night. Nicotrol's patch can only be worn for 16 hours." Superimposed text at the bottom of the screen reads: "Use anytime. Use as directed." The announcer then states: "So much for flexibility," after which the actor chooses Nicorette. The second commercial, "Revised Smart Choice" contrasts NicoDerm and Nicotrol, based on several criteria involving consumer preferences. At the end, the announcer states "more doctors prefer the patch that gives you the choice."

Pharmacia went to court seeking to stop the ad campaign, claiming that GSKCH was violating the Lanham Act. In the case that follows, the court must decide (1) whether it is likely that GSKCH violated the law and, (2) if so, whether the court should preliminarily enjoin the ad, pending a full trial.

PHARMACIA CORPORATION V. GLAXOSMITHKLINE CONSUMER HEALTHCARE

United States District Court, D. New Jersey, 2003
292 F.Supp.2d 594

COOPER, District Judge.

. . . A Lanham Act false or misleading statement may be proved in one of two ways. The plaintiff must show that "the commercial message or statement is either (1) literally false or (2) literally true or ambiguous, but has the tendency to deceive consumers.". . . [In cases of the second kind, plaintiff must show that a substantial portion of consumers actually understand the ad to be making the misleading claim, by producing] evidence that consumers are actually misled by the defendant's statements. . . .

11 Every state has its own laws banning unfair trade and consumer fraud. While federal law must be enforced by the FTC (FTC Act) or by lawsuits brought by an injured competitor (Lanham Act), some state laws, often referred to as "little FTC Acts" allow individuals harmed by false ads to sue. In addition, state tort laws offer remedies to consumers who have been harmed by the way a product has been marketed.

[Discussion of Pharmacia's Likelihood of Success in Proving its Lanham Act Claims]

[The court begins by assessing Pharmacia's claims that GSKCH's ad violates the Lanham Act. The first is that the "Revised Tough Decision" ad makes an expressly false claim about Nicorette:]

While the ad tells viewers that the label states Nicorette may be used any time the consumer needs it, Pharmacia argues, the label in actuality places limitations on when Nicorette may be used. Specifically . . . the label instructs consumers to refrain from chewing Nicorette while eating or drinking . . . cautions users not to continuously chew one piece after another, and not to use more than 24 pieces per day. Pharmacia asserts that these various restrictions render "Revised Tough Decision" literally false because there are significant periods of each day during which a user may not chew Nicorette.

[The court must decide whether the claim is literally false—a "per se" violation—or merely ambiguous.]

. . . If the statement in question does not make an unambiguous claim, there is no Lanham Act violation absent a showing of actual consumer deception. The Court must look at the commercial as a whole when making its assessment. . . . ("A determination of literal falsity rests on an analysis of the message in context.")

The Court finds that GSKCH's statement makes an ambiguous claim . . . "Revised Tough Decision" as a whole conveys the message that Nicorette is a more flexible aid to quitting smoking than Nicotrol. Within this context, we further find that the statement "According to the labels, Nicorette gum can be used whenever you need it, day or night" makes an ambiguous claim. One viewer could understand the commercial to claim that Nicorette's label allows consumers to use Nicorette at times when they would be unable to use Nicotrol. Alternatively, another viewer might conclude that GSKCH is claiming that the label permits users to chew the gum whenever they feel like it, even during a meal. The statement is open to interpretation.

. . . [Without evidence of actual consumer confusion we] will not preliminarily enjoin GSKCH from showing "Revised Tough Decision."

Pharmacia also alleges that "Revised Smart Choice" runs afoul of the Lanham Act because it makes the expressly false claim that doctors prefer NicoDerm [because it] offers the choice of being worn for either 16 or 24 hours. . . .

We find . . . that GSKCH does not have any evidence to support its claim that doctors prefer NicoDerm over Nicotrol because it offers choice, and therefore that claim is per se false.

[Is Pharmacia Entitled to a Preliminary Injunction?]

[Having decided that Pharmacia has made a strong case that GSKCH violated the Lanham Act, the court must decide how fair it is to award a preliminary injunction.]

Harm to Pharmacia

Pharmacia can establish irreparable harm if it can "demonstrate a significant risk that [it] will experience harm that cannot adequately be compensated after the fact by monetary damages. . . . We find that GSKCH's own research demonstrates that a commercial nearly identical to "Revised Smart Choice" was effective at eroding Nicotrol's position in the market in 1996, and that this format was revived because GSKCH believed it would work just as well again. These findings establish a significant risk of harm to Pharmacia, because Pharmacia will likely lose market share if GSKCH is free to air "Revised Smart Choice."

Harm to GSKCH

Pharmacia must also demonstrate that the potential harm it faces without injunctive relief outweighs the harm [GSKCH] will suffer should an injunction issue. . . . To the extent GSKCH is injured by an injunction . . . that injury was caused by GSKCH's own misconduct in making a false claim. The Court therefore discounts any such harm. The likely loss of market share Pharmacia faces without injunctive relief outweighs any harm to GSKCH caused by granting preliminary relief.

Public Interest

The final factor in the preliminary injunction inquiry is whether "the public interest favors issuing the injunction." Pharmacia urges that there is a strong public policy against the dissemination of false and misleading advertising. The Court finds that the case law in the Third Circuit supports this contention, especially in the context of OTC drug advertising. . . .

There is a public consideration that counsels against granting an injunction, however. The public has a strong interest in free competition. . . . The injunctive power of the courts should not be misused by manufacturers attempting to stifle the free market that is the cornerstone of our economy. Courts should therefore be wary of producers' pleas for injunctive relief against the advertisements of their close competitors.

We nevertheless find that "[t]he public interest in truthful advertising is obviously served by a court's prohibition of advertising that is plainly false."

Equitable Considerations

. . . GSKCH asserts that Pharmacia has itself engaged in false advertising, and thus Pharmacia's motion should be denied under the doctrine of unclean hands.

GSKCH argues that Pharmacia comes before the Court with unclean hands because in an October 2002 press release Pharmacia stated that Nicotrol was the only 16-hour patch in the NRT market. GSKCH contends that this statement (which, the Court finds, is false because NicoDerm is also approved for 16-hour use) should preclude Pharmacia from enjoining "Revised Smart Choice."

The Court disagrees. First, GSKCH has not alleged that Pharmacia's statement caused it injury, which is a predicate to application of the unclean hands doctrine. Second . . . the nexus between Pharmacia's statement and GSKCH's claim in "Revised Smart Choice" is too remote. Pharmacia's claim that Nicotrol is the only 16-hour patch was made in a mere press release. The claim did not disparage NicoDerm. In contrast, [the false claim in] "Revised Smart Choice" directly attacks Nicotrol. Further, GSKCH's false statement was made in a recurring television commercial aimed at influencing millions of consumers. This is a far cry from a single press release. Pharmacia's one false statement "does not excuse current deceptive and misleading advertisements to the public."

• QUESTIONS •

1. On what basis does the court conclude that GSKCH likely violated the Lanham Act?
2. What public interests are at stake in this case?
3. In 2004 a dispute arose between competitors in the $15 billion yellow pages industry. Sales tools in this business include self-commissioned surveys demonstrating the popularity of a company's products. Verizon SuperPages sued Yellow Book, a U.K.-based firm, under the Lanham Act, for falsely claiming in its survey material that its yellow pages were more heavily used than Verizon's. At pre-trial discovery, it was revealed that although Verizon's charges were correct, it would have a hard time proving economic harm at a trial. As the court explained:

   > *Damages would [be]particularly difficult to show because the industry as a whole . . . is suffering a gradual decline in revenues. Among the reasons for this decline are: the lack of trust on the part of advertisers in possession and usage figures*

generated by survey research firms hired by individual publishers; the availability on the internet of information previously found only in yellow pages print directories; and the increased reliance by consumers on shopping malls and all-purpose stores such as Walmart and Home Depot, resulting in the closure of many small businesses which traditionally advertised in the yellow pages.

The parties settled. Yellow Book agreed to stop making its false claims and to retrain its sales-force, but perhaps the most interesting aspect of the settlement was the judge's statement that

> *[t]he yellow pages industry requires, if it wishes to remain a healthy competitor with other advertising media, a reliable industry-wide survey procedure which can produce believable comparative and actual usage figures for potential advertisers. The evidence showed that it is entirely practicable to provide such reliable information and that the industry is in a position to adopt such a system. Such a voluntary national system would do more for truth in advertising, protection of the consumer, and the economic health of the industry than any injunction or damages in this litigation.*[12]

Internet Assignment: Find out what progress, if any, has been made in producing "a reliable industry-wide survey procedure."

Industry Self-Regulation

The advertising industry has established a number of mechanisms for self-regulation, and some commentators believe they are more effective than government regulation. For instance, all ad campaigns undergo a review process as they are conceptualized, both by the client (usually represented by a group of lawyers and other technical people) and the ad agency. Concern remains that the nature of the client/agency relationship can complicate thoughtful efforts to monitor the line between truth-telling and deception. Think of the way Perez interacted with Klavir in the *Silueta* case.

The National Advertising Division (NAD) of the Council of the Better Business Bureau is the official self-policing mechanism of the advertising industry. Set up in 1971 to preempt what might have been harsher government interference, NAD investigates about 180 disputes annually and resolves ninety-eight percent of them. In about half the cases the challenged company is let off the hook, and the rest of the time the client company changes or agrees to stop the ad. The two percent of cases not resolved are appealed to the National Advertising Review Board (NARB), which uses standards close to those of the FTC and Lanham Acts. Although NAD and NARB have no enforcement power, they can threaten to send a case to the FTC for government investigation, and they have been successful in stemming the flow of the most openly deceptive and misleading advertising.

In 1990, the American Association of Advertising Agencies adopted the following revision of its own guidelines.

Standards of Practice

We hold that the responsibility of advertising agencies is to be a constructive force in business.

We hold that, to discharge this responsibility, advertising agencies must recognize an obligation, not only to their clients, but to the public, the media they employ, and to each other. As a business, the advertising agency must operate within the framework of competition. It is recognized that keen and vigorous competition, honestly conducted, is necessary to the growth and

12 *Verizon Directories Corp. v. Yellow Book USA Inc.*, 338 F.Supp.2d 422 (E.D.N.Y. 2004).

health of American business. However, unethical competitive practices in the advertising agency business lead to financial waste, dilution of service, diversion of manpower, loss of prestige, and tend to weaken the public confidence. . . .

To these ends the American Association of Advertising Agencies has adopted the following Creative Code as being in the best interests of the public, the advertisers, the media, and the agencies themselves. . . .

Creative Code

We the members of the American Association of Advertising Agencies, in addition to supporting and obeying the laws of legal regulations pertaining to advertising, undertake to extend and broaden the application of high ethical standards. Specifically, we will not knowingly create advertising that contains:

a. False or misleading statements or exaggerations, visual or verbal
b. Testimonials that do not reflect the real opinion of the individual(s) involved
c. Price claims that are misleading
d. Claims insufficiently supported or that distort the true meaning or practicable application of statements made by professional or scientific authority
e. Statements, suggestions, or pictures offensive to public decency or minority segments of the population

We recognize that there are areas that are subject to honestly different interpretation and judgment. Nevertheless, we agree not to recommend to an advertiser, and to discourage the use of, advertising that is in poor or questionable taste or that is deliberately irritating. . . .

• QUESTIONS •

1. Television advertising for children has come under attack for many reasons. One is that small children have difficulty distinguishing between program content and advertising. When commercials for Nintendo's Pokemon video game punctuate the television cartoon show "Pokemon," small viewers are in effect absorbing 30-minute ads. There are also concerns that children are exposed to too much—to an avalanche of ads. In the late 1970s, the FTC recommended a series of changes, including banning all television advertising directed at children under the age of eight, and banning all television advertising for sugared food products directed at children between the ages of eight and twelve. This proposal was withdrawn after critics dubbed the FTC "National Nanny."[13] Do the AAAA Standards above address this issue?

Internet Assignment: Find a set of industry standards that address advertising targeting children. What are the recommendations? Compare them to those you find on a consumer protection site like http://www.consumersinternational.org/homepage.asp. What similarities do you note? Differences?

2. **Internet Assignment:**

a. Update the FTC's efforts to regulate advertising directed at children. Have there been any recent initiatives?

13 A bill decreasing the number of commercial minutes permitted in shows directed at children, vetoed by Reagan, was passed by Congress during the Bush administration. It limits these commercials to 10.5 minutes per hour on weekends and 12 minutes per hour on weekdays.

b. Can you find recent statistics regarding the number of television ads that a typical child is exposed to in the United States?

3. In the mid-1970s, most Saturday morning children's television commercials were for sugary cereals and candy. Today, while sugary cereals are still prominent, there's an added emphasis on fast food, and on large-sized kid's portions.[14] Given the obesity epidemic in the United States, should government take a stronger role in controlling these messages?

Market Manipulation

The Tobacco Story

The authors of the next excerpt ask whether the free market is not in fact prone to distortions caused by advertising and marketing techniques that influence how consumers perceive risk. They focus on the tobacco industry as an example of this syndrome for several reasons. "Firstly, the industry's enormous cash flow from repeat purchases of tobacco products allows the industry to spend unparalleled amounts of money on the tools of manipulation–including marketing research, promotion, public relations, and advertising. Second, the public has for some time been aware that tobacco products may pose serious health risks. That awareness, coupled with the fact that cigarettes are far and away the most dangerous consumer product marketed today, means that the incentive for manufacturer manipulation of risk perceptions is perhaps nowhere more strongly felt than in the cigarette industry. Third, the concentrated nature of the industry might have a catalytic effect on the industry's ability to manipulate."

A Case Study in Market Manipulation: The Tobacco Industry

Jon D. Hanson and Douglas A. Kysar[15]

Creating Demand

A major and constant challenge for cigarette manufacturers has been to create demand for their products among non-smokers—no easy task at the beginning of this century, when the tobacco industry was insignificant, cigarettes were sparse, and ours was not yet a smoking culture. . . . [T]he cigarette culture was itself an industry-nurtured phenomenon, a combined product "of corporate capitalism, technology, mass marketing, and, in particular, the impact of advertising."

. . . Cleverly targeted ad campaigns, such as the now-famous Marlboro Man, succeeded in creating demand for Marlboros and other cigarettes by conveying to smokers a sense of independence, autonomy, and sexuality. Not surprisingly, consumers soon associated cigarettes with desirable, abstract traits of the sort that they almost certainly would not have perceived absent effective advertising.

. . . "As long as there have been cigarettes there has been concern about their impact on health." The nature and degree of that concern, however, have changed dramatically over time. During the early part of this century . . . the health concerns that were articulated tended to involve

14 http://www.pbrc.edu/pressArticle.asp?id=3. Last visited December 24, 2004.

15 Jon Hanson is a professor at Harvard Law School; Douglas Kysar is a graduate of Harvard Law School. This excerpt is from their article "Taking Behavioralism Seriously: Some Evidence of Market Manipulation," 112 *Harv. L. Rev.* 1420 (May 1999).

relatively trivial issues, such as whether cigarettes decreased smokers' "mental efficiency" or stunted smokers' growth. Nevertheless, the issue was significant enough for manufacturers to turn to the emerging advertising and public relations industries for assistance. . . .

[T]he health-oriented campaign by R. J. Reynolds Tobacco Company (RJR) for Camel cigarettes in the 1930s revealed the enormous potential of an aggressive, multi-faceted advertising strategy. Some campaign advertisements directly refuted potential health risks—"[Camels] don't get your wind" and "So mild . . . you can smoke all you want." Others ads portrayed Camels as a soothing health aid: "Get enough sleep and fresh air—find time for recreations. Make Camels your cigarette. You can smoke as many Camels as you please." RJR sometimes reinforced bold assertions like these with meaningless appeals to science ("A [fact]: Science Advances New Data That May Completely Change Your Ideas of Cigarettes") [and] through endorsements by the medical establishment itself. RJR reassured the public that "[d]octors recommend Camel." Regardless of their veracity, these sorts of advertisements appear to have been extremely successful. By the end of 1937, Camels were outselling the main competition, Luckies and Chesterfields, by approximately forty percent. . . .

Following increased public awareness of the dangers of smoking in the 1950s, manipulation of consumer risk perceptions became a much more complicated process for cigarette manufacturers. A favorite tactic was the development of "revolutionary" new types of cigarettes that could be positioned as "safer" cigarettes. . . . Recently released documents regarding a conference of tobacco company scientists in 1968 demonstrates that several of the scientists at the conference emphasized the distinction between a "[h]ealth image" or "health reassurance cigarette," such as a "low tar-low nicotine cigarette which the public accepts as a healthier cigarette," and a "[h]ealth-oriented" cigarette, which is intended to be truly safer. . . .

Filter-Tipped Cigarettes

In the early 1950s, the cigarette companies marketed filters as "trapping the dangerous components of cigarette smoke but letting the 'flavor' through." Ironically, the most successful early filter, touted quite explicitly for its health protection properties, used asbestos as the filtering agent. . . . However, in reality, to compensate for the taste that was lost to the filter, the new brands used stronger tobaccos that contained about as much tar and nicotine as the unfiltered brands, rendering the filters essentially "cosmetic mouthpieces."

Affording smokers an apparent alternative to quitting, filters rapidly became the dominant product on the market. Indeed, their introduction and marketing quickly reversed the two-year decline in per capita cigarette consumption in 1953 and 1954, which had resulted from new evidence linking lung cancer to smoking. Because the manufacturers provided a new type of cigarette, consumers could reasonably assume that the risks of the old type of cigarette and the studies indicating the dangers of that cigarette were irrelevant. The industry was able to offer, in other words, the mechanism through which the smoker could find "self-justification" for his or her behavior. . . .

Low-Tar and Low-Nicotine Cigarettes

The industry's next technological "fix" was the low-tar and low-nicotine cigarette, which was marketed, often explicitly, as a viable alternative to quitting for health-conscious smokers. [B]y 1980, over fifty percent of cigarettes sold were "low-tar." Those health reassurance cigarettes quickly accomplished their aim: the public grew to view them as important, safer alternatives to "regular" cigarettes. . . . Cigarette companies even attempted to persuade physicians to prescribe their use for patients unable or unwilling to quit. . . .

The industry has made . . . efforts to ensure that smokers, although believing that they are smoking "safer" cigarettes are, in fact, maintaining their addiction to nicotine. Specifically, the industry has manipulated the nicotine content of health reassurance cigarettes to provide the enhanced pharmacological effect that ensures even health-conscious smokers will remain addicted to the product.

. . . Cigarette manufacturers have also accomplished this enhanced nicotine content by developing raw tobacco with higher nicotine delivery. Testifying before the Subcommittee on Health and the Environment in the Summer of 1994, then FDA Director Dr. David A. Kessler described a program undertaken by B & W, which developed a tobacco plant known as "Y-1" with more nicotine content. Over ten years, B & W secretly produced a genetically engineered plant with more than twice the level of nicotine found in regular tobacco. To conceal its work, B & W patented the plant in Brazil and shipped millions of pounds to the United States for use in five B & W brands, including three identified as "light" cigarettes. . . .

[V]arious other forms of nicotine manipulation persist. For instance, all American cigarette manufacturers except Liggett add ammonia compounds to their tobacco. . . . According to John Kreisher, a former associate scientific director of the Council for Tobacco Research, "[a]mmonia helped the industry lower the tar and allowed smokers to get more bang with less nicotine. It solved a couple of problems at the same time. . . ."

Recruiting New Smokers

. . . [The]1970s became a period of marketing innovation for the more aggressive among them. The paramount goal of the industry changed from maintaining the existing smoking population to recruiting new smokers, especially young new smokers. . . . Indeed, examination of industry documents reveals a near obsession with marketing to the "pre-smoker."

The industry's chief strategy for capturing this "pre-smoker" market is pervasive, relentless advertising. Cigarettes are among the most promoted consumer products in the United States. The FTC reported to Congress that domestic cigarette advertising and promotional expenditures rose from close to $4 billion in 1990 to more than $6 billion in 1993. Tobacco imagery—product brand names, logos, and advertising messages—is ubiquitous. It can be found on or in everything from billboards to magazines, and from city buses to race cars. The effect is to convey the message "to young people that tobacco use is desirable, socially acceptable, safe, healthy, and prevalent." In fact, young people tend to buy the most heavily advertised cigarette brands, whereas many adults buy more generic or value-based cigarette brands, which have little or no image-based advertising. . . .

In 1967 . . . new advertisement campaigns [such as Philip Morris' for Virginia Slims] specifically targeting young girls coincided with a 110% jump in twelve-year-old starters. . . .

In the spring of 1972, Dr. Claude Teague, then assistant chief of research and development at RJR, wrote a memo discussing what motivates different groups of smokers to smoke, including the marketing of cigarettes to youths. The memo describes the profile of an ideal cigarette for a beginning smoker (between ages thirteen and seventeen) as mild tasting so as not to put them off in the beginning, containing lower-than-normal nicotine because children's bodies have not yet acclimated to nicotine, and being promoted with a simultaneous emphasis on togetherness and individuality. The new campaign that RJR established as a result was Joe Camel. . . . The smooth character appears to have appealed to underage consumers. Studies published in a 1991 issue of the Journal of the American Medical Association found that Joe Camel is almost as familiar to six-year-old children as Mickey Mouse, that the campaign has enticed thousands of teens to smoke the brand, and that Camel's popularity with twelve-to seventeen-year-olds has surged. . . . In three years, the brand jumped from three percent to over thirteen percent of the market, and its consumer niche shifted from the over-fifty smoker to the under-twenty-one smoker.

None of those practices was permissible under the industry's self-imposed regulatory scheme—the Cigarette Advertising Code (the Code)—which was adopted in 1965 and was purportedly intended to restrict advertising to target only persons over twenty-one. The Code prohibited advertising in comic books, school papers, and children's television and radio programs, forbade distribution of samples to the underaged, and disallowed the use of models under the age of twenty-five in commercials or advertisements. But the Code had no real effect. Because of loopholes in its language, millions of children and teenagers watched programs sponsored by cigarette companies and read magazines filled with cigarette ads. A July 1995 report by the California Department of Health Services that surveyed tobacco advertisements in or around almost six thousand stores found that on average there were slightly more than twenty-five tobacco advertisements per store. The report also found that stores within one thousand feet of a school had significantly more tobacco advertising and promotions than stores that were not near schools. Not surprisingly, [the most frequently advertised and promoted brands,] Marlboro and Camel, are the leading brands smoked by children.

Despite these disturbing statistics, each of the cigarette manufacturers involved maintains that the effect of its pervasive advertising and promotion of cigarettes is limited to maintaining brand loyalty and that it has no role in encouraging adolescents to experiment with smoking. That public position, however, is belied by the industry's private practices. Consider the fact that, unlike the health reassurance cigarette described above, tobacco products aimed at minors are not positioned as safer or less risky than other cigarettes. . . . There is growing evidence that cigarette warnings may actually give the product an enhanced gloss in the eyes of young consumers. Several studies have demonstrated a forbidden fruit appeal from television parental advisory warnings for violent shows. Similar studies on the labeling effects of alcoholic versus nonalcoholic drinks also suggest that the warning itself may enhance the attractiveness of the product. Tobacco industry executives seem to have been well aware of that possibility. . . .

[When, at mid-century, news of the health dangers associated with tobacco reached the popular press, the industry made a decision to appear concerned and cooperative, meanwhile organizing itself, with the help of skilled public relations advice, in an "extraordinary decades-long campaign . . . to foster and perpetuate 'controversy' over whether cigarettes cause disease and, more recently, whether they are addictive." Here, the authors explain how this process began—with a proactive, not just a defensive, strategy.]

. . . [T]he chief executive officers of the leading cigarette manufacturers met on December 15, 1953 at the Plaza Hotel in New York City. Also in attendance was the public relations firm Hill & Knowlton, which was to play a central role in formulating and executing the industry's response. . . .

Just one week after the meeting, Hill & Knowlton presented a public relations proposal . . . [which] emphasized that . . . the industry would have to gain the public trust and avoid the appearance of bias. Two key public relations goals for the industry, therefore, were to maintain the appearance of a "controversy" regarding the health effects of smoking and to pledge to consumers (and lawmakers) their own fidelity to consumer health in their own research into this "controversy."

[Within three weeks of their initial meeting, the tobacco manufacturers placed a full-page ad in 448 newspapers around the nation, with total circulation of more than 43 million people in some 250 cities. This ad was entitled "A Frank Statement to Cigarette Smokers."] The Frank Statement included the following reassurances:

Recent reports on experiments with mice have given wide publicity to a theory that cigarette smoking is in some way linked with lung cancer in human beings. . . . We accept an interest in people's health as a basic responsibility, paramount to every other consideration in our business.

. . . We always have and always will cooperate closely with those whose task it is to safeguard the public health. . . .

1. We are pledging aid and assistance to the research effort into all phases of tobacco use and health. . . .

2. For this purpose we are establishing a joint industry group consisting initially of the undersigned. This group will be known as TOBACCO INDUSTRY RESEARCH COMMITTEE.

3. In charge of the research activities of the Committee will be a scientist of unimpeachable integrity and national repute. In addition there will be an Advisory Board of scientists disinterested in the cigarette industry. A group of distinguished men from medicine, science, and education will be invited to serve on this Board. . . .

By the Spring of 1955, it was fairly apparent that Hill & Knowlton's self-defense strategy had been successful. According to one 1955 memorandum, "Suspicion is still widespread but the lynching party seems to have been called off. . . . Even adverse stories now tend to carry modified statements. . . ."

Internal documents seem to demonstrate that the joint industry research efforts undertaken through TIRC and the Council for Tobacco Research (CTR) were self-consciously designed to promote favorable research, suppress negative research where possible, and attack negative research when it could not be suppressed, all in order to assuage smokers' fears. Perhaps the most succinct statement of these objectives comes from a memorandum, believed to have been written by J.V. Blalock, B & W's director of public relations: "Doubt is our product since it is the best means of competing with the 'body of fact' that exists in the mind of the general public. It is also the means of establishing a controversy."

Creating and sustaining controversy over the risks of smoking became standard practice in the industry.

• QUESTIONS •

1. According to the authors, how did the tobacco industry manipulate adults regarding the dangers of smoking? How did it manipulate young smokers?
2. Many argue that, because the health dangers associated with cigarettes are obvious and/or have been known for a long time, when people smoke, they are merely exercising their freedom to choose. How would the authors respond to this claim?
3. Should there be special restrictions on the advertising and marketing of products that are lethal? If so, which products qualify? What restrictions should exist? How might a legal challenge be mounted in opposition to such restrictions?
4. How would a free market thinker view the history of the tobacco industry described by the authors? A utilitarian? A Kantian? A communitarian?
5. **Internet Assignment:** The first world treaty dealing with public health will go into effect in February 2005. The Framework Convention on Tobacco Control bans all tobacco advertising, promotion and sponsorship. Find out which forty countries ratified the treaty. Is the United States a signatory? Why or why not? What can you find out about the likely effectiveness of this global effort to reign in tobacco marketing?

Direct-to-Consumer Pharmaceutical Advertising

The following case was brought by a group of women who had experienced problems with the contraceptive Norplant. Norplant is an FDA-approved reversible contraceptive that can prevent pregnancy for up to five years. Its maker, Wyeth Laboratories, marketed Norplant heavily to women rather than doctors, advertising on television and in women's magazines such as *Glamour, Mademoiselle* and *Cosmopolitan*. The plaintiffs claim that these ads touted the convenience and simplicity of Norplant, and that none carried warnings of side effects, which, as enumerated by the majority judge in this appeal, included "weight gain, headaches, dizziness, nausea, diarrhea, acne, vomiting, fatigue, facial hair growth, numbness in the arms and legs, irregular menstruation, hair loss, leg cramps, anxiety and nervousness, vision problems, anemia, mood swings and depression, [and] high blood pressure." In addition, there were complications with removal of the Norplant device. Plaintiffs point to research published in medical journals. One study reported that Norplant removal was difficult for one-third of women and painful 40 percent of the time. Another found that doctors experienced difficulty in removing the implant in more than half of all instances.

SARAY PEREZ V. WYETH LABORATORIES INC.

Supreme Court of New Jersey, 1999
734 A.2d 1245

O'HERN, Judge.

Our medical-legal jurisprudence is based on images of health care that no longer exist. At an earlier time, medical advice was received in the doctor's office from a physician who most likely made house calls if needed. The patient usually paid a small sum of money to the doctor. Neighborhood pharmacists compounded prescribed medicines . . . It is safe to say that the prevailing attitude of law and medicine was that the "doctor knows best."

Pharmaceutical manufacturers never advertised their products to patients, but rather directed all sales efforts at physicians. . . .

For good or ill, that has all changed. Medical services are in large measure provided by managed care organizations. Medicines are purchased in the pharmacy department of supermarkets and often paid for by third-party providers. Drug manufacturers now directly advertise products to consumers on the radio, television, the Internet, billboards on public transportation, and in magazines. . . . The question in this case, broadly stated, is whether our law should follow these changes in the marketplace or reflect the images of the past. . . .

Direct-to-Consumer Advertising

It is paradoxical that so pedestrian a concern as male-pattern baldness should have signaled the beginning of direct-to-consumer marketing of prescription drugs. Upjohn Company became the first drug manufacturer to advertise directly to consumers when it advertised for Rogaine, a hair-loss treatment. The ad targeted male consumers by posing the question, "Can an emerging bald spot . . . damage your ability to get along with others, influence your chance of obtaining a job or date or even interfere with your job performance?". . .

Advertising for Rogaine was the tip of the iceberg. . . . [The court later mentions medicine for allergies, nail fungus, hypertension, and depression.]

Pressure on consumers is an integral part of drug manufacturers' marketing strategy. From 1995 to 1996, drug companies increased advertising directed to consumers by ninety percent. In 1997, advertising costs of pharmaceutical products surpassed the half-billion dollar mark for the first time, "easily outpacing promotional efforts directed to physicians. . . ." These efforts . . . [have been] extremely successful. . . . As of December 1998, "because of its testimonials" in print and broadcast media by renowned personalities, sales of a product that treats male impotence had increased to $788 million, with approximately 7.5 million prescriptions having been written.

[To highlight why the medical establishment has been troubled by DTC advertising, the majority next quotes from the 1999 *Harvard Law Review* article we have just read on market manipulation:]

> *The American Medical Association (AMA) has long maintained a policy in opposition to product-specific prescription ads aimed at consumers. A 1992 study by the Annals of Internal Medicine reports that a peer review of 109 prescription ads found 92 per cent of the advertisements lacking in some manner.*
>
> *The difficulties that accompany this [type of advertising] practice are manifest. "The marketing gimmick used by the drug manufacturer often provides the consumer with a diluted variation of the risks associated with the drug product." Even without such manipulation, "[t]elevision spots lasting 30 or 60 seconds are not conducive to 'fair balance' [in presentation of risks]." Given such constraints, pharmaceutical ads often contain warnings of a general nature. However, "[r]esearch indicates that general warnings (for example, see your doctor) in [DTC ads] do not give the consumer a sufficient understanding of the*

risks inherent in product use." Consumers often interpret such warnings as a "general reassurance" that their condition can be treated, rather than as a requirement that "specific vigilance" is needed to protect them from product risks.[16]

[Traditionally, companies had a legal duty to warn consumers directly of dangers associated with their products. An exception developed however, in the area of pharmaceutical drugs: manufacturers do not have to warn consumers as long as they have warned physicians adequately. This **Learned Intermediary Rule** made sense in the "doctor knows best" world described at the start of this case, a setting where consumers are dependent upon their doctors for advice and information about prescription drugs.]

[T]he respected Judge John Minor Wisdom explained the rationale behind the learned intermediary doctrine. His perspective reflects the then-prevalent attitude about doctor-patient relationships:

> *This special standard for prescription drugs is an understandable exception to the Restatement's general rule that one who markets goods must warn foreseeable ultimate users of dangers inherent in [the] products. . . . Prescription drugs are likely to be complex medicines, esoteric in formula and varied in effect. As a medical expert, the prescribing physician can take into account the propensities of the drug, as well as the susceptibilities of [the] patient. [The physician's] task [is to weigh] the benefits of any medication against its potential dangers. The choice [the physician] makes is an informed one, an individualized medical judgment bottomed on a knowledge of both patient and palliative. Pharmaceutical companies then, who must warn ultimate purchasers of dangers inherent in patent drugs sold over the counter, in selling prescription drugs are required to warn only the prescribing physician, who acts as a "learned intermediary" between manufacturer and consumer.*
>
> *Reyes v. Wyeth Labs, Inc.* 498 F.2d 1264 (5th Cir. 1974)

A more recent review summarized the theoretical bases for the doctrine as based on four considerations.

> *First, courts do not wish to intrude upon the doctor-patient relationship. From this perspective, warnings that contradict information supplied by the physician will undermine the patient's trust in the physician's judgment. Second, physicians may be in a superior position to convey meaningful information to their patients, as they must do to satisfy their duty to secure informed consent. Third, drug manufacturers lack effective means to communicate directly with patients, making it necessary to rely on physicians to convey the relevant information. Unlike [over the counter products], pharmacists usually dispense prescription drugs from bulk containers rather than as unit-of-use packages in which the manufacturer may have enclosed labeling. Finally, because of the complexity of risk information about prescription drugs, comprehension problems would complicate any effort by manufacturers to translate physician labeling for lay patients. . . .*

These premises . . . are all (with the possible exception of the last) absent in the direct-to-consumer advertising of prescription drugs.

First, with rare and wonderful exceptions, the "Norman Rockwell" image of the family doctor no longer exists. . .

Second, because managed care has reduced the time allotted per patient, physicians have considerably less time to inform patients of the risks and benefits of a drug. "In a 1997 survey of

16 Jon D. Hanson and Douglas A. Kaysar, "Taking Behaviorism Seriously: Some Evidence of Market Manipulation," 112 *Harv. L. Rev.* 1420 (1999).

1,000 patients, the FDA found that only one-third had received information from their doctors about the dangerous side effects of drugs they were taking."

Third, having spent $1.3 billion on advertising in 1998, drug manufacturers can hardly be said to "lack effective means to communicate directly with patients," when their advertising campaigns can pay off in close to billions. . . .

. . . Concerns regarding patients' communication with and access to physicians are magnified in the context of medicines and medical devices furnished to women for reproductive decisions. In *MacDonald v. Ortho Pharmaceutical Corp.*, 475 *N.E.*2d 65 (1985), the plaintiff's use of oral contraceptives allegedly resulted in a stroke. The Massachusetts Supreme Court explained several reasons why contraceptives differ from other prescription drugs and thus "warrant the imposition of a common law duty on the manufacturer to warn users directly of associated risks." For example, after the patient receives the prescription, she consults with the physician to receive a prescription annually, leaving her an infrequent opportunity to "explore her questions and concerns about the medication with the prescribing physician." [And] because oral contraceptives are drugs personally selected by the patient, a prescription is often not the result of a physician's skilled balancing of individual benefits and risks but originates, instead, as a product of patient choice. Thus, "the physician is relegated to a . . . passive role."

. . . When a patient is the target of direct marketing, one would think, at a minimum, that the law would require that the patient not be misinformed about the product. It is one thing not to inform a patient about the potential side effects of a product; it is another thing to misinform the patient by deliberately withholding potential side effects while marketing the product as an efficacious solution to a serious health problem. Further, when one considers that many of these "life-style" drugs or elective treatments cause significant side effects without any curative effect, increased consumer protection becomes imperative, because these drugs are, by definition, not medically necessary. . . .

The direct marketing of drugs to consumers generates a corresponding duty requiring manufacturers to warn of defects in the product. The FDA has established a comprehensive regulatory scheme for direct-to-consumer marketing of pharmaceutical products. . . .

[The majority holds that the plaintiffs can argue in tort that the manufacturers of Norplant misinformed them, substantially "contributing to their use of a defective pharmaceutical product. . . ."]

POLLOCK, Judge, dissenting.

Norplant is not an over-the-counter drug; it can be obtained only with a doctor's prescription. To insert Norplant, a physician or other health-care professional anesthetizes an area in a patient's upper arm, makes a one-eighth-inch incision, and implants six capsules just below the patient's skin. Similar surgery is required to remove the capsules.

The use of Norplant thus requires the significant involvement of the prescribing physician. Even Norman Rockwell would recognize the procedure as one performed in accordance with the traditional physician-patient relationship. . . . The invasiveness of the Norplant procedure, moreover, would give any patient pause and a physician cause to evaluate the risks. . . .

The majority identifies four premises underlying the learned intermediary doctrine that it asserts are inapplicable when a manufacturer advertises the drug directly to consumers. . . . Contrary to the majority, those four considerations remain relevant to the implantation of Norplant.

First, the Norplant System must be implanted surgically. Implicit in the performance of a surgical procedure is respect for the physician-patient relationship. "[T]he physician is in the best position to take into account the propensities of the drug and the susceptibilities of the patient, and to give a highly individualized warning to the ultimate user based on the physician's specialized knowledge." Second, the physician is the only person who can communicate with the patient to obtain the patient's informed consent to the procedure. Third, a pharmaceutical company, such as Wyeth, cannot provide an adequate warning to each individual consumer about the potential side-effects and risks associated with the device. Each patient has individualized risks associated with surgical procedures. Lastly, the Norplant implant, far more than other birth control devices, is a complex contraceptive system that requires detailed instructions and warnings.

• QUESTIONS •

1. What is the Learned Intermediary Rule? Explain the context in which it became law.
2. On what legal grounds does the majority believe that the Learned Intermediary Rule does not apply where drugs are advertised directly to consumers? How does the dissent view this issue?
3. Beginning in the 1990s, with their research pipelines drying up, the major players in the pharmaceutical industry moved to sustain profits by fighting to extend patent periods, by advertising direct-to-consumers, and by raising drug prices. The facts of a case filed recently in California reflect a blend of these strategies: As the patent for AstraZeneca's blockbuster drug for acid reflux, Prilosec, ran out, the company spent millions to persuade consumers that their new and eight times more expensive product, Nexium, was more effective in treating acid reflux than Prilosec in its generic, over-the-counter form. As of late 2004, Nexium was AstraZenenca's best selling product, ranked seventh among all prescription drug sales in the United States. With a $257 million blitz to promote Nexium, the "purple pill," in 2003, the company outspent all other pharmaceutical drug campaigns that year. AstraZeneca was sued by a coalition including senior citizens groups and the A.F.L.-C.I.O., the first time the union joined litigation aimed at controlling health care costs. The plaintiffs argued that the Nexium ads were deceptive. **Internet Assignment:** Find out what happened in this case.
4. One theme of the *Perez* case is the degree to which consumers today are active, aware, and taking responsibility for their own health, rather than passively in awe of medical expertise. Direct-to-consumer advertising—estimated at $3.8 billion as of 2003—is premised on the notion that consumers will be driven to want certain prescription drugs, and to ask for them by name when they see their doctors.
   a. From a consumer perspective, what are the pros and cons of DTC advertising?
   b. Who are the major stakeholders in the pharmaceutical direct-to-consumer scenario? Does this type of marketing create "the greatest happiness for the greatest number," in utilitarian terms? What might a deontological thinker say about DTC marketing?

Fighting Spam

In 2003 it was estimated that 40 percent of all e-mail was spam—unsolicited commercial e-mail—two-thirds of which were false or misleading in some way. That same year, the cost to businesses of spam was estimated at $10 billion annually. According to one Internet marketing researcher, some 206 billion spam items will be sent to American consumers by the year 2006—a figure which means every Internet user will receive 1,400 spam e-mails, twice as many as were received in 2003. Spam clogs ISP networks, undercuts the legitimacy of genuine online marketers, and burdens ordinary consumers with staggering amounts of often creepy message content—typical spam entices the recipient to bank millions in Nigerian oil money for ex-dictators, or offers magical sex cures.

Anti-Spam Legislation and the First Amendment

The Electronic Frontier Foundation, a nonprofit organization that advocates a range of policies affecting the Internet, is concerned that any federal law to prevent spam should not interfere with the ability of nonspam political messages to be communicated online. The following policy statement was posted by the EFF in October 2001.

ANTI-SPAM MEASURES

Electronic Frontier Foundation[17]

While members of the EFF staff and board find this unsolicited e-mail to be as annoying as everyone else, we believe that the two most popular strategies for combatting it so far—legislation and anti-spam blacklists—have failed in their fundamental design. Anti-spam bills have been badly written, are unconstitutionally overbroad, and frequently wander into areas where legislators have no expertise, such as the establishment of Internet standards. And anti-spam blacklists, such as the MAPS RBL (Mail Abuse Prevention System Realtime Blackhole List, the most popular), result in a large number of Internet service providers (ISPs) surreptitiously blocking large amounts of non-spam from innocent people. This is because they block all e-mail from entire IP address blocks—even from entire nations. This is done with no notice to the users, who do not even know that their mail is not being delivered.

The focus of efforts to stop spam should include protecting end users. . . . Specifically, any measure for stopping spam must ensure that all non-spam messages reach their intended recipients. Proposed solutions that do not fulfill these minimal goals are themselves a form of Internet abuse and are a direct assault on the health, growth, openness and liberty of the Internet.

E-mail is protected speech. There is a fundamental free speech right to be able to send and receive messages, regardless of medium. Unless that right is being abused by a particular individual, that individual must not be restricted. It is unacceptable, then, for anti-spam policies to limit legitimate rights to send or receive e-mail. . . .

The Two Extremes of the Current E-mail Battlefield

The legislative proposals that have dominated the anti-spam policy debate for the last several years have failed, and rightly so. The several existing state laws against spam are of questionable constitutionality, too hard to enforce even if they should be enforced, and have done nothing to stem the tide of spam. National legislation will not solve the problem either, while creating a morass of unintended consequences. Serious problems with the anti-spam legislation we have seen to date include:

- misdefinitions of key terms and concepts, including "commercial," "list," and "spam" itself;
- technology-specific requirements that will be rapidly obsolete;
- a focus on punishing expression rather than protecting privacy;
- the giving of broad power or obligation to ISPs to control the private e-mail of their customers;
- jurisdictional problems;
- unnecessary and excessive criminalization of private, civil disputes;
- requirements with which senders will find it impossible to comply;
- and a clear pattern of providing a defense for ISPs in the form of immunity from the simple realities and responsibilities of the marketplace, rather than one of enabling individuals to protect themselves. . . .

The search for a nonexistent, and ultimately impossible, legislative or ISP-level blacklist "magic bullet" solution has actually distracted the Internet community for the last five years from the real solution: better voluntary user-end filtering and/or voluntary, informed and flexible ISP-level

17 Archived at http://www.eff.org/Spam_cybersquatting_abuse/Cybersquatting/ (Last visited July 21, 2003.)

filtering. Only an end user-controlled solution will uphold the rights of the end users while serving to deter spam by removing most of the audience and making it unprofitable to continue junk e-mailing.

The Right Way to Look at Spam

Until we include the free speech rights of all end-users instead of trying to stop a few wrongdoers at the cost of innocent users, any solution for dealing with spam will be fundamentally flawed. End users, known as "customers" to ISPs, should demand that none of their wanted e-mail be censored in attempts to filter out unwanted messages. In addition, Netizens should express their dismay at spam by boycotting products advertised with spam.

On a larger scale, EFF supports combatting spam by providing end-users with adequate tools to filter unwanted messages on the receiving end. We also support the development of more robust and subtle technology for this purpose. Brightmail, for example, has created a system that does a good, if still imperfect, job. Others that attempt to do this are listed at http://spam.abuse.net/tools/mailblock.html.

From a technical standpoint, we would like to see the development of better filtration software on servers, something that could work interactively with the mail recipient in defining what he or she regards as spam using pattern recognition. That is, every time somebody gets a message of a sort he or she does not want, s/he could send it to the filter, thereby making that filter smarter over time, as well as giving it the ability to "learn" as spam techniques develop.

The rights of users to send and receive e-mail must not be compromised for quick and dirty ways to limit unsolicited bulk e-mail. Neither misguided and ignorant legislation, nor collusive, high pressure protection schemes, have a legitimate function or place in our online future. The Constitution, and the promise of a free, open Internet that exists for and is controlled by its participants, requires us to do better.

• QUESTIONS •

1. **Internet Assignment:** The Controlling the Assault of Non-Solicited Pornography and Marketing Act, or CAN-SPAM, was signed into law late in 2003. (a) Find out its major provisions. Would the EFF approve? Why or why not? (b) Find out if it has made a difference. Has the amount of spam been reduced since CAN-SPAM?

2. Consider the various stakeholders in the spam situation: spammers, legitimate online marketers, consumers, ISPs. Think of utilitarian ethical analysis. How do the harms and benefits fall among them?

3. Months after CAN-SPAM was passed, the amount of junk e-mail flooding the Internet remained as strong as ever. The goal of Project Slam-Spam, an unusual teaming of the FBI and other federal investigators with private investigators hired by the Direct Marketing Association, was to generate a sweep of spam prosecutions by the end of 2004. **Internet Assignment:** Was Project Slam-Span a success? Why or why not?

4. How do the efforts to limit spam compare to those aimed at direct marketing by telemarketers? In 2003, the FTC and FCC joined to create the National Do Not Call Registry, aimed at commercial telemarketers. (a) **Internet Assignment:** Assess the success of the Do Not Call Registry to date. What do critics say? (b) Telemarketers have gone to court, claiming the registry violates their Constitutional rights, in part because it places no limits on political or charitable solicitations. Find out what happened in *Mainstream Marketing Services Inc. v. FTC*, 358 F.3d 1228 (10th C. 2004).

Global Issues: Marketing on the Internet

While advertising online offers a global reach, complex ethical issues can surface where cultural values—like freedom of expression—and historical experience differ. In the spring of 2000, Yahoo's auction Web site posted Nazi and Ku Klux Klan memorabilia for sale. Yahoo has a policy against offensive material, but would not enforce it unless a user or watchdog group complained loudly enough. No U.S. law prohibits the advertising of such products (the First Amendment and the *Central Hudson* case would likely not allow one to stand), but in France, Germany and other European nations, it is illegal to advertise Nazi paraphernalia. A French court ordered Yahoo to pay fines of $13,000 per day unless the company installed technology to shield French users from seeing Nazi items on auction sites. In December 2000, Yahoo sites still listed more than 1,000 items related to the Klan or to Nazism, including knives, robes, and daggers, but by January 2001, Yahoo had installed a monitoring program that reviewed information sellers planned to post online and sent rejection messages to sellers whose submissions violated company standards.

THE BRANDING OF CULTURE

In her provocative book *No Logo,* journalist and media commentator Naomi Klein claims that a fundamental shift has occurred—from marketing as advertising of products to marketing itself as the product—to the pre-eminence of "the brand." She sees this shift as having profound consequences for every aspect of our culture.

NO LOGO

Naomi Klein

The astronomical growth in the wealth and cultural influence of multinational corporations over the last fifteen years can arguably be traced back to a single, seemingly innocuous idea developed by management theorists in the mid-1980s: that successful corporations must primarily produce brands, as opposed to products.

Until that time, although it was understood in the corporate world that bolstering one's brand name was important, the primary concern of every solid manufacturer was the production of goods. This idea was the very gospel of the machine age. . . .

[By the 1980s] a new kind of corporation began to rival the traditional all-American manufacturers for market share; these were the Nikes and Microsofts, and later, the Tommy Hilfigers and Intels. These pioneers made the bold claim that producing goods was only an incidental part of their operations, and that thanks to recent victories in trade liberalization and labor-law reform, they were able to have their products made for them by contractors, many of them overseas. What these companies produced primarily were not things, they said, but images of their brands. Their real work lay not in manufacturing but in marketing. . . .

The Beginning of the Brand

It's helpful to go back briefly and look at where the idea of branding first began. Though the words are often used interchangeably, branding and advertising are not the same process. . . . Think of the brand as the core meaning of the modern corporation, and of the advertisement as one vehicle used to convey that meaning to the world. The first mass-marketing campaigns, starting in the second half of the nineteenth century, had more to do with advertising than with branding as we understand it today. Faced with a range of recently invented products—the radio, phonograph, car, light bulb and so on—advertisers had more pressing tasks than creating a brand identity for any given corporation; first, they had to change the way people lived their lives. Ads had to inform consumers about the existence of some new invention, then convince them that their lives would be better if they used [it].

[Klein explains how, in the ad campaigns of the late nineteenth and early twentieth centuries, ads were more descriptive than persuasive, and rivals were not mentioned in the copy. Then things began to change.]

By the end of the 1940s, there was a burgeoning awareness that a brand wasn't just a mascot or a catchphrase or a picture printed on the label of a company's product; the company as a whole could have a brand identify or a "corporate consciousness," as the ephemeral quality was termed at the time. . . .

The search for the true meaning of brands—or the "brand essence," as it is often called—gradually took the agencies away from individual products and their attributes and toward a psychological/anthropological examination of what brands means to the culture and to people's lives.

[She goes on to tell how, for companies like Nike, Apple, the Body Shop, Disney, Levi's and Starbucks, the branding process was becoming more important than the actual products.]

They integrated the idea of branding into the very fabric of their companies. Their corporate cultures were so tight and cloistered that to outsiders they appeared to be a cross between fraternity house, religious cult and sanitarium. Everything was an ad for the brand: bizarre lexicons for describing employees (partners, baristas, team players, crew members), company chants, superstar CEOs, fanatical attention to design consistency, a propensity for monument-building, and New Age mission statements. . . .

[As Klein sees it, the new marketplace is marked by two important developments: "The deeply unhip big-box bargain stores that provide the essentials of life and monopolize a disproportionate share of the market (Wal-Mart, et al.) and the extra-premium 'attitude' brands that provide the essentials of lifestyle and monopolize ever-expanding stretches of cultural space (Nike, et al.)." Here she gives some examples of the "attitude" brands in action:]

The Starbucks coffee chain, meanwhile, was also expanding during this period without laying out much in advertising: instead, it was spinning off its name into a wide range of branded projects: Starbucks airline coffee, office coffee, coffee ice cream, coffee beer. Starbucks seemed to understand brand names at a level even deeper than Madison Avenue, incorporating marketing into every fiber of its corporate concept—from the chain's strategic association with books, blues and jazz to its Euro-latte lingo. What the success of . . . Starbucks showed was how far the branding project had come in moving beyond splashing one's logo on a billboard. Here (was a company) that had fostered powerful identities by making their brand concept into a virus and sending it out into the culture via a variety of channels: cultural sponsorship, political controversy, the consumer experience and brand extensions. Direct advertising, in this context, was viewed as a rather clumsy intrusion into a much more organic approach to image building. . . .

Interestingly, before moving to Starbucks, Bedbury was head of marketing at Nike, where he oversaw the launch of the "Just Do It!" slogan, among other watershed branding moments. In the following passage, he explains the common techniques used to infuse the two very different brands with meaning:

Nike, for example, is leveraging the deep emotional connection that people have with sports and fitness. With Starbucks, we see how coffee has woven itself into the fabric of people's lives, and that's our opportunity for emotional leverage. . . . A great brand raises the bar—it adds a greater sense of purpose to the experience, whether it's the challenge to do your best in sports and fitness or the affirmation that the cup of coffee you're drinking really matters. . . .

[Klein next describes how a new breed of companies style themselves as "meaning brokers" instead of "product producers." The actual product takes a back seat to the real product, the "brand."]

The Brand Expands

The effect, if not always the original intent, of advanced branding is to nudge the hosting culture into the background and make the brand the star. It is not to sponsor culture but to be the culture. And why shouldn't it be? If brands are not products but ideas, attitudes, values and experiences, why can't they be culture too? . . . This project has been so successful that the lines between corporate sponsors and sponsored culture have entirely disappeared . . . What was once a process of selling culture to a sponsor for a price has been supplanted by the logic of "co-branding"—a fluid partnership between celebrity people and celebrity brands.

The project of transforming culture into little more than a collection of brand-extensions-in-waiting would not have been possible without the deregulation and privatization policies of the past three decades. In Canada under Brian Mulroney, in the U.S. under Ronald Regan and in Britain under Margaret Thatcher (and in many other parts of the world as well), corporate taxes were dramatically lowered, a move that eroded the tax base and gradually starved out the public sector. As government spending dwindled, schools, museums and broadcasters were desperate to make up their budget shortfalls and thus ripe for partnerships with private corporations. It also didn't hurt that the political climate during this time ensured that there was almost no vocabulary to speak passionately about the value of a non-commercialized public sphere. This was the time of the Big Government bogeyman and deficit hysteria, when any political move that was not overtly designed to increase the freedom of corporations was vilified as an endorsement of national bankruptcy. It was against this backdrop that, in rapid order, sponsorship went from being a rare occurrence (in the 1970s) to an exploding growth industry (by the mid-eighties). . . .

[Klein goes on to discuss the notion of "cool," a perfect way for product-based companies to move into branding. Cool is a concept that "applies equally to the forty-seven-year-old baby boomers scared of losing their cool and the seven-year-olds kick-boxing tots watching the Backstreet Boys."]

Designers like Strussy, Hilfiger, Polo, DKNY and Nike have refused to crack down on the pirating of their logos for T-shirts and baseball hats in the inner cities and several of them have clearly backed away from serious attempts to curb rampant shoplifting. By now the big brands know that profits from logo wear do not just flow from the purchase of the garment but also from people seeing your logo on "the right people," as Pepe Jeans' Phil Spur judiciously puts it. The truth is that the "got to be cool" rhetoric of the global brands is, more often than not, an indirect way of saying "got to be black." Just as the history of cool in America is really (as many have argued) a history of African-American culture—from jazz and blues to rock and roll and rap—for many of the superbrands, cool hunting simply means black-culture hunting. Which is why the cool hunters' first stop was the basketball courts of America's poorest neighborhoods. . . .

Tommy Hilfiger: To the Ghetto and Back Again

Tommy Hilfiger, even more than Nike or Adidas, has turned the harnessing of ghetto cool into a mass-marketing science. Hilfiger forged a formula that has since been imitated by Polo, Nautica, Munsingwear (thanks to Puff Daddy's fondness for the penguin logo) and several other clothing companies looking for a short cut to making it at the suburban mall and inner-city attitude.

. . . Hilfiger ads are a tangle of Cape Cod multiculturalism: scrubbed black faces lounging with their windswept white brothers and sisters in that great country club in the sky, and always against the backdrop of a billowing American flag. "By respecting one another we can reach all cultures and communities," the company says. "We promote . . . the concept of living the American dream." But the hard facts of Tommy's interracial financial success have less to do with finding common ground between cultures than with the power and mythology embedded in America's deep racial segregation.

Tommy Hilfiger started off squarely as white-preppy wear in the tradition of Ralph Lauren and Lacoste. But the designer soon realized that his clothes also had a peculiar cachet in the inner cities, where the hip-hop philosophy of "living large" saw poor and working-class kids acquiring status in the ghetto by adopting the gear and accoutrements of prohibitively costly leisure activities, such as skiing, golfing, even boating. Perhaps to better position his brand within this urban fantasy, Hilfiger began to associate his clothes more consciously with these sports, shooting ads at yacht clubs, beaches and other nautical locales. At the same time, the clothes themselves were redesigned to appeal more directly to the hip-hop aesthetic. Cultural theorist Paul Smith described the shift as "bolder colors, bigger and baggier styles, more hoods and cords, and more prominence for logos and the Hilfiger name." He also plied rap artists like Snoop Dogg with free clothes and, walking the tightrope between the yacht and the ghetto, launched a line of Tommy Hilfiger beepers.

Once Tommy was firmly established as a ghetto thing, the real selling could begin—not just to the comparatively small market of poor inner-city youth but to the much larger market of middle-class white and Asian kids who mimic black style in everything from lingo to sports to music. Company sales reached $847 million in 1998—up from a paltry 53 million in 1991 when Hilfiger was still, as Smith puts it, "Young Republican clothing." Like so much of cool hunting, Hilfiger's marketing journey feeds off the alienation of the heart of America's race relations: selling white youth on their fetishization of black style, and black youth on their fetishization of white wealth.

• QUESTIONS •

1. How does Klein distinguish the following: marketing, advertising, branding? Which does she view as dominant today?

2. Compare Klein's article to the Galbraith reading at the beginning of this chapter. To what extent does Klein's analysis overlap or support Galbraith's? Does it contradict Galbraith in any way?

3. Klein attributes Tommy Hilfiger's financial success to the "power and mythology embedded in America's deep racial segregation." What does she mean by this? Can you argue against that view?

4. Is there anything unethical about a marketing strategy that exploits racial or gender stereotypes, or that turns racial/gender realities upside down?

   One of Klein's concerns is the blurring of the distinction between advertising and media content. Recent Nike commercials, for example, are lengthy MTV spots that appeared to be music videos. In April 2001, one such ad ran for two-and-a-half minutes with a funk-music sound track. Further confusing the sponsored/nonsponsored divide, the basketball players in the ad are both professional and so-called streetball players. The commercial has nothing in it that is overtly selling, in fact. For just one moment a player thrusts a basketball with the Nike swoosh logo at the camera. "It doesn't have any shoe shots," says the creative director of this ad. "It's more about celebrating the game. We were interested in something that would turn kids on to basketball so they would pick up the ball and play. We wanted to communicate that basketball is a game about freedom and self-expression and individuality."

   What, if anything, is wrong with a marketing strategy like this? Do any ethical issues occur to you?

5. Recently, famous actors like Rob Lowe, Kathleen Turner, Lauren Bacall and Danny Glover have appeared on talk shows to discuss different medical problems, and to recommend

particular drugs to treat them. Viewers never hear that the entertainers are actually paid by pharmaceutical companies to make these statements. Is this anything to do with the branding of culture? Why or why not? Is it ethical?

CHAPTER PROBLEMS

1. What of the "aesthetic appeal" of advertising? Consider this:

> *During recent years, in certain circles, the surest way to silence a would-be critic of advertising has been to cite its artistic achievements. Whatever we may think of the products or the sponsors, this argument runs, we have to admit that those creative types in the agencies are . . . clever, sometimes even brilliant. The only influence—far from sinister—they have exercised has been to enliven our cultural atmosphere with staccato visual and verbal rhythms of the commercial vernacular. . . .*
>
> *Since the late nineteenth century, advertising has given people who like to write, draw, or shoot film the opportunity to get paid regularly (maybe even well) for it. The industry has attracted many extraordinarily talented people. These artists and writers have served, in a sense, as emissaries between social universes, the agency-client world and the wider population; art and big business; museums and commercial culture. They have worked various boundaries, sometimes creatively reconnecting aesthetics and everyday life, more often conforming out of the necessity of agency organization. Whatever their accomplishments, they deserve more than a passing glance. . . .*[18]

And this:

> *Like advertising, poetry's purpose is to influence an audience; to affect its perceptions and sensibilities; perhaps even to change its mind. . . . [P]oetry's intent is to convince and seduce. In the service of that intent, it employs without guilt or fear of criticism all the arcane tools of distortion that the literary mind can devise. Keats does not offer a truthful engineering description of his Grecian urn. He offers, instead . . . a lyrical, exaggerated, distorted, and palpably false description. And he is thoroughly applauded for it, as are all other artists, in whatever medium, who do precisely the same thing successfully.*
>
> *Commerce . . . takes essentially the same liberties with reality . . . as the artists, except that commerce calls its creations advertising. . . . As with art, the purpose is to influence the audience by creating illusions, symbols, and implications that promise more than pure functionality. . . .*[19]

Is certain advertising art? Is all advertising art? None of it?

18 Jackson Lears, *Fables of Abundance: A Cultural History of Advertising in America* (New York: Basic Books, 1994), pp. 261–262.

19 Theodore Levitt, "The Morality (?) of Advertising," *Harv. Bus. Rev.* 48 (July–August 1970), p. 85.

2. In 1998, Coca-Cola held a contest inviting high-school students to devise promotional ideas for the company. A prize of $500 would go to the school with the best PR strategy. Greenbriar High in Evans, Georgia, was the winner. On "Coke Day," students were to attend lectures from visiting company executives, wear Coke t-shirts to school and pose for a group photograph, spelling out the word Coke with their bodies. Senior Mike Cameron decided to play a prank. Just as the group formation photo was about to be taken, he removed his outer shirt to reveal a Pepsi t-shirt. He was suspended for being rude and disruptive. The principal explained: "We had the regional president of Coca-Cola here and people flew in from Atlanta to do us the honor of being resource speakers." Is there anything ethically troubling about this story? Is there a distinction between paid advertisements in schools and corporate sponsorship of the content of education?

3. Should advertisers be allowed access to young students through the schools? (a) What do you think about advertising on school Web sites? About Channel One, the pre-packed current events and commercials "newscast" sold to high schools around the United States, along with "free" television sets, satellite receivers and other equipment? Are they more—or less—ethical than the "exclusive contracts" that high schools and universities sign with the vending companies that supply certain brands of soft drinks or other items in the schools? (b) **Internet Assignment:** What other examples of corporate sponsorship of educational content can you find? Use what you find to write an essay addressing these questions:
   (i) Does the assistance offered to schools by companies come with strings attached?
   (ii) Is corporate involvement a welcome and often crucial helping hand?

4. Back in the 1980s, marketers did not perceive children as a target audience for advertising. Apart from Saturday morning television, which was basically an excuse to show children ads for cereals and toys, children were not noticed by them. Then—big changes. Demographically, the traditional nuclear family model gave ground to the single-parent model, and old-style parenting faded into a baby-boomer philosophy that was more "laid back" about wielding authority. The result: "a much more influential kid," as Paul Kurnit, the president of a Madison Avenue ad agency puts it. In the late twentieth century our economy went through an extended period of growth, and the purchasing power of children increased enormously. At this point, children can influence their families' purchasing decisions—not just of breakfast cereals, but of "cars, vacations, computers." Today's children, according to Kurnit, are "getting older younger."

   In "The Selling of the Clickerati,"[20] reporter Bob Thompson tells this story about 12-year-old Tori Clifford.

   > *One day last spring . . . [s]he was looking through a magazine—she thinks it might have been Seventeen—and her eye was drawn to a blurb about a new Web site. It offered a way for kids like her, who are too young to have their own credit cards, to complete purchases online. "It was like, 'iCanBuy.com, your parents can give you an allowance and you can just go buy whatever you want.' And I said, 'Ooh, that sounds cool!'" She told her mother about it and they checked out the site together. Pretty soon she had an iCanBuy account with a $100 balance. Every time she signed on, she was greeted by a purple screen that proclaimed itself "Tori's Room" and reminded her how many days it was until her birthday. She began to compile an iCanBuy wish list, so people interested in buying gifts for her would know exactly what she wanted. On May 23, she made her first purchase: a purple-blue synthetic Vee Luv sweater from MXG with cranberry and gray stripes. It cost $32, plus $4.99 for shipping.*

   What are the ethical implications of "marketing in kidspace"?

---

20 *The Washington Post,* October 24, 1999.

5. Within the high-stakes $400 billion pharmaceutical industry, about twice as much is spent on marketing as on research. Lately many of its marketing practices have come under scrutiny. In May 2004 Pfizer paid a $430 fine and pled guilty to criminal charges over the marketing by its subsidiary Warner-Lambert of a drug called Neurontin. While it is illegal for a drug company to market a medicine for uses that have not been approved by the FDA, physicians can prescribe for their patients in whatever manner they think best. The Warner-Lambert marketing strategy was to pay doctors tens of thousands of dollars each if they would agree to give talks to groups of other doctors, explaining that Neurontin, which had been approved for epilepsy, could be prescribed for several other ("off label") uses. One of these physician/lecturers was paid more than $300,000; others, including some from prestigious medical schools, received more than $100,000 each. Neurontin became a top-selling drug, producing $2 billion in sales as doctors prescribed it for a range of maladies, including bipolar disorder and restless-leg syndrome.[21]

In 2004, another drug company, Schering-Plough, sent unsolicited checks for $10,000 to doctors, seeking their agreement to take part in clinical trials (for which no real work was required)—and to prescribe its Hepatitis C drug.

By 2004, a government crackdown on the marketing techniques of the pharmaceutical industry was underway, with nearly every global drug company receiving subpoenas.

What would an ethical analysis of these marketing strategies look like from a free market perspective? From the point of view of a utilitarian? A deontologist? A virtue ethicist? A proponent of the ethic of care?

6. In 1980, roughly one-third of all biomedical research was funded by the pharmaceutical industry; as government support declined, the industry stepped in, and by 2000 it funded nearly two-thirds of such work. The industry also provides much of the advertising that supports the publication of professional medical journals, such as the *New England Journal of Medicine.* A 1998 study of medical journal editorials about a controversial group of blood pressure medications found that those who favored the drugs were much more likely to have (undisclosed) financial ties to the drug manufacturers than those who were critical. The industry is also entwined in the regulatory apparatus: In the summer of 2004 a federal panel recommended that Americans at risk of heart disease should radically reduce their cholesterol levels from previous estimates. Most of the members of the panel had financial ties to the pharmaceutical companies that make "statins," new drugs that lower cholesterol.

(a) What ethical concerns do these links between industry, the medical profession, and government raise? Can you think of any ways to protect consumers from any harms that might result? (b) **Internet Assignment:** Find out what reforms have been proposed by Public Citizen. Find out what you can about Public Citizen (who supports it, what is its record, etc.). (c) Find out who opposes the efforts of Public Citizen and why.

7. By the year 2030 tobacco will be the biggest cause of death, killing about 10 million people annually. The fastest growing population of smokers exists in the developing world. In China, for example, there are an estimated 300 million smokers—one-third of its adult population and triple the number of 20 years ago. In the Philippines, 73 percent of adults and half the children ages 7 to 17 smoke. Africa has never been thought of as a primary growth region for smoking, but Philip Morris' profit there has been increasing at the rate of 20 percent a year. And in India, where only 12 percent of people smoke, both R. J. R. Reynolds and Philip Morris are now a presence, trying to tap the last major virgin market for tobacco

21 "I want you out there every day selling Neurontin. . . . Pain management, now that's money. We don't want to share these patients with everybody, we want them on Neurontin only. We want their whole drug budget—not a quarter, not half—the whole thing. . . . Hold their hand and whisper in their ear: 'Neurontin for pain, Neurontin for everything.' I don't want to see a single patient coming off Neurontin before they've been up to at least 4,800 milligrams a day. I don't want to hear that safety crap, either. Have you tried Neurontin? Every one of you should take one just to see there's nothing. It's a great drug!" (Transcript of a whistleblower lawsuit filed against Pfizer and Warner-Lambert in 1996, and unsealed in 2003.)

consumption. What ethical considerations arise when tobacco companies market their products in developing countries?

8. The chic political and cultural Web logs (blogs) run by Gawker Media receive some 400,000 to 700,000 visitors monthly. Recently Gawker began blogging on behalf of big advertisers like Nike. For its advertorial blog "The Art of Speed," Nike provided several short films on the theme of speed and Gawker contributed commentary and layout. A Nike representative called the Gawker blog audience "the right community. It may be small but it's an important and influential group." **Internet Assignment:** Find any blog site containing advertising. What kind of buzz is the sponsor trying to generate? How would you describe the connection between the company's branding and its blogging?

9. New York's Metropolitan Transportation Authority proposes to sell naming rights to bridges and to rail and subway stations to corporate advertisers. Meanwhile, in Rome, city planners have been very successful raising funds for restoring ancient buildings and monuments by selling advertising space. Billboards hang on scaffolding while a structure is being renovated. As of 2004, 50 important sites with aging facades were available to the highest advertising bidder—including the Pantheon—while a huge (and very suggestive) billboard advertising Glam Shine lipstick hung over the Spanish Steps. Is this a win-win situation? What are the ethics of mixing public and private imperatives in this way? Where should the line be drawn?

10. A young, attractive couple is hanging around in Times Square. They are wearing backpacks, and they have a Sony-Ericsson cellular telephone with them, one of the new ones with a digital camera attached. Approaching a passerby, the young man of the couple smiles and says: "Would you take a picture of me and my girlfriend?" Almost everyone is willing to do so, and as they do, he explains how the new gadget works. "It's easy. Look. Just push this button. This is so sweet. I just got it. . . ." Soon the passerby is intrigued with the cell phone too. And although she'll never find out, the passerby has just had an encounter with two paid operatives in what is called a "viral marketing" campaign, promoting a product like a virus spreads disease—silently but very effectively.

    Gary Ruskin, executive director of Commercial Alert, has two big objections to this type of strategy. First, he calls it deceptive. "People think these are tourists but really they are corporate shills. Second it's intrusive. It's like telemarketing in your face."

    Do you agree? How would you feel if the pretty woman flirting with you at the bar, asking for a light for her new cigarette, turned out to be hawking that new cigarette? Does stealth marketing seem unethical to you?

Chapter Project

Legislative Hearing: Hard Liquor Advertising on Network Television

Guidelines in Appendix F

In 1948, the makers of distilled spirits placed a voluntary ban on television ads. In 1996, the industry lifted its ban, and in December 2001, a spot promoting designated drivers on behalf of Smirnoff vodka ran on NBC's "Saturday Night Live." Liquor ads had been appearing on cable and local TV, but this was the first breakthrough into the networks. NBC has its own 19-point guideline for hard liquor ads. They may appear only on shows where at least 85 percent of the audience is 21 years and older; they cannot promote drinking as a "mark of adulthood" or a "rite of passage"; and they cannot show the actual consumption of liquor, for instance. But many are arguing that the stakes are too high to trust industry self-regulation.

You will be representing an interest group testifying before a congressional commerce committee on the question of whether government regulation should control liquor ads on TV.

Spokespeople:

- Seagram's president, representing the industry
- NBC president, representing the networks
- ACLU representative, free speech advocate
- American Medical Association (AMA) president
- Mothers Against Drunk Drivers (MADD) representative
- Reverend Jesse Brown, African-American activist against tobacco and alcohol advertising to blacks
- Republican congressperson
- Democratic congressperson
- Head of the Commerce Committee

Risk Allocation: Products Liability

It would not be possible for Noah to do in our day what he was permitted to do in his own. . . . The inspector would come to examine the Ark and make all sorts of objections.

— Mark Twain, "About All Kinds of Ships" (1892)

Consumers by definition, include us all. They are the largest economic group, affecting and affected by almost every public and private economic decision. Yet they are the only important group . . . whose views are often not heard.

— President John F. Kennedy, declaration to U.S. Congress (1962)

For centuries, the phrase ***caveat emptor*** ("buyer beware") dominated the law in Britain and the United States, warning that most sellers made no promises with regard to the goods they sold. Until the middle of the twentieth century, business could count on common law doctrines and defenses that made it difficult for injured persons to pinpoint a company as having legal liability for harms caused by the products it made and sold.

By slow twists and turns, the laws of contracts, warranty, and negligence began to change. By 1963, when the ***Restatement (Second) of Torts***[1] was adopted, the law had been turned on its head. Injured plaintiffs could look to Section 402A of the *Restatement* to support their arguments that sellers should be liable for harm caused by unreasonably dangerous products. Prosecutors in some states even brought criminal charges against companies that marketed the worst of them.

As if in backlash, an attempted counterrevolution is under way. Recent changes in procedural and evidentiary rules have made it harder for plaintiffs in federal courts to win against sellers of defective goods. Many states have passed laws that sharply curtail damages and foreclose certain kinds of suits, such as those against gun manufacturers. Congress continues to debate proposals for additional tort law "reform." And the common law enshrined in the *Second Restatement* and adopted by courts in most states has been challenged. In 1997, the American Law Institute issued the *Restatement of the Law (Third), Torts: Products,* a document that would rewrite the common law of torts to make it more favorable to sellers. While only a handful of state courts have chosen to adopt the *Third Restatement,* it seems clear that this area of law will be hotly contested for the foreseeable future.[2]

1 The *Restatement* is an attempt by legal scholars to summarize and "restate" the common law based on judicial precedents from around the country.

2 Six states have expressly approved the *Restatement (Third),* three of them by legislation; four have expressly rejected it. See Frank J. Vandall and Joshua F. Vandall, "A Call for an Accurate Restatement (Third) of Torts: Design Defect," 33 *U. Mem. L. Rev.* 909 (2003).

This chapter opens with a Wisconsin tort case that explores two views of the common law. The majority remains plaintiff-friendly, ruling that Wisconsin should stick with the *Restatement Second;* the dissent wants to change Wisconsin's tort rules. Then, we look at punitive damages and the call for tort reform through the eyes of leading litigators. We shift from tort to contract law, as we focus on product liability under the Uniform Commercial Code. In exploring government regulation we look in particular at one of the nation's largest and most controversial industries: pharmaceuticals.

UNSAFE PRODUCTS

Linda Green began her career as a health care worker at St. Joseph's Hospital in Milwaukee, Wisconsin, in 1978. During the course of her employment, hospital rules required Green to wear protective gloves while attending patients. The gloves she wore—cornstarch-powdered latex—were made by Smith & Nephew (S&N).

Today, experts believe that some people become "sensitized" to latex through allergic reactions. Subsequent exposure may cause the person to develop progressively worse reactions, including irreversible asthma. Occasionally hypersensitivity may trigger anaphylactic shock, a life-threatening reaction to even a small exposure.

In 1989, when Green was wearing almost 40 pairs of gloves per shift, the health care community was not generally aware that persons could develop latex allergy. Five years later, Green—certain of her own reaction to the gloves—sued S&N.

Green did not accuse the company of negligence. Instead, her case rested on a claim that S&N should be held "strictly liable" for selling gloves that were unreasonably dangerous and defective in two respects: (1) they contained excessive levels of allergy-causing latex proteins, and (2) the cornstarch with which S&N powdered its gloves increased the likelihood of inhaling the latex proteins and developing a latex sensitivity. The jury found for Green and the company appealed.

GREEN V. SMITH & NEPHEW AHP, INC.

Supreme Court of Wisconsin, 2001
629 N.W.2d 727

WILCOX, Judge.

Background

Prior to 1989, Green never had experienced allergies; however, in 1989 Green began suffering various health problems. Early that year, Green's hands became red, cracked, and sore, and began peeling. In response to this condition, she applied hand lotion, changed the soap she used, changed the type of hand towels she used, and tried various other remedies. Nevertheless, the rash continued.

By September 1989, Green's condition deteriorated. Her rash spread to her upper trunk and neck, and she began experiencing chronic cold-like symptoms such as a runny nose and watery eyes. Green's symptoms grew increasingly severe, eventually culminating in an acute shortness of breath, coughing, and tightening of the throat. As a result, Green spent significant time in the hospital. . . .

After undergoing various treatments and tests, Green was diagnosed in May 1991 with latex allergy. This allergy has compelled Green to avoid contact with latex, thus causing her to change jobs and limit the items she purchases, things she eats, and activities in which she participates. Moreover, Green's latex allergy caused her to develop asthma, thereby further limiting her lifestyle.

Analysis

Strict products liability holds manufacturers and other sellers of products accountable for selling defective and unreasonably dangerous products that cause injuries to consumers. Since 1967, Wisconsin has adhered to the rule of strict products liability set forth in the *Restatement (Second) of Torts* 402A (1965). . . .

[The *Restatement (Second)* did not define "defective and unreasonably dangerous product," so state courts had to create their own definitions. Two different approaches emerged, with some states finding defective designs based on consumer expectations, others weighing the dangers versus the usefulness of a particular design. Wisconsin was among the states that adopted the consumer-contemplation test.]

Under the consumer-contemplation test . . . a product is defectively dangerous if it is dangerous to an extent beyond that which would be contemplated by the ordinary consumer who purchased it with the ordinary knowledge common to the community as to the product's characteristics.

Under [the danger-utility test] approach, a product is defective as designed if, but only if, the magnitude of the danger outweighs the utility of the product. The theory underlying this approach is that virtually all products have both risks and benefits and that there is no way to go about evaluating design hazards intelligently without weighing danger against utility. There have been somewhat different ways of articulating this . . . test. But in essence, the danger-utility test directs attention of attorneys, trial judges, and juries to the necessity for weighing the danger-in-fact of a particular feature of a product against its utility.

S&N . . . contends that a number of policy considerations gravitate against this court's continued use of the consumer-contemplation test. S&N thus argues that this state should abandon its exclusive reliance on the consumer-contemplation test. . . .

[T]his court does not agree with S&N that the consumer-contemplation test unnecessarily eliminates products from the marketplace. An otherwise defective and unreasonably dangerous product may in many cases be made safe for consumer use by means of adequate warnings or instructions. . . . If, even in light of warnings or instructions, a product remains defective and unreasonably dangerous to the ordinary consumer, we see no reason that the product should remain on the market.

[The court goes on to explain the policy reasons behind strict liability. Unlike negligence, which focuses on the behavior of the defendant company, strict liability focuses on the nature of its product. If the product is determined to be "defective or unreasonably dangerous," a plaintiff can succeed in strict liability even without proving that the seller could foresee the risks of harm inherent in its product.]

Several policy considerations [support] our decision to make manufacturers and other sellers of products responsible for placing defective and unreasonably dangerous products into the stream of commerce: (1) the seller of a product is "in the paramount position to distribute the costs of the risks" presented by the products by passing along costs to consumers or by purchasing insurance; (2) consumers have "the right to rely on the apparent safety of the product and . . . it is the seller in the first instance who creates the risk by placing the defective product on the market"; and (3) "the manufacturer has the greatest ability to control the risk created by [its] product since [it] may initiate or adopt inspection and quality control measures thereby preventing defective products from reaching the consumer."

Although products liability law is intended in part to make products safer for consumers, the primary "rationale underlying the imposition of strict liability on manufacturers and sellers is that the risk of the loss . . . should be borne by those who have created the risk and who have reaped the profit by placing a defective product in the stream of commerce. . . ."

[Application of Consumer-Contemplation Test to Facts]

[I]n order to prevail in a products liability case, a plaintiff has the burden to prove that the product at issue is defective and unreasonably dangerous. A product is defective if it is "in a condition not contemplated by the ultimate consumer." A product is unreasonably "dangerous where it is dangerous to an extent beyond that which would be contemplated by the ordinary consumer."

Applying this standard to the facts of the case at hand, we initially conclude that . . . [t]he evidence at trial showed that S&N's gloves were flawed in two respects: (1) they contained excessive levels of allergy-causing proteins; and (2) they were powdered with cornstarch, which allowed the latex proteins to become aerosolized and, consequently, easily inhaled. The evidence further showed that both of these flaws can cause some consumers to suffer injuries—i.e., allergic reactions. Finally, the parties do not dispute that at the time Green became sensitized to latex . . . the health care community was unaware that persons could be allergic to latex; hence, the "ordinary consumer" of S&N's gloves—i.e., health care workers—could not have contemplated at the time of Green's sensitization that S&N's gloves contained flaws that could cause injuries. Based on this evidence, the jury reasonably found that S&N's gloves were in a condition not contemplated by the ordinary consumer—i.e., that the gloves were defective. . . .

[W]e hold that a product can be deemed defective and unreasonably dangerous where that product contains a substance which, unbeknownst to the ordinary consumer, can cause an allergic reaction in 5 to 17 percent of its consumers. . . .

[The decision of the court of appeals upholding the jury verdict is affirmed.]

SYKES, Judge, dissenting.

I respectfully dissent. The majority opinion is seriously out of step with product liability law as it has evolved since this court adopted the *Restatement (Second) of Torts* Section 402A [in 1967]. The majority blurs the distinctions between design, manufacturing, and failure-to-warn product defects. The majority also keeps Wisconsin in the much-criticized and rapidly dwindling minority of jurisdictions that rely exclusively on a consumer contemplation test to determine liability in design defect cases. . . .

Products can be defective and unreasonably dangerous in different ways, and so product liability cases fall into three distinct categories depending upon the nature of the alleged defect: 1) manufacturing defects (arising from a mistake in the manufacturing process); 2) design defects (arising from an unsafe product design); and 3) defects arising from an inadequate or nonexistent warning of a known danger.

In 1997, the American Law Institute issued the *Restatement (Third) of Torts: Products Liability*. . . . I would adopt the *Third Restatement*'s recapitulation of the law as it has developed since the *Second Restatement* . . . especially in the areas of design and warning defects. . . .

Strict liability without fault makes sense in manufacturing defect cases because it is often impossible to prove what went wrong in the manufacturing process to cause the dangerous defect, and because, as between the seller and the consumer, the seller is in a better position to control or distribute the risk of loss through quality control, insurance, and higher prices. . . .

[But] most courts agree that, for the liability system to be fair and efficient, the balancing of risks and benefits in judging product design and marketing must be done in light of the knowledge of risks and risk-avoidance techniques reasonably attainable at the time of distribution. To hold a manufacturer liable for a risk that was not foreseeable when the product was marketed might foster increased manufacturer investment in safety. But such investment by definition would be a matter of guesswork. . . .

Our leading design defect case, *Sumnicht v. Toyota Motor Sales, U.S.A., Inc.* (1984), which declared allegiance to the consumer contemplation test for determining product design defectiveness, represents the minority rule. . . .

Just as there is little justification for imposing liability for lack of a warning absent proof that foreseeable risks could have been reduced by a warning, there is little justification for imposing liability for a product design defect absent proof that foreseeable risks could have been reduced by an alternate design. . . .

In *Sumnicht,* this court adhered to the consumer contemplation test for use in design defect cases, but also outlined a list of factors to assist in the determination of dangerous defectiveness:

The relevant factors are: "(1) [C]onformity of defendant's design to the practices of other manufacturers in its industry at the time of manufacture; 2) the open and obvious nature of the alleged danger; . . . 3) the extent of the claimant's use of the very product alleged to have caused the injury and the period of time involved in such use by the claimant and others prior to the injury without any harmful incident; . . . 4) the ability of the manufacturer to eliminate danger without impairing the product's usefulness or making it unduly expensive; and 5) the relative likelihood of injury resulting from the product's present design."

As the list of factors quoted above and the Third Restatement make clear, consumer expectations are relevant but not dispositive in the determination of whether a product design is defective and unreasonably dangerous. . . .

For the foregoing reasons, I would adopt Section 2 of the Third Restatement and reverse and remand this case for application of its standard of liability. That is, the alleged design defect in the latex gloves that caused an allergic reaction in Linda Green would be evaluated based upon whether "the foreseeable risks of harm posed by the product could have been reduced or avoided by the adoption of a reasonable alternative design . . . and the omission of the alternative design renders the product not reasonably safe." Accordingly, I respectfully dissent.

• QUESTIONS •

1. What tests does the majority identify for determining whether a seller sold a product that is unreasonably dangerous and defective? Which test does Wisconsin use? What arguments does the dissent make for abandoning that test?

2. Presumably, Green sued in strict liability because she did not think S&N had been negligent. In most states, unless a seller is negligent, it is not liable to a consumer who suffers a rare, idiosyncratic reaction to a particular product. In one case, for example, the plaintiff was reportedly the only one to have had an allergic reaction to fingernail glue, although 1,000,000 units had been sold. Why didn't that rule apply here?

3. Is it fair to make legal liability hinge on the damage a product could cause if that damage was not appreciated by either the buyer or the manufacturer at the time the product was made and used? To require an injured plaintiff to show that an alternative design would have been safer?

4. **Internet Assignment:** One of the most controversial sections of the *Restatement (Third) of Torts* involves the design defects that the dissent discusses. This section would abolish the consumer-contemplation test, replacing it with a risk-utility standard that requires plaintiffs to prove the existence of a reasonable, alternative design. Use a source of legal information, such as http://www.lawguru.com/, to find another products liability case in which a judge mentions the new *Restatement (Third) of Torts.* Does the court adopt the position of the new *Restatement*? Why or why not?

Breach of Warranty, Negligence, and Strict Liability in Tort

Modern products liability law evolved from a number of legal theories based on the common law, including breach of contract; warranty claims against those who sold unfit goods; and negligence (tort) claims against companies who breached their legal duty to use reasonable care in the design, manufacture, and packaging of goods.

The early common law had allowed some exceptions to the general rule of ***caveat emptor*** (buyer beware), most notably for food products. In Britain, an Act of Parliament in 1266 made it a crime to sell "corrupt wine and victuals," and American law required those who sold food intended for immediate consumption to ensure its safety or pay damages to anyone injured by it. But, prior to the twentieth century, most people injured by defective goods had little legal recourse.

The most important remedy was a suit for breach of warranty, a legal theory described as a "freak hybrid, 'born of the illicit intercourse of tort and contract,' and partaking the characteristics of both."[3] One defense to breach of warranty suits was especially hard to overcome. For example, in the 1840s, a British driver working for the Postmaster General was thrown to the ground and injured, allegedly as a result of a latent defect in his coach. He sued the coachmaker, only to be told that the manufacturer of a product owed a duty only to the party with whom he contracted. Because the coachmaking company had sold its carriages to the Postmaster General, the coachman himself could not sue. This *Rule of Winterbottom*[4] became the law in most U.S. states, and for more than half a century people injured by dangerous products could only sue those with whom they were in privity of contract. So, for example, when flaws in the flywheel of a machine caused the wheel to explode, killing a man, his widow could not sue the manufacturer because she and her now deceased husband had not purchased the machine themselves, but had only borrowed it from their neighbor.[5]

Gradually, however, that privity bar eroded away. A decision by New York Court of Appeals Justice Benjamin Cardozo marked the beginning of the end of privity in products liability cases. In *MacPherson v. Buick Motor Co.*, Cardozo let stand a jury verdict for the plaintiff on these facts:

> *The defendant is a manufacturer of automobiles. It sold an automobile to a retail dealer. The retail dealer resold to the plaintiff. While the plaintiff was in the car, it suddenly collapsed. He was thrown out and injured. One of the wheels was made of defective wood, and its spokes crumbled into fragments. The wheel was not made by the defendant; it was bought from another manufacturer. There is evidence, however, that its defects could have been discovered by reasonable inspection, and that inspection was omitted. There is no claim that the defendant knew of the defect and willfully concealed it.... The charge is one, not of fraud, but of negligence.*[6]

But proving negligence poses other problems. A plaintiff must establish that the defendant breached its duty of care, creating an unreasonable risk of harm, and that such careless behavior was the proximate cause of the plaintiff's injury. This is often difficult. Generally, a company will not be found negligent if it adhered to industry standards or the "state of the art" with regard to the engineering, selection of materials, production processes, assembly, and marketing of its product. Proof of reasonable quality control procedures is usually sufficient to negate a charge of negligence. A firm can also defend itself or limit the amount of damages it must pay by showing that its negligence was not the only cause of the injury—a car accident caused in part by faulty brakes and in part by drunk driving, for example—or that the plaintiff contributed to her own harm, either by assuming a known risk or acting carelessly.

And then, in 1944, a waitress injured when a bottle of Coca-Cola exploded in her face sued the local bottling company and won. This time, the jury was convinced of the company's negligence, and the California Supreme Court upheld its verdict. The most important part of the

---

3 William J. Prosser, John W. Wade, and Victor E. Schwartz, *Torts: Cases and Materials,* 7th ed. (New York: Foundation Press, 1982), p. 743.

4 *Winterbottom v. Wright,* 152 Eng. Rep. 402 (E.P. 1842).

5 *Loop v. Litchfield,* 42 N.Y. 351 (1870).

6 *MacPherson v. Buick Motor Co.,* 111 N.E. 1050 (N.Y. 1916).

case, however, was the language of concurring Justice Traynor, which foreshadowed the development of the law of products liability:

> *[I]t should now be recognized that a manufacturer incurs an absolute liability when an article that he has placed on the market... proves to have a defect that causes injury.... [P]ublic policy demands that responsibility be fixed wherever it will most effectively reduce the hazards ... in defective products. [T]he manufacturer can anticipate some hazards and guard against the recurrence of others, as the public cannot...*[7]

Eventually, the full California Supreme Court came to agree with Traynor. In a 1963 case, it adopted the rule that manufacturers should be strictly liable for selling defective products.[8] This new legal theory, referred to as the doctrine of strict liability, made it easier for injured persons to sue and harder for manufacturers to defend themselves. Described in Section 402A of the *Restatement of Torts (Second),* strict liability recognizes that there are times when losses must be allocated between two "innocent" parties: the consumer who was hurt while using a product properly and the company that was not negligent in creating it. It places the responsibility on the company for reasons articulated here by Professor Prosser in his noted *Minnesota Law Review* article, "The Fall of the Citadel":

> *The public interest in human safety requires the maximum possible protection for the user of the product, and those best able to afford it are the suppliers.... By placing their goods upon the market, the suppliers represent to the public that they are suitable and safe for use; and by packaging, advertising and otherwise, they do everything they can to induce that belief.*[9]

Restatement of Torts (Second) Section 402A

(1) One who sells any product in a defective condition unreasonably dangerous to the user or consumer or to his property is subject to liability for physical harm thereby caused to the ultimate user or consumer or to his property, if
- **(a)** the seller is engaged in the business of selling such a product, and
- **(b)** it is expected to and does reach the user or consumer without substantial change in the condition in which it is sold.

(2) The rule stated in Subsection (1) applies although
- **(a)** the seller has exercised all possible care in the preparation and sale of the product, and
- **(b)** the user or consumer has not bought the product from or entered into any contractual relation with the seller.

Most states have adopted Section 402A, finding sellers liable for defective product designs, manufacturing ("production") defects, and failure to warn. In each case, the focus is not on the company's behavior (as it is in negligence law), but on whether the product itself is unreasonably unsafe.

For example, a company may hire qualified engineers who design a new car using standard techniques yet produce a model that causes injury. Under the *Restatement (Second) of Torts,* a jury

7 *Escola v. Coca-Cola Bottling Company of Fresno,* 50 P.2d 436 (Cal. 1944).

8 *Greenman v. Yuba Power Products, Inc.,* 377 P.2d 897 (Cal. 1963).

9 50 *Minn. L. Rev.* 791, 799 (1966).

might conclude that there was a design defect because the harmful nature of the product outweighs its usefulness, even if the plaintiff fails to prove that the engineers were negligent.

In other cases, the design of a car may be perfectly safe, but something in the way a particular car is assembled causes injury—an undetected weakness in a sheet of aluminum or a glitch leading to an improperly assembled component, for example. While we expect companies to implement good quality control systems, at the same time we know that some production defects will occasionally slip through the cracks of a manufacturing process. Once again, strict liability burdens the company, not the consumer, with the loss, even though the company was not negligent.

A third kind of defect involves products that cannot be made completely safe, but can be made safer by appropriately warning the consumer. The absence of adequate information about possible side effects of a drug or of potential danger from a particular use of a product (e.g., a child ingesting rat poison) may result in a manufacturer's strict liability for failure to warn. This was one of the problems in *Green* and the main defect in the *Norplant* case discussed in Chapter 7.

In different jurisdictions, interpretations of the *Restatements of Torts* may vary. In every state, a person who claims injury from a defective product must prove that the product was the proximate (or legal) cause of his harm. If the injury results from some alteration in the product (e.g., by the consumer or by someone who serviced it), the seller is not held responsible. While most states allow companies to defend themselves by proving that the plaintiff misused or abused the product in a way that the manufacturer could not have foreseen, there is no consensus as to how a jury should decide whether a product is "defective," or when and how damages should be limited.

> *. . . [The role of tort law in this country] is uniquely American. A mass tort case is a passion or morality play. It speaks to the conscience of the country and asks whether we have gone badly astray. It examines values and probes motives; and when it is completed, it has a cathartic effect. When courts speak of punitive damages as reflecting a sense of outrage, they utter an important truth: when society bears witness to truly outrageous conduct it must react. Swift and certain justice is necessary not only because it will deter future wrongdoers, but also because it substantiates society's intolerance for malevolent corporate behavior that brings injury to thousands.*
>
> — Aaron Twerski, 1994[10]

Punitive Damages

Under the common law of torts, juries are free to award an injured plaintiff all sorts of damages, not only to compensate for damaged property or out-of-pocket medical expenses, but for pain and suffering and, significantly, punitive damages designed to deter similar wrongdoing in the future. It is common for plaintiffs' lawyers to frame their products liability suits as tort cases, claiming that a manufacturer was negligent in designing, producing, or marketing the product and/or that even a nonnegligent manufacturer should be held strictly liable to the injured party, as a matter of public policy. While some state laws limit the amount of punitive damages a jury can award, others leave the jury free to award hundreds of thousands—even millions—of dollars to punish serious wrongdoing.

Among the most widely publicized products liability suits are those involving motor vehicles; they deal with everything from the placement of gas tanks to the choice of tires. In the 1980s, Ford's Pinto and Mustang models were involved in a variety of lawsuits, both civil and

10 Aaron Twerski, Introduction to "Symposium on Punitive Damages Awards in Products Liability Litigation: Strong Medicine or Poison Pill?" 39 *Vill. L. Rev.* 353 (1994).

criminal. In one of the Pinto cases, plaintiffs won not only compensatory damages, but also $3.5 million in punitive damages. The trial lasted six months and included the testimony of a former Ford executive who had been forced into early retirement because he had spoken out on safety. In the following excerpt, the appellate court affirms the verdict against Ford.

Grimshaw v. Ford Motor Company

California Court of Appeals, Fourth District, 1981
174 Cal. Rptr. 348

TAMURA, Acting Presiding Justice.

A 1972 Ford Pinto hatchback automobile unexpectedly stalled on a freeway, erupting into flames when it was rear ended by a car proceeding in the same direction. Mrs. Lilly Gray, the driver of the Pinto, suffered fatal burns and 13-year-old Richard Grimshaw, a passenger in the Pinto, suffered severe and permanently disfiguring burns on his face and entire body. . . .

Design of the Pinto Fuel System

In 1968, Ford began designing a new subcompact automobile which ultimately became the Pinto. Mr. Iacocca, then a Ford Vice President, conceived the project and was its moving force. Ford's objective was to build a car at or below 2,000 pounds to sell for no more than $2,000.

Ordinarily marketing surveys and preliminary engineering studies precede the styling of a new automobile line. Pinto, however, was a rush project, so that styling preceded engineering and dictated engineering design to a greater degree than usual. Among the engineering decisions dictated by styling was the placement of the fuel tank. It was then the preferred practice in Europe and Japan to locate the gas tank over the rear axle in subcompacts because a small vehicle has less "crush space" between the rear axle and the bumper than larger cars. The Pinto's styling, however, required the tank to be placed behind the rear axle leaving only 9 or 10 inches of "crush space," far less than in any other American automobile or Ford overseas subcompact. In addition, the Pinto was designed so that its bumper was little more than a chrome strip, less substantial than the bumper of any other American car produced then or later. The Pinto's rear structure also lacked reinforcing members known as "hat sections" (2 longitudinal side members) and horizontal crossmembers running between them such as were found in cars of larger unitized construction and in all automobiles produced by Ford's overseas operations. The absence of the reinforcing members rendered the Pinto less crush resistant than other vehicles. Finally, the differential housing selected for the Pinto had an exposed flange and a line of exposed bolt heads. These protrusions were sufficient to puncture a gas tank driven forward against the differential upon rear impact.

Crash Tests

During the development of the Pinto, prototypes were built and tested. . . . The crash tests revealed that the Pinto's fuel system as designed could not meet the 20-mile-per-hour proposed [federal] standard. . . . Tests conducted by Ford on . . . modified or reinforced mechanical Pinto prototypes, proved safe at speeds at which the Pinto failed. . . .

The Cost to Remedy Design Deficiencies

When a prototype failed the fuel system integrity test, the standard of care for engineers in the industry was to redesign and retest it. The vulnerability of the production Pinto's fuel tank at speeds of 20 and 30-miles-per-hour fixed barrier tests could have been remedied by inexpensive "fixes," but Ford produced and sold the Pinto to the public without doing anything to remedy the defects. Design changes that would have enhanced the integrity of the fuel tank system at relatively little cost per car included the following: a single shock absorbent "flak suit" to protect the tank at $4; a tank within a tank and placement of the tank over the axle at $5.08 to $5.79; a nylon bladder within the tank at $5.25 to $8; placement of the tank over the axle surrounded with a protective barrier at a cost of $9.95 per car. . . . Equipping the car with a reinforced rear structure, smooth axle, improved bumper and additional crush space at a total cost of $15.30 would have made the fuel tank safe in a 34 to 38-mile-per-hour rear end collision by a vehicle the size of the Ford Galaxie. . . . If the tank had been located over the rear axle, it would have been safe in a rear impact at 50 miles per hour or more.

Management's Decision to Go Forward with Knowledge of Defects

Ford's Product Planning Committee, whose members included Mr. Iacocca, Mr. Robert Alexander, and Mr. Harold MacDonald, Ford's Group Vice President of Car Engineering, approved the Pinto's concept and made the decision to go forward with the project. . . . As the project approached actual production, the engineers responsible for the components of the project "signed off" to their immediate supervisors who in turn "signed off" to their superiors and so on up the chain of command until the entire project was approved for public release by Vice Presidents Alexander and MacDonald and ultimately by Mr. Iacocca. The Pinto crash tests results had been forwarded up the chain of command to the ultimate decision-makers and were known to the Ford officials who decided to go forward with production.

Harley Copp, a former Ford engineer and executive in charge of the crash testing program, testified that the highest level of Ford's management made the decision to go forward with the production of the Pinto, knowing that the gas tank was vulnerable to puncture and rupture at low rear impact speeds creating a significant risk of death or injury from fire and knowing that "fixes" were feasible at nominal cost. He testified that management's decision was based on the cost savings which would inure from omitting or delaying the "fixes". . . .

[The court addresses Ford's claim that the jury should not have been permitted to award punitive damages in this case, because Ford lacked the "malice" required by the California punitive damages statute:]

Ford argues that "malice" . . . requires . . . evil motive, an intention to injure the person harmed and that the term is therefore conceptually incompatible with an unintentional tort such as the manufacture and marketing of a defectively designed product.

[But] numerous California cases . . . have interpreted the term "malice" . . . to include . . . conduct evincing "a conscious disregard of the probability that the actor's conduct will result in injury to others. . . ."

The primary purposes of punitive damages are punishment and deterrence of like conduct by the wrongdoer and others. . . . In the traditional noncommercial intentional tort, compensatory damages alone may serve as an effective deterrent against future wrongful conduct but in commerce related torts, the manufacturer may find it more profitable to treat compensatory damages as a part of the cost of doing business rather than to remedy the defect. . . . Governmental safety standards and the criminal law have failed to provide adequate consumer protection against the manufacture and distribution of defective products. . . . Punitive damages thus remain as the most effective remedy for consumer protection against defectively designed mass produced articles. They provide a motive for private individuals to enforce rules of law and enable them to recoup the expenses of doing so which can be considerable and not otherwise recoverable. . . .

Ford complains that the punitive award is far greater than the maximum penalty that may be imposed under California or federal law prohibiting the sale of defective automobiles or other products. . . . It is precisely because monetary penalties under government regulations prescribing business standards or the criminal law are so inadequate and ineffective as deterrents against a manufacturer and distributor of mass produced defective products that punitive damages must be of sufficient amount to discourage such practices. . . .

[Judgment for plaintiffs affirmed.]

• QUESTIONS •

1. Why did the jury award punitive damages against Ford? On what basis does the court uphold the punitive damages award? Ford argued that the amount should be limited by the California and federal guidelines setting maximum fines for selling defective products. Can you think of any other arguments against leveling large punitive damage awards? What arguments can you make for and against an award of punitive damages in the latex glove case?

2. An internal Ford memo, entitled "Fatalities Associated With Crash Induced Fuel Leakage and Fires," estimated the "benefits" and "costs" of design changes as follows:

   Benefits: Savings—180 burn deaths, 180 serious burn injuries, and 2,100 burned vehicles

   Unit cost—$200,000 per death, $67,000 per injury, $700 per vehicle[11]

   Total benefits: 180 × ($200,000) plus
   180 × ($67,000) plus
   2,100 × ($700) = $49.53 million

   Costs: Sales—11 million cars, 1.5 million light trucks

   Unit cost—$11 per car, $11 per truck

   Total costs—11,000,000 × ($11) plus
   1,500,000 × ($11) = $137.5 million

   Assume you are a safety engineer at Ford consulted as to the wisdom of adding $11 to the cost of manufacturing the Pinto. What recommendation would you make? Can you make use of ethical theory to argue in defense of it? Against it?

3. Suppose the jury had the option of putting Lee Iacocca, Robert Alexander, and Harold MacDonald in prison for their decision regarding the Pinto design. What are the pros and cons of meting out criminal sentences as compared to issuing punitive damage awards?

4. **Internet Assignment:** In November 2004, the Supreme Court of Florida agreed to review a class action lawsuit against the tobacco companies. After a full hearing involving three cancer patients, the trial court allowed the jury to award punitive damages for all smokers. The result: a $145 billion jury verdict, the largest in American history. Find out what happened to this case on appeal. Does the high court set new parameters on punitive damage awards in Florida?

5. **Internet Assignment:** In 1979, Ford was indicted for manslaughter, one of the first corporations to face such charges based on a defective product. In the mid-1990s, the crash of a ValuJet airplane in the Florida Everglades again led to criminal charges. This time, however, the defendant was not the airline or its manufacturer, but SabreTech, a maintenance company. SabreTech was charged with mislabeling hazardous waste (used oxygen generators) and delivering it to the plane that crashed. What happened in these cases? Find any other criminal cases brought against companies. What happened to the company?

---

11 The $200,000 value attributed to the loss of life was based on a study of the National Highway Traffic Safety Administration, which included in its estimate such items as medical costs, pain and suffering, funeral expenses, and lost productivity.

THE DEBATE OVER TORT REFORM

For the past decade, lawyers, legislators, consumer advocates, and the business community—particularly the insurance industry—have debated the need for reform of the tort system. Some changes have already taken Congress, for example, passed the Class Action Farmers Act of 2005, and Federal courts tightened the rules for expert testimony, making it harder for plaintiffs to win suits against sellers. In recent years, the number of lawsuits filed by persons injured by defective products has declined, even as the amounts that juries award to successful plaintiffs have risen.[12] The next readings present two sides of the debate. Fred Baron was the president of the American Trial Lawyers Association when he wrote about Firestone/Ford. His remarks are followed by a reading from two leading proponents of tort reform, Victor Schwartz and Mark Behrens, partners in a large law firm that represents business defendants.

FIRESTONE/FORD MAKES THE CASE FOR THE TORT SYSTEM

Fred Baron[13]

The Firestone/Ford human tragedy tally is now reported to be over 100 fatalities and more than 300 serious, life-threatening injuries caused by tread separation in Firestone tires used with the Ford Explorer. These numbers eclipse the death and injury tolls of the 1970s' Firestone 500 debacle and the infamous Ford Pinto exploding gas tank cases combined. In fact, they are higher than the total U.S. troop casualties reported in both the Bosnian conflict and the Persian Gulf War.

The question surely arises as to what, if anything, we have learned over the past 30 years about protecting consumers and families in America and what we can do to prevent future unnecessary loss of life and human suffering. . . .

As we craft our arguments in state and federal lawmaking bodies against limiting access to justice, we must continually emphasize the following points, made so clear by this sad saga of shredding tires:

Federal regulatory bodies are toothless. The National Highway Traffic Safety Administration (NHTSA) has no way to track safety-related problems unless the affected industry chooses to notify the agency of a problem. Since neither Firestone nor Ford shared information about their tire failure experience with NHTSA until they had been repeatedly sued, the subsequent recall was too little too late, particularly for the affected families. The likelihood of an automotive company voluntarily turning over consumer complaint information in a timely fashion is in the range of zero.

The tort system works. An unfettered civil justice system roots out dangers, holds people and corporations accountable for creating those dangers, compensates those who are victimized, and prevents others from being harmed. Dangerous products are removed from the marketplace as a result of thorough investigative inquiries in civil litigation.

Punitive damages serve an important purpose. NHTSA cannot seek criminal penalties for even the most callous disregard for human life. Indeed, the steepest fine that may be levied for flagrant disregard of regulatory standards is $925,000, hardly hefty enough to deter a multi-billion-dollar corporate enterprise. The threat of civil punitive damages serves to punish and deter outrageous misconduct. Particularly because of the absence of real criminal penalties for corporate wrongdoing, punitive economic sanctions levied in the most egregious cases often serve as the only effective means of changing inappropriate behavior.

---

12 Greg Winter, "Jury Awards Soar as Lawsuits Decline on Defective Goods," *The New York Times*, January 30, 2001.

13 Fred Baron, "President's Page: Firestone/Ford Makes the Case for the Tort System," 36 *Trial* 9 (Nov. 2000).

Secrecy kills. With benign complicity by courts and legislative bodies, tortfeasors routinely seek to seal court records and discovery documents. Firestone/Ford is the latest example of the harm to the public from privatizing the civil justice system. Bogus claims of "trade secrets" notwithstanding, this pernicious practice should be eliminated by enactment of statutes and court rules creating significant presumptions against secrecy. Undoubtedly, if Firestone and Ford had been successful in their efforts to forbid plaintiffs and their lawyers from revealing anything about settled lawsuits, the death toll would be significantly higher. . . .

Beware of the small print. If Firestone and Ford had mandatory arbitration agreements in their consumer purchase contracts, as increasing numbers of businesses do, and those agreements were held to be binding, it is entirely possible that we still would not know about defective tires and sport utility vehicles.

Let's face it, the reason that the civil justice system is under attack all over this country by corporate entities is because it is still effective in carrying out its twin missions: to compensate victims and deter misconduct. Every time that effectiveness is compromised by legislative restrictions, the public will be forced to look only to government agencies to protect the safety of their families.

A Proposal for Federal Product Liability Reform

Victor E. Schwartz and Mark A. Behrens[14]

. . . Federal product liability reform legislation is needed because the current state-by-state product liability system is unnecessarily costly, inequitable, and unpredictable. The patchwork state system has stifled innovation, kept beneficial products off the market, and handicapped American firms as they compete in the global economy. Here are some specifics.

Pregnant women no longer have access to a drug once widely prescribed to treat "morning sickness," in part, because of the manufacturer's legitimate concern about overkill in our liability system. A chief executive officer of a biotechnology company has stated that his company decided not to pursue research into the development of an AIDS vaccine because of the current product liability system. A manufacturer of protective sporting goods equipment has said that raw material suppliers are reluctant to sell to her company because of concerns about "deep pocket" liability. As a result, the company was unable to obtain the raw materials needed to produce and market a new baseball safety helmet that functioned well in prototype testing. The company later chose not to produce hockey helmets, even though interest in the sport has grown substantially in the United States. "In the final analysis," the company's chief executive officer told Congress, "we felt we could not pursue this market because of the additional, uncontrollable liability exposure it would create."

Federal product liability reform can right the scales of justice, preserving the tort "punch" while eliminating overkill caused by excessive and uncertain liability. After twenty years of exhaustive study, the time for meaningful reform is now. . . .

The Need for Federal Product Liability Reform

Congress is uniquely suited to enact a national solution to provide predictability in the product liability system. Predictability reduces unnecessary legal costs and enables consumers to know their rights; it also allows manufacturers to understand their obligations. State product liability

14 "A Proposal for Federal Product Liability Reform in the New Millenium," 4 *Tex. Rev. L. & Pol.* 261 (2000). Victor Schwartz and Mark Behrens are partners in the Washington, D.C., office of the law firm of Shook, Hardy & Bacon, LLP.

legislation, though useful, cannot solve the national product liability problem because a state cannot regulate product liability problems outside its borders. United States Department of Commerce data indicate that, on average, over seventy percent of the goods that are manufactured in a particular state are shipped and sold out of that state. Insurers recognized this fact years ago and set insurance rates based on country-wide, not individual state, data.

In that regard, one can contrast product liability with workers' compensation. When a worker is injured because of employer fault or neglect, all the relevant facts usually occur in the same state. For that reason, workers' compensation rates vary from state to state and are based on intrastate data. Putting all this in practical form, if a company moves from State A to State B, its workers' compensation insurance costs will change, but its product liability insurance costs will not.

Because of the interstate nature of products liability law, the National Governors' Association (NGA) has called upon Congress to enact federal product liability legislation . . . [as has the American Legislative Exchange Council (ALEC), a bipartisan organization of over three thousand state legislators from all fifty states, formed in principal part to protect states' rights. . . .

A new trend at the state level reinforces the need for federal product liability reform legislation. [As a result of plaintiffs' challenges to the constitutionality of state tort reform legislation, t]here are now over ninety state court decisions striking down state tort reform laws over the past fifteen years. . . . Trial lawyer attempts to overturn state legislative tort policy decisions generally rely on obscure provisions of state constitutions, such as "right to remedy" and "open courts" provisions, that have little historical explanation and no "companion" in the United States Constitution. . . . By relying solely on state constitutions, contingency fee lawyers are able to preclude any appeal of an adverse decision to the United States Supreme Court—there is no federal issue. Federal legislation may be the most direct way of responding to the problem of judicial nullification of state tort law. A federal product liability law could not be nullified under a state constitution. . . .

The fact that tort law has long been the province of the states does not mean that it should be off-limits to any reform at the federal level. Federal legislation can provide an effective means of addressing liability problems that are rooted in interstate commerce and national in scope.

Product Liability Reform Proposals

Barring Claims Because of a Person's Abuse of Alcohol or Drugs or Criminal Acts

In about eleven states, a person who is inebriated or under the influence of illegal drugs can recover in a product liability action even if that illegal condition was a substantial cause of the harm. Some states even permit a felon to recover in a product liability action if he or she was injured while fleeing the scene of a violent crime. . . .

Federal legislation barring product liability claims because of a plaintiff's abuse of alcohol or drugs or felonious behavior would implement sound public policy. It would tell persons that if they are drunk or on illegal drugs and choose to get behind the wheel of a car or operate some other product, they will not be rewarded through the product liability system if they injure themselves. . . . At the same time, law-abiding citizens would be relieved from paying more for the products they purchase in order to subsidize the illegal and irresponsible misconduct of others.

Statutes of Repose

Statutes of repose place an outer time limit on liability involving old products. Like a statute of limitations, a statute of repose specifies the time within which a claimant must file his or her action. The difference is that, in product liability cases, a statute of repose starts to run when the product is sold, not when there has been an injury. The purpose of a statute of repose is to eliminate the heavy burdens presented by claims that can arise many years, even decades, after a product has been sold.

Common sense experience indicates that if a product has performed as intended, day in and day out, year after year, for many years, and a harm occurs, the most likely explanation is that the product wore out, was not properly maintained, or was misused. It would be highly unusual for the harm to be the result of a product defect after many years of reliable use.

Not surprisingly, manufacturers almost always win cases involving old products when they go to trial. The cost of defending such claims, however, can be substantial. . . .

Our nation's principal international competitors, the European Community, Australia, and Japan, have adopted ten-year statutes of repose for all products. These laws reinforce a significant competitive disadvantage that American manufacturers face in the global marketplace. . . . With a lower-cost home market as their base and fewer transaction costs here in the United States, foreign manufacturers have greater resources available to pursue new technology and are able to offer goods in the United States for less than their American competitors. . . . Enactment of a federal statute of repose would help level the playing field between American businesses and their foreign competitors.

Basic Rules for Punitive Damages

. . . Consistent with the United States Supreme Court's recognition that punitive damages are a form of punishment, federal legislation should establish the burden of proof necessary for punishment and make the punishment proportional to the "offense.". . .

Federal legislation should . . . put reasonable parameters on punitive damages to make the punishment fit the offense.

For example, Congress could provide that punitive damages may be awarded against larger businesses in an amount up to twice the claimant's economic and noneconomic losses, or $250,000, whichever is greater. Furthermore, Congress could provide that the maximum single punishment against an individual or small business could not exceed two times the amount awarded to the claimant for economic and noneconomic losses, or $250,000, whichever is less (i.e., $250,000 would be the maximum). This lower limit would reflect the practical reality that a punitive damages award exceeding $250,000 would bankrupt most individuals and small businesses. . . .

Several Liability for Noneconomic Loss

. . . The rule of joint liability, commonly called joint and several liability, provides that when two or more persons engage in conduct that might subject them to individual liability and their conduct produces a single, indivisible injury, each defendant will be liable for the total amount of damages. Joint liability is unfair and blunts incentives for safety because it allows negligent actors to under-insure and puts full responsibility on those who may have been only marginally at fault.

• QUESTIONS •

1. What arguments do Schwartz and Behrens make to support their call for national legislation? What would Fred Baron likely say in response?

2. Pressure for national tort reform has come largely from Republican legislators and presidents, who are generally strong supporters of states' rights. Why do you think they have taken this position on tort reform? For opposing views on tort reform check out the American Tort Reform Association at http://www.atra.org and the Association of Trial Lawyers of America at http://www.atla.org.

3. Opponents of federal laws that would limit tort damages or otherwise change state laws point out that the U.S. Supreme Court has narrowed its interpretation of congressional

legislative powers. In a 1995 case, *United States v. Lopez,* the Court overturned the federal Gun-Free School Zones Act of 1990 as an abuse of congressional power to regulate interstate commerce. Would a law limiting punitive damages in a products liability case be different? How?

4. Some states have adopted split-recovery laws, which allocate part of punitive damage awards to state treasuries or, in some cases, to specific programs. Look at a split-recovery law. What advantages and disadvantages do you see to these statutes? How does this approach compare to legislation capping such damages? From an ethical point of view, which seems best?

5. **Internet Assignment:** (a) Find out about existing or pending legislation on punitive damages in your state. (b) In some states, tort reform has been challenged as violating state constitutional rights. Find out if there have been similar challenges in your state. (c) In recent years, the Supreme Court has indicated that excessive or arbitrary punitive damages are impermissible violations of the constitutional right to due process–where, for example, punitive damages were 145 times the amount of generous compensatory damages. *State Farm Mutual Automobile Insurance Company v. Campbell,* 123 S.Ct. 1513 (2003). Find out how this precedent has been applied by the lower courts.

U.S. Stands Alone

In 2002, legal scholar Mathias Neiman surveyed the laws of forty nations on five continents, searching for current trends in the law of civil liability for harm caused by unsafe products. Here, he summarizes his findings:

> *If one had to group the product liability systems of the world, the most important distinction would be between the United States and all other jurisdictions. It is true that today, the United States shares the principle of liability without fault or contract with a huge and growing number of other countries. But it stands apart in almost all other regards, for better or worse. It is virtually the only country with a full-fledged product liability law that shows no signs of European influence whatsoever. It is the only country [in which]: product liability is still a domain of case law, not of statutes; there is no special treatment of consumers or consumer goods; and liability standards have recently become less, not more, severe because curbing liability, not expanding consumer protection, is currently the primary agenda. The United States is the only country where juries routinely decide product liability cases, where discovery rules are merciless, where the plaintiffs' bar is as specialized as it is resourceful, and where product liability is a major issue of public debate. As a result, it is the only nation where victims sue in product liability by the tens of thousands every year, where million-dollar awards are becoming routine, and where punitive damages are a real threat to defendants. In short, the United States is still the only country where product liability really matters on a grand scale.*[15]

15 Mathias Reimann, "Liability For Defective Products at the Beginning of the Twenty-First Century: Emergence of a Worldwide Standard?" 51 *Am. J. Comp. L.* 751 (2003).

The Uniform Commercial Code

On June 9, 1986, Nancy Denny slammed on the brakes of her Ford Bronco II in an effort to avoid a deer that had walked directly into the path of her vehicle. The Bronco rolled over and Denny was severely injured. She sued Ford, asserting negligence, strict product liability, and breach of implied warranty under the Uniform Commercial Code. The jury came back with a mixed verdict; the Bronco was not unreasonably dangerous and defective, so there was no tort liability. But, they found, Ford had violated the implied warranty of merchantability by selling Denny a vehicle that was not fit for its ordinary purpose.

In the excerpts below, the highest court in New York has to decide whether the two legal theories—a tort action for strict product liability and a contract action for implied warranty—are really one and the same.

Denny v. Ford Motor Company

Court of Appeals of New York, 1995
639 N.Y.S.2d 250

TITONE, Judge.

The trial evidence centered on the particular characteristics of utility vehicles, which are generally made for off-road use on unpaved and often rugged terrain. Such use sometimes necessitates climbing over obstacles such as fallen logs and rocks. . . .

Plaintiffs introduced evidence at trial to show that small utility vehicles in general, and the Bronco II in particular, present a significantly higher risk of rollover accidents than do ordinary passenger automobiles . . . [and] that the Bronco II had a low stability index attributable to its high center of gravity and relatively narrow track width. The vehicle's shorter wheel base and suspension system were additional factors contributing to its instability. Ford had made minor design changes in an effort to achieve a higher stability index, but, according to plaintiffs' proof, none of the changes produced a significant improvement in the vehicle's stability.

Ford argued at trial that the design features of which plaintiffs complained were necessary to the vehicle's off-road capabilities. According to Ford, the vehicle had been intended to be used as an off-road vehicle and had not been designed to be sold as a conventional passenger automobile. Ford's own engineer stated that he would not recommend the Bronco II to someone whose primary interest was to use it as a passenger car, since the features of a four-wheel-drive utility vehicle were not helpful for that purpose and the vehicle's design made it inherently less stable.

Despite the engineer's testimony, plaintiffs introduced a Ford marketing manual which predicted that many buyers would be attracted to the Bronco II because utility vehicles were "suitable to contemporary life styles" and were "considered fashionable" in some suburban areas. According to this manual, the sales presentation of the Bronco II should take into account the vehicle's "suitab[ility] for commuting and for suburban and city driving." Additionally, the vehicle's ability to switch between two-wheel and four-wheel drive would "be particularly appealing to women who may be concerned about driving in snow and ice with their children." Plaintiffs both testified that the perceived safety benefits of its four-wheel-drive capacity were what attracted them to the Bronco II. They were not at all interested in its off-road use.

Although the products liability theory sounding in tort and the breach of implied warranty theory authorized by the UCC coexist and are often invoked in tandem, the core element of "defect" is subtly different in the two causes of action. . . . [T]he New York standard for determining the existence of a design defect [in strict liability cases] has required an assessment of whether "if the design defect were known at the time of manufacture, a reasonable person would conclude that the utility of the product did not outweigh the risk inherent in marketing a product designed in that manner." This standard demands an inquiry into such factors as (1) the product's utility to the public as a whole, (2) its utility to the individual user, (3) the likelihood that the product will cause injury, (4) the availability of a safer design, (5) the possibility of designing and manufacturing the product so that it is safer but remains functional and reasonably priced, (6) the degree of awareness of the product's potential danger that can reasonably be attributed to the injured user, and (7) the manufacturer's ability to spread the cost of any safety-related design changes. . . . The above-described analysis is rooted in a recognition that there are both risks and benefits associated with many products and that there are instances in which a product's inherent dangers cannot be eliminated without simultaneously compromising or completely nullifying its benefits. . . . In such circumstances, a weighing of the product's benefits against its risks is an appropriate and necessary component of the liability assessment under the policy-based principles associated with tort law.

[T]he risk/utility balancing test is a "negligence-inspired" approach, since it invites the parties to adduce proof about the manufacturer's choices and ultimately requires the fact finder to make "a judgment about [the manufacturer's] judgment." . . .

It is this negligence-like risk/benefit component of the defect element that differentiates strict products liability claims from UCC-based breach of implied warranty claims. . . .

While the strict products concept of a product that is "not reasonably safe" requires a weighing of the product's dangers against its over-all advantages, the UCC's concept of a "defective" product requires an inquiry only into whether the product in question was "fit for the ordinary purposes for which such goods are used." . . . The latter inquiry focuses on the expectations for the performance of the product when used in the customary, usual and reasonably foreseeable manners. The cause of action is one involving true "strict" liability, since recovery may be had upon a showing that the product was not minimally safe for its expected purpose without regard to the feasibility of alternative designs or the manufacturer's "reasonableness" in marketing it in that unsafe condition.

[Next, the court explains the distinction in terms of the history of the two doctrines: Implied warranty originated in contract law, "which directs its attention to the purchaser's disappointed expectations," while tort actions have traditionally been concerned with "social policy and risk allocation by means other than those dictated by the marketplace."]

As a practical matter, the distinction between the defect concepts in tort law and in implied warranty theory may have little or no effect in most cases. In this case, however, the nature of the proof and the way in which the fact issues were litigated demonstrates how the two causes of action can diverge. In the trial court, Ford took the position that the design features of which plaintiffs complain, i.e., the Bronco II's high center of gravity, narrow track width, short wheel base and specially tailored suspension system, were important to preserving the vehicle's ability to drive over the highly irregular terrain that typifies off-road travel. Ford's proof in this regard was relevant to the strict products liability risk/utility equation, which required the fact finder to determine whether the Bronco II's value as an off-road vehicle outweighed the risk of the rollover accidents that could occur when the vehicle was used for other driving tasks.

On the other hand, plaintiffs' proof focused, in part, on the sale of the Bronco II for suburban driving and everyday road travel. Plaintiffs also adduced proof that the Bronco II's design characteristics made it unusually susceptible to rollover accidents when used on paved roads. All of this evidence was useful in showing that routine highway and street driving was the "ordinary purpose" for which the Bronco II was sold and that it was not "fit" or safe for that purpose.

Thus, under the evidence in this case, a rational fact finder could have simultaneously concluded that the Bronco II's utility as an off-road vehicle outweighed the risk of injury resulting from rollover accidents and that the vehicle was not safe for the "ordinary purpose" of daily driving for which it was marketed and sold. . . . Importantly, what makes this case distinctive is that the "ordinary purpose" for which the product was marketed and sold to the plaintiff was not the same as the utility against which the risk was to be weighed. It is these unusual circumstances that give practical significance to the ordinarily theoretical difference between the defect concepts in tort and statutory breach of implied warranty causes of action. . . .

SIMONS, Judge, dissenting.

In my judgment, the consumer expectation standard, appropriate to commercial sales transactions, has no place in personal injury litigation alleging a design defect and may result in imposing absolute liability on marketers of consumers' products. Whether a product has been defectively designed should be determined in a personal injury action by a risk/utility analysis. . . .

[T]he word "defect" has no clear legal meaning. . . .

The jury having concluded that the Bronco II was not defective for strict products liability purposes, could not logically conclude that it was defective for warranty purposes. . . . The warranty claim in this case was for tortious personal injury and rests on the underlying "social concern [for] the protection of human life and property, not regularity in commercial exchange." . . . As such, it should be governed by tort rules, not contract rules. . . .

Accordingly, I dissent.

• QUESTIONS •

1. What did Nancy Denny think she was buying? What did she buy?

2. Elsewhere in the decision, dissenting Judge Simons argues that the majority imposes a kind of absolute liability on a manufacturer. Is he right? What might Ford have done differently?

3. Compare this case to the *Norplant* case in Chapter 7. What similarities/differences do you see in the marketing campaigns? In the lawsuits?

As the majority in the Denny case notes, the modern law of contracts is found in the **Uniform Commercial Code (UCC),** adopted by every state in the United States as the basic law governing the sale of goods. Under the UCC, every merchant who sells a product automatically promises that it is fit for its ordinary purpose.[16] Food should not be contaminated, hair dye should not cause one's hair to fall out, rungs of ladders should not splinter, televisions should not explode. A merchant[17] who does not intend to make such a promise must adhere to specific rules in order to disclaim that implied warranty of merchantability.[18] In addition, the old defense of privity is no longer a bar to claims under the UCC.[19] Today, a seller's promise that goods are fit for their ordinary purpose can be enforced not only by the purchaser, but by members of her household as well. In some states, the warranty extends even further, protecting not only the purchaser, family, and household, but "any person who may reasonably be expected to use, consume or be affected by the goods and who is injured" as a result of the breach.[20] And the injured party is no longer forced to sue only her immediate seller; manufacturers can be sued, as can retailers.

Despite the seeming overlap between tort and contract, there are differences between the two bodies of law that remain important. Contract law is primarily designed to encourage

16 UCC 2-314.

17 Under the UCC 2-104, a merchant is a person who deals in goods of the kind involved in the sale, for example, a car manufacturer or a car dealer when he or she sells cars; or a person whose occupation indicates that she has special knowledge or skill regarding goods involved, for example, an optometrist selling glasses; or someone who hires a merchant to act on his behalf, such as a middleperson.

18 UCC 2-316, and Magnuson-Moss Warranty Act, 15 U.S.C. 2301 *et seq*.

19 Ten days after her husband presented her with a new car, Henningsen heard a "loud noise," lost control of the car, and struck a brick wall, sustaining serious injuries. The vehicle was demolished, making it impossible to identify any defects in parts or workmanship or otherwise prove negligence, and the injured lacked privity with the defendant car company. Nonetheless, the Supreme Court of New Jersey allowed a jury verdict in her favor to stand. *Henningsen v. Bloomfield Motors,* 161 A.2d 69 (N.J.1960).

20 UCC 2-318.

commerce by assuring those who freely enter into agreements that the law will protect their expectations. If one side reneges on its bargain, the other can go to court to seek a remedy giving her the benefit of the bargain struck.

Tort law has other functions. With respect to product liability, the focus is on safety. Lawsuits compensate those who are hurt, and punish companies who disregard safety, creating incentives to make safer products.

This difference is reflected in the remedies available to potential plaintiffs. Contract disputes rarely trigger the large damage awards often permitted in tort cases. Suppose Company A has agreed to buy 10,000 packs of FunSoftware from Company B, to sell along with its laptop computers, but then enters a slump period, and cannot sell its computers. Company A may decide not to honor its obligations under the contract with Company B—not out of carelessness, reckless disregard, or maliciousness—but because the breach makes good business sense. Courts deal with breach of contract "dispassionately," giving the injured party the financial benefit it expected under the agreement—a combination of what are known as general, special or consequential, and incidental damages[21] but not compensating it for pain and suffering, nor awarding it attorney's fees or punitive damages.

Transport Corporation of America, Inc. (TCA) operates a national trucking business out of Minnesota. In 1989, TCA decided to update the computer system it used to process incoming orders, issue dispatching assignments, and store all distribution records. TCA purchased an IBM computer system for $541,313.38 from ICC, a company that produces software and resells IBM computers. A year after the system was installed, it failed. Although it was ultimately repaired, TCA was without it for almost 34 hours, and sued both the manufacturer (IBM) and the seller (ICC) on various tort and contract theories.

The lower court dismissed the suit before trial, finding that the economic loss doctrine barred the tort claims, and that the plaintiff was not entitled to any damages for breach of contract, because the computer had been repaired. The appellate court agreed, explaining why in the following excerpt.

TRANSPORT CORPORATION OF AMERICAN V. IBM

U.S. Court of Appeals, Eighth Circuit, 1994
30 F.3d 953

MCMILLAN, Circuit Judge.

On December 19, 1990 . . . the computer system went down and one of the disk drives revealed an error code. TCA properly contacted IBM, and IBM dispatched a service person. Although TCA requested a replacement disk drive, the error code indicated that the service procedure was not to replace any components but to analyze the disk drive. TCA had restarted the computer system and did not want to shut it down for the IBM service procedure. IBM informed TCA that replacement was not necessary under the limited warranty of repair or replace, and agreed to return on December 22, 1990, to analyze the disk drive. On December 21, 1990, the same disk drive completely failed, resulting in the computer system being inoperable until December 22, 1990.

TCA alleges that the cumulative down-time for the computer system as a result of the disk drive failure was 33.91 hours. This includes the time to replace the disk drive, reload the electronic backup data and manually reenter data which had been entered between 2:00 a.m. and the time the system failed. TCA alleges that it incurred a business interruption loss in the amount of

21 In some cases, one who breaches a contract must pay consequential damages covering the costs that are a "consequence" of the breach, such as lost profits while a business is shut down because the seller failed to deliver a machine.

$473,079.46 ($468,514.46 for loss of income; $4,565.00 for loss of data and replacement media).

Economic Loss Doctrine

Minnesota courts have consistently held that the UCC should apply to commercial transactions where the product merely failed to live up to expectations and the damage did not result from a hazardous condition. . . . Because failure of the disk drive was contemplated by the parties and the damage was limited in scope to the computer system (into which the disk drive and its data were integrated), TCA must look exclusively to the UCC for its remedy.

IBM's Disclaimer of Implied Warranties

TCA next argues that because it was not a party to the negotiations between ICC and IBM, it is not bound by the terms of the remarketer agreement, including IBM's disclaimer of implied warranties. . . .

The UCC as adopted in Minnesota has a privity provision that operates to extend all warranties, express or implied, to third parties who may reasonably be expected to use the warranted goods. . . . The seller can disclaim implied warranties . . . [and these disclaimers] are extended to third party purchasers [like the plaintiff]. . . .

The remarketer agreement between IBM and ICC included a disclaimer of "ALL OTHER WARRANTIES, EXPRESS OR IMPLIED, INCLUDING, BUT NOT LIMITED TO, THE IMPLIED WARRANTIES OF MERCHANTABILITY AND FITNESS FOR A PARTICULAR PURPOSE." As the district court correctly noted, this language complies with the requirements of [the UCC] (that is, it was in writing, conspicuous and mentioned merchantability) and thus effectively disclaimed all implied warranties.

IBM's Limited Remedy of Repair or Replace

Under Minnesota law, "[a]n exclusive remedy fails of its essential purpose if circumstances arise to deprive the limiting clause of its meaning or one party of the substantial value of its bargain." . . . A repair or replace clause does not fail of its essential purpose so long as repairs are made each time a defect arises. . . .

ICC's Disclaimer of Consequential Damages Liability

[Under the UCC a] seller may limit or exclude consequential damages unless the limitation is unconscionable. . . . The UCC encourages negotiated agreements in commercial transactions, including warranties and limitations. . . . An exclusion of consequential damages set forth in advance in a commercial agreement between experienced business parties represents a bargained-for allocation of risk that is conscionable as a matter of law. . . .

In the agreement between ICC and TCA, TCA expressly agreed to an ICC disclaimer that stated in part "IN NO EVENT SHALL ICC BE LIABLE FOR ANY INDIRECT, SPECIAL OR CONSEQUENTIAL DAMAGES SUCH AS LOSSES OF ANTICIPATED PROFIT OR OTHER ECONOMIC LOSS IN CONNECTION WITH . . . THIS AGREEMENT."

[T]he disclaimer of consequential damages was not unconscionable and . . . the damages claimed by TCA, for business interruption losses and replacement media, were consequential damages. Furthermore, TCA and ICC were sophisticated business entities of relatively equal bargaining power. ICC's disclaimer was not unconscionable and TCA is therefore precluded from recovering consequential damages. . . .

[Judgment for ICC is affirmed].

• QUESTIONS •

1. On what grounds did the court determine that the plaintiff was not entitled to money damages? What should the plaintiff have done to better protect itself?

2. While it is common for businesses to limit damages, as IBM did in this case, the Uniform Commercial Code makes it unconscionable (shocking to the conscience) to limit damages for personal injury in the sale of products to consumers. So, for example, Ford could not give a warranty that limited its responsibility for injuries caused by a defect in one of its vehicles. Does it seem fair to distinguish consumer from commercial transactions in this way? To allow courts to "rewrite" a deal that two parties freely entered?

3. **Internet Assignment:** Courts may refuse to enforce any clause in a contract it finds to be unconscionable or to violate public policy. As the judge in this case indicates, courts are more protective of consumers than of commercial parties to a contract. Consider Terminix. Before the company provides pesticide services, it asks customers to sign their standard contract in which they agree to forego the right to sue in the event of a dispute. Instead, the parties agree to submit controversies to arbitration under conditions spelled out in the contract. One provision limits the arbitrator's power to provide remedies: she can order Terminix to "re-treat" the house; she cannot order payment of any damages under any circumstances. Despite a strong policy in Pennsylvania in favor of honoring agreements to arbitrate, the court in one case refused to compel arbitration in a case where parents and their four children claimed to have suffered permanent injuries as a result of Terminix' negligent application of pesticides. Because an arbitrator would have no authority to order Terminix to pay damages, the court found the clause to be unconscionable and unenforceable against public policy. *Carll v. The Terminix International Company, L.P.,* 793 A.2d 921 (Pa. Super. 2002).

   Find a case from your state that invalidates a contract clause on grounds of unconscionability or public policy. Does it involve a consumer? If not, does the court find disparity of bargaining power between the two parties?

4. From a consumer's perspective, what are the pros and cons of resolving disputes involving defective products by means other than litigation? From a seller's perspective? From a public policy perspective, do you see any difference between agreements to arbitrate controversies that arise out of the sale of a product and employment discrimination claims?

GOVERNMENT REGULATION OF PRODUCT SAFETY

St. John's Wort doth charm all witches away,
If gathered on the saint's holy day.
Any devils and witches have no power to harm
Those that gather the plant for a charm.
Rub the lintels with that red juicy flower;
No thunder nor tempest will then have the power
To hurt or hinder your house; and bind
Round your neck a charm of similar kind.
— Anonymous, c. 1400 A.D.[22]

22 From St. John's Wort, Avery 1998, cited in Michael T. Murphy, "Battling the Blues with St. John's Wort," *Better Nutrition,* February 1998, p. 14.

Some government agencies, such as OSHA, are located within a particular executive department like the Department of Labor, headed by persons who serve at the pleasure of the president. These are known as executive agencies. "Independent administrative agencies" are not within any particular branch of government. They are considered independent because they are headed by a board of commissioners who are appointed for a specific term and can be removed early only for cause defined by Congress.

The record of direct government regulation of product safety by the major independent agencies—the Environmental Protection Agency (EPA), Consumer Product Safety Commission (CPSC), and Food and Drug Administration (FDA)—is spotty at best. And, not surprisingly, they are often caught in a crossfire of criticism from both consumer groups and business interests.

While the Internet is beginning to change the public face of the agencies,[23] it remains to be seen whether easier access to agency records, the status of actions, and advice to consumers and businesses alike will lead to greater confidence in their regulatory work.

Environmental Protection Agency (EPA)

When the EPA was created in 1970, responsibility for oversight of pesticides shifted from the FDA to the new agency. Today, the EPA is responsible for licensing and registering pesticides, herbicides, and rodenticides for use in "strict accordance with label directions, based on review of scientific studies." By law, pest-killers must not pose unreasonable risks to human health or the environment. FDA power under the Federal Insecticide, Fungicide, and Rodenticide Act (FIFRA) is understood to be a general regulation derived from the EPA's power to approve the adequacy of labels and warnings.

National Highway Traffic Safety Administration (NHTSA)

Created in 1970 as part of the U.S. Department of Transportation, the NHTSA's mission is to reduce deaths, injuries, and economic losses resulting from motor vehicle crashes by setting and enforcing safety performance standards, investigating defects, conducting research, and educating the public. Despite this broad mandate, its specific powers are limited, as we read in Fred Baron's account of the Bridgestone/Firestone tire debacle, and by its own admission traffic deaths remain a serious problem. For instance, 43,320 people died in traffic accidents in 2003, the most since 1990. Recently, the NHTSA reported the results of its first-ever track tests, ordered by Congress in 2002 and finally conducted in 2004: large (15 passenger) vans, the kind used by many schools, are unstable and prone to roll-overs when driven above 50 miles an hour—in short, they are too dangerous to transport students. And, the best-selling sport utility vehicle in the United States, the Ford Explorer, was among those that tipped up on two wheels when tested. Joan Claybrooke, once head of NHTSA and later of the consumer advocacy group Public Citizen, has been lobbying Congress to respond to known safety concerns by passing legislation that would make SUVs less likely to roll over, and vehicle roofs stronger. Check out http://www.nhtsa.dot.gov for complete safety reports and the latest recommendations, and http://www.publiccitizen.org for critics' perspective.

---

23 For example, figuring out which government entity has responsibility for a particular kind of product once made it difficult to get information on product recalls. Today, recall information is easily accessed on http://www.recalls.gov which links to those agencies with statutory authority to issue recalls, the FDA, CPSC, EPA, National Highway Traffic Safety Administration (NHTSA), U.S. Coast Guard, and Department of Agriculture.

The Consumer Product Safety Commission (CPSC)

The Consumer Product Safety Act of 1972 created the CPSC as an independent federal regulatory agency to protect consumers from unreasonable risk of injury, illness, or death from unsafe products. Underfunded by Congress (which has funded only three of five potential commissioners since 1987) and unsure of its mission, the agency was described by consumer advocate Ralph Nader as "dormant for 15 years." That changed in August 1994 when then-commissioner Anne Brown issued a recall of a popular but flammable skirt—even though there had been no known cases of injuries. Public appearances and frequent press conferences, a new award to recognize consumer-friendly products, and aggressive enforcement led to a high profile for the agency during Brown's seven-year tenure. And, in 2001, the CSPC joined with the Department of Justice to bring the first-ever government lawsuit against a retailer for not reporting defective products: Wal-Mart was charged with failing to fully report some 41 injuries caused by exercise equipment it sold between 1996 and 1999.

Today, the CPSC has jurisdiction over more than 15,000 types of consumer products and a hot line for reporting dangerous products and product-related injuries. Check out the agency's Web site at http://cpsc.gov for more on its current concerns.

Food and Drug Administration (FDA)

The FDA, created by the 1906 Pure Food and Drug Act to prevent illegal distribution of misbranded and adulterated food and drugs, today oversees the approval of new drugs and medical devices and monitors the safety of cosmetics, dietary supplements, food additives, blood products, and radiation-emitting products such as microwaves and cell phones. Most of the expansion of the agency's role over the years has come in response to widespread demand for change. In 1938, for example, an early "wonder drug"—Elixer of Sulfanilamide—marketed for strep throat in children and laced with a chemical used in antifreeze, killed 107 people. Public outrage led Congress to expand the FDA's responsibilities to include oversight of cosmetics and therapeutic devices, and to authorize the agency to require companies to prove the safety of drugs before they could be marketed.

The most recent overhaul of the FDA became law in 1997, creating an accelerated review process for new drugs and giving the FDA power to review the health claims of food products. Since then, the FDA has posted guidelines for health claims on its Web site and pulled more than a dozen prescription drugs with dangerous side effects from the market.

The debate about the agency's effectiveness in fulfilling its mission to "protect public health by helping safe and effective products reach the market in a timely way and monitoring products for continued safety" is still lively. In the autumn of 2001, the Public Citizen Health Research Group petitioned the FDA to issue a consumer warning and ban dietary supplements that contain Ephedra, citing 1,398 adverse reactions reported between January 1993 and February 2001, ranging from high blood pressure to 81 deaths.

In 2003 Americans spent some $216.4 billion on prescription drugs—more than double what they spent in 1990—and the FDA approved 21 new medicines. Under U.S. law, prescription drugs are only legal if they are licensed by the FDA and sold by a pharmacy licensed in the United States. Yet, as drug costs have soared, large numbers of Americans have been re-importing drugs originally made in the United States and sold in Canada, where government controls keep prices 30 to 50 percent lower than in the United States. By the end of 2004, governors and legislators in almost half of the states had given some consideration to buying from Canada to keep down the costs of medicines for their residents. At the same time, the FDA has been trying to stem re-importation by shutting down illegal Web sites and warning consumers that they risk buying counterfeit or unsafe drugs.

Antidepressants

The FDA has been widely criticized for its action—and inaction—with regard to antidepressants, a $12 billion (worldwide) business. In 2002 almost 11 million prescriptions were dispensed to patients under 18 years of age in the United States alone. Spending on drugs to treat behavior-related disorders in children and adolescents rose 77 percent from 2000 to 2003. Despite the popularity of these drugs, questions about their safety continue to surface.

GlaxoSmithKline's Paxil was originally approved and marketed for adults. In the mid-1990s, SmithKline Beecham conducted two sets of studies on the effects of Paxil on adolescents, one set ("Study 329") at various hospitals and medical centers in the United States, the other ("Study 377") in Canada, Mexico, Europe, South Africa, and the United Arab Emirates. When Study 329 suggested Paxil might help depressed adolescents, its results were presented at professional conferences in 1999 and submitted for publication in professional journals. The results of Study 377, more negative, suggested that Paxil was not effective. There were no press releases, no publications of its results.

The public first learned about the secret Study 377 in 2003, when British regulators asked drug companies for unpublished data concerning antidepressant use among children and teens.

In response, the FDA initiated a review of antidepressants. In June 2003 the agency issued a "Public Advisory" of possible increased risk of suicidal thoughts and attempts in children taking Paxil for major depressive disorders.

Then, in December 2003, British health authorities issued a stark warning: Doctors should not prescribe most new antidepressant drugs to children because the risk of suicidal thoughts, self-injury, and agitation outweighed the benefits.[24] Two months later a scientific advisory panel to the FDA held public hearings, with emotional testimony from parents and children, including a man whose son hanged himself while on Zoloft. The agency's top expert did not testify, because his conclusions that antidepressants cause children to become suicidal were considered to be "alarmist" and "premature." Some who treat adolescents warned that depression is a serious mental illness, and that suicide rates had declined since drugs had become available.

Short of banning a drug, the strongest possible FDA action is to require boldface, black-bordered information sheets to warn doctors and patients of a drug's risks and side effects. In October 2004, after a year of intense controversy, the FDA ordered pharmaceutical companies to add such black-box warnings to antidepressants.

Not all negative side effects of antidepressants are psychological. In 2003, Sidney Wolfe of Public Citizen sued the FDA to force a ban on a Bristol-Myers Squibb (BMS) product, Serzone, known to cause liver failure in some patients. BMS finally pulled Serzone from the U.S. market in May 2004—almost a year after it ended sales in Europe and Canadian regulators had banned the drug. At least 55 cases of liver failure, including 20 deaths, had been reported to the FDA since the drug hit the market in 1994, causing the FDA to add its strongest warning about the liver risk in 2002, but allowing BMS to continue to market the drug.

A government study funded by the National Institute of Mental Health (NIMH) released in May 2004 reported that Prozac helps teens overcome depression far better than talk therapy. At its annual meeting in June, the American Medical Association (AMA) urged the government to create a public registry of clinical drug trials—an idea

24 Only Prozac was still recommended for youngsters (see http://www.mhra.gov.uk).

immediately supported by Merck, one of the world's leading pharmaceutical companies, and by a few members of the U.S. Senate. Some suggested expanding http://www.clinicaltrials.gov, which links to published results of completed trials under a 1997 law directing the NIH to make the public aware of drug trials. (The law did not require companies or academic institutions to post trial results). Major medical journals—including *JAMA, The New England Journal of Medicine,* and *The Lancet*—announced that they were considering a requirement that trials be listed in a registry before the results would be considered for later publication.

In June, New York State Attorney General Eliot Spitzer made headlines when he sued GlaxoSmithKline for consumer fraud for failing to disclose all of its data on Paxil. Days later, the company released on its Web site all the reports of tests of Paxil in children and adolescents, and announced that it would create a company Web site that would publicly list all clinical trials on its marketed drugs. **Internet Assignment:** Check out the website posted by the Pharmaceutical Research and Manufacturers of America, the industry's trade group. Which companies have posted trial findings? Update developments in the FDA's regulation of mental health drugs and in public disclosure of clinical trials.

In 1973, the FDA approved the use and sale of fenfluramine, an appetite-suppressing diet medication that had been tested, manufactured, and packaged by A.H. Robins. Fenfluramine was sold under various names by Wyeth-Ayerst, a division of American Home Products Corporation. Demand soared during the mid-1990s, when people began using fenfluramine along with phentermine in a diet drug combination known as "Fen-Phen." The FDA never approved this combination. By some estimates, there were some six million Fen-Phen users by 1996.

In response to reports linking fenfluramine consumption to an increased risk of serious heart valve problems, the FDA called for, and got, a voluntary withdrawal of fenfluramine from the market in September 1997. Since then, many medical studies have confirmed the relationship between fenfluramine use and heart valve abnormalities.

In November 1999, American Home Products settled a nationwide class action suit brought on behalf of those who had taken Fen-Phen. The company agreed to pay damages to those who suffered valve damage, and to provide medical screening for those who might develop health problems in the future.

Erma Rae Wood—who took Fen-Phen for seven months in 1998—was among those who "opted out" of this settlement. Her reason: It specifically excluded claims for primary pulmonary hypertension, an often fatal disease stemming from decreased blood flow between the heart and lungs. Instead, she brought her own case.

WOOD V. WYETH-AYERST LABORATORIES, DIVISION OF AMERICAN HOME

Supreme Court of Kentucky, 2002
82 S.W.3d 849

GRAVES, Justice.

. . . In recent decades, the issue of present physical injury has intersected with an emerging family of tort cases based on exposure to toxic or otherwise harmful substances. The most significant of these cases, *Capital Holding v. Bailey, Ky.* (1994) remained true to traditional tort law requirements, holding essentially that even where exposure and negligent conduct could be proven, a case must be dismissed if the plaintiff can prove no present physical injury. . . .

We cannot distinguish the exposure to asbestos in *Capital Holding* from the exposure to Fen-Phen in this case. In both instances, the plaintiff was exposed to an agent that had the potential to result in serious future medical consequences, but which had not produced actual physical harm at the time of the suit.

. . . [Wood argues that she has] "indeed suffered a present injury or 'harmful result'" [namely]" the financial expense of the medical monitoring that [she] has been medically advised to undergo." [But her] body has not yet been impaired by her ingestion of fenfluramine, and the only tangible property in question is [Emma Rae Woods'] money, which likewise has not been expended. . . .

As [she] has sustained no present physical injury, her claim cannot stand under existing Kentucky tort law.

. . . Courts in some states . . . are venturing into uncharted territory as they create medical monitoring causes of action and make available medical monitoring remedies that do not require a showing of present physical injury. In these states, the costs of diagnostic testing can be recovered before they are actually incurred on a mere showing of exposure coupled with increased risk of injury. In the name of sound policy, we decline to depart from well-settled principles of tort law.

We are supported in rejecting prospective medical monitoring claims (in the absence of present injury) by both the United States Supreme Court and a persuasive cadre of authors from academia. These authorities explain that, while well-intentioned, courts allowing recovery for increased risk and medical screening may be creating significant public policy problems. The U.S. Supreme Court [addressed the issued in] *Metro-North Commuter R.R. Co. v. Buckley* (1997). . . . Although *Metro-North* had to do with a federal worker's compensation statute, the Court was clearly speaking to the more general issue of medical monitoring when it pointed out that

> *tens of millions of individuals may have suffered exposure to substances that might justify some form of substance-exposure-related medical monitoring. . . . And that fact, along with uncertainty as to the amount of liability, could threaten both a "flood" of less important cases (potentially absorbing resources better left available to those more seriously harmed) and the systemic harms that can accompany "unlimited and unpredictable liability."*

. . . [Henderson and Twerksi, scholars who wrote the *Restatement Third,* suggest four potential benefits from medical monitoring remedies:] (1) allowing recovery fosters access to medical testing and facilitates early diagnosis and treatment; (2) recognizing such claims deters irresponsible distribution of toxic substance; (3) early monitoring may prevent future costs and reduce the potential liability of the tortfeasor; and (4) it satisfies basic notions of fairness by assuring that wrongfully exposed plaintiffs recover the costs of medical treatment.

Weighing these benefits against the potentially negative effects . . . however, the authors conclude that more convincing public policy arguments support the rejection of such claims. For example, courts will inevitably run into problems in determining how to distribute medical monitoring awards. Lump-sum awards might not actually be used for medical costs, especially if a recipient has insurance that will cover such expenses. Monitoring funds to be used by large numbers of people . . . requires administration and does not guarantee that potential victims actually get tested. These remedies are economically inefficient, and are of questionable long term public benefit. Furthermore, defendants do not have an endless supply of financial resources. Spending large amounts of money to satisfy medical monitoring judgments, will impair their ability to fully compensate victims who emerge years later with actual injuries that require immediate attention. . . .

The major argument against medical monitoring discussed in another article, by Victor E. Schwartz *et al.*, is that such a remedy is best left to the legislatures [because] legislatures are in a better position than courts to acquire all of the relevant information in making such a complex and sweeping change to traditional tort law; second, legislatures' prospective treatment of medical monitoring awards would provide fair notice to potential tortfeasors; and third, claims involving collateral compensation demand careful consideration from the legislature. These authors also point out that medical monitoring claims will potentially clog the courts as contingency fee lawyers use consumers as vehicles for enormous awards; furthermore, money awarded for the purpose of health care will go in large percentage to those same lawyers, not the exposure victims. . . .

We are mindful of the predicament in which our decision places [Erma Rae Wood] and others in similar situations. Those who have ingested fenfluramine, but in whom no disease is yet manifest, will be forced to either forego medical evaluations or proceed with them at their own cost. Nevertheless, any other outcome would result in inordinate burdens for both the potential victim and the alleged negligent party.

Granting [her] request for medical monitoring costs absent a showing of physical injury, would require AHPC to finance diagnostic testing for a large number of past fenfluramine users. If each were actually tested, and the results of the tests showed no physical disease, the negligent party will have paid large sums of money despite having caused no physical injury. If, in contrast, the tests revealed the presence of physical disease resulting from the drug ingestion, a strong argument could be made that the victims are precluded from recovering additional damages because they have already recovered on the claim of negligence.

Requiring prospective victims to finance their own testing, and when such testing demonstrates the presence of disease, the victims will then be able to prove a physical injury such as will support a cause of action. If negligence is proven, those victims will be able to recover all of the money spent on testing as well as damages for the injury and future expenses. For those who pay for their own testing but never find disease, we regret the economic expense but suggest that they have paid for a service and received the benefit thereof—in this case, a clean bill of health and the accompanying peace of mind.

From a policy standpoint, this outcome should act as a sufficient deterrent to those who would negligently produce and distribute harmful substances, for they shall still have to compensate victims for any injury caused. Likewise, recognizing only claims supported by physical injury will prevent the potential flood of litigation stemming from unsubstantiated or fabricated prospective harms, thereby preserving judicial and corporate resources to compensate actual victims who develop injuries in the future.

[Judgment dismissing the complaint is affirmed.]

• QUESTIONS •

1. Since, as the court suggests, court-ordered medical monitoring in the absence of actual physical injury inevitably foists unfair costs on either the company or the persons suffering toxic exposure, can you think of any better alternatives?

2. Of what significance is the fact that the FDA approved the marketing of Fen-Phen?

3. **Internet Assignment:** Find out how your state deals with toxic exposures. Compare the circumstances under which a person can sue with the Kentucky rule set forth in *Wood v. Wyeth-Ayerst.*

4. **Internet Assignment:** In April 2004, a jury awarded $1 billion to the family of a woman who died from a lung disease blamed on Fen-Phen. At the time, Wyeth faced dozens of other Fen-Phen lawsuits, and had already financed a $3.75 billion trust to pay those who suffered heart valve damage from the drug. Find out how the company has been managing its Fen-Phen litigation since the verdict in the *Cappel-Coffey* case.

Manufacturer Liability for Consumer Uses

In most states, a seller can defend itself by proving that the consumer's use of its product was an abnormal one, unanticipated by the seller. As you read the next case, ask yourself: Was this an unanticipated "abuse" of an otherwise safe drug?

OxyContin is an opium derivative ("opioid") first approved by the FDA in 1995 for the treatment of cancer pain.

Foister v. Purdue Pharma, L.P.

U.S. District Court, Kentucky, 2003
295 F.Supp.2d 693

REEVES, District Judge.

Background

. . . OxyContin is a prescription narcotic intended to help individuals with moderate to severe pain. . . . It is illegal to use or sell OxyContin without a valid prescription.

. . . In 1994, the Department of Health and Human Services issued clinical guidelines encouraging the use of opioids to treat pain in cancer patients. A year later, the FDA approved the use of OxyContin to treat moderate and severe pain. . . .

[But some individuals learned that by crushing the pills they] were able to unlock the full narcotic effect of the [opioids in OxyContin]. . . . As word of this procedure spread, abuse of OxyContin proliferated. Abuse of the drug in this manner has been particularly problematic in remote, rural areas such as Eastern Kentucky . . . [because] they're home to large populations of disabled and chronically ill people who are in need of pain relief; they're marked by high unemployment and a lack of economic opportunity; they're remote, far from the network of Interstates and metropolises through which heroin and cocaine travel; and they're areas where prescription drugs have been abused—though in much smaller numbers—in the past . . . (cites omitted).

As discussed below, the plaintiffs used OxyContin at various times for both legitimate and illegitimate purposes. . . . All purportedly suffered serious and debilitating side effects; namely, addiction to the drug. Two claim that their relatives were killed by OxyContin. They allege, *inter alia,* that Purdue did not adequately warn them of the side effects.

. . . Rodney Howard ("Howard") is 30 years of age and is also a resident of Pathfork, Kentucky. After working for six years in the coal mines and two years operating a logging business, Howard became gravely ill with Crohn's disease. His pain is severe and his prognosis is grim. In treating his pain, Howard has been prescribed Lorcet, Tylox and Demerol.

Howard was first prescribed OxyContin in January 2000. A month later, he began ignoring his doctor's order to take only two pills a day and began increasing his dosage. By March of that year, he was taking OxyContin orally every 60 to 90 minutes. Around that time, Howard began crushing the pills and taking them intravenously through a portacath that had previously been inserted into his chest to assist in the administration of Demerol. When his doctor discovered that Howard had been injecting OxyContin in this fashion, the doctor ordered the portacath removed. . . .

. . . When Howard's heavy pill habit could not be supported by his prescriptions, he purchased most of his pills illegally. . . .

Amy Foister ("Foister") is a 58-year old resident of Manchester, Kentucky. She was employed as a welder until she sustained a back injury in March 1972. . . . To treat her pain, Foister was prescribed, at various times, Valium, Empirin/Codeine, Tylenol/Codeine, [and beginning in July 2000, OxyContin]. . . . In March 2001, her doctor refused to write any more OxyContin prescriptions due to the "misuse of the meds in our community." In lieu of OxyContin, he prescribed her Valium and Lortab. Foister apparently discontinued her use of OxyContin in March of 2001 and experienced some symptoms of withdrawal for a three to four week period . . . [but] was not "addicted" to OxyContin.

Legal Analysis

As the Supreme Court of Kentucky determined in *Monsanto Co. v. Reed* (1997), "a manufacturer is not liable when the injuries result from the mutilation or alteration of the [product]. Such intervening conduct severs any causal connection between the product and the injury. Here, seven of the eight plaintiffs . . . intentionally altered the OxyContin pills and used them in an illegal and unauthorized manner. These plaintiffs either chewed, snorted or injected their pills . . . overdosed the drug with regularity . . . [and] clearly ignored the directions that accompanied OxyContin prescriptions. At the relevant times, the package insert for OxyContin stated, in bold letters:

> *WARNINGS*
>
> *OxyContin . . . TABLETS ARE TO BE SWALLOWED WHOLE, AND ARE NOT TO BE BROKEN, CHEWED OR CRUSHED. TAKING BROKEN, CHEWED OR CRUSHED OxyContin TABLETS COULD LEAD TO THE RAPID RELEASE AND ABSORPTION OF A POTENTIALLY TOXIC DOSE OF OXYCODONE.*

The warning was repeated later in the insert. Indeed, most of the plaintiffs admitted that they knew that altering the pills could be dangerous.

OxyContin, as approved for use by the FDA, is not unreasonably dangerous when used as directed. Like any drug, however, there are possibilities for abuse. Even "mild" drugs such as aspirin and acetaminophen can be dangerous if used improperly. Such drugs, however, are not unreasonably dangerous simply because they may be harmful if ingested in significant quantities or ingested in an illegal manner. The seven plaintiffs who improperly altered the pills fundamentally changed the characteristics of OxyContin. In effect, they created a different drug. Moreover, in most instances their alteration also included significant overuse of the pills.

The plaintiffs have presented no proof to suggest that the drug would have been unreasonably dangerous absent its illegal alteration. Indeed, the drug's FDA approval indicates that OxyContin is reasonably safe when used as directed. Therefore, the plaintiffs have not demonstrated that OxyContin is the proximate cause of addiction and withdrawal symptoms for people using the drug illegally. The proximate cause of any alleged injury in such circumstances is the alteration and/or abuse of the drug, not the drug itself. . . .

. . . In Kentucky, a plaintiff may not recover in a legal or equitable proceeding when the basis for such an action rests on their own illegal conduct. . . .

[T]he seven plaintiffs that procured and used OxyContin illegally may not recover in this action. These parties . . . are left with the dilemma which they created. . . .

The Learned Intermediary Doctrine

. . . The learned intermediary doctrine provides that once a drug manufacturer has warned physicians of the dangers of the drug, the pharmacy's liability is cut off by the physician's knowledge. . . . In this case, Purdue argues that it warned prescribing physicians of all relevant side-effects and possible abuses. Thus, if the learned intermediary doctrine applies, the defendants' liability is cut-off by the doctor's knowledge.

> *This court agrees . . . that Kentucky will likely adopt the "learned intermediary doctrine," as the* Restatement (Third) of Torts *and numerous other jurisdictions have done. . . .*

The lengthy and technical warnings provided by pharmaceutical manufacturers are much less useful to patients than the considerate, patient-specific instructions offered by physicians. Physicians are in the best position to determine whether the patient understands the benefits and risks and thus is in the best position to provide the necessary warnings. When it is clear that a patient does not understand the risks involved, the physician can explain them in a different manner until it is clear that the patient comprehends the potential complications.

Pharmaceutical companies, on the other hand, have no direct contacts with patients. Indeed, in many instances the patients may not be able to read the printed warnings provided by pharmaceutical companies, either because they cannot read English or because they cannot read at all. In sum, the physician is in the best position to pass on relevant risks. Thus, a pharmaceutical company must simply ensure that the physician is made aware of the known risks. Doing so absolves it of liability for failure to warn. . . .

[Judgment for Purdue Pharma, the maker of OxyContin.]

• QUESTIONS •

1. How do the plaintiffs in the OxyContin case compare to the cigarette smoker who continues to smoke, despite reading Surgeon General warnings, and then develops lung cancer? Are they similar or different in their moral culpability? In their legal rights and responsibilities?

2. Faced with an opportunity to overturn the learned intermediary rule, the Kentucky court chose not to. Compare the court's reasoning to that in the New Jersey case involving Norplant that was discussed in Chapter 7. Which is more persuasive to you? Why? To what extent do the judgments seem to reflect differences in state populations?

3. The attorney general for West Virginia sued Purdue Pharma in 2001, charging the company with aggressively marketing OxyContin and deliberately hiding its addictive qualities from doctors. In November 2004, the parties settled. The lawsuit was dropped in return for Purdue Pharma's promise to spend $10 million on drug abuse and education programs in West Virginia. What argument can you make in favor of injured plaintiffs suing as opposed to suits by state attorneys general? By states? **Internet Assignment:** Find out about other lawsuits against Purdue Pharma. Which outcomes seem preferable from an ethical perspective?

Enterprise Liability

As was mentioned in the essay by Schwartz and Behrens earlier in this chapter, one focus of tort reform is to revise what is known as market share or enterprise liability. Enterprise liability was first used by a California court in a case against eleven of the many drug companies involved in the sale of the synthetic hormone diethyl stilbestrol (DES).[25] Discovered by British researchers in 1937, DES was never patented. In the 1940s, twelve American drug manufacturers agreed to cooperate with each other to bring it to market. They pooled all clinical data pertaining to DES and used literature written by Eli Lilly Company as the model for their package inserts. On the basis of two studies by independent researchers indicating that DES prevented miscarriages in a significant percentage of high-risk pregnancies, Lilly and other drug companies sought FDA approval of the drug. The studies were criticized by some; they lacked controls, later studies could not replicate their findings, and scientists were beginning to discover that drugs ingested by a pregnant woman crossed her placenta and might injure the fetus. Still, none of the drug companies ever used animals or humans to test the effects of DES on the fetus.

Once approved by the FDA, DES was marketed to pharmacists and doctors from 1947 to 1971. It was sold as a generic, because all DES was of identical chemical composition. Druggists usually filled prescriptions from whatever was on hand. Few records were kept, and women

25 *Sindell v. Abbott Laboratories,* 607 P.2d 924 (Cal. 1980).

taking the drug seldom had any way of knowing which firm had manufactured it. During the 24 years that DES was sold for use in pregnancy, approximately 300 makers produced it, entering and leaving the market continuously. Eli Lilly was one of the major producers, selling in bulk to other drug companies for use under their own names and acquiring close to 45 percent of the DES market.

By 1971, studies had established the harmful effects on DES on the daughters of mothers who took the drug. Specifically, tests indicated that DES caused vaginal cancer and adenosis, a precancerous vaginal or cervical growth requiring extensive monitoring. The FDA banned DES.

When Jane Sindell developed adenoids and a malignant bladder tumor, she blamed it on the DES her mother had taken during pregnancy. But her mother had no idea which company had provided the actual dosage she had ingested. On behalf of California girls and women who "may have been exposed to DES before birth and who may or may not know that fact or the dangers to which they were exposed," Jane Sindell brought a class action suit against eleven drug companies, including Abbott Labs and Eli Lilly. The court allowed the suit to go forward, reasoning that it was fair to hold responsible any company involved in the "enterprise of selling DES" that had acquired a substantial share of the national market during the relevant time period; it was not the plaintiffs' fault that they could not pinpoint which company had made which doses of the drug. The court removed from the suit only those market share defendants who could prove that they could not possibly have made the ingested drugs.

Enterprise liability has become particularly controversial because of huge class action suits brought against the asbestos, tobacco, and gun industries. In the next reading, litigator Elizabeth Cabraser speaks out in favor of such suits. The social compact that undergirds our governments, state and federal, is an understanding that "the very powers of the government itself derive from the agreement of the citizens to govern themselves, and universal access to the courts protects against civil oppression by the legislature or private citizens." When Congress and the normal regulatory process fail to restrain harmful industries, Cabraser argues, citizens can still change policy through representative lawsuits. In that way, injunctions and monetary redress thereby become the twenty-first century method of enforcing the social contract.

ENFORCING THE SOCIAL COMPACT THROUGH REPRESENTATIVE LITIGATION

Elizabeth J. Cabraser[26]

These [policy-oriented representative] suits differ, in purpose and magnitude, from more typical "mass tort" litigation, including class action suits arising from specific defective products such as pharmaceuticals and medical devices, because they focus on an entire industry rather than the single manufacturer of a specific branded product and because they are filed against a backdrop of decades of socially-sanctioned promotion and use of the product. Such suits are advanced notwithstanding—or because of—failed or incomplete legislative initiatives to regulate the product or conduct in question.

The classes involved are uniquely large and diffuse. Several hundred thousand persons may be affected by the ingestion of an allegedly defective prescription pharmaceutical, such as the "fen/phen" diet drug combination. Several thousands of persons may have been injured, or placed at risk of future injury, by the implantation of an allegedly defective medical device, such as a fracture-prone pacemaker lead wire. These persons are readily identifiable, self aware, and easily

26 "Enforcing the Social Compact Through Representative Litigation," 33 *Conn. L. Rev.* 1239 (2001).

placed on notice of their claims. They are consumers of a product that has probably been recalled or removed from the market, as was the case in the Diet Drugs and Telectronics litigation. Their claims can be compensated without bankrupting a manufacturer or obliterating an industry. Their cases do not seek to transform the conduct of an industry or the consciousness of the country.

Policy-oriented litigation is both the cause and effect of a fundamental shift in public perception toward a product or practice, informed by a gradual awareness of danger or undesirability, until, in a paradigm shift, a desirable, or at least ubiquitous product becomes suspect, and previously acceptable or tolerated conduct is perceived as violating social norms. The representative suits that accompany such transformation derive their power and legitimacy as much from social attitudes as specific legal doctrine. They are the enforcement mechanisms of the social compact. . . .

Regulation by litigation is designed into our system of government. The social compact is declared by legislation and enforced by litigation. Through direct and representative action in the courts, litigants enforce the reciprocity of rights and obligations that is the animating principle of the social compact theory that in turn was mustered to justify—and mandate—the American colonies' self-conscious creation as sovereign states, their departure from British fealty, and their ultimate union.

The complementary roles of legislation and litigation in the promotion and achievement of progress in the area of civil rights, and now human rights, cannot be gainsaid. Regulation by litigation focuses on correcting transgressions by violators of consensus norms of public health and safety and consumer rights, and is a cost-effective and less intrusive substitute for government regulation. Indeed, litigation does not prospectively regulate corporate behavior; it simply redresses corporate behavior that transgresses the social contract. . . .

Civil litigation, that most democratic of American public activities, is the crucible within which our common law, that most democratic of legal systems, is preserved, evolves and transforms us as it is transformed. . . .

Corporations have economic and political power which distorts and inflates their influence, vis-à-vis that of individual voters, in the executive and legislative branches. This is political reality. The judicial ideal, however, and the charge of the civil litigation system, is to neutralize the effects of social, economic, and political power as between any two litigants before the court. . . .

The civil justice system serves not only to redress private grievances but also to enforce the reciprocity of rights and interests embodied in the social contract to which all individual and corporate citizens are party.

When a single tort, or a course of wrongful conduct, offends societal values because of its purposeful or callous nature, or its harmful impact on society itself, the imposition of punitive damages serves to punish the transgressor, and to deter similar transgressions.

Punitive damages are an invention of the common law, embodying equitable principles, in which the named plaintiffs serve as societal agents to impose a monetary penalty, above and beyond that necessary to compensate the victims, in circumstances in which the compensatory damages recognized at law are considered inadequate, of themselves, to inflict a sting sufficient to bring recognition, remorse, and reform.

Indeed, it may be argued that, in this era of mass production, mass advertising, and multinational corporations, when the impact of a single violation or course of conduct may be visited a millionfold upon one company's customers, the necessity and utility of the doctrine has increased. Notwithstanding attacks upon its underlying rationale, and attempts to find safe harbors from punitive damages in precisely those contexts of mass harm in which it is most needful, the doctrine survives; its constitutionality has been affirmed, and re-affirmed, by our Supreme Court. . . .

Thus, in the case of mass purposeful and intentional harm, such as that exemplified by the tobacco litigation, some procedural mechanism must be applied to protect, reconcile, and harmonize the interests of victims and society in punishment, deterrence, and the equitable use of punitive damages as civil penalties, with the countervailing due process rights of defendants to avoid extinction in the name of atonement. Of all available procedural mechanisms, the class action is the most elegant, comprehensive, and fair.

Class or representative actions arose and developed in the equity practice of this country in the nineteenth century, contemporaneously, and perhaps not so coincidentally, with the rise of corporations. The class action has become the mechanism of choice in consumer, investor, and employment law because it brings economies of scale to numerous similar grievances and provides access to the courts for claims which, absent the representative procedure, individual economic infeasibility would foreclose.

As standard products, including pharmaceuticals, are marketed to increasing millions and are, when defective, associated with mass injury, the class action and the unitary adjudication of similar claims and common issues have and will continue to become more widespread. These principles are controversial, of course, for two reasons: they threaten the viability of corporate strategies of litigation by attrition, and they compete with principles of individual adjudication.

In a perfect world of immediate and cost-effective access to a justice system with sufficient resources to conduct simultaneous trials of thousands of claims in real time, there would be no need to depart from our ideal of the individual jury trial in order to accomplish mass justice. The lawyers and judges of this country must continue to direct every ounce of principled creativity into the development of fair and efficient procedures for the adjudication and the resolution of mass claims in a consistent and economic manner that will sustain public confidence in and reliance on our system of civil litigation. Otherwise, we are likely to see the equally undesirable phenomena of corporate self-interest unchecked by accountability to the community, and individuals who increasingly view themselves as powerless victims, no longer able, and hence no longer responsible, to discharge their affirmative obligations to themselves, their families and to each other. . . .

• QUESTIONS •

1. What is a representative suit? What is the social compact? According to Cabraser, how do representative suits "enforce the social compact"?
2. Was it fair to allow suit against companies based on their "market share" involvement in the production and sale of DES (market share liability)? If not, should anyone be held accountable for the injury caused to DES daughters? Would it be fair to sue all companies who sold DES during this period (enterprise liability)? To sue a company with a share of the market, even if it can prove its product could not possibly have been the one Jane Sindell's mother took?
3. **Internet Assignment:** What suits have been filed in the wake of the collapse of Enron? Are any of them policy-oriented representative suits?
4. **Internet Assignment:** The Class Action Fairness Act of 2005 moves many class action lawsuits out of state courts and into federal. Find out who favored/opposed this law and why. How might it impact on representative suits?
5. **Internet Assignment:** Find an example of a product liability suit brought in your state in which punitive damages were awarded at trial. Was it a class action? How much was awarded? Was the award appealed? If so, was it affirmed, reduced, or eliminated by the appellate court?
6. How would Schwartz and Behrens respond to Cabraser?
7. **Internet Assignment:** In the past decade, states and cities around the country have sued gun manufacturers and their trade associations for reimbursement of the millions of dollars it costs police departments and city hospitals to deal with gun violence. Find out about a

public lawsuit against gun dealers/manufacturers. (a) On what legal theory did the plaintiff sue? (b) What defenses have been raised? (c) What is the current status of the suit?

8. **Internet Assignment:** In November 2004, an appeals court reinstated a suit filed against NL Industries by Milwaukee. The city claimed that lead-based paint sold by the company for use in homes and schools caused toxic poisoning as the paint wore and chipped. A multi-million dollar abatement program had been started, and Milwaukee wanted the industry, not the public, to pay for it. Find out what happened after remand of this case for trial. (b) How does the Milwaukee suit compare to other actions against the paint industry for marketing and selling lead-based paint? (c) In what ways are the lead paint suits similar to those brought against gun makers? How are they different?

GLOBAL PERSPECTIVES

Ensuring the safety of some products—particularly medicines and medical devices—requires extensive testing. For decades, U.S. pharmaceutical companies have conducted many of their clinical trials abroad.

Researchers from the United States traveled to Sub-Saharan Africa in the late 1990s to test what was then state-of-the-art treatment for HIV, including AZT. They were looking for new, shorter drug treatments to prevent mother-to-child transmission of the disease. Negative publicity surrounding the trials—including assertions by leading ethicists that neither the African test subjects nor the African population benefited from them—led to the termination of the studies before completion. The science questions were not the only ones left unanswered.

Today, researchers are once again in Africa, this time with hopes of finding a vaccine that will prevent the disease.

The author of the next reading tackles the ethics of U.S. companies conducting clinical trials in developing nations. Yearby begins with an idea of justice that he traces back to Aristotle. According to Yearby, Aristotle "defined Justice in terms of equality: equals must be treated equally and unequals must be treated unequally." But, he asks, what does that mean in the context of developing new drugs for treatment or prevention of disease?

ARE THE CLINICAL HIV VACCINE TRIALS IN AFRICA UNJUST?

Ruqaiijah Yearby[27]

The U.S. Adopts the Justice Principle

. . . In the early 1970s, the U.S. Senate Committee on Labor and Human Resources held hearings on some of America's most egregious clinical trials, such as the Tuskegee Syphilis Study conducted from 1932 through 1972, in which poor African-American men were denied access to standard treatment. As a result of the hearings, Congress enacted the National Research Act of 1974 . . . created the National Commission for the Protection of Human Subjects of Biomedical and Behavioral Research (Commission) and imposed a moratorium on research conducted or supported by U.S. Department of Health, Education, and Welfare (HEW) until adequate protections for research subjects were developed.

27 From "Good Enough To Use for Research But Not Good Enough To Benefit From the Results of the Research: Are the Clinical HIV Vaccine Trials in Africa Unjust?" 53 *DePaul L. Rev.* 1127 (2004).

. . . [In 1979 the government published the Belmont Report]—the official policy statement of basic ethical principles and [federal] guidelines of HEW regarding research with human subjects. . . . [It] selected Justice as one of the three fundamental ethical principles and defined Justice by first asking the question: "Who ought to receive the benefits of research and bear its burdens?" . . .

. . . [An] injustice occurs during clinical trials when a benefit is denied to a person without good reason or a burden is unduly imposed on a person, "whereas Justice requires that equals be treated equally." In the context of clinical trials. . . :

> *Whenever research supported by public funds leads to the development of therapeutic devices and procedures, justice demands both that these not provide advantages only to those who can afford them and that such research should not unduly involve persons from groups unlikely to be among the beneficiaries of subsequent applications of the research.*

. . . Justice requires that the selection of human subjects for clinical trials be scrutinized to ensure that the population is not selected merely because research subjects are easily available, in a compromised position, or readily manipulated. Moreover, in government-funded clinical trials to develop drugs and vaccines in the United States and abroad, Justice dictates that subjects from vulnerable populations receive a benefit from the results of the trial. . .

History: 1990s Clinical Trials on Existing Drugs to Treat HIV

[Clinical trials conducted in the United States in the early 1990s showed that oral administration of AZT to HIV-positive pregnant women and newborns reduced perinatal transmission of HIV by two-thirds. But the regimen was expensive—$800 per patient—so researchers sought a shorter, less expensive version.]

. . . [E]ighteen clinical trials studying interventions to prevent perinatal HIV transmission were initiated. . . . These studies involved more than 12,000 pregnant women. The primary site of these trials was Africa. Despite the identical purpose of the trials, the structure of the studies conducted in the United States and in Africa were vastly different.

. . . [A]ll the pregnant women who participated in the U.S. study were given some form of treatment to prevent their newborns from contracting HIV . . . [but] researchers gave pregnant African women participating in the study placebos, even though it is widely accepted that placebos cannot be used if a known treatment is available. . . .

. . . The cost of sixty dollars per patient for the short treatment of AZT made the drug accessible to most Americans with or without health insurance. . . . However, the shorter-length treatment of AZT tested in the clinical trials conducted in Africa was not financially feasible to the citizens of Africa and other developing countries.[28]

Many of the [original] African HIV drug trials funded and conducted by the United States were abruptly halted because of pressures placed on researchers and funding agencies to conform to the ethical standards used in the United States.

Are the New Trials to Develop Vaccines to Prevent HIV Unjust?

[In this section, Yearby turns his attention to a new set of clinical trials, designed to find a vaccine that will prevent the disease.]

28 While the United States spent on average $3,000 per person for health care in the 1990s, spending in seven of the eight African countries where HIV trials were held ranged from $5 to $22 per person. Only in Zimbabwe could yearly health care spending—$88 per person—have covered the cost of the HIV treatment being tested.

The purpose of clinical HIV vaccine trials is to develop a vaccine that will either prevent the disease, as in the case of the smallpox vaccine, or slow the progression of the disease, as in the case of the flu vaccine. To develop an effective HIV vaccine through clinical trials, researchers must complete three phases. Phase I [generally uses fewer than] fifty people, to obtain information regarding the safety and effect of the candidate vaccine on human subjects. Information regarding the immune system's response to the vaccine, the effect of the vaccine on different populations, and the effect of different doses on the population is gathered from several hundred subjects in Phase II trials. [Phase III determines the efficacy of the vaccine for preventing disease by following several thousand persons who are given a series of vaccine doses and tested for HIV several months after each dose.] . . .

In 1987, the first Phase I clinical trial for the HIV vaccine was conducted in Zaire. Since 1987, sixty Phase I and II trials have been conducted, testing more than thirty candidate HIV vaccines. Most of the studies have been conducted in the United States and in Europe; and Phase III trials have only been conducted in the United States and Thailand, not in Africa. This is important because only Phase III trials provide information concerning the effectiveness of the HIV vaccine to prevent HIV infection. [In 2003, U.S government-funded Phase I trials began in Botswana and South Africa along with private-funded trials in Uganda].

The [potential] benefit to African society for participating in the three HIV vaccine trials is actual access to a vaccine that will prevent new HIV infections or decrease the number of deaths from AIDS. [But] developing an effective vaccine for Africans is complicated because individual Africans are infected with different types and strains of HIV, [all of which differ from the American strain.] . . .

. . . The HIV trials in Botswana are using the same vaccine currently being tested in trials in Boston and St. Louis. Because these trials are being conducted in the United States and in Africa, positive results from the trials promote the possibility that a multinational vaccine, which would benefit a broader society, would be developed. However, the possible benefits also create ethical dilemmas. There is no guarantee that the company manufacturing the vaccine will price it at a level affordable for the Botswana population. . . . To address this issue of access, the researchers from Harvard University are currently conducting studies in Botswana to create health infrastructures to treat HIV infection and a fellowship program to train scientists to conduct research in developing countries, such as Botswana. . . .

Concerned with reports of vaccine researchers and manufacturers using clinical trials in poor countries to exploit weaker ethical protections for conducting biomedical research, the Ugandan government negotiated an agreement with IAVI [the international scientific, nonprofit organization conducting the trials] that the vaccine, if effective, be accessible to the local population. . . . [But] Uganda does not have the intellectual property rights to the vaccine, the infrastructure to administer the vaccine, or the right to manufacture the vaccine. In 1997, Uganda only spent ten dollars per patient per year on health care; thus, they could ill afford to provide the shorter length AZT treatment at sixty dollars per patient to pregnant women to prevent perinatal HIV transmission. . . .

• QUESTIONS •

1. What are the ethical dilemmas that arise in this situation? How would you resolve them?

2. According to the author, the first HIV vaccine trial was conducted in Africa in 1987 by a French doctor who immunized himself and a small group of Zairians with an investigational HIV vaccine. He chose Zaire because "it was easier to get official permission [in Zaire] than in France," not because the population would benefit from the trials. How ethical was that decision?

3. The Declaration of Helsinki, adopted in 1964 by the World Medical Association, is a set of noncompulsory ethical guidelines for medical research involving human subjects. Since 2000, the Declaration has included the same Justice Principle adopted by the United States in the Belmont report. In 2002, the United Nations Programme on HIV and AIDS (UNAIDS) added the Justice Principle to its Guidance for conducting clinical HIV vaccine trials in developing countries. But Yearby would go further, recommending a compulsory international standard. What would be the advantages of adding enforcement mechanisms? Can you anticipate any problems with doing so?

4. **Internet Assignment:** Find out more about the Tuskegee Syphilis Study mentioned at the start of this article. Who conducted it? How were its shocking circumstances revealed, and when? Were there any reparations made to the black clinical subjects? Find out about the tests conducted on prisoners in Philadelphia in the 1960s, the subject of an exposé *Acres of Skin: Human Experiments at Holmsburg Prison: A True Story of Abuse & Exploitation in the Name of Medical Science* by Allen M. Hornblum. Was the treatment of these prisoners in line with the Justice Principle?

CHAPTER PROBLEMS

1. Talon-G is a rat poison made by ICI Americas and sold only to professional pest control companies. The poison was registered by the EPA and packaged in a container with EPA-approved labeling that displayed warnings cautioning users to keep it out of the reach of children, that it might be harmful or fatal if swallowed, and to store it in its original container in a location inaccessible to children. ICI could have—but didn't—make the poison safer by adding an emetic that would cause any human ingesting it to immediately vomit, thereby expelling the poison (rats do not have a vomit reflex). Alternatively, ICI could have added bitrex, an aversive agent used in a variety of products since the late 1970s that makes the poison taste bad to children but would not keep rats from eating it.
   a. Assume that an exterminator stores leftover Talon-G in an unmarked container. A nine-year-old child finds and eats the poison, thinking it is candy. Several days later, the child dies. On what basis might the child's family bring a lawsuit?
   b. What defenses might be raised?
   c. Assuming that the labels met EPA requirements for warning labels, are there policy reasons for refusing to allow a suit against ICI? See *Banks V. ICI Americas, Inc.* 45 S.E.2d 671 (Ga. 1994).
   d. **Internet Assignment:** Check http://www.epa.gov to find out about the EPA Consumer Labeling Initiative. Is this a good strategy for minimizing harm to humans from dangerous products? What else might be needed?

2. While his mother was sleeping, a two-year-old child retrieved a disposable butane lighter from his mother's purse atop the family refrigerator and used it to start a fire. The child, a sibling, and the sleeping mother were all killed. The lighter had no child-resistant features, and those representing a third child, who managed to escape from the house, brought suit against the maker. Analyze the case using the language of both tort and contract. How does it compare to the Talon-G scenario described above? See *Phillips v. Cricket Lighters*, 2004 WL 1277978 (Pa. Super.).

3. With some 15 percent of American children shown to be overweight, obesity—especially childhood obesity—has become a national health scandal. In December 2003 Xenical became the first drug specifically approved by the FDA for the treatment of obesity in adolescents. In

the past few years lawsuits have been brought—and settled—against McDonalds (for failing to disclose the use of beef fat in its French fries), DeConna Ice Cream Company (for understating fat and calorie content of its ice cream), Robert's American Gourmet Foods (for understating fat and calorie content in its cheese snacks), Kraft (for failing to disclose that Oreo cookies contained trans fatty acids), and the New York City school system for serving non-nutritious food in the schools. **Internet Assignment:** What changes can you detect in the food industry since the spate of lawsuits against them?

4. Can a video game be a dangerous product? On November 22, 1997, thirteen-year-old Noah Wilson died when his friend, identified as Yancy S., stabbed him in the chest with a kitchen knife. Noah's mother, Andrea Wilson, sued Midway Games, Inc., alleging that at the time Yancy stabbed Noah, Yancy was addicted to a Midway video game called Mortal Kombat. Yancy was so obsessed with the game that he actually believed he was the character Cyrax—who kills his opponents by grabbing them around the neck in a "headlock" and stabbing them in the chest. *Wilson v. Midway Games, Inc.*, 198 F.Supp.2d 167 (D. Conn. 2002). (a) Use the language of products liability law to analyze Wilson's claim and Midway's defense. (b) What defense might Midway raise under the U.S. Constitution? (c) How relevant is it that Midway specifically marketed to children by "saturating other industries with products made in the likeness of the characters in the video game," running ads on teen television shows, and supplying Mortal Kombat to video game rental stores and video arcades? (d) Use the language of ethical analysis to decide whether it is ethical to sell violent video games.

5. Is it ethical for a government agency charged with protecting consumer safety to go to court to block lawsuits brought by consumers? In 2004 the FDA did just that, pursuing a strategy consistent with the Bush administration's position in favor of tort reform. A widow, Barbara E. Horn, claimed her husband died because of defects in the design and manufacture of his heart pump. The government filed in support of the manufacturer, arguing that because the device had been produced according to federal specifications Horn should be barred from bringing a product liability suit. **Internet Assignment:** Find out how the federal court ruled in the *Horn* suit. How much importance was placed on the FDA's opinion? Find another product liability suit in which the FDA played a role, and compare it to the *Horn* case.

6. DDT is a cheap way to eliminate insects that threaten crops and people—including mosquitoes that spread malaria. Because it accumulates in the food chain and causes harm to humans and animals, its use has been banned in the United States since 1972. However, 23 nations continue to use it for malaria control, although most countries no longer use DDT for agricultural purposes. Alternative pesticides—such as pyrethroids—are almost two to three times more costly. By 1999, only three nations—China, Mexico, and India—still produced and exported DDT. However, when the United Nations considered a worldwide ban on DDT as part of a plan to minimize the use of 12 toxic chemicals ("persistent organic pollutants"), some members of the public health community were alarmed. There was a resurgence of mosquito-borne malaria, with some 300 to 500 million new cases a year. Drugs to treat malaria are expensive and increasingly ineffective against the disease. Use ethical theory to articulate a response to this dilemma.

7. **Internet Assignment:** (a) Find out what new rules for tire safety have been adopted by the National Highway Transportation Safety Administration since the Firestone/Ford Explorer scandal. (b) By August 2001, some 500 tread-separation lawsuits had been filed against Bridgestone/Firestone. The first suit to go to trial, brought by the family of a woman who suffered paralysis and brain damage in a rollover crash, was settled before verdict when Bridgestone/Firestone agreed to pay $7.5 million. Locate a court case involving Ford Explorer and/or Bridgestone Firestone tires. What was the outcome? (c) Discuss the relative effectiveness of government regulation versus litigation.

8. **Internet Assignment:** Choose one of the federal agencies with some responsibility for monitoring product safety, such as the FDA, EPA, NHTSA or CPSC. Find out about the backgrounds of those persons with policy-making power within the agency, including education, work experience in both the public and private sectors, and political affiliations. Do you detect any potential conflicts of interest? How responsive have they been to public concerns? To issues raised by lawmakers? To problems voiced by the industry they regulate? What guidelines would you suggest for appointments to such positions in the future?

9. **Internet Assignment:** In March 2004, the Environmental Working Group projected that more than 100,000 people in the United States will die of four asbestos-related diseases—mesothelioma, asbestosis, lung cancer, and gastrointestinal cancer—over the next 10 years. Find out what has happened to a bill sponsored by Senator Orrin Hatch that would create a victims' fund supported by asbestos companies and insurers to replace asbestos lawsuits.

10. **Internet Assignment:** In May 2004, a federal court cleared the way for the U.S. government to seek $28 billion in tobacco industry profits as part of its case against cigarette makers in the largest civil racketeering suit in history. The government claimed that the companies deceived the public about the dangers of tobacco and the addictive nature of nicotine, and targeted children through advertising and then lied about it. Find out what is happening in this suit against Philip Morris, R.J. Reynolds, Brown & Williamson, and others.

CHAPTER PROJECT

Mock Legislative Hearing: Dietary Supplements

Description

We will role-play two stages in a legislative hearing on the issue of regulating dietary supplements.

Background

It is estimated that more than 120 million Americans use various dietary supplements, herbal remedies, vitamins, minerals, enzymes, and amino acids—in part because many think of them as safer than pharmaceuticals, an image often fostered by advertising claims.("A hundred percent natural means a hundred percent safe.") However, as we know now Ephedra (used for thousands of years as ma huang), St. John's wort, ginkgo, and ginseng all can cause physical harm under certain conditions.

Under a 1994 law, no safety analysis or FDA approval is required before selling natural ingredients already on the market as dietary supplements, although the agency has the power to remove products that are misbranded or that are shown to "present a significant or unreasonable risk of illness or injury under . . . conditions of use recommended or suggested in labeling." This is what happened when the FDA banned dietary supplements containing Ephedra effective April 2004. By then, they had been linked to heart attack, stroke, and sudden death, and had already been banned in California, Illinois, and New York. Under existing law, producers are allowed to make claims about a supplement's impact upon bodily "structures and functions"—but not to make specific health claims for the product unless preapproved by the FDA. As we know from Chapter 7, the FTC is responsible for policing deceptive trade practices, including false advertising claims.

In June 2004, the U.N.'s World Health Organization (WHO) urged governments to provide insurance for nontraditional therapies and products, see that consumers get information on product efficacy and safety, and ensure that practitioners are properly trained and registered.

Stage 1: The Bills

Two teams of students will draft proposed legislation to present to WHO, addressing concerns regarding the safety and quality of dietary supplements, including those marketed over the Internet, and assigning responsibility for implementing and enforcing their law to appropriate government officials.

Stage 2: Legislative Hearing: See Guideline F

Possible Roles

Legislators:

In addition to a Chair (from the majority party) and senior member of the minority party, legislators should include senators from both parties, with representatives from urban and rural areas. Legislators might also be given the following role enhancements:

a. Receives large campaign contributions from the pharmaceutical industry
b. Newly elected, "liberal"
c. Newly elected, "conservative"
d. "Small government" proponent, elected in the late 1990s
e. Long known as a "consumer advocate"

Public Witnesses:

a. PhMA (The Pharmaceutical Research and Manufacturers of America)
b. Neutraceutical Corp.
c. Weight-Watchers/Jenny Craig
d. PublicCitizen.org
e. Business Round Table (CEOs)
f. Families of Steve Bechler and others whose death and injuries are blamed on supplements
g. Health insurance industry
h. Advertising agencies
i. American Civil Liberties Union (ACLU)
j. Ethicists representing each of the following views: Kantian, utilitarian, communitarian, and feminist
k. People for the Ethical Treatment of Animals (PETA)

Ownership and Creativity: Intellectual Property

If a song means a lot to you, imagine what it means to us.
— Artists Against Piracy

As for piracy, I love to be pirated. It is the greatest compliment an author can have. The wholesale piracy of Democracy was the single real triumph of my life. Anyone may steal what he likes from me.[1]
— Henry Brooks Adams, 1905

In vain we call old notions fudge,
And bend our conscience to our dealing;
The Ten Commandments will not budge,
And stealing will continue stealing.
— Motto of the American Copyright League, 1885

Intellectual property (IP) is the work product of the human mind. Novels, paintings, computer programs, songs, and inventions are all examples. IP differs from other kinds of property (land, buildings, stocks, consumer goods) in several key ways. While often expensive and time consuming to generate, intellectual property can be quickly and easily copied. Unlike tangible items whose use has physical limitations—only one person can drive a car at a time; a pie can be divided into only so many slices—the number of persons who can use intellectual property is boundless. A painting hung in a museum or reproduced in art books or on the Internet can be viewed by many; a poem or song can be endlessly repeated and enjoyed; the same software program can run on computers throughout the world.

The legal framework that protects intellectual property has evolved over the years, as lawmakers sought to promote commercial progress and enrich culture by rewarding inventors and creative people for their efforts.

In the final decades of the twentieth century and continuing into the twenty-first century, IP law has become the focus of controversy, not only in the business and legal communities, but among the general public. As intellectual property has become key to U.S. hegemony in the world economy,[2] legal protections for those owning patents and copyright have been greatly expanded—often in conflict with the norms of cyberspace, whose founders freely shared and borrowed creative works, claiming "information wants to be free." Business interests warn that sharing has economic costs; the Business Software Alliance reported that global losses from

1 Letter, July 11, 1905, to Brooks Adams. *Letters,* Vol. 2, Worthington Chauncy Ford, Ed. (Houghton Mifflin, 1938).

2 The U.S. trade surplus in 2002 estimates included $20 billion in software, $6.5 billion in movie exports, and $2 billion in database services. John H. Barton, "The Economics of TRIPS: International Trade in Information-Intensive Products," 33 *Geo. Wash .Int'l Bx* 473 (2003). Later, when the U.S. ran an overall trade deficit, exports of royalties and other high-tech services still ran $16 billion over imports. David R. Francis, *Christian Science Monitor,* Vol. 96, Issue 131, June 2, 2004, p. 1.

software piracy were just over $13 billion in 2002—a large chunk of the $152 billion global market.[3]

In this chapter, we explore some critical IP issues, beginning with one of the stickiest problems: downloading music from the Internet. The legal background is both traditional copyright law and relatively recent changes under the Digital Millennium Copyright Act. Then we turn to other kinds of IP: trademark, patents, and trade secrets. Conflicting private and public interests underlie the ethical focus of the chapter, which ends with a discussion of the globalization of IP law through the TRIPS agreement and a challenge to western views.

Copyright Law

Article 1, Section 8 of the U.S. Constitution empowers Congress to pass legislation "to promote the progress of science and (the) useful arts by securing for limited Times to authors and inventors the exclusive right to their respective Writings and Discoveries."

The congressional report on the Copyright Act of 1909 articulates the tension underlying intellectual property protection in our legal system:

> *In enacting copyright law Congress must consider . . . two questions:*
>
> *First, how much will the legislation stimulate the producer and so benefit the public, and second, how much will the monopoly granted be detrimental to the public? The granting of such exclusive rights, under the proper terms and conditions, confers a benefit upon the public that outweighs the evils of the temporary monopoly.*

The pull between public and private interests, between desire to encourage and reward individual creators—authors, composers, software engineers—and to use, improve upon, borrow, or critique their works has remained a constant in an otherwise evolving legal landscape.

Music

By now, online music sharing is almost ubiquitous. It began in 1999 when a 19-year-old college dropout, Shawn Fanning, released computer code that allowed his friends to share their collections of digitalized music (MP3 files). By July 2000, some five million users had visited the Napster site, and the Recording Industry Association of America (RIAA) began its campaign to stop it. One tool in its arsenal was to use the copyright law. As federal trial court judge Patel saw it, the RIAA suit to shut down Napster was really about "the boundary between sharing and theft, personal use and the unauthorized worldwide distribution of copyrighted music and sound recordings." While Patel and the federal appellate court in California agreed with the recording industry that Napster illegally contributed to copyright infringement, further appeals and technical difficulties delayed the dismantling of its services.

In the meantime, music swapping had planted itself firmly in the culture. Napster-like Web sites became popular. But the RIAA stood its ground. In the case that follows, the RIAA targets John Deep, founder of Aimster (later renamed Madster). Unlike Napster, which gave its users access to its online clearinghouse containing millions of songs, Aimster itself did not provide a central music "library" but instead allowed those who used its service to receive music directly from the hard drives of other users. Aimster provided encryption software—a free download—to enable users to hide their identity.

3 Douglas Heingartner, "Software Piracy Is in Resurgence, With New Safeguards Eroded by File Sharing," *The New York Times,* January 19, 2004, p. C-9, col. 1.

In re: Aimster Copyright Litigation Appeal of: John Deep, Defendant

United States Court of Appeals, Seventh Circuit
334 F.3d 643 (2003)

POSNER, Circuit Judge.

. . . Teenagers and young adults who have access to the Internet like to swap computer files containing popular music. If the music is copyrighted, such swapping, which involves making and transmitting a digital copy of the music, infringes copyright. The swappers, who are ignorant or more commonly disdainful of copyright and in any event discount the likelihood of being sued or prosecuted for copyright infringement, are the direct infringers. But firms that facilitate their infringement, even if they are not themselves infringers because they are not making copies of the music that is shared, may be liable to the copyright owners as contributory infringers. Recognizing the impracticability or futility of a copyright owner's suing a multitude of individual infringers ("chasing individual consumers is time consuming and is a teaspoon solution to an ocean problem,". . .) the law allows a copyright holder to sue a contributor to the infringement instead, in effect as an aider and abettor. . . .

[Aimster] is a type of Internet file-sharing system that might be created for innocuous purposes such as the expeditious exchange of confidential business data among employees of a business firm. . . . The fact that copyrighted materials might sometimes be shared between users of such a system without the authorization of the copyright owner or a fair-use privilege would not make the firm a contributory infringer. Otherwise AOL's instant-messaging system, which Aimster piggybacks on, might be deemed a contributory infringer. For there is no doubt that some of the attachments that AOL's multitudinous subscribers transfer are copyrighted, and such distribution is an infringement unless authorized by the owner of the copyright. The Supreme Court made clear in *Sony Corp. of America, Inc. v. Universal City Studios, Inc.* (U.S. 1984) that the producer of a product that has substantial noninfringing uses is not a contributory infringer merely because some of the uses actually made of the product (in that case a machine, the predecessor of today's videocassette recorders, for recording television programs on tape) are infringing. . . .

Sony's Betamax video recorder was used for three principal purposes, as Sony was well aware. . . . The first, which the majority opinion emphasized, was time shifting, that is, recording a television program that was being shown at a time inconvenient for the owner of the Betamax for later watching. . . . The second was "library building," that is, making copies of programs to retain permanently. The third was skipping commercials by taping a program before watching it and then, while watching the tape, using the fast-forward button on the recorder to skip over the commercials. The first use the Court held was a fair use (and hence not infringing) because it enlarged the audience for the program. . . . [B]uilding a library of taped programs was infringing because it was the equivalent of borrowing a copyrighted book from a public library, making a copy of it for one's personal library, then returning the original to the public library. The third use, commercial-skipping, amounted to creating an unauthorized derivative work, namely a commercial-free copy that would reduce the copyright owner's income from his original program, since "free" television programs are financed by the purchase of commercials by advertisers.

Thus the video recorder was being used for a mixture of infringing and noninfringing uses and the Court thought that Sony could not demix them because once Sony sold the recorder it lost all control over its use. The court ruled that "the sale of copying equipment, like the sale of other articles of commerce, does not constitute contributory infringement if the product is widely used for legitimate, unobjectionable purposes. Indeed, it need merely be capable of substantial noninfringing uses. . . .

[Posner applies the *Sony* precedent to Aimster:]

. . . [W]e agree with the recording industry that the ability of a service provider to prevent its customers from infringing is a factor to be considered in determining whether the provider is a contributory infringer. . . .

It is not necessarily a controlling factor, however, as the recording industry believes. If a service facilitates both infringing and noninfringing uses, as in the case of AOL's instant-messaging service, and the detection and prevention of the infringing uses would be highly burdensome, the rule for which the recording industry is contending could result in the shutting down of the service. . . . The fact that the recording industry's argument if accepted might endanger AOL's instant-messaging service . . . is not only alarming; it is paradoxical, since subsidiaries of AOL's parent company (AOL Time Warner), such as Warner Brothers Records and Atlantic Recording Corporation, are among the plaintiffs in this case and music chat rooms are among the facilities offered by AOL's instant-messaging service.

[Turning to the arguments raised by Aimster, the court rejects the idea that to prevail, the recording industry must prove it has actually lost money as a result of the copying that Aimster services facilitate. It goes on:]

. . . [W]hen a supplier is offering a product or service that has noninfringing as well as infringing uses, some estimate of the respective magnitudes of these uses is necessary for a finding of contributory infringement. . . . But the balancing of costs and benefits is necessary only in a case in which substantial noninfringing uses, present or prospective, are demonstrated. . . . [Here, Aimster has not yet demonstrated substantial legal uses of its services.]

We also reject Aimster's argument that because . . . the encryption feature of Aimster's service prevented Deep from knowing what songs were being copied by the users of his system, he lacked the knowledge of infringing uses that liability for contributory infringement requires. Willful blindness is knowledge, in copyright law . . . as it is in the law generally. One who, knowing or strongly suspecting that he is involved in shady dealings, takes steps to make sure that he does not acquire full or exact knowledge of the nature and extent of those dealings is held to have a criminal intent . . . because a deliberate effort to avoid guilty knowledge is all that the law requires to establish a guilty state of mind. . . . In *United States v. Diaz* (7th Cir. 1988), the defendant, a drug trafficker, sought "to insulate himself from the actual drug transaction so that he could deny knowledge of it," which he did sometimes by absenting himself from the scene of the actual delivery and sometimes by pretending to be fussing under the hood of his car. He did not escape liability by this maneuver; no more can Deep by using encryption software to prevent himself from learning what surely he strongly suspects to be the case: that the users of his service—maybe *all* the users of his service—are copyright infringers. . . .

[Posner next rejects Aimster's claim that the existence of a potential lawful use of its service is a defense to contributory infringement:]

We also do not buy Aimster's argument that . . . all Aimster has to show in order to escape liability for contributory infringement is that its file-sharing system *could* be used in noninfringing ways, which obviously it could be. Were that the law, the seller of a product or service used *solely* to facilitate copyright infringement, though it was capable in principle of noninfringing uses, would be immune from liability for contributory infringement. . . .

There are analogies in the law of aiding and abetting, the criminal counterpart to contributory infringement. A retailer of slinky dresses is not guilty of aiding and abetting prostitution even if he knows that some of his customers are prostitutes—he may even know which ones are. . . . But the owner of a massage parlor who employs women who are capable of giving massages, but in fact as he knows sell only sex and never massages to their customers, is an aider and abettor of prostitution. . . . The slinky-dress case corresponds to *Sony,* and, like *Sony,* is not inconsistent with imposing liability on the seller of a product or service that, as in the massage-parlor case, is capable of noninfringing uses but in fact is used only to infringe. To the recording industry, a single known infringing use brands the facilitator as a contributory infringer. To the Aimsters of this world, a single noninfringing use provides complete immunity from liability. Neither is correct. . . . [Instead, Posner finds, a preliminary injunction is warranted since Aimster failed to produce any evidence that its services has ever been used for a noninfringing, lawful purpose.]

We turn now to Aimster's defenses under . . . Digital Millennium Copyright Act (DMCA). . . . The Act provides a series of safe harbors for Internet service providers [such as AOL] and related entities, but none in which Aimster can moor. . . . The common element of its safe harbors is that the service provider must do what it can reasonably be asked to do to prevent the use of its service by "repeat infringers." Far from doing anything to discourage repeat infringers of the plaintiffs' copyrights, Aimster invited them to do so, showed them how they could do so with ease using its system, and by teaching its users how to encrypt their unlawful distribution of copyrighted materials disabled itself from doing anything to prevent infringement.

[The trial court's grant of a preliminary injunction is affirmed.]

• QUESTIONS •

1. Did Aimster directly violate the copyright law? If not, on what grounds does the court issue a preliminary injunction against its services?
2. This case did not end the litigation against Aimster. Judge Posner explained that at a later, full hearing, Aimster will have an opportunity to show that its lawful ("noninfringing") uses to be weighed against illegal, infringing ones. Can you think of other non-infringing uses for Aimster?
3. **Internet Assignment:** As the case against Aimster was working its way through the courts, a parallel suit was brought against other peer-to-peer software distributors. In August 2004, the Ninth Circuit Court of Appeals found that Grokster and Streamcast could not be found guilty of contributory infringement because they had no real way to control the users of their system. The court went on to find that their software was capable of substantial non-infringing uses:

> *One striking example provided by the Software Distributors is the popular band Wilco, whose record company had declined to release one of its albums on the basis that it had no commercial potential. Wilco repurchased the work from the record company and made the album available for free downloading, both from its own website and through the software user networks. The result sparked widespread interest and, as a result, Wilco received another recording contract. . . . [T]he record indicates that thousands of other musical groups have authorized free distribution of their music through the internet. In addition to music, the software has been used to share thousands of public domain literary works made available through Project Gutenberg as well as historic public domain films released by the Prelinger Archive.*
>
> *Metro-Goldwyn-Mayer Studios, Inc. v. Grokster Ltd.,* 380 F.3d 1154 (9th Cir. 2004).

In late 2004 the United States Supreme Court agreed to decide whether distributors of peer-to-peer file sharing are guilty of contributory copyright infringement. Find out how the court ruled on the appeal of *Grokster.*

Online Piracy or Culture Jamming?

> *The enigma is this: If our property can be infinitely reproduced and instantaneously distributed all over the planet without cost, without our knowledge, without its even leaving our possession, how can we protect it? How are we going to get paid for the work we do with our minds? And, if we can't get paid, what will assure the continued creation and distribution of such work?*
>
> —John Perry Barlow

As the practice of music file sharing evolved, so too did efforts to stop it—using technolo law, and the market. The major technology players joined together in various ways to imp what is known as "digital rights management," systems for building copy-protection into CD and DVDs and for providing secure and compensated methods for lawful digital sharing. Sony, Apple, and Realnetworks created Apple iTunes to compete with Microsoft's "Windows Media Rights." Intel and Nokia joined a global consortium to create "Project Hudson," enabling hand-held devices to be used to share movies or music files on a limited basis. All had the same goal: to find a technological solution that would limit what they called "online piracy."

In a wave of lawsuits, RIAA joined with the music industry to sue individual users. Unable to identify them initially, they sent "John Doe" subpoenas to the major Internet service providers—AOL, Verizon, etc.—to learn the names of those who were downloading music. Privacy advocates and cybertarians were alarmed, but the suits had an impact: They alerted parents and school administrators to the practice and within six months, reportedly, the number of people swapping files online dropped by half.

The content providers looked to the market, as well. By late 2001, the five multinational companies that dominated the recording industry had introduced their own online (paid) music services. Some bands even created audio files of their live concerts for their fans. (Live Phish Downloads, established in late 2002, reported in January 2004 that its online files had generated $2.25 million in profits.)[4]

There is, however, another perspective on music downloading, as the next reading demonstrates. The experimental music and art collective known as Negativland has been recording music/audio/collage works since 1980, producing a weekly three-hour radio show ("Over The Edge") since 1981, hosting a World Wide Web site (http://www.negativland.com) since 1995, and performing live on occasional tours throughout America and Europe. They are the authors of Fair Use: *The Story of the Letter U and the Numeral 2* (1995), and *No Business* (2005). In the following reading, Negativland describe their work, and a view of "the world as a freely reusable public domain."

Two Relationships to a Cultural Public Domain

Negativland[5]

As of this writing, it's been over fourteen years since Negativland was sued by Island Records for supposed copyright infringement, trademark infringement, defamation of character and consumer fraud contained in our 1991 U2 single. . . .

Other than the two lawsuits against us in the wake of the U2 single, we've never been sued again. But, surprisingly, we've actually been left alone throughout the 1990s and into the 2000s as we continued to release work that appropriates from privately owned mass media, often times in much more glaring ways than anything we were ever sued over. Perhaps it's because we've been flying under the radar as "alternative" music, or perhaps that highly publicized suit, which we publicly defended as "anti-art" because we couldn't afford to defend it in court as fair use, caused others to think twice before suing us again. Or perhaps, at least these days, it's because, in the wake of Napster, DSL, cable modems, file sharing, and mp3s, the music industry now has much

4 Seth Schiesel, "And the Band Played On, Online," *The New York Times*, January 22, 2004, Circuits, p. 1.

5 Negativland, "Two Relationships to a Cultural Public Domain," *SPG Law & Contemp. Probs.* 239 (2003). This article is also available at http://law.duke.edu/journals/66LCPNegativland.

vorry about than a bunch of underground audio artists chopping up and re-using ...ely owned intellectual property.

...e reasons, Negativland has remained appropriatively unrepentant, and we con... e same ways we always have.

...ued to work this way because we like the sound of it. We like the results. We ...t we find out there, it's simply fun to do, and we sense we are not alone in these ...ptions. In continuing to pursue collage and found-sound as elements in our music, we have set our work out as public examples of how appropriation from our media surroundings is neither culturally harmful nor dangerous to anyone else's business. Instead, it hopefully does represent some interesting art perspectives, as well as cultural commentary and criticism which are well worth having around whether or not our work happens to be "authorized" by our subjects and sources. We consider it to be a matter of free speech.

At this late date in the proliferation of collage, we no longer see this "appropriation" approach as particularly daring, edgy or trangressive, as it once truly was. . . . [Our] own phrase "culture jamming" has been appropriated, commodified and marketed and has entered into routine anti-corporate and anti-advertising activist lingo. We see it in the way collage and its ramifications has become a common subject in courses in film schools, law schools, art schools, and music schools. Even though it's all still tacitly illegal, this way of working is now nothing unusual. . . .

Any argument over what should or should not be considered a public domain for cultural works stems from one of two positions:

Position One: Everything created by humans is "work" that is done to gain income and which cannot continue to be done without that income. Therefore, all pieces of cultural "work" need to be compensated, usually on a per-unit basis, if we expect such work to continue. And, therefore, becoming a "user" of such work without compensating the creators for their work is a theft of the creators' rightful and necessary compensation. This position . . . stems directly from our evolution through pre-digital, hard-copy-based world in which the supply of anything made was necessarily physical and so also supply-limited in nature. The physical supply [copying and distribution] of anything made was controlled by the maker of that thing. . . .

Position Two: Digital technologies of reproduction have dragged the above ethic into a virtual new world of production realities in which there is still the creation of individual "works," but once a digital copy of that work is released, it's up for grabs. Those on the receiving end of it are capable of making their own indistinguishable copies ad infinitum and distributing them ad infinitum as well. And they can do this at little cost as individuals at home using consumer technology available to anyone. In other words, we have begun to allow those on the receiving end of cultural output to put themselves in charge of the reproduction and distribution of that work if they so wish. As music makers, for instance, we are no longer in charge of our own music once it actually leaves our hands in digitized forms. . . . We cannot control the further duplication and distribution of our music by those who receive it. This unexpected and perplexing reality has begun to encourage a different ethic and economic standard for digitized cultural work, one that [evolves out of the old] concept of public domain.

This new digitally-driven ethic of free exchange emerged so easily because the ideal of an unhindered, wide-open, and free cultural exchange has always held a deep philosophical appeal for the receiving end of culture, and the receivers have now suddenly been given an effective technological tool to actually make this happen. . . .

In much earlier times, prior to the corporately driven modern era of hands-off, privately owned and copyrighted cultural material, the natural human approach to our own culture was to participate in it by not only absorbing it as an individual, but also by remaking it—adding to it, removing from it, recombining it with other elements, reshaping it to our own tastes—and then redistributing the adjusted results ourselves. Virtually the whole history of human culture consisted of altering, reusing, and copying from the universal public domain in various re-imagined ways . . . until copyright came along.

Copyright has made true folk music, for instance, illegal and impossible. It is extinct as a process. What's left are professional "singer/songwriters," each one "original," each one intending to remain legal by being lyrically and melodically distinguished from all the others, and all having little to do with any kind of true, evolving "folk" process at all. . . .

Acknowledging the strengths and realities of human nature (monkey see, monkey do) has now become a disrespected practice in our commercialized culture. Nothing is allowed to incrementally evolve through various individuals. Each individual must make a legally defined leap from another's (phony) "originality" to his or her own (phony) "originality."

As for the Net, digital distribution does not remove the right to sue for copying or "unauthorized" reuses of existing work, but it does remove a great deal of practicality in actually enforcing such legal mandates. . . . [But t]he success of Napster . . . showed that the public's desire to engage in cultural reprocessing and trading for their own purposes had not become extinct. . . .

The music industry, in which virtually all mainstream music is at the moment owned and controlled by five transnational corporate entities, screams that free digital exchange will kill music if left to its own home reproduction devices. Well, it could possibly kill their kind of expense-laden music, but their self-absorbed assumption that they are all the music that counts is one of the reasons it is so appealing to subvert their economic grip on music by reproducing it and passing it on for free.

[I]f payment for any and all music significantly diminishes, all the other-than-profit-motivated home studios will hang on and keep producing music a lot longer than the big, extravagant, corporate music factories will ever care to. As economies of scale come into play, the consolidation of the major record labels into fewer and fewer hands creates a gigantic economic infrastructure they simply may not be able to sustain. If their worst case downloading disaster scenario comes true, they may slowly implode under their own size and weight, breaking up into smaller companies with lower overheads.

Of course music will not disappear under these conditions any more than it did throughout most of human history, when no one was being paid to make it. Music may, though, change in nature. The notion that one could run a business or have a career based on selling thousands of round pieces of plastic is a relatively new one in human history and not written in stone. . . . [The Internet may be making the current music industry less lucrative. But to] suggest that all this will automatically be bad for music itself. . . is not that easy to assume. We have become so accustomed to equating something's quality and value with the income it earns, we hardly know what to think about that something when it can't rely on this particular self-justifying link. Negativland, for example, has never made even a decent living off of music, yet we continue to make music. And we're probably not the only ones. . . .

The Internet, however, finally opens up self-production as a significant alternative to the notorious corporate label intimidation that has ruled modern pop music production. . . . The Net's unique ability to encourage the self-control and self-ownership of one's own musical career by utterly bypassing the former only game in town—corporate labels' usurpation of control and ownership rights—is not to be dismissed just because the resulting living may be smaller. . . .

The Net's motto for the future may well be "Get Smart or Get Off." Optimistically, and perhaps naively, we hope that the Net will end up being characterized as a people's medium, primarily designed by and for individuals rather than yet another comfortable bed for the mass culture of corporate marketing, which has so far successfully taken over all other available mass media. . . . The Net could become a simultaneously operating alternative, in which everything that remains is functionally in the public domain and open to anyone's reuse. This is not to assume that there will be no ways for creators to garner individual incomes in a digitized public domain, but those ways will probably be unusual in the history of making livings, perhaps including voluntary payment, and mostly yet to be invented. . . .

Meanwhile, all this has landed us in an era in which the traditional business of culture is in the impossible position of seeing its customer base as criminally dangerous to its business. This paranoia stems from the essence of capitalist logic—charging is good, free is bad. And not just bad—impossible! But in the realm of the Net, cultural materials—text, images, and audio—are all constantly moved around by an online audience operating under the assumption that free is good and charging is bad. Online users express this notion there because, for the first time in their lives, they actually can. And they see how the Net can apparently go on and on this way, that the essence of western civilization is perhaps not so threatened by it, that perhaps it even adds something worthwhile to it, and most significantly, that not one off-line business concern, individual or company, has yet gone out of business because of anything that's happening with online file-sharing.

The Internet was never designed as a commercially structured medium for selling digital data. It was designed as a medium for a free, open, and decentralized exchange of information. This tenacious foundation of technology and software is proving extremely difficult to convert into various forms of toll taking. . . .

• QUESTION •

1. Identify the various stakeholders in the online music-swapping controversy created by Napster and its progeny. How ethical are these services from a free market perspective? A utilitarian or deontological one?

U.S. Copyright Law Highlights

1790: First copyright law; protection available only for "maps, charts and books,"—not music—for a 14-year term.

1831: Copyright Act amended to expand protection to musical compositions.

1909: Compulsory licensing scheme and a royalty rate created for "phonorecords."

1912: Copyright Act amended to expand protection to motion pictures.

1914: ASCAP formed (American Society for Composers and Publishers).

1971: Copyright Act amended to extend limited protection to recordings.

1976: Major revision to U.S. copyright law; protection extended to all creations "fixed in tangible medium of expression"—including radio and television.

1984: *Sony v. Betamax;* Supreme Court rules that use of VCRs by home viewers to "time-shift" television shows is a "fair use."

1994: U.S. signs international treaty, Trade-Related Aspects of Intellectual Property (TRIPS); Congress creates penalties for bootlegging audio recordings of performances and music videos.

1995: Digital Rights in Sound Recordings Act gives exclusive rights to holders of sound recordings to public play of digital versions.

1998: Digital Millennium Copyright Act (DMCA) bans technologies that facilitate infringement.

1998: Copyright Term Extension Act (CTEA) (also known as Sonny Bono Act) extends the period protecting all copyrights twenty years to author's life plus 70 years; longer if holder is a corporation.

TRADITIONAL COPYRIGHT LAW

Our first federal copyright law gave those who wrote maps, charts, and books a 14-year right, renewable for another 14 years. Under today's law, ideas that are "fixed in a tangible medium of expression"—such as photographs, paintings, music, movies, and computer programs—can be copyrighted, and their authors generally gain rights lasting 70 years beyond the author's life.

The right attaches when the author first makes her work public, signing, dating, and using the © symbol to claim ownership—although formal registration with the Federal Copyright Office is required to bring a suit to enforce a copyright. Registration is relatively easy; all that is required is a registration form, a fee, and a copy (or copies) of the material.

A plaintiff can establish a **copyright infringement** by proving ownership (by showing that the work as a whole is original and she has complied with statutory formalities) and that the defendant copied the plaintiff's work. To do this, the plaintiff must show that the alleged infringer had access to the copyrighted work and that the offending and copyrighted works are so similar that the court may infer there was factual copying. The plaintiff must then prove that the copying was so extensive that it rendered the offending and copyrighted works substantially similar.

Fair Use

> *In truth, in literature, in science and in art, there are, and can be, few, if any, things, which, in an abstract sense, are strictly new and original throughout. Every book in literature, science and art, borrows, and must necessarily borrow, and use much which was well known and used before. No man creates a new language for himself, at least if he be a wise man, in writing a book. He contents himself with the use of language already known and used and understood by others. No man writes exclusively from his own thoughts, unaided and uninstructed by the thoughts of others. The thoughts of every man are, more or less, a combination of what other men have thought and expressed, although they may be modified, exalted, or improved by his own genius or reflection. . . . Virgil borrowed much from Homer; Bacon drew from earlier as well as contemporary minds; Coke exhausted all the known learning of his profession; and even Shakespeare and Milton, so justly and proudly our boast as the brightest originals would be found to have gathered much from the abundant stores of current knowledge and classical studies in their days.*[6]
>
> — Justice Story, *Emerson v. Davies*

Under the doctrine of fair use, not every instance of copying violates the rights of the author. There are times when the free flow of ideas requires quoting or otherwise borrowing from a copyrighted work. This can happen, for example, when critics review books, when news reporters use video clips, or when teachers make copies of articles for classroom use. The Copyright Act directs courts to consider four factors in deciding whether "fair use" allows a person to borrow otherwise protected work, even without permission. They are:

(1) the purpose and character of the allegedly infringing use, including whether it is commercial in nature, or for nonprofit educational purposes;

(2) the nature of the copyrighted work (e.g., is the original creative or factual?);

6 8 F.Cas. 615 (Cir.Ct., D. Mass., 1845) (Justice Story).

(3) the amount and substantiality of the portion used in relation to the copyright work as a whole; and

(4) the effect of the use upon the potential market for or value of the copyrighted work.

In the midst of the 2000 election, MasterCard sued Ralph Nader and his presidential campaign committee claiming, among other things, copyright infringement. Nader's defense: fair use.

MasterCard International Incorporated v. Nader 2000 Primary Committee, Inc.

U.S. District Court, 2004
2004 WL 434404

DANIELS, Justice.

. . . Since Fall of 1997, MasterCard has commissioned the authorship of a series of advertisements that have come to be known as the "Priceless Advertisements." At the end of each . . . a phrase identifying some priceless intangible that cannot be purchased (such as "a day where all you have to do is breathe") is followed by the words or voice over: "Priceless. There are some things money can't buy, for everything else there's MasterCard."

[Ralph Nader's 2000 campaign ran a political ad similar to the MasterCard ads. It began with] a series of items showing the price of each ("grilled tenderloin for fund-raiser; $1,000 a plate;" "campaign ads filled with half-truths: $10 million;" "promises to special interest groups: over $100 billion"). The advertisement ends with a phrase identifying a priceless intangible that cannot be purchased ("finding out the truth: priceless. There are some things that money can't buy"). [The ad was shown on television for a two-week period, and also appeared on Nader's Web site throughout the campaign.] . . .

Copyright Infringement

[MasterCard] alleges copyright infringement of its Priceless Advertisements. In response, defendants argue the Nader Ad is a fair use of the Priceless Advertisements because it is a parody of the Priceless Advertisements. . . .

An advertisement which uses elements of a copyrighted work "does not necessarily . . . [infringe] the copyright, if the product that it advertises constitutes a fair use of the copyrighted work. . . .

[The court tests the Nader ad against the statutory fair use factors:]

. . . [The] important question under the first factor, and in fair use analysis generally, is whether the allegedly infringing work "merely supersedes" the original work "or instead adds something new, with a further purpose or different character, altering the first with new expression, meaning or message.". . . If "the secondary use adds value to the original—if [the original] is used as raw material, transformed in the creation of new information, new aesthetics, new insights and understandings—this is the very type of activity that the fair use doctrine intends to protect for the enrichment of society."

One such transformative use that is typically found to be fair use is a parody. . . . [Nader's] argument that his Political Ad is transformative of MasterCard's Priceless Advertisements is as follows: [T]he MasterCard commercials' underlying message is "that MasterCard is the best way to pay for everything that matters. . . ." The Nader Ad, on the other hand, portrays the cold, big-money arena of Presidential politics and contrasts Ralph Nader's "truth" as the remedy for the bought and paid-for positions of others. Through this message, defendants claim that the Nader

Ad "lays bare the artifice of the original, which cloaks its materialistic message in warm, sugar-coated imagery that purports to elevate intangible values over the monetary values it in fact hawks" through parody.

. . . The Nader Ad does add something new and qualifies as a "transformative" work [that parodies MasterCard's message.] The message need not be popular nor agreed with. It may be subtle rather than obvious. It need only be reasonably perceived. . . .

[The court quickly dismisses the secondary factor, "the nature of the copyrighted work," as "without much force" in most cases—especially where transformative uses advance science and art through criticism – and of "slight relevance" here.]

In assessing the third factor . . . the amount and substantiality of the portion used in relation to the copyrighted work as a whole must be examined in context to determine whether the extent of the copying is consistent with or more than necessary to further the purpose and character of the [new work]. . . . In the parody context, this concerns "what else the parodist did besides go to the heart of the original." Although the Ralph Nader Political Ad copied the word "priceless" and the phrase "there are some things money can't buy" and used them in a similar manner, the greater part of the Nader Ad is original—the narration, the supertitles, and the film imagery . . . [and] the substance of the message [are] different from the message communicated by the advertisement it copies. . . .

[Finally the court looks at the economic effect of the Nader ad on the value of MasterCard's slogans:]

[Under precedent cases] . . . if the secondary copied use offers itself as a market substitute and in that way harms the market value of the original, this factor argues strongly against a finding of fair use. In this case, the Nader Ad . . . serves an entirely different purpose than the Priceless Advertisements, a political non-commercial purpose. For this reason, the fourth factor also weighs heavily in the defendant's favor for a finding of fair use.

[After weighing the factors the court concludes that the Nader Ad is a noninfringing fair use parody of MasterCard's Priceless Advertisements under the Copyright Act.]

• QUESTIONS •

1. Why does the court find that Nader's use of the Priceless slogan was a fair use?
2. Determine which of the following would be a fair use of copyrighted material by identifying and weighing the factors in each of the following scenarios:
   a. A 7th grade teacher clips an article from the morning newspaper and makes copies for her class to discuss.
   b. A college professor collects chapters from various books and brings them to the local copy center to have them made into a "Class Anthology." She reuses the same anthology for three years.
   c. Same as above, but instead of going to the local copy center, the professor scans the articles and posts them on the course Web site.
   d. A student selects several essays from an online magazine to include in a 50-page term paper, with no mention of their authors.
   e. Same as above, but the student properly attributes each essay to its rightful author.
3. According to Judge Daniels, there must be a connection between the original work and the parody that borrows from it:

> *[T]he heart of any parodist's claim to quote from existing material is the use of some elements of a prior author's composition to create a new one that, at least in part, comments on that author's works.*

Which of the following should qualify as fair use parodies? **Internet Assignment:** Find out what happened in the actual cases.

a. Artist Mark Napler created a "Barbie" Web site, using digital images and text that commented on Barbie as a cultural icon. In an interactive section, visitors could share what Barbie meant to them as they were growing up. There was also an "Alternative Barbies" section, a behind-the-scenes look at the seamy underbelly of Barbie's world, including digitally altered "Fat and Ugly Barbie" and "Mentally Challenged Barbie." Mattel, Inc., maker of Barbie and owner of the trademark, threatened to sue Napler.

b. From his fake news desk on Comedy Central's *The Daily Show,* Jon Stewart used a six-second excerpt from Sandra Kane's public access TV show to mock public access television, and commented on videotaped clips from network news reports.

4. **Internet Assignment:** Visit three Web sites: a commercial homepage, an advocacy site, and a personal Web page. Identify the elements of each site that appear to be original and those that may have been borrowed from another source. Which elements might you borrow without permission to create your own Web site? Which would seem to be protected by trademark or copyright?

Digital Millennium Copyright Act

Once experts figured out how to digitalize movies, filmmakers found themselves in a quandary. The quality of DVDs is superior to that of videotapes, opening the door to a potentially lucrative market of home viewers. But, just as VCRs make it easy to tape a movie shown on TV, computers make it easy to copy a DVD. As the next case explains, the film industry tried to build digital walls, such as encryption codes and password protections, to prevent piracy. At the same time, they lobbied Congress for laws to make it easier to police the unlawful distribution of DVDs by combating piracy in its earlier stages, before the work was even copied. The Digital Millennium Copyright Act (DMCA) did just what the industry had hoped for: It targeted both pirates who would circumvent digital walls and anyone who would traffic in a technology primarily designed to circumvent a digital wall.

In the next case, eight motion picture studios invoke their rights under the anti-trafficking provisions of the DMCA to stop Internet Web site owners from posting computer software to decrypt DVD movies or from linking to other Web sites that made decryption software available. The defendant, publisher of a hacker magazine and its affiliated Web site,[7] argues that the DMCA violates the First Amendment.

UNIVERSAL CITY STUDIOS, INC. V. ERIC CORLEY

U.S. Court of Appeals, Second Circuit, 2001
273 F.3d 429

NEWMAN, Circuit Judge.

The improved quality of a movie in a digital format brings with it the risk that a virtually perfect copy . . . can be readily made at the click of a computer control and instantly distributed to countless recipients throughout the world over the Internet. . . .

7 The court describes the hacker community as one that "includes serious computer-science scholars conducting research on protection techniques, computer buffs intrigued by the challenge of trying to circumvent access-limiting devices or perhaps hoping to promote security by exposing flaws in protection techniques, mischief-makers interested in disrupting computer operations, and thieves, including copyright infringers who want to acquire copyrighted material (for personal use or resale) without paying for it."

[To minimize the piracy threat, the entertainment industry] enlisted the help of members of the consumer electronics and computer industries who in mid-1996 developed the Content Scramble System ("CSS") . . . an encryption scheme that employs an algorithm configured by a set of "keys" to encrypt a DVD's contents. . . . [For a fee, the studios licensed these player keys to DVD-makers, who were obliged to keep them confidential and prevent any transmission from a DVD drive to any "internal recording device" such as a computer hard drive.]

With encryption technology and licensing agreements in hand, the studios began releasing movies on DVDs in 1997, and DVDs quickly gained in popularity, becoming a significant source of studio revenue. . . .

In September 1999, Jon Johansen, a Norwegian teenager, collaborating with two unidentified individuals he met on the Internet, reverse-engineered a licensed DVD player . . . and culled from it the player keys and other information necessary to decrypt CSS. . . . Johansen wrote a decryption program executable on Microsoft's operating system. That program was called, appropriately enough, "DeCSS."

If a user runs the DeCSS program . . . with a DVD in the computer's disk drive, DeCSS will decrypt the DVD's CSS protection, allowing the user to copy the DVD's files and place the copy on the user's hard drive. The result is a very large computer file that can be played . . . and copied, manipulated, and transferred just like any other computer file. . . .

Johansen posted the executable object code, but not the source code, for DeCSS on his web site. Within months . . . DeCSS was widely available on the Internet, in both object code and various forms of source code.

In November 1999, [Defendant] Corley wrote and placed on his web site, 2600.com, an article about the DeCSS phenomenon. His web site is an auxiliary to the print magazine, *2600: The Hacker Quarterly,* which Corley has been publishing since 1984. . . . [T]he focus of the publications is on the vulnerability of computer security systems, and more specifically, how to exploit that vulnerability in order to circumvent the security systems. Representative articles explain how to steal an Internet domain name and how to break into the computer systems at Federal Express. . . .

Corley's article about DeCSS detailed how CSS was cracked, and described the movie industry's efforts to shut down web sites posting DeCSS. It also explained that DeCSS could be used to copy DVDs. At the end of the article, [he] posted copies of the [computer] object and source code of DeCSS . . . [because] "in a journalistic world you have to show your evidence" . . . [and] links. . . to other web sites where DeCSS could be found. . . .

[In the next section, the court addresses Corley's defense: that the DMCA violates the First Amendment. First, the court must decide whether DeCSS code is "protected speech":]

Communication does not lose constitutional protection as "speech" simply because it is expressed in the language of computer code. Mathematical formulae and musical scores are written in "code," i.e., symbolic notations not comprehensible to the uninitiated, and yet both are covered by the First Amendment. If someone chose to write a novel entirely in computer object code by using strings of 1's and 0's for each letter of each word, the resulting work would be no different for constitutional purposes than if it had been written in English. . . .

Computer programs are not exempted from the category of First Amendment speech simply because their instructions require use of a computer. A recipe is no less "speech" because it calls for the use of an oven, and a musical score is no less "speech" because it specifies performance on an electric guitar. . . .

Having concluded that computer code conveying information is "speech" within the meaning of the First Amendment, we next consider, to a limited extent, the scope of the protection that code enjoys. . . .

[The court then quotes approvingly from the trial judge's opinion that:]

> *Society increasingly depends upon technological means of controlling access to digital files and systems, whether they are military computers, bank records, academic records, copyrighted works or something else entirely. There are far too many who, given any*

> *opportunity, will bypass security measures, some for the sheer joy of doing it, some for innocuous reasons, and others for more malevolent purposes. Given the virtually instantaneous and worldwide dissemination widely available via the Internet, the only rational assumption is that once a computer program capable of bypassing such an access control system is disseminated, it will be used. . . .*

There was a time when copyright infringement could be dealt with quite adequately by focusing on the infringing act. If someone wished to make and sell high quality but unauthorized copies of a copyrighted book, for example, the infringer needed a printing press. The copyright holder, once aware of the appearance of infringing copies, usually was able to trace the copies up the chain of distribution, find and prosecute the infringer, and shut off the infringement at the source.

In principle, the digital world is very different. Once a decryption program like DeCSS is written, it quickly can be sent all over the world. Every recipient is capable not only of decrypting and perfectly copying plaintiffs' copyrighted DVDs, but also of retransmitting perfect copies of DeCSS and thus enabling every recipient to do the same. They likewise are capable of transmitting perfect copies of the decrypted DVD. The process potentially is exponential rather than linear. . . .

In considering the scope of First Amendment protection for a decryption program like DeCSS, we must recognize that the essential purpose of encryption code is to prevent unauthorized access. Owners of all property rights are entitled to prohibit access to their property by unauthorized persons. Homeowners can install locks on the doors of their houses. Custodians of valuables can place them in safes. . . . These and similar security devices can be circumvented. Burglars can use skeleton keys to open door locks. Thieves can obtain the combinations to safes. . . .

Our case concerns a security device, CSS computer code, that prevents access by unauthorized persons to DVD movies. . . . CSS is like a lock on a homeowner's door, a combination of a safe, or a security device attached to a store's products.

DeCSS is computer code that can decrypt CSS. In its basic function, it is like a skeleton key that can open a locked door [or] a combination that can open a safe. . . .

[R]egulation of decryption code like DeCSS is challenged in this case because DeCSS differs from a skeleton key in one important respect: it not only is capable of performing the function of unlocking the encrypted DVD movie, it also is a form of communication. . . . As a communication, the DeCSS code has a claim to being "speech," and as "speech," it has a claim to being protected by the First Amendment. . . . [But] the capacity of a decryption program like DeCSS to accomplish unauthorized indeed, unlawful access to [copyrighted] materials . . . must inform and limit the scope of its First Amendment protection. . . .

[Held: An injunction against posting DeCSS on the Web or linking to other Web sites that contain DeCSS is warranted. The posting restriction is justified because the government has a substantial interest in preventing unauthorized access to encrypted copyright material, and there is no less restrictive way of preventing instantaneous worldwide distribution of the decryption code. The ban on posting links is needed to regulate the "opportunity instantly to enable anyone anywhere to gain unauthorized access to copyrighted movies on DVDs."]

• QUESTIONS •

1. What is DeCSS? What was the defendant's legal claim and why did he lose this case?

2. Is there a difference, ethically, between the copyright infringing activity of a music file-sharing service and those who use it? Between a hacker like Johansen who created DeCSS, Corley who disseminated it, and someone who accesses and uses it to watch a movie? If not, is it fair that copyright law, for the most part, is enforced against the Aimsters and Corleys of the digital world?

3. **Internet Assignment:** Find *2600: The Hacker Quarterly.* Besides accessing copyrighted works, what is it about? How would you describe the values that underlie Corley's magazine?

Joint Copyrights and Collective Rights

American copyright law creates a bundle of rights for the owner, including the right to reproduce, distribute, perform, display, or adapt the work. As with other property, the owner can sell or license some or all of her rights. Unknown authors of new books, for example, may contract to sell their copyright in exchange for royalties paid by a company that publishes the book. Others may agree to give up some, but not all, of their rights.

The copyright statute attempts to divide rights between an individual creator and the publisher of what is called a "collective work." Newspapers, magazines, and this textbook are examples. Angela R. Riley, author of the next reading, retains her copyright interest in the article she wrote, although Thomson Publishing holds the copyright in the overall work, *Law and Ethics in the Business Environment.* Movies, too, are collective works to which musicians, screenwriters, cinematographers, and producers all make varied contributions–with the producer holding the collective copyright, and the composer, for example, retaining her copyright to the background music.

But what if the separate individual contributions to a creation are not so easily teased apart? The author of the next reading tells the "story of one indigenous group's search to recover collectivity" through recognition of their rights, as a tribe, to cultural property.

Recovering Collectivity

Angela R. Riley[8]

In 1996 the German rock group, Enigma, spent thirty-two weeks on Billboard Magazine's International Top 100 Chart, turning the new genre of "world-beat" music into a household name. The United States, quick to recognize the mesmerizing quality and marketing potential of the music, selected Enigma's hit single, Return to Innocence, as the background theme for television broadcast advertisements of the 1996 Olympic Summer Games. Meanwhile, far in the southern region of the island nation of Taiwan, the Ami people, Taiwan's largest surviving indigenous tribe, mourn the desecration and exploitation of a sacred tribal creation which has its roots in thousands of years of Ami tradition.

Lifvon Guo, an Ami tribal elder, has spent most of his life as a keeper of Ami traditional folksongs. Lifvon quit school at the age of ten to tend to the animals and the crops. He then committed his captivating voice to the preservation of the ancestral songs of his culture as a tribal singer for almost seventy years. . . . Because the Ami language has not been transcribed in written form, oral tradition is the only method by which the tribe has transmitted cultural knowledge, religion, stories, and personal narratives for thousands of years. For his continued devotion to the passing down of Ami works, Lifvon is highly renowned within his tribe, but, until recently, he had little contact or familiarity with the world outside his indigenous community. That is, until he received a telephone call from a friend in Taipei, informing him that Taipei radio was broadcasting a song in which Lifvon was singing an Ami chant. Lifvon soon learned that a recording of him singing the Ami *Song of Joy* had been pirated and digitally incorporated into a popular "world beat" tune known as *Return to Innocence,* of which over five million copies were eventually sold world-wide.

With the help of friends, Lifvon struggled to reconstruct the events leading up to the international fame of Enigma, and the Ami "contribution" that had made it possible. The answer lay in a performance invitation made by the Ministries of Culture of Taiwan and France in which Lifvon and his wife, along with about thirty other indigenous singers from Taiwan, were invited to perform their songs in music halls across Europe. For a month they traveled, giving group performances of aboriginal music, which were recorded without their knowledge or consent. The

8 "Recovering Collectivity: Group Rights To Intellectual Property in Indigenous Communities," 18 *Cardozo Arts & Ent. L.J.* 175 (2000).

recordings from the concerts were published on compact disc a year later, and eventually fell into the hands of German music mogul Michael Cretu (known in the industry as "Enigma"), who was scouring recordings of "tribal performances" in hopes of finding the perfect piece to integrate into his own music. Cretu was immediately mesmerized with Lifvon's haunting voice, and he purchased the "rights" to the chant from an arm of the French Cultural Ministry. The Ami people never received recognition or payment for the use of the song. In fact, until the phone call, tribal members had no knowledge the appropriation had ever occurred.

Thus, *Return to Innocence* was created, an ethereal song that mixes the Ami aboriginal chant, sung by Lifvon, and modern dance beats to create a new, cutting-edge sound in the record industry, now known as "world beat." *Innocence* appears on Enigma's second album, *Cross of Changes*.

Though the Ami realize a serious injustice has occurred, they also know that current copyright law offers no protection for communally created indigenous works. As a result, the tribe is constrained to observe a piece of its history and culture slip from its grasp. Not only must the Ami confront the futility of challenging the initial infringement, but they are also powerless to determine the fate of the recordings, reap the rewards of their own creation, or control resulting violations of tribal law and blatant distortions of their work. . . .

[This account] is a complicated commentary on the state of indigenous peoples across the globe, their relationship to formal legal systems, and the resulting gap that lingers between the Indian world view and Western law. Indigenous works fail to fulfill individualistic notions of property rights that underlie the structure of Western law, and these works are thus omitted from intellectual property regimes. The focus of current copyright doctrine on rigid individualism devalues and trivializes conceptions of communal property that are deeply embedded in the institutions and norms of indigenous societies. This flagrant dismissal of non-Western viewpoints in the creation, consideration, and interpretation of copyright law keeps indigenous creations unprotected and vulnerable to mass appropriation and exploitation.

This paper contends that only a group rights model of ownership of intangible property will adequately protect the works of indigenous peoples from an ever-encroaching dominant society. The validation of communal property seeks to bring collaborative, inter-generational tribal creations within the scope of copyright protection. . . .

Copyright protection is geared towards the printed word, and societies that transcend this limitation through oral transmission fall entirely outside the sphere of Anglo-American copyright protection. . . . The very nature of Native artistic expression works that are created inter-generationally, built upon fluid conceptions of revision and creativity, and seldom recorded in a tangible medium (notwithstanding the collective memory of its peoples) precludes copyright protection. The result is an entire body of artistic and literary expression that is being generated by groups already surviving on the very margins of society, prevented from enjoying freedom from infringement, appropriation, and callous distortion.

The Ami's *Song of Joy* must satisfy the Copyright Act's three essential requirements in order to earn protection as a musical composition under the Act. The work must demonstrate originality, production by a clearly defined "author," and must be expressed through a "fixed" and "tangible medium."

Though it is clearly established that to be original, a work need only demonstrate a *de minimis* quantum of creativity, *Song of Joy* nevertheless falls short of the applicable standard. The work simply cannot be said to be "independently created by the author." Placing the question of authorship aside, even if Lifvon created *Song of Joy,* he indisputably did not create it independently. The very essence of the song's communal nature defies the notion of "originality."

The Romantic-inspired conception of "originality" is in strict opposition to indigenous notions of creation. The current law, "with its emphasis on rewarding and safeguarding 'originality,' has lost sight of the cultural value of what might be called 'serial collaborations' works such as those resulting from successive elaborations of an idea or text by a series of creative workers, occurring perhaps over years or decades." For the Ami, ascertaining the creation instance is virtually impossible. The song might have existed for as long as the Ami peoples themselves. Lifvon's purpose is to carry the song to future generations of Ami members, thus conveying its significance and import to those who came after him, just as he learned it from the Ami tribal singers who came before him. Knowledge transmission in indigenous communities, a heritage involving centuries of maintaining culturally revered stories in song, implies that even the most basic elements of copyright law remain unfulfilled.

[I]n the seventy years in which Lifvon has been singing, his esteemed role in the Ami community has been defined not only by his inspiring voice, but by his ability to modify the chants, guaranteeing their endurance through time. . . .

Storytelling to Native peoples is about more than entertainment, or even education. It is a vital and necessary component of continued life, the life of the tribe and the life of the world itself. Creation stories are told ritually to ensure the continued existence of the world. . . . Storytelling in the Indian world occurs through songs, chants, narratives, and ceremonies which are kept sacred in the community, but which are not compelled to remain unchanged. Variation on the storytelling by the storyteller is the work of imagination, not contradiction.

In an indigenous society, concepts of creativity and originality rely on notions of fluidity not seen in the Western world. By its very nature, oral tradition is a passing down, a handing off, of creative expression. A work can be reborn and recreated each time it is sung; it takes on the needs of the tribe, defined and redefined by its keepers and by the purposes for which it is called upon. Without recognition of group rights to communal property, it is virtually impossible to frame indigenous works in the monolithic scheme of current copyright law. . . .

Because only an "author" is entitled to copyright protection, the meaning of the term is of great importance. . . . [T]he Romantic archetype has lent to copyright doctrine a conception of the author as lone genius, whose work breaks from tradition and does not receive increased importance or validity through connections to prior creations. . . .

The resulting definition of authorship exists in direct opposition to the communal methods of creativity symbolizing the structure of Native communities, which place the origins of tribal works in the group, not the individual. . . .

Designating a clearly identified "author" [essential for copyright protection] in the case of Song of Joy, as with most indigenous creations, is inconceivable. . . .

The most likely scenario is that there never existed a clearly delineated "author" or "authors" of the song. In indigenous societies, many members believe that ceremonies, music, and stories are communicated to the tribe by the Creator. . . . Thus, in whatever manner the inspiration for Song of Joy was conceived, known methods of transmission among indigenous peoples indicates that the song does "belong" and has always "belonged" to the tribe as a whole. . . .

[T]he sanctity of the work itself derives, in part, from the import placed on the collective creation of the piece. The group product in the indigenous society is the medium through which all tribal members, living, dead and unborn, speak their voice and become a part of the tribal way. . . .

Denying copyright protection to works not "fixed in a tangible medium" results in the devastating exclusion of an entire realm of indigenous creations, as the use of oral tradition spans almost every Native community in existence. . . .

[Riley recommends legal protection that embraces a "group-rights model" of copyright law that would protect collaborative inter-generational tribal creations.]

To fully embrace the group rights model, implicit in which there is a profoundly non-Western conception of ownership, there must exist a common belief among group members that they are "normatively bound to each other such that each does not act simply for herself or himself but each plays her or his part in effectuating [a] shared normative understanding." For many Native peoples, tribal affiliation is precisely this sort of commitment. . . . For individuals within these distinct groups, flourishing in the world as a person is intimately related to cultural identity.

Identity in the indigenous world is inextricably linked to community structure. But identity for tribal peoples reaches further, to form a forceful nexus between the group and its cultural property. For a tribe, the authority to control that property is essential for group survival, as it links its very existence to collective creations. Cultural property situates indigenous people in a historical context, tying them to the place from which they came and the point of their creation. Tribal members become linked to the goods of the tribe: turtle rattles, trickster narratives, religious bundles often resulting in a commitment to the objects outside of themselves; this commitment is the Native peoples' definition of what life is about.

For a tribe, determining the destiny of collective property, particularly that which is sacred and intended solely for use and practice within the collective, is a crucial element of self-determination. The legal enforcement of a group model of invention and ownership would support self-determination principles, not only by protecting indigenous works from theft and exploitation, but by placing the sanctity of tribal cultural property back into the hands of indigenous peoples, affirming their ability to determine themselves as a people through their culture. When a group has exclusive authority to prescribe the employment of its most valuable creations, the entire community flourishes and benefits. Most importantly, the group-rights model of ownership takes into account the Indian world view by providing a foundation for "intergenerational justice." Preserving the divine nature of cultural works and sheltering them from the market demonstrates Indian respect for those who have walked on, and sets the work aside for use and honor by future generations.

• QUESTIONS •

1. What are the three elements that make a work eligible for copyright? How does the Ami *Song of Joy* fail each?
2. How would Riley modify the law of copyright? Why?
3. Think back to the ethical frameworks in Chapter 1. Which support the legal protection of tribal cultural property? Explain.
4. Suppose that, instead of a single payment to Lifvon for one song, you wanted to set up a system to fairly compensate indigenous people whenever their culture became the basis for a new work of art. What might that system look like? Who should control it?
5. Riley argues that the infringement of collective rights is only the first violation against Native peoples:

   > *Beyond appropriation lies the distortion and misrepresentation of tribal creations as they are freely picked up by non-Natives and openly exploited for capital gain, playing into Westerners' fetish-ism with Native works, but without recognition or compensation going to the Native communities.*

   Compare the distortion that occurs in "borrowing" indigenous work to other kinds of borrowing, such as music sampling or the creation of jigsaw puzzles and mouse pads out of reproductions of well-known paintings.

Public Domain

While Riley looks to create protection for "group" rights, some argue we should be moving in the opposite direction, reducing private control of culture and preserving more for our common, public use. Material that is always freely usable by anyone, without permission, is said to be "in the public domain." Free-floating "ideas"—as opposed to expressions that have been "fixed"—and government writings, such as judicial opinions, are available to anyone. Too, when copyright expires protected works are said to return to the **public domain.**

Lawrence Lessig, author of the next reading, is concerned about the diminishing public domain. After telling two stories, he goes on to explain that we have experienced a "technological inversion," such that the old values embedded in our copyright laws no longer make sense.

The Creative Commons

Lawrence Lessig[9]

Everyone has heard of the Brothers Grimm. They wrote fairy tales. If you are like I was, you probably think that they wrote wonderful and happy fairy tales—the sort of stories children ought to be raised on. That's a mistake. The Grimm fairy tales are, as the name suggests, quite grim: awful, bloody, moralistic stories that should be kept far from any healthy childhood. Yet you are likely to believe that these stories are wonderful and happy, because they have been retold to us by an amazing creator called Disney.

Walt Disney took these stories and retold them in just the way our founders imagined that our culture would grow. He took the stories, and retold them in a way that would speak to his time. And most important for my purposes here, he could retell them because these stories lived in the public domain. Their copyright protections had lapsed. And they had lapsed because copyrights, in America at least, are for a "limited time" only. That limitation in turn builds a kind of creative commons: a resource from which anyone can draw and add and build upon because the Constitution guarantees the law's protection will end.

We can think of this "creative commons," this public domain from which others may draw, as a lawyer-free zone. No one can control what you do with material there, meaning you need never speak to a lawyer to draw material from there. The public domain is thus a resource that requires the permission of no one. And it is a resource that creators throughout history have drawn upon freely.

[But under today's law, with copyright extending 70 years beyond the life of an author, or 100 years if owned by a company as a "work for hire"] . . . no one can do to the Disney Corporation what Disney did to the Brothers Grimm. . . .

[Lessig tells another story, this one about AIBO, a robot dog created by Sony that sells for roughly $1,300.]

. . . As with any dog, ownership gives you the right to take the dog home and teach it how to behave—at least within limits.

One fan of the AIBO dog learned something about these limits. He took his Sony AIBO dog apart to understand how it worked. He tinkered with the dog. And after tinkering with the dog, he figured out how the code instructed the dog to operate, and he wanted his dog to operate in a somewhat different way. He wanted to teach his dog to dance jazz. On his website, aibopet.com, this fan of the AIBO taught others how to tinker with their pet. And one particular bit of tinkering would enable the AIBO dog to dance jazz. . . .

[W]hen the owner of aibopet.com posted this little hack on his website, he got a letter from the Sony Corporation: "Your site contains information providing the means to circumvent AIBO ware's copy protection protocol constituting a violation of the anti-circumvention provisions of a law called the Digital Millennium Copyright Act.". . .

[To understand these stories, Lessig writes, we need to look at the technological inversion that has occurred in the United States:]

. . . [The original values of our copyright law] protected the public domain. They enabled a vibrant cultural commons. Yet changing technology and changing law is increasingly enclosing that commons. Tools built into the architecture of cyberspace are defeating a tradition of balanced freedom that defined our past. Yet the law has not yet recognized this inversion. . . .

The Framers granted authors a very limited set of rights. . . . Our outrage at China notwithstanding, we should not forget that until 1891, American copyright law did not protect foreign copyrights. We were born a pirate nation.

In the first ten years of this copyright regime, there were some 13,000 titles that were published. Yet there were less than 1,000 copyright registrations. The aim of the original copyright

9 55 *Fla. L. Rev.* 763 (2003).

regulation was to control publishers. In 1790, there were 127 publishers. This law was a tiny regulation of a tiny part of early American culture.

Most culture thus remained free of any copyright regulation. You could take a book and write an abridgement . . . translate the book . . . turn it into a play . . . physically write out every word in that book and give it to your friends without any regulation of copyright law. The culture was free in a sense that is increasingly being demanded in debates about culture today: there was a freedom to Disnify culture, as Disney did to the Brothers Grimm . . . and a freedom to tinker with the content that one finds without fear of committing a federal crime, as the fans of the AIBO wanted.

We could say, following a recent Apple ad campaign, that in our past, there was a freedom to "Rip, Mix, and Burn" culture. Regulation protected against unfair competition, but that regulation left people to develop their culture as they wished.

That past has now changed. It first changed because the law has changed. [Today, the law protects] essentially any creative work reduced to a tangible form . . . [and does so] automatically.

More important than these changes in law are the changes effected by technology. Think about the life of a book. . . . The publisher can't control what I do with a printed book because there is no way to control pages separated from the publisher. And not only can they not control what I do physically with the book, the law, copyright law, affirmatively limits the ability of the publisher to do anything to the book, once the book is sold.

But compare then a book in cyberspace. I have . . . in my Adobe eBook Reader . . . *Middlemarch*—a work that is in the public domain. Even though this uncopyrighted book is in some senses free, it's not free in the Adobe eBook Reader. . . . [Limited p]ermission is granted to me to read this book aloud . . . I may copy ten text sections into the computer's clipboard memory every ten days . . . [and] print ten pages everyday using my computer. And here is the most embarrassing example: my most recent book, *The Future of Ideas.* My publisher released it stating I'm not allowed to copy any text sections into the memory, I'm not allowed to print any pages, and don't try to use your computer to read my book aloud, it's an offense of copyright law. Freedoms I would have with a real book get erased when this book is made virtual.

Now what makes these protections possible? In part what makes it possible is just the code built into the Adobe eBook Reader. The technology gives the publisher a control over an eBook that no publisher could ever have had over a regular book. And because of this control, the *use* of an eBook is regulated . . . [instead of] the publishing of copyrighted material. . . .

These controls increasingly mean that the ability to take what defines our culture and include it in an expression about our culture is permitted only with a license from the content owner. Free culture is thus transformed into licensed culture. The freedom to remake and retell our culture thus increasingly depends upon the permission of someone else. The freedom to Disnify is undermined. The freedom to counter-tell stories is weakened. The freedom to tinker, especially for the technologist to tinker, is threatened.

• QUESTIONS •

1. If you had the power to rewrite the law of copyright, would you want to? If so, give it a try. It may be more productive to work with a classmate or two. If not, write a critique of the revisions proposed by one or more of your classmates.

2. **Internet Assignment:** Find out what you can about Lessig. What background does he bring to the debate about expanding or limiting IP rights? Who are his supporters? Detractors?

3. **Internet Assignment:** Digital archivists Bewster Kahle, founder of the Internet Archive, has sued for the right to include out-of-print books and films in his nonprofit archive for educational and research purposes. His argument rests on the claim that recent changes to United States Copyright laws are unconstitutional. How did the courts rule?

Beyond Copyright: Misappropriation, Trademark, Patents, and Trade Secrets

Ours is a highly individualized culture with a great faith in the work of art as a unique one-off, and the artist as an original, a godlike and inspired creator of one-offs. But fairy tales are not like that, nor are their makers. Who first invented meatballs? In what country? Is there a definitive recipe for potato soup? Think in terms of the domestic arts. This is how I make potato soup.

— Angela Carter, novelist

As the reading on collective indigenous culture suggests, not every good idea is—or can be—fixed in the kinds of "tangible expressions" that can be copyrighted. Nor is federal copyright law the only source of protection for intellectual property. The following case involves a claim of misappropriation under California's state law.

White v. Samsung and Deutsch Associates

U.S. Court of Appeals, Ninth Circuit, 1992
971 F.2d 1395

GOODWIN, Senior Circuit Judge.

Plaintiff Vanna White is the hostess of "Wheel of Fortune," one of the most popular game shows in television history. An estimated forty million people watch the program daily. Capitalizing on the fame which her participation in the show has bestowed on her, White markets her identity to various advertisers.

The dispute in this case arose out of a series of advertisements prepared for Samsung by Deutsch. The series ran in at least half a dozen publications with widespread, and in some cases national, circulation.

. . . Each [ad] depicted a current item from popular culture and a Samsung electronic product. Each was set in the twenty-first century and conveyed the message that the Samsung product would still be in use by that time. By hypothesizing outrageous future outcomes for the cultural items, the ads created humorous effects. For example, one lampooned current popular notions of an unhealthy diet by depicting a raw steak with the caption: "Revealed to be health food. 2010 A.D. . . ."

The advertisement which prompted the current dispute was for Samsung video-cassette recorders (VCRs). The ad depicted a robot, dressed in a wig, gown, and jewelry which Deutsch consciously selected to resemble White's hair and dress. The robot was posed next to a game board which is instantly recognizable as the Wheel of Fortune game show set, in a stance for which White is famous. The caption of the ad read: "Longest-running game show. 2012 A.D. . . ."

[The court must determine whether the defendants have violated Ms. White's common law right of publicity, by "appropriat[ing her] name or likeness to [their] advantage, commercially or otherwise" without her consent. Since they had not actually used Vanna White's name or her real likeness in the ad, defendants argued they did not "appropriate" her. But the Court decided not to limit the manner of appropriation in this way.]

[T]he most popular celebrities are not only the most attractive to advertisers, but also the easiest to evoke without resorting to obvious means such as name, likeness, or voice.

Consider a hypothetical advertisement which depicts a mechanical robot with male features, an African-American complexion, and a bald head. The robot is wearing black hightop Air Jordan basketball sneakers, and a red basketball uniform with black trim, baggy shorts, and the number 23 (though not revealing "Bulls" or "Jordan" lettering). The ad depicts the robot dunking a basketball one-handed, stiff-armed, legs extended like open scissors, and tongue hanging out. Now envision that this ad is run on television during professional basketball games. Considered individually, the robot's physical attributes, its dress, and its stance tell us little. Taken together, they lead to the only conclusion that any sports viewer who has registered a discernible pulse in the past five years would reach: the ad is about Michael Jordan.

Viewed separately, the individual aspects of the advertisement in the present case say little. Viewed together, they leave little doubt about the celebrity the ad is meant to depict. . . .

Television and other media create marketable celebrity identity value. Considerable energy and ingenuity are expended by those who have achieved celebrity value to exploit it for profit. The law protects the celebrity's sole right to exploit this value whether the celebrity has achieved her fame out of rare ability, dumb luck, or a combination thereof. . . . Because White has alleged facts showing that Samsung and Deutsch had appropriated her identity, [she is entitled to a trial on her common law right of publicity claim.]

[In the next section, the court dismisses the defendant's claim that their parody is protected under the First Amendment:]

In defense, defendants cite a number of cases for the proposition that their robot ad constituted protected speech. The only cases they cite which are even remotely relevant to this case are *Hustler Magazine v. Falwell* and *L.L. Bean, Inc. v. Drake Publishers*. . . . Those cases involved parodies of advertisements run for the purpose of poking fun at Jerry Falwell and L.L. Bean, respectively. This case involves a true advertisement run for the purpose of selling Samsung VCRs. The ad's spoof of Vanna White and Wheel of Fortune is subservient and only tangentially related to the ad's primary message: "buy Samsung VCRs." Defendants' parody arguments are better addressed to non-commercial parodies. The difference between a "parody" and a "knock-off" is the difference between fun and profit. . . .

[After the appellate decision, and before the trial, the defendants sought a rehearing. They lost, but two justices agreed with them, expressing their views in this dissenting opinion:]

KOZINSKI, Circuit Judge, with whom Circuit Judges O'SCANNLAIN and KLEINFELD join, dissenting.

Saddam Hussein wants to keep advertisers from using his picture in unflattering contexts. . . . Clint Eastwood doesn't want tabloids to write about him. . . . The Girl Scouts don't want their image soiled by association with certain activities. . . . George Lucas wants to keep Strategic Defense Initiative fans from calling it "Star Wars." . . . And scads of copyright holders see purple when their creations are made fun of. . . .

Something very dangerous is going on here. Private property, including intellectual property, is essential to our way of life. It provides an incentive for investment and innovation; it stimulates the flourishing of our culture; it protects the moral entitlements of people to the fruits of their labors. But reducing too much to private property can be bad medicine. Private land, for instance, is far more useful if separated from other private land by public streets, roads and highways. Public parks, utility rights-of-way and sewers reduce the amount of land in private hands, but vastly enhance the value of the property that remains.

So too it is with intellectual property. Overprotecting intellectual property is as harmful as underprotecting it. Creativity is impossible without a rich public domain. Nothing today, likely nothing since we tamed fire, is genuinely new: Culture, like science and technology, grows by accretion, each new creator building on the works of those who came before. Overprotection stifles the very creative forces it's supposed to nurture.

The Panel's opinion is a classic case of overprotection. . . .

The ad that spawned this litigation starred a robot dressed in a wig, gown and jewelry reminiscent of Vanna White's hair and dress . . . posed next to a Wheel-of-Fortune-like game board. . . .

The gag here, I take it, was that Samsung would still be around when White had been replaced by a robot.

Perhaps failing to see the humor, White sued, alleging Samsung infringed her right of publicity by "appropriating" her "identity." Under California law, White has the exclusive right to use her name, likeness, signature and voice for commercial purposes. But Samsung didn't use her name, voice or signature, and it certainly didn't use her likeness. The ad just wouldn't have been funny had it depicted White or someone who resembled her—the whole joke was that the game show host(ess) was a robot, not a real person. No one seeing the ad could have thought this was supposed to be White in 2012. The district judge quite reasonably held that, because Samsung didn't use White's name, likeness, voice or signature, it didn't violate her right of publicity. . . . Not so, says the panel majority: The California right of publicity can't possibly be limited to name and likeness. If it were, the majority reasons, a "clever advertising strategist" could avoid using White's name or likeness but nevertheless remind people of her with impunity. . . . To prevent this . . . the panel majority holds that the right of publicity must extend beyond name and likeness, to . . . anything that "evoke[s]" her personality. . . .

Intellectual property rights aren't like some constitutional rights, absolute guarantees protected against all kinds of interference, subtle as well as blatant. They cast no penumbras, emit no emanations: The very point of intellectual property laws is that they protect only against certain specific kinds of appropriation. I can't publish unauthorized copies of, say, *Presumed Innocent*; I can't make a movie out of it. But I'm perfectly free to write a book about an idealistic young prosecutor on trial for a crime he didn't commit. So what if I got the idea from *Presumed Innocent*? So what if it reminds readers of the original? . . . All creators draw in part on the work of those who came before, referring to it, building on it, poking fun at it; we call this creativity, not piracy.

The majority . . . [is] creating a new . . . right. . . . It's replacing the existing balance between the interests of the celebrity and those of the public by a different balance, one substantially more favorable to the celebrity. Instead of having an exclusive right in her name, likeness, signature or voice, every famous person now has an exclusive right to anything that reminds the viewer of her. . . .

Consider how sweeping this new right is. What is it about the ad that makes people think of White? It's not the robot's wig, clothes or jewelry; there must be ten million blond women (many of them quasi-famous) who wear dresses and jewelry like White's. It's that the robot is posed near the "Wheel of Fortune" game board. Remove the game board from the ad, and no one would think of Vanna White. . . . But once you include the game board, anybody standing beside it a brunette woman, a man wearing women's clothes, a monkey in a wig and gown would evoke White's image, precisely the way the robot did. . . . The panel is giving White an exclusive right not in what she looks like or who she is, but in what she does for a living.

This is entirely the wrong place to strike the balance. Intellectual property rights aren't free: They're imposed at the expense of future creators and of the public at large. Where would we be if Charles Lindbergh had an exclusive right in the concept of a heroic solo aviator? If Arthur Conan Doyle had gotten a copyright in the idea of the detective story, or Albert Einstein had patented the theory of relativity? . . . [I]intellectual property law is full of careful balances between what's set aside for the owner and what's left in the public domain for the rest of us: The relatively short life of patents; the longer, but finite, life of copyrights; copyright's idea-expression dichotomy; the fair use doctrine; the prohibition on copyrighting facts; the compulsory license of television broadcasts and musical compositions. . . . All of these diminish an intellectual property owner's rights. All let the public use something created by someone else. But all are necessary to maintain a free environment in which creative genius can flourish.

The intellectual property right created by the panel here has none of these essential limitations. . . . Future Vanna Whites might not get the chance to create their personae, because their employers may fear some celebrity will claim the persona is too similar to her own. The public will be robbed of parodies of celebrities, and our culture will be deprived of the valuable safety valve that parody and mockery create. Moreover, consider the moral dimension, about which the panel majority seems to have gotten so exercised. Saying Samsung "appropriated" something of White's begs the question: Should White have the exclusive right to something as broad and amorphous as her "identity"? Samsung's ad didn't simply copy White's shtick like all parody, it created something new. True, Samsung did it to make money, but White does whatever she does to make money, too; the majority talks of "the difference between fun and profit," but in the entertainment industry fun is profit. Why is Vanna White's right to exclusive for-profit use of her persona a persona that might not even be her own creation, but that of a writer, director or producer superior to Samsung's right to profit by creating its own inventions? . . .

The panel, however, does more than misinterpret California law: By refusing to recognize a parody exception to the right of publicity, the panel directly contradicts the federal Copyright Act. Samsung didn't merely parody Vanna White. It parodied Vanna White appearing in "Wheel of Fortune," a copyrighted television show, and parodies of copyrighted works are governed by federal copyright law. . . .

Finally, I can't see how giving White the power to keep others from evoking her image in the public's mind can be squared with the First Amendment. . . . The First Amendment isn't just about religion or politics—it's also about protecting the free development of our national culture. Parody, humor, irreverence are all vital components of the marketplace of ideas. The last thing we need, the last thing the First Amendment will tolerate, is a law that lets public figures keep people from mocking them, or from "evok[ing]" their images in the mind of the public. . . .

In our pop culture, where salesmanship must be entertaining and entertainment must sell, the line between the commercial and noncommercial has not merely blurred; it has disappeared. Is the Samsung parody any different from a parody on Saturday Night Live or in Spy Magazine? Both are equally profit-motivated. Both use a celebrity's identity to sell things—one to sell VCRs, the other to sell advertising. Both mock their subjects. Both try to make people laugh. Both add something, perhaps something worthwhile and memorable, perhaps not, to our culture.

Commercial speech is a significant, valuable part of our national discourse. . . .

For better or worse, we are the Court of Appeals for the Hollywood Circuit. Millions of people toil in the shadow of the law we make, and much of their livelihood is made possible by the existence of intellectual property rights. But much of their livelihood and much of the vibrancy of our culture also depends on the existence of other intangible rights: The right to draw ideas from a rich and varied public domain, and the right to mock, for profit as well as fun, the cultural icons of our time.

• QUESTIONS •

1. Is there intellectual property at stake in this case? Explain. How might copyright law apply to the case?
2. Try to articulate the moral judgments each side uses to bolster its legal arguments. Which do you find more persuasive? Why?

Trademarks

Federal trademark law—the Lanham Trademark Act (1946) and the Federal Trademark Dilution Act of 1995—protects a company's ownership rights to the name, logo, or symbol that identifies its products. Nike's swoosh, McDonald's arches, and the Xerox name are all identifiable trademarks. The company has an economic interest in the mark it has created, and a right to prevent competitors from using it for their own benefit or in ways that would harm its rightful owner. Cases involving infringement require a showing that the use of a competitor's mark is substantially likely to confuse consumers about the source of a product, or suggest that the trademark's owner made an endorsement it didn't make. Anyone—even a noncompetitor—can be guilty of dilution if they do something to blur or tarnish a trademark, whittling away its selling power through unauthorized use on dissimilar, usually shoddy, products. In the *Nader* case discussed earlier in this chapter, for example, MasterCard accused the Nader campaign of both infringing and diluting its trademark. The court dismissed both claims. There was no infringement because viewers would not be confused into thinking MasterCard endorsed the Nader campaign, and no dilution because it was a noncommercial use that could not harm MasterCard.

Patents and Trade Secrets

United States patent law protects the rights of those who discover tools, machines, processes, and other "novel, useful and not-obvious" inventions. The range of patentable ideas is enormous—from the chemical method for making pearl ash that won the first U.S. patent, to such recent inventions as Amazon.com's one-click Internet checkout ("business method"), a new variety of hybrid corn, and receptor genes on the human genome sequence. The U.S. Office of Patents and Trademarks initially decides whether a patent should be authorized, but the courts must make a final determination if a competitor challenges its validity.

The patent, once acquired, gives the inventor a complete monopoly for a limited time (20 years), during which no one else may use or profit from the invention without permission. After it has expired, full information about the invention is made available to anyone. Assume, for example, that a pharmaceutical company develops and patents a new medicine that is approved by the FDA. During the patent period, the company ("inventor") has complete control over distribution of the drug, deciding whether and how to license it to other manufacturers. Once the patent has expired, however, the chemical makeup of the drug becomes public information, and generic versions can legally be sold.

One alternative to patent protection is to keep your idea to yourself, and to sue anyone who tries to use it. Under state tort laws, a lawsuit can be brought against someone who wrongfully takes ("misappropriates") a trade secret. You don't register your trade secret as you register a trademark; you don't need to go through a lengthy and costly application procedure as you do for a patent. Suppose, for example, that you create a great recipe for chocolate chip cookies. Written down, the recipe is a "fixed, tangible expression" that can be copyrighted, preventing anyone from reproducing it in other cookbooks without your permission. But the value of the recipe is in the cookies—and even if it remains unpublished, it will lose some of its allure if competitors make the same cookies. If you did not want to go through the patent process, you might still maintain a near-monopoly use of your recipe has long as (1) it has some economic value, and (2) you had taken reasonable steps to keep it secret. In most states, you could sue to stop anyone who wrongfully discovered your recipe from using or disclosing it. Breaching a promise to keep an idea confidential, breaking into a competitor's office, or lying about your identity to gain entry to the kitchen are examples of unfair, inappropriate methods that would be considered wrongful. Figuring out the recipe by taste trials ("reverse engineering") would not be considered wrongful.

Global Intellectual Property Rights (IPR)

We are currently engaged in a global contest over the expansion of IPR. The next reading explores the limitations of using traditional patent law to protect indigenous medical knowledge. Gelvina Stevenson, the author, proposes instead that we look to more flexible trade secret law. Stevenson's article is followed by a reading on a related debate: how to ensure access to modern pharmaceuticals in the developing world, without harming the industries heavily invested in patenting them.

TRADE SECRETS: PROTECTING INDIGENOUS ETHNOBIOLOGICAL (MEDICINAL) KNOWLEDGE

Gelvina Rodriguez Stevenson[10]

There is a growing recognition that plant research will lead to the development of new drugs and that indigenous knowledge of plants will make this research more efficient. Today, most major drugs are plant-derived. It is currently believed that there are approximately 35,000 plants in the developing world that have medicinal value.

The Ottawa-based Rural Advancement Foundation International (RAFI) has estimated that in the early 1990s, germplasm from developing countries was worth at least $32 billion dollars per year to the pharmaceutical industry.

The ethnobiological knowledge of indigenous peoples can be extremely effective in focusing the search for new medicines. It is estimated that, by consulting indigenous peoples, "bio-prospectors" can increase the success ratio in trials for useful substances from one success in 10,000 samples to one success in two samples; . . . [a]pproximately three quarters of the plant-derived compounds currently used as pharmaceuticals were discovered through research based on plant use by indigenous peoples. Potential cures may be lost as rain forest area diminishes. The rainforest is considered a warehouse of valuable compounds which could aid the development of useful new medicines. It is estimated that only 1,100 of the 35,000 to 40,000 plants with possible undiscovered medicinal or nutritional value for humans have been thoroughly studied by scientists. . . . It has been suggested that much of the orally-transmitted indigenous knowledge . . . will also be lost, since it is estimated that 3,000 of the world's 6,000 languages will vanish. . . .

In 1992, the United Nations hosted a Conference on Environment and Development (UNCED) in Brazil. . . . [This] resulted in the United Nations Convention on Biological Diversity [CBD] which commits signatory countries to conserve biodiversity and equitably share resulting benefits. The signatories also agreed that the benefits of utilizing biodiversity, including technology, should be shared with the source country. The CBD has been ratified by 168 of the 177 countries that are parties to it . . . [but has yet to be ratified by the United States.]. . .

Adding to the growing importance of indigenous ethnobiological knowledge are recent advances in microelectronics and molecular biology, which enable companies to screen plants more efficiently. This has made bio-prospecting more profitable. . . .

Recently, companies have been protecting these expanding interests by seeking patent protection for valued plant-derived drugs. This has led to an increase in biotech-related patent claims and caused a backlog at the Patent and Trademark Office.

Using U.S. Patents to Protect Indigenous Ethnobiological Knowledge

A patent is a legal certificate that gives an inventor exclusive rights to prevent others from producing, selling, using, or importing his or her invention for a limited period of time.

While patent law varies somewhat in different countries, it generally protects inventions of a particular subject matter. "Inventions" include machines and other devices, chemical compositions, manufacturing processes, and uses for such inventions that are found to be (1) new,

10 "Trade Secrets: The Secret to Protecting Indigenous Ethnobiological (Medicinal) Knowledge," 32 *N.Y.U. J. Int'l. L & Pol.* 1119, 1122-24, 1131-67 (2000).

(2) non-obvious, and (3) useful. U.S. patent law requires that an invention be new, i.e., not known or used by others in the United States or published in any country. . . .

The non-obvious requirement establishes that, although the claimed invention might add some elements to a prior art reference, the addition of these elements, if they are obvious, will not be enough to warrant patent protection. If the additional elements are obvious "to a person having ordinary skill in the art to which said subject matter pertains," they will not be considered sufficient to meet the non-obvious requirement. In other words, a patent is considered obvious if a person could have easily created the invention from what was already publicly known. . . .

In order to satisfy the usefulness requirement, commonly known as the utility requirement, the invention must be useful to society. The patent applicant must know exactly what the invention will be useful for and must explain in the application how the invention will be useful.

A naturally-occurring subject matter, often called a "product of nature," such as a plant or human cell, is not patentable. However, United States courts have held that the "discoverer" may obtain a patent on the biological matter in a purified, isolated, or altered form. The Supreme Court, in fact, has held that genetically-altered living organisms are patentable as "manufactures" or "compositions of matter." Patent procurement is expensive and procedurally complex. In the United States, the only way that an inventor may obtain a patent is by filing a timely application with the Patent and Trademark Office, a federal government agency. . . . In general, [patents] are awarded to a natural person, but can be, and frequently are, assigned to another party or corporate entity. Patents . . . may be assigned or licensed in exchange for a payment of royalties. . . . A patent owner may file a civil suit for infringement against anyone who, without authority, makes, uses, or sells the patented invention. The infringer need not be aware that he is infringing and is held to infringe even if he achieves the same invention independently. Under U.S. law, possible remedies include injunctions and damages, with a minimum damage award included in the statute, and attorney's fees.

It is difficult for indigenous peoples to obtain a patent on their ethnobiological knowledge for a number of reasons. All of the above mentioned prerequisites for patentability, because they are grounded in Western notions of intellectual property, make it easier for Western pharmaceutical companies to obtain a patent on a modification of indigenous ethnobiological knowledge than for indigenous communities. Perhaps the most fundamental reason for this disparity is that patent law is based primarily on the goal of providing incentives to individuals for commercial innovation rather than the goal of protecting communal knowledge. . . .

[The] rigid requirements that the inventor be known and be the first to invent, or the first to file in jurisdictions outside the United States, in order to receive a patent, pose an immense obstacle for indigenous communities who wish to patent their ethnobiological knowledge. Another problem with awarding a patent to a "medicine man" . . . or even to the indigenous community, is that the same cultural and ethnobiological knowledge is often found among several distinct indigenous societies. . . . It would be unfair if one community were granted a patent, because other neighboring groups which have used the same information for just as long, if not longer, would then be suddenly infringing on a patent while they continued their ancestral practices. Discovering which group was the first to discover the knowledge and first to make use of it is nearly impossible and likely to create societal disruption.

Even if [one indigenous person] were able to show that he was the inventor and were granted a patent, the individualism upon which the patent is philosophically based would still create problems for [his group.] [For example, in] 1992, a British company, The Body Shop, entered into a supply contract with Chief Paulinho Paiakan, a respected leader of the Kayapo. Chief Paiakan agreed to supply to The Body Shop 6,000 liters a year of natural oil to use in hair conditioners in exchange for a small percentage of the profits. The Body Shop gave their payment to Chief Paiakan. [According to] Stephen Corry, an indigenous rights activist and Director General of the organization Survival International . . . "[t]he project has caused deep divisions amongst the Kayapo exacerbated by the way Paiakan has accumulated great personal wealth and power." . . .

A great deal of indigenous ethnobiological knowledge has been published and documented by ethnobotanists and other scholars. . . . This will bar indigenous communities from satisfying the novelty requirement.

An illustration of the barrier that the utility requirement can pose is evident in the problems the National Institute of Health (NIH) has had with the patenting of genes. The NIH failed to receive a patent for gene fragments that are used as markers to aid in the mapping of genes. The Patent and Trademark Office rejected . . . the NIH claim that the gene fragments satisfied the utility requirement by their use as markers in the mapping of genes. . . . The NIH case suggests that although much indigenous knowledge has shown its utility by the simple fact that it has led to the development of products and processes patented by pharmaceutical companies, the PTO may not consider this utility claimable under U.S. standards.

Products of nature, also known as naturally occurring subject matter, are not patentable. . . . [This means that] Western pharmaceutical companies that isolate an active chemical in a plant and create a genetically engineered plant or animal can receive a patent while indigenous peoples, who use the natural form of the plant, cannot. . . .

Traditional knowledge presents unique problems in determining non-obviousness because it is difficult to determine what the prior art might have been. Presumably, the prior art would be knowledge that the indigenous people had prior to the invention. Since both prior art and claimed invention would be generations old, it would be difficult to determine at what point in time an indigenous group had acquired or developed a particular piece of knowledge, i.e., the invention. . . .

And even if patent law was able to conceive of the entire community as the inventor, neighboring communities are likely to be aware of the plant and its use. This will automatically characterize the plant and its use as obvious. Most importantly, the mere fact that indigenous people often will have possessed the knowledge for centuries may further ensure that the knowledge is considered obvious. . . .

Technically, patent holders have the legal right to prevent imports into the United States of products that were created using technology patented in the United States. Thus, an indigenous community in a developing country could be precluded from exporting products that were developed using existing species if that product is patented in the United States. . . .

Finally, once an invention is patented, the characteristics of the invention are made public, enabling others to obtain the knowledge. Some of the knowledge may be sacred to indigenous communities and they may not want this knowledge shared with other cultures. A patent is effective only for [a limited time period] . . . and after expiration, its subject matter is freely available for use by the public.

Using Trade Secrets to Protect Indigenous Ethnobiological Knowledge

If an invention does not meet the requirements for patentability or the inventor simply chooses not to patent her invention, the inventor may still have the option of protecting it as a trade secret . . . [which] enables the inventor to retain control over the invention for as long as it remains secret, instead of solely for the patent period, [and] does not require any government filings or approvals to be effective. . . . Trade secrets may be assigned or licensed. They are protected for as long as the owner successfully prevents the secret from becoming widely known. Anyone who misappropriates knowledge steals it or fails to keep it confidential is required to pay for its use and may even be enjoined from further use.

There are generally three main requirements for trade secrecy protection that exist in virtually every legal system that recognizes trade secrets: (1) the information must be secret; (2) the information must have commercial value because it is secret; and (3) the person claiming the trade secret must have made reasonable efforts to keep the information secret. . . .

Secrecy need not be absolute; all that is necessary is that the holder of the secret make reasonable efforts to maintain its secrecy. "Reasonable" efforts to maintain secrecy include having entered into confidentiality agreements and having disclosed information solely on a "need to know" basis. . . .

While the application procedure for a patent is costly, complex, and time consuming, trade secret protection arises automatically as a matter of law, with no costly or lengthy application process.

The lenient way in which courts in the United States determine what constitutes a reasonable effort to maintain the secrecy of a trade secret suggests that in many situations an indigenous community may be able to satisfy this requirement. . . .

The court's leniency in finding commercial value is illustrated by the fact that all that they require is that the claimed trade secret be valuable to "some" public, i.e., have "potential" value. . . . In addition, courts do not require that indigenous peoples recognize the full value of their knowledge either to themselves or to pharmaceutical companies in order to seek trade secret protection. . . . A trade secret's commercial value will not be negated by the fact that it was inexpensive to develop or easily discoverable.

The owner of a trade secret has the right to prevent the unauthorized disclosure of a trade secret by other parties. Disclosure or use of a trade secret, without the privilege to do so, constitutes misappropriation if: (1) the trade secret was discovered by "improper means" or (2) the disclosure or use of the trade secret breaches a confidence of duty to the party from whom the secret was obtained. . . .

• QUESTIONS •

1. What are the required elements to obtain a patent? Why is each so difficult for indigenous peoples to demonstrate?

2. According to Stevenson,

> *A U.S. patent that was recently granted to two pharmaceutical companies illustrates how the law's preference for pure substances makes it easier for pharmaceutical companies to satisfy the non-obvious requirement and make it difficult for indigenous communities to do so. W.R. Grace and Agrodyne obtained patents for derivatives of the neem plant developed in their laboratories as an environmentally-friendly alternative to commercial synthetic pesticides. Scientists first learned of this drug and its insecticidal properties from farmers in India who had used ground neem seed for centuries as a pesticide. The prior art that the scientists started with was the indigenous knowledge and methods of extraction, identification, isolation, and purification of the active components to develop a pesticide. However, since the companies synthesized the active chemical in the laboratory, and did not merely extract it from nature, a patent was granted to the companies on the neem derivatives. Thus, in spite of the fact that the insecticidal, nontoxic, and biodegradable properties of neem were known to millions of Indian farmers, the seed derivatives were deemed not obvious and the pharmaceutical companies were granted a patent for their derivative of neem.*

(a) Is this ethically acceptable from a utilitarian point of view? (b) **Internet Assignment:** Find out what happened when Grace's neem patent was challenged by the WTO.

3. What values within indigenous cultures make it difficult or impossible for them to secure U.S. patents for their "inventions"?

4. What advantages to trade secret law does Stevenson describe?

Highlights in the Development of International IPR

- **The Paris Convention** (1883). The first international agreement on IPR was founded on the principle of "national treatment." Signatories agreed to provide foreigners the same IPR protection given to their own citizens, but each nation continued to have its own rules as to what was patentable and how. The World Intellectual Property Organization (WIPO), a specialized agency of the United Nations, currently administers the terms of the Paris Convention.
- **Biodiversity Convention** (1992). An outgrowth of the global Rio Conference, the aims of this agreement are to conserve biological diversity and sustain biological resources for future generations. It recognizes states' sovereign rights over biological resources and calls for protection of the rights of communities and indigenous people to the customary use of biological resources and knowledge systems. Signatories agree to facilitate environmentally sound use of their resources by other members and to assist in the transfer of technology to developing countries so that they can capitalize on their own natural resources, even if it requires sharing innovations protected by intellectual property rights. The U.S. has not signed this treaty.
- **Trade-Related Aspects of IPR (TRIPS) Agreement** (1994). Strongly supported by the U.S. and adopted within the framework of the Uruguay Round of Multilateral Trade Negotiations that created the World Trade Organization (WTO), TRIPS incorporates IPR protection into the General Agreement on Tariffs and Trades (GATT). According to TRIPS, "the protection and enforcement of intellectual property rights should contribute to the promotion of technological innovation and to the transfer and dissemination of technology, to the mutual advantage of producers and users of technological knowledge and in a manner conducive to social and economic welfare, and to a balance of rights and obligations."

TRIPS and the HIV Crisis

The Treaty on Trade-Related Aspects of Intellectual Property Rights (TRIPS) is the first international treaty to create minimum national standards for IPR protection, requiring all nations to make patents available for "any inventions"—whether products or processes—capable of industrial application. Despite this broad language, there are some exceptions written into the agreement. Member nations can still decide whether to allow patents on named categories of inventions, such as diagnostic, therapeutic, and surgical treatments; plants, animals, and microorganisms; and "essentially biological processes for the production of plants or animals," for example, cloning.

The public policy exception allows WTO members to "adopt measures necessary to protect public health and nutrition, and to promote the public interest in sectors of vital importance to their socio-economic and technological development." Members can also deny patents for inventions whose commercial use would jeopardize the "ordre public" or "morality" of their nations.

TRIPS is administered by the WTO. Complaints—over refusal to allow or recognize certain kinds of patents, for example—are to be resolved by consultation and mediation if possible, and after a hearing before a Dispute Settlement Body, if necessary.

In 2001, a Ministerial Conference of the WTO meeting in Doha issued an interpretation of the TRIPS agreement that allows developing nations some flexibility in addressing the HIV crisis. Nonetheless, this Doha Declaration on TRIPS and Public Health reasserted the basic tenets of

TRIPS. Some, including James Thuo Gathii, author of the next reading, are critical of U.S. influence over the WTO. Gathii, who teaches law at Albany Law School, is especially skeptical of the way the United States has addressed the HIV epidemic in sub-Saharan Africa. His claim: the highest priority of U.S. policy is to support strong patent protection. And, he argues, that strong pharmaceutical patent protection as well as poverty explain why fewer than 30,000 of the more than 28.5 million Africans living with HIV/AIDS virus in 2001 had access to life-prolonging drugs. Thus he refutes the United States government's claim that poverty alone accounts for lack of access to these drugs.

The Structural Power of Strong Pharmaceutical Patent Protection

James Thuo Gathii [11]

. . . [B]y silencing alternative conceptions of intellectual property rights that balance the rights of patent holders with the obligations patent holders . . . may have to consumers of patented products . . . the law and foreign policy of strong patent protection reflects the relative ability of the United States to impose its will on less powerful countries. . . . [T]he discourse of charity and humanitarianism accompanying the uncompromising support of patents at any cost simply disguises the U.S.'s priorities in ensuring its multinational pharmaceutical companies acquire markets for their drugs without any threat to their profitability even in the face of heart-wrenching human need.

. . . Strong patent protection is founded on the view that patents are private property rights that confer unconditional rights over inventions and discoveries. . . .

This view . . . undervalues the fact that the patent monopoly is granted to an inventor in return for the inventor producing a benefit to the society. In other words, patents have both a private as well as a public essence. To refer to patents only as a form of private property right is therefore to downplay the balance between the interests of the inventor and the public consuming the patented product contemplated in many national jurisdictions. . . .

[Next, Gathii argues that pharmaceutical companies and western governments, such as the United States, have successfully shifted the focus away from the relationship between high drug prices and patents and onto endemic poverty in developing countries.]

. . . Prior to the Paris Convention on Industrial Property, there was a vibrant debate regarding the necessity of a patent regime crossing national boundaries. . . . With the adoption of the Paris Convention on the Industrial Property in 1883 . . . the stakes of the Convention shifted towards whether patents would be viewed as tools of public policy or as private property rights. . . .

With the advent of the TRIPS Agreement, the view of patents as a form of private property prevailed, as is reflected by the exclusive nature of the rights conferred to patent holders in that agreement.

In addition, these rights are further buttressed in a number of ways. First, the World Trade Organization (WTO) has, since 1995, protected patents backed up by a dispute settlement system that is compulsory and binding. This dispute settlement system is capable of sanctioning States that violate the rights protected by this patent regime. Second, the TRIPS Agreement departed from the norm of regulatory diversity underpinning the Paris Convention model under which patent rights were regarded as a national prerogative. . . [U]nder the TRIPS Agreement,

11 "The Structural Power of Strong Pharmaceutical Patent Protection in U.S. Foreign Policy," 7 *Journal of Gender Race & Justice* 267 (2003).

there is now a minimum international substantive regime of what intellectual property rights protections countries should adopt. The requirements of the TRIPS Agreement give countries little choice regarding the scope and extent of the patent rights they can grant. . . . For example, the flexibility to exclude certain inventions, such as pharmaceuticals, from patent protection vanished. The TRIPS Agreement also [requires countries to put into place] judicial and administrative institutions, procedures, safeguards and remedies . . . to further secure the rights protected under the treaty. Only those patents that are capable of industrial application are protected. Further, the TRIPS Agreement is non-derogable—countries cannot make reservations without the consent of all signatory state parties, which seems rather difficult to attain.

. . . To the extent that the Bush administration has been engaged with the HIV/AIDS pandemic in Africa, the issue of access to antiretroviral drugs has been eclipsed by a preference for prevention as opposed to treatment programs. The rationale in favor of prevention is that those already infected will die anyway. . . .

[B]y highlighting prevention to the exclusion of treatment, lack of access to antiretroviral drugs for treatment is banished into the background . . . [although] evidence from Brazil indicates that integrating treatment and prevention saves on cost. . . .

[Gathii identifies U.S. insistence on strong patent protect in the domestic context, citing an example from the 2001 anthrax scare. Even during possible bioterrorism, the American government put patent rights first.]

. . . As soon as the presence of anthrax spores was discovered in the offices of leading news organizations and in the offices of congressional leaders, there were immediate calls for the amassing of Ciprofloxacin, since it is the widely preferred antibiotic for patients infected with anthrax.

One alternative the government had under federal law, besides subsidizing Bayer to stockpile the drug, was using its eminent domain powers to override the patent by issuing compulsory licenses to generic companies to manufacture the drug. The government considered, but did not invoke this power. Instead, it entered into an agreement with Bayer, under which it agreed to subsidize Bayer's production of 1.2 billion Ciproflaxacin (Cipro) pills for stockpiling. This stockpile would, according to Health and Human Services Secretary Tommy Thompson, be adequate to protect at least 10 million Americans on a two-pill regimen for sixty days in the event of a bioterrorist attack. . . .

Notwithstanding Bayer's concession to lowering the price of the drug [from $4.50 to $1.89 per pill], observers have noted that the government shortchanged American tax-payers, since "Indian companies sell a generic version of the same drug for less than 20 cents.". . . Hence, critics of the federal government have argued that it sacrificed public health at the altar of intellectual property rights, by allowing Bayer to continue to be the sole supplier of Ciproflaxacin.

There is yet another consideration that factored into the U.S.'s refusal to issue compulsory licenses over Cipro. The United States does not want to undermine the legitimacy of its negotiating position with developing countries over whether the World Trade Organization treaty, TRIPS, allows these countries to override patents which would enable them to effectively address the HIV/AIDS pandemic. The United States has consistently opposed the efforts of developing countries to override patent protection that would legally allow them to produce generic equivalents of the patented drugs used in the treatment of HIV/AIDS patients. . . .

• QUESTIONS •

1. What does Gathii mean by "strong patent protection"? What evidence does he cite to support his argument that it is a high priority of U.S. policy? How has that perspective become a global standard?
2. How would Gathii revise global patent protection policy?

3. Gathii identified **compulsory licensing** as one way that the United States might have gotten cheaper access to Cipro. TRIPS allows a government that has made reasonable efforts to gain access to a patented drug and failed to seize the patent to use it to manufacture a generic copy, and pay the patent holder a reasonable royalty. (a) Would the HIV pandemic in Africa be the kind of emergency situation that would justify compulsory licensing? (b) Would this be a good alternative for African nations? (c) Would the sale of HIV drugs in the United States provide a good case for compulsory licensing?

4. There are other alternatives not mentioned by Gathii. One is **parallel importing,** a practice that is legal in some countries and illegal in others. It involves the importation of drugs from a country where the patent holder sells them for less. (a) Who benefits from parallel importing? Who might be harmed by it? (b) **Internet Assignment:** In August 2004, the governor of Vermont sued the FDA to permit Vermont to import generic drugs from Canada. Find out what happened.

5. Another way to lower the price of pharmaceuticals is to encourage companies to manufacture generic alternatives to a patented drug. This is legal everywhere once a patent has expired, and in developing countries during a grace period (recently extended to 2016) for full-compliance with TRIPS. Consider the various stakeholders. Who benefits from **generic manufacturing?** Who is harmed by it?

6. Which seems most fair: compulsory licensing, parallel importing, generic manufacturing, or a revised view of patent protection along the lines envisioned by Gathii?

7. Some AIDS activists suggest that the WTO discard global IP protections and replace them with incentive programs. James Love, director of the nonprofit Consumer Project on Technology, would raise investment funds from countries around the world, using them to reward scientists who discover breakthrough medicines that could be made and sold at low prices. What would be the benefits of a research program that relied more on government levies and a "prize" model than private investment? The disadvantages?

8. **Internet Assignment:** Find out about recent efforts to address the urgent need for HIV and other drugs in developing nations.

Chapter Problems

1. The Copyright Act makes clear that "one of the most important purposes to consider is the free flow of ideas, particularly criticism and commentary." With that in mind, which of the following would be considered fair use?
   a. A literary critic quotes from six short stories in a scathing review of a popular author's newest collection.
   b. A painter, inspired by the poetry of a Pulitzer-prize winning poet, shows his work in a gallery installation in which he posts a different poem next to each of his two dozen paintings; the gallery publishes a guide to the show that includes the text of the poems and photos of the paintings.

c. Same as before, except that it is a student visiting an art gallery for the first time who decides to publish online his own "guide to the show."

2. **Internet Assignment:** Apple and Microsoft have copyrighted their operating systems. This means, for example, that a software engineer who wants to write a program to run on Windows must pay Microsoft for a license to use its Windows code. Another operating system, Linux, is not copyrighted and can be freely copied. (a) Visit http://www.gnu.org to find out about the free software movement. What kinds of open sourceware are available to the public? (b) Richard Stallman, a self-styled computer hacker, came up with the idea of a "copyleft" license to perpetuate free software. Find out what is meant by copyleft. (c) Compare the ethics of traditional copyright to those of copyleft.

3. Peter K. Yu, assistant professor of law at Benjamin N. Cardozo School of Law, writes:

> *For more than 2000 years, the Chinese had been heavily influenced by Confucianism, which provided "the blueprint of an ideal life" and the yardstick against which human relationships were to be measured. To the Chinese, the past was not only a reflection of contemporary society, but also the embodiment of cultural and social values. By encountering the past, one could understand the Way of Heaven, obtain guidance to future behavior, and find out the ultimate meaning of human existence. One could also transform oneself and build his or her moral character through self-cultivation. Thus, materials and information about the past had to be put in the public domain for people to borrow or to transmit to younger generations. Because intellectual property rights allow a significant few to monopolize these needed materials, they prevent the vast majority from understanding their life, culture, and society. Intellectual property rights therefore "contradict traditional Chinese moral standards."*
>
> *Unlike Westerners today, the Chinese in the imperial past did not consider copying or imitation a moral offense. Rather, they considered it "a noble art," a "time-honored learning process" through which people manifested respect for their ancestors. At a very young age, Chinese children were taught to memorize and copy the classics and histories. On the one hand, such undertaking would instill in the youngsters familial values, filial piety, and respect for their cultural legacy. On the other hand, copying was practically needed to ensure success in the imperial civil service examinations, which emphasized the knowledge of the Confucian Four Books and the Five Classics. Success in those examinations would not only bring power and glory to the candidates, but would also bring honor to their families, districts, and provinces. . . .*
>
> *Although their unacknowledged quotation may be considered plagiarism today, the Chinese in the imperial past regarded such a practice as an acceptable, legitimate, or even necessary, component of the creative process. Indeed, Chinese writers from early times saw themselves more as preservers of historical record and cultural heritage than as creators. . . .*
>
> *To a very great extent, this compiling tradition was similar to that held by Westerners before the emergence of the contemporary notion of authorship in the eighteenth century. Unlike contemporary writers, "[m]edieval church writers actively disapproved of the elements of originality and creativeness which we think of as essential component of authorship. They valued extant old books more highly than any recent elucubrations and they put the work of the scribe and the copyist above that of the authors.". . . Rather, like the Chinese people, they regarded imitation as the sincerest form of flattery and a necessary component of the creative process. . . .*
>
> *Finally, the Chinese subscribed to the Confucian vision of civilization. Under this vision, the family constituted the basic unit of human community, and the world was an outgrowth of this basic unit. Emphasizing familial values and collective rights, the Chinese did not develop a concept of individual rights. They also did not regard*

> *creativity as individual property. Instead, they considered creativity as a collective benefit to their community and the posterity. Having a strong disdain for commerce, they greatly despised those who created works for sheer profit....*
>
> *[Under Communism] many Chinese believed it was right to freely reproduce or to tolerate the unauthorized reproduction of foreign works that would help strengthen the country. Some of them also believed that copying was needed, or even necessary, for China to catch up with Western developed countries. Thus, one could easily find bookstores containing "special" rooms selling pirated works from Western publishers. One could also find Reference News (Cankao Xiaoxi) providing translated excerpts from foreign news materials published abroad. Even today, the Chinese sometimes refer to pirated computer programs "as 'patriotic software,' out of a belief that it speeds the nation's modernization at little or no cost."...*

a. How does Chinese history and culture attach value to intellectual output?
b. Identify clashes between Chinese traditional values and western rules governing IP.
c. **Internet Assignment:** Entry to the WTO means that China will have to comply with TRIPS. What can you find out about changes in Chinese IP policies in recent years? Can you find any evidence that Chinese values are influencing TRIPS?

4. **Internet Assignment:** Misappropriation of trade secrets has been a federal crime since passage of the Economic Espionage Act (EEA) of 1996. (a) Find a criminal case involving wrongful taking of a trade secret in violation of this law. What kind of secret was taken? What was the outcome of the case? (b) Find a civil action for wrongful taking of a trade secret under state tort law. What kind of secret was taken? What was the outcome of the case?

5. Paid subscribers to an expensive, exclusive seminar training program known as "Executive Success" have access to a copyrighted course manual that is not available to the general public. Rick Ross works for a "cult deprogrammer" and also runs nonprofit Web sites that provide information to the public about controversial groups that have been accused of mind control. A one-time Executive Success participant gave Ross a copy of the training manual, which Ross then gave to two "experts" for analysis. When their analysis was posted on the Web site, it included large sections from the copyrighted manual. (a) On what basis might the XIVM, the company that runs the seminar, sue Ross? How might he defend himself? (b) **Internet Assignment:** Find out how the Second Circuit Court of Appeals ruled in the actual case, decided in 2004.

6. Copyright law recognizes two distinct copyrights in a "collective work," such as a newspaper or magazine. Rights in the original, separate contribution vests in the author, while the publisher acquires a copyright in each issue of the periodical as a "collective work." Prior to a lawsuit filed by Tasini, it was common for freelance writers to sell their stories to major newspapers and magazines based on verbal agreements as to topics, deadlines, length, and fees, with little or no reference to copyright. When *The New York Times, Newsday,* and *Time, Inc.* licensed their publications to computer database companies, they did so without asking their freelance authors. The writers sued claiming the Copyright Act preserved their right to sell or re-sell their articles.[12] (a) **Internet Assignment:** Find out why the court ruled in favor of the authors. Based on this ruling, advise the owner of an electronic database how it might continue to operate after this case. What advice would you give to a freelance writer? To a newspaper publisher? (b) Consider the various stakeholders affected by the *Tasini* ruling. Who is helped by it? Hurt by it? (c) **Internet Assignment:** Courts in France, Belgium, the Netherlands, and Norway, applying their domestic copyright laws, have also concluded

12 *New York Times Company, Inc. v. Tasini,* 121 S.Ct. 2381 (2001).

that Internet or CD-ROM reproduction and distribution of freelancers' works violate the copyrights of freelancers. Find out how these issues have been addressed in other nations.

7. In 2002, in what is known as the Sonny Bono Act, Congress extended copyright term to last seventy years beyond the author's life, or one hundred years in the case of copyrights on "works made for hire" and owned by companies. (a) What are the benefits of this law? What do you think of this criticism of it?

> *If current copyright law had been in effect a hundred years ago, the U.S. government might have had to pay royalties to use the image of Uncle Sam, and so would anyone who wanted to depict a jolly red-suited Santa Claus. (Both were created by the cartoonist Thomas Nast, who died in 1902.). . . In 1995, ASCAP tried to get summer camps to pay licensing fees for the songs the kids sang around the campfire. Disney went after day-care centers in Florida that had crude murals of Mickey and Goofy on their walls. . . . The once open fields of culture are increasingly fenced in. . . .*[13]

(b) **Internet Assignment:** Find out what happened in the Supreme Court when the Bono Act was challenged as unconstitutional.

8. How should international conflicts over public domain be resolved? Consider Project Gutenberg, a volunteer effort to put the world's literature online. In Fall 2004 its Australian branch posted the 1936 novel *Gone With the Wind* on the Internet. The book is in the public domain in Australia, where copyrights expire after 50 years. In the United States, however, the copyright will not enter the public domain until 2031, so the owners of the copyright demanded that the Gutenberg Project remove the novel.

9. **Internet Assignment:** In October 2003, the Federal Trade Commission recommended changes in the law to promote innovation, concerned that too many questionable patents had been issued and that the extremely high cost of patent litigation was forcing too many alleged infringers to pay for licenses on patents of debatable validity. Find out what has happened to these recommendations.

10. **Internet Assignment:** Visit the WTO (http://www.wto.org) to interact with the organization on a number of topics, or to listen in on ministerial meetings through live audiostream.

11. **Internet Assignment:** In 2003, Maine passed the Unfair Prescriptive Drug Practices Act to regulate the processing of prescription drug claims and services by insurance companies. The insurers, "pharmaceutical benefits managers" or PBMs, were required to disclose details about their various contracts with drug manufacturers, pharmacies and with the persons and companies who bought their prescription drug insurance policies. (a) Is there any kind of intellectual property are at stake in this scenario? (b) What claim can the PBMs make that they should be protected against disclosure? (c) The PBMs sued to enjoin Maine from implementing its law. Find out what happened in *Pharmaceutical Care Management Association v. Rowe,* 307 F. Supp.2d 164 (D.Me. 2004) and on any subsequent appeals.

12. While the TRIPS agreement requires members to protect copyrights, it makes no similar provision for requiring an international fair use exception to copyright law. Does this matter? Who would benefit from such a requirement? Who would be hurt by it?

13 James Surowiecki, "The Talk of The Town: Righting Copywrongs," *The New Yorker,* January 1, 2001.

Chapter Project

Ethics Roundtable: Protecting Collective Property

1. Preparation

Read through the "Tivas Scenario." Students will be assigned to consider it from an "ethical perspective" or a "national perspective."

Tivas Scenario[14]

Tivas is a hypothetical indigenous community in southern Mexico that predates European contact. It is home to the Tivani people, who have had little interaction with Western industrial society. Its members maintain most of their traditional way of life. While treatments for common afflictions are generally well-known to all members of the community, the methods of preparing plants to treat serious illnesses are known solely by the community's respected "medicine man," M. For example, many members of the community know that toenail and fingernail fungi should be treated with the green, oval shaped leaves that grow abundantly near the river. They also know that the leaves with the thickest veins and a reddish tint found primarily in the fall treat the affliction best. However, they do not know how M prepares the leaves to make the cream he applies to the nails. That secret is known only to M and other medicine men in a few neighboring indigenous communities.

The United States pharmaceutical company "BioCo," like many of its peer companies, has committed research and development money to study plants to identify useful new medicines and chemicals. It has determined that it would cut costs in half by studying the plants already used by indigenous communities to treat various afflictions. Looking specifically for medicines that treat nail fungi, and having read an article in Natural Geographic about the traditional medicinal practices of the Tivani (including their treatment of nail fungi), BioCo sends "Botanist" and "Chemist" to southern Mexico.

Botanist and Chemist move to a hotel in a small city an hour's drive from Tivas. They drive into the community and attempt to establish a relationship with M. Sensing that M is wary of them, they explain that they are looking for a medicine that will treat people in the United States who are afflicted with nail fungi and that they understood that the Tivani had identified a plant that treats the fungi. They explain that if this plant proves useful, it will help many people. M emphasizes that the plants, and the way in which he prepares them to treat fungi, have been passed down for generations through the chain of medicine men and are extremely sacred. He does not share with them any information about the spiritual value of the plants, but does give them general information about the plant and brings the scientists directly to the anti-fungal plant.

The scientists stay for a couple of months, testing and collecting the anti-fungal and other plants. They eventually return to the United States, thanking M for his help and promising to be in touch. Upon their return, BioCo invests considerable time and resources into their efforts to isolate "frungoid," the active chemical in the newly "discovered" plant, Frundanialosis, which is actually the plant that M showed them.

14 This Tivas Scenario was derived from the Tivas hypothetical written by Gelvina Rodriguez Stevenson as part of "Trade Secrets: The Secret to Protecting Indigenous Ethnobiological (Medicinal) Knowledge." Reprinted with permission from 32 *N.Y.U.J. Int'l L. & Pol.* 1119, (2000) 1122–24.

After two years, BioCo isolates the active chemical, frungoid. BioCo immediately files for a patent at the United States Patent and Trademark Office (PTO). A year later they are granted a patent for frungoid and after frungoid receives FDA approval, they begin to market it. They are assured protection for their patent in all countries that are signatories to the General Agreement on Tariffs and Trade (GATT), and in Mexico and Canada under the North American Free Trade Agreement (NAFTA).

Within a year, BioCo has made $1 million in profits. BioCo sends a one-time check to M for $10,000, 1 percent of the first year's profits. M has received more money than he has ever had, but this creates a number of problems.

2. The Ethical Roundtable

The Ethical Roundtable will take place as a fishbowl exercise. Teams of two students role-play each of the following perspectives in a discussion of the scenario:

- Global free marketers
- Utilitarians
- Deontologists
- Virtue ethicists
- Tivani people
- Bio Co. shareholders
- M.
- Botanist
- Chemist

3. Response

The rest of the class will be assigned to represent different nation-members of the World Trade Organization (WTO) as it considers policies governing intellectual property. After listening to the Ethical Roundtable, WTO members will discuss their responses from the perspective of the nation they represent.

APPENDIX A

EVALUATING INTERNET SOURCES

Many college and university libraries have compiled guidelines for assessing the worth of online sources. One of the best, offered by librarians Jan Alexander and Marsha Ann Tate, provides an extensive checklist for identifying and evaluating different kinds of Web sites:

- Advocacy (usually, ending with domain .org),
- Business/marketing (.com or .net),
- Informational (.edu or .gov),
- News (usually .com) and Personal.[1]

Alexander and Tate created the following criteria:

- **Authority/Objectivity:** Look for Web sites that give the author's name, title, organizational affiliation, and contact information. This will help you identify biases as well as expertise. Government and educational sites, along with online scholarly journals, provide such indices of authority and objectivity. Traditionally, publications that have undergone peer-review or are published in scholarly journals (such as law reviews) are given greater weight than those published by the author ("vanity publications").
- **Accuracy:** Pay attention to whether information sources are cited, to how well the page has been edited for grammar/spelling, and to whether the information on a Web site can be verified by referring to other sources.
- **Currency:** Check when the Web site was last revised. Outdated links are a sign that a Web site is not current. (Laws change when amendments, new laws, or new court interpretations have occurred since a Web site was last revised.)

Another excellent place for advice about Web site evaluation is http://www.rhetorica.net.[2] Some ideas from it include:

- **Beware persuasive writing:** Written advocacy for a particular view can be flawed by illogical reasoning. Learn some basics of logical analysis to monitor this. For example, check that the premises (underlying assumptions) of an argument are logical; if not, the rest should not be considered persuasive. And look for a logical connection between premises and conclusions.
- **Rev up your bias-detector:** If you identify bias, you might not necessarily dismiss a Web source as useless. But potential bias is another factor in helping you decide how to evaluate a particular Web source.
- **Notice the "spin":** There are many subtle ways to put a spin on information. Pay special attention, for example, to the use of labels, euphemisms, and metaphors. What impression is

---

1 Called "How to Evaluate and Create Information Quality on the Web," the online version can be found at http://www2.widener.edu/Wolfgram-Memorial-Library. Alexander and Tate include links to additional sites with Web evaluation materials.

2 Check out "Critical Questions for Detecting Bias," at http://www.rhetorica.net/bias.htm.

created by the title or headline? By the writer's tone and word choice? What details are included, and do they support the overall analysis? If the text is not clear, ask yourself: Is this a deliberate attempt to confuse?

- **"Unpack" visual and audio elements:** Suppose you read a story posted on a Web "news site." Note how it is designed, its placement (front page? buried?), and the kind of material that surrounds it—textual, visual, audio, advertising. What do all of these elements—and the way they are joined—tell you about the intended audience? The point of view of the author? Consider the message being sent by such things as color choices, relative size, and the particular juxtaposition of images and text.

Web sites—or Web news sources—are posted by a person or an organization of some kind. It makes sense to find out what you can about the individual or organization in order to best evaluate what they have created online.

Art Silverblatt, Julie Ferry, and Barbara Finan, in *Approaches to Media Literacy,* provide excellent tools for helping readers become more sensitive to the prevailing ideology in a media presentation. They make the following suggestions:

- **Identify ownership patterns** in the media, generally, to assess how they affect media content.
- **Analyze an organization** (e.g., CNN, Fox News) to see how the ownership, resources, and internal structure (e.g., decision making) of a particular media organization influence the content of its products.
- **Uncover the "World View"** of a particular media presentation (such as a Web site) by thinking about the types of people who are depicted within it. Are characters presented in a stereotypical manner? Are they in control of their own destinies, or under the influence of others? Is there a supernatural presence in this world? Stories—and ads—reveal a world view by the way they portray what it means to be successful, how success is achieved, and what kinds of behaviors are rewarded.
- **Unpack an individual author** by finding out what you can about his or her expertise or educational background (is it relevant to the topic at hand?), employment or professional experience, and membership/leadership role in organizations or political/advocacy groups. Look for clues as to who funds/publishes his or her research. If he or she has been honored or recognized in a special way, by whom?

APPENDIX B

An Introduction to Legal Research

I. Major Sources of U.S. Law

Under the U.S. Constitution, our government is both centralized and uniform at the national level, and decentralized and differing at the state level. As the following chart indicates, each source of law at the federal level has its counterpart at the state level.

Federal	**States**
Constitutional: U.S. Constitution	50 state constitutions
Statutory: Laws passed by the U.S. Congress	Laws passed by 50 state legislatures
Case Law: Judicial opinions of the Supreme Court, federal Circuit Courts of Appeals, and federal District (trial) Courts	Judicial opinions of state court judges
Administrative Law: Federal regulations passed by federal agencies	State regulations passed by state agencies

For a fuller introduction to the American legal system, check out the American Law Sources On-line Web site at http://www.lawsource.com/also. This site compiles links to free legal sources online, including amicus curiae briefs, law reviews, and periodicals.

II. Citations Matter

A legal citation is an abbreviation that allows us to locate and identify legal documents—cases, laws, or articles from legal journals, for example. The same citations are used in printed materials and online.

Reading the Citation to a Statute
There are three parts to a citation to a statute: an abbreviation representing the set of books (series) in which a law is published or the database in which it can be found online; a number representing the title of the law, which helps you to find the appropriate volume in the library or to identify its subject matter online; and a number that refers you to the particular section of the law you are citing. Because every title contains many laws passed at different times, the section identifies a particular part of the law within that title.

Consider the citation: 42 U.S.C.A. 2000e, et seq.

Series/Database
U.S.C.A. is the abbreviation for United States Code Annotated. Most law libraries contain this set of books, which is a compilation of all of the laws passed by the U.S. Congress, arranged according to broad subjects. If you are searching online, U.S.C.A. tells you that you are looking for a federal law (i.e., one passed by the U.S. Congress).
Note that each state has a set of books containing state laws. The formal citation to a state's laws requires a particular abbreviation for the series. For future reference, write the abbreviation for the series that collects your state laws.

Title
The number preceding the series is called the title number. In our example, 42 is the title number for laws relating to Public Health and Safety.

Section
Finally, the numbers after the series (in our case, 2000e, *et seq.*) refer to the section(s) of the law. In this example, *et seq.* is used to refer to sections that begin at 2000e and continue through the end of that particular civil rights law (2000f, 2000g, etc.). For online research, the easiest way to locate a specific law is to enter the database (e.g., federal statutes, or particular state statutes) and then search using the correct title and section number.

III. Locating Statutory Law

To locate the text of a statute, start by considering the information you already have.

A. Locating a Statute Using Its Legal Citation

Suppose you already have a legal citation to a particular statute. For example, assume that you know that a law prohibiting racial discrimination has the following citation: 42 U.S.C.A. Sect. 2000e-2000e-17.

On the Internet
There are a number of ways to access statutes online, and it is relatively easy if you know the citation. One of the best free online sites is the legislative service of the Library of Congress. It contains the full text and Congressional record of federal statutes, along with proposed legislation (bills) and their current status. The URL is http://thomas.loc.gov. Because our citation is to a federal law, this URL is a good place to start. By searching the federal laws for 42 U.S.C.A. 2000e, you should be able to find the full text of the law. Other user-friendly sites where you can find federal statutes as well as state laws include:

http://lawcrawler.findlaw.com
http://www.lawsource.com/also/
http://www.lawguru.com

B. Locating a Statute by Analyzing a Legal Problem

Suppose you don't have any citation or reference to a particular law. Instead, you have a problem to solve, involving discrimination in the workplace. You have heard that there are laws prohibiting such discrimination, but you have no idea where to find the text of such a law. How can you find it?

On the Internet
It can be time-consuming to try to locate a particular statute online without its citation because key words or phrases often appear in dozens, sometimes hundreds, of statutes. One of the best places to start is with a Web site that organizes American law by subject (e.g., alternative dispute, commercial law, environmental law). One such site is http://www.lib.uchicago.edu/LibInfo/Law/subject.html.

C. State Statutes

The above methods work equally well for locating state statutes. Most college libraries contain the statutes for their home states, and occasionally for those of neighboring states. For online searches, be sure you enter the database for the appropriate state.

IV. Locating Case Law

A. Case Reporters

The law is found not only in the text of statutes passed by Congress and state legislatures, but also in the written opinions of federal and state judges explaining their rulings in particular cases. Edited versions of such judicial opinions are found throughout this book. To find the complete case opinion and other case opinions, it is necessary to learn something about Case Reporters—books that collect judicial opinions—and online searches for case law.

B. Locating a Case Using Its Legal Citation

Under the uniform system for referring to judicial opinions, each case is identified by the names of the parties, followed by a citation containing three parts: an abbreviation for the Reporter (or series of books in which the opinion is published) and numbers to identify the particular volume and page number where the case was published. Here, the series or Reporter corresponds to a database when searching online.

Suppose you want to read the full opinion in a Chapter 1 problem case, *Fried v. Archer,* 775 A.2d 430 (Md. 2001). You can find it online or in the library using the names of the parties (Fried and Archer) or the citation (775 A.2d 430).

In a library, you would find the case by looking at volume 775 of a set of books called the Atlantic Reporter (abbreviated A.), Second Series (2d.) (Note: Each volume of each set of reporters is numbered, beginning with 1. When the numbers get too high, the publishers begin a second series of the same Reporter, and then a third series.), and turning to the page 430.

Online, you can use any case citation to locate the full text of the opinion through any of the following sites:

http://www.lawsource.com/also/ (ALSO: American Law Sources On-line)
http://www.lawguru.com (Internet law library that enables you to search for cases and statutes by state)
http://lawcrawler.findlaw.com
Westlaw
Lexis-Nexus

C. Common Traps to Avoid

- Be sure you are using the right database—state or federal cases, trial courts (such as the federal District Courts), appellate courts (such as the federal Circuit Courts of Appeals), or the Supreme Court. (Our example is of a Maryland state court case, so you would want to be sure to use the database that includes state court cases.)
- Consider how new/old your case is. Some databases will require you to identify the time period (within two years? before 1945?) to be searched.
- If you are searching by the citation, be sure you have entered each element correctly (volume number, series, page number), paying particular attention to whether the series is the first (letters only), second (letters followed by 2d) third, etc.
- If you are searching by names of parties, be sure you are spelling the names correctly.

D. Locating a Case by Analyzing a Legal Problem

Suppose you have no particular case in mind. Instead, you know that you want to find out something about wrongful discharge of employees. You looked in your state statutes and you couldn't find any statute dealing with wrongful discharge. You know from the chapter on whistleblowing in this text that wrongful discharge is a kind of tort and that tort law is mostly judge-made law (case law). How can you find a case about wrongful discharge (or any other topic)?

Once you have located an appropriate database—federal cases if you are searching for opinions interpreting the U.S. Constitution or federal statutes; state case law in most other instances—you can search for cases by key words or phrases (such as wrongful discharge, tort, employment-at-will). As you become more experienced in reading and researching case law, you will learn to refine your search terms.

E. Locating Cases that Interpret a Particular Statute

Using an appropriate database (e.g., state case law), use the citation as a keyword to find cases that have cited and interpreted the case. In some cases, such as Westlaw, you will need to put quote marks around the citation to do this search. Learn the best method for whatever search tool you use most often.

V. Administrative Law

The rules and regulations promulgated by government administrative agencies are also published so that anyone can find and read them. When first adopted, they are all published in the newspaper, for example, in the *Federal Register.* Of course, a chronological list of the latest government rules and regulations is not the easiest resource to use. Like federal statutes, federal regulations are codified (or arranged by subject) in the Code of Federal Regulations (CFR). This code can be used in the same way as the United States Code or any state law code.

On the Internet

The complete Code of Federal Regulations can be accessed online through http://www.access.gpo.gov/nara/cfr/cfr-table-search.html.

State Administrative Law

Most states have a similar codified version of regulations adopted by state administrative agencies. Check your library to see if there is a copy of the state code of administrative rules and regulations. If there is, note here the form for citing it:

Check a government Web site for your state to see if the administrative code is available online.

VI. Common Abbreviations

Federal Statutory Materials

U.S.C. United States Code (the official codification of laws passed by Congress)

U.S.C.A. United States Code Annotated (U.S.C.A. contains the text of statutes, followed by notes of relevant cases and references to other materials related to the topic.)

State Statutory Materials

Check to see if your library contains a copy of your state statutes. If so, locate the correct abbreviation (citation form) for the series by turning to the front of any volume to find "Cite as (abbreviation for series). (Full name of state statutes)."

Federal Case Law

1 S.Ct. 99 means: volume l, Supreme Court Reporter, page 99

U.S. Supreme Court cases can be found in each of the following:

U.S. United States Reports (official version)

S.Ct. Supreme Court Reporter (Annotated case reporter)

L.Ed. United States Supreme Court, Lawyer's Edition (Annotated case reporter)

Other federal court cases can be found at:

F., F.2d, F.3d Federal Reporter (oldest cases), Federal Reporter, Second Series (more recent cases), and Federal Reporter, Third Series (most recent cases) from federal Circuit Courts of Appeal)

F. Supp., F. Supp. 2d Federal Supplement (contains decisions of federal trial courts, called District Courts) Federal Supplement, Second Series (more recent opinions of federal trial courts)

State Case Law

A. Atlantic Reporter, (Conn., Del., Me., Md., N.H., N.J., Pa., R.I., Vt., D.C.Munic. Ct.App.)

A.2d Atlantic Reporter, Second Series

Cal. California Reporter

N.E. North Eastern Reporter (Ill., Ind., Mass., N.Y., Ohio)

N.E.2d North Eastern Reporter, Second Series

N.W. North Western Reporter (Ia., Mich., Minn., Neb., N.D., S.D., Wis.)

N.W.2d North Western Reporter, Second Series

N.Y.S. New York Supplement

N.Y.S.2d New York Supplement, Second Series

P. Pacific Reporter (Alaska, Ariz., Calif., Colo., Haw., Id., Kan., Mont., Nev., N.M., Okla., Ore., Utah, Wash., Wyo.)

P.2d Pacific Reporter, Second Series

S.E. South Eastern Reporter (Ga., N.C., S.C., Va., W.Va.)

S.E.2d South Eastern Reporter, Second Series

So. Southern Reporter (Ala., Fla., La., and Miss.)

So. 2d Southern Reporter, Second Series

APPENDIX C

STAKEHOLDER ETHICS ROLE PLAY

A person faces a business ethics dilemma, with a tough decision to make. In this exercise, students play the roles of a decision maker and of several "stakeholder" advisors. After the stakeholders offer their points of view, the decision maker makes a choice and explains the reasons behind it.

The role play can done in a "fishbowl" format, with the decision maker and the various advisors in a circle in the middle of the room and with the rest of the class arranged in a larger circle around them, observing. Or, to involve more participants, the decision maker and the different stakeholders can be represented by small groups. (Recommended size of groups is three to six students.) In another variation for even more participation, students can replicate the same exercise in separate groups, each of which would have one decision maker being advised by several stakeholders.

1. First Plenary: Introduction

The decision maker defines the problem and explains the process of the role play to all.

2. Break-Out #1: Stakeholders Meet Separately

Students in each stakeholder group meet to identify their own interests and to articulate how they want to see the problem resolved (or, if they represent an ethical perspective, to articulate the direction their approach to ethics dictates and the reasons for it). Each group should appoint a "scribe" to take notes and another student to lead intra-group discussion. A "reporter" arranges the points into a cogent argument. Meanwhile, the decision maker can meet with the instructor to prepare questions for the stakeholder groups at the plenary session.

3. Plenary Session

The decision maker moderates a plenary session, asking each stakeholder representative to offer advice. As they present their interests and preferred outcomes, the decision maker asks questions to clarify or challenge a point of view. This phase of the exercise may evolve into a free-form discussion among the various stakeholders, with the decision maker acting as facilitator/referee, and with the stakeholders querying and challenging each other. The goal is that the class achieve a refined sense of the different perspectives.

Next, the decision maker should lead a brainstorming session on options, with anyone free to suggest a means of resolving the dilemma and with no discussion of whether any one suggestion is either wise or practical. Roles are irrelevant here—the goal is to unlock creative approaches, to bring a full range of ideas to the surface. The resulting list of options should be placed on the board/screen or printed out before the session ends.

4. Break-Out #2: Stakeholders Regroup

While the decision maker takes time to think about what has just transpired and to weigh options, the stakeholder groups reconvene to discuss solutions and decide which to recommend, given the information they now have regarding all the stakeholder concerns.

5. Final Plenary

The decision maker asks each group to report back its final recommendation and then explains to the class how he or she will deal with the dilemma, and the reasons for this choice.

6. Individual Follow-Up Memo

One way to allow each student to participate more fully is to assign a brief memo, in which each person (regardless of role) recommends and justifies a solution to the dilemma.

APPENDIX D

Mock Trial Materials

Order of Representation

1. Opening statement by plaintiff's attorney
2. Opening statement by defendant's attorney
3. Plaintiff's case: Direct examination of plaintiff's witnesses by plaintiff's attorney, followed by cross-examination by defendant's attorney
4. Defendant's case: Direct examination of defendant's witnesses by defendant's attorney, followed by cross-examination by plaintiff's attorney
5. Closing statement by plaintiff's attorney
6. Closing statement by defendant's attorney
7. Trial judge charges the jury
8. Jury deliberates and returns a verdict

Directions for Attorneys

You have the important responsibility of making sure that your team pulls together to prepare a strategy and materials for the trial and to present your case. Be sure to collaborate on all of this. Exchange telephone numbers and/or e-mail addresses and develop a schedule of regular meetings.

You control what the jury will learn about the case from your client's perspective, depending on how you deliver both the opening and closing statements and how you handle the questioning of witnesses.

Preparation

Read the witness statements in the chapter project carefully and reread the chapter.

Opening Statement

First introduce yourself and your client to the judge and jury and then briefly explain how you view the facts of the case. An opening statement is to the evidence later given at the trial as the picture on the box of a jigsaw puzzle is to the pieces inside the box; you are giving the jury a thumbnail sketch of what's to come. As you tell what happened from your client's point of view, use language and emphasis to try to build sympathy toward your client and against the other side. Be clear and speak audibly. Practice will greatly improve your delivery. Rehearse—with your teammates, with anyone who can stand to hear you, alone in front of a mirror—as much as possible.

Direct Examination of Your Own Witnesses

Let your witness tell the story. Questions should be short, simple, and understandable, and your witness should be doing most of the talking. Your job is to keep your witnesses on track, to help them remember every detail you want the jury to hear, and in the right order. If the witness rushes through or mumbles something important, be sure to go back to it. You might say, "Excuse me, Mr. Witness, but I don't believe the jury heard that last remark. Would you mind repeating what you just said?" Remember that the jury knows nothing about this case beyond what it hears at this trial. As your witnesses testify, they should tell the story in ways that put the best possible spin on the facts from your client's perspective. A witness may embellish the facts, but if he or she contradicts or changes them, your opponent is free to use the witness role description to show that the witness may be lying. Practice with your witnesses.

Cross-Examining a Hostile Witness

Again, questions should be simple and understandable. Prepare by making a list of the crucial facts you want the witnesses to admit. Then build up to each one in small steps, with questions that a person can't waffle around on. Your questions might begin with, "Isn't it true that . . . ?" You might tell the witness you are going to ask a few simple questions, and ask leading questions that require a simple "yes or no" answer. Then, if the witness tries to explain further, interrupt politely but firmly: "Yes or no please."

At the trial, pay close attention to the direct questioning of the witness you are about to cross-examine. Be ready to make changes in your prepared questions at the last minute, depending on what actually happens on direct examination.

If a witness says something that contradicts an earlier statement (in the text), emphasize the discrepancy by asking the witness; "Did you make this statement earlier?" Show the witness the statement; ask him or her to read the relevant portion to the jury. This is a very effective way to challenge the credibility of a hostile witness.

Take your time. You have the upper hand psychologically, because a hostile witness has no idea what you might ask. If a witness doesn't give you the answer you had hoped to hear, it is probably a good idea not to linger too long on that particular point, but to keep moving to another line of questioning. What you don't want to do in cross-examination is allow a hostile witness to offer long-winded explanations, or to repeat something you wish the jury had never heard in the first place. Try to end with something punchy, so when you say "No further questions" you will sound appropriately dismissive.

Objecting to Evidence

Listen carefully as your opponent asks questions. You may interrupt the trial with objections for any of the following reasons:

1. Irrelevant: The question strays too far from the issues of the trial.
2. Badgering the witness: The opposing lawyer is being rude or overbearing to your witness.
3. Speculation: Your witness is being asked to offer an opinion but does not possess the appropriate expertise to answer.
4. Asked and answered: Your witness has already been asked and has already answered the question.

Be ready to object and to justify your objections. The judge will sustain or overrule them.

Communicating with Your Teammates

During the trial, you may confer with your teammates. In fact, you should be helping each other as the trial unfolds. This means you may whisper helpful comments or pass notes. Try not to disturb the proceedings, however. You may also, as an attorney, interrupt the trial to confer with another attorney on your own team as she is questioning a witness.

Closing Statement

Make a persuasive summary of the evidence you have presented and describe the weaknesses in your opponent's case. If there were some items that you couldn't effectively deal with during the Q&A of trial testimony, now is your chance to "clean it up"—to revisit parts of the case.

The closing statement is also your opportunity to go beyond the particular facts of the case, and to explain to the jury the **policy reasons** that support a win for your side. Policy reasons address what is good for society in general. Policy concerns the long-term consequences—to all of us—of a certain decision. Although policy is not the same as law, law is in part based on what is considered good for society overall. For the policy portion of your closing, ask the jurors to think of the ramifications of this case for the future. Help them imagine how a ruling in this case might affect every workplace. Talk about why a decision in your favor will be good for society, and/or why a decision in favor of the other side will not. Examples will help clarify your points. The "slippery slope" argument might come in handy.

Stay away from the law in the closing statements. For purposes of the mock trial, the jury will decide what the law will be. (In an actual trial, the judge would instruct the jury as to the rules of law to be applied.)

Directions for Witnesses

Read the witness statements very carefully, especially your own. Think about your character from your team's point of view. What spin will you put on the facts? You may stretch or exaggerate to make the story sound more sympathetic to your side, but if you contradict any fact given in the witness statements you may be impeached on cross-examination. In other words, be creative, but don't lie!

Work with your team to decide what you will be asked and how you will answer during "direct examination"—the friendly questioning by your own side. You and your team need to decide exactly what questions you should be asked, so that you have the maximum opportunity to develop the story from your team's point of view. You should do most of the talking, not your lawyer. The lawyer for your team should be asking you questions that are "prompts" that allow you to explain each part of the story fully.

You and your team should also try to determine what would be the approach of the opposition to your character during cross-examination. What questions are they likely to ask you? Anticipate as fully as possible and plan how you want to answer to minimize the damage. There may be certain points that are likely to hurt your side on cross-examination. Decide with your teammates whether you want to address those issues on direct examination in order to eliminate the surprise factor and maintain more control over what the jury hears.

Directions for Jurors

In the mock trial, as in the real world, jurors should learn about the case only through the trial itself. That means that you should not read anything prior to the trial.

Listen carefully as the trial unfolds. You will be asked to reach a verdict based on your reactions to the dispute as you understand it, and on the persuasiveness of the final arguments as you understand them. Keep in mind that your decision affects not just the parties in this case, but others in similar situations in the future.

When you go into deliberations, first select a foreperson. The foreperson should facilitate an open discussion in which everyone participates. Once all opinions have been aired, try to reach consensus. If this is not possible, take a vote. The foreperson reports the verdict to the judge.

APPENDIX E

ALTERNATIVE DISPUTE RESOLUTION

Since the early 1970s, the time-consuming and expensive process of litigating business disputes has been increasingly replaced by different forms of alternative dispute resolution. ADR has been embraced by the Supreme Court, which has ruled that courts must refuse to hear lawsuits when a commercial contract calls for arbitration,[1] and by Congress, which has authorized federal agencies and federal courts to use informal alternatives to litigation such as mediation, conciliation, and arbitration.[2] In fact, to circumvent costly litigation, more and more companies have inserted binding arbitration clauses into employment contracts, so that disputes over pay, discrimination, misconduct, and other matters must be resolved not in court but by a panel of arbitrators.

Win-Win or Principled Negotiation

When opponents in a dispute focus only on their ultimate goals and approach one another with a "winner take all" attitude, the resulting agreement is too often one-sided and short-lived. In contrast, the concept of principled negotiation is that there is a better way, a way to reach a lasting agreement, satisfying at least some of the interests on each side. The leading resource for learning about principled negotiation is Roger Fisher & William Uri, *Getting to Yes* (1991). These points summarize the process they recommend:

@ Separate the people from the problem. Deal with the relationships among the parties separately from the merits of the dispute.

@ Focus on interests, not positions. For example, *being comfortable* may be the interest at stake, not whether a window needs to be open or closed.

@ Invent options for mutual gains; be creative.

@ Where thorny disagreements remain, move to objective neutral criteria to ensure a fair resolution.

@ Before negotiations begin, each side should develop its BATNA (best alternative to a negotiated agreement). In a legal dispute, this almost always means that if settlement fails, a party can file suit. It requires both sides to consider what they are likely to win—or lose—if the case goes to court.

Preparation for Arbitrators and Mediators

In preparation for your role, learn more about alternative dispute resolution from one of the following:

@ The Beginner's Guide to ADR, available through the Web site of the American Arbitration Association, http://www.adr.org

@ National Arbitration Forum resources at http://www.arb-forum.com

@ Arbitration: the WWW Virtual Library's section on Private Dispute Resolution, http://www.interarb.com

---

1 *Southland Corp. v. Keating,* 465 U.S.1 (1984).

2 *Administrative Dispute Resolution Act of 1990* and *Alternative Dispute Resolution Act of 1998.*

Negotiation Exercise

Preparation

Read through your assigned witness statements carefully to understand the "facts" and to get a feel for your character. Try to identify his or her real needs and interests, so that you can be open to resolutions that will best satisfy those needs. Consider both long- and short-term interests, both economic and relational, business and family concerns. Rank your interests. Decide on your BATNA.

First Round

Meet with the opposition. Try to follow the rules of principled negotiation. Explain your side's interests. Listen to and question the other side carefully to develop as complete an understanding as possible of their interests.

Break-Out

Split sides apart before you reach an agreement. Develop an offer. Develop a back-up offer.

Second Round

Meet with the opposition. Exchange your offers and discuss them. If you have difficulty forming an agreement, try brainstorming alternatives.

Repeat Rounds

Continue the process of meeting with the other side and alone with your team until the negotiation is complete.

Debrief with the Whole Class

Compare the various negotiated agreements. Which one identified the largest area of mutual interest? Which one was the most balanced? Which is most likely to survive into the future? Vote for the best agreement, giving reasons for your vote.

Mediation/Arbitration

While a negotiated agreement is arrived at by opposing sides on their own, a mediator or an arbitrator is a neutral third party who is actively involved in the agreement-making process. A mediator listens carefully to both sides, and then helps them discover their mutual interests, close their differences, and think of creative ways to craft an agreement. An arbitrator is more like a judge. An arbitrator listens to arguments made by each side, asks questions of each side, and then acts without further input to craft an agreement that both sides must then accept. (Before an arbitration, both sides agree that they will accept the terms of the agreement that will be decided for them.)

Comparative ADR Role Play

Using a single dispute, some students role play as opponents, while other students role play mediators and arbitrators. The class is evenly divided among negotiating, mediating, and arbitrating teams.

Once all the agreements have been finalized, the whole class debriefs by studying the results and discussing the comparative strengths and weaknesses of the three processes for reaching agreement.

APPENDIX F

LEGISLATIVE HEARING

In this exercise some students role play legislative committee members hearing testimony on a piece of controversial proposed legislation, while other students role play public witnesses offering their views on the proposed law.

The legislative committee sits as a panel facing the public witnesses in the middle of the room. If the class is large, the rest of the class surrounds them, listening in, making a "fishbowl" set up.

A committee chair calls each public witness, one at a time. After each speaker has finished a brief opening statement of opinion, legislators can ask a few questions of that speaker. When all of the speakers have been heard, the whole class votes on the bill as a full legislature.

Legislators/Legislative Aides

Depending on class size, some students may be assigned to role-play legislative aides.

Before the Hearing

Prepare for your role by forming your political position on the bill (for or against it), considering your own opinion and also what your "constituents" are likely to think. If you are uncertain of either, find online news coverage from your part of the state/country. (If the class is large enough to allow for legislative aides, yours can do more extensive research into your position.)

Write a list of questions to ask the various public witnesses. Try to make them provocative and interesting. Suggestions: Hypothetical questions are often very effective, setting up examples that sharpen points of disagreement. Consider asking about the long-term consequences (on business, the nation, on particular constituents, etc.) of the proposed legislation; how new laws will impact on existing state or national laws; and how proposed legislation will be implemented and enforced.

During the Hearing

Listen carefully to each speaker. Be prepared to vary or adapt a planned question to fit the situation at hand. Try not to give speeches during the hearing itself, as your goal is to elicit input from the public.

After the Hearing

You will have an opportunity to articulate your position for or against the proposed legislation, giving your reasons and referring to testimony that supports your position.

Public Witnesses

Remember that you are playing a role; stay in it. Avoid drifting into advocating your real-life position on the issue.

Before the Hearing

Think about the position a person in your role is likely to take on the proposed legislation, regardless of what your personal opinion may be. Online, find out more about the group you represent.

At the hearing, you will begin by giving a short (5 minute) statement explaining your view and the reasons for it. Practice a clear and crisp opening statement before class. Prepare for questions by thinking ahead about what you are likely to be asked and how you will answer.

During the Hearing

You will need to pay careful attention to other public witnesses as they may raise points you had not considered. Be prepared to address those points when it is your turn, as part of your opening statement, since you will not be able to directly question or engage with the other public witnesses. Your interaction will be limited to speaking to the legislative panel, and responding to the questions they pose to you.

Writing Exercise

Students who do not serve as either public witnesses or legislators can be given written assignments as editorial writers covering the hearing for a newspaper or magazine or as members of the larger Assembly/Senate. In their editorials or absentee ballot reports, they will articulate their opinion on the proposal and their reasons for it, based on observing the legislative committee proceedings.

Glossary

A

Abusive discharge – a tort, recognized in some states, committed when an employer discharges an employee in violation of a clear expression of public policy, also referred to as "wrongful discharge"

Administrative law – the rules and regulations established by government agencies, as opposed to law created by courts and legislators

Affidavit – a written declaration or statement of facts, sworn before a person who has the authority to administer such an oath

Affirm – the ruling by an appellate court that agrees with a lower court decision and allows the judgment to stand.

Alternative Dispute Resolution (ADR) – the resolution of disputes in ways other than through the use of the traditional judicial process; mediation and arbitration are examples of ADR.

Amicus curiae – Latin for "friend of the court"; an individual or entity that petitions the Court for permission to file a brief because of strong interest in the case

Answer – the pleading of a defendant in which he admits or denies any or all of the facts set out in the plaintiff's complaint or declaration

Appeal – the process by which a party to a lawsuit asks a higher court to review alleged errors made by a lower court or agency

Appellant – the party who appeals a case to a higher court

Appellate court – a court having jurisdiction of appeal and review

Appellee – the party in a case against which an appeal is taken; that is, the party with an interest adverse to setting aside or reversing a judgment

Arbitration – a process in which a dispute is submitted to a mutually acceptable person or board who will render a decision to which the parties are bound

Arbitrator – a disinterested party who has the power to resolve a dispute and (generally) bind the parties

Assumption of the risk – in tort law, a defense to negligence when a plaintiff has voluntarily exposed herself to a known risk

B

Bill of Rights – first ten amendments to the U.S. Constitution adopted in 1791; sets forth specific individual protections against government intrusion

Bona fide – Latin for "in good faith"; honestly, sincerely

Brief – in litigation, a formal legal document submitted by attorneys for both sides of a dispute outlining the issues, statutes, and precedents that make up the legal arguments of each side

Burden of proof – proof in a civil case by a fair preponderance of the evidence; proof in a criminal case beyond a reasonable doubt

C

Case at bar – the particular case that is before the court

Case of first impression – a lawsuit raising a novel question of law; without precedent in the particular jurisdiction

Case law – the law created when an appellate court issues a written opinion in a lawsuit. Sometimes referred to as common law. CONTRAST: statutory law

Cause of action – the facts, which evidenced a civil wrong, thereby giving rise to a right to judicial relief

Caveat emptor – Latin for "let the buyer beware"; the concept that the buyer bears the loss if there is anything defective in the goods she purchases

Cease and desist order – an order by an agency or court directing someone to stop an unlawful practice

Certiorari – a means of obtaining appellate review; a writ issued by an appellate court, such as the Supreme Court, to an inferior court commanding the record be certified to the appellate court for judicial review

Chattel – personal property; tangible property that is mobile

Class action – a suit brought by or against a group with common interests in resolving particular issues of law or facts. Sometimes called a "representative action." The named plaintiff in a class action is a representative of the group.

Claim – a cause of action

Collective bargaining – the process whereby union representatives bargain with management on behalf of employees concerning wages, hours, and other terms and conditions of employment. The result of this process is a collective bargaining agreement.

Collective works – under U.S. copyright law, collective works are those that originate from more than one author

Comity – respect or deference; the doctrine that allows an administrative agency or court to defer to the actions or decisions of another body

Commerce clause – the clause in Article II, Section 8 of the Constitution that gives Congress power to regulate commerce among the several states

Commercial speech – speech that proposes a commercial transaction; the Supreme Court has interpreted the First Amendment as giving more limited protection to commercial speech than to political speech

Common law – also called case law or judge-made law; as distinguished from law created by the enactments of legislatures, the common law is comprised of the principles and rules that derive solely from custom and from judgments and decisions of courts

Communitarianism – the belief that individual liberties depend on the bolstering of the foundations of civil society: families, schools, neighborhoods. It is through these institutions, according to communitarians, that we acquire a sense of our personal civic responsibilities, of our rights and the rights of others, and a commitment to the welfare of the whole of society.

Comparable worth – the idea that jobs should be evaluated on the basis of the education, experience, skill and risk involved so that different jobs of similar worth receive similar compensation; sometimes referred to as "pay equity."

Compensatory damages – money that compensates an injured party for the injury sustained and nothing more; such compensation as will simply make good or replace the loss caused by a wrong or injury

Complaint – the first pleading by the plaintiff in a civil case. Its purpose is to give the defendant the information on which the plaintiff relies to support its demand. In a complaint, the plaintiff sets out a cause of action, consisting of a formal allegation or charge presented to the appropriate court.

Concurring opinion – with reference to appellate court cases, a concurring opinion is one by a judge who agrees with the majority opinion's conclusions, but for different reasons, and who therefore writes a separate opinion. CONTRAST: dissenting opinion, majority opinion

Consent decree – a court decree entered by consent of the parties. It is not a judicial sentence, but is an agreement of the parties made under the sanction of a court.

Consumer Product Safety Commission (CPSC) – an independent federal agency created in 1972 to protect the public from death or serious harm caused by dangerous products

Contract – a legally enforceable agreement between two parties

Copyright – protects the original work of authors, painters, sculptors, musicians, photographers, and others who produce work of literary or artistic merit

Corporation – a legal entity created by statute authorizing its officers, directors, and stockholders to carry on business

Cost-benefit analysis – a way to reach decisions in which the costs of a given action are compared with its benefits

Counterclaim – a claim presented by a defendant that, if successful, defeats or reduces the plaintiff's recovery

Criminal law – a set of laws, the violation of which is an offense against society. Crimes include both minor crimes (misdemeanors) and more serious felonies.

D

Damages – a monetary award granted by a court to a winning party.

Declaratory judgment – a judicial opinion that declares the rights of the parties or expresses the court's interpretation of a law without ordering anything to be done

Deep ecology – an ethical belief system based on ecological concerns that begins with the premise that the biotic community in which we find ourselves has intrinsic value

Defamation – the disparagement of one's reputation; a civil action (tort) involving the offense of injuring a person's character, fame, or reputation by false and malicious statements

Default – omission to perform a legal or contractual duty; the failure of a party to appear in court or defend an action after being properly served with process

Defendant – the party against whom an action is brought in a civil case; the accused in a criminal case

Defense – an assertion offered by a defendant who, if successful, relieves her of liability, reduces the plaintiff's recovery, or defeats a criminal charge

Deontology – the study of duty; as developed by Immanuel Kant, the notion that there are certain moral rights and duties that every human being possesses, that ethical choices derive from universal principles based on those rights and duties

Deposition – a pretrial discovery process of testifying under oath (but not in open court) and subject to cross examination, where the testimony is recorded and intended to be used at trial

Design defect – in product liability law, the concept that a seller should be liable for harm caused by a product that was not well designed

Dicta/Dictum – Latin; an abbreviated form of *obiter dictum* ("a remark by the way"); An observation or remark made by a judge in pronouncing an opinion in a case, concerning some rule, principle, or application of law, or the solution of a question suggested by the court, but not necessarily involved in the case or essential to its determination

Disclaimer of warranty – seller's claim that no promises (warranties) were made when goods were sold

Discovery – pre-trial processes that allow each side to obtain information about the case from the other side for use in preparing for trial or settlement. Discovery devices include pre-trial depositions, motions to produce documents or to inspect premises, written interrogatories, and pre-trial medical examinations.

Dissenting opinion – in appellate courts, an opinion written by a judge who disagrees with the result reached by the majority, as well as its reasoning. CONTRAST: concurring opinion

Disparate impact discrimination – in an employment context, discrimination that results from certain employer practices or procedures that, although neutral on their face, have a discriminatory effect. For example, height and weight requirements for all applicants are not discriminatory on their face, but will have the effect of excluding more women than men.

Disparate treatment discrimination – in an employment context, any practice or decision that treats applicants or employees differently depending on their race, sex, religion, or national origin

Due process – a concept embodied in the Fifth and Fourteenth Amendments to the U.S. Constitution, meaning fundamental fairness. Due process mandates that government may not take life, liberty, or property from citizens unless they are given notice and a fair opportunity to be heard.

Duty of care – in tort law, all persons have a duty to exercise reasonable care in their interactions with others

E

Economic loss doctrine – a common law rule, followed in some states, that holds that a person harmed by another's breach of contract may not bring a tort action unless there was injury to a person or property other than that which was the subject of the contract

Eminent domain – the right of the government to take privately owned land for public use, paying the owner a just compensation

Employment-at-will doctrine – the common law rule that holds that whenever an employment relationship is of an indefinite duration, either party–the employer or the employee–may terminate the relationship at any time, for good cause or bad, in good faith or with malice

En banc – where most appellate cases are heard by only some of the judges, a decision en banc is one heard by the full court

Enterprise Liability – legal theory that allows a plaintiff to sue every company within a particular enterprise if plaintiff cannot identify the particular firm that caused her harm.

Environmental Protection Agency (EPA) – federal agency established in 1970 to oversee national environmental policy and laws

Equal Employment Opportunity Commission (EEOC) – five-member commission created in 1964 to administer Title VII of the Civil Rights Act by issuing interpretive guidelines, investigating, holding hearings, and keeping statistics

Equal protection – a concept embodied in the Fifth and Fourteenth Amendments to the U.S. Constitution that government cannot treat persons in similar situations differently

Equity – a system of justice that developed in England separate from the common-law courts. Few states in the U.S. still maintain separate equity courts, although most apply equity principles and procedures when equitable relief is sought. A broader meaning denotes fairness and justice.

Exclusivity rule – Under workers' compensation laws, the exclusivity rule provides that workers compensation is the only remedy available for some injuries.

Executive branch – branch of the U.S. government that includes the president and is charged with enforcing the law; the powers of the president as established in Article II of the U.S. Constitution. Also used to refer to the governor of a state

Expert testimony – trial testimony from an authority recognized by the court as having special knowledge

F

Fair use – under American copyright law, the right to use limited portions of a copyrighted work, without permission, for education or criticism

False Claims Reform Act – a federal statute that allows citizens to file a civil suit against any company known to be defrauding the government; also referred to as *qui tam*

Federal Register – a publication providing notice of rule making by federal agencies

Federal Trade Commission (FTC) – a bipartisan, independent administrative agency authorized by Congress to prevent unfair methods of competition and unfair or deceptive trade and advertising practices

Federalism – the Constitutional relationship between the states and federal government whereby responsibility and autonomy is divided between them

Feminist ethics – the notion that the right thing to do stems from a sense of responsibility for one another based on caring relationships, rather than from allegiance to abstract principles. CONTRAST: utilitarian analysis of consequences or deontological universal rights/duties

Fiduciary – a person having a legal duty, created by his or her undertaking, to act primarily for another's benefit. For example, corporate officers are fiduciaries with fiduciary duties to their shareholders; lawyers have fiduciary duties to their clients.

Fiduciary duty – the legal duty that arises whenever one person is in a special relationship of trust to another

Food and Drug Administration (FDA) – federal regulatory agency responsible for overseeing safety of food, drugs, and cosmetics sold in the United States

Fundamental freedoms – those rights given special priority and protection under the U.S. Constitution, including the right to free speech, free religion, free press, the right to vote, and the freedom to travel

G

General Agreement on Tariffs and Trade (GATT) – created in 1948 as an agreement; GATT grew to be both an agreement and an organization that negotiated international trade and tariff rules. In 1995, GATT was replaced by the World Trade Organization (WTO).

Gross negligence – a conscious or reckless act or omission that is likely to result in harm to a person or property; a higher level of culpability than simple negligence

I

Implied warranty – a warranty or promise that arises by law, although the seller did not express it. For example, an implied warranty of merchantability indicates that a good is fit for its ordinary purpose.

Indictment – a formal accusation made by a grand jury that charges a person has committed a crime

Infringement – violating the exclusive rights of a copyright or patent holder by using the protected work without permission or license

Injunction – a court order directing someone to do or not to do something

Instructions to the jury – directions that a trial judge gives to the jury explaining the law to be applied to the facts that the jury finds

Intellectual property laws – copyright, patent, trademark, trade secret, and other laws that protect intangible property that is the work product of the human mind

Intentional torts – a category of civil wrongs giving redress to the victims of willful wrongdoing. Wrongful or abusive discharge of an employee, misappropriating a trade secret, and battery are all intentional torts.

International law – law considered legally binding among otherwise sovereign, independent nations. Treaties are a form of international law.

Interrogatories – a discovery device consisting of a series of written questions directed to the opposing party, to be answered in writing, under oath

Intrusion – an intentional tort, committed when one party intrudes on the solitude of another in an overly offensive way. Sometimes referred to as invasion of privacy.

Joint and several liability – a rule in the tort law of some states that when two or more defendants are each partly responsibility for harm to the plaintiff, the plaintiff can demand payment from any one of the defendants

Judgment – official ruling by a court

Judicial branch – branch of the U.S. government that consists of the federal courts and its powers as set forth in Article III of the U.S. Constitution; sometimes referred to as the judiciary

Judicial review – the process whereby a court reviews legislative action to ensure that it was Constitutional or administrative agency action to ensure that it was Constitutional, legal, and in compliance with the agency's enabling legislation

Jurisdiction – the power of the court or a judicial officer to decide a case; the geographic area of a court's authority; the power of a court over a defendant in a lawsuit

L

Legislation – the act of passing laws; the making of laws by express decree; also used as a noun to mean a statute or statutes adopted by a legislative body. CONTRAST: case law

Learned Intermediary – a person with special training and expertise, such as a doctor, who stands between the seller of a product, such as a prescription drug or medical device, and the patient on who uses it.

Legislative branch – branch of the U.S. government that consists of Congress and its powers as set forth in Article I of the U.S. Constitution. Each state also has a state legislature that is the body of government that enacts state laws.

Legislative history – the background and events leading up to the enactment of a statute

Lobbyists – those who attempt to influence legislators to pass laws that favor special interests

M

Magnuson-Moss Warranty Act – federal statute designed to prevent deception in sales contracts by making warranties easier to understand

Mediation – an alternative dispute resolution process in which a neutral third person attempts to persuade disputing parties to adjust their positions to resolve their differences. Unlike judges or arbitrators, mediators do not impose solutions on the parties.

Misappropriation – a wrongful taking of something belonging to another, as illegal taking of a trade secret or benefiting economically from the use of another's name or likeness, thereby misappropriating his right of publicity

Motion – a request to a judge or court for a rule or order favorable to the petitioning party, generally made within the course of an existing lawsuit

N

National Labor Relations Act – also known as Wagner Act; federal statute enacted in 1935 that established the rights of employees to organize unions, engage in collective bargaining and to strike

National Labor Relations Board (NLRB) – federal agency created by Wagner Act to oversee union elections to prevent unfair and illegal labor practices

Negligence – voluntary conduct that foreseeably exposes the interests of another to an unreasonable risk of harm; also the name of the civil (tort) action brought by a plaintiff injured by the negligence of another

NGOs – non-governmental organizations or NGOs are voluntary and charitable not-for-profit associations, such as the Red Cross and Public Citizen.

Nominal damages – minimal damages awarded for a breach of contract or technical injury, but where no actual harm was suffered

Non-delegation doctrine – interpretation of the U.S. Constitution that stops Congress from delegating too much of its power to another branch of government or to an administrative agency

Nuisance – improper activity that interferes with another's use or enjoyment of his property

O

Occupational Safety and Health Act of 1970 – federal statute that requires health and safety protections for employees at their places of work

Occupational Safety and Health Administration (OSHA) – federal agency that promulgates and enforces workplace health and safety standards, conducts inspections and investigations, keeps records, and conducts research

Order – decision of an administrative law judge; final disposition of a case between the government and a private party

P

Patent – the exclusive right or privilege to make, use, or sell an invention for a limited period of time, granted by the government to the inventor

Pay Equity – the idea that jobs should be evaluated on the basis of the education, experience, skill and risk involved so that different jobs of similar worth receive similar compensation; sometimes referred to as "comparable worth."

Per curium – Latin; "by the court"; used to indicate an unsigned opinion by the entire court rather than a single judge; sometimes refers to a brief statement of the court's decision unaccompanied by a written opinion

Petitioner – a party that files a petition with the court, applying in writing for a court order; a party that asks a court to hear an appeal from a judgment; a party that initiates an equity action

Plaintiff – a person or entity that brings an action or complaint against a defendant; the party who initiated a lawsuit

Pleadings – the formal allegations of the parties of their respective claims and defense, including the plaintiff's complaint, defendant's answer, and plaintiff's reply

Police power – the legal right of government to legislate for the public health, welfare, safety, and morals

Precedent – a previously decided court case that serves to notify future litigants how subsequent similar cases will be resolved

Preemption – in federal-state relations, the concept that where there is a direct conflict between federal and state actions, the federal law will have priority and the state action will be void

Prima facie – Latin; "at first sight"; a fact presumed to be true unless disproved by evidence to the contrary

Privilege – in tort law, the ability to act contrary to another person's right without that person having legal redress for such actions. Privilege is usually raised as a defense.

Privity of contract – the relationship that exists between promisor and promisee of a contract

Probable cause – reasonable ground for supposing that an individual has committed a crime

Procedural law – that part of the law which concerns the method or process of enforcing legal rights

Products liability – the legal liability of manufacturers and sellers to buyers, users, and sometimes bystanders, for injuries suffered because of defects in goods sold. Liability arises when a product has a defective condition that makes it unreasonably dangerous to the user or consumer. Sometimes referred to as "strict liability."

Promissory estoppel – a doctrine that applies when a promisor reasonably expects a promise to induce definite and substantial action or forbearance by the promisee, and that does induce such action or forbearance in reliance thereon; such a promise will be enforced if necessary to avoid injustice

Proximate cause – event(s) or action that, in natural and unbroken sequence, produce(s) an injury that would not have occurred absent the event(s) or action

Public Domain – in copyright law, creative or government works that can be freely copied and used by anyone without asking permission are said to be "in the public domain".

Punitive damages – awards unrelated to the victim's injuries that are designed to punish the wrongdoer; damages awarded to a plaintiff that are greater than the amount necessary to compensate her loss; generally granted where the wrong involved intent, violence, fraud, malice, or other aggravated circumstances

Q

Qualified immunity – protection from being sued that is available that is limited to certain circumstances

Qui tam – suit brought by whistleblowers under the federal False Claims Act against those who are alleged to have defrauded the government

Quid pro quo – Latin, "this for that"; the giving of one thing for another

R

Remand – to send back; the sending of a case back to the same lower court out of which it came for the purpose of having some action taken. For example, appellate courts often reverse a finding and remand for a new trial.

Remedies – the aid that a court gives to a party who wins a lawsuit

Remedies at law – court award of land, money, or items of value. CONTRAST: Remedies in equity

Remedies in equity – relief deemed to be appropriate, based on fairness, justice, and honesty to remedy a situation, such as an injunction, restraining order, specific performance, or the like. CONTRAST: remedies at law

Respondeat Superior – Latin, "Let the master answer." Doctrine which makes an employer ("master") responsible for the acts of an employee ("servant") committed within the scope of the employment.

Respondent – the party that contests an appeal or answers a petition

Restatement – a book published by the American Law Institute consisting of its understanding of the law created by the judiciary throughout the country; each volume of the Restatement covers a different area of law, such as agency law, contracts, torts.

Restitution – equitable remedy in which a person is restored to her original position prior to loss or injury, or is placed in the same position she would have been in absent a breach

Reverse – decision of an appellate court to overthrow, vacate, set aside, void, or repeal the judgment of a lower court

S

Shareholder – a person who owns stock in a corporation

Sovereign immunity – doctrine preventing a litigant from asserting an otherwise meritorious claim against a sovereign (government)

Standing to sue – the legal right to bring a lawsuit; in order to have standing, an individual or group must have a personal stake in the outcome of the suit

Stare decisis – Latin, "Let the decision stand." Doctrine under which courts stand by precedent and do not disturb a settled point of law. Under stare decisis, once a court has laid down a principle of law as applied to a certain set of facts, the court adheres to that principle and applies it to future cases in which the facts are substantially the same. (Stare decisis does not mean "the decision is in the stars.")

State action – in Constitutional law, the term is used to designate governmental action necessary to bring a constitutional challenge to such action

Statute – an act of a legislature declaring, commanding, or prohibiting something; a particular law enacted by the legislative branch of government. Sometimes the word is used to designate codified law or legislation as opposed to case law.

Statute of limitations – a statute prescribing the length of time after an event in which a suit must be brought or a criminal charge filed

Stay – a court order to stop, arrest, or forbear. To stay an order or decree means to hold it in abeyance or to refrain from enforcing it.

Strict liability – liability without fault. A case is one in strict liability when neither care nor negligence, neither good nor bad faith, neither knowledge nor ignorance will exonerate the defendant.

Strict Scrutiny – In Constitutional law, government actions or laws that discriminate on the basis of race or ethnicity, or that infringe on fundamental freedoms like free speech are closely scrutinized by the courts to see that there is a compelling reason to justify the discrimination or infringement.

Subpoena – a writ ordering a person to appear and give testimony or to bring documents that are in his or her control

Substantive law – that part of the law, which creates, defines, and regulates rights. CONTRAST: procedural law

Summary judgment – a pretrial decision reached by a trial court after considering the pleadings, affidavits, depositions, and other documents, on the ground that no trial is needed because no genuine issue of fact has been raised

Supremacy clause – a clause in Article VI of the U.S. Constitution which provides that all laws made by the federal government pursuant to the Constitution are the supreme laws of the land and are superior to any conflicting state law

Supreme Court of the United States – highest level of the federal judicial system, with nine justices appointed by the president of the United States for life

Suspect classification – in Constitutional law, differentiating between persons based on their race, national origin, or religion

T

Takings – term referring to government seizure, regulation, or intrusion on private property for which the owner is entitled to compensation under the Fifth Amendment to the U.S. Constitution

Title – ownership of property

Tort – French word meaning "wrong"; a civil wrong or injury, other than a breach of contract, committed against the person or property of another for which a civil court action is possible. Assault, battery, trespass, and negligence are all examples of tort actions.

Tortfeasor – a person who commits a tort

Trademark – a distinctive mark, logo, or motto of stamp affixed to goods to identify their origin. Once established, a trademark gives its owner the right to its exclusive use.

Trade-Related Aspects of Intellectual Property Rights (TRIPS) Agreement – a treaty adopted in 1994 that incorporates protection for intellectual property into GATT

Trade secret – something of economic value to its owner (e.g., an unpatented formula, a client list) that is protected by law because its owner has taken reasonable steps to keep it secret

Treaty – an agreement or contract between two or more nations that must be authorized (ratified) by the supreme power of each nation to become international law

Trespass to land – entering onto or causing anything to enter onto land of another; remaining on or permitting anything or anyone to remain on land owned by another

Trespass to personal property – sometimes called trespass to chattels; unlawful injury to (or other interference with) the personal property of another that violates the owner's right to exclusive possession and enjoyment of her property

U

Unconscionability – against public policy; unduly harsh and one-sided; shocking to the conscience

Uniform Commercial Code (UCC) – a comprehensive code, drafted by the National Conference on Commissioners on Uniform State Laws, which has been enacted in all the states. It includes articles governing the sale of goods, commercial paper, banking, and other commercial laws.

Utilitarianism – an approach to ethical reasoning in which ethically correct behavior is not related to any absolute ethical or moral values but to an evaluation of the consequences of a given action to those who will be affected by it. In utilitarian reasoning, a good decision is one that results in the greatest good for the greatest number of people affected by it.

Verdict – the answer of a jury given to the court concerning the matters of fact committed to their trial and examination; it sets no precedent, and settles nothing but the specific controversy to which it relates. It is the decision made by the jury and reported to the court, such as guilt or innocence in a criminal trial or whether the defendant is liable to the plaintiff in a civil case and the amount for which she is liable.

Virtue ethics – the ethical theory, derived from Aristotle, that our moral abilities (or virtues) are a matter of good habits, developed through training and repetition, within communities

Void – null; ineffectual; having no legal force

W

Warranty – seller's assurance to the buyers that the goods sold will meet certain standards

Warranty of merchantability – seller's promise to the buyer that goods sold will be fit for their ordinary purpose

Whistleblowing – an employee's reporting an employer's illegal or unethical acts

Worker's compensation – a program under which employers are required to make payments to employees who are injured during the course of their employment, regardless of negligence or fault

World Trade Organization (WTO) – created by the Uruguay Round of GATT in 1994 to administer GATT and to resolve disputes

Writ – a commandment of a court given for the purpose of compelling a defendant to take certain action, usually directed to a sheriff or other officer to execute it; a court order directing a person to do something

Writ of certiorari – an order of a court to an inferior court to forward the record of a case for reexamination by the superior court. Cases are often brought to the attention of the U.S. Supreme Court when the losing party applies for a writ of certiorari. If the writ is granted, the Court agrees to allow an appeal.

Wrongful discharge – see Abusive discharge

Z

Zoning – restrictions on land use imposed by state or local government

Index

A

D

E

F

G

H

I

M

N

O

Q

R

S

T

U

Y

Z